MRS. DRED SCOTT

MRS. DRED SCOTT

A Life on Slavery's Frontier

Lea VanderVelde

OXFORD
UNIVERSITY PRESS
2009

OXFORD
UNIVERSITY PRESS

Oxford University Press, Inc., publishes works that further
Oxford University's objective of excellence
in research, scholarship, and education.

Oxford   New York
Auckland   Cape Town   Dar es Salaam   Hong Kong   Karachi
Kuala Lumpur   Madrid   Melbourne   Mexico City   Nairobi
New Delhi   Shanghai   Taipei   Toronto

With offices in
Argentina   Austria   Brazil   Chile   Czech Republic   France   Greece
Guatemala   Hungary   Italy   Japan   Poland   Portugal   Singapore
South Korea   Switzerland   Thailand   Turkey   Ukraine   Vietnam

Published by Oxford University Press, Inc.
198 Madison Avenue, New York, NY 10016

www.oup.com

Library of Congress Cataloging-in-Publication Data
VanderVelde, Lea.
Mrs. Dred Scott: a life on slavery's frontier / Lea VanderVelde.
p.   cm.
Includes bibliographical references and index.
ISBN 978-0-19-536656-3
1. Scott, Harriet, d. ca. 1870.
2. Scott, Dred, 1809–1858—Family.
3. Women slaves—United States—Biography.
4. Slaves—United States—Biography.
5. Scott, Dred, 1809–1858—Trials, litigation, etc.
I. Title.   II. Title: Misses Dred Scott.
E444.S38V36 2009   973.7′1 15092—dc22
[B] 2008027920

9 8 7 6 5 4 3 2 1

Printed in the United States of America
on acid-free paper

For Harriet's children, my children, and all of our children

CONTENTS

Dramatis Personae

Harriet Scott

Dred Scott

Eliza and Lizzie Scott

Lawrence and Elizabeth Dillon Taliaferro

George Catlin

Clara Catlin

Joseph Nicollet

George
Featherstonhaugh

Henry Hastings
Sibley

Henry Dodge

Gideon and Samuel Pond

Steven and Mary Riggs

Steven Bonga

George Bonga

William Bonga

Jacob Fahlstrom   Roswell Field   Dr. Nathan Jarvis

Joseph R. Brown   William Beaumont   General D. C. Buell

Major E. A. Hitchcock   Pierre Chouteau, Jr.   Julia Chouteau,
baby Ben Sanford

John F. A. Sanford

Elizabeth Irene Sanford
Emerson Chaffee

Dr. and Congressman
Clifford C. Chaffee

B. S. Garland

Lucy Berry Turner Delaney

Hiram Rhoads Revels

Reverdy Johnson

Montgomery Blair

Henry S. Geyer

Only Justices McLean and Curtis dissented from the majority opinion, although all nine justices voiced opinions. Curtis resigned from the court in protest after the decision, so he was no longer a U.S. Supreme Court justice by the time the daguerreotypists came in to take their portraits.

Chief Justice Roger Taney

Justice John McLean

Justice Benjamin Robbins Curtis

Justice James Moore Wayne

Justice John Archibald Campbell

Justice John Catron

Justice Peter Vivian Daniel

Justice Robert Cooper Grier

Justice Samuel Nelson

MRS. DRED SCOTT

Introduction

THIS HISTORICAL NARRATIVE is different from most other biographies because of what it attempts to undertake and the methods used. Neither Dred Scott nor his wife, Harriet Robinson Scott, could read or write, and yet this book undertakes to be the biography of Harriet. There are no letters that reveal her innermost thoughts. Writing a biography of an illiterate person is daunting, but it must be done if we are to understand our common history, and particularly if we are to have any account of significant efforts by subordinate individuals to influence the circumstances of their lives. That, after all, was the point of the Dred Scott case. We must attempt to look at the case from their perspective. Both Dred Scott and his wife Harriet sued to establish their freedom and, derivatively, the freedom of their daughters. To win that freedom, they brought suit against one of the most commercially influential persons in the United States at the time.

No Supreme Court decision stands in greater infamy to this day than *Dred Scott v. Sandford*.[1] The Court ruled that the Scotts were not citizens and could not be citizens because of their race. The Supreme Court of the United States stated that as black persons, they had no rights that white men were bound to respect. The Court endorsed racial inequality and denied their freedom claims in sweeping language. The opinion preempted Congress's power to make laws to improve their condition of enslavement. And thus, their case prompted a constitutional crisis. This family's lawsuit demonstrated that the American Constitution as interpreted by the Taney Court was inadequate to bring about slavery's end, except through the actions of individual states. Because the notorious Supreme Court decision influenced much of what came after,[2] it set the stage for the Lincoln-Douglas debates.[3] Dred Scott's name became famous and famously synonymous with injustice. When the Reconstruction Congress later passed three broad-reaching amendments to the Constitution, it did so because the Court's opinion in the Scotts' family case had denied Congress the power to act. Further reforms were pressed and continued until the enslaved were declared emancipated and slavery was abolished by law. Upon this family's life story, the U.S. Supreme Court rendered its bitter ruling and from it the nation learned a lesson about the importance of human dignity and freedom. Who could have imagined that in the long run, this lawsuit would influence the legal evolution of human liberty—not by winning the day but actually by focusing national attention on the losing claim? The Scotts' very public loss at the Supreme Court gave the struggle for freedom an object lesson.

By refusing to surrender their claim, the Scotts focused the nation's attention on slavery and raised the issue that ultimately changed the course of American history. Although this family's fate was at stake, those who sat in judgment of them knew little of the circumstances of their lives. To this day, Dred is described by historians as a somewhat mysterious figure.[4] Even less has been known about Harriet, although she was a party to the suit and, legally, her status was key to determining the fate of their daughters. She was considered merely as a procedural paragraph in the notorious opinion, and her distinctive experiences were so deeply buried in the procedural technicalities of the case to have been lost from view. With so little known generally about slaves suing for freedom, the Dred Scott case has been a notorious case without a center, without a means of comprehending the human beings whose fates lay in the balance of the court decision and the sequence of personal events that brought them to the highest court of the land.

In fact, the story of the Scotts' life makes little sense from the Court's account of the stipulated facts. Some of the justices of the Supreme Court even expressed bewilderment about the sequence of facts that brought the litigants before them.[7] If the Scotts valued their freedom and lived in free territory, why did they ever return to a slave state? Why did they continue to live in a slave state for six years before filing suit? Since St. Louis was just across the river from the free state of Illinois, why didn't they attempt escape in that six years if they were not always chained?

The lives of subordinate people are consistently erased by time and memory. Servants, such as Dred and Harriet Scott, who sued to improve their lowly status, are partially hidden in history because they could not leave letters and writings. This is generally true of servants, who performed their work without being seen or noticed, and it is especially true of slaves, who were legally forbidden from learning to read. No historian will ever be able to use Harriet or Dred Scott's own words to reveal the stories of their lives or the sequence of events that brought them to the highest court of the land. Nonetheless, their efforts to resist domination and assert their independence are important and subject to more complex and conditional motives because resisting and losing are often fraught with great consequences. Thus, examining the circumstances in which these subordinate persons turned to the courts to petition for relief must be examined in the context of the specific circumstances that confined them. If we are to recover an understanding of their efforts, other measures must be used to reveal their important stories. This technique is not widely used, though it has been utilized by other historians attempting to reclaim an understanding of the nature of the lives of slaves and Native Americans.[8] Other new scholarship has demonstrated more systematic ways that the perspectives of subordinate people differ from dominant accounts.[9] This research tradition de-centers formal legal institutions and procedures and takes seriously the idea that ordinary people of subordinate status can be legal actors.

There is yet a third way that this narrative differs from other historical slave biographies. It portrays the life of a frontier slave. Although there is a very important increasing body of scholarship about antebellum southern slavery[5] as well as about the status of free blacks in the northern states before and after slavery became illegal,[6] there has been very little scholarship about frontier slaves. Because the material circumstances were so very different on the northern frontier, it would be a mistake to think that the patterns of antebellum southern states, in slave law and customs, simply carried over to become the conditions of slavery on the northern frontier.

This historical biography is different from most because it must take a more anthropological approach to revealing what can be known about the lives of Harriet and Dred. This book carefully constructs the historical time and place where Harriet and Dred lived: first, in one of the most remote regions of Indian territory and later in the frontier city of St. Louis, Missouri. As frontier slaves the Scotts' lives were different in several ways from those of the slaves in states where rules of law were well established and slavery had been entrenched for some time. The research has been a challenge. In reconstructing their lives, I first had to place them chronologically and geographically by reading all the available documents together. Wherever possible I checked for corroborating evidence of the Scotts' whereabouts. One difficulty in interpolating across multiple documents is that the individual documents were not written for the purpose of revealing the details of a subordinate's life. Much of what one can know of Harriet's existence comes from public sources like the census, where she was counted, but not necessarily named, and from the court records, which reveal the way that a series of lawyers attempted to construct a version of her life in terms of the elements they thought convenient or necessary to win the case. Nonetheless, it is still possible to attain a surprising degree of corroboration by reading multiple sources side-by-side. Where reports were contradictory I have presented the evidence and attempted to deduce the more reliable source.[10]

Because Harriet and Dred lived in the households of highly influential persons, who did leave written records, more can be deduced about them than about many antebellum frontier slaves. The journals and letters of Harriet's owner, Lawrence Taliaferro, are particularly revealing because both Harriet's role in the case and the significance of Taliaferro's diary have been overlooked by every previous historian of the Dred Scott case.[11] The very simple, almost obvious, idea that a wife's life circumstances were as significant to the context of the family's struggle for survival as her husband's has opened several additional avenues of archival research never before explored by historians of the famous case. Lawrence Taliaferro, who gave Harriet in marriage to Dred, was a faithful diarist, and his journals detailed many of the events that shaped the Scotts' lives on the wilderness frontier—and presumably influenced the development of Harriet's character.

Writing the life of an unlettered servant at a frontier fort is slightly easier because the Army and the Indian Agency meticulously documented names and events. Thus, arrivals and departures of most settlement people at the fort were recorded. Each settlement person arrived at a particular time, at an ascertainable age, usually with a specific assignment or mission, and in an ascertainable chronology. Each male resident did or did not bring along wives, children, and servants—which further dictated their household needs and structure. Local trading houses, of which there were only two (and occasionally a third), kept purchase lists of items bought by each household, and some lists exist of what was shipped to the frontier and what was shipped out.[12] Thus, the purchase by a particular household of a pair of children's shoes suggests a child lived in the household and census documents and genealogical records, especially of the army personnel and early settlers, corroborate the child's name and the names of his or her siblings as well as dates of births, deaths, and marriages. Black servants were often identified by status but not by name. Through these multiple sources, chronologies can be developed and the identities of unnamed persons, like black servants, can be inferred by processes of elimination. There were never more than 20 African Americans at one time in the immediate area where Harriet lived in the 1830s.

I have intentionally chosen Harriet, who was, after all, a co-litigant as the biography's subject. Her life path further highlights the significance of the newly discovered evidence. Women's history is often necessary to complement the many histories that have been written about men. Dred's life story has been told effectively by Walter Ehrlich, in *They Have No Rights*,[13] but Harriet's life story was missed. Moreover, Harriet's is the contrasting element in this story. She grew up on the frontier. Therefore she was more susceptible to its influence than was Dred, who arrived as a mature adult, after having already been exposed to the ravages of institutionalized southern slavery. His experience was more typical of southern slaves. Prior to arriving at a frontier fort, he lived in Virginia, Alabama, and the slave city of St. Louis; he had been married and lost his wife to sale; and he himself had been sold from his family of origin into the service of Dr. John Emerson. Harriet came to the frontier just out of childhood, and with the freshness of adolescence, she was more likely to absorb the frontier experience. In centering this biography on Harriet, I need not take into account all the many life experiences and acculturations that had already shaped the older, more worldly wise Dred.

Writing a life of an illiterate servant also requires a careful reconstruction of the material culture. Performing household tasks within the strict material constraints of her life dictated most of Harriet's daily efforts. Drawing water, chopping firewood, cooking, cleaning, doing laundry, and caring for her babies were all-consuming daily exertions for a person in her situation. In frontier Minnesota, the weather, especially the winter cold, was a pervasive factor in the Scotts' lives, and the harsh nature of the environment served as something of a leveling device in the experiences of all who wintered over at the fort.

Harriet's frontier experience as an antebellum slave is worthy of depiction because it runs so counter to the predominant slavery narrative. The tensions of enslavement on the frontier are set against a wilderness background of states coming into being rather than in a setting of cultivated fields, fences, boundaries, patrols, and established legal systems.[14] I start her story with her arrival as a girl by steamboat in wilderness Minnesota rather than her birth in Virginia, or her short time in Pennsylvania about which little of the particulars are known.

The challenge of interpretation has been to create a place for a black servant woman and her husband in the phenomenal surrounding tableau. Learning, for example, that the Scotts were both present and situated among perhaps only 50 settlement people at the tumultuous Ojibwa treaty of 1837 (which involved more than 2,000 Indians) required me to consider what role each would have been assigned in the social organization of the event.

Although the trail of Harriet's existence is often lost, the continuity of her life emerging at different historical junctures ties the story together. Even if the subjective details of her particular life can never be completely known, informed speculation can be based on close study of the documentation of others most similarly situated. I am acutely aware that in this anthropological reconstruction, as in others, the direct evidence is sometimes very minimal. Nonetheless, until more is found, it is all that we have. Over the course of my writing this book, the *New York Times* made their archives searchable, and as a result an extensive interview with Mrs. Emerson, the real defendant in interest, about the Dred Scott case came to light. It had been there all the time, but since it did not appear on an anniversary or in an obituary, no historian of the case had ever incorporated it into the mosaic of known facts. No doubt, more documents will come to light with time.

In keeping with the traditions of legal research, I have not been content to report the evidence with the ubiquitous "may." Many things may have happened, and if the possibility is that slight, I neglected to speculate on possibilities that seemed improbable. Instead, I have attempted to assess probabilities in terms of "undoubtedly" when it cannot reasonably be assumed otherwise, "probably" because all evidence that we have points in that direction, but my assessment suggests the degree of confidence gained from looking at other, similar instances. We have no alternative but to speculate on these lives using the best means possible. Otherwise, we leave them unimagined and thereby risk, as a result of the silence inflicted upon them, creating the false impression that only the lettered contributed to history.

One can fairly assume that others' reports of events in the small, closed community were well known within the community and accurate. Commensurately, knowing the chronological order of events and physical constraints of Harriet's life, first as a slave on the northern wilderness frontier and then as a washerwoman in St. Louis, we can rule out certain other life experiences as displaced by what we do know. Harriet did not flee to Canada nor did she ever experience slavery in the plantation South or the travails affecting most field hands. In chronologically stringing together the events of Harriet's life it is impossible to totally rule out improbable events, but we can presume that she lived within the frame of behavioral norms, acceptable for a subordinate servant woman. Otherwise, her actions would have been noted as curious by one of the several journal-writing people around her.[15] Moreover, had she not conformed to expected norms of subordinate survival behavior, she might not have survived a departure from expectations. Slaves who acted out were removed from their domestic situations or did not live long, as the story demonstrates.[16] From careful reading of all the texts available it appears that Harriet did not attempt to run away. Slave attempts to escape generally left some written report in newspapers, letter files, or official reports. I've attempted to generate a comprehensive list of all runaways advertised in the *Missouri Republican* during the time that Harriet lived in St. Louis, and her name is not among them, nor is her demographic profile.

A writer engaging in a biography of illiterate historical figures must adhere to certain strict conventions of methodology because the fiction writer's technique of invention is impermissible. The search is for what *can be* known about what actually happened and what *can be* deduced from the evidence. Thus, the only dialogue involving Harriet or Dred in this work occurs in the first chapter and is taken from a newspaper account of an actual conversation with Harriet. The dialogue of other persons, where it appears, is also verbatim. Second, rather than resort to fictional conventions that wrap things up neatly, one must be committed to following the story wherever it leads. Some things can never be known for sure because the evidence is contradictory, such as whether Harriet or Dred ever reached Louisiana in 1838.

This particular account is a meticulous marshaling and juxtaposing of the documented facts, and from those facts a subjective life comes into focus; though without letters, diaries, or speeches to draw on, the biography of an illiterate person cannot be the account of a deep inner life. That degree of privacy will always remain hers. Harriet left no first-person account of what she thought to be the critical turning points in her life. The reader who seeks such a definitive narration will be disappointed. Still, those persons who surrounded her contributed recorded discourses that must inevitably have shaped her impressions of the world. These rich discourses provided her with a language to organize her understanding of the world, whether that world was frontier Minnesota or antebellum St. Louis.

Read carefully the list of citations, notes, and appendices to judge whether the implications have been fairly drawn. I had faith that unembellished facts would turn out to be as fascinating as fiction, and I was delighted to discover that the fully verifiable elements of this story had an almost epic quality. Reality, when fully assembled, is at least as remarkable as fiction.

The accumulated evidence suggests a common woman of considerable gumption. When asked about the infamous case, her response was to ask the journalists to leave her husband alone.[17] By considering the actions that only she could have taken in advancing the case (or actions taken with her consent and continued participation), one must suppose that she thought about these events and reflected on their consequences for her family. From the journalist's visit we observe a shred of character, a person who is fully aware of her surroundings, and a person who provides for her immediate family with a strong sense of independence. From the fact that she did not surrender through 11 years of litigation, one must deduce that she had more fortitude than the many who brought freedom suits but did not persevere.

Because she did survive, we must presume that she had the basic set of emotional responses to her circumstances necessary for her to survive. To do less inferring of normal emotions and thoughts would deny her subjectivity. We can reasonably assume that she was caught up in the excitement of the community in which she lived when those communities were threatened by Indian wars, fires, and pestilences of epidemic proportions. We can reasonably assume that like most sentient beings, she felt apprehension entering a strange new environment, sadness when people living close to her were seriously injured or died, and comfort when she was shown small gestures of kindness. The birth of a child usually changes the psyche of a woman to that of a mother, and Harriet's recorded willingness to provide for her children and take steps to hide them during the trial implies that she bonded with her children and cared about their well-being.

At the point in the story that Harriet left Minnesota with Dred for the frontier city of St. Louis, their story must be told within the contours of what is known about the lives and obstacles to survival for similarly situated persons in the same community. The discovery of almost 300 other slave petitions for freedom was another important piece of information in the story. I began the search for these cases in the backrooms of the St. Louis courthouse more than a decade ago with Ken Kaufman and Melvina Conley.[18] The search was taken up as well by Ken Winn, the Missouri state archivist of extraordinary vision, by Mario Favazzo, and by Mike Everman. Washington University in St. Louis has now given the world access to the files by placing them on the Web.[19] Researching the context cannot provide definitive answers to all the case's mysteries, but it provides insight into the most bedeviling questions such as why the Scotts returned to a slave state after living in free territory and why they chose their timing when they did.

As Harriet's legal status was far more uncertain than that of slaves in the plantation South, based on her residence in Indian territory of the Northwest Ordinance, so too the changing circumstances in St. Louis cast further doubt on her status. This biography is set against two different, but both (at the time that she lived in them) evolving, conditions that throw her status into question: the increasingly settled, regulated, enclosed, and contested frontier, and St. Louis, where inhabitants became more and more hostile to the liberties of free blacks. The northern wilderness and the frontier city of St. Louis were as central to her life struggle as the conditions that led her from one place to another.

As a subordinate woman who invoked law to achieve her freedom, what did Harriet's life mean? Her life was an anomaly to the American perception of the frontier as a place of personal freedom and lawlessness, her life shows the contradictions inherent in setting up a new legal order on the frontier. She lived as a slave in a territory with few laws, except the most basic territorial law expressly prohibiting slavery. As such, her life also demonstrates the difficulties in breaking dominant patterns and enslavement. By persisting in the quest for freedom, her life reveals the simple heroism of ordinary people. Examining her experience renders the important abstract principles of slavery and freedom more concretely human and real.

The themes of this life are belonging and usefulness. It was because slaves were useful that they were brought to the frontier. On the frontier, she belonged to the settlement community. Once she returned to St. Louis in the slave state of Missouri, because she was no longer useful on the frontier and could no longer belong or survive there, she encountered a culture in which her belonging was increasingly subject to question. Even the language of Justice Taney's notorious opinion plays belonging and usefulness off against race to conclude that African descendants, though useful as slaves, could never belong to the American polity and were less useful to it free than enslaved.

Until now, this law suit has been a historical moment without a center. This is the story of one of the lives at its center and an account that provides answers to some of the mysteries.

CHAPTER 1

Wife of a Celebrity

ONE SUMMER DAY in 1857, as a freedwoman was ironing in her own front room on an alley in St. Louis, she saw a pair of white men approach. Her two daughters were busy assisting her, stoking the fire and moving the heavy irons from stove to ironing board so they would be hot enough to smooth the wrinkles from the freshly laundered clothes. At the back of the room, behind another ironing board, her elderly husband was asleep.[1]

The laundress watched cautiously as the white men came nearer. When they reached the wooden porch, they called out to her, "Is this where Dred Scott lives?" Her husband was now famous; his name was known across the country.

She hesitated. "Yes," she said.

"Is he at home?" This wasn't the first time people had come looking for him.

"What's the white man after that Negro for? Why don't the white man tend to his own business, and let that Negro alone?" she replied. The freedwoman was a respectable, smart, tidy-looking black woman in her 30s, the men later wrote. From the spirit of her answer they knew her to be Dred Scott's wife and nobody's slave.

There was a rustling at the back of the room. From behind the second ironing table, an old black man raised himself to see the visitors. He recognized them. He assured her, "It was all right." He'd met the gentlemen before.

"One of these days they'll steal that Negro," she continued, but she yielded as the white men entered the house, encouraged by Dred's acknowledgment.

The men were journalists from *Frank Leslie's Illustrated Newspaper*, and their account of Harriet Robinson Scott is the only existing first-person description of her by anyone who ever actually met her. The journalists had approached Dred at the fairgrounds a few days before and asked to interview him and take his picture. When he didn't show up at the photographers' studio, they found him through his lawyer, obtaining a letter of introduction and his address.

Dred explained that more interviews would just bring him bad luck. The white men pulled out the lawyer's letter to show the Scotts, and although neither could read, they knew the signature. Dred then told them that he would do whatever his lawyer suggested because he was his friend and "knows best what I should do."

Harriet listened to everything attentively, though she wasn't impressed by the strangers. She had seen others react to her husband's celebrity. She repeated, "One of these days they'll steal that Negro. What do white men come after that Negro for?" She warned that "the devil was at the bottom of it."

The men insisted that they meant no harm and only wanted Dred's picture. Harriet was leery because she knew other white men had tried to get her husband to come away with them. Freedmen had been kidnapped and sold down the river into slavery from St. Louis.[2] There were also men who had promised to give her husband $1,000 a month if he would travel through the North. They said that the American people wanted to see him. Despite the offer of a fortune, Harriet had insisted that Dred refuse. She'd always been able to earn her own, honest living, thank God, and she didn't want money gotten in that way. No good would come of it. It appeared that Harriet had persuaded Dred against showing up for the picture.

The newsmen took a different tack and began to flatter Harriet. As they later wrote in the newspaper, they could see that she was the old man's "real master."[3] They complimented her on her fine appearance, asking if she too would sit for a portrait. Although she said that she didn't want to be made "Tom fool of," she seemed to reflect on the possibilities and added, "How can I give a daguerreotype when I'm not fixed up or anything?"[4] Something about the offer appealed to her, and she began to bargain with the visitors over the terms. She took out her finest dress to show them.[5] Harriet Scott finally agreed that Dred could have his picture taken, and she and the girls would come along and have theirs, provided the men gave the family some pictures for themselves. It was a deal.

The next day each of the four Scott family members, wearing their best clothes, sat stiffly before the lights to have their portraits taken: Dred and Harriet, each individually, and the girls together. That picture, subsequently engraved for the newspaper, is the only remaining likeness of Harriet. It shows a very dark-skinned, dark-eyed woman with high cheekbones. Her thick, curly hair was pulled neatly back and she wore gold hoop earrings. She bears a pleasant, but unsmiling and slightly apprehensive expression. Her eyes are focused straight at the camera. Dred's eyes stare off as if he had shifted his attention during the long sitting that the photograph required.

Pictures of the entire family appeared on the front page of the nation's leading weekly. After that moment of national fame, Harriet and her daughters faded again from public view. Harriet didn't seek publicity; in fact, she tried to avoid it. She merely wanted to be left alone to live in peace, earn her own living, and raise her children. After a lifetime of adventure, she apparently welcomed the return to the quiet, respectable work of doing laundry and attending church.

Hers was a life that could be equaled by few that century. She had lived for several years surrounded by Sioux and Objiwa people who spoke languages at first unknown to her. She endured brutally cold Minnesota winters. She traveled the extent of the nation on the steamboat, the most advanced means of travel of the time. She had served some of the century's most important, best-educated, engaging, and ambitious men at her master's table. She returned as a free black person to live in a slave state that increasingly turned to law to circumscribe her personal liberties. She nursed her aging husband and kept her family intact through fires, floods, and epidemics. She sat silently beside her husband in the courtroom and hid her children for their safety, while holding out for her family's freedom in a hostile environment for more than a decade, a legal battle that extended to the highest court of the land.

This modest, ordinary, low-born young woman accomplished something extraordinary. From all evidence, it was her idea to bring suit, and her determination carried her family through. Harriet didn't set out to change the world; she only sought to free her family and herself from slavery. Though illiterate, black—and hence perceived as different in the racial caste system of the times—the mother of two young children, and desperately poor, she challenged the claim that she and her family were slaves.

The lawsuit, in turn, pitted her family against one of the wealthiest, most powerful families in America: the financial power broker, John F. A. Sanford of the American Fur Company. She and her husband ultimately lost the most important and dramatic lawsuit in the history of the U.S. Supreme Court. When the high court took up her case and rejected her claim of freedom, it convulsed the entire system of law and justice.

Although Harriet lived her life at the turning point in constitutional history, she was an outsider almost all her life and her history is virtually unknown. As a slave on the frontier, she lived outside the main fort in a household surrounded by Indian tribes often at war with each other. Later, as a servant within the fort's walls, she was surrounded by a finely regulated military social system that minutely measured the status distinctions between soldiers and different grades of officers in their clothing and privilege. As a servant, her place was at the bottom of the register but outside the system of official rankings. She could be considered invisible and as such ignored.

As a slave, she was excluded from most social communities. And yet, from the margin and from persons regarded as marginal, so very much can be learned about how a nation is forged and who is considered as belonging or useful.

The social isolation of the frontier must have forged her bond to her husband and taught her the self-reliance and perseverance to endure for eleven years of litigation. She sustained her spirit when many others gave up. Her persistence in her quest for independence—the act of filing and maintaining such a momentous lawsuit, particularly given the conditions of her life—reveals heroism.

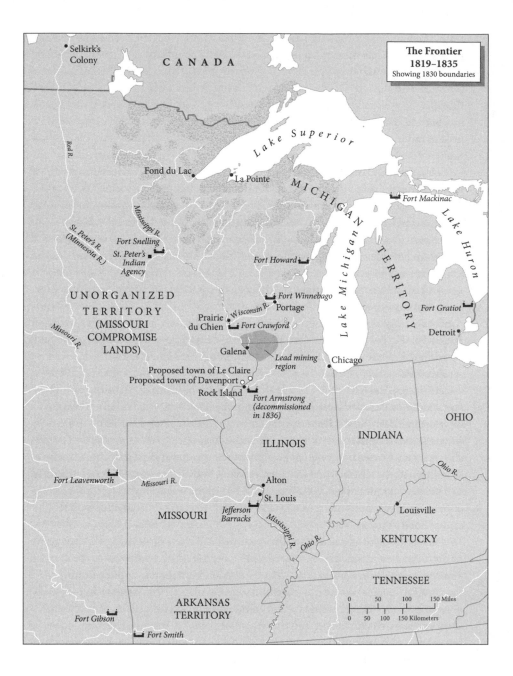

The Frontier
1819–1835
Showing 1830 boundaries

Selkirk's Colony

CANADA

Lake Superior

Fond du Lac
La Pointe

MICHIGAN

Fort Mackinac

Lake Huron

Red R.

St. Peter's R. (Minnesota R.)

Mississippi R.

Fort Snelling
St. Peter's Indian Agency

Fort Howard

Fort Gratiot

Lake Michigan

TERRITORY

Detroit

UNORGANIZED
TERRITORY
(MISSOURI
COMPROMISE
LANDS)

Fort Winnebago
Wisconsin R. Portage

Prairie du Chien Fort Crawford

Missouri R.

Galena

Lead mining region

Chicago

Proposed town of Le Claire
Proposed town of Davenport
Rock Island

Fort Armstrong
(decommissioned
in 1836)

ILLINOIS

INDIANA

OHIO

Ohio R.

Fort Leavenworth

Missouri R.

Alton
St. Louis

Louisville

MISSOURI

Jefferson Barracks

Mississippi R.

Ohio R.

KENTUCKY

TENNESSEE

Fort Gibson

ARKANSAS
TERRITORY

Fort Smith

0   50   100   150 Miles
0   50   100   150 Kilometers

CHAPTER 2

1835: Arriving on the Frontier

WATER SPLASHED REGULARLY off the steamboat *Warrior's* big paddle wheel propelling the ship up the Mississippi River as it carried a small slave girl deep into the North American interior.[1] This new mechanical technology was a marvel. Travelers to remote western rivers no longer depended on the strong arms of young Creole voyageurs to paddle supply boats upstream.[2] Steam engines had replaced the muscle of men.

As the big wheel churned the foam, the 14-year-old servant girl had time to sit and simply watch the wheel's inevitable drive. She had few chores since the *Warrior* had stewards and cooks to meet the master's needs. The master's entire household was traveling west, so the young girl traveled with the other black servants on the lower deck just above the water, carried along with boxes and barrels of cargo and the large valises destined for the frontier.

The master, Lawrence Taliaferro (pronounced "Tolliver"), U.S. Indian Agent to the Sioux nation,[3] had made this trip through the river highways that comprised the heart of the country each year for more than a decade. This was the first trip for Harriet, the youngest servant girl in his entourage. It is uncertain whether Harriet first went west with Master Taliaferro in 1834 or 1835, but his route was always the same. She did make the trip in spring 1835 as the entire Taliaferro household was moving to St. Peter's Agency, in Indian Territory, after President Andrew Jackson had reappointed Taliaferro to another term as Indian agent to the Sioux, a post he had occupied for more than a decade.[4]

The Taliaferros were building a new, very large, and very grand house back in Bedford, Pennsylvania, the peaceful mountain spa resort that was their permanent home.[5] Having already served several terms as Indian Agent, Lawrence Taliaferro, now 41, had considered simply resigning.[6] But serving as Indian agent to the Dakota was his life's work. Perhaps the tumultuous events of the preceding summer of 1834 had impressed upon him how much he was needed at his agency full-time. Who else could be trusted to ward off the unscrupulous fur traders who threatened to introduce more whiskey to the Dakota Indians? Who else could maintain the fragile peace between the two Indian nations competing in the same hunting grounds? At any rate, he resumed his calling, agreeing to serve for another four years. This time he brought along his wife, his brother-in-law, and more black servants, planning to stay at the wilderness outpost through the winter.

Setting out on the river highways, the Taliaferro entourage consisted of three primary members: the master, the mistress, and her brother, Horatio Dillon, a young gentleman without portfolio, and half a dozen slaves or "servants," as Taliaferro always referred to them.[7] The servant group included 14-year-old Harriet, 18-year-old Eliza, perhaps one of Eliza's babies, and some slave men. Taliaferro owned 21 slaves over the course of his life, but usually only six or seven at a time.[8]

When she left Bedford, Harriet couldn't have known that she would never see the Allegheny Mountains again. The Taliaferros' wintering over would extend through two full years, and by the time her master returned to winter again in Bedford, the servant girl Harriet would be married, remaining in the West with her husband, Dred Scott. River traffic opened earlier on the Ohio than it did on the upper Mississippi. The trip west took six weeks in all, requiring a stagecoach ride and at least three steamboat transfers to traverse half the continent—that, at the time, constituted all of the American nation, 1,600 miles along the river corridor from western Pennsylvania to St. Peter's Agency.[9] In St. Louis, the party changed boats and took passage on the *Warrior*, the largest steamboat ever to have plied the waters of the Upper Mississippi. This very boat had recently done service in the Blackhawk War, firing cannon on the dispirited band of Sac and Fox Indians as they swam across the river in their final retreat. Now the *Warrior* carried passengers up the Mississippi as far north as St. Peter's Indian Agency.[10]

Every evening the steamboat moored along the shore for the night. The stokers let the engine fires burn out and the engines went silent. The cabin boys lit the lanterns in the private cabins and the great common dining room. More glowing lanterns were suspended from poles leaning over the river's dark waters.[11] The lanterns, dangling like great fireflies reflected in the river, gave the steamboat the aura of floating fantasy.

Two days out from St. Louis, the *Warrior* stopped at Fort Armstrong, on Rock Island, on the Illinois side of the river. There Taliaferro visited the local Indian agent, George Davenport, at an impressive house that could be seen for miles on the steamboat's approach. If Harriet left the steamboat or met anyone at Fort Armstrong, it would have been Davenport's black indentured servant woman, Charlotte.[12]

Living at Fort Armstrong at the time was the man who would become Harriet's husband: Etheldred, the post doctor's slave. They probably didn't meet then because their masters were neither acquainted nor had business with each other. The man slave Etheldred had been purchased in St. Louis and taken to Fort Armstrong in the supposedly free state of Illinois to serve the fort's doctor.[13]

Another two days and the *Warrior* stopped at either Julien Dubuque's lead mines on the western shore of the river or at the muddy little lead mining town of

Galena, set slightly back from the Mississippi on the Illinois side. The lead tailings ran down the tributary and into the main current of the great river. Journeying upstream in spring was like traveling backward in time. Although the trees were in full foliage in St. Louis, the buds were just popping out in the north country. The nights grew cooler again. It was not unusual to see even a late April snowstorm at St. Peter's. In another two days, the ship reached another fort, the landing in Prairie du Chien. There the *Warrior* remained longer, as it was the last place Captain Throckmorton could get the additional cordwood needed to power the engines for the remainder of the trip upstream. There would be no settlement or cabin in the 300-mile stretch between Prairie du Chien and their destination, St. Peter's.

The sleepy village of Prairie du Chien, with its rough log houses and mud roads, was poorly situated with respect to the river's erratic flood waters. The village was inhabited principally by descendants of early French fur traders, who preserved the voyageurs' language and customs. Adjoining the village was a wooden fortification, Fort Crawford, which stood on an even less desirable site than the town, built on an island that flooded each spring, bringing miserable inconvenience and dysentery to the soldiers.

At Prairie du Chien, Taliaferro was surely greeted by his good friend, the local Indian agent, Joseph Street.[14] The Streets often asked the Taliaferros to stay with them when the steamboat stopped for the night. The servants probably went ashore when the rest of the passengers did. At the Streets' home, they could visit the slavewoman Patsey and her five children to exchange news. Meanwhile, their masters upstairs enjoyed the dinner that Patsey had spent the day preparing.

The Streets' house was already legendary as the place where Chief Blackhawk had recently surrendered.[15] Although his people had been decimated in the battles, Blackhawk had evaded capture and refused to be taken. He would surrender to only one man, the Indian agent, and only at the agent's house—not to the generals at the fort. Those were his terms, the only terms on which a man who had lost the war could insist. Such was the importance of an Indian agent, the representative of the U.S. government both in war and peace and in all diplomatic dealings with the tribes in Indian territory.

By the summer of 1835, Street, who formerly was agent to the Winnebago nation, was reassigned to the Sac and Fox Nation. Street was embroiled in difficulties with the American Fur Company, and his troubles foreshadowed the difficulties that Taliaferro would encounter over the next years. Harriet would watch as the sequence of events on the advancing frontier would take a similar toll on her master, agent to the Dakota.

The Winnebago had suffered from longer contact with the encroaching settlement in their area than the Dakota, to whom Harriet's master was assigned; for the Dakota, there was still hope of achieving health, stability, self-sufficiency, and a measure of independence.

In 1835, Agent Joseph Street was being hounded by the men of the local American Fur Company for doing his job.[16] Street had earned a reputation for resolutely opposing company policies when they encroached on the Indians' legitimate claims to the local resources of furs, woodlands, and lead.[17] Whiskey was already a chronic problem at Prairie du Chien, and on this issue, Street had also antagonized the community's French population, who considered whiskey the elixir of life.[18] Now that the Sac and Fox tribes had been roundly defeated in war, the fur company was seeking to remove Street and his Indian agency from Prairie du Chien. Since the Indian nation had ceded the land in defeat, the fur company claimed, there was no longer need for an agency there. The fur company men were pressing for Street to be reassigned downriver to Rock Island. Although Harriet's master already had his own difficulties with the fur company men, Street's situation was more acute. Taliaferro had tangled with fur company men in his area when they tried to bring whiskey into his jurisdiction the preceding summer and he had won. During the embargo incident a shootout had erupted on the river between drunken soldiers, fur company men, and Taliaferro's agents as they confiscated the contraband whiskey. Having prevailed in that skirmish, Taliaferro operated with greater confidence now than did his friend Agent Street in Prairie du Chien where the battle to keep out whiskey had already been lost.

Strategically, removing Street's agency from Prairie du Chien would weaken Taliaferro's, since it was the nearest agency for relaying information or supplies and maintaining the influence of government policy. The two agencies were four days' travel apart, and moving Street's agency further south or west into Iowa would stretch the travel distance to more than a week. As a result, more Indians would gravitate to Taliaferro for help, and their dependency on the fur company would increase. Lawrence Taliaferro shared Street's view that the Indian agency was needed to moderate the American Fur Company's opportunistic influence over the Indians.

As the master's fortunes determined the lives of everyone within his household, Patsey, the Streets' bound servant, may have shared his apprehension about the relocation. That she had no control over the matter wouldn't necessarily eliminate anxiety.[19] Patsey may have invited other bonded servants—some who had indenture papers, others who did not—over from the fort for the evening. By means of late night meetings after chores, slaves maintained the network of personal support by which they could survive. The visiting servants would have needed to set off in the early, predawn morning to walk the three miles back to the fort in order to arrive before the white people woke.[20]

The morning after the steamboat had arrived at Prairie du Chien, the ship's bell signaled that it was time to set off.[21] A half day upstream the *Warrior* steamed past Bad Axe Creek, the site of the final bloody battle in the Blackhawk War. So many of Blackhawk's people had been killed there that there were too few survivors to bury the dead, and wolves had pulled the bodies apart. All that remained of the vanquished people was a bone field, partially covered with grass. The steamboat *Warrior*'s captain was proud of his role in firing on the fleeing Indians. It was said that during the battle the muddy river ran red.[22] The few survivors who made it across the river were set upon by Dakota warriors, the Sac and Fox tribe's sworn enemy who entered the war at the government's request. Master Taliaferro saw this as bad policy. Urging the Dakota to enter the U.S. war against the Sac and Fox only stirred up intertribal hatred,[23] and he took no pleasure in this result.

A full day upstream, the *Warrior* stopped at the first Dakota village it encountered to allow Agent Taliaferro to confer with the chief.[24] Chief Wabasha's village was located north of the neutral ground, an expanse of land west of the Mississippi, set aside by treaty to keep distance between the hostile Dakota and Sac and Fox nations. Whenever news came from below—of a steamboat, of killings, or an epidemic—Wabasha was the first Dakota chief to know about it and to send word to Agent Taliaferro.

The master usually dressed in full regalia for meeting with chiefs. Discussing relevant news and monitoring the barometer of tribal relations were his most important tasks as Indian agent. He was aware of the value of an entrance and usually prepared himself to meet the chiefs after his winter absence.

Harriet may have been curious to see the Indian village as the boat docked, but she also must have been apprehensive. She had never encountered Indians before, either in Virginia, her birthplace, or in Pennsylvania. She had no way to speak to these strangely clad people. Even the master for all his 15 years as Indian agent could speak to them only through his métis translator, Scott Campbell, who no doubt had joined the voyage by now.

The ritual greeting never varied.[25] Indian agent and Indian chief sat together, smoked tobacco from one of the carved red stone pipes that the chief's pipe bearer produced, and held council. The pipe bearer provided the pipe, but after a winter of depleted supplies, Taliaferro usually provided the tobacco. The pipe was offered to the four compass points—north, south, east, and west—was smoked by Taliaferro and Chief Wabasha, and then passed from man to man around the circle. Then they would talk, Scott Campbell interpreting. The lesser men leaned in to listen as the principal men exchanged news.

Wabasha was probably groomed and painted for the occasion, having anticipated the boat's arrival for several days. He wore a medal around his neck, adorned with some president's profile and suspended on a ribbon. Agent Taliaferro gave the chiefs these medals bearing the image of the Great Father in Washington as a talisman of allegiance.[26] Wabasha was older than Taliaferro, although the two men had been friends for 15 years.

After sitting together in the council, the agent customarily distributed gifts and annuities. The moneys, paid annually, were the result of an early treaty with the Dakota that Taliaferro had helped negotiate.[27] In addition to money, the treaty provided the tribes some livestock, food stores, and the services of a blacksmith, known as the treaty blacksmith. This year, however, the money failed to reach St. Louis before Taliaferro set out for the north. This placed him in the awkward situation of explaining the delay. It would not do for him to arrive empty-handed, so he usually brought some small gifts of his own to give to the principal men. This system of exchanging gifts cemented the bonds between the agent and the chiefs.[28] The chief customarily gave the agent gifts in return, typically a long-stemmed red stone peace pipe.[29]

It was the end of May by the time the steamboat *Warrior* rounded the bend of Oliver's Grove, 25 river miles below the fort. The previous year Agent Taliaferro had prevented a trader named Joseph Brown from building his cabin at that very spot when the Indians complained that it was one of their traditional hunting grounds.[30] Settlers often saw as unoccupied sites that the Indians had long recognized as desirable hunting and camping grounds in their regular seasonal migrations. It was hubris for settlers to believe that they were the first to discover them. The crew and passengers were probably in high spirits, knowing their destination was close. Rounding the bend, the passengers took in the full panorama of their surroundings. Every traveler seemed to remark upon their first glimpse of the fort.[31] Like a medieval stone castle, the sand-colored fort was prominently positioned on the bluff above the valley where the two rivers met. The sheer stone wall facing the river rose a full 130 feet from the dock, where people surely had gathered to meet the *Warrior*.

Arriving steamboats, particularly the first one of the year, were springtime's most important occasion. Maj. Bliss, the commandant of the fort, was there with a military delegation to greet the boat. The garrison's tiny band of musicians usually played a rousing song as the steamboat maneuvered to dock. The handful of families that lived in the surrounding area gathered as well because the entire community had awaited this day for months. The steamboat brought them news, diversion, and, after the long winter, much needed food and supplies. If the Sac and Fox regarded the *Warrior* as an instrument of death, to those who had endured seven months of winter isolation this first steamboat of the season must have seemed like both Christmas and the circus come to town.[32]

A long, inclined wagon path wound around the sheer stone wall, linking the steamboat dock to the prairie plateau above. From there the wagons entered the fort through the sentried gate that faced out onto the prairies.

There were few buildings on the prairie plateau outside the fort's massive stone walls—only the stables and garrison gardens were nearby. A quarter mile from the stone fort stood the small handful of agency buildings that would become Harriet's home. But as the travelers emerged from the river valley, they saw that the plateau was not empty. Farther back from the cliff and away from the fort, many other pairs of eyes had watched the big boat's arrival. Surveying the situation from various high points on the river and from teepees pitched around the agency house were hundreds of watching, expectant Indian people. The Indians had known for some time that the agent was arriving. Ever since the boat had left Prairie du Chien, groups of Indians were spotted along the river's banks, and runners went from village to village with the news of its arrival.

They were waiting for Harriet's master. They called him *Muzzah-Bak-sah*, meaning "the iron cutter." They knew that the steamboat carried the man who called himself their father.[33] Muzzah-Bak-sah brought iron, which the treaty blacksmith forged into hoes, spears, and traps for them; thus Muzzah-Bak-sah brought the Dakota into the iron age. He also brought fresh tobacco, barrels of food, tools, and the annuity payments that would further open the traders' storehouses to them.

The several hundred waiting Dakota who were encamped around the agency compound made this tent city of lodge-poled teepees more populous than the fort.[34] It was usually a noisy, active place. The women performed almost all the labor of carrying, building cooking fires, and hauling water, while the men talked, smoked, gambled, and went to council with the agent to talk about war and peace and the tribe's material needs. Children roamed freely, exploring wherever their interests led them. Some Sioux had horses that could carry the tent poles as travois, but there were also always packs of dogs. The Sioux kept great numbers of dogs,[35] that wandered freely around the temporary village. In the middle of this bustling temporary tent city stood the lone stone house that would be Harriet's home for the next few years.

If arriving by boat at the first Indian village had heightened her sense of apprehension, walking from the dock up the path to see the agency compound completely encircled by tepees, except for the steep bluff side, must have required all of her courage. Unlike the fort, the agency house had no protective fortification or guards or even a fence; it was exposed—to the sky, to the prairie, to the high bluff drop off, and to the Indian village that now surrounded it.

The tiny agency compound was the nerve center of communication for the north country's many tribes. The landmass of prairies, lakes, and forests would eventually become five American states.[36] Over the next two years, a diverse group of visitors would make the trek to Harriet's master's front door for all manner of reasons. She would likely come to know their nations, tribes, and some of their individual identities, and, with time, even learn to distinguish their personal agendas as seen through the eyes of the master she served, Agent Muzzah-Bak-sah.

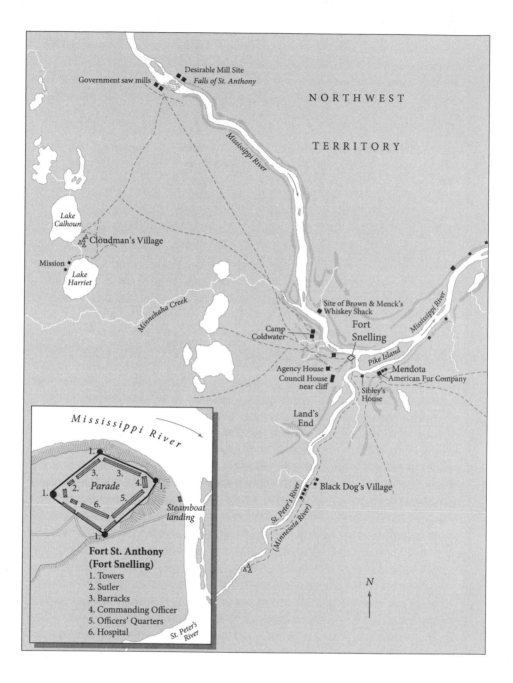

NORTHWEST

TERRITORY

Desirable Mill Site
Falls of St. Anthony
Government saw mills

Mississippi River

Lake Calhoun
Cloudman's Village
Mission
Lake Harriet

Minnehaha Creek

Site of Brown & Menck's Whiskey Shack
Camp Coldwater
Fort Snelling
Pike Island
Agency House
Council House near cliff
Mendota
American Fur Company
Sibley's House
Land's End

Mississippi River

Black Dog's Village

St. Peter's River
(*Minnesota River*)

N

Mississippi River

1.
3.   3.
2.   *Parade*   4
6.   5.
1.
Steamboat landing
1.
1.
Fort St. Anthony (Fort Snelling)
1. Towers
2. Sutler
3. Barracks
4. Commanding Officer
5. Officers' Quarters
6. Hospital
St. Peter's River

CHAPTER 3

Settling In

T HE ARRIVING TALIAFERRO party stayed at the commandant's quarters in the fort while the mistress and servants set up the agency household. Each morning, the servants left the fort to walk through the village of teepees. The well-used hides that formed the exterior walls of the teepees carried symbolic markings and were darkened from smoke on the inside and dirt and grime outside. Small bundles of sacred heads and feathers called "medicine" dangled from the tepee door flaps to protect the inhabitants.[1]

The servants aired out the stone house and made it livable. The primary purpose of bringing slaves to the frontier was to make their master's living circumstances more habitable. The slave men tended to the livestock that had endured the long river passage and unpacked the heavy furniture including Mrs. Taliaferro's piano.[2] Eliza and Harriet set up a workable kitchen in the underground space and cleaned the house of the insects and prairie animals that had burrowed into the shelter in their three-season-long absence.[3] Harriet and Eliza stretched stiff new hemp rope between the hollowed out holes of the wooden bedsteads in the master's second floor bedroom. The agency house, with its central door, four pairs of windows, and pair of chimneys flanking each of its sides was in a sad state of disrepair.[4] The master had written to the superintendent of Indian affairs, complaining that when it rained, the "hired man and I have not a dry spot in our houses."[5] The house had to be made winter-tight during the short Minnesota summer. The master also directed that the grounds around the agency buildings be enclosed with split rails. The fence separated the land claimed by the agency from the endless prairie plateau that often served as the campground for traveling Native peoples. The rail fence also protected the agency garden from the cattle that grazed freely on the plateau during the summer. A fence kept the grass around the buildings from being trampled into mud and dust like a common cattle yard. Although the entire territory was under his jurisdiction, the master set his personal boundaries.

Once the house was in order, Eliza and Harriet probably prepared the garden for planting. The agency's garden was patiently replanted each year with anything the master thought might grow in Minnesota's short growing season. With more people to feed this year, a larger garden was needed, and there was no time to delay. Any extra produce that could be grown would be preserved for the winter to come.

Within 20 paces of the house stood the two-story council house where the master met with the tribes. The agent added repair of the partially burned, partially rebuilt council house to the list of summer tasks. The original council house had been a source of pride for him. The central hexagonal tower, with two wings spanning 70 feet, stood impressively like a gigantic eagle on the edge of the bluff, overlooking the deep river valley. Its central tower echoed the fort's six-sided gun towers. In the early 1830s, the building was set ablaze by an angry Indian.[6] Though it was partially rebuilt, it did not match its previous grandeur. The building's second story was inhabited by Scott Campbell, the agency interpreter and his large Métis family. Part Scottish, part Sioux, Campbell was the master's right-hand man and key to communicating with the Sioux tribes. In the evenings, Campbell sat on the council house porch watching the river and smoking his pipe.[7]

About a mile distant from the agency house was another set of tumbledown buildings, where the blacksmith lived and kept his forge. A stable was probably still standing, ready to receive whatever livestock the Taliaferros brought along.[8]

This painting of Fort Snelling, a view from Mendota, depicts the agency house to the left of the fort (surrounded by a fence). The stables can be seen between the agency house and the fort. The Indian Council House does not appear in the painting and may have been washed off the bluff by the time this rendering was painted. Sibley's house is the large house in the foreground. This Edward K. Thomas painting is dated between 1836 and 1842. *Minnesota Historical Society.*

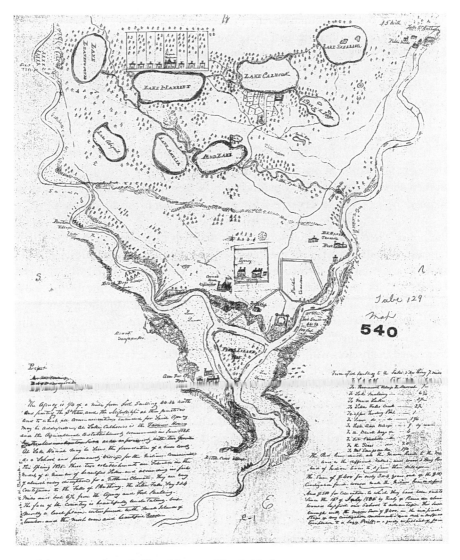

Hand-drawn map of Fort Snelling. *Minnesota Historical Society.*

Within this handful of run-down buildings on the vast, treeless prairie bluff high above the river, the bound servants sought their own private spaces. If there had been a shed to house the servants, it was least likely to have been kept in repair. It may well have been salvaged as plank by 1835 when Harriet arrived at St. Peter's Agency.[9] The slave men and boys probably slept in the stable, with the horses and cows. Assigning a servant to bed down near the livestock was prudent. Local settlers sometimes lost animals to theft. The master trusted that the Indians would not bother *his* animals,[10] but there were other predators on the prairie. That slave men and women slept in different places was merely a function of their division of tasks. The women weren't protected from the heavy work or cleaning the barn. It was simply expedient that slave women like Harriet, slightly over five feet tall, were replaced whenever someone larger or stronger was available for the heavier tasks.

Slaves not assigned to the stables usually slept in the basement kitchen on a common pallet of rags, set out each night in front of the open fire. This way they could tend the fires early in the dawn to warm the house, especially when the weather was particularly cold.

The below-ground kitchen of the agency house had its own separate entrance, located at the bottom of a set of steps that descended into the ground.[11] The servant women shuttled prepared food outdoors, up these stairs, around the back, and in through the back door to serve the Taliaferros their dinner in the dining room.

Although the design was intended to keep smoke and cooking odors out of the house, there were gaps, at some points one-half inch wide, in the floors that separated the basement from the first floor. The raw boards, laid sufficiently far apart to accommodate shrinkage and expansion, were then covered with carpets. For the serving women who lived below, the gaps in the floor meant that dust showered down on them whenever anyone walked overhead. Moreover, sound was apt to travel between the floors as easily as within the same room. Downstairs servants soon learned from their masters above to be quiet. But the masters rarely concerned themselves with the fact that the downstairs servants might be able to hear every word they said.

Mrs. Taliaferro was mistress of the household, director of Harriet's daily tasks, and the person whose comfort justified bringing the maid servants west. Harriet and Eliza were there to cushion her from the hardest or least desirable tasks that the frontier demanded for survival. Few gentlemen or officers brought wives to the frontier without also bringing servants to allow their wives to live as befitted their status as ladies.[12] Frontier officers often sought black servants from the St. Louis slave market when they married or traveled to remote posts with their families.[13]

Elizabeth Dillon Taliaferro, the agent's wife, had fair skin and dark eyes. She was pretty, well-mannered, and wore her long glistening black hair in loopy sausage curls that framed her face.[14] Though she was demure, she enjoyed riding and had brought her lady's sidesaddle as well as her piano. As a Pennsylvania innkeeper's daughter, she received many compliments on her table and her household's organization.[15]

The serving women were as much involved in grooming their mistress for the day as in the household chores. The mistress probably preferred long-serving Eliza to Harriet for the personal matter of dressing. Servants were called upon to brush their mistresses' hair, roll it in rags, fuss with the many troublesome hooks that did up their dresses, and lace their waists into stays before they could descend the stairs to their breakfast tables.[16] Contemporary etiquette books stated, "It is not good taste for a lady to appear at the table in the morning without being laced at all; it gives an air of untidiness to the whole appearance."[17] Nothing about the mistress tolerated untidiness.

What little ladies' society existed at St. Peter's was composed of only four women: Mrs. Taliaferro; the equally genteel commandant's wife, Mrs. Bliss; the stolid captain's wife, Mrs. Loomis; and her newly married, 16-year-old daughter.[18] Miss Loomis was married by a Presbyterian missionary minister who arrived with the Taliaferros aboard the *Warrior*, seeking to establish a church in the area. As the only marriageable young lady at the fort full of officers and soldiers, Miss Loomis had had her pick of beaus the previous winter. Her father's subordinate, Lt. Ogden, had faithfully attended the prayer meetings that her father led and submitted to baptism in order to win her favor and her father's approval.[19] By virtue of her new stature as a married woman, the new Mrs. Ogden was now mistress of her own household and initiated with new respect into the ladies' society while the three senior married ladies could be expected to instruct her in the dimensions of her new status. Ladies were always addressed with the "Mrs." preceding their name. In speaking of their husbands—as the ladies' circle inevitably did—good manners required them to use their own husbands' formal title: "the major" or "the captain."[20]

The commandant's wife welcomed Mrs. Taliaferro's return. Mrs. Bliss saw herself stranded at this remote outpost with only her young son for company. With well-trained servants in both households to undertake the most burdensome chores, the ladies could manage their days and still enjoy some leisure in visiting, reading, working needlepoint, or playing the piano. When the mistress joined the other ladies at the post, she brought the gift of news, gossip, new recipes, and fashions from the East.[21] Each tidbit of news could be delicately tasted, savored, examined, and discussed over tea and cakes served by one of the ladies' black maids. The arriving domestics soon noted the absence of Fanny, the "high yellow" slave woman from the commandant's household. The Bliss boy told them that Fanny had become too much the favorite of the enlisted men, who had begun to hang around the commandant's kitchen. The commandant sent Fanny back to St. Louis to be sold.[22] This must have served as a warning to adolescent Harriet to avoid becoming too familiar with the soldiers. It also indicated the limits of behavioral norms, even on the wilderness frontier. Certain license would not be tolerated.

The Blisses' other manservant, Hannibal, had experienced his own misadventure over the winter. He had brewed a batch of beer from the buds of spruce trees and sold it to the soldiers. When the beer was discovered, both his master and the fort's sutler, who held the only legal franchise to sell alcohol at the post, were infuriated. For his enterprise, Hannibal was confined to a large pit in the ground for two days. Post commandants were nicknamed by the men for the kinds of disciplinary punishments they meted out, and behind his back, Major Bliss was known as "the black hole." He meted out the same punishment to Hannibal that he did to a soldier for insubordination.[23]

Over the winter that Indian Agent Taliaferro had been absent, two incidents had occurred that demanded his immediate attention. Although not a law man in the conventional sense, the Indian agent was called upon to dispense whatever frontier justice was possible. His effectiveness was determined by whether the rules he laid down were followed. The resolution would be a success if the disputants accepted his decision and he managed to avoid further bloodshed. Success was measured in peace and stability. Though vested with official government author-ity, he had no means to enforce his decisions nor any authority over the troops at the fort. He could request military involvement when he could persuade the commandant who controlled the troops. The first matter pressing for the agent's attention was the more significant as it threatened war between the Indian nations. Open hostilities had broken out again between the Sioux and the Chippewa. As the two tribes hunted together in an area of contested grounds near Lac qui Parle, the Sioux had killed several Chippewa. The Ojibwa chief arrived with a delegation of his people in a magnificent flotilla of birch bark canoes to report his views of the hostilities.

The Chippewa chief, Hole-in-the-Day, was an elegant and well-mannered spokesman for his people. Although still a young man, he had already been chief for five years.[24] He was not particularly tall, and as an Ojibwa, shorter than most Sioux. He also dressed plainly, unlike the young warriors who festooned them-selves with eye-catching paint and feathers. Rather, his personality made him stand out. He was intelligent, clear of focus, and ambitious, but his true effective-ness lay in his oratory. He could dominate any ritual performance with eloquence and passionate delivery. On one memorable occasion, he had responded crisply to Governor Cass that the Ojibwa claimed the Sioux lands by right of conquest, just as the Americans had won land from the British. This quickness of wit, analogy, and oratorical skill made him leader of his tribe.[25]

This day, Chief Hole-in-the-Day described the Sioux attack. He said that although the two nations had hunted together and shared meat with each other, "When [most of] our people had left to return home and we were few in num-ber, they came and killed us. The trader, Mr. Renville has been there."[26] As the Chippewa chief spoke, the local Spirit Lake band of Sioux, who were present in council, listened attentively. The Ojibwa chief tactfully emphasized that the local tribe was not to blame. It was another band of Sioux, the Wahpeton, who had killed seven of his people.[27]

After Chief Hole-in-the-Day presented his grievance, he proposed, "Our lines ought to be run in peace.... [O]ur people's hearts are sore and they don't know but what they will go to war. It is a good thing to have our lands marked off."[28] Indian Agent Taliaferro acknowledged the Ojibwa chief's report, assured him that a gov-ernment surveyor was coming soon to mark a boundary between the two nations and gave him some trade goods to acknowledge his visit.[29]

The killings had taken place near the house and trading post of Joseph Renville, a well-established French Métis man with a large family. Like most French traders, Renville was part Indian. His trading post at Lac qui Parle was always surrounded by loyal Dakota tribesmen who were his kin and who as hunters had helped him develop a small commercial empire.[30] The seriousness of the incident required Mr. Renville's side of the story, and he arrived in a few days' time.[31]

Chief Hole-in-the-Day was direct in proposing reciprocity: "Let us give up a man for a man, a woman for a woman. If we kill the Sioux, take our people. If the Sioux kill us, they must give them up." The chief implored the Indian agent, "This is the only way to stop the spilling of blood. You can never keep the peace [otherwise]." To Renville, the chief demanded, "Deliver up three of your people to be punished."[32]

Mr. Renville remained silent. A Sioux partisan who expected to be on the receiving end in this round of retribution responded in favor of boundaries, voicing the usual Sioux complaint that the Ojibwa were the intruders on Sioux lands. "We can never have peace until each stays on his own land. I am a soldier. I claim the land as my father did. I will do the work of a soldier regarding those lands."[33]

Agent Taliaferro always heard everyone out and waited until last to speak. Rising to his feet, he addressed the gathering with characteristic solemnity. "I hold the treaty in my hands which you all made in 1825."[34] He paused for emphasis. "The Sioux have done wrong and deserve to be punished....A man for a man and a woman for a woman. Let each nation surrender and then we may have a firm peace. Sioux, you have endangered the life of your friend, Mr. Renville. He has been of great usefulness to you, but the Indian agency may now have to remove his trade."[35]

To remove a licensed trader was one of the strongest sanctions that an Indian agent controlled and a powerful threat to keeping the tribe in line. (Tribes had come to depend upon their traders to supply them with Western goods.) Taliaferro agreed that the best long-term solution was to divide the nations' territories and keep a neutral ground (with as much distance as possible) between them. Just such a neutral territory was established to the south to separate the Sioux nation from the Sac and Fox. A similar boundary between Sioux and Ojibwa lands had been contemplated for some time, though the survey party was slow in coming.

Maintaining the peace with Indian nations was the agent's primary mission, but his day-to-day work consisted of regular contact with the chiefs, delegations, and individuals, listening to the grievances of anyone who came to complain and supplying visitors with the goods they were entitled to under the treaties. This duty, that he called "carrying on the trade with the Indians," meant enforcement of the intercourse acts, making sure that trade with the Indians was carried out according to U.S. laws.[36] Beyond the internecine trader dispute and the possibility of an impending war between the Sioux and the Ojibwa, Harriet's master, the de facto law maker for the region, was also called upon to settle domestic matters of civilians in the area. His advice was sought whenever disputes arose.

After the Ojibwa left, two of the local bands of Spirit Lake Sioux asked him to mediate a dispute over a woman. Some men from the Sixes band had forcefully abducted a Little Crow woman. Both sides turned to the agent, Harriet's master. Like resolving an argument over a horse, he announced an amicable resolution allowing the woman to live with one tribe and threw in 25 plugs of tobacco and one blanket to assuage the other tribe.[37]

Over the next four years, watching her master mete out justice, Harriet probably came to see how the principal actors in this new place regarded him. The Sioux customarily gave people multiple names, so in addition to Muzzah-Bak-sah, "Iron Cutter," they called him "Four Hearts."[38] The four hearts represented his concern for the four peoples resident in the area: the two Indian nations, the Métis settlers, and the American soldiers. It is reasonable to assume that Taliaferro was Harriet's first tutor in the expectation of fairness, prudence, and the limits of law. She had to follow his direction, not only because she was his slave and his servant but also because her survival depended upon his success in navigating the strange environment surrounding them. She opened the agency door to gentlemen and strangers who called at the house, and she must have learned to distinguish the many Indians who frequented the agency. As she was his dependent, it was imperative that she adapt to his proper protocol so that she did nothing that interfered with his mission and so that she maintained his favor. He was also a man who could not help but bring his concerns home, and as he discussed daily events over the evening fire, she probably heard him expound through the gaps in the dining room floorboards.

The second matter pressing on the master's attention was minor, but it would bring the man he would come to see as his nemesis to his door. When a hired man named Wells distributed traps left at the government sawmill to Indians, the American Fur Company accused him of theft. The fur company's new manager came to see Agent Taliaferro to file a complaint against Wells. If the claim was true, Taliaferro would require Wells to pay for the traps. The new company manager, however, wanted more: revocation of the man's trading license, which would put him out of business completely. The American Fur Company systematically discouraged any other independent traders who might cut into their profits and by now they had successfully eliminated their principal institutional competitor, the Columbia Fur Company.[39]

The company's new local manager, 24-year-old Henry Sibley,[40] paid his first visit to the agent demanding that the offender's license be revoked. Sibley's liquid eyes and passive countenance gave him the appearance of sincerity. Like Taliaferro, he had a stately bearing and was meticulous about his appearance.[41] This was the agent's first opportunity to take the measure of the enterprising young man who would rival his authority in the region.

Sibley had arrived in the area the preceding October, after Taliaferro had left for the winter. He had been handpicked by the company's principal men to replace the increasingly troublesome local manager Alexis Bailley.[42] While Bailley wouldn't sell out to other company men, Sibley had succeeded in cajoling Bailley into selling him his shares of the company. Sibley split the profits with the company's principal men and became a junior partner in the American Fur Company.[43]

Three men, Sibley near Fort Snelling, and Joseph Rolette and Hercules Dousman in Prairie du Chien, now controlled the company's regional franchise. The company headquarters was in New York City, though its domain spread from Detroit to the Oregon coast. John Jacob Astor, the company's founder, having made his vast riches, had sold out to Ramsey Crooks, who succeeded him as managing partner and ran the company from New York for the next decade.[44] Sibley could not have become the local manager without New York approval.[45] The company groomed ambitious young men like Sibley for positions of higher management. Meanwhile, another ambitious young man, John F. A. Sanford, the man Harriet would eventually battle for freedom, was also moving up in the ranks of the powerful company.[46] For the time being, Harriet had no relationship to Sanford, but young Sibley and the company would come increasingly within the household's focus of attention in the next few years.

Young Sibley was accustomed to the good life that his social position offered. Born in Michigan territory, the son of a justice of the Michigan Supreme Court, he had received a classical education and studied law, but he decided that he preferred hunting and a life of action in the outdoors. He smoked cigars, but only good ones. An opportunity to prepare the books for the American Fur Company at Sault Sainte Marie fell into his lap and, succeeding at that task, he was recruited to replace the troublesome Bailley as manager of the fur collection post on the upper Mississippi River.[47] After Sibley bought out Bailley, he commissioned a large stone house to be built at a place called Mendota, on the river's west bank, across the valley from the fort and the agency, and he developed a network of fur trade contacts. Each year, thousands of fur pelts from the upper Mississippi were collected, counted, sorted, and packed there before they were shipped downriver to St. Louis. At Mendota, Sibley began building a bachelor's domain, a sort of empire for himself in the wilderness. Throughout his life, Sibley maintained the aura of someone "to the manor born," even if that manor was located on the frontier.

The matter of the stolen traps was Sibley's first encounter with Taliaferro. Sibley was savvy enough to realize that his predecessor's whiskey fiasco the previous year reflected badly on the company and threatened the warm relationship that the company enjoyed within the fort's protection. Soldiers drunk on the company's whiskey had threatened mutiny. In the present situation, Sibley needed to make a gesture that was both law-abiding and insisted on justice for his own interests. A calculated offense was a good defense, taken, in this case, against a weaker interloper like Wells. Sibley was a very skilled chess player[48] and apparently brought the same sense of strategy to his business dealings. Sibley visited Taliaferro several times that month to press the matter. After each visit, a perceptive servant might have observed the way the visitor behaved after leaving her master's presence, reading an emotion from a sly smile, a twitch, or a shrug of the shoulders as the visitor mounted his horse and rode away—perhaps gleaning more than her master could see. Whether Harriet or Eliza held the door, they might have discussed the day's visitors at their own late evening fireside. Did they sense early on what a formidable force Mr. Sibley would become in their master's plans for Indian autonomy and well-being?

Through these visits, the young company man established his own credibility with the Indian agent and distanced himself from his predecessor's mismanagement. From Prairie du Chien, the ousted Alexis Bailley filed suit against the agent for seizing his whiskey shipment. The other company partners quietly informed Taliaferro that they did not intend to join the suit and were willing to set Bailley adrift, and the whiskey fiasco with him.

During one visit, Sibley tactically asked whether the government intended to continue the previous year's practice of searching the company's boats for whiskey. Schooled in the code of honor among Virginia gentlemen, Lawrence Taliaferro responded accordingly. "Your word of honor, Mr. Sibley, that the law shall not be violated by the introduction of prohibited articles and you may rest assured of never having a visit from me or by my authority."[49]

Mr. Sibley replied, "I should be pleased at all times that you will communicate with me in case of any reports of our people or if you hear of any improper proceedings at any time in the country."

"I shall certainly do so."[50]

With this gentlemen's agreement, the two men resolved the first move of what would become a match of deepening intensity. At stake in the coming years was the fate of the Indians and the measure of influence wielded by the company within the territory. Master Taliaferro, a proper Virginia gentleman, expected much of this gentlemen's agreement with the young company partner. On the other hand, Henry Sibley, student of law and son of a territorial judge, knew that legally the agreement promised nothing. Sibley had managed to secure the guarantee that boats bringing him supplies would not be inspected for liquor. Whether Sibley did import liquor for the Indians, the Fur Company was not averse to asking him whether he could help find someone to smuggle liquor into the United States for the Indians when it later suited their purposes.[51]

Henry Sibley, who managed the fur company in the Minnesota region was the first fur company man whom Harriet encountered, but he would not be the last. Ultimately, Harriet's lawsuit for freedom would pit her against Sanford after he became the company's New York power broker, more important in the company than even Sibley, and, as she watched events transpire between her master and the American Fur Company, she might have gained some sense of the power associated with the name Sanford: John F. A. Sanford. Like her master, her strength would be a guiding sense of justice.

CHAPTER 4

Entertaining Guests at the Indian Agency

ARRIVING WITH THE Taliaferros aboard the *Warrior* was the Reverend Thomas Williamson, an ordained Presbyterian missionary who had contacted Taliaferro months before, offering his services to teach the Indians. He arrived in advance of his family to check the location. Taliaferro decided that a minister in residence at Lac qui Parle would be a reliable source of information in monitoring the conflict between the two Indian nations. To pursue this course of missionary "diplomacy," the agent needed the cooperation of the trader Joseph Renville, who maintained a large household at Lac qui Parle.

Within a few days, he invited Mr. Renville to dine with him. The evening's purpose was to persuade him into extending his protection to the missionary's family. This was the first of many formal dinners that Harriet and Eliza prepared for the master's guests. Mr. Renville was, of course, flattered by the invitation and well pleased to be offered a dinner prepared with provisions brought from below. As innkeeper, Humphrey Dillon's daughter, the mistress took special pride in her hospitality.[1] The serving women must have labored all day below ground to prepare a feast from the precious stores and whatever fresh meat was available. The master usually served Madeira wine that he kept on hand for special occasions.[2]

As the Taliaferros plied their guest with imported foods, different communities took their repast at different places on the prairie. Just below the bluff, on the banks of the St. Peter's, some 12 lodges of Sioux from Lake Calhoun had pitched their tepees to subsist for a time on the ground potato, a root they gathered from the beds of shallow waters. At the fort, the soldiers ate the same meal served them every day: meat, gravy soup, and flat bread. For Harriet and the other servants, their own meal had to wait until they had cleared, washed, and put away the dishes and remaining food; only then were they free to cook their ground cornmeal and pork fat. Foods prepared for the main table were saved for the principal persons of the household; it was not customary for slaves to share in the main table's leftovers.[3] Each group on the prairie met its common hunger separately, subsisting on the different grades of sustenance within its access, occupying different niches in the food chain. The wide open new American frontier was already stratified by consumption patterns. To find her way, Harriet needed to discern her place and its limitations within the existing social structure.[4]

The dinner appeared to achieve its purpose because Joseph Renville welcomed Reverend Williamson to settle near him at Lac qui Parle. Reverend Williamson's was only the second missionary initiative in the area and the first one backed by an established church.[5] Religious evangelism was booming in America in the mid-1830s—at Fort Snelling as elsewhere.[6] The previous year two idealistic young men, the Pond brothers, had paddled up to St. Peter's to begin a lay ministry to the Sioux. Taliaferro had sponsored them at Cloudman's village, the Indian agent's agricultural experiment, where he hoped to convert the nomadic Sioux into yeoman farmers. The elder Pond brother, Samuel, was taller and skinnier, and the scholar of the two. The Indians called him "Red Eagle." They called younger, stronger, and rounder Gideon "Grizzly Bear."[7]

During their first year, the Pond brothers had impressed the local people with their boyish sincerity, if not necessarily the prudence of their endeavor. The fort's surgeon described them as "thorough Yankees from Connecticut." "They appear to have but little education and from their appearance have just left the plough to embark on this design. They have no connection with the missionary societies, but have engaged on it on their own bottom.... They have taken up their abode with a band of Indians at Lake Calhoun, living like them on boiled corn with grease or tallow or in the absence of that on dogs' meat, roasted ground hogs, muskrats, or raccoons...anything that is found in earth, air or water."[8] Still they had built a cabin, killed several wolves, and stuck it out through a particularly long hard winter. For Taliaferro, the arrival of these young idealist men, who were a positive influence for the Dakota, was a dream come true.

The Taliaferros were Presbyterians like Reverend Williamson,[9] but Taliaferro seemed virtually untouched by the spiritual revival that animated others to come west as missionaries. Harriet's master kept Sabbath when he could, although not as strictly as some. He was a pragmatic man, and he noted that often the most important transactions seemed to occur on Sundays.[10] He may have been present when the church formed at the fort, although a diary entry suggesting that 70 Indians appeared at his door requesting council that day may have kept him otherwise occupied.[11] He supported most missionary efforts to the Indians. The Ponds, the Williamsons, and later other Protestant missionaries all received his permission and encouragement to settle in the area, but his emphasis was less one of encouraging religious conversion than it was of mediating against the dominating suasion of the other, more renegade white men, particularly the fur traders. He saw missionaries as a positive civilizing influence, who helped improve the material conditions of those individuals he called "his children."

The agent wrote extensively in his diary about politics and hunger, but rarely of religion, except for rather standard invocations of God. The only concession in Taliaferro's diaries to the religious fervor during this period is his reference to Indian persons, particularly in times of suffering or death, as "souls." "Souls" were synonymous with human beings in his eyes.[12] The term connoted a certain respect and the innate spiritual worth of the people he called his children.

Harriet too was a Christian woman and at some point, she joined the African Baptist church. The African church in Bedford, Pennsylvania served the 57 colored people in the town. Attending church was a privilege allowed to both indentured servants and free blacks in Bedford. On the frontier, those living on the edge of survival—the Métis families, servants, and slaves—could not necessarily afford the privilege of resting on the Sabbath. To spend an entire Sunday at rest was a luxury, whereas survival required continual effort. In later decades, when individuals from the area's small black population did join churches, they tended to form their own separate churches rather than join the established Presbyterian church of Sibley, Reverend Williamson, and the Pond brothers.[13]

For all their efforts to convert the "heathen savage," the missionaries showed little interest in the black servant population. Most of this wave of New England–born missionaries neither brought slaves with them nor sought to acquire them, like many of the New England–born military officers did. This was either a matter of economy or faith.[14] The domestic labor necessary to maintain the missionaries was done, for the most part, by missionary wives and by unmarried sisters brought along to maintain the household.[15] When the missionary women later sought to teach Indian women to assist them in housework, they met with much frustration and little success.[16] One missionary stated the dilemma: "No good, decent [Indian] woman could be found willing to do for white people what they did not do for themselves."[17] Black servants brought west were accultured to settlement habits and skills and often excelled at them.

As the summer days passed, the Indians encamped around the agency awaiting the steamboat with the annuities. The ship had not returned.[18] By the second week of June, when the season's supply of ground potato had run out, the Indians complained of hunger. They begged for food at the agency house every day. Word arrived from downstream that the *Warrior* had reached Prairie du Chien again but had turned back without proceeding on to St. Peter's. This was more than a slight setback. Taliaferro dug into his private household stores to try to alleviate the Indians' hunger. At his directive, the servant women probably fetched the rations from the basement pantry. This was another way that Harriet and Eliza may have been integrated into their master's specialized mission of caring for the Indians. It was unthinkable that a genteel lady like Mrs. Taliaferro would fetch food rations for the Indians. The agent reported issuing 59 rations of pork and 59 pounds of flour.[19] Each ration was exactly measured and counted: exactly 59 portions, not 60. The household food stores were probably kept in the basement kitchen separate from the other agency commodities because food was such an immediate target for hungry people.[20]

No steamboat meant no annuity at the usual season. The Dakota had expected their hunting supplies to be replenished by the end of May, in time to hunt buffalo on the western plains. Delay disrupted their hunting cycle and jeopardized their annual pattern of sustenance. The Indians could borrow only by incurring debt from the traders, which they would have to make up for out of furs that they brought in later in the year. The agent was running out of excuses as more Indians showed up at the agency in search of the long overdue supplies. Every day, Indians appeared at the door imploring him to produce the boat. Taliaferro wrote in his diary that "To go out to hunt is for them to go off to starve."[21]

In June, Wah-paa-koota's tribe of 80, who were encamped nearby, performed the buffalo dance.[22] Taliaferro regarded the dance primarily as diversion for the Indians from their incessant hunger. For the dancers, the buffalo dance was intended to compel the spirits to send them food.[23] The dancers danced, and still the steamboat did not come.

The Indians' starvation must have disturbed the servants, since their own daily rations were more at risk than food for the household's principal members. The servants, like the enlisted men, received a single ration a day. Even more worrisome, extreme hunger sometimes drove people to extreme behaviors. It was said that a starving, emaciated Dakota woman had once grabbed the flesh on the arm of a black woman servant menacingly. An officer who chanced to witness the incident spread the story that the hungry Dakota woman was driven to cannibalism.[24]

Rain continued through June that year, requiring the maidservants to keep fires in the house. On the 18th, such a hard rain fell that the master even allowed some Indians to sleep in parts of the house. This was an extraordinary gesture for Taliaferro, since he was a man of considerable reserve and generally preferred to keep more distance between himself and the tribes. He usually encountered the Indians at his office, the council house, or the doorway threshold. Indians were sometimes known to enter cabins unannounced,[25] ignoring the privacy signaled by a closed door and startling the occupants—a practice that the agent didn't want to encourage. Still, offering them a dry place to spend the night must have seemed the smallest of comforts he could provide in the absence of food.

With so many hungry Indians milling around the place, dissatisfied over the annuities delay, Harriet and Eliza may have found it unsettling to have them sleeping in the house. Living in the low basement kitchen, the servants must have been acutely aware of the activity upstairs. The kitchen's separate entrance allowed the servants to keep the Indians and other dangers at bay. But now the Indians actually slept overhead.

With nothing more to offer the tribes encamped on their doorstep, the Taliaferros went riding into the countryside. The agent rarely traveled far from the agency compound while he was in residence. He preferred to be ready at the agency, should anything arise. He depended on informants and the steady stream of visitors for news about what was going on in the Indian territory. The rare times when he left the compound were one-day excursions to picnic and fish at the Falls of St. Anthony or to inspect the progress of the Dakota at the nearby agricultural community. At these moments he derived some distance, some perspective from the incessant press of human want that often confronted him at the agency. There he could also check in on Mary, his only child and the daughter of an Indian woman. Mary was just turning seven.

Taliaferro's journal was notably circumspect on the subject of his daughter. The little girl was the grandchild of Chief Cloudman, the hunter turned farmer whom Taliaferro had designated as chief. Only occasionally did he write about "certain children" at the lakes although never about her mother, his former lover. It was a subject that embarrassed him,[26] although he accepted responsibility for his daughter. Seven-year-old Mary was one of several children left with their Dakota mothers when their officer fathers transferred out.[27] Taliaferro felt honor-bound to serve as guardian for all of them. He wrote to their fathers, sometimes informing them of their children's circumstances and sometimes seeking special support for them.[28] Thus, he looked in on them whenever he rode out to the agricultural settlement.

On the ride that summer day in 1835, he espied several Indian women at work in the fields and challenged them to a friendly competition. He promised to reward with a new blanket the woman who had the cleanest field; each of the others would receive a present as well depending upon their efforts. This was the kind of role that Harriet's master enjoyed most: rewarding his children for the merit of their industry.

TWO LONG-EXPECTED ARRIVALS at the agency finally put the household at ease. The first was a government survey party prepared to set a boundary between Sioux and Ojibwa lands.[29] It was hoped that the survey would bring peace. More important, the steamboat *Warrior* finally returned with the necessary supplies and an entire load of passengers. A light rain fell as it maneuvered to the landing but this was not enough to dampen the curiosity of its passengers. On the upper deck stood a group of young ladies with their umbrellas, excited to catch a glimpse of the fort.[30] The young ladies, who were from the Jacksonville Boarding School in Jacksonville, Illinois, were making a pleasure cruise.[31] The chugging noise of the big ship also called forth some 60 Indians who anticipated finally receiving their promised annuities and other provisions. The Indians regarded the young ladies on the deck with as much curiosity as the young ladies regarded them.[32]

In the ship's hold were the Indians' provisions and supplies of iron for the agency forge, as well as provisions for the fur company outpost across the river at Mendota. Taliaferro lost little time in distributing the goods to the waiting Indians. His rulered lists, written on long sheets of paper, were ready, scrupulously maintained and organized by tribe. He personally handed the appropriate sum to each Indian man who was recognized as the head of a household, had the man make his "x" in the space provided for him, and shook his hand. The custom of shaking hands was relatively new to the Dakota, but they soon learned this settlers' custom.[33]

The *Warrior* also brought the extensive supplies that Henry Sibley had ordered to outfit his new store at Mendota. He planned to outdo his predecessor with a larger store of food supplies and equipment sufficient to last his men and customers all winter: barrels of New Orleans sugar and sticky molasses, salt, dried peaches and apples, 33 barrels of a commodity called "one hog pork," bacon and hams, kegs of lard and tallow, hundreds of sacks and bushels of corn, coffee in bags, and a cracker barrel. For trading with the Indians, Sibley kept entire bales of textiles: woolen blankets, strouding, gaudy colored cloth, guns and traps, and tinware. He also ordered luxury items: a box of single cavendish tobacco, among several kegs of common plug tobacco; British soap for those who did not make their own; 12 barrels of port wine; and five demijohns of sperm oil, a product of whaling ships sent out from Nantucket.[34]

As the soldiers worked alongside the crew to unload the cargo, the tourists disembarked from the upper decks. Tourists were a new phenomenon for St. Peter's. Few had previously ventured north, since the area was considered dangerous during the Blackhawk War. As Indian agent, Taliaferro had to be officially apprised of everyone entering Indian territory, so the steamboat's captain provided him with the roster of arriving passengers. The St. Louis newspapers had recently touted the idea of river travel for pleasure, calling it "the fashionable tour."[35] But never had so many visitors, and particularly so many ladies, journeyed this far upriver.

Among the tourists were one gentleman and lady of particular note: George Catlin, already widely known as *the* famous painter of the West,[36] accompanied by his wife, Clara. Catlin had cultivated an impressive patronage, including William Clark, the superintendent of Indian Affairs and Pierre Chouteau Jr., the St. Louis head of the American Fur Company. Catlin had developed his reputation as the painter of Indian tribes through his early association with John F. A. Sanford, the same man who would become Harriet's adversary in the fight of her life. Three years earlier, the artist had accompanied Sanford, who had been an Indian agent to the Mandan Tribe and stationed on the Missouri. As host, Indian Agent Sanford introduced him to various tribal members, providing him with the inspiration for what would become his life's work: painting portraits of Indians throughout the West.[37] Since then, the painter had visited several different outposts to sketch Native American peoples in their variety. This was probably the first time that Sanford's name was mentioned in the Taliaferro household (and perhaps the first time Harriet would hear of him), a name dropped by Catlin as he socialized with Harriet's master that summer.

Catlin sold images of the West to Easterners and even to Europeans, who sought to see the human face of the frontier savage. As a matter of masculine bravado and self-promotion, he made a point of informing the public that the West was no place for ladies.[38] He said he was accustomed to traveling the wilderness by himself, but in actuality he usually accompanied others such as Sanford, Chouteau, and Henry Dodge on their various forays into Indian country. As a storyteller, he recounted these expeditions, telling of narrowly escaping death and witnessing exotic ceremonies that were inappropriate for the delicate eyes of ladies. Like many frontier entrepreneurs, he promoted his brand by rendering the West wilder and woollier in telling the story.

The new convenience of steamboat travel meant that the upper Mississippi was a destination that ladies could comfortably visit. Thus, it was no coincidence that Catlin was joined on this trip not only by his wife, Clara, but also by a bevy of young school-aged ladies on a summer pleasure cruise from school, chaperoned by respectable matrons. No doubt, the group included several slave women, necessary to attend to their mistresses' trunks, tresses, and dressing. Though slavery had been illegal in the territory since 1789, families of this status, like the Joseph Street family of Prairie du Chien, customarily retained black servants indentured for life.

When the ship docked, the ladies went ashore to explore the port of call. Primary among the attractions at St. Peter's was the impressive stone fortress, "the Colossus of the River," the only one of its kind on the Mississippi, and the beautiful sheer drop falls of St. Anthony. What the waterfalls offered in natural wilderness appeal, the agency offered in exotic local culture. At the agency, travelers could see Indians still living in much the customary way.[39] Even though the local Mdewakanton tribes no longer wore handmade leather garments, the tribal peoples at St. Peter's Agency were as close to living their traditional lifestyles as any within reach of steamboat. On the lower stretches of the great river, like Prairie du Chien, most tribes had already become dependent supplicants, living at the edge of forts and towns. Now destitute, as beggars they had lost their appeal.[40] The St. Peter's Agency offered contact with that more picturesque independent Native American lifestyle that Americans envisioned as representing the true West.[41]

George Catlin came both for pleasure and business. The Catlins disembarked so that George could have a month of painting to complete his visual compendium of Indian portraiture. The commandant's wife, delighted to have company, invited them to stay at the commandant's quarters at the fort.

Taliaferro was also very much taken with the artist and his project. He wrote that Catlin would "open the sluicegates of knowledge" about the Indians to the nation and the world.[42] To assist him, the agent introduced Catlin to the Indians as a powerful medicine man. The artist set up his easel and began work painting some Ojibwa men who were visiting the agency and seemed flattered to have their portraits done.

Catlin basically selected his subjects by their dress and adornment. One of his subjects, an Ojibwa warrior, whom he deemed a dandy,[43] appears to be specially groomed for the sitting: bare-chested, wearing bead necklaces and, of course, a large medal bearing the image of a president's head. His shoulder-length hair and bangs are slicked down with red paint and his arms are painted with red symbols. His headdress has feathers pointing straight up and two plumes curling provocatively forward over his head like a rooster's comb. Another day, Catlin painted the Black Dog, a local Mdewakanton chief. The old chief stares out sadly from his painting. His eyes stand out because the lower half of his face is blackened and fades from view. His face paint highlights searching eyes beneath drooping heavy lids—earnest, sad, doubting, but also hoping to believe. Around his neck he too wears the ubiquitous president's medal of loyalty.

While Catlin painted, his wife sat quietly at his side. Learning that she was *enceinte* (as the French said) with their first child, she restricted her activities. When Mrs. Catlin walked between the fort and the agency, Ojibwa women crowded around her, offering cones of maple-sugar for sale.[44] One woman carried a baby, strapped to her back in a bentwood cradle. A crosspiece protected the baby's head and held beads to entertain the child. The Dakota also strapped their children on their backs, but with less access to wood on the prairie, they were more apt to fashion their carriers from softened leather hides. It may have been Clara Catlin, pregnant for the first time, who persuaded her husband to paint the Ojibwa mother and child. George Catlin even purchased a cradle from an Indian mother and engaged in an extensive description of them in his notes.[45]

George Catlin's Ju-ah-kis-gaw, Woman with Her Child in a Cradle. (Ojibwa tribe). 1835. *Smithsonian American Art Museum, Washington, DC / Art Resource, NY.*

Catlin did not paint any Eastern Dakota women, whose dress he found uninteresting. The local Dakota women dressed more plainly than the men, covering themselves simply with close-fitting coats of printed cloth, blue broadcloth skirts, and large blankets year-round. Their government-issued blankets embroidered with colored ribbons, folded and sewn on in zigzags and stripes, were not sufficiently interesting for the widely traveled artist.[46] The Eastern Sioux had already traded away most of their authentic clothing and prized handcrafts to collectors like the post doctor, Dr. Jarvis, for food and medicine.[47] Even Dr. Jarvis now found Eastern Dakota crafts uninteresting. He wrote, "Among the Indians immediately around here, little can be procured in the way of curiosities. Their weapons and utensils, such as they are, are made by the blacksmith of the Indian agency or procured from the Indian traders."[48] The doctor had already obtained many of the Sioux treasures that were not easily replaced. Catlin was so impressed with Dr. Jarvis's collection that he offered to buy it. Each article had been manufactured by hand from raw materials, a process that took an enormous amount of time and concentrated effort. The fur company now bought almost all the furs the Indians captured, so it was a matter of simple economy that they sold the bounty of their hunts and bought cloth to outfit themselves. The nomadic Sioux always seemed to live in the short term.[49]

Catlin's preoccupation with his subjects' appearances drew attention to the details of Indian dress.[50] Harriet must have been struck by how very different their clothing was from her mistress's or even her own. The Dakota women decorated their blankets with bright ribbons and beads. Harriet's own clothes were plainer in color, probably made from a dove-colored, serviceable material called "Negro cloth."[51] In charge of washing the mistress's wardrobe, Harriet and Eliza knew every hook and eye, and dart, of her elaborate dresses, which had to be repaired if they came undone in the washing. The various outfits were sufficiently complicated that the mistress required another person's help when she dressed. Harriet's own tight-waisted dress had far fewer fastenings than her mistress's.

For the Fourth of July, the master sent runners to the nearby villages inviting the Sioux to dance in order to furnish the artist with action scenes. By custom, the runners' message was accompanied by the gift of a plug of tobacco. The agent informed the villages that the great medicine man, Mr. Catlin, would fire the big gun 21 times in honor of the dancers. The fort always celebrated the Fourth of July with a 21-gun salute, so the Indians would not be disappointed.[52]

During the glorious long days of midsummer, couples began to present themselves at the agency, requesting that Taliaferro marry them.[53] Although the Indian agent had licensing authority over civilians entering Indian territory, his legal authority to marry couples was uncertain. Taliaferro had long troubled over whether it was appropriate for him to preside over weddings, given his official charge.[54] Yet, at 2 P.M. on July 3, he decided to perform the first of several weddings at the agency office, as he would eventually marry Harriet to her husband. This day, one of Mr. Sibley's hired men married the Métis daughter of another voyageur. Taliaferro was someone who always rose to the occasion, and he probably improvised remembered elements of his grandfather's Presbyterian preaching style.

On the Fourth of July, several Sioux villages convened at the agency compound to play a competitive ball game for the amusement of Taliaferro's guests. The fort cannon was fired in salute. The Indians greeted each bang with whoops and calls of "waukon"—which meant "marvelous," or "magic."[55] Catlin was already familiar with variations of Indian ball games played by tribes in different parts of the country, and he sketched a couple of players while the game progressed.[56] As an expert observer, he studied what differentiated this locale's custom from others he had seen.

At the game's conclusion, Catlin presented the ballplayers with a barrel of flour, some pork, and tobacco as if they were trophies. Then the Sioux danced in front of the agency. The dances were distinct to the experienced observer, and, by longer exposure, Harriet undoubtedly came to know them. Her master narrated them for Catlin. That day the Sioux performed the beggar's dance, which was usually performed when they were very hungry. Dressed in wolf and dog skins, men, women, and children sang as they sniffed for food among the audience. When it was produced, they danced in gratitude, while some dancers gathered the food in their skirts to be divided for eating later. Catlin stopped sketching briefly during the dance of the braves, which differed from the other Sioux dances because it did not have repetitive steps. Instead, the braves' dance was a free-form expression intended to relate the tribe's history and their current state of existence. The dancers improvised movements, investing them with meaning.[57]

The following week, when another steamboat brought more tourists, the Indians danced the beggar's dance again, sniffing out the new visitors for gifts of food.[58] They also offered to perform the dog dance if the officers gave them two dogs that could be sacrificed. This dance entailed butchering the dogs and placing their hearts and livers on sticks. Only braves who had taken scalps of their enemies' heads could participate. Each danced forward, boasting of his fearlessness, and bit off pieces of the uncooked dog's hearts.[59] Later, 25 Ojibwa arrived in birch bark canoes and danced for the artist outside the agency house. As host of the event, Taliaferro blushed to note that "all things [were] in a state of nature. Nothing on in the shape of dress except their breech clothes and there were...ladies present."[60]

The bands of the Ojibwa nation set up their rounded bark lodges on another stretch of the prairie plateau. Their summer houses were customarily made of bark mounted on portable stick frames, which could be rolled up and repacked for travel.[61] With the Ojibwa's arrival, the Sioux had new competitors for a ball game. Wagers on the outcome sharpened the competition because each village bet so much of their precious goods on the win that neither side could afford to lose. The Sioux staked guns and blankets, while Chippewa wagered bark canoes and sugar.

The Taliaferros considered the many steamboat tourists as their guests, and they gave a grand party in their honor. Such an elaborate affair required several days for the servants to prepare.[62] This was an evening for using the finest glassware, the linen tablecloths, and, of course, Mrs. Taliaferro's black-and-white china, which they had painstakingly transported from Bedford. This was the opportunity for the Taliaferros to entertain in style. Outside of an occasional dinner guest, there were few opportunities for a party. The servants washed and ironed the linens to set the fine table. The silver had to be polished, the table knives sharpened, and the sideboard set with whatever delicacies the frontier and the pantry had to offer. The servant women probably collected the garden produce and baked specialties such as buttermilk biscuits or molasses or fruit sweets for the occasion. The staple of any frontier feast was a buffet of several varieties of meat such as smoked game hens, pheasants, fish, fresh ham, or even homemade sausages.[63]

Social protocol dictated that the evening begin with a series of toasts, each followed by a musical flourish performed by the tiny military band. Etiquette required the host to toast his guests, and in turn they offered toasts to him, to the president, and to the nation. Then came the songs "To the Spirit of '76," followed by "Yankee Doodle," and a toast to the Constitution of the United States followed by the "Star-Spangled Banner." Knowing the protocol of these routines bonded gentlemen strangers.[64]

Harriet likely watched from the sidelines, poised to serve lemonade and strawberries and dressed in her best starched apron.[65] What did the lofty words of the Constitution mean to her? As the household's domestic servant, she probably poured the guests more wine when their glasses needed filling and served out the tiny wild strawberries on Mrs. Taliaferro's well-patterned black and white china. Among the men, Mr. Catlin was brimming with amusing anecdotes gleaned from his extensive travels. The steamboat captain, who was also in attendance, was a talkative man and likely to repeat the story of his role in the Blackhawk War.[66] Visiting tourist General Patterson and Taliaferro shared memories of the War of 1812, a war too early for most of the younger officers to appreciate. Captain Loomis interposed comments on the state of religious revivals in the country. In this way the social groups defined themselves by demography, geography, and affinity of experience.

As the fine summer evening drew on, the guests could drift between the drawing room, dining room, and splendid wooden porch that ran the length of the house—even strolling out onto the grassy bluffs overlooking the river as the sun lingered late into the evening on midsummer nights.

Two days later, the *Warrior* prepared to depart.[67] Aboard were most of the summer visitors, including Mrs. Catlin. Her husband had decided to stay on and paddle downstream in a handsome birch bark canoe he had bought from the Ojibwa. As the summer visitors said their farewells, the agent presented one of his distinguished guests with an Ojibwa peace pipe from his collection.

Indian pipes drew Catlin's attention, since he had observed that similar red stone was used for pipes among many tribes. Wherever he had traveled throughout the West, he noticed that shapes, sizes, and adornment differed, but the pipe bowls were always carved from the same red stone, though he had never seen the source of this particular stone. He fancied himself an amateur geologist.[68] This suggested that the source was in some remote site and was traded throughout Indian territory, implying that all the Indian nations were part of a larger trading network.[69]

Taliaferro knew exactly where the red stone came from. The Sioux revered the red stone quarry as a sacred place. Although he'd never been there himself, it was within his agency's jurisdiction, not too many days' ride west across the plains. Catlin was so struck by the news that he considered setting off to see the quarry, but because his wife was expecting him to meet her downstream, he resolved instead to return another time to see the quarry.[70]

The painter stayed another nine days. Before embarking, Catlin asked the agent to authenticate the portraits he had painted there. It confounded him that he could not get the Indians' names straight. "No Indian will ever volunteer his [own] name.... And most chiefs have a dozen names, which they use according to caprice or circumstance."[71] Catlin didn't realize that the Dakota used personal names differently than did the settler culture. Beyond the handful of common names designating birth order and sex, each member of the tribe acquired a new name with each new distinguishing life circumstance. Persons did not choose their own names but were named by other members of the tribe. They didn't even speak their own names.[72] Names were used in the village discourse to note new achievements of community members, and an individual's multiple names taken together told the story of his life. This living, changing, inventive system didn't fit Catlin's need for taxonomy.

During his month in residence at the agency, at this confluence of waters, the traditional homeland of the Eastern Sioux, Catlin actually painted more Ojibwa. He completed 12 portraits in all, four Sioux and eight Ojibwa, including the mother

George Catlin's Big Eagle (or Black Dog), Chief of the O-hah-kas-ka-toh-y-an-te Band. Eastern Sioux (Dakota). 1835. *Smithsonian American Art Museum, Washington, DC / Art Resource, NY.*

and child. Catlin described the Eastern Sioux as "a sorry contrast" with the Western Sioux on the upper Missouri. "[T]hey're poorly clad and fed." Catlin's mission was to show the world the finest specimens. Agent Taliaferro provided the names that he knew. "He Who Sits Everywhere," "He Who Travels Everywhere," "The Otto-way," *Kaw-baa-mab-ba*," and the local Sioux chief "Black Dog" all became part of Catlin's summer legacy.[73]

The harsh imperatives of tribal economy were not the subject of George Catlin's focus. He painted interesting surfaces. Yet his presence may have given Harriet new insight in observing these new peoples. For example, one could usually distinguish Ojibwa from Sioux by the puckered moccasins they wore.[74] As an impressionable young girl thrown into a puzzling new environment, Harriet may have brought some focus to her perceptions by watching Catlin's attention to details.

Then the painter, accompanied by a corporal as escort, set off slowly paddling the white birch bark canoe with the easy downstream current. At one point, as a final gesture of incongruous domesticity in the wilderness, the artist and the corporal unfurled a large umbrella, held it forward over the bow of the canoe, and let the wind carry the white canoe with the umbrella as a sail.[75]

CHAPTER 5

Late Summer Harvest

NOTHER COUPLE ASKED the agent to marry them in late July. The bride was the eldest daughter of a man named Perry, whose family members were early refugees from the failed utopian community founded by Lord Selkirk on the Red River in Canada, to the north and west.[1] Ten years earlier, when the first refugees had arrived from the Red River, dragging their possessions across the plains, the fort commandant had taken pity on them and allowed them to build cabins and remain, even though the environs were supposed to be a military reserve. Over the intervening decade, a cluster of cabins had been built near the Coldwater Spring, a few miles from the fort. Old man Perry, Abraham Perry, who maintained a large herd of cattle, was regarded as a patriarchal figure in the settlement. His wife was useful as a skilled midwife.[2]

The occasion uniting Sophie Perry in marriage with an enterprising young man drew all the neighbors since there were few reasons for celebration in their hardworn lives.[3] Before the ceremony concluded though, it was interrupted by a large contingent of uninvited guests. Arriving across the prairie were more than a hundred new refugees from the failing Selkirk community. They too had made their way from the Red River, across 700 miles of grass wilderness, to reach St. Peter's Agency.[4] Most were bound even further, for Indiana. This caravan of sunburned and blistered refugee men, women, and children, oxen and sometimes half-tamed buffalo drawing wooden carts, diverted the wedding guests' attention. The Perrys and most of their neighbors had made the same trek with their children a decade earlier. They may even have recognized some of the sojourners. The wedding celebration, further enlivened by the new arrivals, turned into a reunion of kindred spirits, refugees from a similar western ideal. The night was marked by fiddle music, dancing, and large bonfires in the encampments to celebrate both a wedding and the wayfarers' happy arrival at a place of civilization.[5]

It was late before the music finally ended. In the quiet of the night, the cattle and horses were skittish. Then there was a great commotion just outside the agency house. The master's Newfoundland dog barked loudly. The servants may have been the first to see the intruder in the enclosure. The master was roused just in time to grab his rifle and save the dog from attack by a panther.[6] Panthers were very rare indeed in the area. The large cat must have been trailing the trekking refugees, their slow-moving oxen, and large-wheeled carts, circling their camps at night and hoping for carrion or animals left behind. The panther's night visit was a reminder that there were unseen predators following the weak. The maidservants probably tightened the bent-nail latch on the cellar door before returning to their sleeping mat on the kitchen floor.

Just three days later, a second larger caravan of 200 Canadian refugees arrived. This traveling party was composed mostly of Scots. They joined the other wagon team encamped near the fort to rest and water their livestock until they were strong enough to proceed further. St. Peter's was only the second settlement that the trekkers had encountered in several weeks of walking through the high prairie thatch. After traveling for weeks in the wild, the remote fort must have seemed like high civilization: it was a place to make repairs, find a doctor or a sutler with necessary stores, and a source of fresh water and news from the wider world. One Scotsman was dressed in complete highland costume, plaid kilt and bonnet. The curious local Indians, drawn by the prospect of trading with the refugees, reacted with delight that his colorful skirt resembled their own breechcloths.[7]

Across the valley, Sibley hired a refugee couple as domestics. He complained in a letter to his mother that he had to do all of his own cooking and pickling. "Scarcely a day passes that the agent of the Grand Co." as he referred to himself, "is not seen with sleeves rolled up & towel in hand, washing castors or dishes, while his head is busy in devising means to get something to eat." Sibley was not altogether content with his new Canadian housekeepers. He wrote, "the woman is dirty and so are her two small children, whose cries not infrequently go far to disturb the equanimity of even as old a bachelor as myself. In truth, I begin to think seriously of taking unto myself a wife."[8] He dismissed the couple shortly. He later obtained a mulatto man, who he occasionally beat when he was displeased, to cook for him.[9]

In early September, the Taliaferros rode out to the lakes again where a few hundred people of Chief Cloudman's band had taken up farming, now with the Pond brothers' assistance. To Harriet's master, the Pond brothers' arrival was an answer to a prayer. They were hardworking, honest, sincere, and as reform-minded about the Dakota as was he. He arranged for them to teach Big Thunder to plow, a task which they accepted as an ideal entry into the community.[10]

That fall the Pond brothers were joined at the lakes by yet a third missionary venturer and his family. Although the elder brother, Samuel Pond, was making some progress in learning the Dakota language, he did not get along with the newly arrived Reverend Stevens. The learned, officious minister frequently pointed out to the Pond brothers that he was schooled in divinity and they were not.[11] Samuel planned to venture off with the Sioux on their fall deer hunt to learn their language by immersing himself in their survival routine and to get some distance from Reverend Stevens.[12] The Sioux language was a complete enigma to the settlement people. No one at the fort knew even the most basic words without the help of a Métis translator.[13]

One last summer visitor to pass through the Agency was an English geologist, who was leading a small American-sponsored expedition in search of mineral deposits. George Featherstonhaugh (pronounced "fanshaw") made a trip up the St. Peter's River, which the Sioux called the "Minnaysoter."[14] Like the artist Catlin, this geologist was a man of grand ambition. Featherstonhaugh advocated a revolutionary notion for the times: that geology was the science of nature, not of any particular country. He was convinced that American rock formations correlated to those in England.[15] The idea that geology was history rather than national geography was revolutionary.

Featherstonhaugh was accompanied by an American army officer named Lt. Mather, and the two were hardly a compatible team. The disagreements, fueled by the Englishman's sharp tongue and the lieutenant's stubborn stoicism, had grown into true enmity by the time they reached St. Peter's Agency. Mr. Featherstonhaugh sought more comfortable quarters in the fort while Lt. Mather preferred to part ways and camp alone down by the boats. While Featherstonhaugh, a tall, imposing Englishman given to slighting side comments, was a big thinker and man of the world, his military escort, described as a man of solid, good sense, attended to the practical necessities of wilderness travel. The two had disagreed initially on what was necessary to equip the expedition and just about everything that came after. Featherstonhaugh viewed his escort as a puritan Bible-thumper.[16]

One evening in mid September, the Taliaferros invited Featherstonhaugh to dinner. The mistress again took pains to serve their important and worldly guest her table's best. As usual, the servant women spent the day preparing dinner in the basement kitchen and ran out-of-doors between the two floors to serve it.

The master and his guest did not take to each other. For one thing, the War of 1812 stood between them. Taliaferro held a lifelong enmity toward the English, and Featherstonhaugh was "an Englishman in the full force of the term."[17] For another, the geologist had recently visited Henry Schoolcraft, agent to the Ojibwa. Any praising mention of Schoolcraft's name usually raised the master's ire.[18] Still, the geologist traveled under the auspices of the American government and, by his education, he was clearly a man of substance. They talked of Virginia friends they had in common and whom the master had not seen in a long time.[19] The host probed his guest for information from Virginia, a world quite distant. The geologist had also passed through the mistress's home of Bedford Springs on his voyage west, stopping to examine its interesting mineral waters.[20] Stories and information about public opinion and the state of the world were part of the treasure that a traveler brought with him to make himself a welcome guest at far-off settlements.

Perhaps at least as much to show his own importance as to be helpful, the master offered to provide the geologist with letters of introduction to both Mr. Renville, the trader at Lac qui Parle and the missionary whom the master placed nearby. (One can assume that a servant was sent for the quill, the inkwell, and paper so that Taliaferro could write the notes for his guest.) The Englishman was not impressed, later describing Taliaferro as having "less information at the service of the traveler going amongst the Indians than any person I had yet met with occupying his official situation."[21]

Although the English geologist was critical of the master, he praised the mistress as having "a very fair share of personal beauty"[22] and the Taliaferros' household as very comfortable, warm, and welcoming, bestowing further compliment on his hostess. But the mistress could never have accomplished such a living standard on her own without the full-time labors of the two servant women. Domestic servants provided the margin of hospitality and comfort on the wilderness frontier. That night when Featherstonehaugh stumbled off to the fort to sleep he found there was no bed, only a table in an empty spare room. The commandant's wife apologized the next morning that they could not offer him better accommodations because she was temporarily without a domestic servant.[23]

That summer, the master and mistress were at their sociable best. As summer yielded to autumn, the master mused on the summer's visitors: an artist, an industrialist, and a geologist: "We attend to gentleman fond of field sports & good hunting. We are decidedly averse to black legs, steam doctors, pick pockets, Abolitionists, kidnappers, & whisky introducers." In 1835, abolitionists, in the master's mind, were charlatans like the rest.[24]

In early autumn, Taliaferro learned from the commandant something about one of his dinner guests that shocked him. The depth of his reaction reveals how his beliefs about race permeated his judgment. Major Bliss had ascertained that Joseph Renville, the supposed half-French, half-Dakota fur trader with the large house and following at Lac qui Parle, was, in fact, as the master wrote in his diary, "a full Indian."[25] Renville wasn't French at all; he just passed as French. The bond, the co-conspiracy of race, that the master thought he shared with Renville as partners in cultivating Western civilization among the Dakota dissolved instantly with this information. The Taliaferros had invited him to a splendid dinner to get him to protect the Reverend Williamson's mission. They didn't invite "full Indians" to dine at their table. The master had discussed the Lac qui Parle Dakota—the "other"—as a people to be encouraged but, like wild things, regarded with some distance and watched carefully. Now that Taliaferro knew that Renville was "one of them," he saw the folly of his threat to remove Renville's trading post from the Lac Qui Parle tribe—as if Renville was a white man who could be pulled if the Indians misbehaved. A Dakota man neither needed a trading license nor could be removed from his own nation. Renville had passed so successfully that Agent Taliaferro now considered him an impostor. Embarrassed by his own mistake, the agent shifted his reliance to the Reverend Williamson in dealing with the Dakota in that critical area. Race made all the difference in how much he trusted someone with his agenda.

The season's last keelboat arrived on September 27, bringing up Lt. Storer's and the sutler's families—who planned to stay the winter. Both of the wives were from fur trade families. Lieutenant Storer's bride was the youngest daughter of the principal French trader at Prairie du Chien.[26] They were married by a priest in Prairie du Chien shortly before the groom was detailed to accompany the government surveyor marking the Sioux and Chippewa line. Lt. Storer escorted his pregnant bride to her new northern home and brought along a black servant named Betsy.[27] The Mirees, the second family, were undoubtedly accompanied by their old slave, Hannah, who was among the first to die when winter set in. The keel-boat's departure was also the last chance to leave. After that, anyone who remained in St. Peter's would be there for the entire winter, unless they braved the chilling waters with a Mackinac boat or canoe trip of at least 14 days. Only the postman regularly risked long-distance exposure, trekking the distance on snowshoes or by dogsled during the winter.

At first, the autumn days were deceptively similar to the summer's. The corn, planted in rows in the fields at the lakes, was coming into milk. Enormous flocks of blackbirds from all across the continental interior were drawn to the ripening corn. The settlement people fended them off with gunshots.[28] The Indian women built scaffolds in each field to guard the corn. The Dakota women and children climbed the scaffolds and, from atop the towers, they waved their arms and gave an alarming shriek at the flocks' approach.[29] The women and children had to be vigilant because the troublesome birds withdrew only temporarily. Whatever the crows devoured diminished the tribe's harvest and hastened the days of hunger that always came long after the crows had abandoned the north. The ripening corn attracted bears one day, and the Dakota killed ten discovered in their cornfield. This meant a feasting day, especially for the young men who killed their first bear that day. The claws were strung into necklaces as laurels for the successful hunters.

Adapting to one technology, replacing handheld hoes with a plow, required yet another technological innovation for the resulting larger harvest. Storing the harvest was a serious problem for a people without warehouses or barns. Traditionally, the Sioux hid their surplus corn by burying it in small bark containers to be dug up when needed after the January deer hunt. Once snow covered the ground, only their owners could find the caches. But this year's bumper crop was harder to contain and conceal, so the agent gave the Indians any empty barrels he could find, sending them with a servant from the agency, driving the oxcart seven miles to Lake Calhoun.[30] Every material thing that came by steamboat was pressed to serve a longer life of usefulness on the frontier.

At the end of October, an old Indian woman hurried to the agency house seeking help for her pregnant daughter, who was in labor with a difficult birth. Despite all the chants and rituals, the baby did not emerge. Dr. Jarvis, the military surgeon, was trained to treat soldiers, but not mothers.[31] In his matter-of-fact way, Dr. Jarvis declared the situation hopeless.[32] Since nineteenth-century doctors had little obstetrical training, Jarvis may never have delivered a baby in his life, much less by caesarean section. No one mentioned calling Mrs. Perry, the midwife, or maybe she did not attend native women in labor. When the woman died, her life-less pregnant body, together with the cradle she had prepared for the arrival of her baby, were placed on the scaffolds on the hill at Pilot Knob. Death often visited young women in childbirth, and it would claim more over the winter.[33]

The winter of 1835–36 was undoubtedly Harriet's first at St. Peters. The previous year, Master Taliaferro had vacated the agency in autumn. This year, the household remained to see the full cycle of a northern autumn and winter unfold around them.

As the sumac turned bright red with the first frost and the days grew shorter, the pace of activity around the fort increased. With winter approaching, there was little time to waste. Much of the time was occupied in winter preparation, securing the house, and harvesting the garden's bounty. Vast pots of water were usually boiled to scour all the available earthenware vessels and sear the vegetables for pickling. The odor of vinegar solutions permeated the house. The mistress probably supervised, with Eliza and Harriet performing most of the work. The master built an underground ice house with a hired man and an unnamed "servant," a term that was usually used to describe bound black slaves brought to the frontier. The pit had to be dug before the ground froze, so that[34] slabs of ice, cut from the frozen river in winter and drawn up the steamboat ramp on sleds, could be stored below ground to last until summer. Everything at this latitude took long-range planning and many steps.

The master always played the role of worker ant to the surrounding community of grasshoppers. "It is hard to get labour here & when obtained it is at the highest possible rates," the master recorded. "All like to live without exertion here."[35] Hard work was a recurrent theme for Harriet's master. Sufficient firewood, food, and weatherproof shelter had to be secured for the winter, which lasted more than half the year. Dozens of trees had to be felled in distant groves, chopped up, and hauled back to the enclosure by the oxcart before winter in order to keep the fires burning and the house habitable.

There was considerable anxiety about going into the long winter unprepared. Both as the agent and as the head of the household, the master felt personally responsible for his immediate family, his several slaves, and his three hired men and their families. Between the interpreter's family, the blacksmith's, the striker's, and his own, there were 28 people living at the agency to feed over winter.[36] Winter meant the end of both sources of food: the short growing season and the steamboats' cargo. Whatever they laid aside now had to last them until the river ice broke in April, or they would starve. Only meat could be killed year-round. Potatoes, onions, and turnips were stored in boxes of sand in the cellar to keep from freezing. Rows of earthenware pots and jars sealed the fruits of the women's canning efforts. Even salt, basic for pickling vegetables and curing meats, came by steamboat. The master surveyed the food stores and calculated and recalculated the amounts needed to feed all of his dependents at the agency.

There was talk among the hired men of leaving the agency due to lack of sufficient food stores for the winter. "Money will not buy provisions," the master noted. With winter coming on, the lieutenant, designated as the fort's commissioner of subsistence, was ordered to stop selling food to the civilians. "So we are left unexpectedly destitute & at a season when indeed they must leave this place or starve."[37] Having endured Minnesota winters before, the master knew that the climate showed no mercy.

Due to the shortage of hired men, the servant women probably undertook the messy task of mudding the house. This process of insulating the house was done by boiling chunks of mud and wood chips and plastering the mixture into any exposed gaps between the stone, the door, and the window frames. Mudding the house was hand-chapping work, but necessary to do before winter set in.[38]

As one by one the household tasks were completed, the Indians' seasonal cycle would have become apparent to the young slave girl. Their customs of setting up camp one day and moving on without notice the next, walking single file, dressing, and eating would no longer seem as strange. With longer exposure, she would come to know and even anticipate their seasonal life, much as her master did. Her knowledge of Indian life, so far gleaned through summertime's bright lens, was likely deepened to give her an understanding of how Sioux endured the winter. The agency people weren't the only ones concerned about food shortages—Indians visited regularly pleading for food. The master again dug into his personal stores to provide what he could. "I could not listen to such plain truth evident to my senses...& refuse a small item of comfort to these destitute people.[39]

It is also reasonable to surmise that the forcefulness of her master's agenda sharpened her observations, since the Indians' well-being was his primary objective. It was why he was there, it occupied most of his thoughts and plans, and she, like the other servants, was there to serve him, his wife, and his purposes.

One evening, the Indians celebrated the crisp fall nights with dances and bonfires, within view of the house. The Spirit Lake Sioux danced between light and shadow.[40] There was a desperation in the dance that night that haunted the observers. Normally, there were rigid formalities about who participated in which dance, but this particular autumn night, the lines between the social roles dissolved. Men and women, boys and girls, performed the dance with bits of other ceremonies intertwined. The dances were performed frantically, exuberantly, as if this were the last dance before the long winter set in, a winter, they knew from experience many would not survive.

By the first week in October, once the corn was harvested, the Dakota men set out on the fall fur hunt. Although pelts were the thickest in the spring, the Dakota increasingly hunted muskrat in fall as well in order to satisfy their fur trader creditors. Some of the women accompanied the hunters in order to carry the loads, set up the tepees, make fires, and cook. Most women, though, and a few men headed for the cranberry bogs and rice lakes. The cranberries brought in by Dakota women were a rare sweet taste in the Indians' diet, which was composed primarily of smoked meat and bitter roots.[41] Harriet's master always bought a barrel full of cranberries from the Indian women. With the local tribes dispersing, the agency would be quiet for several weeks. Once the hunters returned from hunting muskrats, they would set off again for deer.[42]

During the fall of 1835, Henry Sibley toured the far flung fur-trading posts of his newly acquired empire. Sibley had sufficiently set up his living quarters to write with satisfaction, "I am at length cleverly ensconced in my bachelor's den, but time alone will determine how I will succeed in getting along."[43] Now, like a prudent general, he toured his subordinates in the field. He had placed Joseph Brown, a man whom the Indians complained tried to occupy their favorite hunting spot, at Lake Travers. Brown owed the company a considerable debt, and he signed on with them to work it off. He would later become one of Sibley's primary henchmen, but in 1835 he was just another low-level trader who had gone to work for the company after failing as an independent.[44] Joseph Renville, the "full Indian" passing as a Frenchman, continued trading at his large house at Lac qui Parle. Sibley's other lieutenants, mostly men with French names, operated out of small cabins in the wilderness, where they collected furs from the Indians.[45]

The days grew rapidly shorter and colder before the geology expedition returned and Mr. Featherstonhaugh came to dinner again. He had not found any copper deposits.[46] Still, he brought stories from his travels. The geologist fancied telling one particular story of a white-haired Indian maiden with particular relish and he undoubtedly shared this story at dinner. He claimed it was his most vivid memory of the trip.[47] The story of racial contrast and cultural belonging may have struck a receptive chord with the adolescent Harriet, listening in between serving dinner and cleaning up. Featherstonhaugh had seen a beautiful young Indian girl with fine flaxen hair, running among the trees along the banks of the river. He was "very much struck" he said, "with the flaxen-haired beauty, whose unusual appearance so much contrasted with the…others."[48] When he next met the tribe, he asked about her. She was known as *Pah-kah-Skah* or "White Hair." She was the daughter of a fur trader named Robinson, who had abandoned her, her mother, and brother when he'd moved on. (Harriet may have pricked up her ears on this point, since her own last name was Robinson. Was she kin to the fur trader? How much did this adolescent girl know about her origins and the likelihood of coincidence?)[49] Pah-kah-Skah's brother fit better into Sioux society, but Pah-kah-Skah's appearance set her apart. If the slave girl reflected upon the story, she might see in it comparison to her own situation, living among a people with whom she shared a culture but bore a distinctively different appearance.

When the geologist next saw the girl, he was surprised at her unkempt appearance and dirty clothes. Clearly, grooming was an important component of his sense of beauty. He called to her, and though she understood no English, he thought he detected "a modest feeling" about her, something he declared lacking among the tribe's other girls. He claimed to be "touched with the hopelessness of her condition…which seemed to implore the protection of the race she had sprung from."[50] (Featherstonhaugh would not have known that the master, too, had a Métis daughter.)[51]

And so the English geologist gave the blonde Indian girl presents of food and a bright colored handkerchief. The other Indian women pressed him for gifts like the scarf. He explained that he gave that gift only to Pah-kah-Skah because she belonged to his race, but he gave them some pork and biscuits asking that they be kind to her.[52] When Featherstonhaugh asked what would become of her, his Indian hosts teased him for his interest, suggesting that he marry her. Yet her image stayed with him, and because this Indian girl looked white, among the social background of the Dakota tribe, the Englishman felt a stronger obligation to her.[53]

This time the Englishman slept at the commandant's house. (The commandant's wife must have acquired a servant in the meantime.) But given the imminent cold weather, he could not linger or he would have to stay the winter.[54] The expedition set off downstream in Mackinac boats for the lower country, with the Blisses' son in their company. His mother, who had long anticipated the day that her son would have to leave for school, waved in tears as her only child set out with the expedition in a Mackinac boat powered by the great river's current and steered by French voyageurs, singing and rowing their way downstream.[55]

November was ideal to haul wood. Once the ground froze, oxcarts rolled over the surface without bogging down in mud. Still, the master reported difficulty finding a woodcutter. "No Frenchmen to be had for money to do any labour— for want of provisions. None to be had at the Post. A long winter before us & no means of rendering ourselves comfortable."[56]

In mid-November, one of the bridegrooms whom the master had married that year came to the door to consult him about a debt. Everyone in the community turned to Harriet's master to resolve their disputes. It seems that since the wedding, the groom had worked for his father-in-law, old man Perry, without being paid. He wanted fair wages for his months of work,[57] but his father-in-law refused to pay him. Taliaferro sympathized with the young man but explained patiently that he had no authority to recover the debt for him. The young bridegroom could easily have earned good wages, with labor in such short supply. There simply was no legal procedure in the area. He told him that the customary method for settling such as dispute was for creditors to seize one of their debtor's livestock.[58] Since old man Perry had a large herd, the master advised him to take a cow against the debt and sent the young man on his way.

Word came later from the village at Coldwater Spring that the son-in-law had indeed levied his debt. Instead of a cow though, he had slaughtered one of Perry's prized oxen. The master said nothing about killing the animal, and an ox was more useful to the entire community on the hoot to draw wagons than slaughtered for meat. This act of spite impoverished everyone.

CHAPTER 6

Wintering Over at
St. Peter's Agency

B Y MID-NOVEMBER, ICE blocked the river, making it completely impassable by
boat. The community was sealed in, bound together, encircled by ice for better
or worse for the next six months.

Although the coming of winter in Minnesota is marked by the first snow, it
is the first snow that actually stays on the ground that really counts. The snowfall on the day that the Mackinac boat left melted in a few days time. By mid-
November, however, another six inches of snow had been laid down. The dull
brown prairie grass was now covered with a thick, bright white blanket. The
world was reborn as fresh and new. Within two weeks though, the temperature
fell to 10 below zero, too cold to snow. The soft-fallen snow became crusty as
sugar that remains too long in the bowl. The ice on the rivers was solid, eight or
nine inches deep.[1]

That fall, the sutler's old slave woman, Hannah, died. Old Hannah and Horace
were owned as a couple. There is no indication that they were formally married,
but they may have formed an attachment, in the manner of servants forced by
their captivity to live in close proximity. An attachment was a means of accommodating their circumstances, of mutual survival, or simply a human response to
the isolation they experienced from other social ties in their lives. Horace had died
only a short time earlier, and often when one life mate passes on, the other dies
shortly thereafter. Or perhaps Hannah had simply caught a chill spending so many
days exposed to the elements and sleeping on the wet ground on the open keelboat
trip from Prairie du Chien.

On the night that the old woman died, the northern lights came again. Watching the skies that night, one observer at the fort described the phenomenon: "Broad
sheets of light shot from the zenith directly overhead to the edge of the horizon in
every direction…illuminating the heavens like noon day.…the Aurora was tinged
of a most beautiful orange color from the reflection of the immense fires on the
prairies."[2] Each community of people imposed their own interpretation on the

phenomenon. The Indians thought that the northern lights represented ghosts of various totems.[3] The people close to Hannah may have taken it as a sign that Hannah's soul was released from this world. The people of St. Peter's did not know (indeed, no one on the planet then knew) what caused the northern lights every 11 years. The next time the solar wind blew over the earth's poles to display the aurora borealis, Harriet and her husband Dred Scott would make the momentous decision to seek their freedom together in the St. Louis court.

Late in November, too late for regular travel, a man named Stambaugh arrived to assume the position of new sutler for the post.[4] Samuel C. Stambaugh, it seemed, was rewarded with the sutlership for delivering his state's votes to Andrew Jackson. Foolishly, he set out too late in the season and his keelboat was locked in the ice of Lake Pepin. Soldiers had to be sent to rescue the boat, or at least salvage what they could of its valuable stores. The men were ill-equipped for the 20-mile trek through deep snow and several suffered frostbite.

Taliaferro invited the new sutler and several officers to dinner. As Harriet shuttled the warm food from the basement kitchen outdoors to the dining room, wolves could be heard howling in the distance.[5] Everyone was interested in the new man, but each was also curious to learn how he had secured his appointment. Being appointed sutler at a military post was a patronage privilege that many officers, and even Indian Agent Taliaferro, were interested in securing when their military service ended.[6] Though no one locally knew of this relationship, Stambaugh had already made plans with Henry Sibley to set up a more permanent presence in the territory. Stambaugh had shown himself amenable to fur company interests in earlier dealings. The company men realized that sutlers were "always inclined to dispute Indian trade with the company,"[7] so they sought to influence their selection. To ensure that Stambaugh was amenable to the company's interest,[8] the company, through Sibley, negotiated a deal, with Stambaugh.[9]

Each night, the wolves circled the fort, and they moved closer. In late November, there was a great barking of dogs on the plateau prairie near the fort. Numerous greyhounds and mutts were let loose to chase down a wolf, which they caught and killed. Another wolf was soon trapped in an improvised pen.[10]

The winter months changed the servants' routine. No day began without their building fires in the fireplaces and no day ended without seeing them banked and put out. To keep the house habitable, fires had to be fed all day long. The time and attention expended for fire tending punctuated all the day's other tasks. Harriet's long winter was measured in fires built and tended.[11]

Keeping a fire going required skill and continual monitoring. Although novice fire builders wasted wood, the experienced knew how to cultivate each different fire for optimal burning. New logs were needed every 10 minutes, each one chopped into pieces no larger than the fireplace opening. Each task required a different fire: hot fires for boiling laundry, constant fires for cooking, slow fires of coals and embers for baking and heating the room. At midday, one could best afford letting the fire go out to sweep the day's accumulation of ashes from the five fireplaces into the ash barrel to be saved for making soap in the spring.

The winter diet depended heavily on meat, flour, and fat. Bread could be purchased from the fort's bake house and household bread was usually baked in a cavity built into the chimney of the kitchen hearth. The day's main meal was usually served at noon to the three principal members of the Taliaferro family. The servants also slaughtered and dressed animals. As long as the cows produced milk, it was unwise to slaughter them. Chickens and other wild fowl needed to be plucked, singed of feather stubble, gutted, and hung to dry. The servants would necessarily become well acquainted with handling wild grouse, partridge, and wild turkey. Everything else had to come from the pantry's dwindling reserves or the sutler's equally dwindling storehouse. Although the servant women prepared all the meals for the main table, they themselves subsisted on three variations of the common staple of cooked corn meal called johnnycake, cornpone, and dodger for variety.[12]

Winter also made the daily task of hauling water more of a burden. The agency house, high on a bluff set back from the river, had no known spring nearby. Though the fort had a deep well, it's not clear whether water was hauled from the fort or the agency house had a separate well or cistern. The most convenient source of water was snowmelt, provided one could keep supplying the bulk of snow needed to produce a trickle of water.

Like the other servants, Harriet lived close to these primal elements of fire, wood, ashes, water, meat, and fat, handling them, touching them with calloused, chapped, and bare hands so that her mistress was spared. That was her role for the winter, and the winter chores were unrelenting.

Visitors to the agency dropped off with cold weather. Then came the slow realization that everybody one saw was locked together, in captive companionship, for the duration. There would be no new faces for at least six months. It is at this point in the human experience that the distinct habits of different individuals become very noticeable. The way an officer presented himself, the way someone walked, carried a rifle, or wore his hat would become recognizable at 200 feet. Who among the community was an early riser and who took late afternoon rides on the prairie became familiar. Indians lingering in the neighborhood instead of accompanying their tribes on their autumn hunts assumed recognizable identities. As the days grew colder, fewer people ventured out. With more work done indoors, the rare silhouettes of those seen outdoors appeared in starker contrast against the empty wilderness landscape. Routines, that bare skeleton of time, revealed their gaunt regularity.

During the winter, the agent spent a good deal of time writing letters, reports, and his daily diary. By November, he was writing with a strained penmanship. On December 1 he noted, "The weather almost too cold to write in the office. I am preparing letters and documents for the intended express."[13] The following day, he entered only the words: "Too cold in office—retired to my private residence."[14]

Christmas and New Year's were the liveliest winter festivities of the long, dark, cold months. Although Christmas trees were yet to be introduced in America, the house was cheerfully lit. In the Virginia tidewater, where the master and the slaves came from, slaves customarily had free time around Christmas for drinking and visiting kinfolk at other plantations. There was no thought of visiting kinfolk at St. Peter's, 300 miles from anywhere, and the servants couldn't leave their winter chores of fire tending for more than an hour. But the one tidewater slave tradition that was most likely to have been maintained in the Taliaferro household was the Christmas box. In the Christmas box, servants received their annual allotment of new cloth or clothing. The ritual was for the servants to surprise their master with the cry of "Christmas box," to which the master was expected to produce gifts for his dependents. A shift, a length of calico, or worsted cloth that the servants could sew into their own clothing was the prize.[15]

How curious this frontier Christmas must have seemed to Harriet! At previous Christmases at Mr. Dillon's famous inn in Bedford, the festivities were elaborate. There servants answered the door to friends and acquaintances who came calling, taking their hats and coats, showing them into the front sitting rooms, and announcing their arrival. The innkeeper hosted elaborate Christmas dinners for friends and travelers making their way through the mountain valley. Humphrey Dillon was famous in Bedford for being the first person ever to serve strawberries and cream at Christmas. He had found a way to raise the strawberries indoors as houseplants.[16] Here on the frontier, no fruit was fresh. But even with limitations, the settlement community tried to reproduce the customs of remembered Christmases. Carols played on the mistress's square piano set the tone. Potatoes from dark winter cellars were mashed to be eaten with meat gravy. Christmas justified slaughtering a pig and devoting an entire day to roasting meat on a spit. Venison sausage, onion soup, wild rice dressing, boiled turnips, and cabbage were local delicacies. Molasses was more available for sweets than refined white sugar, and there were the cranberries purchased from the Indian women in the fall.

On Christmas day, settlement and Indian people alike engaged in the custom of paying social calls on the community's few principal men, where they could expect to be received in the warmth of a fire. Well-wishing visitors called upon the agent at his house and the commandant and the sutler at the fort; and many crossed the frozen river to call upon Mr. Sibley at Mendota. The Indians expected small gifts of food or tobacco at each stop.

Harriet probably opened the door to the expectant visitors as they arrived and shut it firmly after them to keep out the winter cold. There was no thought of taking hats and coats. Small portions of food, like gingerbread, were divided in advance.[17] The aspect of "calling" that the master detested, however, was the kissing. Each of the many blue-blanketed Indian women who came to call expected to kiss him, slapping an affectionate smooch on his face. The kissing custom was carried over from the region's previous French occupants. The proper Virginia gentleman really did not approve of the custom, but he was too much the diplomat to suggest to the Indians that it be discontinued. At day's end, he registered in his diary, "This day passed off quietly with the usual employments of the season."[18] New Year's Day followed the same calling routine with the principal men again receiving visitors at their warm houses.

With the close of the holiday season, the settlement people fell into a stable routine built on simply enduring the long winter yet to come. At the 45th parallel, January days lasted only a few hours. The sun barely came out at all some days and it remained above the horizon hardly long enough to raise the temperature. The heavy curtains were rarely opened to allow in the daylight. Indeed, full shutters were needed night and day to keep out the drafts. The difficulty of keeping warm exceeded the inconvenience of being deprived of sunlight. So many days were spent, like the evenings, inside by the fireplace. Candles and glass-chimneyed hurricane lamps provided some light, but only the post's commandant could afford the expensive spermaceti candles; the rest of the officers made do with the cheaper tallow ones. In the basement kitchen, the servant women depended upon the firelight or smoky lard lamps, like the soldiers did. Still, people at the settlement were better off than the Indians in their lodges and tepees, who had only the smoky central firepit for heat and light.[19]

The settlers dispensed with laundry in the wintertime, thereby relaxing one of the community's primary markers of social standing. Anything washed between December and March would never dry but simply freeze stiff. Fireplace drying racks were needed for boots and outer clothing that regularly got wet by contact with the snow. Clean laundry had to wait until some chance break in the weather, which often didn't happen until April. As Featherstonhaugh's account of Pah-kah-Skah illustrated, grooming and clean clothes were the visible standards that the settlement community used to distinguish themselves from the native tribes and lay claim to superiority. Gentlemen and ladies washed with imported milled soap, fur traders with homemade soap, and the Indians, it was said, bathed in lakes and streams and wore their clothing until it rotted off their backs.[20] After New Year's, however, even officers went without shaving for the warmth of a beard, and the ladies took to wearing pleated housecaps all day long. It was more important to be warm than to keep up appearances. The wind and cold cut right through the tightest woven cloth. Fur hides were really the only suitable clothing material at those temperatures, but wearing fur made the settlement people resemble the Indians even more closely.

Every act of exertion took longer in the winter. One of the servants, and at different times probably each one, had to tend to the animals and milk the cows. Morning and night, someone had to see that they had enough hay and that the ice was chopped clear from the water trough. There were at least two calves in the stable, and calves meant there was milk. Harriet and Eliza must have followed the milking routine with separating milk from cream, washing up the milking buckets, and, in the evenings, churning the cream into butter, which kept longer than cream in the pantry.[21]

Winter curtailed one's range of senses as well as one's activities. Going out of doors to milk or feed the chickens or even for a breath of fresh air chilled one's lungs. The outdoor daylight was blinding in contrast to the dim interiors where one spent most of the time. If one had to walk very far it was possible to become susceptible to snow blindness and lose one's way. By the third week of January, the snow was 16 inches deep but blowing and drifting into deeper piles in places. Each morning, the doorsteps and paths from kitchen to backdoor and from house to barn to woodpile had to be shoveled out. The unbroken wind blowing across the prairies created virtual snow bluffs, several feet high and crusted over in some places; the wind swept the ground bare elsewhere. The wind and snowdrifts made the quarter-mile distance between the agency and the fort seem even farther.

Surviving the winter was the end in itself. The French had a name for those hardy individuals who braved the northern winters to trade with the Indians for furs. The French called them "hivernants," meaning winter people. This word may have come closest to recognizing the type of discipline that winter imposed on survival itself.[22]

Surviving the winter reduced the dimensions of social status at St. Peter's. With many of the rituals and distinctions completely relaxed, winter pressed down upon them all, reducing the common interest to the most basic necessity of keeping warm and fed. There was community among those warming themselves at the same fires, and sincere welcome for the rare winter visitor: a new face that one had not seen for a while. Certainly between the Taliaferros, neither the master nor mistress chopped wood or did the messier work when a servant was available to do so. Yet except for the handful of principal men who had servants to take over the routine work for them, Harriet's chores were not significantly different from those done by most ordinary settlement people. The enlisted men, the settlers at Coldwater, and the Métis fur trade community, all worked as continuously as she did and experienced the same cold and dark. In this respect, though her status was that of a slave in free territory, her life conformed to the norm of local settlement culture. Her workday life was more "typical" of free persons at St. Peter's than it would have been if she had been enslaved in the plantation South with its rigid and highly differentiated social privileges and grades.

In fact, she inhabited a household that enjoyed much greater comfort and means than most. In the agency household, she was better equipped with labor-saving devices than the poorer settlement families in the area. If any kitchen in the area had a cookstove, butterchurns, a mangle for squeezing the water from laundry, and even a complete collection of kitchen utensils it would have been the Taliaferro household. In the warmth of the agency house, she lived more comfortably than the enlisted men in their barracks or most settlers in their cabins or shanties. And although the difference could be seen in the freedoms, privileges, and luxuries of the people at the top—some households had ladies, such as her own mistress, who engaged in the leisure of needlepoint and playing piano—the winter cut through social standing. Even the mistress suffered the cold and had to pick up an iron tongs to tend a dying fire when necessary. The house belonged to the Taliaferros, however, as had Harriet herself, at least before she came north, and whatever similarity her workday bore to the workdays of Métis women, or the enlisted men's wives, it was still a fact that neither Harriet nor the other slaves owned their own cabins. Like the soldiers, whatever private space or moment of peace they found for themselves within the basement kitchen could be shattered at any moment by the arrival of one of the Taliaferros with a task for them to fulfill.

CHAPTER 7

Winters Deep

IX OR SEVEN people living in close proximity in the small agency house meant that, inevitably, each person learned to recognize the others' movements by the distinctive way that a floorboard creaked, or by a sniffle or a cough. The sounds of the maidservants' movements were muffled in their basement domain while the three upstairs dwellers' movements—the master, the mistress, and her brother, H. N. Dillon—were amplified down into the kitchen from above. All of the house's inhabitants were drawn into even closer proximity by their need to share the fires' warmth.

The over-familiarity of one's household mates was combined with an urge to seek out like-minded souls. Winter's isolation produced the general longing for companionship, and different sets of social cohorts formed among the settlement peoples at St. Peter's. The master usually visited three men who were about the same age and station: the commanding officer Bliss, Dr. Nathan Jarvis, and Mr. B. F. Baker, who ran a trading post independent of the American Fur Company.[1] Taliaferro and the doctor regularly rode their horses through the deep snow the half mile to Baker's stone trading house, near the Coldwater settlement. Thus, Bakers' store became their gentlemen's club. The other officers, Dr. Jarvis wrote, were "agreeable men, although too much addicted to cards,...the prevailing vice in all these outposts when men are shut out from amusements during the long and severe winters."[2] As they sat or stood around the stove at Mr. Baker's store and discussed the issues of the day, they formed opinions about the world outside St. Peter's. As an independent trader, Mr. Baker was not beholden to the company, so Taliaferro favored him with his patronage. After visiting Mr. Baker's, the agent undoubtedly repeated what he'd learned to his wife and brother-in-law at dinner. Gossip and opinions broke the winter's monotony for the Taliaferros, as they had little to do but refine their views on the world as they considered their isolated place in it. Always within earshot, and equally removed from her origins and other influences, teenage Harriet must have absorbed these views of the world.

For Harriet and the other servants, who could not read, all new information came from what the master read and spoke aloud.

On those rare occasions when the military courier arrived with the mail, Taliaferro spent the entire day reading the papers.[3] With so little information penetrating the wilderness isolation, the mail's arrival provided hours of study and discussion. The news from the papers was never fresh; it had been several weeks in coming, carried by steamboat as far as possible, and then by keelboat, and finally over land by snowshoe or dog train, but it took on a new currency when it reached the secluded post. One could never anticipate when a new burst of letters would arrive to inform their isolated encampment in Indian country about what was occurring in that area called the United States, which they had left behind.[4] But the mail arrived only sporadically, so, for the most part, the only community that mattered at St. Peter's was the local one. Although the agent sought out social contact with peers, he never mentioned discussions with servants in his journal. They did not count in the formation of local opinion because, by their status alone, no one bothered to consider what they thought. But then such engagement was not to be expected: the commandant never asked the enlisted men for views either.[5]

So eager was Taliaferro for conversation, he sometimes discussed current events with the chiefs in council. "It is amusing at times to learn the state of the news floating among the ignorant Canadians and French," he wrote. "They have it that [a]s between the Indians and whites in the south, all the whites were killed. [The Chiefs] were pleased at my confidence and unreserve [sic] in them."[6] Conversation bonded the participants. On one occasion, as if leading a class, he recorded the Chiefs' political opinions and reactions.[7]

Item 3 the Great fire in New York: The Indians thought "Did not the people of New York run away at the cause of the loss of so many fine houses?"

Item 4 U.S. Tension with France: "They could not see how two such friendly nations as the U.S. and France could go to War or have any difficulty."[8]

Given the close quarters of winter confinement, the servant women and their mistress were like fellow prisoners isolated by cold and snow drifts. They must have been just as glad when the master and brother Horatio left for a few hours because it gave each of them a little more room to themselves.

While there were a sufficient number of settlement men at St. Peters to form different social cohorts based on age and class, there were very few settlement women, and even fewer for whom English was their first language. Within the Agency household, Harriet and Eliza at least had each other to confide in, but Mrs. Taliaferro had only the trio of officers' wives a quarter mile distant at the fort, a circumstance which might have meant that Mrs. Taliaferro became closer to Harriet and Eliza than their formal status would otherwise dictate. Especially during the prolonged very cold spells, the distance to the fort was simply too great for a lady to venture. Other winter accounts detail stretches of time lasting days and weeks when even hardier pioneer women found that travel as far as a quarter-mile to the next neighbor was simply impossible.[9] Many settlement women living on the frontier recount that the physical isolation from social contact, and especially from other women, was one of the most difficult psychological burdens of surviving the winter.[10] As if to underline the difficulty, narratives of life at frontier forts of this era routinely mention the tiny number of ladies as a significant feature of community social life.[11] At these times of extreme social isolation, Mrs. Taliaferro may have turned to the servant women to share her confidences. We have no direct evidence about their relationship, and a search for letters by Mrs. Taliaferro has come up empty, but other ladies with serving women in Wisconsin Territory do recount forming stronger personal attachments to their servants. Mrs. Kinzie, living in similar circumstances at Fort Winnebago, describes taking an interest in the edification of her black indentured servant girl Louisa.[12] When Elizabeth Dodge married and moved with her husband to the Blue Mounds in Wisconsin territory, she said that during the first 18 months she spent there, the only company she had was her husband and her two black servant women.[13] In the frontier's isolation, slave women provided their mistresses with some female companionship in a manner not necessary in the antebellum South or at military posts where there were numbers of ladies present for the winters.

In February, Madeliene, the daughter of Scott Campbell the Métis interpreter, married a hired man employed at Mr. Sibley's.[14] Madeliene was Harriet's age and had lived in the second story of the council house, only footsteps away from the agency house, since Harriet arrived. The wedding must have been of considerable interest to adolescent Harriet and may have spurred her to reflect on her own future. Would she ever marry? It wasn't an impossible idea. The one other independent black woman in the community was part Ojibwa and she had a husband and family. Marguerite Bonga was the descendant of former slaves brought to the area by a British officer and also the granddaughter of an Ojibwa chief. She had married Jacob Falstrom, the Swedish immigrant and refugee from the Selkirk community, and the Falstroms now lived with their Swedish-African-Ojibwa children at the Coldwater Spring.[15]

As Métis wives, Madeliene and Marguerite Bonga Falstrom survived in much poorer material circumstances than the Taliaferros or even the Taliaferro servants. The Campbells and the Falstroms survived without a stove, candles, an ice house, or more important, regular supplies of goods from the St. Louis markets. Thus, for Harriet, to marry a Métis man would have meant adjusting to a more primitive standard of living than she enjoyed while a slave in the Taliaferros' household.

Moreover, if Harriet were to marry, she'd look for a husband in the settlement community rather than among the Dakota. Having grown up accustomed to settlement living standards, like any other daughter of the community, she would likely have found it unthinkable to take an Indian husband and follow his way of life. The life of Dakota wives was known as one of misery and extreme servitude.[16] How could she, Harriet, who knew how to iron a tailored shirt and set a proper table with linen, consider moving into a wigwam where the primary food was dogs, muskrats, and vermin much of the year? She had traveled on the most modern conveyances of the time: stagecoaches, steamboats, and even railroads. She had seen strawberries raised in a hothouse in winter. Among those marriages occurring between tribal and settlement peoples, the Dakota spouse was invariably the wife. There was no known example of a Dakota man taking a settlement wife, black or white, free or slave. Such a husband could not provide sufficient supplies of settlement goods.[17]

Race and status hindered relationships between slave women and enlisted men. Fanny had been sold for her liaisons with soldiers. And Harriet was still under her master's control, his slave and his dependent, even though living in a free territory. Any marriage required his approval. A generation earlier, slave women in the Northwest Territory had married Frenchmen.[18] It was not that race didn't matter then, but with so few women in the territory in the 1820s, a slave woman knew how to keep a settlement-style household, while Indian women did not. After the wedding, Madeliene Campbell, now Russico, followed her husband across the river to his worksite and bore two children within as many years. Madeliene's first two children were boys, but when she finally had a daughter, she named her Harriet.[19]

As weddings broke February's monotony at the agency, so too, the Dakota devised seasonal entertainment, events that caught the agent's interest. The Indians built sweat lodges, which were used in very private rituals among the Dakota. The most significant winter ritual was the great medicine dance, the ceremony in which elite members of the tribe initiated others into the inner circle.[20] That year almost 200 Indians assembled in response to the invitations, which were small bundles of tobacco. The medicine ceremony recognized the significant social distinctions between the elite in each tribal village—that is, between those who were initiated by the ceremony and those lesser individuals who were not.[21] No one could be invited to join unless his moral standing was excellent.[22] One short February day, the ladies and gentlemen of the post rode out to Pike Island, frozen in the Mississippi, in sleighs to observe the ceremonial dance.[23] By Washington's birthday, the Indians had concluded their medicine ceremonies and were moving off on their hunts again, leaving only the weakest to remain behind. They would be gone from the agency for two months.

Days of quiet followed, during which external stimulation was near zero. The minds of the settlers surely tended to turn inward, as they reflected on previous events and redirected themselves toward longer term plans. February was a time of planning for both Taliaferro and Henry Sibley, who increasingly kept his own counsel. The agent's thoughts turned to starting a new school for Indian children at the Lake Calhoun and Lake Harriet settlements. He discussed the idea with the local tribes, in much the same way that he always talked to them about farming as a means to feed themselves in the future. Taliaferro had a particularly personal reason for establishing a school at the lakes.[24] His daughter, Mary, was turning eight years old and approaching the age when further education was important. That summer he had been reminded of the importance of education in several ways. The commandant's son was sent off to school. A steamboat full of giddy girls from the Jacksonville school, where respectable frontier families sent their daughters to be trained in the domestic arts, had visited St. Peter's. It was unlikely that his half-Dakota daughter could attend there, but establishing a school for Indian children in the vicinity was within his authority as Indian agent. Besides Mary, Taliaferro was the guardian of three Métis girls, all daughters of old friends, who had once lived at the fort.[25] Furthermore, Featherstonhaugh's story about Pa-kah-Skah had highlighted the fate of half-breed girls, who appeared to have more difficulty fitting into the Indian culture than their brothers.[26] The school that the agent envisioned was a place where half-breed daughters, trained by missionary women, could learn the skills of proper young ladies, making them suitable for marriage to Métis settlement men.

In his diary, he never mentioned bringing Mary into his home to be educated by his wife. The mistress remained childless, and the master was very discreet about his daughter.[27]

The Reverend Stevens called at the office one day to discuss Indian schools and "certain children." As a family friend, he would normally be expected to come to the house. The fact that they met at the office suggests that "certain children" included the delicate subject of Mary.[28] The Reverend Stevens and his wife spent the following day with both Taliaferros.

Sibley was planning for the future as well. The enterprising company man was angling to be appointed sutler at a yet to be created western fort but, when that didn't happen, he instead cultivated a partnership with Mr. Stambaugh, Fort Snelling's new sutler.[29] Sibley and Stambaugh agreed on a shares provision. In exchange for agreeing not to compete for the Indians' trade, Stambaugh could use the company's credit. Taliaferro knew nothing of the arrangement.

In the six months since they'd met, the agent had not made friends with Mr. Sibley. Their early gentlemen's agreement had not kept the fur company from pressing its advantage vis-à-vis the Dakota in several venues. Sibley's maneuvering had shown him to be in the camp of Taliaferro's old enemies. Taliaferro's hopes that company policies toward the Indians would improve under Sibley's appointment seemed to be dashed as he realized that Sibley was the handpicked representative of Indian Agent Street's longtime enemies.[30]

At his house across the river, Sibley's cohort was composed of the younger, unmarried lieutenants. This group formed a club, calling itself, unexplainably, "the bote-screw."[31] The club consisted of a trio of lieutenants who engaged in practical jokes that bordered on breach of military discipline and measured gambling debts in bottles of Madiera wine.[32] With the river frozen solid and little for the officers to do in the winter, it was difficult, but not impossible, to reach Mr. Sibley's by horse. There Sibley had begun to furnish his new stone house with all the appointments of a manorial estate, including a good library, current periodicals, pictures, and cigars, all the requirements of a cultivated life. He also had his horses and dogs and at least twenty Métis retainers, like Madeliene Campbell's husband, to do his bidding. Though Sibley was wise enough to sufficiently distance himself from implication in the young officers' practical jokes, he fed their vices by providing them with a comfortable bachelor pad away from the commanding officer's scrutiny.[33] Lt. McClure had taken up a relationship with one young Indian woman living among the Dakota encamped around Mendota.

On one occasion, Sibley recounted that an Indian chief appeared in his bedroom, dragging a shy daughter by the hand. The chief offered him the young woman as a wife, hoping to make an advantageous alliance with the powerful head of the fur company. Sibley reported declining the man's offer politely.[34]

Marrying a chief's daughter was an established fur trader custom.[35] The alliance gave the trader protection in the area and ensured that the tribe provided its furs to him. Joseph Brown, for example, engaged in this custom repeatedly and notoriously.[36] From the Indians' perspective, marrying one's daughter to a trader reciprocally helped the Indian family have better access to Western goods and guns. But Sibley, the young lord of the manor at Mendota, head company man, did not need to take an Indian girl as a wife to get on in the fur trade. He owned the contracts of other traders.

Although it wasn't discernible under the mountains of bulky clothing everyone wore, at least four women in the community were approaching their final months of pregnancy by February. The blacksmith's Métis wife was expecting her third child, and Lt. Storer's new bride, expected her first. Lt. McClure's Dakota mistress was pregnant. And in the agency household, Eliza, the Taliaferro's eldest slave woman, was pregnant for at least the second time, with a child she would name Jarvis. Sleeping on the communal palette of rags on the kitchen floor, Eliza must have found it hard to find a comfortable position with her belly expanding. Sharing the same pallet, Harriet slept closely enough to Eliza to feel her discomfort.

With deep snow blanketing the plateau, the weaker Indians who had stayed behind from the hunt moved in close to the fort. Some 40 Sioux lodges clustered like smoking mushrooms next to the fort's high stone walls. Each lodge housed about seven people—totaling almost 300 people encamped there. With the Indians so near the fort, they became occasional targets of drunken soldiers' abuse, the soldiers intent upon finding women or making sport. The Indians brought their complaints to the agent, who relayed them to the officer of the day for reprimand. By day, the Indians trooped down to the river where they crouched on their haunches beside holes in the ice and waited patiently for fish to approach so they could spear them. The catches were good. "Pike, pickerel, black bass & sun fish in all their variety are taken in great abundance."[37] The evening fires carried the smell of roasting fish and the sense of calm of hungry people being fed.[38]

One morning so much snow accumulated that the drifts reached the upper story of the agency house. The master responded with a certain pride of hardiness, commenting that the people from St. Louis, in their comfortable homes, had grown soft and could not survive as he did. Although the snow was too deep to walk to Mr. Baker's house for company, he slogged through on snowshoes with the doctor to visit a hired man who was sick.[39] On February 26, the weather dropped to 10 degrees below zero, and word came from the fort that Lt. Storer's wife had delivered a baby girl. The following day, the baby died. It was 20 below zero, so there was no way to dig a grave for even the tiny coffin. Her body would have to remain in her parent's possession until the weather broke and the gravediggers could thaw the ground with fire. The climate was particularly hard on newborns.

Mrs. Storer was "afflicted" by grief, and over the coming year she succumbed also. Only two of the four babies born in the area that winter survived the year.

The cold weather persisted into March, and it was so intense and prolonged that many cattle died. "Severest winter on record," Dr. Jarvis recorded.[40] "If ever poor devils prayed to be released from captivity, so do we from this dreary reign of an Arctic winter."[41] The weeks between January and March were the time of greatest hunger. When they were unable to spear fish, the few Indians who remained nearby had no providers since their husbands, brothers, and the stronger women were still out on their spring hunts.

Begging Indian women and children appeared at the agency offering to shake hands. When they saw someone approach they said, "*Hirharha nampetchiyuza*," which meant "I give you my hand with pleasure,"[42] and grabbed the hand of the person from whom they begged. Offering gifts was the most dignified way to ask reciprocation in food. One old woman presented the agent with a pipe. The master traded potatoes for the fish offered by another old Indian woman. The young servant girl could not have been immune from this begging, since the Indians besieged everyone who they thought could help them. "*Hirharha nampetchiyuza*." Lingering around the agency, they must have seen Harriet regularly carrying plates of food from the kitchen into the house. The master grumbled that the post was refusing to sell bread and pork to those who would have bought it to give to the Indians. It pained him to refuse them food. "I had recently some 200 or 300 visits of old men, old women and many children.... [c]ompassion had induced me to give until I found my private means could not stand it.... I was sorry to be unable to go further. Indians have already eaten me nearly out."[43] The household was also running low on firewood.[44] Other Indians arrived at the agency requesting coffins to bury their dead. Coffins at least kept their bodies from being torn apart and eaten by hungry wolves when there was no wood to build scaffolds.

Although Taliaferro was generally strong of spirit, he tended to fall ill when the stress of his job proved more than he could endure. The bravado of hardiness that he had expressed a few weeks earlier had worn off in the unending weeks of March. Now he wrote, "For 17 days past I have been confined to the house with general debility of the system. I find this climate has proven an over match for my constitution—full 16 years have I been in this country."

The entries in the master's daybook were increasingly terse when he wrote, "March 5, Very cold this day. Our cattle bleed at the nose and the tips of their tails from frost and cold." Fully one quarter of the community's 200 cattle perished from the cold over that winter. When a servant came in from the barn to announce that another cow had died during the night, the master wrote, "Makes 2 calves and 1 cow this season so far. I may lose more. Hay alone will not support cattle constantly employed in this climate 45 degrees north." He gave each carcass to the hungry Indians for food.[45] The Indian women, who customarily did the heavy work for their people, probably dragged the heavy carcass out of the barn to a place where it could be chopped apart to carry, but the butchering had to be done far enough from the barn that the blood would not attract wolves.

Despite the fierce cold, blowing winds, and drifting snow, one could still make out Indian women huddled over holes in the ice attempting to fish. Taliaferro rode out a mile or two one day and returned to report that "the snow covers the earth everywhere and it is injurious to the eyesight."[46] Through the next two weeks traveling any distance was out of the question. Anyone who ventured out came back suffering the sting and disorientation of frostbite and snow blindness.[47] Despite the hazard, Lt. Wood arrived from Prairie du Chien with mail. He had left to retrieve it five weeks previously, living the entire month in the deep heavy snow and bitter cold. By the in-coming mail, Taliaferro learned that his mother had died weeks earlier in Virginia. He hadn't even known that she was ailing.[48] How far away they were from the rest of the nation!

The mail also brought stimulating news of a major troop transfer for the garrison. The present soldiers were to be ordered out and four new companies were expected in spring. Fort Snelling had been manned by the same troops, virtually without leave, for several years. This rotation of troops was big news. The new troops were coming from Fort Armstrong, situated on the Rock Island downriver in Illinois, a fort that was being decommissioned with the conclusion of the Blackhawk War, and westward movement of the lines of defense.[49]

During a thaw in March, the local Métis people went sugaring, while Harriet probably began the monumental task of washing the household's winter laundry. Both activities could only be done during a thaw and both involved boiling large vats of liquid while standing in the snow melt. Both of these intense, miserable, wet, and cold late-winter activities were considered women's work In their respective communities.[50]

After a winter of making do, the agency household yearned for clean clothes. Laundering took days of effort: sorting clothing, presoaking overnight, and washing the cleanest first to preserve the quality of the water. (Harriet would one day use this skill to feed her family.) Water was drawn and carried by hand, and heated by fires built and stoked by hand. The wet mass was stirred in the oversized container with a laundry paddle and then kneaded against the scrubbing board by hand. With soap in short supply, washing women had to rub the wet clothes clean. Once washed, the sopping, heavy clothing was wrung out by hand and arranged over rope tied in the open air. By the end of the day, Harriet would be wet to the skin from bobbing her arms up to her elbows in the tubs of water. Her hands would be raw from the hot water and lye soap, her back aching from the strenuous work of lifting and bending. Still, the clean sheets, shirts, and trousers signaled a return to civilized living.[51]

When the outside temperature dipped again to six degrees below zero, the slush on the ground froze hard and the master grumbled, "The weather seems pertinaciously determined to keep the ice solid until April."[52] With the cold snap, almost everyone in the agency house, except Harriet, seemed to be ailing, so Dr. Jarvis was called from the fort. The mistress remained in bed with a sore throat. The master asked the doctor to pull one of his molars, a messy procedure done with only a device like a pliers and whiskey. As one of the few healthy people in the house that day, Harriet may have assisted with clean rags and a bowl of packed snow to stop the bleeding.

The third person needing care was the servant Eliza, who was due to deliver a baby within days. The master did not note either her pregnancy or the birth in his diary, which was uncharacteristic of him. He noted having his tooth pulled and the birth of Eliza's other babies,[53] and he did seem to count the months of Eliza's gestation in the margin of his diary.[54]

For Harriet, this birth would have been of supreme importance. She, more than anyone else, was likely to attend her fellow maidservant as she labored in childbirth on the pallet of rags they shared in the basement kitchen. The mistress would be of little help, the doctor knew little of obstetrics, and the area's only midwife, old Mrs. Perry, lived at the Coldwater Spring, which seemed even farther away. In all likelihood, Harriet delivered the baby alone. It is reasonable to assume that it was Harriet who received the wet, wrinkled baby in cleanly prepared cloth and cut the cord with a kitchen knife. Who else but another slave woman could be counted on to attend a slave woman in labor?

No doubt the baby was named Jarvis after the doctor. But why he was so honored remains unknown. Perhaps the doctor was the father. From the time Dr. Jarvis arrived at the fort he lamented the lack of eligible women in the area. He appears to have been one of the few bachelor officers who did not establish a liaison with an Indian woman.[55] The doctor often said that the Indians did not interest him, apart from their artifacts. He may have turned his amorous attentions to his friend's civilized servant woman. No one acknowledged paternity of Eliza's baby, but then that was not unexpected. The father could have been almost any man at the fort, the mistress's brother, a manservant, or even the master. However, chastened by the birth of Mary, his Métis daughter, and with his wife in his company all winter, Taliaferro was least likely to have been the father.[56] Eliza's baby had a hernia and lived only through the summer to the next autumn's frost. His disability probably kept Eliza more occupied with his care than usual.

CHAPTER 8

1836: Spring and the Change of the Guard

THE INDIANS AWAITED the first sighting of a crow in spring to let them know that they had survived another hunger season. The winter that seemed it would never end finally broke on March 24. The household awoke to gentle sunshine. "The genial rays of the sun smile for once upon us this morning," Taliaferro remarked.[1] His journal records a "day so fine inhabitants and military are like bees and ants busy flying about and others sunning and thawing out after a long and tedious winter." The fort's massive walls released their captives to walk out and view again the prairie's broad horizon. "Many straggling Indians also to be seen who are smiling at the prospect of spring and the appearance of wild geese and ducks."[2] The days grew perceptibly longer, quickening the pace of life and bringing the pleasure of renewed sensation.

There had been cracks on the ice for days, but the river ice finally broke on April 11. Within two days, although the snow was still deep, Mr. Baker, the independent trader, left for St. Louis. He floated down the melting river, seeking goods for the Indian trade and carrying his neighbors' mail and special orders. (Sibley as company manager didn't need to make the icy trip; he simply waited at his trading house for his partners to send him the goods he ordered.) Lt. Ogden and his bride left next in a Mackinac boat with a crew of nine boatmen, their first trip out since they had married a year before. The Ogdens' departure made Harriet's master a little resentful.[3] He grumbled about the stingy furlough policy of the Indian agency that kept him in place on the frontier.

April is the cruelest month on the North American plains, at the 45th parallel. Mid-April, several more inches of snow fell. But just the taste of spring renewed outdoor activity. People of all the various prairie communities left the dark interiors of their winter shelters, seeking excuses simply to spend time outdoors. The tempo of life and the rate of social exchange increased with the temperature and the hours of daylight. The Reverend Stevens called at the agency for the horses that had been kept there over the winter, and Mr. Pond came in for the ploughs.[4]

The ground thawed enough that the Indian women could dig roots from the marshes and lake bottoms to feed their families. Standing in the cold, melted waters, they hoisted their skirts and felt for roots in the mud with their bare feet.[5] The agent ordered the blacksmith to make them more functional, iron hoes that were especially long and narrow so they could pry the roots loose.

The end of winter also meant that the tribes extended their wanderings, which brought the possibility of new tensions when different nations encountered each other in contested hunting grounds. By one report, Yankton Sioux were killed by Mandan people on the banks of the Missouri.[6] By another, a Sioux hunting party murdered some Fox Indians they encountered on the neutral ground, that strip of no-man's land intended to separate the Sioux lands to the north from those of the Sac and Fox to the south.[7] Such conflicts between the Sioux and other nations were especially disturbing because Sioux-Ojibwa relations were still on edge. Tribal memories ran long, and a small incident could spark war to avenge unresolved grievances. It was imperative for lasting peace that the previous year's murders at Lac qui Parle be resolved before the Ojibwa acted to avenge them.

The agent pressed the Sioux to surrender the tribesmen who had murdered the Ojibwa. One accused man had already tried to turn himself in during the winter in order to be fed at the fort during the hunger time, but the agent refused to accept the accused one by one. In order to secure the peace, he insisted that the resolution be a collective effort, with other Sioux tribes playing a prominent part in bringing their countrymen to justice. Though Taliaferro had tried working through Joseph Renville, Renville had fallen out with members of his own tribe over how to explain the murders. Some Indians accused Renville of inciting the attack on the Ojibwa and claimed that he prevented those involved from surrendering for fear that he'd lose face. Taliaferro no longer trusted him.[8] Nevertheless, the source of the tension in the territory was the relations between the Indian nations, not Mr. Renville. Taliaferro knew that in this delicate negotiation his own personal influence would be put to the test.[9]

Chief Black Dog of the local Sioux band was now backing off on his promise to turn over the murderers. The old chief spoke in council: "My son, Mah-zah-hoh-tah was rather hasty in saying the people of Sixes Village should produce the murderers when called for by our Father...."[10] Black Dog was never regarded as a strong leader, and age had weakened him further.[11] Background negotiations were taking place at all the campfires of the several tribes, and there was a series of furtive consultations between the various leaders and the agent.

HALF A CONTINENT AWAY, Congress had other designs on the area. United States' interests were focused on the region's timber resources. Washington (then called Washington City) dictated new national policies to the frontier. Congress passed the Indian Removal Act in 1835, intending to clear lands east of the Mississippi of all remaining Native inhabitants.[12] With the Sac and Fox already removed from their Illinois farms, the statute set the stage for the government to remove the Ojibwa to the north next, which by law meant negotiating a treaty with them.[13] The Ojibwa to the north occupied the valuable timber forests of northern Wisconsin.

Following the template set forth in the 14 sections of the Northwest Ordinance,[14] Congress had already carved some new states from the Northwest Territory, an expanse that originally extended from Lake Huron west to the Mississippi. The Northwest Ordinance was the plan for territorial law and governance in the region as well as for the creation of states and procedures of dealing with the Indians. Most particularly to Harriet, the Northwest Ordinance declared that "there shall be neither slavery nor involuntary servitude" in the territory, which meant Harriet's freedom.

With the successively changing boundary line, Sibley wrote that he had been a citizen of Michigan, Wisconsin, Iowa, and the Minnesota Territories without ever changing his place of residence at Mendota.[15] (Harriet, too, residing in geographically the same place as Sibley, west of the Mississippi, was successively resident in Michigan, Wisconsin, and Iowa territories during her time there. Although her citizenship would be an issue in the later freedom suit, no one considered that by living in the same place she too had actually been a resident of so many different territories.)[16]

By 1836, Michigan had become a state, and the upper Midwest was called "Wisconsin Territory." Authorizing territorial government for the remainder of the area was the first step toward eventual statehood for the next designated area. Thus, in April, Congress created a territorial government for the remnant of the Northwest Territory, called "Wisconsin Territory," which included Taliaferro's domain at St. Peter's (even though technically it lay on the river's west bank).[17]

The law also called for the appointment of a territorial governor but, more important to Taliaferro, it transferred regional authority for Indian Affairs from William Clark in St. Louis, with whom the master had a long working relationship, to whoever was appointed as the new governor. As U.S. agent to the Dakota, Taliaferro was now ordered to report to "his excellency" Governor Henry Dodge, former dragoons officer turned lead miner and land speculator in the Prairie du Chien region.

The bureaucratic restructuring was a logistical nightmare from the perspective of St. Peter's Indian Agency. It was hard enough to get reports to General Clark, who at least was reliably to be found in St. Louis and in a better position to respond. Now Taliaferro had to send every message first to Governor Dodge,[18] whose time was spent traveling throughout the region setting up a territorial government and selecting a capital.[19] Taliaferro then had to hope that Dodge promptly relayed them on to the commissioner of Indian Affairs in Washington. The commissioner was not at all helpful in appreciating the difficult logistics of this new order, and he insisted that all Indian agents go through Dodge before reporting to him.[20] This new chain of command delayed communication even more between Agent Taliaferro on the front line and anyone who could respond meaningfully in case of an Indian crisis. During these months, Harriet must have gradually grown aware that her master, who probably seemed omnipotent to her, was beset by his own troubles with the men to whom he reported. Other men's agendas and other forces in play also interfered with his plans for the Indians.

The next step toward statehood required extinguishing all Indians' claims to lands within the territory through U.S. government purchase.[21] In this capacity, the Indian affairs commissioner wrote Governor Dodge, asking him to ascertain the Ojibwa's views about relinquishing the land. The new governor responded truthfully that he had no idea what the Ojibwa thought. He could not know because there was no agent to the Ojibwa in that entire northwestern corner of the territory, and hence no official way to learn their views.[22]

Without an agent of their own, various Ojibwa tribes regularly sought out Harriet's master, though he lacked authority to deal with them officially. Taliaferro had long lobbied that a subagent be assigned to the Ojibwa nation some place south of Lake Superior so that they could more conveniently receive the annuities they were already entitled to by previous treaties. They were also entitled to their own blacksmith. As things stood, the closest Ojibwa agency was Schoolcraft's agency in Michigan, several hundred miles east of where they now hunted. As a consequence of that great distance, they frequented Taliaferro's agency whenever they needed a blacksmith or to communicate with "the great white father."[23] Given the tensions between the two Indian nations, it was imprudent for the Ojibwa to venture repeatedly through Sioux territory, particularly for needs that Taliaferro's blacksmith was never supplied to meet anyway. After a decade of urging the commissioner to create a new, more conveniently located subagency for the Ojibwa, Taliaferro got word that Congress had finally authorized the appointment of a subagent to be stationed near a place called LaPointe on Lake Superior. Buoyed with the news, Taliaferro promised the Ojibwa in council that they would soon have a new father coming to live among them to see to their needs.[24]

However, even with congressional authorization, it was not easy to get a subagent in place. The first person to be appointed resigned after only a few months. He traveled to the spot, saw the decrepit buildings where he was supposed to live, and simply concluded it wasn't worth it and resigned. The second appointee ventured to St. Louis, the nearest city, to obtain necessary supplies, but was instead sternly reprimanded for leaving his post. He was admonished that the law required Indian agents to stay at their posts 10 months a year. The man committed suicide soon after. The third man appointed prudently sought a year's worth of food and materials *before* traveling to the remote station deep in the north woods. He traveled to Detroit, the city nearest the main Ojibwa Agency site. At Detroit, however, he found that no funds had been allocated for him. Moreover, with Michigan now a state and the reassignment of authority over the new Wisconsin territory to Governor Dodge, no one in Michigan could tell him from whom to expect funds.[25]

This bureaucratic bungling incensed Harriet's master. He had promised the Ojibwa that a subagent was on his way for a year and a half, but after three tries, there was still no one equipped to take up the post.[26] This was yet another difficulty of administering the Indian agency at a remote site and over a far-flung region with limited communication and transportation.

A further problem brewing was the settlers, who kept arriving in search of homesteads before the Indians had been removed and the lands opened for sale. The call west had been sounded, and settlers were searching Indian territory for the best lands, building cabins, and attempting to get preemption rights before the lands could be legally claimed. Throughout the territory, prematurely established homesteads caused both legal uncertainty and social instability. The community at St. Peter's anticipated that Indian removal was simply a matter of time but questioned the fate of those who had arrived early and settled without permission. Would the claim jumpers get ahead of everyone else or did they need to take their place in line? The topic was fueled by envy and greed. What to do about early settlers would eventually jeopardize even Taliaferro's safety and test Harriet's loyalty to her master, though for the time being it was simply a topic of impassioned discussion.

The military personnel at the fort favored removing the squatter village in order to create a clean slate for new claimants. They preferred this outcome because many planned to join the land rush as soon as they'd completed their enlistment or when the lands opened for sale, whichever came first. The military personnel worried that the squatters had already gotten the jump on them by staking the best lands.[27] The commander, the junior officers, the politically appointed sutler, the fur traders (even Alexis Bailley, still litigating a suit against Taliaferro over the seizure of his whiskey), and, of course, the squatters wrote their representatives arguing over the fairness of the rules to be laid down.[28] Ironically, from a territory without regular mail service, letters about land policy were streaming in to Congress.[29]

Taliaferro most resented the officers' involvement on the issue because he believed that he was the appropriate authority to inform Washington about national policy from the frontier. The lands were Indian territory after all, and he was the congressionally authorized agent in charge. The junior officers who clubbed together at Sibley's house obviously held different views and they had gotten under his skin.[30]

The greatest security threat to the agency household was the possibility of war between the two Indian nations. If violence broke out, the six or seven people, living exposed as they were on the prairie plateau and surrounded by nothing more than a split rail fence, would find themselves in the middle of an Indian war. The Blackhawk War in which many were killed was recent memory. Nonetheless, little incidents and disputes between the local settlers and the local tribe persistently nagged at the master's attention.

Disputes arose over cattle grazing and firewood. The Indians occasionally seized a free ranging cow belonging to a settler. They saw the seizure as justified since the numbers of wild game had declined and the domestic animals were grazing on Indian land. As one Dakota chief stated: "Our game is gone and a man may starve one and two days and even three but on the 4th he becomes desperate and Kills the first thing that crosses his path—Hence is it surprising our people occasionally Kill an ox or a Horse?"[31]

The Mdewakanton tribe also objected to the settlers taking firewood from their lands. The pockets of softwood timber were being cut down much faster than they could be replenished, and even the soldiers had to travel noticeably farther distances on wood detail to find, cut, and haul enough firewood for the fort.

Still, some miles back from the great river, on the little tributaries in Wisconsin, there were magnificent white pine forests that were just waiting to be lumbered for building the West. These were the splendid forests that held Congress's attention. At both the local and national levels, people fought over the supply of wood, whether scrub firewood at the prairie's edge or the regal timber in the Wisconsin forests.

The agent dutifully consulted with the Dakota about whether the squatters should be displaced before deciding it wasn't yet necessary to do so. At the time, the Mdewakanton expressed no interest in ejecting the families living at the Coldwater Spring. Taliaferro faithfully wrote Washington. "The Indians are not averse to ... the settlement. ... Some have even requested that their friends not be removed."[32] Taliaferro considered the settlers less of a problem to the Indians than the fur traders who were licensed to be there. Still, most conflicts could be avoided, he wrote, by moving everyone not officially licensed or connected with the government east of the Mississippi, leaving only fully licensed fur traders, like Sibley and B. F. Baker, and government personnel on Indian lands. The cabins at the Coldwater Spring were ultimately "of little value," Taliaferro wrote. "They would be as ever satisfied to be permitted to remove [across the river] where they will be in the way of no one."[33] He was gravely wrong in this assessment. The dozen cabins west of the river near the spring were modest, but they were treasured by the families who occupied them. And Taliaferro seriously underestimated their tenacity in defending them. For the families at the Coldwater Spring, these cabins represented all they had after more than a decade of hard living in the north country.

The village of squatters sensed their own growing vulnerability and began to organize in response. One day, they sent a delegation to Taliaferro to discuss petitioning the government.[34] Emotions ran high on the topic, and the situation was personally awkward for Taliaferro. Assembled before him were men who had peaceably been his neighbors and upon whom his household depended for hired tasks. Nothing could be resolved, however, until a treaty was reached.

THE IMPENDING TROOP TRANSFER distracted some attention from squabbles over firewood, cattle, and land. With the Sac and Fox removed from Illinois, the army planned to close the fort at Rock Island, Illinois, and move the line of strategic military defense north and west of the river. Since the army rotated troops infrequently, the transfer was a significant event in community life.

Of the fort's existing officers, only the evangelical Capt. Loomis was scheduled to remain. Master Taliaferro was genuinely disappointed to see his friend Major Bliss leave after so many years spent together at the post. In the hospital quarters, Dr. Jarvis was also planning to depart. During his time there, Dr. Jarvis had accumulated the largest collection of Indian craftsmanship in the Territory, more than many tribes owned collectively. The collection overflowed his rooms at the hospital,[35] and on orders to ship out, he packed everything in crates to send to his family in New York for safekeeping.

Jarvis's collection represented material creations of the highest skills, produced by Dakota and Ojibwa tribes over many years. Each piece had been painstakingly worked from indigenous materials by craftsmen with little leisure to spare. To craft a single piece the tribe had to gather the requisite materials from different sites in their nomadic wanderings over a year of seasons. The Indians customarily presented their traders or the doctor with such gifts,[36] as a way to create lasting bonds, expecting that the recipient would continue to supply them with goods, food or medicine when needed.[37] Jarvis had gotten several of his prize possessions in trade for medical services.[38] Now, however, Dr. Jarvis packed up all the Indians emblems of friendship as he planned to depart.

Jarvis's collection was diverse and extensive. There were 10 pairs of delicately fashioned moccasins, decorated exquisitely with quills in floral patterns; embroidered mittens; buckskin shirts and dresses;[39] unique personal accessories such as five headdresses, some with horns or carved antlers; a bear claw necklace, the trophy of some fortunate hunter; and more than a dozen sacred medicine bags, which were usually so closely identified with their owner's spirit that strangers were generally not allowed to touch them. Pouches like these were *waukon*, great magic. One bag was made of fine eagle skin, decorated with bird feather and porcupine quills dyed different colors. Jarvis owned four quivers for arrows of wolf skin, otter skin, and buffalo hide; a baby cradle; and two tiny model canoes, intricately detailed and perfectly scaled to size. There were saddles and snowshoes, each laced with more than a hundred finely cut sinew thongs, meticulously woven, laced, and tied to bentwood frames like elaborate basketry. There were ornamental mirrors and fantastical musical instruments, including rattles, wooden and reed whistles, drums, and an amazing nine-holed Sioux flute, ingeniously carved from ashwood that had been worked into a twisting, spiraling form to cradle the player's fingers And then there were many, many long carved red stone pipes, each unique.[40]

Shipping his collection out deprived the tribes of the items' *waukon*, as well as the models from which a new generation of artists could reproduce the techniques of their ancestor master craftsmen. The tribe's best specimens of handcraft, traded with the expectation of continued friendship, medicine, and food, were packed in shipping crates bound for the doctor's New York home, to wait in storage while he headed to his next military posting.

The Indians' annual winter collection of furs was also being prepared for shipment east at Mendota by the fur company workmen. It was a good year for the company, with a yield of almost 300,000 pelts from the upper Mississippi Valley.[41] Most of the pelts were destined to be processed into felt hats for the gentlemen of Europe.

As Sibley assessed the year's yield, he too reflected on how the tensions between the different tribes of Sioux had affected "our business." In his letter to New York, Sibley reported. "The lower Sioux, who number by far the best hunters, in consequence of the poverty of their own lands, have long been obliged to visit the hunting grounds of their neighbors, the upper Sioux. The upper Indians have attempted to put a stop to the intrusion. I was obliged to make a special visit [north], to mediate between the parties, and I only succeeded in reconciling them by use of strong threats, that if the lower Indians were not allowed to hunt undisturbed...I would send an order to the different posts to stop the trade entirely."[42] So complete was his control over the Indians that he could order one tribe to permit others to enter their traditional hunting grounds to compete for the fur-bearing animals. No wonder he rivaled the Indian agent's power. Sibley saw his order as a simple imperative to earn the optimum yield for the business, given that the intruders were the better hunters and had already culled the animals on their lands.

THE NEW TROOPS of the Fifth Infantry arrived by steamboat on May 8, 1836, and were received at the dock by a full military delegation and the many customary unofficial onlookers. Among the 140 arriving military men were Dr. John Emerson and his black servant man, then called "Etheldred." The new doctor and Etheldred were hardly noticeable in the disgorgement of troops at the dock. At least five black servants accompanied their officer masters from the supposedly free state of Illinois.[43]

Standing together, the doctor and Etheldred appeared as opposites. Dr. Emerson was a large white man, six feet, four inches tall. As he left the ship, he hobbled slightly, and though he wore the official white surgeon's uniform for the occasion (as he did most every day of the year), he wore only one boot and just a sock on his other foot. He suffered from bunions and could not put on his left boot.[44] Etheldred, by contrast, was almost a foot shorter, very, very dark, and probably neatly dressed in plain-colored clothes. By his status as an officer's servant, he would be well enough dressed for the time in neat and sturdy worsted "negro cloth" and a decent pair of brogan shoes. A servant's appearance reflected on the master's standing, and John Emerson considered his own prospects promising. The two were about the same age, though their life paths had been joined for only about five years, long enough to fall into a pattern of easy familiarity.

Dr. John Emerson, in his mid-30s, was impulsive in spirit and an Irishman by birth.[45] He had attended the Philadelphia medical college on scholarship and then drifted west to St. Louis, seeking to get on the army payroll.[46] At the time, there were plenty of patients sick, with cholera, smallpox, malaria, and all manner of injuries, though many could not pay. The Army Medical Department, however, provided a regular monthly salary for a doctor's services, and the Indian agency paid extra for treating Indians. Dr. Emerson had initially come into the military surgical corps as a temporary replacement. The naturally congenial young fellow worked the social network to get the necessary recommendations for a regular appointment[47] and was assigned to Fort Armstrong on the Illinois side of the Mississippi. Dr. Emerson sought a valet and all-round assistant, and so he bought Etheldred in St. Louis. In all likelihood, Dred was Dr. Emerson's first and only slave.[48] The army paymaster gave doctors and other officers money to hire servants. Under the standard arrangement at the time, an officer was entitled to choose between having an enlisted man assigned to him or receiving a monthly stipend to finance the keep of a slave or hired man of his own. The doctor bought Etheldred just before he took up his first official post at the fort in Illinois.[49]

Doctor Emerson had liked Fort Armstrong, and if he could have, he would have preferred to stay on there. He had two good friends at Fort Armstrong: George Davenport, the sometime Indian agent and full-time fur trader, and his financial backer, the Creole-French Monsieur Antoine LeClaire. Together, the three men had hatched plans—big plans—for the development of towns on the west bank of the great river, once the government opened the land to claims. Each of his friends envisioned a city bearing their names. With their encouragement, the doctor had staked his own acreage west of the river. He had hired a man to build a cabin, raise a few crops, and build a fence so that his claim would be secured when the territory was officially opened to take claims.[50]

Just one thing had interfered with the doctor's plans, however. There was no longer a need for a fort at Rock Island, given the entire removal of the Sac and Fox nation from Illinois in 1834. Without a fort, there was no need for the government to keep a doctor there. So the doctor received transfer orders before his claims could be perfected. With his interests in the hands of his watchful, enterprising friends, he accompanied the troops to the northernmost post on the Mississippi. His Iowa land claims, though, preoccupied his correspondence for the next several years.

While the slave Etheldred served the doctor at Fort Armstrong, he had also served three other junior officers as well. As their valet, Etheldred had prepared their meals, cleaned their quarters, brushed their uniforms, polished their boots, and probably groomed their horses, the expected tasks of an officer's valet.[51] Two of these officers accompanied the troop transfer.

All four officers had collected money from the army by hiring Etheldred. Since the army paid each officer a wage and ration allowance for a servant, all four could collect full reimbursement (in the amount of $14.50 per month) by claiming some manservant, and they all claimed Etheldred. For a lieutenant whose own pay was only $30 a month, this was a sizeable increase. In fact, with four officers collecting the full allowance for him, Etheldred's services cost the U.S. Army more than a second lieutenant, $60 per month, or $720 per year. More important, this amount exceeded his purchase price.[52] Thus, the U.S. Army actually subsidized slave ownership on the frontier.

As a slave, Etheldred was not entitled to any of this sum, though a small allowance may have found its way to his pocket. The officers most likely kept the extra money, paying some to Dr. Emerson by way of hire for use of his slave. So lucrative was this particular scheme that even the one officer who didn't accompany the rest to Minnesota continued to collect money by claiming Etheldred as his servant, though he was now stationed at a different army post 200 miles away.[53]

On May 9, Maj. Bliss officially relinquished command of the post to his successor, Lt. Col. Davenport. Davenport's troops had served under him for several years. The gentlemanly Col. Davenport was regarded as a good commander and a fair-minded, temperate man.[54]

The Blisses were bound for civilian life in Pennsylvania. The army had sought to assign Maj. Bliss to Florida, where hostilities flared with the Seminole Indians but, rather than go to Florida, he resigned, and the Blisses disbanded their household. Since they no longer needed, nor were compensated for, the services of their slave, Hannibal, they gave him his freedom and passage as far as Louisville. It's not clear whether Hannibal could have stayed on in Indian territory or whether he would have wanted to. It was rumored that he, a brewer of spruce beer, eventually became a preacher in Louisville.[55]

Other servants were also shipping out with their officers. The very skilled, large black man named James Thompson was less pleased with the move. He had come to the fort a decade earlier as a sutler's slave and later was sold to a captain. With his master Capt. Day reassigned to Fort Crawford, he was obligated to go along.[56] At Fort Snelling, Jim Thompson had maintained a remarkably independent existence for a decade. He had even taken a Sioux wife, who lived at the agricultural settlement at the lakes, and they had a couple of children.[57] He often did odd jobs for pay, for example, building Agent Taliaferro new office furniture.[58] He was adept at carpentry and equally adept at surviving in the wilderness. His prowess had even impressed the Indians.

With his master's transfer, however, Jim Thompson was being sent to a place where his Sioux family could not go. It was neither safe for them to be in Prairie du Chien, nor permissible, in terms of army policy, for them to live with him at the fort. As Dakota people they would be at risk if they traveled to traditional Winnebago territory. More important, they'd lose the support of their larger kinship network if they moved. Jim Thompson's wife was a daughter of Chief Cloudman, so she and her children remained behind with the rest of her tribe. The parting must have seemed bitter to them and particularly unjust to this man who had long enjoyed his autonomy. But Jim Thompson would find a way back, and when he did return, to what was surely Harriet and the other servants' amazement, he did so as a free man.

The transfers caused commotion at the fort for several weeks. Military doctors usually resided in the post hospital rather than the officers' quarters not only for reasons of convenience but also to demonstrate their semi-independence from the chain of command; their authority stemmed from the surgeon general rather than the local military commander. Thus, Dr. Emerson and Etheldred moved into the fort's hospital, located near the big gate. Dr. Jarvis stayed on for six weeks while Emerson got settled. Of Emerson, Dr. Jarvis wrote: "The new doctor is no chicken, 6' 4" in his stocking feet."[59] That he was "no chicken" may have indicated that even Jarvis could see that his colleague would not back off from a fight. Army life had its own jurisdictional disputes, and when confronted, Dr. Emerson did not back down to a challenge to his authority. He would engage in confrontations more than once over honor and authority during his military career, and he even kept a pair of dueling pistols at the ready.[60]

Dr. Emerson spent the first month organizing the hospital, dealing with the administrative tasks of transferring, cataloguing, and accounting for all the hospital provisions he had brought with him. The Medical Department was extremely strict in accounting for supplies. Every bandage, cot, piece of ginger root, and bead of mercury had to be accounted for or there would be hell to pay. Accounting irregularities ended many military careers, and errors made in performing this tedious task would eventually embroil Dr. Emerson as well.

The doctor immediately complained about the wood supply for the fort hospital as it compared to his previous station several hundred miles downriver. Emerson notified the commander: "Fires are needed day and night and the allowance is altogether insufficient."[61] The same day, he received the commandant's curt response. "Doct. Emerson will perceive that he has received for the present month, the greatest quantity of fuel allowed by regulations."[62] The weather was definitely colder at this latitude, though the military ration was the same. Unfortunately there, on the edge of the prairie, there were fewer additional sources of firewood.

The cool weather delayed the planting of the gardens. As the son of a Virginian farmer, Taliaferro probably supervised as his black servants performed the actual work of planting. He never mentioned plowing or working the ground himself. He noted, "Season backward a few days. Indians preparing to open and cultivate their...fields. I could do great and lasting good to the poorer and more helpless Indian population."[63] Whenever Harriet's master encountered setbacks, he reminded himself of his higher purpose.

Across the plateau and behind the fort, Harriet would be able to see soldiers at work in their own gardens. At the stables, the new officers' valets groomed their masters' horses, which needed to be exercised after being confined in the ship's hold on the trip upriver to the fort. Amid the gardens and the stable there were small numbers of cattle grazing freely on the plateau. One day that spring, perhaps on a gardening day, Harriet must have met Etheldred for the first time. Since Dr. Emerson always kept a horse, Dred may been grooming or exercising the animal.[64] But somewhere in their daily routine, they met. The two servants, one tending her garden and the other with his master's horse on the prairie plateau, may have silently acknowledged each other from a distance and then drawn closer, by curiosity, to talk, either as individuals or as part of a group. Their masters did not make each other's acquaintance for almost another month, though servants had no need to stand upon the formality of proper introduction. Their lives were brought together by their masters' careers, and, as enslaved persons, their masters still determined their residences and their daily routines. But during the early summer months, their masters were fully occupied with their own agendas. Northern summers were tranquil and relatively relaxed. The daylight was long, so there was time and space for the two to meet and develop their own relationship. As long as they completed their chores, they were probably free to walk about the area, as Jim Thompson often had. There was a beautiful waterfall a short distance up the Mississippi and the prairie appeared like a flower bed with wild lilies, roses, sweet Williams and a thousand others,[65] and Dred had a horse to exercise. Though both were deemed slaves (or as Master Taliaferro described them, "servants"), no one was concerned about their running away. There was no place to run away to.

The several tribes of Dakota again began to gather at the agency, anticipating their treaty annuities. Each day more Sioux men and women arrived asking for provisions that still had not arrived.[66] The Ojibwa arrived too, bringing some of their spring maple sugar harvest and asking when their new subagent would arrive. The Ojibwa offered maple sugar to the local Sioux who were present at the council house, a very constructive gesture toward peace.

In council, the Ojibwa chief Peagic began,

If you see us here today, it is distress that brings us.[67] We are worse off than any of our nation above or below us. We were told that you were not our Father.

We went to the [Great] Lakes and when we got there we were asked where we came from and when our answer was given from near this place, we were told to come here and so we returned as we went empty-handed.

You say we shall have a father soon on our own lands. We hope he may come soon for . . . [w]e have been long like dogs—driven from one door to another. But . . . [y]our heart is in the right place, and this my nation well knows for your name is in the mouths of all—even our children smile when we speak of seeing you. . . . My arm is strong, and for 16 years you know my heart. You made me a new heart (indicating the presidential medal on his chest). . . . Our country is barren of game, and we are left without other means of support.[68]

Nadin, the Wind Chief, added: "I followed you to Washington and you have my face in your office."[69] "I hope if you can give us a few hoes and fish spears . . . Also give a little tobacco if you have it. We are like lost children in our nation and our fires burn dimly." Nadin was always poetic but direct in his requests. He would later speak for the Ojibwa nation at the time of the treaty relinquishing their lands.

The master replied, "My friends, I expect your new Father by the next steamboat . . . and it is my determination to turn my children, the Chippewas, over to him clear from all difficulty and bad feelings to the Sioux, and then we will both unite our good deeds and help you and the Sioux to walk on clean land and under a bright sky in all time to come. The Sioux, who murdered your people last year, will be ready to meet the friends of the deceased . . . this month. I have nothing, my friends, but what belongs to the Sioux," the master said, gesturing to the Dakota warriors who were present and listening. "If the Sioux Chief Wah-kon-Tunkah will give you some hoes and fish spears, I shall feel pleased."[70]

On cue, the Sioux chief rose, saying, "We are badly off too. But you are worse off than us. So out of our small annuity I will give you, my friends, a few hoes and fish spears. This is all I can do, but I do it with a good heart."[71]

IT HAD BECOME APPARENT that the Indians were getting whiskey from somewhere. The following week, the agent posted official notice on the sutler's door that soldiers were prohibited from trading whiskey with Indians. It was now obvious to him that Sibley had an interest in the sutler's store, thus doing business on both sides of the St. Peter's river. Though there was no fondness between the men, Taliaferro felt secure in his own authority and believed he could simply ignore Sibley's expanded venture.

It was 10 days before the steamboat *Frontier* came within sight of the bend. When it reached the dock, the word came that it was freighted with cargo for the American Fur Company, but there were no Indian goods on board. The master and the Indians were again disappointed.[72]

Mr. Baker returned aboard the *Frontier*, with his stocks in trade and extraordinary and horrifying news from St. Louis.[73] He had witnessed a black boatman tied to a tree and burned alive by a mob. The brutality of the incident shocked the nation that summer and altered the course of race relations in the West. Reaction to the incident set in motion a chain of events that eventually affected the lives of Harriet and Dred. With everyone talking about the sensational incident, it could not have escaped Harriet's attention.[74] Still, she could never have anticipated that the aftershock from this remote event would affect her life, living in the pastoral setting of a Minnesota summer.

Mr. Baker had witnessed the mob murder with his own eyes. It was not that black men had not been hanged or brutalized in the city before. This incident was a different order of cruelty: the accused man already in custody, without trial, was burned alive by a mob of ordinary citizens, in full view of hundreds of others.[75] It began when a policeman attempted to arrest one black river boatman for some minor offense. As the officer took the man's arm, his shipmate, a man named McIntosh, aided his escape by cutting loose the man's shirt sleeve. The policeman was left foolishly holding the ripped sleeve, so he arrested McIntosh for interfering with the arrest. As McIntosh was escorted to jail, and the streets filled with people returning from work, the clever McIntosh joked with his police escorts about the prank, and they responded in kind, suggesting that the courts might just hang such a prankster. McIntosh panicked, and, still holding his knife, he slashed about wildly, trying to free himself. In the scuffle, he stabbed one deputy in the chest, a wound that proved fatal. The other deputy and the crowd gave chase, and the incident escalated. Seeing the bleeding policeman and fleeing black man, the crowd began to cry for revenge. The mob wrested McIntosh from the custody of jail, and the cry changed to "Burn him!"[76] Some men bound McIntosh to a small locust tree with chains, while others gathered armloads of brush and set it afire. The crowd stood silently by as the pleading McIntosh was burned alive.[77]

Despite the horror of the atrocity, no one was ever prosecuted for McIntosh's torture and murder. Some saw the incident as proof that free blacks simply could not coexist with white people, and hence it energized the efforts to send free blacks back to Africa through a recolonization organization. The violent hatred unleashed was neither spent nor contained. Only one St. Louis newspaper went so far as to actually condemn the mob's actions.[78] The Reverend Elijah Lovejoy, editor of the Presbyterian newspaper, reported the injustice in vivid terms.[79] Vigilantes in turn vented their anger at him, his criticism of the burning of McIntosh, and his plea for tolerance, calling him by the epithet of "abolitionist." Within months they burned his printing press. Within two years time, the smoldering public rage would result in a shootout in the streets of Alton, Illinois, claiming the Reverend Lovejoy's life.

As Lovejoy witnessed the mob's murder of McIntosh, an Alton City attorney would bear witness to another mob's retributional murder of Lovejoy—and then to the impossibility of bringing the mob to justice. That man would eventually file Harriet and Dred's freedom suit as their first attorney. This brutal incident was inextricably linked by two personal choices of conscience to someone who would aid Harriet and Dred in filing for freedom.[80] But we are getting ahead of the story.

On June 1, another steamboat arrived, this time with 30 tourists but none of the Indian goods. Departing on the steamboat were Horatio Dillon, who had spent a year living at the agency house without finding useful employment,[81] and Samuel Pond, who had spent two years trying to learn the Dakota language as a missionary.[82] Not finding his fortune in the West, young Mr. Dillon returned to

Pennsylvania to take over management of his father's inn. Not getting on well with the new minister, who lorded his superior divinity training over the Pond brothers' lay teachings. Pond left to study for the ministry in Connecticut.[83] His younger brother, Gideon, stayed on, however, and Samuel promised to return as soon as he was ordained. Harriet would see both Horatio Dillon and Samuel Pond return.

ON JUNE 3, TALIAFERRO WROTE that the Sioux had surrendered all four men who had murdered the Ojibwa the previous winter.[84] It had taken him a year of continuously entreating the Sioux to persuade them to turn in the murderers. To reconcile the two nations to peace, the surrender was done before an audience composed of some 70 local Sioux tribesmen and the new post commander, Col. Davenport, and his officers. The accused men surrendered peacefully and were placed in the guardhouse. Three other warriors, including Black Dog's son, accompanied them into the fort to see that no harm came to them. The master wrote with no small amount of satisfaction, "I have succeeded in all I desired with these people without resorting to force or calling on the military for aid. It is a feather in my cap—which my enemies would like to pluck from it . . . out of spite."[85]

The following day, when Agent Taliaferro visited the guardhouse to check on the prisoners, he was surprised to find Sibley there, with a sidekick acting as interpreter. Sibley had no business talking to the prisoners. Taliaferro was incensed, and he returned to his office to write a complaint to the officer of the day.[86] As it turned out, one of the junior officers, whose friendship Sibley had cultivated, had given him access to the prisoners. The junior officer was reprimanded, but the agent remained irritated by Sibley's nerve and ability to insinuate himself wherever and whenever he wanted. Sibley could have had little purpose at the guardhouse among the prisoners and their escorts except to enhance his own prestige among the Indians. Thereafter, Taliaferro kept his plans secret. He sought out the commander to discuss a plan to resolve the matter between the Indian nations, and to his satisfaction, Col. Davenport offered him the support he needed. (The household servants probably went about their chores on tiptoes.)

On Monday, June 6, Taliaferro called for the prisoners to be brought to the council house. The commander ordered them released, and when everyone was gathered, the three warrior-escorts spoke:

> Now that all the murderers have surrendered to the great Father, we hope that all persons would be satisfied of the wish of our people to make peace with the Ojibwa. . . . [w]e hold ourselves responsible for bringing forth the prisoners. We stand ready to come to the Agency the moment we received news of the arrival of the Ojibwa. [W]e will give ample satisfaction to . . . the Ojibwa and try for once and again to have clear roads and a bright sky over our people. My father, we promise you this voluntarily and as you know we will perform our words, you need not cause us to sign any papers. We call on the great Spirit to witness our compact and you may feel certain it being fulfilled to you and to our Great Father, the President. [O]ur people did a bad thing, and their being carried into your fort was

proper. My father, we have been released and we now stand all three of us prepared... to fulfill your commands.[87]

The agent believed their sincerity and felt sure he could trust them. With faith in their promises, the council was deemed closed. The Indians returned to their homes in fine spirits.

Taliaferro was even more delighted. He had successfully concluded his long negotiation with the Sioux, they had accepted the resolution, and he had carried it out through his moral influence alone, without a show of force. By his moral suasion, the Indians had conformed to reason and his sense of justice. He had also gotten the new commandant's support in the delicate matter. The release of tension in the agency house that night must have been palpable.

Still Taliaferro was miffed at Sibley's meddling. He considered his enemies as "some or all nearly of the Am Fur Cpy" who were "sorely jealous of his great influence with the Indians."[88] The junior officers were too tight with Henry Sibley. He wrote that the company was disposed to "stop short of nothing in getting me off from this Agency before the treaties are commenced with my Indians. But I feel doubly strong in my integrity. The President nobly sustains me."[89] He underscored the word "nobly" three times. It was perhaps his finest hour.

With the resolution of the Indian crisis, Agent Taliaferro could turn his attention to more minor matters. The trader Joseph Brown visited to discuss the complaints lodged against him by Major Bliss, the previous post commander. With the change of command at the fort, Brown expected old infractions to be forgiven. Taliaferro reviewed the circumstances and determined that Brown had done nothing more than other squatters had done: to build on Indian land. "All must pass free, or all [be] condemned, when all are found in exactly the same position."[90] Equal treatment in administering the rules was a principle Harriet's master articulated and believed in.

Agent Taliaferro was prepared to reissue Brown's trading license, but he probably trusted Brown too much. He had expended considerable energy making certain that the Indian murderers promised to "sin no more," and he had underlined its importance as a norm by a public ritual—but he extracted no similar promise from Joseph Brown to stay clear of the whiskey trade. The master didn't realize what a scalawag Brown would become, or perhaps he wanted to believe that only Alexis Bailley was responsible for introducing whiskey in the imbroglio two summers earlier.[91]

The western Sioux of the far outlying prairies were expected soon for their annual visit to the agency,[92] if they weren't frightened back by news of smallpox. This full assembly of tribes had not gathered at the agency in the year since Harriet arrived. Now the agency house was again becoming the central meeting place and the clearing house for the agendas of almost everyone in the territory.

By June 8, the western tribes were in view. One hundred thirty Yanktons, Sussetons, and Wahpeton were encamped in sight of the agency, and in the evening the chiefs paid the agent a visit. Although Harriet had seen the western Sioux before, it was still undoubtedly intimidating to have such large numbers of painted strangers on horseback approach the house. Yankton Chief Wah-na-tah headed the delegation. After ceremonially paying respects, the western chiefs and head men returned to their encampment on the far side of the Minnesotay river.

Four days later, the Yankton Sioux appeared splendidly attired in beautiful headdresses and other ornamentation and danced for over an hour at the agency house in the presence of Col. Davenport and the new officers and ladies of the post, who had never seen the western Sioux in their finery. More than 500 Indians, mostly men, danced that day.[93] In all likelihood, Harriet waited upon the officers and ladies with refreshments. Afterward, the agent presented the dancers with a barrel of salt pork. Then some 40 mounted Indians amused themselves by causing their stallions to fight. Unlike the local Mdewakanton, who usually traveled on foot and by canoe, the Yankton Sioux were developing a horse culture. The stallions rearing up on their strong hind legs pressed each other against the agency fence to gain advantage. "My enclosure suffers," the master reported, but without a hint of bitterness.[94]

Three days later, many of the Indians became sick on the pork that the agent had given them. (The bad barrel must have been from last year's supply, since the annual supply had not yet arrived.) To make amends, Taliaferro gave them a freshly slaughtered beef.[95]

On June 13, the long-expected steamboat arrived during an important council meeting. News of the ship's arrival broke up the council. The steamboat *St. Peters* had finally brought the payments and goods that the western Sioux had traveled across the plains to the agency to receive. The distribution of annuities could begin at once.

The steamboat also brought news that smallpox had reappeared again at Prairie du Chien.[96] Over the next weeks, Indian messengers reported the scourge's advance: within 10 days, it was as far north as Wabasha's village and within another week just south of the agency. Smallpox had the Indians in fear. The smallpox attacked Indian peoples with deadly effect. "They are flocking in to me from every direction to get vaccinated, the benefit of which many of them have already learnt," the master wrote.[97]

To ward off the smallpox, Taliaferro supervised vaccinations of almost a thousand tribe members, "now up to 967 all tolled by self, surgeon of post and others."[98] Dr. Emerson, the hospital stewards, and Dred (who likely assisted) administered vaccinations to some 300 western Sioux people in a single week.[99] The Indians were orderly in lining up. They lined up to receive their annuity payments each year, and they always walked single file through the tall prairie grass. In all likelihood, Dred assisted in the messy task of vaccinating. An ointment mixed with the mashed crusts of smallpox scabs was smeared into a cut made in the arm of the person to be vaccinated. The Indians were stoic about having their arms cut. Ritual bleeding was a common practice to them.[100] From downriver, when word came that the Black Tomahawk had died of smallpox,[101] the western tribes hastened their departure. The Ojibwa never returned to receive the murderers' surrender because they feared the smallpox.[102]

The Yankton chief called upon the agent to shake hands as he was leaving. In bidding farewell, the several chiefs left 22 peace pipes as tokens of respect.

The agent was expected to reciprocate. Taliaferro gave Chief Wah-na-tah his umbrella at the chief's request.[103] The Chief of the Yanktons left with the master's umbrella tucked under the blanket of his horse. What could a Yankton chief do with this symbol of civilization? Did he use it to keep the rain off, to provide sunshade on the plains, as a rod, a staff, a symbol of authority, or did he keep the umbrella in the same way that Dr. Jarvis collected Indian goods, as a curious contraption of another culture?

With a mixture of pride and shame, one chief bid farewell saying, "My father, I have no pipe to give you, but I know as we are well-acquainted, you do business as well without the ceremony of the pipe."[104] To make a pipe required the red stone that was only available from the sacred quarry, and his band had been hunting in a different region.[105]

On June 24, while the mistress joined some officers and ladies on a ride out to visit the falls, the master stayed behind to confer with the Reverend Williamson, who was down from his new location at Lac qui Parle. The master delighted in discussing matters of policy with men he considered equals. Harriet's master laid out his grand plan for civilizing the Dakota and rendering them self-sufficient. Whether Harriet listened in on the conversation this day or some other, she heeded his words in the long run. This agenda—a mission of independence through self-sufficiency—almost became a mantra that he worked out in virtually every conversation he had with Indians and with settlement leaders alike.

As usual, the master detailed fuller accounts of his own positions in his diary than of his guest's responses. One topic on his mind was the significance of labor in civilizing Indians. Taliaferro maintained, "Labour in the shape of agriculture, teach them the uses and value of property—learn them to feed themselves in abundance first, and after being taught those things fully and their stomachs well-filled, Indians will then be in a situation to attend to all proper admonitions—but not before."[106] The second topic was the propriety of marrying cohabiting couples. It was the reverend's special duty, Taliaferro maintained, to perform the ceremony because the blessing of marriage had a tranquilizing effect on the people of the countryside. He himself had already married several Métis and settlement couples in the area. Within the year, the master would marry Harriet to Etheldred.

These two tenets of his philosophy of betterment, the importance of hard work and the propriety of marriage, must have taken root in the servant girl's consciousness. Her life struggle would be buoyed by the support of a marital union. And the very words she later used to explain to the newspaper men why she was entitled to independence were remarkably close to her master's own mantra: she could work to support herself and her family. By taking in washing, she did not need to depend on anyone else. And that entitled them to be left alone, to be free.

Late June of 1836 marks the first mention in Taliaferro's diary of Dr. Emerson by name. Although the two had labored together to vaccinate the Sioux, there had been little opportunity for formal introduction.[107] Taliaferro's attention was primarily occupied with dealing with the Sioux and Ojibwa, and he was most interested in cultivating his working relationship with the new post commander. Dr. Emerson did not have time to pay a courtesy call on the Indian agent until July 3, when a steamboat arrived with a full berth of tourists, and some called at the agency, as did Dr. Emerson.[108] The two masters would become respected colleagues, and Harriet's master would give her in marriage to the manservant in the doctor's household.

CHAPTER 9

Celestial Explorers

EVERAL OF THE summer's steamboat tourists wished to remain at the agency. Since servants' help was necessary to making the frontier livable, it was also the key to extending hospitality. "[A]s we are not prepared for much company, none remained but a distinguished French gentleman—who had letters to me from my friends in St. Louis," the master wrote.[1] The French gentleman, who was invited to stay, filled the place of houseguest after Mistress Taliaferro's brother departed. Joseph Nicollet remained with the Taliaferros all winter. His was a friendship in which one was invited to visit and remains for the year.[2] The master wrote: "So Monr. Nicollet has comfortable quarters in my family residence and the use of the Agency house to store and carry on his observation at his leisure."[3]

By living in the same household that winter, Harriet came to know one of the century's most remarkable men. The small man with dark curly hair was a brilliant mathematician, and he had already made significant scientific advances in his native France. He also erroneously predicted that the new science of probability could be used to forecast the stock market. Having made some disastrous investment recommendations to powerful friends in Paris, he had had to leave France in disgrace. Setting his sights on America, he had lofty aims; he wished to add to the exploits of the great French explorers and contribute to the record of explorations in the West. Failing at his career, he labored for his posterity. Trained in the highest scientific learning of mathematics, astronomy, geology, and map making, he came to St. Peter's with no less an aim than to measure the heavens and chart the waters of the earth.[4]

When he arrived at the agency doorstep, he brought letters of introduction from influential people in Washington and St. Louis. Nicollet seemed to charm everyone he met.[5] Despite the master's usual distrust of "foreigners," this Frenchman won his complete trust. Nicollet was described as "urbane, forbearing, rounding off obstructions in intercourse; polished and persuasive, and careful of the feelings of others."[6] As Nicollet, the amiable houseguest, seemed to suit his hosts, the Taliaferros, the St. Peter's Agency delighted the French scholar-explorer. He described the area as "the finest site on the Mississippi river; the natural beauties of its environs adding to its importance and grandeur."[7]

Nicollet was equipped with all the latest scientific instruments to explore the new world: sextant, barometer, thermometer, chronometer, pocket compass, and spyglass. He wanted to determine the source of America's greatest river and to be the first to map the stars from this latitudinal position. He wasted no time in getting down to work, measuring the distance from the edge of the moon to the sun, to the stars Spica and Altair on July 5. From the North Star's altitude, he could precisely determine the latitude.[8] "To him an astronomical observation was a solemnity, and required such decorous preparation as an Indian makes when he goes where he thinks there are supernatural beings."[9] His measurements proved to be extraordinarily accurate.

Two days later, the heat of summer came on in full force. The thermometer hit 92 degrees in the shade as the sun shone down on the treeless plateau. The mosquitoes were bad. On such days, the basement kitchen was the most pleasant place to be. The Taliaferros set off for a picnic to the falls of St. Anthony with their French guest, the commandant's wife, and the few remaining officers. The explorer scientist was delighted with the spectacle of "its waters, rebounding in jets from the accumulated debris at its foot, its ascending vapors, and the long and verdant island that separates the two portions of the falls, with the solitary rocky island that stands in front."[10] After lunch, Taliaferro fished for sunfish and perch in the pools around the falls, while Nicollet climbed around gathering rocks and classifying them. "*Strophomena, Orthis*....Crinoidal remains of peculiar forms, one resembling lipocrinites."[11] Each sample was patiently recorded in his notebook. Nicollet's erudition impressed his hosts, although that did not appear to be his aim. His command of scientific matters was as seamlessly a part of his character as pointed remarks and sharp edges were of Featherstonhaugh's. The Frenchman was "in truth [the master] of a hundred cases or categories, receptacles of mind, subdivisions for convenience, in which, from a full experience, [he] pigeonholed" rocks, fossils, plants, animals, stars, and even "his fellow mortals with a hand as free as that of a compositor scattering type."[12] The rocks, flora and fauna of the unknown American West were a playground for his active mind.

After three weeks at the agency house, Nicollet, carrying all his instruments as well as his powder flask, shot bag, gun, and umbrella, set out to find the headwaters of the great river. He was guided by a Sioux man and his son. Henry Schoolcraft claimed to have found the headwaters in a lake he named "Itasca."[13] Already Taliaferro resented the public claims that his rival Indian agent Schoolcraft made as the "first" to discover the Mississippi's source. He hoped that Nicollet would prove his rival to be wrong.

More important, Nicollet's quest for the headwaters of the Mississippi underlies an important point about the geographical location of St. Peter's Agency. In many ways the people at St. Peter's were not entirely clear where they were in the wilderness. Nicollet discovered for them that they were at the 45th latitude. Although Schoolcraft had claimed to have found the river's headwaters, the agency existed at a place where the river met, but at a place that had never been mapped. Over the course of the next two years, Nicollet would be the first to provide a scientifically accurate map of the region.

By July, when the local Indians had again set off for their hunts, it was particularly quiet at St. Peter's. After the Fourth of July holiday, most officers and their families departed for Prairie du Chien, leaving behind only Dr. Emerson and a small detail of officers in charge of the men. The fort's officers were ordered to sit in court-martial on another officer. Since the accused was entitled to a jury of his peers, that meant calling in almost the entire officer corps of the upper Mississippi valley.[14] The families went along to go visiting, which usually meant servants traveled as well. The fort seemed almost deserted when a census taker came upriver to count the settlement inhabitants.

Censuses were taken often in the territory in the 1830s, anticipating the point when the population would reach a sufficient size for statehood. Indians were not counted in the census because they were not considered residents for citizenship purposes. This gave the impression that the area was sparsely populated. Slaves were counted, though under the constitutional rule that the state's population was composed of all of the free population and a fraction for each slave. Surprisingly, Dred Scott is listed by name in the July 1836 territorial census. The census listed only heads of households and enumerated their dependents. In this way, his listing supports the assertion that he had lived as a free man in free territory.[15]

Despite the midsummer idyll, the continued violent reverberations from the boatman burned alive in St. Louis reached even St. Peter's Agency. In late July, the Reverend Lovejoy, who had been most critical of the murder, had his printing press burned by an angry mob for the first time.[16]

On July 23, Taliaferro asked Dr. Emerson to cross the St. Peter's River to treat an ailing Indian woman, though he arrived too late to save her life.[17] Thereafter Dr. Emerson wrote his superiors requesting formal permission to furnish medicines to the Indians.[18] At this time in his career, the doctor played entirely by the book. A recent court-martial may have made him particularly conscientious in dispensing army material. The unfortunate quartermaster, charged with converting military property, had done little more than sell off empty barrels and a reclaimed stray horse, but he was found guilty and discharged from the army.[19] The tension between strict army accountability and charity to the Indians would eventually prove to be Dr. Emerson's undoing.

George Catlin returned that August to explore the red stone quarry. (His wife Clara had lost the baby.) He resumed his quest, accompanied by an English traveling companion.[20] From their parallel sets of papers, it is evident that Sibley knew Catlin was on his way well before Agent Taliaferro did.[21] Sibley seemed to be informed of all comings and goings in the territory, often before the agent knew of them.[22] Catlin and his companion left for the quarry on horses he borrowed from Sibley.

Even Catlin realized that the red stone quarry was the Dakotas' most sacred site. This was part of the allure that drew him there. It was the heartland of Indian legend and myth. The Indians told that in ancient times, the Great Spirit had called all the Indian nations together there. The Great Spirit broke off a piece from the red rock wall, made a huge pipe by turning it in his hand, and taught the people (a term synonymous with the Dakota in the language) how to smoke the ritual of peace. This ritual they would use in encountering each other. He told them that this red stone belonged to them all as their flesh—to use for pipes of peace. No war club or scalping knife could be raised at the sacred red stone quarry.[23] The quarry's lure was irresistible to Catlin.

August 21 brought an early frost to end what had been a very short, cold summer.[24] Large flocks of passenger pigeons were flying every morning. The Indian women were busy building scaffolds where they could take their places as human scarecrows. [25] The corn harvest was good enough, but the growing season was slowed by the cold rains and the late spring, so the melons never ripened at all. The gardens were picked over for whatever could be preserved before it blackened and shriveled from the frost. Along the river bottoms the first frost changed the sumac bright red, the willows a golden yellow. Still all of the year's annual treaty provisions had not arrived. "We look now daily for a steamboat with public stores due since June....Causes of delay—none assigned," Taliaferro wrote in his journal.[26]

When Catlin returned to St. Peter's with rock from the red stone quarry, he recounted meeting opposition from the Indians, but he had pressed on anyway. About 150 miles before the quarry, they met mounted warriors, who tried to turn them back. The Indians surrounded Catlin and his companion and alternately cajoled and threatened them to give up their pursuit. "No white man has been to the red pipe and none shall go," one warrior solemnly told him. "You see that this pipe is a part of our flesh....If the white men take away a piece of the red pipestone, it is a hole made in our flesh, and the blood will always run. We cannot stop the blood from running."[27] The warriors failed to persuade Catlin, who had no intention of turning back. He was even more intrigued by the challenge than ever, seeing himself as bravely overcoming Indian resistance in the name of science rather than as someone desecrating a sacred place.[28] After camping for the night, the two explorers simply rode through their Sioux guards in the morning without further incident.[29]

The quarry was an anomaly in nature. The stone bore the high polish and surface luster of melted glass in a stratum about two feet thick, overlaid by hard red sandstone. Herds of buffalo poured through the small valley on their annual migrations, exposing the surface.[30] Catlin believed, correctly, that the red stone was a new variety of steatite, not known in geological circles.[31] About the quarry's spiritual significance, Catlin said only that the Indian spirit was "palpable" there (much as he had described the Dance of the Braves). Then he filled his saddlebags with specimens and returned to the east and St. Peter's by a different way than he had come.

The agent had already received protests from the Indians by the time Catlin returned.[32] "The Sioux look with a callous and watchful eye on all who attempt to visit the pipestone quarry...The Sioux were very much incensed at the determination of Mresses. Catlin and Wood."[33] Still, Catlin had won the agent over to his scientific justification."[34] Catlin left the frontier, taking his rock samples back to

institutions of higher learning for chemical assay and his own geological recognition and personal fame. Subsequent analysis in scientific journals confirmed his
hunch, and the stone was named "catlinite" in his honor.[35] The Dakota prediction
also proved to be true. Within a few years of his visit to the sacred quarry, the
Dakota, as a people, were in complete disarray. As the Sioux guards predicted, the
flesh of the red men already suffered from the running of blood from the hole that
white men had made. In the future, even Harriet's master with all his diplomatic
skill, could not keep the blood from running.

The well-respected Dakota chief Wabasha died that summer.[36] He was Taliaferro's most important ally. He was the first chief the agent visited on his arrival
for the year and the last one he bade farewell to when he traveled downriver. The
68-year-old chief was an unchallenged voice of authority among the eastern Sioux
tribes.[37] Whenever collective decisions needed to be made, it was Wabasha who
sent forth runners to the other tribes to issue invitations bidding their chiefs to
come together to deliberate.[38] Wabasha's death signaled a generational turnover.
The first chiefs that Taliaferro had recognized 15 years earlier and even played a
role in appointing were now aging.[39] With their passing, younger Dakota men were
asserting their own places in a new social order with a symptomatic breakdown
of discipline within some tribes. The recent rash of attacks by younger Indians on
the settlers' cattle was something the old chiefs could have discouraged. Taliaferro
recorded that: "The young Indians are somewhat mischievous this season—an
arrow was shot into a cow...near the fort."[40] Even his own cattle were injured
by the young Indians' pranks. A milk cow returned home from grazing with an
arrow stuck in its side, and by week's end, some pigs had been stolen. When the
Ojibwa Chief Hole-in-the-Day arrived at the agency, he too had been shot at. He
held in his outstretched hand two arrows that were fired into his canoe as he portaged around the falls of St. Anthony on his way downstream. The agent sent Scott
Campbell to find out which young men were responsible. When he returned, he
informed Taliaferro of more thefts: all the firewood, some 48 cords collected for
the agency at Mud Lake, had been stolen.[41]

On September 9, 1836, there was a killing frost. That day Eliza lost her baby son
Jarvis, not yet six months old. He died of a hernia, most likely a condition of birth.
Taliaferro had a small coffin made, and Eliza's baby was buried near the pine tree in the
garden near the house.[42] Losing her baby must have thrown her into a depression and
saddened the whole household. The tone in Taliaferro's diary became more somber.[43]
For Harriet, who had likely been there at the birth and who shared the sleeping pallet
with mother and baby every night, it must have been an indescribably sad time.

THE INDIANS' CORN HARVEST this year was too large to store in leftover barrels.
After one chief had decided to deposit his plow at the agency during the previous
winter hunt, others decided it would be wise to store their corn with the agent
as well. Throughout October, Indians brought their corn and other items to the
agency before going off on their hunts. The council house that had once been
the master's pride now became a grainery.[44] Taliaferro noted the various tribes'
deposits in his daybook: three pipestems, a buffalo scalp, a plough, and a chain.[45]

The season was turning. The Indian women brought cranberries to sell at the fort, and the tribes divided again as most men left on their autumn muskrat hunts and the women searched for wild rice.[46]

The October 1836 papers were full of election news. Harriet's master favored Van Buren for president, though the Galena paper (the only one in the upper Mississippi valley) was decisively against the man. The paper painted him as unworthy primarily because he favored extending the vote to free blacks.[47] The words "FREE NEGROES" were printed in all capital letters for shock value. The article warned that if Van Buren became president, free Negro suffrage would follow. His vice-presidential candidate was accused of miscegenation.[48] "If these men be elected, how long before poor white girls will become the waiting maids of sooty wenches. And the whole population will become one huge mass of...mulattoes."[49] The vice president was even said to favor "white slavery."[50] These articles lambasting Van Buren were bound to raise the master's ire. Taliaferro would never have considered himself an "abolitionist," but this race-baiting of his candidate crossed the line. Did Harriet react if she heard the words, "sooty wench" read aloud? Or was she numb to this style of language?

THOUGH CATLIN HAD ENTERED sacred ground by pushing past the Indian sentries, several miles farther north, Nicollet had encountered tribes and their customary practices very differently. Nicollet sought out various chieftains for conversation, to learn what they could teach and to make friends. His impending return from the wilderness was heralded by a letter, a custom practiced by one attuned to the refinements of being a guest.[51] At noon, on September 28, the welcome guest returned to a house that had sunk into gloom of grief since his absence.

The French explorer brought with him the Ojibwa Chief Flatmouth and 10 of his men. At Otter Tail Point, he met the acerbic Ojibwa chief who recited a litany of grievances against American policy. The Frenchman knew that these matters were significant to his host, Agent Taliaferro, so he persuaded Chief Flatmouth to return with him to St. Peter's and speak them to the agent directly.[52]

Presumably Chief Flatmouth told Taliaferro the same things he had said to Nicollet because the two accounts are quite similar, but Taliaferro's report of Flatmouth's council is far less complete and nuanced than Nicollet's record. Flatmouth may have spoken differently to the agent, but Taliaferro was also not the astute listener that Nicollet was.[53] Again, Taliaferro recorded more of what he told the Ojibwa chief than what the chief said to him.[54] According to Nicollet's account, the chief told him: "I say what I think....I have been listening to the American [Taliaferro]. He has a fine body, a fine mouth. He speaks well. He has eyes with which he sees well, but he looks askance as his mouth speaks, and when his mouth speaks, his heart is mute."[55]

Flatmouth's dissatisfaction with the Americans was explicit:

Do they think they can amuse us with medals and flags?...Such things are for children. If these medals were dollars I would find them useful. But I cannot make dollars out of them. [T]hey are useless.

See how miserable my people look.... See how the Americans treat us: They always say they want to help us, and yet we never see them. They abandon us to the mercy of merchants who trade at a price three times above that ever asked by the French [or] English and in return supply us only with bad merchandise, thus making the price six times higher. And these traders, well do they know the American government is not capable of either helping or protecting us. They do with us what they please, and if in these times when they force us to go naked and starve, we beg for justice, not charity, they threaten to leave.

We are endlessly told to bury the war hatchet, and if we dig it up we are threatened with rods and ropes, or with being placed under the ground...[56] Thus the Americans plan to treat us as they treat their black people. They do not come to see how we are in our homes, to find out about us, to help us....I know why they do not come. It is because we are poor. But when they shall be poor as we are, then they shall come to take our land, not to till it with us, but to drive us west. We shall not go west! We shall not sell! We shall not surrender our land, not until every one of the warriors you see around me has been killed.

...I am not an animal. I am not like those in the East whom they call their children and whom they treat like three- or six-year-olds, a rod in their hand. They purchased their lands, and now they hold them prisoner and treat them as slaves. When they talk to me of buying our soil, I know what I have to say. But were I to give consent to the sale with the approval of my men, can our Great Father in Washington afford to pay? He may well pay for a handful of soil, and then for another; he may well pay for a tree; but our country.[57]

Chief Flatmouth, like all of his fellow Ojibwa chiefs, would sell his country during the treaty the following year, despite his deep reservations. He left after spending a week at the agency, with gifts, but not much more satisfied than when he arrived. Taliaferro reported simply, "Indians complaining and many go off dissatisfied with everybody and everything."[58]

The agent was stewing over his own set of complaints. He was still beset by the problem that the Dakotas' provisions had not arrived, and he listed the other things his agency lacked:

1. 6 months full without foods of any kind. 2. Treaty stipulations for 1836 not fulfilled. 3. Smith's shop stationary for want of steel. 4. Stationary, books. 5. No pay for the hired men of the Agency. 6. No contingency funds to meet any purpose. 7. No funds for repairs of Agency, though promised 8 or 10 months ago.[59]

In the morning chill, a Mackinac boat arrived with cargo for the American Fur Company's store, but although the small boat brought the bills and invoices for the Indian goods, the necessary goods remained behind at Prairie du Chien, where the larger steamboat had broken her shaft. "There remains no visible means or chance of getting the articles up this winter.... "[60] The company-chartered boat had not extended the courtesy of carrying the mail. Taliaferro accused the company men of being "particularly selfish and unaccommodating... They are ready, however, to ask for all such attentions and think it hard, if refused."[61] Basic reciprocity between the gentlemen was obviously lacking, though the agent was now in a state of mind to see every omission as a slight. When mail finally arrived, it brought further upsetting news from Pennsylvania that the mistress's mother was not expected to live and she was asking to see her daughter for the last time. In the lateness of the season, it was impossible. "We are 1600 miles from our family and with no chance of transport?"[62] The household entered the coming winter with a grim aspect. They had witnessed the death of Eliza's baby and anticipated the death of another loved one far away, and they lacked the basic provisions necessary to ensure their survival with any comfort through the winter months.[63]

The first snow fell followed by another hard frost. The leaves had all turned color, fallen, and blown away. Thirty Dakota returned from the rice swamps with a large number of teal ducks they had caught. Taliaferro hired some Indian women to dig up the remaining potatoes. There was more work than the servants could do, and everyone's spirits were low. The ice began to form along the river banks.[64] By November 1, winter arrived.

Nicollet settled in to work on his writings. "I squat in a little house prepared for me, wrapped in a bearskin, my head covered with a wool cap, to receive visitors, who come to me from Ft. Snelling or the Sioux." He also seemed happy alone in his own thoughts. "Study, calculations, editing will make the hours fly."[65]

In describing the Sioux, the observant Nicollet engaged them on what he thought to be their own terms. Nicollet was deeply insightful on the difficulty of actually knowing another people's culture.[66] He usually used the word "sauvage," taken from Rousseau, to refer to the Indians. "The names under which we know the sauvage nations are scarcely ever the names which the nations give to themselves," he wrote, noting what had eluded Catlin entirely. "Since we never arrive at these nations, except by passing through others, the names that we receive are those which their neighbors give [them].... [These names] are as variable as the routes that lead to a nation, and the name, thus, depends on the side from which one arrives."[67] He was also skilled at ethnology. He recorded considerable new detail about words, customs, and meanings of Dakota life.

In all of his perceptive notes about various tribes, he never mentioned the slaves who made his existence possible in St. Peter's that year. The slave women's contributions were elided as he described their efforts in the passive voice: "the little house that had been prepared for me."[68] There is little question who prepared the house for his comfort every day: Harriet and Eliza; the mistress merely ordered it done. Like Featherstonhaugh, he attributed the conveniences of his existence to his hosts' generosity, not to the efforts of the individuals they held as slaves. Rousseau's language gave Nicollet a context for understanding the Sioux as part of "the family of man"—as a people in their pure and natural state. But Nicollet seems to have held no parallel fascination for African Americans, forced to perform the labor that supported his travel and his scientific advancements.

That Nicollet did not notice the servants does not mean that they did not observe him. How could Harriet not give thought to the man who remained with her master and mistress during that long northern winter? As he was the third principal person of the household, she would have done his laundry, changed his sheets, made his bed, emptied his chamber pot, and cooked the wild rice and milk broth on which he subsisted when his malaria flared up.[69] She furnished the wood and prepared the fires, both in his bedroom in the main residence and in the little house to which he retreated to write and study.

ON NOVEMBER 8 Taliaferro noted, "Wolves come into our enclosures for something to eat. The season is hard upon them."[70] At night, one would be able to hear their howls, calling to each other. Also on that day, the oxcart, on which so much depended, broke down under a load of wood. With one wheel irreparable, another way had to be found to haul the wood.[71] Without a cart, the oxen were useless, so the master gave one team to Jacob Falstrom, the Swede, and the other to another settler at the Coldwater Spring.[72] At least the servants wouldn't need to feed the oxen over the winter.

That November, when the fort's officer in charge of subsistence auctioned off the stores of surplus pork, it was discovered that many of the barrels had gone bad. To everyone's amazement, even the rotten pork sold at high prices.[73] "Necessity has no law," Harriet's master commented.[74]

Before the local Mdekatowan Indians left for the annual deer hunt, some stopped to ask the agent about plans for the sale of lands.[75] Specifically, the Indians wanted to know whether the government had agreed to their terms.[76] The agent assured them: "my nation is disposed to see your people do well and the more happy you become the better pleased we shall be.... You say you respect me and listen to my councils, then be at peace and labour for the support of your growing families. You say you wish to live like the whites and dress like them. If so, you must consent to labour as they do and you will be satisfied." The agent used almost every opportunity to repeat his mantra: hard work will make you free.

A week later, an incident occurred at the fort that drew the attention of everyone within earshot on the plateau.[77] Sentences were carried out on several soldiers convicted of desertion by the court-martial. The sentences were heralded by the drum corps. Some of the convicted soldiers were flogged 50 times, and others 100 times. Then, with shaved heads, they were drummed out of camp. The drum corps escorted them through the fort's gates and down the incline to the dock. Thus publicly shamed, the men headed downriver.

Ironically, expulsion was the area's ultimate penalty.[78] Expelled from the shelters and food stores in the dead of winter, the convicted soldiers had to either find their way to the next outpost down the frozen river channel or beg someone in the area to let them stay. To be expelled from the community during this season was the worst penalty of all, even worse than the whipping. This was freedom at a high price.

In early December an incident far to the north triggered the territory's first murder trial. A fur trader named Aitkin kept a trading post at Sandy Lake, where he traded principally with the Ojibwa. In keeping with the traders' custom he had taken an Ojibwa wife. Their adult son was killed fighting another Ojibwa man named Che-ga-weye-cum. Aitkin and his friends later pursued the man and captured him.

Since only the Ojibwa Indians were involved in the incident, and no Sioux, prosecution of Che-ga-weye-cum fell outside of Taliaferro's jurisdiction. Had it been a killing between tribesmen, the victor would simply have taken the victim's scalp. A missionary accompanying the group persuaded them to take Che-ga-weye-cum somewhere where he could be tried under laws of the land.[79] The nearest court sat in Prairie du Chien, 300 miles downriver. The last boat on the river had gotten stuck, and it was hard enough for a mail carrier to get through on snowshoes during the winter. So it was decided to bring Che-ga-weye-cum to Fort Snelling, 100 miles from the site of his capture, to remain in the fort's custody for the winter. The fort only had military authority, so it could not try Che-ga-weye-cum. All the while that the accused was held and fed, court-martialed soldiers continued to be prosecuted and expelled from the fort. This was the first lesson of criminal trials and legal process on the frontier.

On December 24, the thermometer registered zero at sunrise. The Taliaferros celebrated Christmas with Monsieur Nicollet. The mistress and the French house-guest played Christmas carols on the piano and violin, and the servants received their Christmas boxes. Sunday, Christmas day, the master wrote, "A number of Indians called to pay their respects to me at the office and had, of course, to undergo various salutations on the cheek from many and old as well as young women—a custom derived from our Canadian population. Not a very agreeable one."[80]

The master's outlook was decidedly less rosy than earlier when the weather was fine, and, accordingly, everyone in the house must have been aware of it. "My life has thus far been a laborious one of 24 years in the public service and I find that after so many years of privation and hardship at an extreme remote post I shall at last die poor as poor indeed."[81] Around him he saw poor persons buying rotten pork for food. "The prices paid by poor people for every article necessary to their comfort—150 percent more paid by them than by men of capital. One half of the world lives by fleecing and plucking others."[82] However, he was cheered by Van Buren's election.

In succeeding days Taliaferro's diary entries were reduced to almost telegraphic notes, written in haste due to the extreme cold temperatures. "December 26—30 degrees below zero at sunrise. Some more snow at 9:30 this morning. 6 inches has fallen. December 27, 25 below zero at sunrise. Three suns reflected this morning. Such brilliant beauty as the sun reflects of a cold morning is beyond description or the painter's art."[83]

At year's end, on December 30, the agent joined a party riding out to the lakes to inspect the progress at the Indian school. His daughter Mary was there, now eight-and-a-half-years-old, perhaps missing her front teeth, and taking instruction from Miss Stevens, the minister's niece. Light-hearted, witty, and strikingly beautiful, Miss Stevens had also become more fluent in the Dakota language, because she came to the Dakota young enough to learn their language easily.[84] As the leading Christians at the fort, the Loomises and Ogdens rode along with the party, as did the tall doctor. However, Dr. Emerson's ulterior motive for accompanying the group was probably his interest in the young schoolteacher.[85]

On December 31, 1836, the agent once again received almost 150 calls by old men, women, and children. He was kissed by at least 50 of them. "A disagreeable ceremony for a busy man at the end of the year," he recorded. "On tomorrow it will be worse unless I can get off and out of sight."[86]

CHAPTER 10

The Call of the Wood as a Prelude to Treaty

I N THE 1830S, great primal forests of tall white pine timber situated along Lake Superior's southern coast in Wisconsin territory were an even more significant natural resource to the nation than lead or furs. These white pine forests no longer exist, but in the 1830s the fate of national expansion depended on them and their fate was to be decided by a treaty at St. Peter's.

Wood was as necessary for building the frontier as it was rare. At that time, all lumber destined for St. Louis and other upper Mississippi towns had to be shipped in from mills located in the East. This shortage was felt even at the agency.[1] Westward expansion had reached the continent's central river, but west of the Mississippi the lands were mostly treeless prairie. Those trees, running along creek beds and river valley pockets, were the shorter, scrubbier softwood varieties, unsuitable as building materials. But south of Lake Superior there were tall straight pine forests. These northern Wisconsin forest lands were the richest source of good timber anywhere within range of water shipment. The lands belonged to the Ojibwa, and the Northwest Territory Ordinance required the Indians' consent if they were asked to cede their lands, so the U.S. government had to make a treaty with them to get them to relinquish their forest lands.[2]

The American Fur Company saw the occasion of an Indian treaty as an opportunity to acquire cash, something always valuable and in short supply. To make the most of this financial opportunity, the company's objective was to get between the government and the Indians. The federal government was willing to pay the Indians substantial amounts of monies for the land, but, because the fur company had advanced them traps and other Western goods, the fur company held debts against the tribes. If the company could leverage the Indians' dependency properly, it could slice off shares of the largest, most important and expensive real estate deals of the century, and be paid promptly in cash. The fur company intended to collect the Indians' debts against the monies allotted to them for sale of their lands. Some government officials supported the maneuver. Territorial Governor Cass favored the idea of using the Indians' debt load as a way to persuade them to relinquish their land.

The fur company had learned to monitor the government's every move in western expansion in order to actively intervene in successive treaty negotiations.[3] Assigned to this task was John F. A. Sanford, who would become the Scotts' notorious adversary. Sanford had married the daughter of the St. Louis head of the American Fur Company and advanced to become their most effective Washington lobbyist. The former Virginian, who was now favored son-in-law to the Chouteau fur-trading family, would not come into direct relation with Harriet for several years, but he was already involved in some of the larger frontier policy issues that affected her household and her community at St. Peter's. Sanford increasingly traveled between St. Louis, New York, and Washington City to peddle the company's influence. The company had an extraordinarily good communication network between the fur trade captains in the field and company headquarters, and John F. A. Sanford was often in routine contact with the Commissioner of Indian Affairs in Washington.[4]

The company's policy of leveraging the Indian debt in treaties was at odds with Taliaferro's vision for the Indians. In the year that followed, Taliaferro found himself increasingly out of the loop of information, particularly given that his outgoing reports needed to go to the territorial governor before they could be forwarded to Washington. Governor Dodge's home was a day's ride from Prairie du Chien, but no permanent capital had yet been established for the territory. Hence, Dodge continually traveled around the territory, conferring with residents in far-flung settlements who hoped that their village would be chosen as the new site of government.

Late in 1836, Taliaferro received a copy of a new treaty with the Eastern Ojibwa tribes of Michigan negotiated by his fellow agent Henry Schoolcraft. Outraged at what he read, he declared it to be "Fraud!" in large block letters in his diary.[5] The treaty's first priority was paying the fur traders' claims against the Indians.

Years before, when the federal government abandoned its monopoly on buying furs from the Indians, private companies moved in quickly, becoming the sole recorders of the Indians' debt. The Indians had no records of their own, and debts were recorded on ledgers that the Indians could not read. Though the Indians were not unsophisticated in bartering with traders, they were regarded as notoriously easy marks in deals structured in U.S. currency. The Indian chiefs acknowledged this weakness themselves.[6] There was no check whatsoever on the debit sums the traders named. Moreover, debt and gift were culturally blurred concepts in trader-Indian exchanges. To cultivate Indian loyalty, the traders regularly gave them gifts and held feasts as well as extending credit against future fur hunts. Gifts and hospitality purportedly offered "in friendship and goodwill" could later be claimed as Indian debt, and unscrupulous traders had incentives to inflate amounts or even claim debts that were never incurred.

"If the government continues to recognize this gratuitous practice of permitting the treaties with Indian tribes to recognize the payments of traders and other adventurers among them for goods and credits said to be lost in their trade with said tribes," Taliaferro wrote, "it will take millions out of the treasury."[7] He highlighted a subtle legal point. The Indians never pledged their land or monies derived from their land to the traders to secure their debts.[8] Moreover, the amount at stake was enormous. The treaty with the Eastern Ojibwa proposed to release $300,000 of government currency directly to the traders.

It particularly rankled him to learn that these exorbitant sums were to be awarded to the American Fur Company traders under a new treaty while the Indians often starved while waiting for their portion in the form of late-arriving annuities. This inequity was more than Taliaferro could bear, particularly while the Sioux at his agency still waited empty-handed for overdue annuities promised under a treaty that was more than a decade old. He stalled the Sioux with excuses and attempted to ward off their hunger by digging into his own reserves. Not only was he alive with the sense of injustice, he was in the best position to know what was happening in the field. Yet his reports could not even get through to Washington expeditiously.

Simultaneously, entrepreneurial businessmen seeking early permission to build sawmills were already visiting the area seeking prospects well in advance of new treaties. Most speculators scouted every possible authority, pursuing permission wherever they could find it. Agent Taliaferro denied one man permission to build a sawmill, so he contacted the Indians directly. The Indians then sought the agent's advice. Ultimately, the man approached Col. Davenport for permission. This circular method was typical of policy making in the territory.[9] Each issue bounced between different jurisdictions of civil and military government at far ends of the country. The split of official authority on these matters hindered the development of a unified and coherent policy. Not only was jurisdiction divided between the Indian agency and the military but the two different chains of command also spanned the nation, from the northern woods to the territorial government (which changed location yearly) and on to Washington City, with its two different federal bureaus. Coordination would have been a nightmare even if the public objectives had been unitary, which, of course, they weren't.

The commissioner of Indian Affairs in Washington wrote Governor Dodge asking what the Chippewa wished to do about selling their land and lumbering rights. Although assigned the obligations of Indian superintendent within the territory, Governor Dodge knew no more about the Indian nation than did the commissioner, as he lived hundreds of wilderness miles south of the Ojibwa north woods. "As to the wishes of the Chippewa Indians relative to the establishment of mills in their country," Governor Dodge wrote back, " I am unable to state what [they] may be. The death of Mr. Sinn prevents my ascertaining the wishes of these Indians officially at this time."[10] (This second man appointed subagent had committed suicide.) Nonetheless, the governor offered an opinion that the commissioner surely wanted to hear: "I think the Chippewa Indians may be benefitted by the erection of sawmills in their country." Dodge's advice was to purchase from the Chippewa and the Sioux Indians "all their pine country east of the Mississippi River, as early next season as [they] could be convened." "The country," he wrote "abounds in pine, is barren of game and unfit for cultivation, and valuable alone for its lumber materials.... [I]t would not be difficult to effect a purchase of that whole pine region of the country. The Chippewa Indians are poor and in want, and in justice to them...the sooner the pine country can be purchased the better. Both for the Indians and the citizens of this territory."[11]

Sensing the opportunity, the regional fur company partners sought lumber and sawmill sites as well. Their objectives were as singular in making money as the government's were diverse. One company partner pressed the Ojibwa to sell milling rights on the primary tributary of the upper Mississippi, but Ojibwa leaders "consistently turned down the offer until 'the wine arrived.'"[12] Dodge was aware that a deal was under way[13] and he advised Washington that the amount the company proposed to pay was "*entirely too small.* [The Company manager] wants the privilege of occupying the better part of the pine region of country [which] would give him a complete monopoly of all the advantages…on that river."[14]

Even the small military sawmill at the Falls of St. Anthony behind the fort was coveted by the Fort's sutler, Mr. Stambaugh. This little sawmill, built by the army, produced all the plank necessary for the fort and the agency, for buildings, furniture, and even for coffins. Sutler Stambaugh attempted to claim the mill and the exclusive right to mill lumber as part of his sutlery franchise to supply material to the post. To secure this claim, he traveled to Washington to meet his political friends face-to-face. He reached the capital at a bad time, however, because the men he hoped to persuade were away on extended trips. Instead, the official he did meet doubted the authority to dispose of government property and refused him the privilege of controlling the sawmill.[15]

News of this scheme didn't reach Taliaferro or the commandant, frozen in only three miles from the site, for several more months. Only then could they speak against it. When Col. Davenport heard about it, he saw through the sutler's objective immediately. He had witnessed private claimants move in quickly when Fort Armstrong was decommissioned. If Stambaugh acquired the sawmill while he was sutler, he could attempt a preemption claim against the future time when the military withdrew from the area. Stambaugh would then be in a position to claim the most desirable mill site in the area.

Both Agent Taliaferro and Col. Davenport were shocked by Stambaugh's audacity. Each wrote his respective superior in Washington: "We are upon Indian land," the Colonel protested in his letter, "and [we] cannot, consistently, grant any part of it to any person, whatever for his private use.[16] Surely the interests in the military sawmill could not be transferred to this man!"[17] The sutler's temerity in pursuing his own advantage would surprise and disappoint Taliaferro further. Sutler Stambaugh, awarded by President Jackson with the post of sutler, played by the rules of the spoils system.[18]

Everyone in the region seemed to be aware that the government was moving toward acquiring all Indian land east of the Mississippi. As Agent Taliaferro described the national stakes, geography dictated destiny. "A glance at the map is sufficient to convince all as to the future importance of this post to the U.S., in an efficient government of the northern and western tribes. An entering wedge is now absolutely requisite to secure a stronger interest with the neighboring Sioux, and a timely liberality would secure to us the most happy results. I have some experience, and the Government may yet profit by its application. LT."[19] The master held repeated councils with the Sioux to divine their wishes regarding the lands. He was hopeful when he received mail that the governor might visit him the following spring. "I wish he may. Then he can see and judge for himself as to...this country and learn my true course of policy with the Indians of this vast region."[20]

By Christmas 1836, Henry Sibley too knew that an important treaty was planned for the coming summer, and he advised the company's New York headquarters. "It is of great importance to us that Major T[aliaferro] not be appointed a commissioner," Sibley wrote.[21] "He is known to be inimical to the Am. Fur Co....[H]e has repeatedly declared that if appointed commissioner at any treaty, he would not allow anything [to the Company] for Indian credits." Putting the matter directly, Sibley wrote, "I would recommend that some competent person, (yourself, if possible,) should proceed forthwith to Washington, and endeavor to defeat the appointment of Major T. and procure the assent of Governor Dodge to act in lieu of him." As commander of the fort at the time, Col. Davenport was also a likely candidate for treaty commissioner. He had stood with Taliaferro, both in the matter of Sibley's access to the Indians in the guardhouse and on the sutler's attempt to take over the sawmill. Sibley wrote, "Col. Davenport is a fair and honorable man, but our Agent has too long had his ear to make his appointment as commissioner a very profitable one to us. If Gov. Dodge should be directed to act as sole Commissioner, I should much prefer it."[22] In response, Ramsey Crooks, the New York manager of the American Fur Company lobbied to see that Sibley's hopes were realized.[23]

As Sibley sat writing to company headquarters from the hillside at Mendota, Taliaferro recorded in his journal: "Sharp Cold: Dec. 27, inkstands and bottles burst with expanded liquid."[24] One of the servant women probably cleaned up the spill of congealed, crystallized ink and broken glass. Harriet may not have been attuned to all the nuances of the contest under way, but her master was not given to silent travail. Everyone in his household had to be aware of his reaction when he perceived injustice, just as certainly as they'd know the direction of the wind.

This was the larger constellation of forces and actors swirling around Harriet's North Star. The affairs of masters were necessarily the subject of discussion by their servants. The servants' tenuous position meant that they had to be alert to the countervailing moods and opinions of the principal people they served so closely. With virtually unlimited access to every household member (servants needed to keep the fires stocked and continually tended), the servants must have known everything.

On long winter evenings, to pass the time, Nicollet, the house guest, and the mistress played duets: he on the violin, she on the piano. The talented violinist knew classical songs as well as the street melodies of Paris, Creole New Orleans, and St. Louis, where he had been the guest of fur baron Pierre Chouteau Jr. The sweet violin and piano music must have wafted through the house from where the master sat reading or musing by one fireplace and through the floorboards to the basement kitchen, where Harriet and Eliza washed up, tended the late night kitchen fire, knitted socks for the family, and prepared their own meals of coarse ground corn and animal fat. After the evening music sessions, the mistress called to the servant women to make Monsieur Nicollet a late supper. He liked a broth of warm milk and wild rice before going to bed. All the candle lamps and most of the fires were extinguished and all would retire. With this last command of the day, Eliza and Harriet could settle in and lie down to sleep on their rag pallet before the kitchen fire's embers.

Given her proximity, Harriet may have been able to observe the successive events from the vantage point of her master, who regularly sought to promote distributive justice. Taliaferro's perceptions, passions, and views of independence and the value of marriage and labor, and even his tendency to repetition, were not intended to tutor her understanding of the world, but they must have had that effect, nonetheless. They must have conditioned this young slave woman to expect justice. Her later tenacity in preserving her family's independence could have sprung uninspired from her heart, but it is more likely that it was nurtured by her life's experience—and the person who shaped that experience most forcefully these formative years was Lawrence Taliaferro. It appears reasonable to assume that the lessons learned through her observation of Taliaferro fortified her to eventually go the distance in the constitutional lawsuit.

What Harriet could not yet have known was that John F. A. Sanford, the engineer of the company machine, increasingly well-tuned with each successive turn of government treaty making, would be the very man she would encounter in the fight for the freedom of her family. At this time, he worked the levers and peddled influence for the American Fur Company, which was the most powerful company in the nation and in Washington City.

THAT YEAR, during their first winter at the 45th latitude, Dr. Emerson and Etheldred experienced the true cold of the North. Three times each day, the tall doctor stepped outdoors to record the temperature, as he was required to do by army regulations. The extreme cold must have frosted his glasses, clouding his vision as he peered at the thermometer to obtain the necessary reading. In this Minnesota winter, the air would freeze in a person's nostrils with each breath. Never having enough warm clothing to keep some part of the body from being chilled, one might sit wrapped in blankets or fur pelts, hoping for the warmth to return to fingers or toes so these could move again. Such were the conditions with which Emerson and Etheldred contended, and their quarters were doubtlessly less well insulated than the Taliaferros' house at the agency.

Visitors to the hospital brought Dr. Emerson a steady stream of colds and sore throats. This was particularly true of the enlisted men, who bunked together in close quarters to keep warm. All-in-all, however, the men were fairly healthy and the hospital was rarely filled. Occasionally, the doctor journeyed across the river's hard ice to Mendota, where the bachelor fur baron Henry Sibley lived. There he would pull teeth or treat any ailments of the retainers living around the fur company buildings.[25]

Reacting to the harsh winter conditions, Emerson wrote the first of his many letters requesting transfer. Usually he pled his case in terms of some illness, which he thought might justify reposting. "Having suffered severely this last winter...with a rheumatic affliction in my left arm and left lower extremity, the joint almost useless, I dread the ensuing winter.... While writing this, I am suffering severe pain."[26] He also confided, "When last in Philadelphia, I contracted a venereal disease for which I had to take mercury rather freely and which...aggravates my rheumatic affliction."[27] Barring a transfer to a warmer climate, the doctor wrote the surgeon general asking to take the medical exam for promotion. He even bought a carpet bag from the sutler in anticipation of the trip. A few weeks later, he returned the carpet bag when no invitation to sit for the exam materialized.

During the winter, Harriet was most apt to see Etheldred when she went to the sutler's shanty because it was situated inside the gate just opposite the post hospital. Waiting as the sutler's hired man filled the order, they would have an hour or so to gather news about the goings-on within the fort.[28] The errand gave the agency servants the excuse to see the other servants in the area.[29] About 200 men were stationed at the fort that winter, but one rarely saw them outside the high walls. While the men marched on the parade ground, officers' servants often went out to watch them.[30]

Etheldred might find a reason to visit the sutler's store, too. Dr. Emerson had a sweet tooth, and he regularly charged apples, currants, and raisins. Canned peaches were his favorites.[31] Inside the post, Washington's Birthday was generally celebrated with a ball, and the sutler sold tickets for the event.[32] That year, Dr. Emerson bought two tickets for the ball. The only two unmarried women in the area were the young missionary, Miss Stevens, whom the doctor quite fancied but who may have been unable to attend from her mission home seven miles away, and Miss Mix, the stout sister of Mrs. Loomis. Some officers teased the doctor about the portly Miss Mix. Of course, Emerson might have been happy to sleigh out to Lake Harriet to pick up the entire Stevens family for the event.

When the river ice finally broke in May, a group of soldiers set off downstream escorting the accused Che-ga-weye-cum to a court in Prairie du Chien. The Mackinac boat contained two men involuntarily bound together by the murder: the accused and the victim's father.[33] Che-ga-weye-cum had remained in the guardhouse prison since December. The grieving father, having nursed his vengeance all winter, was now prepared to see his son's murderer taken to court.

Crossing their path and traveling north against the current, was a delegation of missionaries paddling a heavy dugout canoe. Navigating the party was someone Harriet may have never expected to see again: none other than Capt. Day's slave, James Thompson. Thompson had returned, and he was now a free man. The travelers arrived at St. Peter's with plans to set up a Methodist mission. Thompson had been purchased and freed by the head of the Methodist missionary delegation. The minister needed a Sioux language interpreter to establish his mission to the Dakota, and Jim, as Brunson called him, had accomplished what few English speakers had: he had mastered the elusive language, in part with the help of his Sioux wife. Now his language facility gave him the means to return to her.[34]

The Methodist minister had published a call in the denomination's newspapers for the faithful to contribute money to help purchase Jim's freedom. The appeal tapped both the ideas of Christianizing the heathen Indians and freeing a slave to do so. With an outpouring of donations across the country, Brunson paid Capt.

Day the exorbitant sum of $1,200 for Jim, claiming that Jim's emancipation was divine providence.[35]

What Jim Thompson had accomplished must have astounded the other black servants. Though his master had taken him away as a slave, separating him from his wife and children, he had returned a free man, navigating his own way home. Knowing the surrounding area better than anyone, the freedman navigated the delegation upstream, hunting deer for food, when necessary. Jim Thompson had remained faithful to his Indian wife, while the officers who had taken Indian lovers had transferred out, never to return.[36] Jim Thompson not only attained freedom but his wilderness survival skills also ensured his continuing independence. The six foot, 200 pound mulatto man seemed to move easily through many different communities.[37] The newly freed Jim Thompson worked side-by-side with the white missionaries at the lakes.[38] Nonetheless, on the account books at Mendota, he was always listed by race as "James Thompson, a negro and a black man."[39]

As the other missionaries before him, the Reverend Brunson consulted with Taliaferro about the best location for a mission[40] before deciding to locate the Methodists at a place called Kaposia, the traditional home to Big Thunder's band.[41] Consistent with his worldview, the Methodist missionary sought to position himself and his church between the government moneys and the recipient Indians, much like the fur company did. He saw the treaty monies as an opportunity to support the Methodist mission to the heathen. He urged that the Indian annuities be paid to missionaries like him who labored to domesticate the Indians rather than to the Indians themselves.[47]

CHAPTER 11

1837: A Treaty Made before Her Eyes

THAT SUMMER THE PROSPECT of a treaty drew many different people to St. Peter's Agency, where the Minnesota River met the Mississippi. The official treaty party set out by steamboat from Dubuque to rendezvous with the Indians with the intent of buying the northern half of Wisconsin.[1] The Ojibwa had been notified to arrive at the agency sometime between July 1 and 20. Taliaferro had sent runners with messages of invitation and small packets of tobacco to all the Ojibwa villages.

Lush, deep green virgin pine forests extended from Lake Superior through the Chippewa River Valley to the Mississippi.[2] If the government could open those lands to lumbering, the river's current would aid shipping to downstream customers throughout the entire central continental area. These, the only major forest lands within 500 miles, were claimed by the Ojibwa, who had already pushed the woodland Sioux farther west—as they themselves had been pushed from the Great Lakes by earlier waves of settlement and Indian removal.

Through its maneuvering the company had successfully seen to it that neither Taliaferro nor Colonel Davenport was named as commissioner. The two-person treaty party, which arrived aboard the Steamboat *Irene*,[3] consisted of Territorial Governor Henry Dodge, who was a former dragoons officer, Indian fighter, lead miner, and now a frontier statesman, and Verplanck Van Antwerp, a New York lawyer who served as secretary of the commission. A third commissioner failed to arrive in time to catch the steamboat and it left without him.[4]

Less than a month before the treaty was scheduled to start, a subagent to the Ojibwa was finally appointed. However, when the subagent, Daniel Bushnell, arrived for the first time at his new post, none of the Indians with whom he was supposed to establish ties were around because they were out on the annual buffalo hunts.[5] Bushnell could hardly obtain the Ojibwas' views, let alone their confidence, in this short month before they were to make the most important treaty in their people's history, signing away their interest in almost three million acres of land. Bushnell barely had time to wait for whoever showed up at his subagency before enlisting them to walk south with him to the anticipated rendezvous point. During the negotiation, some Ojibwa looked instead to the man they knew and had trusted before, Harriet's master, agent to the Dakota. Although he was passed over for appointment as treaty commissioner, he had the Indians' confidence.

The spread-winged council house was too small to accommodate the hundreds of people expected for this momentous public occasion. Tradition required that Indian treaties be negotiated publicly in the open air so that everyone could observe the proceedings. But they also needed to be conducted under some sort of canopy. The soldiers constructed a shade bower from branches and saplings torn from the river banks. The bower, built along the outside of the fort's wall, was the stage for the pageantry of treaty making in the shadow of the imposing fort.

By June 30, many tribes had already gathered in anticipation. The temporary village of bark lodges housed 1,300 people, making it more populous than any town within hundreds of miles. Just 10 days before the treaty was to begin, as the Indians gathered, most of the troops under Col. Davenport were ordered to depart to aid in a crisis with the Seminole Indians in Florida.[6] Although a new command had been ordered to the fort, it would be weeks before they could arrive, so when the treaty began, there was only a skeleton staff of 19 soldiers manning the fort.[7] Since military surgeons were posted independently of the command, Dr. Emerson, and accordingly Etheldred, stayed on to attend the incoming company of men.

Col. Davenport's reassignment to the Seminole war was a stroke of luck for Sibley and the company. Without a steadfast troop commandant at his side, Taliaferro lacked an ally for his position of ensuring distributional fairness to the tribes. Capt. Scott, who was left in command, was a skilled soldier but no statesman. Even the doctor outranked him. Capt. Scott could not be counted on to take the high ethical ground in opposing fur trader claims.[8]

Just as Sibley had wished, the commission was a one-man show, and although Van Antwerp served as secretary, Henry Dodge was clearly the man in charge. At 55, Dodge was clean-shaven, fit, and robust, with a towering reputation. He had come to the territory as a squatter on Indian lead mines, but by evading eviction he had become a successful lead mining businessman;[9] he was also a territorial legislator and a veteran of two Indian wars. He still carried the laurel of "war hero" among the settlers for his leadership in the Blackhawk War. Even his interests in mining lead for munitions were considered patriotic in the territory. To the northern Indian nations, his warlike feats in conquering the Sac and Fox made him an estimable person.[10] (The northern Indians hated the Sac and Fox.) Now as territorial governor,[11] he was also Taliaferro's superior, the superintendent of Indian affairs for the territory. As the event's undisputed leader, Governor Dodge did not really negotiate: he listened to the Indians and then essentially set the terms. As a former captain of the dragoons, he knew how to give orders. He announced the government's policy and eventually determined several treaty terms almost by directive.

Although Dodge was now governor of a free territory, his family still held several persons as slaves at his home near Prairie du Chien. He had brought five slaves into Wisconsin from Missouri. One particular slave man, Toby, usually accompanied him in his travels and was probably the unnamed slave who attended him now.[12]

The commission's secretary, the tall, skinny New York–born Dutchman named Verplanck Van Antwerp, had a great thatch of auburn hair and wore tiny, rectangular spectacles perched on his nose. As secretary of the commission, it was his task to actually write the treaty and serve as scribe to Dodge's commanding performance. What Dodge provided in age, frontier experience, and political negotiating style, Van Antwerp balanced with scrupulous attention to legal detail. The young Van Antwerp had risen in the world rapidly through his friendship with the president's son. From his own accounts, Van Antwerp was clearly in awe of Dodge, and he probably played the part of an admiring sycophant toward the imperial Dodge—an attitude that enhanced the governor's prestige further in the Indians' eyes.[13]

The commissioners stayed and took their meals at the agency house with the Taliaferros.[14] The master had looked forward to this opportunity to spend time with the governor since he saw it as his chance to influence him on Indian policy.[15] The table probably included seven persons: the master; the mistress; Governor Dodge; Van Antwerp and his cousin; perhaps the Dakota subagent, Miles Vineyard; and, of course, Monsieur Nicollet, who was still a houseguest. Dr. Emerson, who witnessed the treaty and outranked the captain temporarily in command, would logically be invited to join them, completing the table for eight. With so many houseguests, Harriet and the other servants would have been busier than usual. But each evening, she may have overheard discussions of the day's events as she waited on the commissioners.

At Mendota the fur company men eagerly anticipated the treaty.[16] Since the Ojibwa were both the company's trappers and their customers, whatever concerned them was of interest to the company. Sibley entertained several company men, including Hercules Dousman, his senior partner from Prairie du Chien, who had come for the event. Also waiting at Sibley's house for the treaty's completion was a group of men, financed and outfitted by the company and ready to set out for the best mill sites as soon as they received the go-ahead. The law required that the Indian agent be apprised of every visitor to Indian territory, but Sibley neglected the protocol by failing to register his guests. Taliaferro sent him a curt letter of reminder.[17]

On July 20, with some 1,300 Ojibwa assembled to participate and 700 Sioux looking on, the council began under the bower in the shadow of the fortress. The Ojibwa chiefs in attendance included Hole-in-the-Day; his brother, Strong Ground; as well as the ascerbic Chief Flatmouth, who had complained about the Americans and not wanting to sell his land when visiting Taliaferro with Nicollet the previous summer. Several other tribes were represented by orators and leaders, including Nadin, Pei-ya-jik, and the Buffalo, who were already known to Taliaferro's household from their regular visits to the agency.

In keeping with ritual, the council began by smoking the long red stone peace pipe. It was offered to the four points of the compass, smoked first by Governor Dodge, and shared by all the chiefs present.[18] Then each chief had a chance to speak. The day ended with Dodge urging the Ojibwa to remain at peace with the surrounding Sioux during the treaty-making time.[19]

Each day, after Etheldred prepared the doctor's white dress uniform, he would have little to do but to wait on his master. Each principal man present at the treaty council had his own attendant standing behind him. In the proper hierarchical order of things, even the young secretary, Van Antwerp, had his younger cousin[20] with him to see to his personal arrangements. These sets of hierarchies and sub-hierarchies seemed to define social organization on the frontier in the absence of the more formal sets of hierarchies existing among the army inside the fort. Thus, instead of meeting as common men on equal footing (such as would be akin to the two nations making a common constitution), each nation resorted to a hierarchy of principal men and subordinate men in the proceedings. Moreover, women were not in attendance on either side. The women's places in both cultures were similarly limited to the housekeeping and food preparation, which allowed the men to appear independent. The Ojibwa and the Sioux women remained at their respective encampments during the treaty, performing all the work necessary to maintain their people for the duration. No woman signed the treaty, and no woman's voice was recorded in the transcriptions. It's quite likely that there were no women present under the treaty bower at all.

Accordingly, Etheldred, but not Harriet, probably witnessed firsthand the daily deliberations and the craft of each day's negotiation. Everything was stated twice, once in English and once in Ojibwa. The interpreters, who spanned the spectrum of frontier ethnicity—from Scot-Dakota to African-, Irish-, and French-Ojibwa—translated. No one translated for the hundreds of Sioux who looked on from farther away.[21] But even for those who didn't sit close enough to hear, the proceedings were demonstrated in ritual and public display.

On the second day, the Ojibwa failed to appear at the bower. A messenger reported that the chiefs wanted more time to talk among themselves.[22] When the council began again the following day, several chiefs submitted requests. One chief was deaf and wished to sit closer. Some wanted better accommodations. Another wanted more tobacco and more food. "My father, your children…wish you to give them four times more tobacco than you have given them. My father, what has happened to you? Have you cut off your breasts, that you cannot suckle your children? If you did so, it would render them more pliant and ready to yield to your wishes."[23] The chiefs cajoled the government representatives because whatever their people received now did not have to be negotiated for later. There was no reason to hasten the process while their people were fed well. The longer the treaty process, the longer the feasting time.

Taliaferro used his time with Dodge to warn him about the company's practices. In a letter, he released the full depth of his anger so completely that he overstepped the bounds of reason in his perorations on the subject. His letter was an unmitigated tirade against the American Fur Company. Everything that he had wanted to tell the governor about the company's bad actions and misfeasance during the past was poured into the letter. Unfortunately, by venting his anger in such a white heat, in such an unrestrained way, he played into the hands of those who sought to discredit him as an intemperate zealot.

"This Company is becoming a giant, and is in full array against the government in all that concerns the welfare of our Indian relations. [It threatens]...to break down all competition in the trade and to enslave the poor Indian body and mind to their dictatorial will. In all this, they have sought...the cooperation of the public authorities, and when not obtained, these have been threatened with the malediction of the Company and with removal from office."[24] (Agent Street's early warning of the company's enmity had come to rest at Taliaferro's door. In fact, Taliaferro should have remembered that his friend Agent Street had had a showdown over lead mining rights and Indian claims with Henry Dodge, the very man who presided over the treaty for forest lands now.) Taliaferro urged that the government reestablish its exclusive fur trading franchise with the Indians, which it had abandoned in 1820 at the American Fur Company's urging.[25] "However badly the former system...it was nothing in comparison with the amount of funds fraudulently extracted from the Treasury by the American Fur Company for lost credits in their trade with the Indian tribes."[26] Taliaferro urged Congress to act now to "save from certain, and rapid destruction a people justly entitled to our sympathies, and protection—yes more, we are honor bound to do so as a nation of civilized beings."[27]

The governor took Taliaferro's letter and dutifully forwarded it on to Washington, though it does not appear from his records that Taliaferro ever received a response.

On Monday, July 24, the council proceeded with introductions. One by one, each chief stood up, addressed the audience, identified himself and his authority, and recounted the history of his particular band. Each speaker claimed authority to speak either through linkage to some noteworthy Ojibwa or claim of personal honor, thereby justifying his people's particular relation to the land in question.[28] "I only wish to tell you who my ancestors were. I am the son of...one of the greatest Chiefs of our nation."[29] Still others based their claims on lands they presently held. Gesturing to the east, the Spruce claimed, "It is only I who can tell you the truth about the lands where I live. Although I am but a child, you shall hear straight about my lands, because I am the master of them."[30] Chief Flatmouth explained his rise to chief as based on the merit of his own acts, although his ancestors were chiefs.[31] Each speaker then took his seat on the ground surrounded by his pipe bearers, principal warriors, and adult sons. With a quill pen, Van Antwerp recorded much of the proceedings.[32]

Unlike most Americans, Dred, and occasionally Harriet, were eye-witnesses to this history of nations transpiring at St. Peter's Agency. As servants they played only a supportive role in the drama, but from their stations of service, they could observe every play. They could watch the impressive, dignified governor prevail over a thousand Indians just by holding out for what he wanted. As Nadin told the governor, "Your look is so firm that I think it would not be possible for you not to do what you wished."[33] Holding out was a winning strategy that would eventually sustain Harriet and Dred through their lawsuit as well.

The Buffalo and Nadin advanced together to the governor's table. (Harriet may have recognized Nadin, the skilled orator named for the Wind, from the portrait of him that hung in the master's office.) Shaking the governor's hand, the Buffalo joked that he would shake hands with all of those present, but his arm was too short. Then he yielded to Nadin.

"We are a distracted people, and have no regular system of acting together," Nadin began.[34] Then he asked for more food; "You have everything around you and can give us some of the cattle that are around us. At [the last treaty, 1825], we were well fed."[35] Taliaferro responded by ordering that more food be provided. There would be no treaty until the Indians' bellies were full.

Absent from the gathering was the Pillagers Band, so named for their particular fearsomeness. It is unclear that they were invited; their lands might or might not have been east of the Mississippi River—but invited or not, the other chiefs expected them.[36] On the treaty's fifth day, the Pillagers arrived, disrupting the proceedings. Harriet's master described their arrival in alarming terms as "so many black devils" directed to force the commissioner to give the trader Lyman Warren $20,000. Lyman Warren rushed into the arbor and seated himself, fanning himself with his hat. Almost 100 Indians rushed into the arbor with him, causing a commotion. At the rear was their brand-new subagent, Daniel Bushnell, no doubt confused by everything and probably at a loss as to what to do. He arrived at the scene in the traveling company of a trader, who, it seemed, was not welcome at the gathering at all.[37]

Taliaferro drew his pistol and took aim at Lyman Warren. Chief Hole-in-the-Day declared, "Shoot, my father!" But the governor, standing next to Taliaferro, stopped him.[38]

"Very well, sir," the agent replied, "I only hold for the first overt act of hostility, then I sell my life, if need be, after the fall of the dastard who has attempted to intimidate this Commission."[39]

The next day, the governor reassigned the interpreters. One Sioux chief stated his great confidence in the gathering and that he and his men "will set far off and listen."[40]

On July 27 the talks deadlocked. Ma-ghe-ga-bo, a Pillager warrior who was designated to speak for the group, advanced to where the governor stood and pointed at a map between them. Ma-ghe-ga-bo was highly decorated for the occasion with red paint, a coronet of bald eagle feathers and several medals around his neck. "My father," he said, "when we first met here, we smoked and shook hands together. Four times we have gone through the same ceremony, and now, on the fifth, we have come to give you an answer. I stand here to represent the chiefs of the different bands of my nation, and to tell you that they agree to sell you the land you want."[41]

"The being who created us, made us naked. He gave you and your people knowledge and power to live well. Not so with us; we had to cover ourselves with moss and rotten wood. You must show your generosity towards us. My father, in all the country we sell you, we wish to hold on to that which gives us life—the streams and lakes where we fish, and the trees from which we make sugar. [We] will now show you the tree we wish to preserve." Someone handed him a small branch and he placed the sprig upon the table. "It is a different kind of tree from the one you wish to get from us. Every time the leaves fall from it, we will count it as one winter past."[42] The Indians knew that the government sought the tall pines rather than the broadleaf trees.

Ma-ghe-ga-bo continued, "We have understood you will pay us in goods and money for our lands, and we wish to know now how much you will give us for them."[43]

The governor, an artful negotiator, declined to name an amount. He directed his interpreter to ask the Indians to set the first figure: "As the land belongs to you, I wish you to tell me what you wish me to pay you for it." This response was doubly clever: the first sum named would set the negotiation ceiling. Further, the Indians had no words in their vocabulary to describe the sums appropriate for purchasing 28,000,000 acres of land.

Ma-ghe-ga-bo replied equally deftly by constructing a figure larger than the Ojibwa language allowed. "My father, if you offer us money and goods, we will take both. You see me count my fingers (counting six). Every finger counts ten. For so many years we wish you to pay us an annuity. After that, our grandchildren, who will have grown up, can speak for themselves.... My father, you will now see all your children in whose behalf I speak. All the chiefs who agree to sell you the land will now rise." At his signal, some 30 chiefs stood up. Ma-ghe-ga-bo then raised the piece of paper that he had placed over the map, signaling agreement. Taking the governor's hand he said, "My father, I will not let go your hand until I have counted the...villages." Nineteen village tribes were counted as Ma-ghe-ga-bo held the governor's hand to identify the village chiefs among the throng seated under the bower.

"We do not wish to disappoint you and our great father beyond the mountains in the object you had in coming here. We therefore grant you the country you want from us." Retaining in his hand another piece of paper, he said, "This piece we will keep, because we wish to say something more on it. At the conclusion of this treaty, you will ask us to touch the quill, but, no doubt, you will grant us what we ask before we do so. At the end of the treaty I will repeat what the chiefs have to say to you, and keep this paper for that purpose."

The Indians had wisely offered the government only the land's use for three generations, retaining title and preserving their grandchildren's opportunity to renegotiate the terms thereafter. The U.S. government, however, wanted full title, free from lingering interests by the Ojibwa so that they could remove the Ojibwa permanently and give title to settlers. The governor's reply was so lawyerlike that it may have been coached by Van Antwerp, the lawyer. "Your great father never buys land for a term of years. [Y]ou shall have the free use of the rivers and the privilege of hunting on the lands you are to sell, during the pleasure of your great father. If you sell these lands, you must sell them as all the other Indian nations have done."

Government Indian removal policy dictated that the many children of Indian mothers and white fathers, called "half-breeds" by the government, had to leave their homes on the land as well. The Indians expressed much greater concern about these children than did the white commissioners. "Our women have [borne] the half breeds among us. They are poor, and we wish them to be provided for....We wish to divide with them all....What you propose to give us, we wish to share only with [them]. My father, we...recommend our half-breed to your kindness. They are very numerous. We wish you to select a place for them on this river, where they may live and raise their children, and have their joys of life."

"It is a good principle in you to wish to provide for them," Dodge replied. "But you must do so in money, and cannot give them land." Dodge then proposed that annual payments be paid for only 20 years, rather than 60. The day concluded with two prices and two sets of terms, but with agreement that the tribes were willing to sell.

After the opening rituals on Friday, Chief Flatmouth, who had been absent the previous day, took his turn to address the crowd. He spoke "with no sugar in his mouth." Nicollet had encouraged him to trust Taliaferro the previous year. "We are pleased that our agents may estimate the value of our lands....We will wait to hear what you offer for the lands, and will then make you our answer. We will depend upon our two fathers (the Indian agents) to interest themselves for us; and we will submit it to them whether what you offer us is enough."[44]

Governor Dodge repeated the demand that the sale must be final, though the Indians did not need to leave the lands until white settlers moved in. "My friends, I will make known to your Great Father your request to be permitted to make sugar on the lands, and you will be allowed during his pleasure to hunt and fish on them. It will probably be many years before your great father will want all these lands for the use of his white children." He offered them $800,000, to be paid over 20 years, and promised to provide them with blacksmiths.[45] The assembled people retired to consider the terms.

Only 20 chiefs arrived for council the following day.[46] As always, the council began by passing the peace pipe. When a suitable time had passed, the governor asked whether the Ojibwa would accept his terms? No one replied. No one took the floor. The chiefs whispered among themselves too quietly to be heard for translation.

After half an hour had passed, two warriors emerged from the Ojibwa encampment, carrying two flags—the Ojibwa war flag and the stars and stripes—and dancing to beating drums. Behind them several hundred braves, all elaborately painted and waving tomahawks and spears, danced in a parade.[47] The parade drew everyone's attention. Seeing the throng of Indians in full battle dress, Capt. Scott ordered the fort's gates be closed and the 19 soldiers to stand at alert.[48]

The spectacle could be seen from the agency house, so Harriet and the other members of the household may have been drawn out to watch by the beating drums. When the parade reached the bower, Mage-ga-bo and the other lead warrior approached the governor to shake hands and began to speak. The grand entrance was orchestrated to announce the Indians' assent to the terms. The Indians would accept what the governor offered. Then some 300 warriors dressed in their finest costumes danced. While they danced, Van Antwerp drew up the document, with the governor announcing that all would meet "to touch the quill" the following day.

As the Ojibwa danced and recounted their deeds of bravery, it was inevitable that their prowess would be extolled in the number of scalps taken from their primary enemy, the Sioux. The local Sioux present paid close attention whenever an Ojibwa warrior gestured to the Sioux scalps on his belt.[49]

For the signing, the secretary wrote out the names of some 40 chiefs and warriors, leaving parentheses for each to make his respective "x"-mark. Each picked up the quill and touched it to the paper.

As the several servants looked on, their masters became signatories of the Treaty of 1837. In all, 12 white men signed, including Maj. Taliaferro, Capt. Scott, Dr. Emerson, and Nicollet. Five of the signers were company men: Sibley, and four of his partners. The four interpreters, whose heritage was as mixed as the nations', signed the paper as well. They were the French-Ojibwa Dube, Irish-Ojibwa Quinn, Scots-Sioux Campbell, and, finally, the African-Ojibwa Bonga.[50] After Governor Dodge and Van Antwerp signed with matching solemnity, 1,400 Ojibwa feasted on 10 beef cattle furnished by Taliaferro and slaughtered by the hired men. In the treaty's final terms, Lyman Warren, the unwelcome fur trader, received an undeserved $20,000 bonus, according to Taliaferro.[51]

And so, the great pine forests of northern Wisconsin were secured for building the frontier. The treaty was negotiated on an almost treeless prairie under a bower of softwood saplings. Harriet and Dred had likely watched as the terms were set for one of the largest land transfer deals in American history: more than 2.8 million acres east of the Mississippi River.[52] The Indians had spoken in the language of conciliation, accommodation, temporary government use, and partial ownership, wishing to retain negotiating rights for the next generation. Governor Dodge had insisted on permanence and complete and exclusive ownership, conceding only the right to hunt, fish, and collect maple sugar. The Indians, by turn, spoke of sharing the wealth with the half-breed children of both peoples. Governor Dodge referred to them as "your half-breeds," deducted their share from the Indians' allotment of money, and denied them any place to remain east of the river.

Like Taliaferro and Sibley on their first meeting, both sides thought they had reached agreement and won their point in the extended ritual. What the Ojibwa told their followers was less clear than what Van Antwerp recorded as the settlement interpretation. In drafting the agreement in the best lawyerlike fashion, Van Antwerp eliminated what ambiguity he could. The treaty still needed to be approved by Congress. Ultimately, its interpretation would be left to the courts of the same federal government that had appointed Dodge as negotiator, the same courts that ultimately determined Harriet and Dred's fate. But before even two years had run, even before Harriet and Dred had left the area, the Ojibwa would come to regard the treaty as inadequate to guarantee them what they were promised. The treaty would come back to haunt Taliaferro, too.

As the Ojibwa danced at the treaty closure, the men waiting at Mendota lost no time in launching their expeditions. Sibley's senior partner, up from Prairie du Chien for the important event, bought two dozen cigars.[53] He and Sibley sent off the waiting expedition to stake early claims in the woodlands that the Ojibwa had just ceded. The team engaged boatmen, axmen, loggers, and mechanics to occupy a site at the falls of the Chippewa River for a sawmill.[54] So rapid was their response that all the available refugees passing through from the Red River settlement were hired in the speculators' service.[55] For his part, Dr. Emerson saw the treaty as a pending investment opportunity too.

Having concluded their business, the commissioners' party found themselves without a steamboat. Captain Scott had the soldiers fit up a Mackinac boat for their use, furnished with a sail made from a tent. The treaty commissioners disembarked for home, floating downriver with the current. In the decades to come, all of the tall pines of Wisconsin would be cut by avaricious lumbermen, creating one of the most severe ecological changes in the area. None of the forests were replanted, and the barren soil would become the sand that Aldo Leopold tried to reforest when he wrote *A Sand County Almanac*.[56]

WHILE ATTENTION at the fur company compound focused on seizing the area's best lands, at the agency, Taliaferro was quietly making plans to convey a Sioux delegation to Washington. A similar treaty was planned for Sioux claims east of the Mississippi. By negotiating far from the frontier, Taliaferro hoped that the Sioux nation would be able to negotiate terms without the fur company's influence. The governor had approved the plan while at the agency, and the agent had already written to engage a steamboat for the delegation. By planning the trip in secret, he sought to avoid the company's usual efforts to divert amounts to their own benefit in the deal.[57] But first he had to make sure that the Obijwa left the fort peacefully. August turned hot. When the last of the food provided for the time of treaty making was consumed, the Ojibwa departed for their summer villages. Monsieur Nicollet also bid farewell to the Taliaferros, with whom he had spent the year, and headed north to Lake Superior.

By the time that the steamboat *Ariel* arrived at the dock, Agent Taliaferro had the delegation ready to depart. The servants at the agency had to be entrusted with knowledge of the impending departure, but they could tell no one. Harriet packed him for the trip in secret. The steamboat "was prompt, the traders [were] astonished at the coup d'etat. My interpreters and employees conducted their friends on board, and with steam up off glided the steamer downstream."[58] The boat stopped at Kaposia briefly for Big Thunder, passed on to Red Wing, and finally to Wabasha's village, picking up chiefs and tribesmen on the way. The agent was concerned not only about evading the fur traders but also assuring the Sioux delegations' safety aboard ship. The last time he led a delegation to Washington, one chief changed his mind and decided to abandon the long journey, jumping from the stern of the steamboat. He made his way alone from Kentucky, almost reaching his own nation, only to be murdered as he traveled through hostile Sac and Fox territory.[59]

With the departure of the Sioux delegation, life at St. Peter's fell quiet again. The fur traders were off staking claims for mill sites and prime woodlands in the newly relinquished territory. The remaining Sioux returned to their fields to guard their corn from the crows, and the tiny vestige of army troops stationed at the fort raised and lowered the flag in the rhythm of garrison life. The treaty bower was dismantled, to be used for firewood. No one remained at the agency in August. The mistress had left for Bedford by this time, taking Eliza and the other servants.[60] Scott Campbell's large family had abandoned the top floor of the crumbling council house and now lived across the river, on land they hoped to secure under the upcoming treaty (as he was half Dakota). Taliaferro had promised them a plot of their own land for their long loyal service.[61]

CHAPTER 12

Marriage: Together Alone

T̲H̲A̲T̲ ̲L̲E̲F̲T̲ ̲H̲A̲R̲R̲I̲E̲T̲. Though she was surely occupied with the guests during the treaty making, she didn't leave with either the master or the mistress. At some point in these last busy weeks, Harriet was married by her master to Etheldred, the slave of Dr. Emerson, in the same manner that he performed other weddings at the agency. (It was said that several marriages were performed that summer in anticipation of legitimating the children who would be eligible to take shares under the treaty.[1]) In Taliaferro's autobiography, Harriet's master mentioned their wedding last of several he conducted.[2] Taliaferro indicated that he performed the ceremony himself and that he gave her to Etheldred, the slave, in marriage.[3] Accordingly, Harriet moved into her husband's lodgings at the fort.

The wedding ceremony must have been extremely significant for her, since it paralleled important rituals practiced by the other residents of the community and it signified her release from her master.[4] We cannot know whether Harriet Robinson loved Etheldred, but she later came to care for him. Etheldred loved her, according to Taliaferro, who wrote how happy Dred was to take young Harriet as his wife.[5] Dred had been married before in St. Louis, and his wife had been sold away from him.[6] Now he received Harriet as his wife, given by her master in marriage. At the time, Dred was already 40, but Harriet was only 17. They remained mates for life. In the years to come, Harriet bore Dred four children. Even when the Mexican War campaign separated them, Dred found his way back to her. At the very least, marriage offered Harriet some security, protection, and a degree of independence. Taken to the frontier as an adolescent, she may have experienced the sexual vulnerability that threatened many enslaved women.[7] She found an older protector in Dred. Given their ages, he could have been her father. In marrying him, she entered not only his protectorate but that of his master, Dr. Emerson.

What was Harriet's status at this point? Surely, by marrying her to Dred and then leaving, Taliaferro intended to relinquish any claim he had to her or her services. Did this act emancipate her? Or was a specific act emancipating her even necessary—that is, had she been free since she took up residence at St. Peter's under the auspices of a slave master whose domicile was the now free state of Pennsylvania? What determined her status legally at the time? There are several aspects complicating what should have been a straightforward answer.

First, geographically, the specific locations where she lived—the quarter mile between from the Agency house and the fort—could not have been closer to the border margins of legal jurisdiction, unless she had resided on a houseboat in the middle of the Mississippi. (Incidentally, that would be where her first child would be born.) The Northwest Territory, governed by the Northwest Territorial Ordinance, banned the existence of slavery.[8] The Northwest Territory was thought to extend only as far as the Mississippi River, but even the location of the origin of the Mississippi River was in question at the time. Until Nicollet produced his important map, while Harriet lived in the region, the exact location of the river system that surrounded them was unknown to the settlement community and lawmakers in Washington.[9] Because there was little settlement on the west banks of the Mississippi River north of the state of Missouri, the settled western bank of the river, including the entire stretch of river from Burlington, Iowa, to Sibley's home at Mendota,[10] was conventionally considered as being part of the Northwest Territory. There was simply no other governmental apparatus of which it could have been considered a part.

According to law, slavery was banned in the Northwest Territory as well as in states expected to emerge from the Louisiana Purchase north of the Missouri Compromise line.[11] That meant that both banks of the Upper Mississippi river were legally deemed to be a free territory. What enforcement existed for either of these provisions was less clear. Slaves such as Rachel, who had preceded Harriet in service in the area, had succeeded in establishing their freedom in the Missouri courts when they were taken back to St. Louis.[12] By implication this meant that Harriet was free by the simple act of residing in free territory, even before her marriage to Dred, as was Dred, although Dr. Emerson continued to regard him as a slave. Each should have been able to redeem his or her freedom whenever they moved to the proximity of a settled court of law.

Second, although Taliaferro could no longer have claimed her services based on a slave status in the territory, while she resided in his household she was still subject to his control under the common law, which was also referenced as the law in the Northwest Territorial Ordinance,[13] and by extension, probably thought to have extended to the Missouri Compromise lands. As a domestic in his household, under the common law and as an underage girl, the law did allow him to chastise her (had he had the inclination), and by striking her, he could require her to obey him. And he probably had a say in when and whom she would be permitted to marry.[14] Thus, notwithstanding the clear statement of federal law that slavery was not permitted on either side of the river, certain prerogatives of householding were accepted as custom and even authorized by the common law. Notwithstanding these prerogatives of control, she could not be sold by him. Under the common law, only slaves could be sold by masters, not servants, not apprentices, nor household dependents.

When Taliaferro relinquished Harriet's services and she left his disassembled household, he could no longer exercise even those householding prerogatives over her. After she left Taliaferro's household and with his permission married and entered that of another, even these aspects of his control over her would expire. She was no longer obligated to obey him, or subject to his control, whether verbal or physical. Thus, to a great extent nothing held her to Taliaferro thereafter, neither as the slave master who originally brought her to free territory, nor as the head of the household in which she lived.

Every indication suggests that Taliaferro relinquished claim to her services, but did he sell her to Dr. Emerson? His own statement, recorded long after the event, was that he gave her to Dred, Emerson's slave, or former slave, while in free territory. There is no evidence in either his contemporary papers or Emerson's suggesting an attempted sale. More important, even if there had been evidence of an attempted sale, the sale of a human being in free territory where slavery was abolished would have been illegal, either void or voidable anyway.

From Taliaferro's viewpoint, marrying Harriet to Dred was a necessary convenience, as Taliaferro closed down his household and planned to depart for the winter. From his perspective, he fulfilled his obligation by placing his dependent in a household where she would have adequate food and shelter. One could not simply let a former slave woman face winter alone, any more than one could let a child or a horse fend for itself.[15] Only soldiers were set free in the dead of winter, and that expulsion was a severe punishment. It was almost impossible to survive the winter independently—that is, without ample store of provisions or a social network. On the social level, a slave woman at a military fort presented a special difficulty. The experience of the "high-yellow" woman, Fanny, proved that. Women needed households for their survival and males to protect them from other males. Given the numerous single men at the post, a free young servant woman was considered an attractive nuisance. By marrying her to Dred, her master was assured that a man was designated to look after her and that she would have the material needs of survival.

What it appears that Taliaferro did not do, however, was to engage in some manumission proceeding or give her written freedom papers. Then again, Taliaferro was the person representing civil law in the vicinity. There were no courts established anywhere within 300 miles where such a proceeding could have occurred. Instead, in the absence of notaries and courts, legally significant events were concluded by publicly recognized custom. Treaties were conducted this way; marriages were performed this way. Taliaferro did conduct a publicly recognized marriage of Dred and Harriet that even officers of the Fort thereafter recognized by referring to her as "Har. Etheldred."[16] Had Taliaferro been exceptionally scrupulous in guaranteeing Harriet's freedom, he might have given her a written statement of her freedom. In the context of his situation, where even paper and stationery had run out, even this act would have been difficult.

Third, philosophically, the question of whether Harriet was free at this time runs even deeper. What determines whether a person is free or enslaved in a wilderness area where purportedly no law keeps slavery in place and what law there is forbids slavery but with weak legal enforcement?[17] Do actions of intention of the slave master govern this status? That evidence suggests Harriet was free. Do actions of independence taken by the subjugated person govern this status? What actions of independence, autonomy, or resistance are necessary for a person who needs to eat? The evidence that exists seems to suggest that at the time Harriet was a free person, married to a man whose own household master still regarded him as a slave.

Two days after her master left Harriet with Dred, Dr. Emerson made an unusual purchase, for a bachelor, at the sutler's store. He bought a "straw bonnet," two yards of bonnet ribbon and a length of calico cloth. Most likely the bonnet was a woman's hat, and the ribbon was for a crown and a tie.[18] Calico cloth could be used to make a new dress or apron.

These purchases suggest two possibilities. There was talk that Emerson was attempting to court the beautiful young schoolteacher at the mission—with little success. But a woman's bonnet was quite a personal gift. It was something a young missionary woman might buy for herself or that a father might buy for his daughter, but still an object that carried extra signification if offered to a young woman by an eligible and clearly interested bachelor.[19]

If the gifts weren't intended for Miss Stevens, they were probably intended for Harriet as a wedding present. Whether Emerson regarded himself as her owner, her master, or merely her patron, a new outfit of clothing was an appropriate gesture for Etheldred's master to give to Etheldred's bride. What was too forward a gift if offered by a gentleman to a young white woman was a generous gesture in this context. For Harriet, whose only real possessions were the clothes she owned, a bonnet, ribbon, and calico cloth would represent important symbols of Emerson's willingness to provide for her.[20] Such purchases honored the Scotts' marriage.[21] Thus, as Dred's wife, and with his master's apparent acknowledgment, she moved into Etheldred's quarters in the basement of the stone hospital. There she probably expected to live in service to the doctor.

Her master's steamboat had barely departed when the doctor received transfer orders himself. His frequent requests for transfer away from the cold winters were finally granted, and in late August, he was ordered to proceed to St. Louis. He was to leave as soon as another doctor relieved him. What Dr. Emerson had planned for the Scotts is unknown, but by the time someone arrived to relieve him, it was much too late in the season for them to accompany him by canoe. The hospital basement would be their home for the ensuing winter.

As Harriet moved from the agency house to her place beside her husband in the post hospital, a new set of rhythms surrounded her. She no longer had regular contact with the families of the hired men at the agency or the families at the Coldwater spring. She now met those who lived outside the walls only in the punctuated times—at intervals of weeks or months—when she left the self-contained world of the fort. Harriet might walk past the guardhouse sentry to garden or wash clothes down at the river. But most of her daily activities were circumscribed by the thick stone walls, which undoubtedly muffled her perception of the events transpiring outside among the Indian peoples. No longer did she greet Indian visitors at the door. The dozens, often hundreds, of Dakota and Ojibwa peoples who frequented the agency, who danced the ceremonial dances and who sought daily gifts, advice, and iron repairs, must have become familiar to her by now. She may have been able to distinguish many by name, by family, and by tribe, particularly the members of the local Spirit Lake bands. One can assume that she knew their stories: who had lost a wife, a child, or been shot in the shoulder. The tribal people continued their existence in their nomadic cycles outside the fort, walled off from her view.

The social world that surrounded Harriet at the fort was minutely ordered by military regulation. From the commander on down, there were captains, first and second lieutenants (some brevetted, and some not), sergeants, corporals, privates, and musicians. Even Doctor Emerson held a specific place in the social hierarchy—above the enlisted men and most officers, but below the commander. Before she moved into the fort, she might have seen him only as the tall doctor who treated the Indians. Now she could observe that people saluted him when he walked by. As a servant woman she didn't need to bother herself with these distinctions in rank, and for the most part, the officers and men probably took no notice of her.

The rhythm of days at the fort was set by the trumpeting of reveille and the blowing of taps. Harriet's life may have never been so attuned to the hours of the clock. Every day proceeded in the same manner, beat out in regular time by the tiny band of army musicians—every day, that is, except Christmas and New Year's. At daylight, the bugler, two drummers, and a fifer marched the length of the barracks to awaken the military community. All the garrison soldiers turned out on the broad parade ground. Breakfast was at 7 A.M., followed by work detail, when groups of men went off to assigned tasks until noontime dinner. Parades and drilling filled the afternoon interval. Retreat beat at sundown.[22] The signal to head for bed was sounded at nine o'clock. After that the band played some favorite tunes, and the soldiers returned to their bunked beds. Only the officers stayed up as late as they pleased. Harriet lived at the very edge of this routine, both as a servant woman and in the doctor's household and Dr. Emerson was making plans to leave almost as soon as she moved in.

Her only peers were the few other officers' servants, though Harriet was the only black woman at the post that winter. The others had left with the departing officers.[23] Two black men, in addition to her husband, lived and served inside the fort: Jack, Capt. Martin Scott's longtime slave, and a man named Bill Johnston, owned by Lt. Reid. Outside the fort, the newly freed Jim Thompson worked at the Methodist mission out at Kaposia, so Jim and his Sioux wife had moved from the lakes. Despite having freed him, the Reverend Brunson still placed claims on Jim to fulfill the work of interpreting for the missionaries.[24] Only the African Ojibwa Mrs. Fahlstrom remained nearby at the Coldwater Spring, with her Swedish husband and children. Sometimes her brothers, the Bongas, visited her, but for the most part they traded with the Ojibwa tribe farther north. But Mrs. Fahlstrom had no reason to venture inside the fort, and Harriet had no authority to permit anyone to enter the fort to visit her.

As the sole servant woman, Harriet found her housekeeping services were in demand. She worked for three different officers that fall, until the commandant's wife laid exclusive claim to her services. Harriet is listed on bachelor Lt. Whitehorne's servant account,[25] and Lt. Thompson's wife, Catherine, claimed that Harriet worked for them as well.[26] Catherine Thompson later played an important role as a witness in the Scotts' trial, verifying their residence in the North.

This officer, Lt. James L. Thompson (who shared the same first and last name as the newly freed slave), had brought his family to Fort Snelling at the end of May from Fort Winnebago on the Wisconsin River. His wife, Catherine Hamilton Thompson, was an impulsive young woman who had married him against the wishes of her military family by eloping with him to a justice of the peace at a former post. Catherine's family opposed the marriage because they found Lt. Thompson was intemperate. They had forbidden her from seeing him before the couple secretly eloped.

Catherine liked such luxuries as cologne, stylish prunelle shoes, and a looking glass, all bought from the sutler's store. From their purchases, the Thompsons must have had at least one child, since they bought toys and children's shoes and socks.[27] (A later census gives the name of their child as James L. Thompson, Jr., then four years old.)[28] Though Catherine later testified that Harriet worked for her, at the time Lt. Thompson never listed Harriet as servant on his pay slips. He claimed someone named "Catherine," the same name as his wife.[29] It would have been illegal to hire his own wife as a servant, but by this arrangement, the couple could keep the money allotted to an officer for a housekeeping servant. The impulsive Catherine and the intemperate Lt. Thompson divorced after a scandal at Fort Snelling the following year.[30]

On August 20, 1837, after only two months as acting commandant and during the critical time of treaty making, Capt. Martin Scott officially turned command of the fort over to Maj. Joseph Plympton, who finally arrived from Wisconsin with his troops. The Plymptons moved into the commandant's quarters at the top of the diamond and sought Harriet's assistance. Mrs. Plympton gave birth to their fifth child that month.[31]

The Plympton family had lived in the stone fort before when the officer was a young lieutenant. Now he returned as its commander. Plympton looked the part of a man in command. He carried himself well and was strikingly handsome, with a high forehead, dark blue eyes, and steel gray hair.[32] But his style with the Indians was quite different from Harriet's former master's. He did not like to sit with them, and he was sometimes impatient in hearing them out. "There is no use for long speeches—come at once to the point," he would insist. "I want a straight-forward answer."[33] His manner with soldiers and servants was probably similarly direct. Maj. Plympton had an agenda for the next stage of frontier development: professionally, he intended to clear the immediate military reserve area of settlers. Personally, he planned to stake land claims of his own as soon as the lands were opened for sale. His combined official and personal agendas set a course in direct conflict between the fort personnel and the people living at the Coldwater Spring.

Mrs. Plympton had an even more impressive pedigree than her handsome husband. She was a Livingston, and among her extraordinarily well-connected relatives were governors, senators, congressmen, and ambassadors. Elizabeth Plympton grew up served by black servants, perhaps even slaves, on the Hudson Valley family estate at a time when slavery was legal in New York and common among the gentry.[34] Nonetheless, the Plymptons brought with them no servants of their own.

The month the Plymptons arrived they hired one of the Perry girls,[35] but the tension between the Coldwater squatters and the garrison may have already been evident, since Rose Perry worked for them only one month. (Rose Perry's fiancé was the most outspoken of the Coldwater group.) The following month, Plympton looked for a servant from within the fort and took Harriet. A decade earlier, as a junior officer there, Plympton had approached Taliaferro, asking to buy Eliza as a slave. Then the Plymptons had only two children.[36] The master had recorded: "Capt. Plympton wishes to purchase Eliza. I informed him that it was my intention to give her her freedom after a limited time. But Mrs. P. may keep her for 2–3 years."[37] Eliza did not remain that long with the Plymptons. (Nor had she formally been freed in the intervening time. Eliza remained with the Taliaferros, 11 years after the master wrote those words.) Now, again seeking household help, the Plymptons turned to Taliaferro's former slave, Harriet. By November, the 17-year-old servant bride was working in the commandant's large house with the Flemish gables. She had probably heard about the Plymptons from Eliza.[38]

The commandant's house was the grandest residence in the fort. It occupied the keystone position at the far end of the diamond-shaped parade ground, farthest from the fort's gate. Here again Harriet navigated both the public and the private worlds of the house, the upstairs and the downstairs. She was most at liberty, however, in the basement kitchen with its stone hearth and oven that filled an entire side wall. Hollowed out of the wall was a small larder, with a little spring that kept it cool. She performed the many housekeeping tasks for a family of seven, as she had for the Taliaferros. In this family with many children there was even more to do, and she was their only servant woman.

While Agent Taliaferro was away in Washington, with the Sioux delegation, the commander laid the groundwork for removing the squatters, including the Perrys, from the area around the fort. To ascertain how many settlers were out there, he commissioned a lieutenant to conduct a survey and a census of all the white people in the area surrounding the fort. The survey also sought to identify the sites of natural resources, along with their exact distance relative to the fort and the area's most desirable lands. Completed in a matter of days, the survey listed 157 white persons living on the reservation land: 82 at the Coldwater Spring and 25 on the far side of the river at Mendota, with the rest at fur trading outposts farther away.[39] Altogether there were 200 horses and cattle in the vicinity.[40]

Major Plympton sent one copy of the report to Washington and presumably retained the other for his own use. Then he waited for news that the Sioux had signed over their lands and that Congress had approved the terms.[41]

At the fort, as long as the river was open, the community received sporadic news from the outside world. From Prairie du Chien came the news that Che-ga-weye-cum had finally been indicted by a grand jury. But the land rush, spurred on by the Ojibwa treaty, had delayed his trial because even the victim's father, Mr. Aiken, had set out to stake land claims. So Che-ga-weye-cum spent another winter awaiting trial, this time in the jail at Prairie du Chien.[42]

The Sioux delegation's arrival in Washington was reported to have created a sensation,[43] and a treaty was signed before 400 spectators at a church in the nation's capital. The social dynamic was very different from the Ojibwa treaty, where the ratio of Indians to settlement people was reversed.

Despite Agent Taliaferro's covert departure, Sibley and two other traders hurried to Washington to secure their own interests as soon as they heard that a treaty was planned.[44] Sibley wrote New York headquarters reporting the treaty's terms, with mixed approval. The moneys allotted were generous, and the company would get a sizable cut. But Sibley was irritated by the news that the Métis interpreter Scott Campbell was to get an annuity and land grant on the Mendota side of the river near his own fur trade buildings. "You recollect...that I thought Scott Campbell had received something by way of bonus, or he would not be so pliant in the hands of our friend, the Major," Sibley wrote cynically.[45] The treaty provided Campbell with 500 acres and an annuity that Sibley described as "a very snug sum!" "I wonder they did not grant him our [buildings]," Sibley remarked. In the larger battle for Indian influence, if the agent was effective in securing land for his interpreter, his power was enhanced, and accordingly, the company's power diminished. The company lobbyists set to work to try to eliminate Scott Campbell's promised allotment before Congress ratified the treaty.

The legal significance of reserving lands for the Indians, for military or any other government purposes, was to declare them permanently closed to private claimants and homesteading. Clearly, the government would designate the land of the promontory between the rivers on which the fort stood as reserved for military purposes. Just where the lines were drawn, however, implicated the cabins built near the Coldwater Spring. All the talk about drawing the reservation boundaries had made the 82 settlers living there increasingly edgy. They could be evicted from the cabins and homesteads that they had built if the land was reserved. They saw other men beating a path into the Wisconsin woods to stake out the best sites, while the security of their own homesteads seemed to wane.

The settlers banded together for mutual protection, convinced they had earned the right to stay. Most had been there for almost two decades, with the permission of the former commandant. They had invested their sweat equity in building cabins and sheds, cultivating gardens, and enduring the harsh conditions. Their children, now intermarried, had begun a third generation, hoping to build cabins of their own. Now in command, Major Plympton was clearly signaling a position hostile to their interests, even though he had known them since his superior had permitted them to build cabins and stay. The settlers at the Coldwater Spring felt betrayed.

Now Maj. Plympton wrote Washington urging that the military reserve be expanded due to the difficulty getting wood for the garrison.[46] Removing the settlers would eliminate them as competitors for the limited supply of firewood. The claim was somewhat disingenuous because there was little timber nearby, except for softwood scrub. Washington responded by requesting Plympton to mark off the lands he believed necessary to be reserved on the map. He marked off the entire village of eight homesteads as reserved as military land—foreclosing the area from homesteading.[47]

Meanwhile, the commandant and the officers hatched plans of their own to stake claims based on the newly proposed boundaries. Doctor Emerson joined in despite being under orders to leave. Waterpower sites were the most valuable, and like the sutler Stambaugh, the officers especially coveted land near the sawmill site at St. Anthony Falls.[48]

Two different doctors were ordered to Fort Snelling to relieve Dr. Emerson, but neither of them had yet arrived by October. On October 8, 1837, an impatient and increasingly frustrated Emerson wrote the surgeon general, "As yet, Wright has not arrived." He feared the exposure of a long, cold canoe trip, once navigation had closed, if he got out at all. Several days later, Dr. Wright finally appeared, having paddled up from Prairie du Chien, with a junior officer escort, under way for two solid weeks in an open canoe. From Emerson's perspective, it was none too soon. Emerson gave notice of his imminent departure: "I have this day turned over the Assistant surgeonship to Dr. J.J.B. Wright all the hospital stores, bedding, medicines, &c."[49] (Even in his haste it was important to execute the proper paperwork.) He had but a day to settle his personal accounts at the sutler's store and at Sibley's fur trading store across the river.[50] He departed the same way that his relief had arrived, by canoe with the officer escort, leaving Dred and Harriet behind with his horse and his medical books. He couldn't very easily take them with him in the canoe, but he didn't indicate that he intended to abandon them any more than his other belongings.

With Emerson's departure, Harriet and Dred were together alone for the entire winter but in service to other officers at the fort. As servants of different masters, but owned by none of them, they enjoyed slightly more personal autonomy, within the generally highly regulated order of life at the garrison. Thus, the newly married couple began their first year of life together.

When Harriet came to work at the commandant's home she was already recognized as a married woman by dint of a last name. Most slaves had only a single name: a first name. The Plympton pay slip listed her as "H. Dread," or "Har. Dread," signifying her status as related to Dred, taking his name, a married woman. Her husband continued to be inscribed simply as "Etheldred," or "Dred."[51] It's not clear that she was paid; instead Plympton probably credited Dr. Emerson for her services. An entry registered in the sutler's account books, where all small debts were recorded, debits Plympton $16 to be paid to the account of the absent Dr. Emerson.[52] This figure corresponds appropriately to a servant's wages for four months. Nor is it clear who provided for the Scotts over the winter. Bread rations drawn from the bakehouse were charged to the doctor's account.[53] Even slaves, used to living on little, had to eat.

The Plympton family was far wealthier than the Taliaferros, as their purchases indicate.[54] Plympton had business acumen, and he had expected to become a West Indies merchant before he was caught up on the War of 1812. Once he received an officer's commission, he stayed on in the army.[55] He was not averse to making a profit, however, and with the shrewdness of a Dutch mercantilist, he saw business possibilities for land claims in the area. The Plymptons seemed to live above the fray, insulated from the problems of the local people, so Harriet was probably less exposed to the political currents of the territory than she was when she lived at the Agency.

Agent Taliaferro did not bring the Indian delegation home until mid-November.[56] The damaged steamboat *Rolla* barely limped to the dock.[57] On the last leg of its journey, one of its boiler flues exploded, killing a black boatman and a horse, being transported in the hold.[58] To the agent's relief, however, none of the Sioux were injured by the accident—nor prompted to jump overboard. Maj. Plympton greeted the delegation at the dock, telling Taliaferro, "I feared for you, and you were wise in your plans." Plympton was aware of the hostility that the American Fur Company harbored against the Indian agent, but he didn't say just what he feared. Harriet probably saw her former master again as a guest at the commandant's house, but he had little time before he left again and made no notation about her. With ice freezing in, the boat captain was anxious to get the damaged boat south to warmer waters.[59]

The *Rolla* also brought the second medical doctor dispatched to relieve Emerson.[60] This man, the 34-year-old Dr. Erastus B. Wolcott, hired Dred to work for him from his November arrival through March.[61] Dr. Wolcott's wife and infant child remained where he had been stationed earlier, at Mackinac Island in Lake Michigan. When he was transferred to Prairie du Chien, they could not accompany him, and he found it so miserable living apart from them that he tried to resign. The surgeon general replied with a sharply worded letter that he could not resign and furthermore reassigned him to Fort Snelling, even farther away from his family. Disgruntled and exhausted, Dr. Wolcott arrived after being in transit continuously for three months under orders he had attempted to relinquish. Adding injury to disappointment, it was probably his horse that was killed in the steamboat explosion.[62] Both doctors were unhappy to be ordered to Fort Snelling. Dr. Wright had lived apart from his wife for some years,[63] and with these urgent orders, he had no time to bring her to the frontier. On Christmas Day, back in Pennsylvania, she gave birth to a son, whom she named after his father. Thus, the hospital was staffed over the long northern winter by two doctors, both miserable over being separated from their wives and infant children. Both doctors saw their double assignments as pointless.[64] Small wonder that Dr. Wright, in particular, began to build resentment at Emerson, whom he had been ordered to relieve.

Serving in the commandant's house, Harriet must have prepared the Christmas meal for the family as well as the expected annual Christmas banquet for the handful of officers and wives. "'Twas the Night before Christmas," written by a cousin of Mrs. Plympton's, was circulating at the time.[65] Harriet must have conceived a child around New Year's.[66] Like most women she was probably unaware of the early stages of her pregnancy.

Inside the fort's high stone walls one only knew as much of the season as the color of the sky and the snow that fell. The fort balanced at the crown of the bluff, linking water, stone, and sky, but the high stone walls blinded residents to the spectacular view. Harriet could only glimpse the world beyond the walls when she climbed the rickety stairs of the latrine to empty the families' chamber pots over the fort's wall. There alone, from the height of 100 feet above the shore, could the panorama of the joined rivers beneath her reveal itself. Inside the fort there was little vegetation and no trees. Even the grass of the parade ground was beaten into dust and mud by the routine marching of the men.

With no view of the horizon and a monotonous routine, day in and day out, attention focused instead on one's fellow residents. During the long winter months together, the more dramatic life stories of the fort's inhabitants were gradually revealed. There was little else to talk about. News rarely broke the ice lock from the outside world, and the doors and the windows all faced inward on the parade ground; the fort was surrounded by a high stone wall fortified against anything of interest taking place in the surrounding territory. No one in the fort bothered to monitor the Indians' daily activities.

Stories about the reigning officers were probably the most interesting to subordinates. Most of the men had served together before, but the presence of newcomers—the doctors and Harriet and Dred—meant there was someone who hadn't previously heard the all stories. At the fort hospital, there was a whole winter as time to pass. Only half of the eight officers, not counting the two doctors, were married.[67] The most notorious officers that winter were Lt. Thompson and Catherine for their elopement, the expert marksman Capt. Scott, who had temporarily commanded the fort during the treaty time; and Lt. E. K. Smith, the army's prodigal son. At 49, Capt. Martin Scott, the oldest bachelor officer,[68] neither gambled nor drank (at least not that winter) preferring coffee instead.[69] His passion was hunting and he kept a kennel of hunting dogs and a slave man named Jack, who cared for the dogs. Jack had been with him for years in the Northwest territory.[70] Once, upon returning home to Vermont, the captain had Jack dress in livery and drive him in a carriage to see his brother—all in an effort to impress him. In order to display his legendary shooting skills, Capt. Scott regularly required poor Jack to prop an apple on his head so that he could demonstrate his ability to shoot it off Jack's head with a pistol.[71] Luckily for Jack, the captain's marksmanship was good.

Lt. E. K. Smith was famous for having revived a destroyed army career. The West Point–trained officer from an Army family had been court-martialed and expelled from the army for striking an insubordinate soldier in his command. Smith's famous officer father and uncles had lobbied to have him reinstated, into the same infantry unit from which he had been dismissed, arguing that the rules on striking soldiers had recently changed so that Lt. Smith's violation of the rules should not have resulted in his dismissal.[72] Lt. Smith was reinstated, an army turn-about that almost never happened. His reputation had been tarnished.[73]

In early March, a seasoned roustabout from the outside world brought the fort terrible news of tribal warfare. Philander Prescott came in from his remote trading post to see the fort's doctor.[74] He reported an Ojibwa attack on the Sioux. After being treated to a feast by the Dakota, some of Chief Hole-in-the-Day's men had committed an unforgivable act of treachery—the Ojibwa had risen in the night and murdered their Dakota hosts as they slept.[75] This treachery could only be avenged by blood. The Ojibwa had broken the peace and the trust that Taliaferro had worked so hard to knit together. Word of the treachery spread throughout the Dakota nation. It was reported that the Sioux had even served the Ojibwa their dog meat, which was considered the highest honor for guests.[76] Major Plympton received the news but did nothing, waiting for Agent Taliaferro to deal with the matter when he returned in spring.

Across the river at Mendota, the company men were seeding further distrust of Agent Taliaferro among the Sioux. Since the treaties gave the traders moneys to satisfy the Indians debts, the chiefs thought they would be warmly treated by the company head men.[77] They weren't. When a chief named the Good Road visited Mendota, Dousman (Sibley's partner who was standing in for him in his absence) persuaded the chief to sign a paper renouncing the treaty and requesting Taliaferro removed as Indian agent. Another chief was insulted when he visited the company's trading house, being told, "You sold your land and what did you get for it? You ought to have asked more. Then you could have paid up more of your old debts to your traders. You ought to have listened to your traders.... they would have gotten more for your lands.... You sold your lands and were bribed by the medal you wear. What is it worth? Will that cover your people? You have fooled away your lands."[78] Chief Big Thunder had expected gratitude for signing the treaty and agreeing to the inclusion of the trader's debts; instead he was insulted as a fool.[79]

Scott Campbell managed to convey these reports to Taliaferro back in Bedford.[80] He wrote back that "I feel confident that before this summer is over The Good Road will change in my *favour*." "The Sioux treaty will no doubt be ratified.... I yet believe all will go well.... I regret to hear of the condition of *our* people. I feel for them, but as I often told them and they now see, and feel it. Their treaty stipulations is all that will save them from starvation and want in future.—I know it will be a death blow to the influence of the traders. They are doing all they can to defeat its ratification by the Senate, but it won't all do. We will succeed & our 'poor foolish Indians' will be happy at last."[81]

CHAPTER 13

Traveling the Length of the River

J UST WEEKS AFTER arriving in Louisiana, Dr. Emerson was already complaining and again seeking reassignment. His letters suggest that he made considerable effort to avoid being assigned to the swampy Sabine River, with its insects, snakes and malaria.[1] Although his rheumatism had subsided in the warm climate, he now reported difficulty breathing, along with his usual chronic complaints of syphilis and liver disorder.[2] "No other medical officer in the army would attempt to do duty if suffering as much as I have for more than twelve months. My distracted state of body and mind has entirely unfitted me for duty."[3]

Much more to his liking, he was assigned to accompany a detached party destined for Natchitoches, an old French town in Louisiana, where he soon found a bride, despite his many ailments. The doctor was introduced to a sister-in-law of one of the officers, Miss Irene Sanford from St. Louis, who was visiting her sister, Captain Bainbridge's wife. Irene Sanford and the Bainbridges would play major roles in the Scotts' lives.

The doctor lost no time in courting the young lady, who it seems was there in search of a husband. Within the month, her brother, John F. A. Sanford in St. Louis was apprised of the impending marriage, remarking, "Irene had lost little time finding herself a husband."[4] On February 6, 1838, Dr. John Emerson and Elizabeth Irene Sanford were married in Natchitoches.[5]

With a wife to provide for, the doctor must have thought more seriously about sending for Dred and Harriet to come to Louisiana. Slaves were necessary to uphold a suitable standard of living, especially in the South.[6] As a lady, his new bride couldn't be expected to do all the housework herself. Emerson had little reason to believe that word would get through to the frozen fort so far upriver. Still, it seems he made some effort to communicate with the Scotts, telling them to come to Louisiana, and his message seems to have reached them because they did leave Fort Snelling—but they could not have done so until the spring thaw.

The evidence shows that by March neither Harriet nor Dred was listed on the pay slips of any Fort Snelling officer.[7] The Plymptons replaced Harriet with a woman named Nancy, and at the end of March, Dr. Wolcott replaced Dred with Jack, Capt. Scott, the marksman's slave.[8] Even if the Harriet and Dred were indeed released from employment by other masters, they still couldn't depart until the ice broke. Catherine, Lt. Thompson's estranged wife, later testified that they left in April.[9] Whenever the date of their departure,[10] it must have been that spring because there is corroborating evidence that they returned to Fort Snelling from St. Louis with Emerson later in the fall.[11]

How far south they traveled is further confused by Emerson's letters and his fickle plans.[12] Emerson repeatedly requested to be reassigned north again, even before the river opened and the Scotts could depart. "[M]ay I be ordered to Snelling?" he wrote, "Climate does not agree with me."[13] If Emerson expected to return, he had little reason to pay their passage downriver.[14] Nonetheless, they probably set out on the season's first steamboat.[15] Arriving that spring was Agent Taliaferro, facing what would be a summer of increasing tensions and conflict.[16]

For the Scotts, it must have been exhilarating to travel downstream on a large steamboat in the spring. It had been three winters since Harriet had left the immediate vicinity and two for Dred. During the last winter the thermometer had stayed below zero for an entire month, keeping everyone shut in.

The river highway broadened out before them, and the weather grew warmer. At every port the captain gathered news of the changes occurring in the seasons and further stages of settlement along the river frontier. The Scotts may also have made this trip with the hope of finding opportunities for themselves. By now the couple must have been aware that Harriet was carrying their child. At some level, they must have been conscious of seeking a stable home.

African Americans traveling the western waters were not unusual, since many worked on the riverboats as firemen, stewards, and chambermaids.[17] So Harriet and Dred would not have seemed out of place on the steamboat. One newspaper alluded to "that numerous class of free colored people on the western waters."[18] Yet African American travelers occupied a different status from that of whites. Sometimes slaves traveling with their masters and mistresses slept on trundles in their owner's private cabins, where they could take care of errands. But a free black person attempting to book a cabin would have difficulty, so they usually traveled on the lower deck. The irony of domestic servitude was that in slave status, black persons were admitted to places where they'd never have been allowed had they been free. The first-class rooms and passageways that Harriet and Dred walked freely when in the service of their masters were now off-limits to Mr. and Mrs. Etheldred traveling together.[19]

Some of the black boatmen were free while others were slaves, hired out by their masters to work steamboats. The captains obligated themselves to return these slaves.[20] Some owners even bought insurance in case their slaves attempted to escape while working on the river. Black cooks, stewards, chambermaids, and even barbers attended to travelers' comforts. Stevedores, deckhands, and engine stokers performed the heaviest tasks of actually moving the cargo and firing the lumbering boats up the great rivers.[21]

African Americans working the boats aroused some suspicion for the easy way they moved in and out of towns.[22] Francis McIntosh, the man burned alive in St. Louis, had worked on the river. That April, as the Scotts descended the upper river, a black cook suspected of rape had his hands tied and was deliberately thrown overboard to drown by the passengers.[23] Most suspicion was directed at single black men; a couple traveling together wouldn't seem so threatening. Still, the knowledge that even free black men, if accused, could be killed was frightening.

Apart from the fear of being mobbed, traveling by steamboat carried considerable risk. There was always the chance of falling overboard since the decks had no guide rails and few people knew how to swim.[24] Steamboats hit snags and ran aground on sandbars; their engine boilers exploded with some regularity. Deck passengers like the Scotts were especially at risk because the lower deck was so close to the engines—though most explosions occurred on the upstream voyage when captains pushed their boats' boilers to dangerous levels going against the river's current. Exploding steamboats were a national calamity that year, with eight boats destroyed by explosion or fire in just six months. More than 700 people died in such accidents on the Mississippi River alone.[25]

Nonetheless, after a long winter of confinement, the steamboat ride must have felt like freedom to Harriet and Dred, even though they were actually responding to a master's call. At night, when the captain could no longer see from his perch to navigate the river's vagaries, the *Burlington* tied up along shore and the engines went silent. Then, after the lanterns were lit and dinner served to the white passengers in the dining room, the black boatmen retired to communal pallets on the lower deck floor where the Scotts were encamped.

The steamboat stopped at every port of call. At most ports, the passengers disembarked long enough to walk about the town, and by walking around, the Scotts could observe other living situations. At Fort Crawford in Prairie du Chien, where the boat stopped, Dred and Harriet had known a few people—though an unfamiliar black couple attired as servants may have been stopped at the gate.[26] Although Agent Joseph Street had been transferred downriver, his family maintained a home in Prairie du Chien, including Patsey, indentured-for-life to the family. By now, Patsey's oldest children had been given to the Streets' oldest children, with promises of freedom when they reached age 21.[27] But who knew the value of these promises?[28] Governor Dodge had finally set his five slaves free, including the man who had accompanied him to the agency house during the treaty-making session.[29] When he finally manumitted his slaves, after they had worked for him without pay in free territory for more than a decade, the governor stated that it had been simply "*inconvenient* to do so until now."[30] In some ways this was neither more nor less than southern slave masters did in releasing aging slaves from service when they were no longer useful.[31] Nonetheless, Dodge's five slaves were able to keep their own cabin, which was something.[32]

The big news at Prairie du Chien was that Che-ga-weyes-cum had been acquitted of murdering Mr. Aitkin's son. He was tried shortly before the *Burlington* arrived.[33] The jury deliberating his fate had even heard testimony under oath from an African-Ojibwa man called as witness for the prosecution.[34] (The man was

John Bonga, Marguerite Bonga Fahlstrom's brother.) In the custom of frontier juries, after three days of trial, the jury retired to a small storeroom and drank a little "quelquechose."[35] The jurors expected alcohol for their service. After enough drinking, the jury concluded that Che-ga-weyes-cum's act wasn't really murder— it was just two Indians fighting over a woman, settled in the traditional Ojibwa way (the victim, Mr. Aiken's son, was half Ojibwa). The steamboat left Prairie du Chien, alive with the gossip of the trial's conclusion. News like this was customarily called out from the bridge even to shoreside cabins where the boat did not dock.

The acquittal was a huge disappointment for the upriver community, who expected greater satisfaction for the effort taken in bringing Che-ga-weyes-cum to trial.[36] The accused was taken to Prairie du Chien to be tried when he could have been killed on the spot, as Mr. Aiken, the victim's father, had wanted. What did it accomplish to feed him for two winters, spectators reasoned, just to release him again? The verdict undermined their faith in the law's ability to deliver justice. The Métis community was insulted that the jury could not distinguish them, with their settlement ways, from a full-blooded Indian.[37] Wasn't a white trader's half-white son, who lived like the western settlers, entitled to full justice? Wasn't his white father entitled to retribution?[38] Frontier justice was divided along a racial edge between settlement culture and Indian ways, and the Métis, who were necessarily divided in their loyalties, were not seen as clearly belonging to either group.

Still farther downstream, the *Burlington* reached the disbanded fort where Dred had once lived. But on the opposite side of the river, a new town bearing the name of Emerson's friend Davenport was just being established. The doctor's other friend, LeClaire, was engaged in building a new hotel. Dr. Emerson himself still retained a hired man to hold his staked claims until the land sale. Further south, at Burlington, the temporary territorial capital (and the steamboat's name-sake), the territorial legislature deliberated over land sales. Complicating the issue was a currency shortage due to the nation's recent depression. There was too little money circulating for settlers to pledge the purchase money needed to hold their land. Governor Dodge recommended delaying sales until the situation changed, though claimants all over the territory were anxiously watching for the dates.[39]

At Alton, Illinois, another episode of mob violence had claimed the life of the Reverend Lovejoy, the religious newspaper publisher who became an abolitionist after witnessing the burning of the black man McIntosh. The Alton city attorney attempted to bring Lovejoy's murderers to account, but without result. There was no doubt who had participated in the murder, as several gentlemen even claimed credit for the act. Despite his best efforts, the attorney could not get a jury to convict anyone in the mob.[40] Most people believed that Lovejoy had gotten what he deserved.[41] In abolitionist circles outside the region, however, Lovejoy was becoming a martyr.

The Alton city attorney quietly resigned, closed his Illinois law practice, and moved across the river to St. Louis. This disillusioned lawyer, Francis B. Murdoch, would later file Harriet and Dred's lawsuit for freedom.[42] Whether the servant couple encountered Murdoch that summer is unclear, but when they were ready to sue, he would file the papers in the courthouse for the slavery trial of the century.

It was June 10 by the time the *Burlington* arrived at the St. Louis docks, which was the central terminus for all steamboat travel on the western rivers. Anyone traveling onward had to change steamboats there. Dred and his pregnant wife disembarked at the St. Louis docks with no definite place to stay. They had camped out on the lower deck of the big steamboat, barely above the water's surface, for 14 days. Like the biblical Joseph and Mary, carrying their few belongings, they arrived in the crowded city seeking a place to sleep. Porters, meeting arriving passengers who would hire them, could see that the couple had no trunks to carry and would pass them by. Vendors selling milk and fresh food to the weary passengers pushed their way through the dockside crowds, hawking their wares. Dred may have asked someone for directions to a safe place to sleep for the night. There were boarding houses that catered to black boatmen and black travelers. Leah Charleville was a washerwoman who kept such a house not far from the docks.[43] The Scotts might have gotten a mattress at Leah's or taken a meal there. Any black boatman could have shown them the way. But Leah charged by the night, and the couple may not have had the money to spend.

Travelers without a specific destination usually return to places familiar to them. As Harriet had passed through the town only briefly en route from Pennsylvania to St. Peter's, she had no St. Louis base to which to turn. Dred, however, knew the Blow family, who had brought him west from Virginia and then sold him to the doctor. The remaining Blows lived at the Charlesses' residence as one of the older daughters, Charlotte Blow, had married into the Charless family. Dred could probably have expected there the charity of a meal or a place to sleep for a night.[44] Charlotte was regarded as a generous soul, and she took pride in the fact that she and her husband did not turn the needy away.[45] There is no evidence, however, where the Scotts landed when they reached St. Louis.

In St. Louis, there were many things about the institution of slavery that Harriet had probably never seen, and some Dred hadn't witnessed for a long time. One was patrols instituted at intervals by the city to sweep the streets of vagrants. The slave couple walking along, carrying their few belongings, would have had to avoid the patrols or they would have found themselves stuck in jail as presumed runaways until Dred's owner could come to bail them out.[46]

There were also temporary holding pens for slaves in the city. These small courtyards were surrounded by buildings and closed off by gates of iron bars. The slaves slept in the buildings at night and were turned out into the yards during the day.[47] Here they awaited sale or transport, or they were simply held in storage, so to speak, until their masters' return. Harriet and Dred would undoubtedly try to avoid these places. The mayor had the power to sign a warrant for the arrest of any slave thought to be on the loose. The slaveowner had to pay charges to reclaim a slave held in jail or one of the pens, or the slave would be sold at auction in due course.[48]

Rabid dogs roamed the city's dirt streets that summer. Five or six had been shot, and the mayor finally ordered the capture of all dogs running loose.[49] The summer rolled out hot and dry and the unpaved streets of St. Louis were pulverized to dust.

However Dred and Harriet made their way through the streets of St. Louis, one place that they might have found refuge was at the African church. On Sundays, the word on the street would direct people to the church,[50] which was headed by the Reverend Meachum, a self-made free black man about Dred's age. He was a minister by spirit and a successful barrelmaker by trade. It's likely that slaves like Dred and Harriet, seeking temporary assistance, found their way to his church. The church minister advocated gradual emancipation but stressed buying one's freedom legally rather than suing or escaping.

THE SLAVE COMMUNITY of St. Louis had been buzzing with the topic of abolition since the burning of McIntosh,[51] which had occurred just two years earlier. The charred locust tree where McIntosh was burned alive still stood at the corner of 7th and Chestnut Streets, now tied with yellow ribbons; it had become a tourist attraction for persons traveling west.[52]

Another topic of interest among the slave community—and to the traveling Scotts as they contemplated a home—was whether conditions were better or worse in St. Louis than in Virginia. Some thought that slavery was at its most barbarous in St. Louis.[53] There were stories to support this claim. One St. Louis military officer had whipped a slave woman to death in the street.[54] Others maintained that however unfavorable St. Louis might seem, slavery was mild here compared to the sugar and rice plantation states to the south. Everyone knew someone who'd been sent south, and few ever returned.[55]

People in the business of selling slaves down the river were called "soul-drivers" by the slave community.[56] On the boat, the men and women were coffled two-by-two and kept on the lower deck, guarded so that they did not get loose. Sometimes slaves slipped off their chains and escaped at landing places while boats were taking on wood, or they jumped into the open water. One observer noted that a woman, taken from her husband and children, "having no desire to live without them,...jumped overboard and drowned herself."[57] Slaves resisted being sent south at all costs whenever possible. Even slaves assured by their masters that they wouldn't be sold feared for their security when they were required to go south.[58] Many of the decade's several freedom suits were triggered by the threat of being shipped south.

The record is unclear as to whether the Scotts remained in St. Louis or traveled on to Louisiana as the lawsuit later maintained.[59] It is stipulated in the lawsuit that Harriet journeyed on to Louisiana, in a claim that was not made, or perhaps not necessary, in Dred's parallel case.[60] But other evidence suggests that once they'd arrived in St. Louis, despite its perils, one or both of them simply refused to embark for Louisiana. That summer, Dr. Emerson acknowledged learning of some resistance in a letter; he wrote, "Even one of my negroes in St. Louis has sued me for his freedom."[61] There is no record of such a suit in the St. Louis court files, however, and Dred was the doctor's only slave by all accounts. Technically, perhaps, Harriet was "one of his negroes," as his slave's wife.[62] Dr. Emerson's reference to "one of my negroes," rather than "slaves" casts doubt on who Dr. Emerson was referring to. The language, "his freedom," could mean Dred specifically, or it could have been just a generic reference. If one of the Scotts had threatened suit, it would be extremely unlikely for either of them to have embarked for the South: Dred, because he was suing, and Harriet, because, as a free person, she had no reason to abide Emerson's call if her husband resisted. Every day Harriet's belly grew bigger with the child she carried. She could gradually loosen her apron stitches to cover her expanding figure. Finding food would occupy much of their attention.

Down in Louisiana, Dr. Emerson persevered in his efforts to be transferred north.[63] His primary concern seemed to be securing the land claims he had had staked in Iowa, opposite the decommissioned fort. Emerson wrote:

> While stationed at Ft. Armstrong, Illinois, I entered considerable land on the east side of the Mississippi and purchased a claim of 640 acres on the west side in the immediate vicinity [which] have become very valuable since my arrival at this post. Suit has been commenced against me for the purpose of getting possession of my place by persons…thinking I could not defend myself.[64]

In mid-July he begged to be transferred north again.[65] Finally, late in the summer, the doctor got his wish and received orders back to Fort Snelling.[66] Just in time—if he read newspapers reporting that land sales were expected to begin within two months.[67] He planned to look after his land interests.

That summer was so dry that the water level was falling on all rivers west of the Alleghenies, and boats from the east had difficulty reaching St. Louis. In the drought, there were daily reports of steamboat mishaps on the shallows during what should have been their busiest transport season.

The St. Louis newspapers posted the usual announcements of slaves for sale and rewards for runaways. Pierre Chouteau Jr., of the American Fur Company and St. Louis's richest man, posted notice of a reward for the capture of a girl named Mary Ann who had absconded. "It is presumed that she will endeavor to get into Canada, by the way of Cincinnati, or Illinois river," the announcement continued. Chouteau promised not only the $100 reward but also to pay all expenses if she was delivered to him in St. Louis or kept in any jail so that he could retrieve her again.[68] Dred and Harriet had no reason to be wary of the Chouteaus or John F. A. Sanford yet. They could not have known that the powerful fur trade family was kin to their master's new bride. Doubtless, the Chouteaus paid no attention to them.

That year, John F. A. Sanford, the man who would eventually become their nemesis, became a partner in the powerful firm belonging to the close-knit Chouteau family.[69] The ambitious Sanford had demonstrated great usefulness to the company by successfully lobbying Indian treaties through Congress. These treaties gave company men credit for debts they claimed were incurred to them by the Indians, the very policy that Agent Taliaferro had found most objectionable. Sanford was even on hand in Washington to cash several I.O.U.s from the treasury issued to James Wells, Scott Campbell, and others for services rendered in conducting the Sioux treaty.[70]

That summer, as Sanford made partner in the mercantile firm, the tribe that he once served as Indian agent was devastated by an outbreak of smallpox. News reached St. Louis that thousands of Mandan Indians had died in what was to be the greatest known epidemic devastation of an Indian people. It was said by some that blankets infected with smallpox had been delivered to the Mandans. Others said that some Mandan went aboard a Missouri River steamboat to obtain whiskey, contracted the disease, and spread it far and wide.[71] Whether the mode of transmission was whiskey or blankets, Sanford's firm was implicated. Almost all provisions sent west were furnished by Chouteau and Co., Sanford's firm, on Chouteau steamboats.[72] Sanford had lived with the Mandan as their Indian agent for almost five years. A Mandan woman had been his lover[73] and may even have borne him children. However, the virtual extermination of the Indian people he had lived with garnered not a line in his extensive correspondence.[74]

In September, John F. A. Sanford's first mentor, the aged Gen. William Clark, explorer of the West, died. Sanford had learned his first important lessons from Clark—including the practice that masters did not relinquish their slaves. William Clark freed none of his slaves at his death.[75] Clark, who liked to be known as friend of the Indians, was not an emancipator of slaves. He had resisted even York, the enslaved man who traveled with him and saw him through the famous pioneering exploration west. When York claimed that he had earned freedom for the deeds that he accomplished in the service of the great exploration of the continent's interior, William Clark ordered him locked up until he learned to behave more tractably.[76] Clark had been Sanford's first mentor.

On September 18, the sunlight grew strangely dim at midday in a solar eclipse[77] as the Emersons were returning to take the Scotts north. By September, Saturday slave sales, suspended over the summer, recommenced on the courthouse steps.[78]

The Emersons arrived in St. Louis on September 21 and spent only five days in the city.[79] During this time, the bridegroom could be expected to meet his new in-laws. His father-in-law, Alexander Sanford, had recently settled on a large farm northwest of the city. Anticipating Fort Snelling's remote location, Irene would want a new trousseau and home furnishings before they went north. And at some point the doctor took charge again of Dred and his pregnant wife.

How did he find them? Why did they resume service with Dr. Emerson? Perhaps they had no choice. Or perhaps within the circumstances it was the best opportunity they had. They were hardly in a good position to launch a lawsuit for their freedom with Harriet pregnant and without a support system in St. Louis other than each other. Moreover, Harriet may have desired to go north in order to bear her child in free territory. The importance of the free state boundary was well known. One might not be treated any better in Alton, in the supposedly free state of Illinois, where the mob killed Lovejoy, but state borders had consequences for slavery and freedom. The river was considered its own jurisdiction, as almost a legal neutral ground beyond the clutch of enslavement or state jurisdiction.[80] A child born in the North had a much better chance of being declared free. In any event, when the doctor needed to press on upriver, the Scotts were again in his company and in his service. The Emersons and the Scotts traveled aboard the *Gypsey*, departing the port of St. Louis on September 26, at 8 A.M.[81] Also taking passage was Reverend Brunson, the Methodist missionary who had freed Jim Thompson. Reverend Brunson had come to St. Louis to buy supplies for the mission.[82]

Although the *Gypsey*'s small size allowed it to travel more easily over the shallows, it was cramped and uncomfortable and lacked the comforts of bigger ships. Because it was one of the few shallow draft boats expected to make the trip, it was also crowded with passengers and dragged a small barge in tow. Other boats, like the *Burlington* that had brought the Scotts downriver, could accommodate 30 cabin passengers, with "individual staterooms...calculated to render the passenger comfortable and agreeable."[83] The *Gypsey* had no private cabins at all and only two group cabins, one reserved for ladies and the other for gentlemen.[84] The sternwheeler was more of a tugboat than a pleasure ship. One river traveler described these small boats as "Hell afloat." In these

> small high-pressure steamboats in the summer months...the sun darting his fierce rays down upon the roof above you, which is only half-inch plank, and rendering it so hot that you quickly remove your hand if, by chance, you put it there; the deck beneath your feet so heated by the furnaces below that you cannot walk with slippers; you are panting and exhausted between these two fires, without a breath of air to cool your forehead. Go forward, and the chimneys radiate a heat, which is even more intolerable. Go aft but there is nowhere to go, except overboard, and then you lose your passage. It is, really, a fire furnace.[85]

In this hot, noisy, steam-powered environment, the time of Harriet's parturition drew near. As the *Gypsey* drew nearer St. Peter's, so did the birth. The place of her baby's birth would be a critical fact in the later freedom suit, and Dred and Harriet would call the *Gypsey*'s captain as a witness. The court documents state that their oldest child was born "on board the Steamboat *Gipsey* north of the north line of...Missouri" and upon the Mississippi River. The uncomfortable expectant mother may have paced back and forth below deck in the unbearable heat of the wood furnaces and steam engines like a trapped animal on the crowded little ship. Where aboard ship could she actually deliver her baby when the labor pains came? Below deck, she had no privacy, unless she could find a secluded corner behind the barrels of cargo and bales of blankets destined for the Indians. There were some berths in the separate ladies' cabin, but was she welcome there, indisposed to serve as she was? The situation posed a new dilemma of cultural manners on the crowded boat. If the other ladies were mothers, they might understand her travail and allow her into the ladies' cabin; few would be of much assistance though. Ladies knew little of midwives' work, and there was surely no midwife on board. Even Dr. Emerson may not have known how to deliver a baby. A birthing slave woman might be considered a nuisance by the ladies, and in her discomfort, be made to feel their hostility. Dred could not enter the ladies' cabin. Somewhere on the *Gypsey* Harriet endured the hard labor of bearing her first child.

It was a girl! A healthy baby girl! They named her Eliza. Someone probably brought Harriet fresh river water, skimmed from the surface to avoid the sand, and more water to bathe herself and her newborn.

Some historians interpret the baby's naming as a tribute to Emerson's new bride, Elizabeth Irene Emerson.[86] However, Mrs. Emerson almost never used the name Eliza, preferring Irene. Moreover, virtually every white mistress in Harriet's life was named Elizabeth: Mrs. Taliaferro and Mrs. Plympton as well. More likely, the baby was not named after a white mistress but instead for Harriet's friend, the slave Eliza, from Taliaferro's household.[87] Living together in the agency house in the wilderness, sharing the chores and the same sleeping pallet, Harriet would have been as close to her sister servant as anyone. Over the next years, some significant portion of Harriet's life's energies would be occupied with pregnancies and babies, but this was her first child.

The *Gypsey* arrived at Rock Island, Illinois, where the doctor and Dred had lived before and where the doctor had land claims staked. Court records place both the Emersons in court in Davenport on October 3, 1838. Dr. Emerson must have had a confrontation with his former attorney, whom he accused of cheating him, and whose conduct vis-à-vis his land claims had troubled Emerson for some time. The confrontation must have been heated because Emerson later found it necessary to apologize for his behavior.[88]

Back aboard the chugging little sternwheeler, past the mouth of the Fever River leading to Galena's lead mines, past Dubuque, to Prairie du Chien, the passengers arrived at the last settlement before the long stretch of wilderness. The governor observed the boat's slow progress: "Steamboat passed this place yesterday having on board the goods for the Upper Indians, but from the low stage of the river above this, it will probably take from 8–10 days before her arrival at St. Peters."[89]

Completing the last leg aboard ship were a large number of Canadian lumberjacks heading north, seeking work in the new logging camps on what had been Ojibwa forests. At the entry of the St. Croix River, the *Gypsey* paused to discharge cargo near the place that Mr. Aiken, the Ojibwa trader was building a sawmill and cursing the courts for setting his son's murderer free.[90] Finally, after almost a month crowded on that floating furnace, the passengers of the *Gypsey* arrived at the dock of St. Peter's. It was still October, but the ground was covered with seven inches of snow. The Scotts had returned aboard the *Gypsey* to the place they had left that spring.[91]

CHAPTER 14

A New Baby in a New Land

HE SIGNIFICANT PERSONAL change for Harriet and Dred was that now they held a new baby in their arms. They had a new mistress, a new bride who surely gazed up at the impressive stone fort, as all newcomers did, a fort that would be her new home for the next two years.

The freedman Jim Thompson met the steamboat at the dock, sent by Agent Taliaferro with a message for the Methodist missionary.[1] The freedman had done work at the agency during the Reverend Brunson's absence.[2] Jim Thompson may have been baby Eliza's first visitor. Who could fail to be charmed by a tiny baby and her proud parents? Jim's Dakota wife had also recently had another baby.[3] Blessed by the dockside visit of the lucky freed man, the new parents carried baby Eliza onto snow-blanketed, solid ground to her new home in free territory.

The quiet of the first night back was disrupted when a large group of Canadian lumberjacks, who got drunk at the little steamer, fought "a royal battle...like so many wolves."[4] The Indians watching the drunken brawl were amused because a late night brawl was still a source of curiosity. But in the winter to come, drunken soldiers would become almost a regular evening occurrence.

Dr. Emerson and his lady moved into his old surgeon's quarters, displacing Dr. Wright, who was now very reluctant to leave. For their part, the Scott family probably moved back into the basement of the hospital wing, where their newborn wouldn't disturb the Emersons. The two new household members occasioned social introductions. Doctor Emerson proudly introduced his bride, whose maiden name, Sanford, was familiar to officers who had served in the West. Her brother was once the Mandan Indian agent, but, more important, was now known for his connection to the wealthy Chouteau trading firm that supplied so many of the fort's material needs. The hospital quarters were the new bride's first real home of her own. She must have settled in to build their nest with things they had brought with them, since they purchased relatively little from the sutler. Brother

John F. A. Sanford was pleased to have married off the second to last of his five sisters and offered to pay for a silver set sent from New York.[5]

The white mistress and black servant had much in common, despite their relative status. They were roughly the same age and both were married to men considerably older than they were. Both women, born in Virginia, had been brought west through fates and fortunes of the men who headed their households. Even if Harriet was no longer technically a slave, Mrs. Emerson was still her husband's master's wife, so Irene was now her new mistress. Although Mistress Irene had no claim of ownership over her, it would be Mrs. Emerson first, and then her influential brother, John F. A. Sanford, against whom Harriet would eventually wage her battle for freedom. At this time, however, their lives ran parallel, and there was no signal of anything but harmony between them. Each had their own bright future in the domestic realm, the nineteenth century's highest calling for womanhood; only Harriet was married to Dred, a man still regarded as a slave.[6]

There were few old friends for Harriet to show the baby to. Mrs. Plympton had already left for the East with her five children and didn't plan to return all winter. Catherine Hamilton Thompson, whom Harriet had served, had left as well in the company of Lt. Tappan in the most salacious of circumstances.[7] Upon some officers' suspicion that she was having an affair with Lt. Tappan, she was discovered in Lt. Tappan's quarters hiding under his bed by an investigating group consisting of her outraged husband, Capt. Scott, and Dr. Wolcott.[8] Finding his wife under the bed, Lt. Thompson threatened to kill Lt. Tappan. Capt. Plympton then issued the summary order to expel both Lt. Tappan and Mrs. Catherine Thompson from the fort the following day, accepting Tappan's resignation in lieu of a court martial. Although there was no steamboat at the ready, a boat was fitted for them and Lt. Tappan left without settling his accounts, and Catherine Thompson was expelled leaving her young son behind with her husband. It was said that the pair floated past Prairie du Chien as well, too ashamed to go ashore.[9] Lt. James Thompson secured a divorce in the Wisconsin Territorial Courts the following month, one of the first divorces ever sought in the area.[10]

The community to which the Scotts returned was much as they'd left, only more so. Every antisocial tendency evident on the surface before had deepened over the intervening summer. Land speculation had so intensified that everyone suspected someone else of sharp dealing. The settlers at Coldwater were even more defensive about the prospect of losing their homesteads. And the summer had been a disaster for Indian relations and for Harriet's former master, Agent Taliaferro.

Over the summer, the government had begun the process of adjudicating the amounts to be paid to each specific tribe for their respective share of treaty payment. Speculators had often stepped in to seize the cash as soon the amount was determined.[11] The sutler Stambaugh had left, having proven himself to be a scoundrel. This man of many schemes had been appointed trustee for the orphan Métis children of officers previously stationed in the area. He used his position to abscond with more than $5,000 of their money.[12] It infuriated Taliaferro to see the Indians exploited in this way, but he seemed to be alone in his indignation at the profit takers. The stories of some successfully getting away with large sums of money seemed to feed the greed of others. The officers, Major Plympton and marksman Capt. Martin Scott had formed partnerships for land claims with both the reluctantly departing Dr. Wright and with the eagerly returning Dr. Emerson.[13] Each group of claimants waited and schemed in their readiness to pounce once the lands were opened for legal claim. Financial partners negotiated, maneuvered, and hired grubstakers to do the actual work of building a cabin and holding the land in exchange for financing. And each stakeholder maneuvering for his own interest seemed to suspect everyone around him. No one wanted to miss out on the riches, though no one knew when the land would be open for sale.

Sporadic attacks by Indians on settler's livestock had become almost routine. From the Indians' point of view, with much of the wild game gone, the free roaming cattle on *their* land were fair to kill for food—while the settlers viewed the Indians' acts as theft. Taliaferro failed to resolve the conflicts to anyone's full satisfaction. He tried docking the Indians' annuities for the cattle they killed, but then he had to determine who had done the killing and which tribe to charge for the loss. For every missing cow, an angry owner approached the agent demanding recompense.[14] Taliaferro tried to get the settlers to keep closer track of their livestock by posting a guard.[15] The settlers, already on edge about possibly losing their homesteads, complained that Taliaferro wasn't doing enough to stop the cattle raids, complaints that he earnestly denied.[16]

The summer had also been fraught with more disastrous incidents between the Indian nations. Ojibwa Chief Hole-in-the-Day had barely escaped with his life during a visit to the Ojibwa interpreter who lived at the Coldwater Spring. The Sioux had lain in wait for him practically in the shadow of the fort. Moreover, the traders continued sowing discontent among the nations about the treaties they had signed. The tribunal meeting to pay out the half-breeds' claims had embarrassed Taliaferro by drawing attention to his paternity of a "half-breed" child. Lt. Thompson had gone so far as to publicly humiliate Agent Taliaferro at the officer's mess by contesting his authority to embargo alcohol, so the agent had ceased taking his meals with the other officers.[17] Furthermore, the master's most loyal aide, his interpreter Scott Campbell, had learned that he would not receive his promised land allotment. (The American Fur Company had succeeded in getting Campbell's allotment struck from the treaty before ratification.) Campbell had turned to drink; sometimes he appeared drunk in his official duties, leaving the agent without a dependable translator in delicate tribal negotiations. Taliaferro left St. Peter's Agency as deeply disappointed as he had ever been[18] but resolving not to resign until all treaty stipulations were fulfilled for the Indian people he called "his children."[19] Agent Taliaferro departed for the winter when the *Gypsey* left.[20] His attention was so completely absorbed with other worries that he did not note the new arrivals in his diary.

With the onset of winter, when the post's inhabitants mentally began to tally the identities of those who remained to be their companions for the wintering in, it became clear that there were few ladies and, accordingly, few domestic servants at the fort. In the officers' wing, the handsome Col. Plympton alone occupied the headquarters at the top of the diamond, with his entire family back east for the winter.[21] Most of the nine officers were either single or living apart from their families that winter.[22] In fact, there may have been no other officer's lady at the fort to keep company with the new mistress. Since black domestic servants like Harriet were usually brought to the frontier when an officer married and needed a servant to help his wife, there was no peer in Harriet's station either. There were even fewer servants of African descent this winter. Only Jack, who continued to run Captain Scott's hunting dogs, remained.[23]

The charges for sewing supplies and sweets on Dr. Emerson's account paralleled the charges on Lt. Thompson's. This may suggest that Mrs. Emerson provided a motherly touch for Lt. Thompson's young son after his mother had been banished from the fort.[24]

The garrison's population was larger than before, with 177 men and even more on detached service, at the sawmill or in the countryside gathering wood. Most were Irish immigrants recruited at the New York docks, fresh from their arrival.

This winter's set of officers were more mature and settled than in the years past. Instead of hanging around Sibley's house planning practical jokes and carousing with Indian women, two lieutenants formed a thespian society.[25] The doctor and Maj. Plympton played cards.[26]

Harriet's thoughts were probably absorbed with her newborn during her first months as a mother. The high stone wall surrounding the fort blocked any view of the surrounding prairie plateau; a sunset, the frozen river, or even the northern winter sky, which lit up but a few hours a day, was circumscribed by the wall. The snows of 1838–39 sealed Harriet's family within the fort this fourth winter in the North. She may have been content in the hospital basement: her husband and her infant drawing her attention inward. There were three in the bed to keep warm. Through the wall that separated their basement room from the hospital stable, they probably heard muffled sounds as the large animals moved around. Still nursing, at three months, baby Eliza would begin to smile. There was probably no internal stairwell, but they must have had their own fireplace hearth.[27] Dred may have assumed some of the heavier daily chores to allow Harriet more time with the baby.

A new officer who had arrived with them aboard the crowded *Gypsey* suffered from some mysterious ailment. Second Lt. William Darling spent most of November on sick leave in the officer's area of the infirmary, and he stayed on for December and January, taking up permanent residence in the hospital. Second Lt. Darling must have taken a particular liking to Dred because he hired him as his servant, too.[28]

Late fall brought the first test of military discipline under Plympton's command, when a court-martial was invoked to deal with deserters. This was Harriet's first opportunity to view military justice from inside the fort. By tradition, the fort doctor was assigned the role as the accused's defense counsel in the proceedings. Post doctors were selected as defense counsel because they stood outside the military chain of command. There was less potential conflict of interest within the military command structure if the doctor defended the accused. Although the doctor was an officer, he did not command men. He was the man one turned to for a toothache, a fever, or a sympathetic court-martial defense. Ironically, in case of conviction, the doctor was also required to see that the man did not perish under the infliction of the customary sentence of flogging. Thus, the Scotts probably heard about the court-martials from the defense counsel perspective.

Of the almost 200 soldiers on site that winter—mostly immigrants—few could list skills or a trade.[29] More than half were from Ireland, born in places like county Limerick, county Cork, or Tipperary. They were part of the great Irish migration spurred on by the terrible potato famine. They arrived at the docks of Boston or New York looking for work. There they'd been found by army recruiters, prowling the docks and seeking to enlist soldiers for the frontier. Before they knew it, they were enlisted and placed on steamboats headed down the Ohio for the West.[30] When the harsh winter set in, several tried to leave.

In one sense, these men were a source of kinship for Dr. Emerson; he, too, was born in Ireland. On the long winter nights, soft fiddle music and singing could be heard coming from the wooden barracks on the far side of the parade ground. He knew the melodies, but in another sense, to be Irish, or perceived as Irish, was unpopular in America and particularly unpopular for an officer who wished to move up in his station, as Dr. Emerson did. In the official records, Emerson was circumspect about his birthplace.[31] There was, of course, good reason for him to be careful. A quartermaster once gave him trouble about it, calling into question how an Irishman had ever been allowed to become an officer. No, it was better to pass as a Pennsylvanian than to be recognized as Irish.[32] If the brogue that the soldiers spoke and the tunes they played resounded in his memory, he was careful not to openly disclose it. Of course, as an officer, the surgeon was forbidden from fraternizing with the soldiers anyway.

This year, with so many fresh recruits, many of whom were surprised at the circumstances they found themselves in, military discipline was hard to maintain.[33] In November, eight privates were held in the brig. It was not hard to apprehend deserters. Everyone who left headed south. The frozen river was the only trail out. Despite several years in the service, Assistant Surgeon Emerson had attended a court-martial only once before. In the coming year these trials would occur with regularity.[34] Most men charged with desertion were found guilty, and there was often little Dr. Emerson could offer by way of defense. Nonetheless, anticipating the uncomfortable spectacle of the convicted soldier's flogging must have been a disheartening prospect for the doctor.

The first sets of court-martial were held in mid-December.[35] Two convicted deserters were given the customary sentence: their heads were shaved, they received 50 lashes on their bare backs, and they were drummed out of the service. All sentences had to be approved by headquarters at Jefferson Barracks, so the privates were returned to the brig to await approval of their inevitable fates.[36] The numbers of men imprisoned for drunkenness and desertion increased with each month over the winter.

For Christmas that year, Dr. Emerson bought yards of cotton and linen,[37] and something special: two shawls. One was a plain shawl that cost $1.12, and the other, listed as "fine," cost a full $6. The fine shawl was certainly for Mistress Irene and the plain one was probably given to Harriet. This gift would have been a true kindness to use to keep herself warm and wrap around the baby. Lt. Darling, who employed Dred, bought a pair of suspenders, either for himself, though he seemed to spend most of his time in bed, or as a gift for Dred.[38]

Although Christmas meant the custom of calling, no one remained at the agency to receive the Indians, so they only visited the fort commandant and the company man at Mendota. As the Indians were permitted to troop through the gate past the hospital to the far end of the parade ground, Harriet may have greeted some of them as well. It is likely that she knew these Dakota visitors better than anyone in the fort. She too had come to the frontier young enough to have acquired some of their language. They probably begged her for food, if she had any to give. "*Hirharha nampetchiyuza*," or "Greetings, my friend, I give you my hand in pleasure," was the usual prelude to a request for food.[39]

Lt. Darling, by now the hospital's permanent patient, was eventually relieved of duty on the doctor's recommendation. Since the ailing man did not need his boots polished or his uniform brushed, Dred probably attended him as a hospital orderly.[40] No one quite knew what afflicted him. His mind was very much disordered, the doctor said, from something he had contracted while serving in Florida.[41] No doubt Dr. Emerson tried the full range of treatments on Lt. Darling, possibly directing Dred in their application. Heating small glass cups over a flame and then applying them to the torso to suction out bad vapors was thought to help most abdominal ailments. If cupping didn't work, the doctor had leeches and a scarification device to bleed the patient. The little mechanical box of razor blades cut the skin in six parallel slits when the lever was released. Nothing seemed to help Lt. Darling, however, and, by midwinter, he was sufficiently incapacitated not to be able to ride his horse, which he sold to the doctor.

Most important to Dred, however, the ailing lieutenant paid him. The sutler's accounts list a $7.50 debit on Lt. Darling's account "to pay Dread."[42] The entry is clear: Lt. Darling did not pay Dred's master; it says "to pay Dread." This princely sum of $7.50, two months' wages, was the only entry crediting pay to any of the fort's slaves.[43] Dred also had credit at the sutler's.[44] Since he was able to charge there, he must have been accumulating cash of his own. Between Lt. Darling's payments and the sutler's credit, the Scotts managed a tiny household economy in their own names. This privilege alone distinguished them from most slaves. Once the Scotts were paid for their services (as they were by 1839), they probably sought extra jobs. A small amount of their own savings gave them the beginnings of a base of financial independence.

Most talk among the officers, as they played cards that winter, revolved around their plans to stake land claims in the new territory. The doctor wrote letters urging his friends to protect his Iowa claims, which amounted to some 640 acres.[45] Emerson was almost paranoid about a rumor he'd heard that Dr. Wright was angling to return to Fort Snelling, so he wrote the medical corps to make sure it wasn't true.[46]

By pooling their earnings, Dr. Emerson and several officers hired Philander Prescott and outfitted him to stake a claim for them near the mouth of the St. Croix River. Philander Prescott, the hardy soul who had trekked down to the hospital the previous winter to bring news of the Ojibwa treachery, was certainly able to survive at the site by himself over the winter, having run trading houses in even more remote locations. The greatest risk in hiring a stakeholder was that he would leave the place, but the honest, hardworking Prescott was a reliable man.[47] Dr. Emerson and his partners paid him $1,000 to build a cabin and furnish a small trader's store. Under the arrangement, Prescott would get one-eighth interest in the land claim, and the officer partners would get the rest. By November, Prescott had left for the site.[48] Agent Taliaferro was also interested in the site and disappointed to learn, when he returned, that the officers had already staked it.[49]

The mouth of the St. Croix River was a site second in value to only, perhaps, the Falls of St. Anthony. At the Falls of St. Anthony the Mississippi River dropped a full 50 feet, creating a greater falls than those upon which Massachusetts mill towns had been built.[50] Almost every entrepreneur in the vicinity of the fort, including the post officers, coveted that waterpower site.[51] The half section nearest the falls, on the river's east bank, was already held by Stambaugh, along with his new partner in the sutler's trade and the absent Dr. Wright. Another section was held by the partnership of Major Plympton, Capt. Scott, and Dr. Emerson.[52]

The setting of a boundary line distinguishing the federal reserve land from the land that would be opened to private claimants under the homestead acts was the most contested policy in the area. As Plympton wrote to his superior, the secretary of war, to set the reservation's boundaries in consonance with his official agenda to eject the squatters from Indian land, Dr. Emerson wrote to his superior, the surgeon general in what appears to have been a coordinated effort aimed at removing the squatters from their homes—and therefore from making a claim against the falls. Plympton's and Emerson's common theme was that all settlers be evicted from the military reserve because they sold whiskey to the soldiers and thus undermined garrison morale.[53] The commander couched the theme in terms of military defense while the doctor phrased it around the soldiers' health and well-being. Plympton made no attempt to hide his financial self-interest, however.[54] In fact, he openly stated his request as a favor from his superiors. Plympton wrote as if making a personal profit was simply his prerogative as commandant. "[My property] would be greatly enhanced in value, by a military reserve, which would place our claim most contiguous to the fort."[55]

His blatant self-dealing was obvious to the watchful settlers, causing heightened tension between the fort and its neighbors. Stambaugh, who had been rebuffed from seizing the little sawmill near the falls outright as his prerogative as sutler, disputed the major's line-drawing as "awkward and unnatural" in another letter to the secretary of war. He too pointed out that the officers benefited most from such a boundary.[56] For his part, Stambaugh tried to argue that a steamboat landing and hotel, which he was prepared to build, were what was necessary, and that the line-drawing disadvantaged him. When Maj. Plympton posted an eviction order informing the Coldwater Spring settlers that the government regarded them as "squatters" and they should prepare to move, Stambaugh joined forces with the squatters in a common cause against the officers' interests. In April, Abraham Perry's third daughter, Rose, who had once done housekeeping for Plympton, was married at her father's house to James Clewett. Clewett, as one of the few persons outside the fort who was able to read and write, also took up the cause of letter writing on behalf of the Coldwater Spring residents.[57]

The first sign of spring to be noticed inside the fort was the slushy thaw underfoot. The stone walls held on to the cold even on the brightest sunny day. Then one day, overhead, there was the first glimpse of a chevron of flying Canada geese, honking their distinctive calls. By April, the freezing temperatures and the fierce winds subsided. Outside the walls, the Indian women left for sugaring, but with no one at the agency, no one really noticed they had gone until the blue-blanketed women appeared outside the gate again with cones of maple sugar to sell.

CHAPTER 15

The Deteriorating Community

AFTER THE ICE cleared sufficiently on the rivers,[1] the first steamboat arrived.[2] Agent Taliaferro arrived alone this time, bringing only his large black dog, Nero. He did not intend to winter over. This was to be his last summer at the St. Peter's Agency, his final hurrah. He was there simply to see that the treaty was carried out and that justice was done to the Indians who had sold their land by treaty. Mrs. Taliaferro remained in Bedford, and without a lady in the household, there was no need for him to bring servants.

Over the winter, disaster had struck his father-in-law's famous hotel in Bedford when a fire swept through the town. Harriet must have known that misfortune like this usually meant even greater insecurity for the servants than for their masters. A master's financial catastrophe usually meant that some servants were not needed. When cash was needed, servants would be sold. Pennsylvania was in the process of gradual emancipation, but Humphrey Dillon, the mistress's father, still had two black indentured servants.[3]

Horatio Dillon, the mistress's brother, who had spent an entire year at the agency without finding his fortune, had only recently taken over the hotel before the fire. He had endeavored to raise its level of culinary specialties,[4] advertising a diverse, high class of service. With the hotel now a total loss, he was again without portfolio. And so, Taliaferro planned to bring him west again. Taliaferro's old friend, the independent trader B. F. Baker, had taken over as sutler with Stambaugh's departure, but in his declining health, he needed a young man's help.[5] Dillon, who stayed in St. Louis to buy supplies for the trading post, would arrive later.

Arriving without servants of his own meant that the agent had to arrange help for the simple day-to-day matters of housekeeping. After the unpleasant treatment the officers had given him the previous summer about his Métis daughter, the agent no longer felt comfortable dining at the officers' mess. It is possible that he turned again to Harriet to serve as his housekeeper.[6] She was the logical choice.

Although she was still caring for nine-month-old Eliza, she would have been considered available for labor. Servant mothers simply adapted to their responsibilities as the tasks and their teething babies demanded. Moreover, once the slave to a master, the enslaved person was always susceptible to his call. Taliaferro knew and trusted her. She'd been trained in his household and would know exactly how he liked things: his tea served, his boots brushed and blacked, and his shirts starched. Whatever the form of the arrangement, calling upon her would have been consistent with the master's view that a man's former slaves were always part of his family and that the master's personal relationship to slaves endured longer than the property relation. If, in his own mind, he had freed her, then there was all the more reason for him to feel entitled to call on her services again as a favor, believing that she was indebted to him for the "gift" of her freedom.[7] If, on the other hand, he had sold or bartered her services to the doctor, then he would feel it appropriate to ask the favor of her service from him. There is no direct evidence revealing who worked for Taliaferro this summer, but someone he referred to as a "servant" did, and it was a servant who was tied to Dr. Emerson. This "servant" would also save Taliaferro's life.[8]

One of the agent's first tasks was to hire treaty farmers so the tribes could begin plowing. These were men paid by the government to do farming for the Indians, as part of the treaty terms. The work was hard and did not appeal to most settlers in the area. Each treaty farmer labored alone, plowing the fields on tribal land, building storehouses for the tribe's corn, and breaking bullocks into a team. The younger Pond brother agreed to continue to serve as Indian farmer at the lakes, using the pay to support his missionary work.[9]

Before the 1837 treaty, Indian chiefs, including Big Thunder, showed some interest in plowing. But after the treaty, which promised to provide them farmers, none would touch the plow.[10] There were several reasons for their reluctance. Indian women performed the heavy work in Sioux culture and they also, traditionally, did smaller scale corn planting. Indian men saw such tasks as women's work, even though generally Indian women could not shoulder the heavy iron plow.[11]

In addition, the Indians were astute in observing that the other important men in the settlement culture—Sibley, Major Plympton, and Taliaferro (i.e., men with whom they dealt, made treaties, and wished to be respected as equals)—did not personally shoulder the plow. Instead, they had other hired men, and sometimes even slaves, to work for them. The Indians sought parity with the leaders of settlement culture. Accordingly, they looked to the treaty farmers they were promised to raise their crops for them. This meant that Taliaferro had to find several men who would be willing to work for pay for the Indians rather than working their own land stakes. They would also have to be willing to live near the fields at some distance from other settlement people. "Many seem ill-disposed among our own citizens to be Indian slaves,"[12] the agent observed. It was one thing to provide the tribes with blacksmiths; it was quite another to find farmers. Blacksmiths held a social standing in their trade and independence in their duties, and they worked their own forges, located in the company of other settlement peoples. A farmer, stationed out with the Indians, tilled soil that belonged to the Indians.

The Indians had their own ideas about who they wanted to be their farmers.[13] When Big Thunder learned that the government paid farmers a couple hundred dollars a year, he urged the agent to appoint one of his Métis cousins to the job. Taliaferro was not at all sure that the man Big Thunder wanted for the job would actually do the work for the money. The chief took the agent's rejection of his man as a personal slight, and in his pique, went out and killed one of his tribe's own oxen for spite. Just as Abraham Perry's son-in-law had retaliated, Big Thunder had chosen to kill an ox. Spite seemed to be a recurrent theme when men were frustrated in achieving satisfaction in social dealings.[14]

The American Fur Company also sought to have their retainers appointed as treaty farmers. For much the same reason that the agent placed missionaries among certain tribes to secure loyal influence, the company was interested in seeing one of their men get the job as the Indians' treaty farmer. The company men knew by this point that Taliaferro wasn't receptive to their suggestions, so they used the Indians to lobby for their choices. Taliaferro had a particularly difficult time finding a farmer for Black Dog's band. The previous farmer refused to stay on, saying that the band had repeatedly harassed him. Mah-zah-Hoh-tah brought the agent a note, written by Sibley, nominating one of Sibley's men for the position. Initially, the agent deemed the man ineligible, as a foreigner. A few weeks later, he wrote despairingly that he might have to take him because no one else was willing. Only the Pond brothers seemed to enjoy the job, though even they noticed that their fellow government farmers had as little to do with the Indians as possible.[15]

It never occurred to Taliaferro to employ slaves as farmers in the way that he and the officers imported them for household chores. The proposition was unthinkable, in part because the treaty provided wages to the man directly and not to some master for his slave's hire as the army paid out servant stipends. The economics were such that slaves strong enough to engage in heavy agriculture were considerably more expensive to employ than the domestics whom officers purchased in St. Louis to run their households.[16] Though Taliaferro hired the freedman Jim Thompson for carpentry, even when he was a slave, he never offered him the contract as treaty farmer.

Thus, Taliaferro's bright vision of Dakota self-sufficiency through farming was failing as a consequence of the labor terms. The Virginia planter's son refused to believe it at first. The solution to the Indians' hunger seemed so clear to him. He was so convinced it would work. His dream of giving the Dakota the means by which they could feed themselves was dissolving, in part, over the issue of who shouldered the plow. The Indians sensed that having others plow for them was even better than learning to plow themselves. They understood that Taliaferro wanted them to adopt settlement habits. "I want to be a civilized man. I wear a hat," one chief told him to please him.[17] Taliaferro's main message was hard work: labor will make you free from hunger now that your game is gone and the trading company is taking advantages.[18] From later developments, it seems that Harriet was paying attention to the message.

On June 1, the master was surprised to receive word that the Ojibwa Chief Hole-in-the-Day and his people were on the move, traveling in his direction. The

Dakota, photographed with stovepipes, on a visit to Washington in 1858. Almost two decades after Taliaferro resigned as Indian Agent, Joseph R. Brown took the next generation of Dakota leaders to Washington. Blankets and cut hair became symbols of distinction among the Dakota at the time between those who retained the old ways and those who had adopted settlement ways. *Charles DeForest Fredericks / Minnesota Historical Society.*

Dakota, photographed with headdresses, on a visit to Washington in 1858. Joseph R. Brown, on the far left, and his half-brother Nathaniel Brown, on the right, are pictured among the Delegation. Among the Métis in the picture is Scott Campbell's son, Antoine Joseph Campbell, who renewed his father's request for the land allotment promised his father by Taliaferro. The promised allotment was stricken from the 1837 treaty by representatives of the American Fur Company, at Sibley's insistence. Antoine Campbell is identified on the picture as seated near Joseph R. Brown, with Brown's hand on his shoulder. *Charles DeForest Fredericks / Minnesota Historical Society.*

Catlin first began Indian portraiture on a visit to the Mandan people on the Missouri River in 1832. At the time, their agent was John F. A. Sanford. Catlin's painting of Pigeon Egg going to and coming from Washington, D.C., became iconographic of images of Indian delegations when it was reprinted by Currier and Ives. Sanford escorted the delegation, of which Pigeon Egg was a member, in 1832. Catlin portrayed Pigeon Egg as wearing the wrong dress in each setting (a Washington building is featured where Pigeon Egg wears traditional dress, while tepees form the background where he wears a stovepipe and officer's uniform and carries an umbrella and a fan). *Smithsonian American Art Museum, Washington, DC / Art Resource, NY.*

Ojibwa chief declared that he was coming to Fort Snelling to see Governor Dodge because his people were upset that LaPointe on Lake Superior had been designated as the place for payment of their annuities.[19] Chief Hole-in-the-Day refused to take his people there because the greater distance was just too far. The children would starve on the way, he claimed. So the Ojibwa were on their way to St. Peter's Agency to register their complaint at the place where the treaty had been made. Taliaferro never expected the Ojibwa to visit Fort Snelling that year. Not only were Ojibwa annuities not expected there, but Governor Dodge was not in the vicinity, and the Sioux annuities had not even arrived.

Agent Taliaferro sent a message to the chief to head off the Ojibwa.[20] Taliaferro's messenger was the African Ojibwa Steven Bonga, whom Taliaferro described as "a half-breed Negro of the Nation." (The description finessed the issue of what nation Bonga belonged to, whether Ojibwa or American.) Bonga was Mrs. Fahlstrom's brother, and he probably lived with the Fahlstrom family at the Coldwater Spring.[21] Bonga was often called on as an Ojibwa interpreter. Taliaferro wrote, "Though a smart man, his English is African dialect. Hard to connect so as to make sense."[22] On his way to deliver the message, Bonga stopped at Sibley's store to buy crackers.[23] Sibley probably learned of his mission thereby.[24] The company man seemed to know everything.

The message Bonga relayed urged Hole-in-the-Day to stay where he was and not to bring his people to St. Peter's. He was still hated here by many Sioux for betraying his hosts while they slept. He had narrowly escaped attack when he'd visited the agency the previous year, and the Sioux would probably try again to kill him. The deep animosity between the two nations remained, and the most recent incident had not been smoothed over. The Ojibwa had to be persuaded to stay away while there were so many Sioux at the agency, especially when the Sioux were hungry, dissatisfied, and still angry with Hole-in-the-Day.

A Sioux man came, for the third time in two years, to ask the agent for a coffin for one of his children.[25] "The Indians are starving. I am compelled to ask favors in order to carry on friendly intercourse," wrote the agent.[26] In this stage of desperation, Taliaferro probably sought food donations and aid from every imaginable source. Only a few individuals in the area had substantial food stores to lend: Sibley, B. F. Baker, the quartermaster in charge of all the army stores, and the doctor.

The trading houses had goods, but they charged them on credit. The quartermaster was necessarily a stickler for detail and no easy hand in sharing army supplies.[27] The doctor, though, was entitled to a separate, regular allotment of food for the hospital, and he managed the accounts himself. Under military regulations, Dr. Emerson was entitled to draw, from the quartermaster, a supply of pork and flour for the hospital every month, regardless of the number of people sick at the hospital—and there were never that many sick at this fort. That gave Emerson a surplus. Like the post surgeons before him, Dr. Emerson had gotten into the regular habit of drawing the full food supply whether he used it up or not; he sold or traded the surplus for other things that the hospital needed.[28] Taliaferro must have prevailed in persuading the doctor to donate some of his surplus. Shortages in Emerson's hospital account books and accusations that he gave the Indians food gave him trouble later on.[29]

How could the doctor refuse? He had checked about permission to dispense medications to the Indians. How could someone who ministered to the ills of Indians in time of disease, fail to see that they were slowly dying of starvation and malnourishment? Who would be the wiser if a couple barrels of pork or flour were turned over to the Indian agent to distribute for this good purpose? The agent made these entreaties in the interests of humanity and the U.S. government—the same U.S. government that the doctor served. Though Emerson later denied giving away entire barrels of food to the Indians, it seems likely that he supplied the agent with some of his extra food. When he was later accused, he denied doing anything wrong, but he didn't deny the accusation categorically.[30] He simply minimized how much he had given away. This act of charity, whatever its true extent, would eventually cost him his military career. A few years later, Surgeon's Corps officials would charge him with mismanagement. His concession was that sometimes when a starving Indian reached his door, he sent down to the kitchen (probably to Harriet) for a little left-over meat or bread for the hungry person.

This fateful move would redound upon the Scotts in the way that a master's misfortune often became his servants' misfortune. Dr. Emerson would react to his military discharge by turning the Scotts out to fend for themselves. The Scotts too may have been implicated in the fateful act of charity: Dred to take the barrels to the agency in a cart. Harriet may have broken them open to hand out the measures of food for the supplicants as she was bidden.

Despite Taliaferro's best efforts to head off the Ojibwa, they arrived at the agency anyway. Chief Hole-in-the-Day descended the river, accompanied by 500 members of his tribe traveling in canoes and on foot. With Taliaferro's message delivered but unheeded, the messenger, Stephen Bonga, descended the river with them.[31] The chief said that he was already below Rum River before he received the message so he couldn't turn back. Now he asked only to stay at the agency for three days' time before he and his people returned upriver. All he asked was that the agent keep the Sioux from interfering with his people, and he and his people would be quiet in turn.

In the circumstances, the agent first had to consult the Sioux. They acquiesced: there would be no harm if the Ojibwa stayed three days and left. The agent then prepared to hold a separate council with the Ojibwa the following day. Although the master could rely on the chiefs' word, it was the young warriors and lesser men who were most apt to break discipline and breach the peace. Only by a nationwide meeting could their compliance be ensured. Given the military implications, the agent asked Major Plympton to attend as well.

Every day, Harriet probably walked the quarter mile to the agency house, through these two uneasy camps, to see to Taliaferro's meals and housekeeping. The interpreters were kept busy shuttling messages to and from the separately encamped nations that the agent was trying to keep at peace.

A canopy of saplings had been hastily prepared along the fort's outer wall, mimicking the treaty canopy two summers earlier. There would be no beef provided at this meeting.[32] The canopy council was barely 100 feet from where the post hospital stood just inside the gate. The agent met with the Ojibwa at 10:00 one morning in a public council that must have attracted the attention of everyone within the fort, including the women and children.[33] Harriet and her family must have been drawn to it along with the others. From a further periphery some 150 Sioux watched.

Chief Hole-in-the-Day had a speech to deliver. Holding the treaty in his hand, he addressed the Indian agent, the commander, and the assembled peoples with full dramatic solemnity. It had been two years since the treaty was signed at this very place and the Ojibwa had relinquished their lands east of the great river, he said. He recounted what he believed to be his people's understanding under the treaty. His people were now located north and west of the Mississippi. They could not travel as far east as La Pointe to receive their annual payments each year.

"We cannot go.... You see your own women and little children here near as this day," he said, gesturing to the assembled crowd.[34] "You wish to keep those children from harm. We have our own children and wish not to see them starve. We cannot go to LaPointe," the chief implored. "We should starve on the way. I tell you this day if we [have not] sold our lands, we have it yet and we will never go to La Pointe."[35] The implication was that if the Ojibwa were dissatisfied with the Americans' performance of the treaty terms, they would reclaim their lands. Other Ojibwa, lesser chiefs than Hole-in-the-Day, took their turns to speak, all dissatisfied with the government's compliance with treaty's terms.[36] One speaker declared that he wished to see the man with the big feather, Governor Dodge. He would tell him his mind and what he expected about payment.[37]

The Ojibwa had a legitimate grievance. It was folly to expect them to trek every year on the white man's schedule to pick up their annuities and have their tools repaired. The agent asked Mr. Aitkin, who traded exclusively with the Ojibwa, to advance them 12 days' provisions. The agent offered them ammunition and corn that they could take to go to LaPointe or to return to their lands.

During the day, more bands of Ojibwa arrived. Word had spread through the larger Ojibwa nation to rendezvous at St. Peter's, where, after all, they had gathered before. The tribes came from three directions, over rivers and by land. The important men rode horses. By the end of the day, 40 more canoes had arrived, bringing the accumulated Ojibwa population to 750. The Ojibwa women busily constructed the summer travel shelters, turning the plateau into a segregated village of two nations again.

Somehow the agent had to hold the peace between the Ojibwa people and an equal number of hungry Sioux subsisting on marsh potato and waiting for the rest of their own provisions to arrive. Surrounding the agency house, at campfires all across the prairie, were more than 300 shelters—deerhide tepees and bark tents. Around each fire, hungry Indian families spent the nights waiting for the U.S. government to supply the annual provisions that had purchased their lands. None of the promises were completely fulfilled. All had reason to be dissatisfied with the government and Harriet's master.

With the great gathering of peoples, incidents were bound to occur. When the agent was not resolving the large questions of concern to the Indian nations, he was asked to settle family affairs and straighten out the possession of livestock. In one incident, a sorrel horse, assigned to Wabasha's Band, had fallen into the possession of Black Dog's Band.[38] In another, a Sioux woman who espied her son living with the Ojibwa band approached the agent to get him back. The woman had married an Ojibwa being held prisoner by her people. Two years before, after her husband's death, she had given their son to his Ojibwa uncle to raise. Now that he was older she wanted him back to support her. The boy had become attached to the Ojibwas, however. The agent advised her to not try and call him back. She ought to let him stay where he was best satisfied. Nonetheless, within both tribal cultures, the hold that a mother had on her son was lifelong. The mother insisted, and fearing a disturbance, the agent ordered the boy to return to his mother. He noted that the parting was hard on the boy and his Ojibwa uncle.

Breaking the tension a little, the Sioux men played a ball game at the prairie near the bluff's edge. The Emersons rode their horses out to watch them play.[39]

At the Ojibwa camp, the people seemed to be packing to leave. In previous years, such a meeting of councils would have been the occasion for presenting medals. For decades, the Indian agents had ritually bestowed upon the chieftains medals newly minted with the profile of the current American president, or, as the Indians referred to the president, the great father in Washington. More important chiefs were given medals larger than those given to less important chiefs.[40] Lately, however, presidential medals had fallen into disrepute among the Indians, as Flatmouth had reminded the agent before. The American Fur Company had mimicked the government practice, handing out medals bearing the profile of its founder, John Jacob Astor.[41] So many medals had been distributed that they had lost their importance. At this gathering, the agent recollected the discredited indicia of the great father, and blamed Schoolcraft, the official Indian agent to the Ojibwa, for cheapening their value by giving them out to unworthy individuals.[42]

CHAPTER 16

Battles and Baptisms

VEN AS THE Ojibwa prepared to depart, more Indians arrived. The numbers of Sioux at the agency doubled as western bands came in expectation of their annuities. In total, more than 2,000 Indians, 846 Ojibwa, and 1,250 Sioux now camped on the plateau.[1] Those chiefs who brought along their horses raced them back and forth through the tent city to demonstrate their prowess. Chief Strong Ground was thrown from his horse and bled considerably, requiring Dr. Emerson to bind his wounds.[2]

Hole-in-the-Day told the agent: "Now I report my earnest desire to go to see the president."[3] The Dakota had visited Washington to negotiate their treaty. The Ojibwa chief was now ready for *his* grand tour of the country. Hole-in-the-Day didn't realize that for the Americans, treaty making was a one-time deal. Once the tribe had surrendered its lands by treaty, the American president had no further interest in seeing him or hosting his warriors on a trip to the nation's capital.

A steamboat arrived with H. N. Dillon, Taliaferro's brother-in-law, and the stores destined for the sutler's shanty at the fort. Since Mr. Baker suffered from consumption, Horatio Dillon had arranged the annual spring purchase in St. Louis.[4] But the remaining treaty goods that the Sioux expected were not aboard.[5]

Amid the encampments of the two Indian nations, about 50 pullcarts of settlers arrived from the northeast, fleeing from the hard living conditions at Selkirk settlement on the Red River of Manitoba.[6] With eviction pending at the Coldwater Spring, these new refugees found only temporary hospitality. Those who had preceded them by a decade feared being turned out from their homes,[7] and the arrival of the new refugees underlined the squatters' continuing insecurity.

The *Ariel* arrived next, with stores for Mendota and a passenger purveying whiskey and defective goods.[8] The agent used the steamboat's departure to send an emergency allotment of flour, corn, and pork to two different bands of Sioux farther south on the river. (This large allotment may have come from Dr. Emerson's supply at the post hospital, since no new stores had yet arrived for the agency.)[9]

The sharp-dealing passenger, who came and departed on the *Ariel*, had succeeded in selling a barrel of whiskey to Scott Campbell. One night, several drunken Indians were seen emerging from Campbell's house. "I have some reason to think Mr. Campbell somewhat culpable," Taliaferro wrote.[10] But upon searching his house, the agent found that Campbell's whiskey barrel was unopened.

Jim Thompson, the freedman, reported that another trader had whiskey on the west bank, the Indian side of the river.[11] The soldiers sent by Major Plympton to investigate reported finding nothing. Dissatisfied with the report, Agent Taliaferro went himself with a party of men, and finding the contraband, he knocked in the barrel heads and poured out the whiskey.[12] Taliaferro concluded that the soldiers could not be trusted to enforce the whiskey embargo.

As the population increased and the summer temperature rose, the situation became even more unstable. Like the rising barometer before a storm, everyone sensed some coming conflict, but no one knew how or when it would break. Jacob Falstrom reported that his heifer had been killed by Indians from Black Dog's village. He brought the fresh bones to show the agent.

Through sequenced negotiation the agent managed to bring the two Indian nations together to talk in council for several hours. The peace pipe went round, and to Taliaferro's satisfaction, both parties promised to keep the peace for one year.[13] Perhaps something good had come of the Ojibwas' arrival at St. Peter's after all. It was a fragile peace, but it was a truce for the time being. Now fully packed, the Ojibwa set off for home.

On the morning of the first day of July, Mr. Campbell knocked at the door of the agency house before daylight. With no servant in the house, Taliaferro himself opened the door to find before him about a dozen Mdewakanton men. Hah-kee-parc-tee said that a group of his people had gone off to the falls to attack the Ojibwa and that his party was on their way too. They had stopped to ask Taliaferro's opinion. Agent Taliaferro erupted, bluntly calling them "a pack of fools." He said, "You smoke the pipe of peace yesterday and this morning seek blood? No wonder the Chippewas say they can have no confidence in you."[14]

His strong, stern response seemed to inhibit them from joining an attack. The Sioux groups that had set off earlier did encounter the Ojibwa as they portaged the falls, but they smoked together, and then both left the falls without coming to difficulty. Hearing the news the next morning, the agent sighed, "The Chippewa are all off. 890 souls."[15] The thermometer reached 91 degrees that day.

On the heels of the Ojibwa departure, the bishop of Dubuque arrived by canoe. Bishop Loras, the first church official of such high stature to visit St. Peter's, was accompanied by a young priest and an interpreter; their aim was to establish a Catholic mission there.[16] While he was in the area he intended to perform sacraments for the Métis Catholics. He'd been offered accommodations at Scott Campbell's house across the river.[17] Ordinarily, Taliaferro would have welcomed another civilizing influence in the outlying area—someone who could aid with the Indians' farming and education. But placing a church near the fort did not serve the agency purposes of providing influence to counter fur trade influence in outlying areas and would complicate matters by providing an additional reason for the Métis squatters at the Coldwater Spring to wish to remain near the fort. Rather than involving himself in the discussion, he politely referred the bishop to the commanding officer, cynically noting in his diary that it was "Laughable: should the agent discharge his duties and be found fault with."[18] He planned to let Major Plympton handle the bishop's request.

Very early July 3, four Ojibwa men broke from the main group peacefully traveling north and crossed over to the agricultural mission village at Lake Harriet where the Sioux lived. Minutes after sunrise, the four men shot and scalped a respected Sioux leader who was peacefully searching for a stray horse in the brush. The Ojibwa were so intent on scalping their victim that they overlooked a young boy, also searching for the horse. The boy ran back to the village and gave the alarm.[19]

The Pond brothers were at the village to witness the panic, and recorded the events thus:

"The Chippewas! The Chippewas have surrounded us! We shall all be butchered! The Badger is killed. There across on the other bank of the lake. There he lies all bloody. The soul is gone from the body, escaping through that bullet hole; the scalp is torn from the head." Every warrior, young and old, uttered his determined vow of vengeance as Red-bird, the medicine man, stooped to press his lips on the yet warm, bleeding corpse, cursing the enemy in the name of the gods.[20]

The runners sent out in all directions brought back warriors from other tribes in an hour or two. The arriving warriors were painted and armed for the warpath. This further act of Ojibwa treachery required a significant counter-response. Two other Sioux bands, the Wahpekuta and Little Crow's people, went in pursuit of yet a different party of Ojibwa, who were passing up Lake St.Croix bound for La Pointe. That traveling group, having left the post only the previous morning, was only a day away. They would be moving slowly, with the women—accompanied by children—carrying all of their belongings. They did not know of the attack on the Badger and would be unaware that a war party was pursuing them.

The Reverend Stevens brought Agent Taliaferro the disturbing news that 150 Sioux warriors had set off after the Ojibwa. Taliaferro predicted there would be a "severe and bloody conflict" and quickly notified the commandant.[21] All he could do then was wait for news.

The agent sent Scott Campbell to check on things at Lake Calhoun. The people of the fort waited tensely throughout the day. Scott Campbell returned at nightfall with a little Métis girl (one of Taliaferro's wards), who had been left wandering about in the confusion. Her mother, once the mistress of an army lieutenant, was the Badger's widow. She followed the avengers out of respect to her murdered husband, leaving the girl behind. With no men remaining at the lakes and many Indian women and children left unprotected, the agent asked Major Plympton to send some soldiers over to protect them.[22]

On Wednesday, July 3, 1839, the two largest battles in Sioux-Ojibwa history occurred where the Sioux war parties met the departing Ojibwa.[23] One hundred warriors from Little Crow's band attacked the Ojibwa at the St. Croix to the east, an encounter that resulted in at least 25 deaths. Another battle was waged to the west, near Rum River.[24]

The agent waited until midnight for the details of the skirmishes. As he waited, he wrote in his journal, "Momentous day on Indian concerns. No news up to 10 p.m. this night as to the 280 Sioux, who went in pursuit of the Ojibwa.... I told them not to come."[25]

The next day, the Fourth of July, passed without celebration. Instead of 21-gun salutes, band concerts, and Indian ball games, the soldiers were on high alert, anticipating the worst. Everyone remembered the bloody Blackhawk War five years earlier. With two Indian nations at war, this could be worse.

In the early morning came a shrill wailing.[26] It was the Sioux death song. Canoes of wounded Sioux came down the placid river from the falls. The wounded brought the report of more violence near Rum River. In both battles, 124 people lay dead ("124 souls," the agent wrote) and more were wounded.[27] The doctor probably treated the wounded at the agency.[28]

The agent sent out messengers to seek help from the trading companies in stabilizing the situation. Mr. Aiken had offered the Ojibwa traveling supplies; now Taliaferro looked to Sibley to wield influence with the Sioux. Sibley, after all, had recently been appointed justice of the peace in the new territorial reorganization.[29] He had at least two dozen men in his service, and, as the local company manager, the Indians respected his influence. The messenger returned to say that Mr. Sibley had left his house a few minutes before the messenger arrived. The agent received the news and wrote, "I am disappointed."[30] He would get no help from Sibley. He suspected Sibley had tried to avoid his appeal by absenting himself. Sibley knew every move in the territory as soon as, if not sooner than, the agent himself did.

Major Plympton dispatched a detail of men to investigate one battleground. The detail was likely to encounter survivors, though none of the soldiers could speak the language. Lt. McPhail asked Taliaferro to assign an interpreter to accompany them. Neither Scott Campbell nor Peter Quinn wanted to go. Quinn was fearful because his wife was Ojibwa and he was too deeply embroiled in the vengeance pattern already. His house was the site of the previous year's attack on Hole-in-the-Day.[31] Scott Campbell couldn't leave that evening because the bishop planned to baptize his family the next day. So Capt. Scott, Lt. McPhail, and their men rode off without an interpreter, knowing that they would be unable to communicate with anyone they encountered—the injured, survivors, or witnesses.

From the St. Croix River came the intelligence that more shooting had occurred. Mr. Aitken and Mr. Brunet had been shot at while at work building their sawmill. The Sioux had caught up with the Ojibwa a second time near the men's lumber site and wounded more Ojibwa. Mr. Aitken was furious. He told the messenger to say that he damned them all—the agent, the interpreter, the Sioux, and the Ojibwa—for his misfortune.

Now the agent insisted that Mr. Quinn ride to catch up with Lt. McPhail's men on their way to the St. Croix battleground to see the Ojibwa and to learn from

Mr. Aitken whether he needed assistance. They were to provide whatever help they could to the wounded.[32]

The agent sent an urgent express to Dakota Chief Big Thunder to see him by 10:00 the following morning to find out whether any of the chief's people were still in pursuit. If so, the chief was to recall them immediately. Big Thunder came at his request. "This killing of the Badger has brought heavy consequences. 101 souls killed for the loss of one man and it is distressing to think that they were mostly women and children," wrote the agent.[33]

The bishop had designated July 5 for baptisms. The Campbells brought all of their children, as did the blacksmith. Altogether 56 people were anointed with oil and water. The bishop's visit had little effect on the fort's predominantly Presbyterian officers, now served by an army chaplain.[34] The following day, the bishop blessed the marriages of the Campbells and the Massees, who had never been married in a church, and gave communion. One would think that the visit of such an important personage as a bishop would have induced Dr. Emerson to take communion as well, but his name doesn't appear in the bishop's notes.[35] Besides, he was probably occupied dressing the wounds of the battle survivors.

As if the situation at St. Peter's was not already sufficiently confused, a cattle drive interrupted the holy sacraments—as well as the procession of survivors returning from the Indian battles. Two men, who regularly crossed the plains from the Red River, passed through the valley with a drove of 150 cattle and a two-wheeled cart pulled by bison calves and loaded with dried buffalo meat.[36] When they offered the meat for sale from the rear of the cart, parishioners left the mass early to buy pemmican. St. Peter's, where the rivers joined and a place that was so isolated during the winter months, had become the frontier crossroads of several conflicting agendas.

Three days later, the military detail returned from the St. Croix battleground, along with a drunken deserter they had rounded up on their ride. McPhail reported seeing almost 40 bodies at the site, but he estimated there were more dead. Most still lay where they had fallen while seeking cover in the ravine, but some had not had time to get out of their canoes and their bodies still lay by the water where they had died. The baking heat of July had hastened the bodies' decay and the stench deterred the soldiers from approaching the bloodiest site of the conflict in the ravine; they gave no thought to burying the dead.

Although the Ojibwa took more casualties than the Sioux (the Sioux returned with 95 scalps),[37] the officers said that the Sioux were beaten back. On their retreat, they were heard crying, fearing that their wounded would be taken from them as captives. Capt. Scott called the Sioux cowardly.[38] Still, the scene of the battle was so affecting that even the hardened Capt. Scott became sick with fever and spent the rest of the month recuperating in the hospita, where the Scotts would be able to hear him retell his version of the scene. A month after the battles, when the Lake Calhoun Sioux finally returned to the battleground to collect the bodies of their people, they had no bodies to bury. The dead had been dragged off and pulled to pieces by wolves and vultures.[39]

Having completed their mission, the bishop's party started for home by canoe. The agent sent a report of the battles with him to give to the governor. Since the territorial jurisdiction had shifted again, St. Peter's was now in Iowa territory.[40]

The consequences of the battles continued to spin out. More reports came in of casualties, as those wounded eventually succumbed to death. A minor chief died of wounds from the St. Croix battle, so the agent had to name a new chief to succeed him.[41] The weather turned exceedingly hot and the river levels fell rapidly. There was little prospect of a steamboat bringing annuities anymore this year. It was the driest summer ever known, even worse than the previous year. The garden's crops and the Indians' corn had all but burned up in the blazing sun. Dr. Emerson wrote his friend in Rock Island to send 50 bushels of corn from his farm on a shallow draft vessel. He reiterated his concerns about bidding for his land when it came up for auction.[42]

On July 15, Harriet may have noticed that her former master was particularly somber. That day, after the 27 years that he described as "arduous service,"[43] he officially resigned his post. The battles weighed heavily on him, no doubt, but even in his personal journal, he didn't blame the tribes, whom he continued to regard with affection. Of the Indians he wrote, "[They] are a people who only look for today. Tomorrow provides for itself. But in this idea, much real want and misery is of expedience and felt."[44] As his reason for quitting he stated simply, "I can no longer endure [the] machinations of traders."[45] For months, he had noted his frustration at the canny ability of the fur company men to outmaneuver him at every turn. When he needed their help to bring calm to the warring tribes, they could not be found. They were always two jumps ahead of him and never seeking the same objective of a stable future for the Dakota. "No move is made or directed at Washington, whether it is in regard of our Indian Affairs, Army, or other matter, but it is known to the American Fur Company."[46]

The company's letters indicate that he was right. The company was extremely efficient in directing and organizing its interests, whether in Washington, in St. Louis, at Mendota, or Traverse de Sioux. Traders brought Sibley reports of what was happening among the six or seven outposts within the region under his direction. Even the agent's own messengers could be tempted to divulge information when they stopped by Sibley's store. The information gleaned from Sibley's informants was routinely sent on to New York, coordinated, and relayed back to other managers all through the territories. If lobbyists were needed in Washington, the company sent someone with very good connections. There was little that one man stationed at St. Peter's could do for the Indians in the face of such an efficient machine, well oiled with information and money and directed by the single purpose of generating influence and wealth.

A tenth steamboat was spotted on the river, but again it arrived without the Sioux annuity. "I never saw people more vexed than the Indians seem at this tenth disappointment this season."[47] The boat remained only a couple of hours at the landing before leaving again. With water levels as low as they were it was necessary to keep moving. On the evening of July 19, 1839, a storm came bringing high winds and ominous thunder. The following morning was interrupted with showers again, though still not enough for the parched gardens and cornfields to revive. Two days later an eleventh boat arrived, finally, mercifully carrying the long-awaited annuity for the Sioux and several wedding guests. As the *Malta* docked at the fort, the agent tried to figure out how to unload the supplies. The courts-martial were interrupted for the wedding of one of Taliaferro's cousins, sister of Captain Hooe, at the officers' barracks. That day Captain Hooe's youngest sister married a young man from Dubuque. There would be a feast with drinking and toasts and even dancing into the evening, such an irony after the recent tragedies. Since the bride was a cousin, the agent would attend, of course, along with the entire complement of officers and their ladies. Harriet probably ironed the dress uniforms of both the doctor and the agent as well as Mrs. Emerson's dress.

After the wedding day festivities, the guests took the steamboat on an excursion to the St. Anthony falls. Afterward, the steamboat set out to see the place of the Indians' slaughter. Like the locust tree in St. Louis where McIntosh was burned alive, the battleground had become a tourist attraction for steamboat passengers. When the festivities were over, the post's officers reconvened the dreary task of court-martial. Below the fort at the river's dock, Taliaferro returned to the job of moving the Indian provisions up the ramp to the agency. It rained heavily that day, drenching the flour sacks and bales of cloth standing out in the open. "Beautiful mode of doing business," the agent grumbled. "Not one cent of funds for transportation and no storehouse for property. My interpreter a little drunk, as is too often the case with him."[48]

In July,[49] the post's officers sat in another series of courts-martial. There had never before been so many pending disciplinary matters, with 17 soldiers in the brig[50] and two more missing as deserted. The officers were duly sworn, and Dr. Emerson was again appointed to defend the accused. True to frontier priorities, the court adjourned temporarily when the quartermaster was going to sell some surplus food.[51]

In the court-martial proceedings, several privates were convicted for habitual drunkenness. Some had already spent half of their time in service confined in the brig. Drunkenness rendered them worthless. The usual severe sentence—head shaving, flogging the bare back, and a drumming out of service—didn't seem to deter the privates from drinking, so the officers tried something new. They decreed that each convicted man's identity be furnished to every post so he couldn't reenlist again and ordered each to be marked indelibly on the left hip with a "D" for drunk. That way if the man tried to reenlist, the surgeon would recognize the mark during his physical exam.

The idea of tattooing a soldier with a mark of shame reflected the officers' frustration at the widespread use of alcohol and breakdown of order among the troops. Before any punishments could be imposed, however, they had to be approved by division headquarters in St. Louis. The sentenced men were sent to the brig to await word from St. Louis.

At night the Scotts may have overheard the doctor tell his wife about the poor sots whose defense he was obligated to prepare and whose sentences he would have to witness. Even later in the night, both the Emersons upstairs and the Scotts sleeping in their basement room would be able to hear the sentries attempt to quell the nighttime commotion as more soldiers returned home drunk. Soldiers were regularly observed crossing the Mississippi to reach a whiskey shop set up by Joseph Brown and Henry Menck on the opposite shore.[52] With as many as 20 to 50 soldiers confined in the guardhouse at night, little work could be done at the fort. The strength of the troops was divided between those under detention for drunkenness and those needed to arrest them and keep them in the brig.

Agent Taliaferro spent the next few days drying bales and packages soaked by the rain. Scott Campbell sobered up enough to help, and he brought with him an insolent young Métis man. The three men hauled the packages from the docks to the agency compound and stacked them in the hallway of the house, where they would be safer. As Taliaferro labored to move the cargo, he began to hear ominous rumors. One teamster he employed told him that an Indian named Hee-pee had sworn to murder him. There was no apparent reason for this (Hee-pee stated no grievance against Taliaferro), but the Indian claimed that he had had a dream that he must kill the agent.[53] The man must have been going mad. Hee-pee's third child had died a few weeks earlier, and the agent had given him a coffin for her. Still, even rumors had to be taken seriously.[54]

CHAPTER 17

Taliaferro's Last Stand

I F HARRIET DID attend to Taliaferro's housekeeping that last summer, she would have walked the quarter mile to the agency house to clean and bring him meals each day. The weather had become so hot that the agent declined to ride out to the lakes.[1] The master had no horse that summer, and even his black dog was missing. When the mail carrier arrived, he said he thought he had seen the master's dog in the possession of a lumberman at the St. Croix camp.[2]

The Mississippi was low, and the waiting Dakota were uneasy with the heat and the prolonged delay of this year's annuities. Despite occasional rains, the heat was taking its toll on the very young and the old. The sawmill had difficulty providing a sufficient amount of plank for the coffins that were requested. "More deaths than births among the Indians this year," the agent recorded. "Things bad as they are."[3] The scorching heat had turned the prairie thatch to straw so the prairie couldn't be used as pasture. The Indians brought their horses across the river to feed on the corn they had planted—the corn crop that was intended to tide the Dakota themselves over the winter.

The heat took its toll on people's tempers as well. Mrs. Campbell and her husband, the interpreter, fought, and they lately engaged in outright brawls. The interpreter increasingly turned to alcohol, drinking during the day as well as night. Much of the couple's problems stemmed from the financial setback they had suffered when the company succeeded in eliminating their promised land allotment from the treaty. (Sibley had requested that Taliaferro's promise to Campbell be scratched from the treaty before congressional ratification.) But it was Mrs. Campbell who had the upper hand in these noisy arguments, and she beat her drunken husband quite severely. The agent remarked that wives were "not justified in knocking out their husband's brains to enforce their commands."[4]

Taliaferro wrote, "Massey lost his child and buried it in my garden's graveyard."[5] The Masseys lived at the Coldwater Spring and often helped the Agent. This small private funeral was attended by those who felt closest to the Masseys, including Dred, Harriet, Mrs. Mortimer, and the Emersons—all of whom Massey had worked with in the post hospital. "The bones of my friends are in my private cemetery. Seven bodies. Enclosed neatly in my garden," wrote Taliaferro.[6] Eliza's infant son, Jarvis, was also buried there near a cedar tree planted in the center.

August was the time that the blackbirds from all over the central continental plain sought out the Indians' cornfields. This year, however, the Sioux women did not bother to set up the traditional scaffolds. "Corn season and black birds to guard against,"[7] the agent noted in his diary. Not only had the horses eaten into the corn harvest but the crows were taking the remainder. "Your corn is being destroyed by the black birds and you sit still," he exhorted a group of Sioux the following day.[8] "Wild rice you fear to gather with your women." At the rice marshes the Sioux were likely to encounter the Ojibwa again. The Sioux explained, "[We are in] a poor way to defend ourselves against the Chippewa in case we are attacked."[9]

The sustained heat wave seemed to make people do crazy things. Little Crow's band killed one of their largest work cattle for food. "They now have but six left," the agent noted. "The wild condition of the northwestern Indians tends to render them reckless as to future prospects of realizing benefits from ownership of property."[10] A little later, Gideon Pond sent a note that the Indians at the lakes had also butchered one of the work oxen. "'No heed of tomorrow' is the Indians' motto," the master remarked sadly.[11] The young Métis man named Benjamin, who had helped move the Indian stores to the agency, took a horse and led him straight through the doorway and into the agency house. Then he mounted the horse in the narrow hallway and tried to ride amid the Indian goods stored there. This oddity was the last straw for the master. He ordered the interpreter to discharge him.[12]

On August 15, the *Ariel* was in sight. "Another disappointment after thirteen arrivals would be the devil among the Indians." There were goods, but no invoices with the goods. "Aug. 17, 100 degrees in shade. Some of the annuity goods were stolen for want of storage room in the Agency house."[13]

The agent had reached the conclusion that more distance was necessary between the Sioux and the settlers. The number of attacks by the Sioux on settlers' cattle was ratcheting up the conflict between the two peoples. Although he had tried to compensate the settlers from the Sioux annuities, the annuities themselves were so slow in coming that every barrel was needed for the Indians' survival. The Métis involvement with the tribe's decision making was its own problem, since, he concluded, the Métis had urged the Sioux to attack the Ojibwa.[14]

On August 19, Taliaferro posted a public notice of land reservation that included the Coldwater Spring settlement. No action that he could have taken would have enraged the settlers more. At the time, he was more concerned with the deficits of his own office, however. He reflected: "It is hell on the agent here. The neglect of the Indian office. One year, this agency has been without funds of any description."[15]

The chiefs of all the Sioux villages called on the agent and repeated their request to be given the goods now stored in the agency house. Since Taliaferro was uncertain how much more would arrive, he attempted to hold off distribution until he knew that he could divide the shares equitably. Eventually, he yielded to the chiefs and asked his cousin, Capt. Hooe, whom he could depend on, and his nemesis, Sibley, whom he distrusted most, to witness the food distribution.[16]

He also still needed to make some arrangements for his daughter's future. Now that his plans for an Indian school had been rejected, he wrote a touching letter to his longtime friend Samuel Pond.

> My dear Sir
>
> If you can prevail upon Mary (and she seems so willing) to remain with you, and Mrs. Pond—it would afford me consolations, and pleasure. I should be willing to pay you and her for your trouble including her board, clothing, and tuition. In time she may from habit and instruction in household matters be able to assist Mrs. P. The indolent habits and aversion to light labours will have to be gotten over with these Half breeds by flattering their vanity—small rewards, etc.
>
> We will after she consents to stay—talk over together our further understanding and arrangements for the future. Mary's mother, grandmother, and others are about to leave for the Lake to get wild rice, and they now seem willing to let her stay with you.
>
> Yr friend & obt sert, Law Taliaferro.[17]

By September, Taliaferro's friend Mr. Baker, who had taken over the sutler position, was fading rapidly. He planned a final trip to St. Louis to make arrangements for his family, leaving the sutler enterprise in the hands of young Horatio N. Dillon.[18] Even Dillon received a share of the personal antagonism directed at Taliaferro. His presence caused jealous speculation that Taliaferro intended to move into the private sector and perhaps even become a competitor for land claims.[19] One day, a drunken clerk at Dillon's shanty disclosed how deeply the officers resented him. Some had urged their men not to pay up their accounts in the hope that it would adversely affect the sutler business.[20]

Direct threat against Taliaferro was also rumored. The word around the fort was that "Menck will grab him at the Prairies" when he left for the winter.[21] The agent was mildly amused at the threat, and wrote it off as idle talk. Menck, the whiskey seller, was, in Taliaferro's estimation, a fool. He had been scared out of his house by some Sioux seeking whiskey, and in the incident Menck had been made a laughingstock.[22] The Indians had found a small opening in the roof of his house and crawled in from the top. Having scared him off, they helped themselves to a couple of gallons of whiskey. Menck had come to Taliaferro to collect for the loss of his whiskey, as the settlers routinely did when the Indians killed one of their cows. Taliaferro would not help the man. Later, a small party of Sioux destroyed the whiskey shop owned by Menck and his partner, Joseph Brown.[23] One Indian involved was rumored to have claimed that the agent sent him to destroy the shop.[24] The agent denied this, but he was smugly pleased at the way the incident had turned out. No wonder the coward Menck was making threatening noises. The agent couldn't see that the whiskey seller posed any threat to him, not realizing that even a coward could turn if he was sufficiently embarrassed.

Taliaferro closed out his accounts, planning to leave St. Peter's Agency that Saturday. All of the men who served the agency in various roles came round for their pay and to say goodbye, including the Pond brothers, Philander Prescott, the blacksmith, Mr. Massee, Scott Campbell, and even Dr. Emerson. As a sentimental gesture, the agent gave each of the men presents.[25]

When Dr. Emerson and Major Plympton visited him to say goodbye, they let slip information about some of Sibley's planned land dealings. The agent finally realized that Sibley had moved beyond furs and that he too was buying up the land claims awarded to Métis Sioux. The agent recorded: "Sibley is feeling his way to fortune."[26]

The word around the fort was that a former soldier named Hays was missing. It was known that Hays had money socked away[27] and some suspected that another ex-soldier, named Phelan, knew something about his disappearance. The two men lived together in a house that Jim Thompson, the freedman, had built for them. That day, a party of Indians arrived to announce they had discovered Hays's body near Carver's cave. Dr. Emerson rode out to the site with a few men to examine the body and retrieve it for burial. The doctor concluded from the injuries that Hays had been murdered. The suspect, Phelan, was brought to Sibley's trading house for questioning. In his new role as justice of the peace, Sibley formally placed him under arrest and had him confined to the guardhouse until the next steamboat could take him downstream for trial.[28]

Monsieur Nicollet, who had been surveying the upper reaches of the river that summer with his engineering apprentice, John C. Fremont, and the freedman, James Thompson, left on schedule. But still the agent stayed on, hoping to catch up with Nicollet downriver.

EARLY OCTOBER BROUGHT the smoky weather of Indian summer. That month, baby Eliza turned one year old. Harriet probably continued to walk the quarter mile to the agency house, where her former master grew increasingly isolated and embittered.

On a cloudy Saturday, October 5, the agent was attacked from a quarter he didn't anticipate. That morning, he was ambushed—not on the river, as rumored, but in his own bedroom. In the early morning hours, with no one else in the house, Taliaferro was taken by surprise. His attacker was Henry Menck, the man who ran the destroyed whiskey shack where the soldiers drank.[29] Menck had been threatening with bravado to "grab him at the prairies" when Taliaferro traveled south. Now, without warning, Menck confronted him with a gun in his own bedroom as he lay sleeping in his nightclothes. Menck probably could not have gotten into the house if the agent's dog or any servants had been present.

Menck declared that he held him personally responsible for the Indians' destruction of his whiskey shack and wanted to arrest him. He claimed that he operated under the auspices of a lawsuit. He kept Taliaferro hostage at gunpoint for nine hours, brandishing his weapon as if he would kill him. What angered the gunman was the agent's apparent pleasure over what the Indians had done. He blamed Taliaferro for urging them on. Hadn't Taliaferro laughed when he'd heard about the melee? Menck also mentioned James Clewett, of the Coldwater settlers, who was aggrieved about the proposed eviction.

Taliaferro later recorded that he was surprised in his morning dress, thrown on the floor, a pistol put to his ear, and kept in this position with Menck's knee on his stomach, demanding $280 cash as recompense for the destruction of his shop.[30] Taliaferro did not have that kind of cash on hand. Menck certainly intended to torment Taliaferro and may have eventually intended to kill him. After nine hours of this standoff, an innocent intervention apparently interrupted the hostage situation. Taliaferro's two accounts are somewhat confusing as to what occurred after his nine hours of being held by Menck. A servant apparently happened upon the situation in progress and ran back to the fort for help. It may very well have been Harriet, making a routine afternoon trip to bring Taliaferro his supper, as he said he was in his sick bed, and stumbling upon the hostage situation taking place upstairs. In the circumstances, Harriet, more than anyone else at St. Peter's at the time, would have been likely to bring him supper. She would be considered as "one of his servants."[31] By 1839, the practice of bringing black slaves to Fort Snelling had almost completely fallen away such that Harriet and Dred were two of the last former slaves still there.[32]

Taliaferro indicates in one account that he sent a message to the fort.[33] Who but a servant would have been available in his house to take such a message? The messenger brought back Dr. Emerson. This also suggests that it was either Harriet or Dred who discovered the situation. Emerson heeded the call. When the doctor arrived, he tried to reason with Menck and to get him to put down his gun. He offered him what he considered his most valuable asset—his claim to 640 acres of Iowa land—as security for the agent's release.[34] Menck refused, insisting on cash.

Somehow the kidnapping came to an end without bloodshed. The officers sent Menck away for failing to have a passport for Indian country. A shaken Taliaferro described his captor as "a brute and an assassin" in every respect. It seems that Harriet may just have saved the life of the man who had freed her. Any debt of gratitude for her release from bondage by him would have been more than repaid.

All summer long Taliaferro had been making his plans to leave St. Peter's. Now he needed no further inducement. For the remaining two nights until he left, he could have sought refuge by sleeping at the hospital. But Taliaferro was as vain as he was self-righteous and would have regarded such a gesture as a capitulation to thugs. He would not want to give the officers the satisfaction of thinking that he was afraid. The brave, unflappable master whom Harriet had served was now a shaken man.[35] He had prided himself on the fact that, until this year, no hungry Indian had ever bothered his livestock. Warring tribes had come to his house, at his bidding, to make peace. But one whiskey-selling rogue had held him hostage at gunpoint for hours in his own bedroom and shaken his sense of security to its core.

Two days after his ordeal, Taliaferro made his final entry in the remarkable daily journals that he kept for almost two decades. It simply said, "Steamer *Des Moines* saves me a canoe trip down,"[36] and he took his final leave of St. Peter's.

Harriet never saw Taliaferro again. Departures of people close to her were a fact of her life. Many people simply fell away. Most of the other servants who made up her immediate social community—Eliza and Jack, the marksmen's slave—had left or had been stripped away from her from time to time, just as her own family had been. She had come of age as Lawrence Taliaferro's servant, listening to his lectures and noting his agenda: "Hard work will make you free." His presence was the only remaining tie to her birthplace of Virginia and her mother. He had also married her to a husband and relinquished his claim to her. Still, he left his influence on her and the others at St. Peter's.[37] Everyone knew him to be incorruptible.[38]

The whiskey seller Menck never followed up by suing Taliaferro.[39] With the agent out of the territory, there was no one against whom to levy a claim. But Alexis Bailley, who had crossed the agent by importing whiskey five years earlier, still nursed his grudge and pursued it to legal completion. Ten years after the event, the stubborn Bailley succeeded in getting a default judgment entered against Talia-ferro. The court in Prairie du Chien ruled against the former agent for failing to appear, but by the time Alexis Bailley received his default judgment, Taliaferro had been gone from the territory for five years.[40]

CHAPTER 18

Leaving Minnesota and Its New Tribunals

FTER TALIAFERRO LEFT St. Peter's Agency, the full void of his absence was felt. The center did not hold. People who had been part of the agency community for years began to simply drift away. The battles between the Mdewakanton Sioux and the Ojibwa had destroyed the stability of the settled farming communities at the lakes. The Sioux now feared a counterattack from the Ojibwa if they remained there. They gathered their corn, taking what they could carry and leaving what they couldn't in storage with the Pond brothers. The agricultural communities, so patiently built over several years with Taliaferro's encouragement, simply dissolved in the aftermath of the Indian battles. With no settled group of Indians at the lakes, it was pointless for the Pond brothers to stay there. Nonetheless, they had promised to care for the Indians' farm animals over the winter, and the Ponds always kept their promises. Taliaferro's now 11-year-old daughter also remained with them.[1]

By the time Agent Taliaferro left, the Methodist mission effort had all but collapsed as well. After the Reverend Brunson selected a site, with the idea that Jim Thompson, the freedman, would serve as the mission's permanent translator, he installed another minister to head the mission and left. None of the missionaries he brought in stayed long, however. At some point, the freedman and his Dakota wife moved on too. Jim was free, after all, which meant that he could come and go as he pleased. He did not need to rely on the mission pay; he could provide for his family in many other ways. When he left, the Reverend Brunson accused him of laziness and ingratitude, throwing in the gratuitous charge of whiskey selling as well, although there was no evidence of this. Ultimately, Brunson blamed the mission's failure on the freedman's departure.[2]

Things continued to go poorly for Taliaferro's brother-in-law, H. N. Dillon. It's unlikely that the young man lasted the winter. At the end of summer, his terminally ill partner died in St. Louis. Without either Taliaferro or Mr. Baker to back him, and with his authority undermined by both the officers' enmity and the insubordination of his employees, Dillon was an easy target. Sibley quickly moved in to dispossess him of the sutlership.[3] The business owed more than $21,000.[4] Sibley wrote to a St. Louis partner, "I have the impression that neither Taliaferro nor Dillon are popular at the garrison, so I judge that neither will get the appointment of sutler." Sibley had the power to crush Dillon by simply seeing that he received no further credit for business debts. Sibley took legal possession of the remaining goods in the sutler's store, and by the following spring he had installed his friend Franklin Steele as the new sutler at the post. Steele was the same man who had slickly outmaneuvered the commandant to stake claim to the sawmill property.

Sibley's power expanded as magistrate. The seat of justice for the civilian community had moved from the agency house to Sibley's house at Mendota where Sibley was an official magistrate, but Sibley grew tired of the official tasks and appointed his employee, Joseph Brown, co-owner of the destroyed whiskey shack, to serve as magistrate instead. In a turnabout of fate, the scoundrel whiskey seller, Indian woman two-timer, repeatedly sanctioned by the former commandant and by Agent Taliaferro, had become the magistrate. In the years to follow, Joseph Brown would even be appointed Indian Agent and take a delegation to Washington. On the frontier, one decade's scoundrels became the next decade's public officials.

With the onset of winter,[5] the quartermaster distributed the stoves among the officers' households. This winter Lt. McPhail served as quartermaster. The small, scrawny man who had served valiantly on express duty and in reconnoitering the battleground, had never before been quartermaster. Cast-iron stoves had only recently become available to the army, and they were an immense improvement for surviving Minnesota winters. Unlike a fireplace, a free-standing stove, set away from the wall, could radiate heat around the entire room. In the annual distribution, the doctor requested two stoves, one for his own quarters and an additional one for Dred, Harriet, and the baby. The rookie quartermaster refused, saying there weren't enough stoves. The doctor took umbrage and insinuated that the young lieutenant was lying.[6] McPhail's best defense was an offense, so he struck the first blow; he hit the doctor between the eyes, breaking his glasses and bruising his nose. Although Emerson was a head taller than McPhail, he didn't strike back immediately. Instead, he walked determinedly to his quarters, returning shortly with a brace of dueling pistols. He brandished the pistols at the quartermaster, which was the gentleman's method of escalating a dispute. At the sight of the pistols, the small quartermaster began to run across the wide parade ground, in full view of all the residences, with the doctor following and cursing at him.

When another young lieutenant appeared to take McPhail's side,[7] the dispute became a free-for-all. The commander came onto the scene, armed with a cane. Major Plympton was the only man at the fort who outranked the assistant surgeon, and so he arrested him. The episode created a great commotion in the garrison for several days, but Dr. Emerson was never officially reprimanded, according to the records. The doctor may, in fact, have prevailed. His account with the sutler that year indicates that he paid for two stove pots, presumably one for each stove.[8]

Harriet and her husband must have been grateful for the doctor's gesture. He had risked his personal honor to obtain a stove to get them comfortably through the winter. Dred would have known that this wasn't the first time his master had been arrested by a post commander.[9] Emerson stood up to authority when he believed he was justified. The fact that the doctor had stood up for the Scotts suggests that he protected and provided for them.

With a stove in one's sleeping quarters, a person would not have to lie near the fireplace and rise continually during the night to bank the blaze just to keep warm. A stove also meant independent quarters at the garrison, where soldiers huddled together for warmth. Enlisted men slept without stoves, two to the bed, four to the bunk, three bunks to the barracks rooms in the Minnesota winters. The fact that stoves were generally distributed only to officers and enlisted men who had wives suggests that Dr. Emerson placed the Scott couple on a par with these free families. Most settlers and Métis people in the community surrounding the fort couldn't afford stoves. With a stove, the Scotts could establish a more comfortable household of their own, in their own space, in the hospital basement. Baby Eliza, most susceptible to the winter cold, could be kept in the rooms of her parents, and none of them would freeze. There were plenty of rooms at the large fort, but having a stove meant the family could enjoy its own privacy in relative warmth.

The episode echoed another incident that would occur later in Florida after the Scotts had ceased serving Dr. Emerson. This incident established him as a man who was a better master to his slaves than most.[10] The doctor, then served by a different slave man, placed his servant in the hospital when he fell ill with fever. The bed that his slave took had been occupied by a soldier. That post's quartermaster lodged a formal complaint against Emerson for allowing a slave to recover in a bed intended for soldiers.[11] As with the stove incident, the good doctor defended his actions and eventually won.[12]

THE COMMANDER PURSUED his agenda to remove the settlers at the Coldwater Spring from their cabins. Taliaferro had once provided a common reference point and sympathetic ear for the people of Coldwater Spring. Although he had become alienated from both sides, his departure hardened the lines between the two groups. Few families at the Coldwater Spring had made provisions to leave,[13] still hoping to remain where they'd built, lived, and arranged their lives for almost two decades. It would take more than a written order to get them out.

The secretary of war sent orders to the U.S. Marshal in Prairie du Chien to remove them—by force if necessary. But the marshal couldn't arrive during the frozen winter months.[14] The settlers' meetings continued at the house of old man Perry. James Clewett was selected as chair and Henry Menck, the whiskey seller who had held Taliaferro hostage, was secretary. More written petitions were sent to the government attesting to the "many evils endured by the citizens from the oppressive conduct of the military officers stationed on this frontier and the many disadvantages" they had experienced as settlers.[15]

Other petitions sent to Washington protested the attempts of "quarter-blood" Metis persons to share in the treaty dispositions. Scott Campbell, Philander

Prescott, and several "half-blood" children including Taliaferro's daughter Mary, signed to a petition arguing that quarter-bloods had signed their interests over to Samuel C. Stambaugh and Alexis Baily and that the half-bloods were being "defrauded out of our just rights by bringing in improper persons and throwing the country open to the inroads of the whites."[16] (Almost all of the signatories were men or children of men connected to Agent Taliaferro, Campbell, Lamont, Ortley, Wells, Cratte, his own daughter, but he was no longer there to advise them.) The irony of the letter was its attempt to pit one group of Métis against another by virtue of proportion of blood heritage.

The winter drew Dr. Emerson into a series of formal trials: first court-martials, in which he had to defend the accused; then a murder trial, in which he had to identify the body and the cause of death; and finally a civil suit before the new local magistrate as an interested party in a land claim.[17] From her time with Master Taliaferro, Harriet had probably absorbed at least some of the former agent's advice on self-sufficiency, along with what he considered to be justice and how he carried out those judgments. She had been present as a series of disputes and crises prompted the making of frontier law and order. Initially, her master's agenda had been to keep the peace between warring tribes and to solve grudge vendettas, along with deciding the custody of women, children, and horses. Each time a different kind of dispute threatened the community's social fabric, it called for a different order of resolution and the invention of an appropriate response, authority, fact-finding mission, or trial. All was done within the constraints of what was possible in the small community without a state. When faced with the crisis between the Indian nations, her master had attempted, with considerable success, to direct the warriors away from the practice of avenging honor with blood. This had been a significant accomplishment, since the taking of scalps continued to be the mark of manhood among the Sioux: taking a scalp permitted warriors to engage in the honor of the Dog Dance as well as to be eligible to take a wife.[18]

When the Ojibwa Che-weyes-ca-gum killed a Métis Ojibwa man in a dispute over a woman, the community responded by sending him to Prairie du Chien where he would be given the due process of the formalities of a trial. Now the majority of disputes that threatened the civil order and stability of the community were over land. But they were occurring between the settlement people themselves with resort to a justice of the peace.

This year, Harriet observed how a different master assumed different roles in a series of courtroom dramas. From scraps of information, the former slave-servants could form an understanding of the agendas at play in the community. From their position of subservience, such information was as necessary to understanding the forces that affected them as it was self-preserving. In this new series of disputes, Dr. Emerson acted as defense counsel, expert witness, and finally litigant of his own self-interest. For each trial, Harriet probably pressed the doctor's military uniform, with its double rows of brass buttons.

In late November, there was another series of courts-martial.[19] Again, all were found guilty and sentenced to the usual sentence of 50 lashes on the bare back with a cowhide whip well laid on. They were to forfeit all pay and allowances and be drummed out of the service.[20] Additionally, a letter "D," one inch in diameter, was to be tattooed on the right hip of each. With so many drunk and deserting, the officers of the courts-martial at Fort Snelling attempted to increase the penalty. Desperate times required desperate measures.

The army's commanding general eventually disapproved the punishment of being marked with a tattoo as not authorized by law. The general wrote that it was "repugnant to the spirit of our free institutions."[21] The general directed that such a sentence was not to be imposed in the future because it was "discreditable to the Republic, and to the age in which we live, [almost as discreditable] as if the soldiers were sentenced to be mutilated....If a soldier is of any value to the service, he cannot but know that his officers can in no case inflict degrading punishment not expressly prescribed by law, without themselves committing a dangerous violation of that law which we are all sworn to support."[22]

By December, there was apparently a pending pregnancy in the Emerson household. A letter that Henry Sibley wrote to the New York Fur Company headquarters in December 1839 bears evidence of a birth of a child to the Emersons.[23] The birth was never recorded in the family histories, so it is uncertain when it occurred or how or if it affected the Scotts.[24] Sibley wrote New York headquarters that Dr. Emerson wanted "a child's cup to be made of the best material."[25] The cup to be made of silver was intended for Emerson's "little one." The request was relayed to Irene's brother, Sanford, who offered to pay for it. Sanford had given the Emersons a silver service for their wedding previously. The silver child's cup added symbolically to the family silver. From the letter's phrasing, it seems likely that a child had already been born to the Emersons.

Yet, there is no further reference to a child in the Emerson family these years. The child may have died soon afterward, causing grief to overshadow the baby's birth[26] and preventing the Emersons from mentioning it publicly.[27] But without more specifics the event cannot be placed into a chronology or even a seasonal context. Child mortality was particularly high on the frontier.[28] Many babies seemed to succumb in the coldest months.[29] As a doctor charged with saving life, Emerson would have taken such an event hard; to the mother, it would have been crushing.

THE SETTLERS' ANGER at the prospect that they would be displaced played itself out in every civil engagement between the fort and the settlers. Even Dr. Emerson replaced his hospital steward, George Massey, who came from the Coldwater community, with a soldier from within the fort.[30]

As Dr. Emerson planned for the future, he hoped to move up in the army's service. He wrote to his superiors again, raising the question of his advancement. He requested permission to sit for a board examination for promotion to surgeon.[31]

Across the river at Mendota that winter, Sibley became involved with a young Dakota woman from Black Dog's band. She was known as "Red Blanket Woman," a name that may have signified her association to Sibley. Dakota names changed, reflecting some new characteristic distinguishing the individual. Most Dakota women wore blue blankets, provided by the annuities or bought from the traders. That this woman wore a red blanket set her apart. Sibley stocked blankets, some certainly different from the government-issued ones. He probably provided the red blanket, which gave the woman status in the Indian community as his wife. Within the year, she bore him a child.[32]

There were still 12 privates in confinement in February. The officers court-martialed four privates who had deserted from the wood gathering detail.[33] March 1840 was a particularly bad month for drunkenness, resulting in an additional 26 in confinement. Another seven men were listed as deserted but not yet found. Even a noncommissioned officer, an ordinance sergeant, disappeared one evening and was supposed to have drowned falling through the ice.[34]

In March 1840, Philander Prescott sued a man named Foote for jumping his claim.[35] Dr. Emerson and other officers had an interest in the case because they had staked Prescott to establish the claim. The trial took place at Mendota, where the former whiskey-seller Joseph Brown now served as magistrate. Foote moved in and took possession of Prescott's claim, while Prescott was absent on an extended errand. If Prescott lost the claim, the doctor and his partners would lose as well.

The jury was drawn from people living at the Coldwater Spring, people who were also about to lose their homes due to the federal eviction order. The jury heard the case, but could not agree on a decision. The case was tried a second time, again resulting in a hung jury. Although Prescott had solid evidence to prove his claim, the settlers had become so hostile to the officers who they knew were Prescott's backers that they refused to vindicate Prescott. A victory for Prescott was a victory for the men who planned to benefit by evicting them from their land. Prescott reported,

> I found that every influence possible was working against me. [Joseph Brown] would like to see my claim taken from me because the officers...owned near the whole. Brown felt sore about the whisky shop being broken up, for it was a source of quite a little income to him, and he would like to see the officers injured in return...He done all he could to get a jury that would decide against me, but my proof was too strong, and the work showed too much for any just jury to decide against me. But there were enough always to make a split jury and keep me in expense, which [was] over $200.[36]

Stymied by two hung juries, Prescott offered the claim jumper a compromise: he offered up half the claim if Foote would yield the other half. The two men settled by splitting the claim. Prescott reported, "This the officers did not like, but it was the best I could do, and so it stood."[37] Within three days of the resolution, the post officers signed another letter urging the settlers' removal, writing that the squatters were, first, foreigners and, second, whiskey sellers—no doubt referring to the magistrate, Joseph Brown.[38]

Having lost half his investment in Prescott's stake at the St. Croix river, the doctor wrote his Iowa friends again, urging them to journey to Dubuque for the upcoming land sale.[39] Emerson's letters to LeClaire were almost predictable indicators of his other financial circumstances. Each time his life took another turn, he wrote his friend in Iowa to secure his interest.[40] The doctor still hoped to be sent to New York to take the exam for promotion.

It was only a matter of time until the territory's U.S. marshal came from Prairie du Chien to act on the order to evict the settlers, but in the dead of winter nothing moved. The deputy marshal could only journey upriver to carry out the orders after the Mississippi ice broke. In the meantime, the season's first steamboat brought Dr. Emerson orders to leave Minnesota and to report to Florida for the Seminole War.[41] He had a month to put his affairs together. Most of the garrison—more than 200 men—were shipped out for Florida that month. The garrison dropped from 342 to 108 men.[42]

As the Emersons prepared to leave, the U.S. marshal closed in on the settlers. On May 1, 1840, the deputy marshal arrived and immediately gave notice. No one moved. The marshal had been instructed to seek any necessary military help from the garrison. On May 6, the deputy led a group of soldiers to the settlement at the Coldwater Spring to drive off the residents by forcibly removing their belongings, removing the roofs, and burning the cabins down.[43]

The soldiers attacked house after house, tearing off the roofs and setting the cabins ablaze to prevent the settlers from attempting to return. Every cabin—the homes of almost 100 people—was in flames in a scorched earth policy.[44] The settlers were forced to evacuate after witnessing the destruction of the homes they had built and called home for more than a decade. Some relocated themselves as far downriver as they could walk, driving their cattle with them.

Dred and Harriet must have witnessed the fires, the community's destruction, and the exodus. The smoke from the fires was visible from the wall of the fort. If the Scotts had had any hope of staying on in free territory, it would be among the people in the Coldwater community. There, with the Fahlstroms or some other family, they might have found shelter for the winter, and perhaps work. Once Dr. Emerson and most of the officers transferred out from the fort, there would have been no way for the Scotts to stay on in free territory. Now the community among whom they might have found a home was in crisis. The Coldwater refugees now scrambled to construct shelters for themselves during the short summer months before winter set in.

By May 20, Dr. Emerson had settled up his accounts and collected the money for services he had rendered to the fur company men at New Hope. In this cash-poor society, his accounts were settled by Sibley, as owner of the trading post, advancing him cash for his services against the debts of all the fur trade people.[45] Dr. Emerson was also given a $5 credit for a "string of bells" (presumably sleigh bells)[46] that he wouldn't need in Florida. On May 29, 1840, Dr. Emerson ended his tour of duty at Fort Snelling.[47] The Seminole War withdrew most of the military from the country's northern forts. The only soldiers permitted to remain at Fort Snelling were the commandant, two junior officers, and fewer than 100 men.[48]

The Scotts accompanied the Emersons when they left because there was virtually no other option open to them. Saying goodbye to free territory was probably not as difficult for Harriet as one might expect. Almost everyone she knew, except the Plymptons, had already left or was leaving.[49] There was simply no place to stay.

Without the doctor's help, the servant family could not expect even the comfort of a stove during the coming Minnesota winter.

The Falstroms were moving off to join another missionary settlement. Jim Thompson, the freedman, had work building new houses for the Coldwater refugees, south of the reservation. He had the skills to feed his family by hunting and fishing, if needed. In times of real desperation, he could fall back on the help of his wife's Dakota kinship. But only someone with the survival skills of Jim Thompson could stay on in the territory. For independence one needed the material goods of survival. Neither Dred nor Harriet had such materials or the skills necessary for survival in the harsh climate.

The Pond brothers and their families left the lakes and moved temporarily into Baker's old house, which had been vacated by the unlucky Dillon.[50] (The stone house, perhaps the only one left standing, was not torched because it was a licensed Indian trading house, enjoying the same status to remain on the reservation as Sibley's buildings at Mendota.) In spring 1840, the fires were still smoldering over the ashes of the Coldwater settlement, blowing a bitter soot into the air. Two steamboats, the *Tennessee* and the *Omega,* simultaneously arrived at the dock to pick up the soldiers and carry them south.[51] Harriet had spent five winters in Minnesota, and Dred had been there for three. Their daughter, born aboard a steamboat, was now two years old and walking with unsteady steps when they again took a steamboat south to St. Louis.

At the same time, traveling north aboard the steamboat *Malta,* were a fashionable party of St. Louis residents enjoying a pleasure cruise up the Mississippi. The tourists crossing their path included the influential Chouteau family, proprietors of the American Fur Company and Mrs. Emerson's brother and sister, John F.A. Sanford and Mary Bainbridge.[52] Fate would later bring the Scotts within their circle of influence.

CHAPTER 19

While the Doctor Was Away: St. Louis, 1840–1843

AND SO, HARRIET and her family returned to a slave state with the Emersons. No one needed to kidnap them or force them aboard the ship. All of the civilian housing in the immediate vicinity had been burned to the ground. There was nowhere else for them to go. The only settlements on the upper Mississippi were forts, like Fort Snelling, where Dred, at least, would have been regarded as the servant of another military officer. Chicago was little more than a settlement, and the other tiny river towns were hardly places for an African American family without money or farming experience.[1] Reassigned to the Seminole War,[2] Dr. Emerson traveled south along the river highway with the redeployment of almost the entire military contingent of the upper Mississippi Valley. He left the Scotts in St. Louis with his wife. By the end of June, he'd reached the fort at Tampa Bay.[3] It is unlikely that either of the Scotts went to Florida during the three years the doctor served there. At first, Emerson listed Etheldred on his Florida pay slips, but he later named a different slave man. Dred's name did not appear on the doctor's pay slip again.[4] Most likely, Emerson listed him in order to claim his allowance until he lined up another servant. After all, there were plenty of slaves available in Florida.[5]

Instead, the Scotts probably remained in the St. Louis area for the next four years, where the events of their day-to-day lives drop into obscurity. There was no conscientious diarist in Harriet's new household, so it's not clear how long the Scotts remained with Mistress Irene at her father's farm. Yet their experiences were bounded initially by Mistress Irene's direction and the Sanford farm—and later by the constraints that the regional community imposed upon all bound servants.

The St. Louis the Scotts entered in 1840 had changed little from the river town they had visited two summers earlier. Rows of moored steamboats and the boatyards lining the shore were the first thing one saw when approaching the town by water. Behind the boatyards, low, wooden warehouses laden with goods stretched the shore's length. Higher on the hill, one could see the cupola of the courthouse, amid church spires and trees in full leaf. The season was much more advanced at this latitude than it had been at St. Peter's.

Standing on the levee and observing the crowds of people flocking to St. Louis by every boat, it seemed that the "world and his family" were coming to town.[6] Crowds of people thronged the streets near the docks. Every boat brought 100 or 200 new people and more cargo that would be piled high along the wharf. There were black stevedores hoisting the crates and barrels, black servants selling drink and foodstuffs to the arriving travelers, and black draymen waiting with horses and wagons to deliver arriving passengers to their destinations. The city's hotels and boardinghouses were so overcrowded that many hotels had beds in the hallways.

Country merchants were in town, visiting the low warehouses along the docks to buy their stores of goods for the season,[7] but most new arrivals came from more distant parts of the Union. Some came seeking employment and some hunting after debtors. Compared to the rest of the country, St. Louis was flourishing. The pressure of poor financial times in other quarters induced many to travel west in hopes of bettering their condition.[8]

The town hugged the shoreline. St. Louis was still a town of primarily low brick buildings and shambling wood-frame houses, stretching along the shore's lower reaches. There were few buildings more than four streets back from the river, and none over two stories high. The city's business district extended only six or seven blocks along Main Street, parallel to the river and just behind the warehouses.[9] Four blocks back from the river, on a small rise, stood the courthouse, which was the city's primary landmark. During the next two decades, whether crowned with a cupola or, later, a rotunda dome—whether built of brick or limestone—the courthouse would be continually under construction to accommodate its increasing business and to project the imperial vision of a series of architects. All buildings in town were described in relation to the courthouse. Along the same rise, across the street from the courthouse, the city's first grand hotel, the Planters' House, was under construction as well.[10] When completed, the lavish hotel provided a clublike atmosphere for private elites, banquets, and formal dress balls, complementing the more populist gatherings that occurred across the street at the courthouse. Behind the courthouse stood the jail.

The sheer brutality of the city's race relations had given St. Louis a reputation for mobs and lawless violence. Incidents such as McIntosh being burned alive and the repeated armed assaults on Lovejoy's printing press had been reported widely. To disabuse Easterners of this reputation for lawlessness, newspaper articles tried to promote the idea that the city had become more civilized. "We have noticed …the improvement of the moral feeling, and hence the diminution of riots and similar scenes of violence and outrage,"[11] one newspaper reported optimistically. Although the Reverend Lovejoy was driven out of St. Louis by violence, St. Louisians assumed no responsibility for his eventual murder at the hands of a mob, since it occurred across the river in Alton, Illinois. Besides, most city residents thought the man was a provocateur and got what he deserved for talking abolition.[12] Nonetheless, the next violent public spectacle would occur the following year, when four

St. Louis Birdseye, 1859, shows the city wharf district rebuilt after the 1849 fire. *Library of Congress.*

black boatmen were publicly hanged after being convicted of robbery, murder, and arson.[13]

St. Louis was a major national slave market as well. At the east door of the courthouse, facing the river, slaves had been sold routinely for decades. Standing on the steps, facing the surrounding crowd and the river beyond, black people were auctioned for labor. Human beings, ranging from seven-year-olds to old men and women, were displayed for sale and sold to the highest bidder. Children younger than seven were usually sold packaged with their mothers to avoid the burden of motherless slave children.[14]

The greatest human indignities were visible on the courthouse steps. Prospective customers poked and prodded the persons to be sold. Potential buyers thrust their fingers into the mouths of confined individuals and examined their teeth as if they were horses. Adult men and women could be ordered to strip naked for inspection.[15] There were few bids for slaves who were too old to work. Owners blackened the elderly slaves' heads with dye or plucked out their grey hairs to conceal age.[16] Slaves offered for sale were coached to appear lively and happy while on view. This puppet show of frenetic animation masked the true tragedy of slave lives and obscured the fact that their family ties were being severed without their consent and against their will. Slaves had no ability to resist or direct the sales. Owners expected them to participate in their own sales by personally describing— bragging if they would—their initiative, skills, and abilities.[17] Afterward, collections of purchased people were coffled together for transport to their destinations. Those who stumbled or could not walk were simply dragged along mercilessly with the rest.[18]

St. Louis Levee with Steamboat. *Library of Congress.*

St. Louis's slave market cornered the traffic in human beings brought to the city from the east, north, and south. Few of the city's enslaved were born in Missouri. The majority had been brought west by their migrating masters. Sometimes traveling by steamboat down the Ohio River from Virginia, Maryland, and Kentucky, sometimes around Florida by steamer to Mobile and up the great river from New Orleans, surplus slaves were brought to St. Louis for sale and then shipped to destinations beyond.

Moreover, with currency in short supply, transporting slaves was one way to transfer wealth west. On reaching St. Louis, many cash-poor masters either sold or hired their slaves out to work for cash wages so that ultimately the masters could move their families from lodgings in cramped and crowded rooming houses to places of their own.[19] The work and wages of slaves enabled their masters' upward mobility once they arrived in St. Louis. Dred had come west this way. The phenomenon of white migrants bringing slaves west with them as portable wealth was prevalent enough to have a name. New arrivals who brought nothing with them but slaves were called "slave-poor," as they were poor but for the slaves they owned. The Blow family, Dred's original owners, had arrived in the city that way.[20] They were "slave-rich" really, bringing their wealth only in the value of Dred and some other enslaved individuals.

Some things had changed in the two years since the Scotts had visited the city. By 1840, individual slave dealers developed their businesses into partnerships and more established firms built outdoor slave pens.[21] When money was tight, people tended to sell their slaves, flooding the slave labor market. It was hard to sell slaves at a profit in bad times. William Walker, the city's most infamous slave dealer had gone bankrupt and left town, pursued by bad debts.[22] But other dealers in human property had replaced him. In the coming decade, Reuben Bartlett,

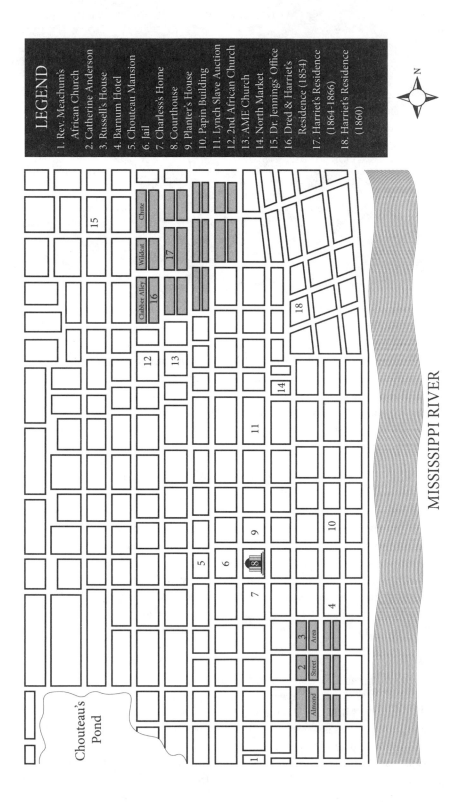

MISSISSIPPI RIVER

Chouteau's Pond

N

LEGEND

1. Rev. Meachum's
   African Church
2. Catherine Anderson
3. Russell's House
4. Barnum Hotel
5. Chouteau Mansion
6. Jail
7. Charless's Home
8. Courthouse
9. Planter's House
10. Papin Building
11. Lynch Slave Auction
12. 2nd African Church
13. AME Church
14. North Market
15. Dr. Jennings' Office
16. Dred & Harriet's
    Residence (1854)
17. Harriet's Residence
    (1864-1866)
18. Harriet's Residence
    (1860)

Clabber Alley

Wildcat

Chute

Almond   Street   Area

Bernard T. Lynch, and the partnership of Blakey and McAfee would become the most feared traders. Given their notoriety, these names were certainly known to the Scotts.[23]

Although St. Louis society consisted of several different social communities in 1840, race slavery was an accepted practice in all of them. The leading members of the old French fur trading community, the new industrialists, military officers, Indian agents, and the Catholic Church all held slaves and depended upon them as house servants. All five sectors not only engaged in the practice but also publicly defended slaveholding.

The city population of 17,000 was roughly equal to the population of the surrounding county. There were eight times as many white inhabitants as blacks in the county, with black persons disproportionately located in the countryside rather than the city. Although the black city population, numbering about 2,000, was two-thirds slave and one-third free, it totaled less than half the number of enslaved persons in the surrounding county. On the farms, almost none of the black population were free.[24]

Although the city was not yet large enough to have wealth-segregated neighborhoods, it was already segregated to some extent by race. Most city slaves lived near their masters, either in the cellars or attics of houses or in shanties near the outhouses on the alleyways. A growing community of free blacks had begun to form in different pockets of the city, usually on the least desirable land. Not all city blocks had alleys, but those that did attracted communities of free blacks and slaves.[25] Alleyway slave quarters paralleled the big houses that lined the main streets. Ramshackle wooden structures were added in the alleys wherever there was space.

The social mix of free blacks living together with slaves disturbed the city's white communities. The white slaveholders feared that slaves would take on airs and learn dangerous attitudes of independence from the free blacks. Still, there were few other places where free blacks could live.[26]

Although much of St. Louis society was highly transient and fluid, race slavery was an almost insurmountable barrier to black advancement. A poor white man migrating from Kentucky or Virginia, or even an immigrant newly arrived on the continent, could reach St. Louis and, if he was lucky and astute, make a fortune to secure his children's future. But the opportunities for black families, free or slave, were limited. Unlike the hundreds of other immigrants arriving at the docks daily, the Scott family was black, so their race distinguished them more than even their legal status, which was uncertain after living in the free North. In this otherwise fluid, mobile society, they were limited in the relatively few roles and occupations they could assume. The various St. Louis households through which they navigated for the next decade—country gentry, military, and urban merchants—saw them first and foremost as black persons and, by legal presumption, as slaves.[27]

The mistress's father, Col. Sanford, probably waited with a buggy and driver to fetch them from the steamboat landing. Mistress Emerson, now 25 and married for only two years, returned with the Scotts to live in her father's household, on the large farm northwest of the city, pending her husband's return. Her experience in the North had changed her from a new bride to a married woman to a mother, though it's unclear whether the Emersons' child, who did not survive infancy, survived long enough to be brought to Missouri.

North of the city, the Missouri River dumped its western waters into the Mississippi mainstream. Flowing from the west, the Missouri River made a little French curl before entering the north-south stream of the Mississippi. The Sanfords' farm lay within that curl of the rivers. The 380-acre farm was a full 15 miles northwest of the city, on the St. Charles Road. As the crow flies, the farm was closer to the city of St. Charles, just across the Missouri River's southern branch, than it was to St. Louis. However, to get to St. Charles required a ferry crossing.[28]

It must have been a shock for the Scotts to move to the Sanford farm after living in the North. On farms like the Sanfords', slaves did not work for the obvious household necessities of survival but for their masters' consumption and enrichment. The basic constraints of climate and hunger did not drive the slaves' work as much as overseers' demands. Most work was directed at producing an agricultural product for sale by the master—the proceeds of which the slaves would never see. Slaves were driven to labor by the whistle and whip. At Missouri farms, some white members of the master's family did not appear to work at all.[29]

This deep and profound racial divide must have jarred the couple's senses after their years of living at Fort Snelling. There, the predominant racial divide was between native and settlement peoples. Within that chasm in the social order, the Scotts clearly belonged to the settlement peoples. By their language, their culture, their dress, their habits, and their home within the fort, they were aligned with those identified as white.

The northern agency and fort had been Harriet's home for five years, since her early adolescence. No doubt, after years of enjoying the simple privileges of settlement community life, she had become accustomed to the freedom that the situation permitted her. Although she'd known Virginia slavery as a child, she may have forgotten or as a child been shielded from the more painful memories of slavery there. It had been years since she'd lived in a community where her race made such an enormous difference. She may have quite reasonably believed from her vantage point that during the years she lived in the North, the institution of slavery had changed as well. Slavery was on the way out when she left Bedford, Pennsylvania, with Taliaferro.[30] In Pennsylvania, the subject of conversation was the gradual emancipation of all the state's slaves. As her own personal circumstances had evolved for the better, she may have expected the outside world to have improved accordingly. Yet, in St. Louis, time had stood still in this respect. If anything, race slavery had become more entrenched. Over the next two decades the oppressive trend would continue.

Certainly life at the northern fort was no picnic. Harriet had had physically taxing work to do, requiring long hours most of the year. She worked for others, following their directives. But the work that she was directed to do was aligned with the household's survival, and she could probably appreciate its purpose. Without hard work, the house froze, there was nothing to eat, and the livestock would die.

Hunger and cold were felt, understood, and shared by all. Thus, everyone in the community worked sometimes to ensure survival. The harshest constraints on the Scotts' freedom were material and climatic. With a stove and quarters of their own, Harriet and her husband were in no way the worst-off in the northern wilderness.

Of course, the Scotts were held to the discipline of labor, but no more so than most settlers in the area and all the fort's soldiers. In some ways, the Scotts were less regimented than most at the fort. Slaves could not question their orders, but neither could soldiers. The reasons for the Scotts' labors were more immediately apparent than some military commands. Also like the soldiers, the servant couple received occasional pay for their labors and kept their own account at the sutler's store.

But within the constraints of the necessary tasks, Harriet could walk around as she pleased without patrols, licenses, or complicated sets of rules constraining her liberty. There were no jails or slave pens. There was only the brig where the commander sent the drunken soldiers and Indians accused of murder. Harriet may even have persuaded herself that she and her husband belonged to the community, just as the Swede and his African Indian wife were accepted. Or just as George Bonga, who described himself as white though his skin was very dark, was likewise accepted.[31] Why wouldn't she hope that the outside world had kept pace with her lived experience and with her own emergence as an increasingly independent adult? Harriet had enjoyed some significant experiences of independence in Minnesota: she was able to direct the regime by which she fulfilled the responsibilities of her workday, and she enjoyed the privilege and privacy of a family of her own.

Her return to St. Louis quickly dispossessed her of the illusion that she belonged like everyone else. In Missouri, unlike the wilderness frontier, there were no Indians—there were merely black folks and white folks. Some black folks were slaves, and some were free, as she may have regarded herself. None were nearly as free as the whites were, however. In St. Louis all sorts of race-based distinctions were in place, and that year there was even talk in town of establishing a workhouse to confine anyone found idle on the street.[32]

Moreover, unlike Minnesota, where there was a Native American majority, in St. Louis, the white residents seemed focused upon have exaggerating the racial differences between black and white Americans. These differences were posed as sharp contrasts and presented as markers of inferiority. White St. Louisians relished an almost prurient belief that African descendants, particularly in Africa, were inherently depraved and degraded.[33] Africans in America were believed to be better trained than those remaining in Africa. But white St. Louisians believed that even the best were bound to regress to their primitive ways from time to time—a belief reinforced through sensational newspaper accounts of slaves' crimes. Slaves who ran away were thought to be afflicted with an illness.[34] Ungrammatical speech—probably indistinguishable from the southern drawl spoken generally—was mocked and attributed exclusively to black folk. In the North, black folks were praised for their abilities to master and interpret Native American languages.

In St. Louis, white people believed blacks were unable to master common English.[35]

Nor did anyone question this way of thinking. It was illegal in Missouri to advocate abolition.[36] Anyone who questioned slavery openly was called an abolitionist—an epithet in St. Louis.[37] Not even the most progressive local newspapers had defended the Reverend Lovejoy's exercise of free speech. If a respectable white man was accused of abolitionism, he would demand a public apology, and make some statement to demonstrate his alliance with the norm of racist thinking. During the 1840s, there were no true abolitionists in St. Louis, and local hostility to abolitionism continued for the entire length of the Scotts' trial. But St. Louis geography influenced its destiny. The city lay at the crossroads of the nation in the development of its national identity. Geographically, it was the West. The river was the official frontier boundary and the national artery that marked the division between the settlement lands on its east bank and the vast West, where settlement was thought destined to occur over the next two decades. The great river's waters contained most settlement expansion until the time that all Indian claims were extinguished and the Indians removed. North to south, St. Louis was at the river's midpoint between its headwaters and the delta lands south to New Orleans.

East to west, St. Louis was a point at the imaginary extension of the line surveyed by Mason and Dixon. The Mason-Dixon Line was drawn from the national capital, along the Pennsylvania-Maryland boundary, and extended along the line of the Ohio River, which emptied into the Mississippi south of St. Louis. The path of extension westward was like an arrow that pointed directly at the emerging city of St. Louis. For this dividing line to continue west, St. Louis was the location to control. The nation had called its planned extension of slave and free states "the Missouri Compromise" after all. Harriet and Dred had returned to live at that place at the crosshairs of the aim site. Their lawsuit would unravel the Missouri Compromise and eventually lead to the unraveling of the Union itself.

ACCOMPANYING THE YOUNG MISTRESS to her father's house, the Scotts entered Col. Sanford's domain. This family's members, one after another, would assert dominion over the Scotts for the next 20 years—until ultimately John F. A. Sanford asserted control over them.

The Sanford farm was extensive, with more than 300 acres of rich farmland, orchards, and timber.[38] If Sanford had owned more slaves, the expanse would have been considered a plantation. With only six, however, it was more of a farm. Col. Sanford raised racehorses, hogs, and other livestock and some cash crops, though he had not lived there long and he didn't even own the farm. It was not the mistress's childhood home; in fact, she had never lived there before, but had only visited while on her honeymoon trip north.

Her brother, John F. A. Sanford, actually owned the farm. He bought it for his father, as he bought the stock, the equipment, and the racehorses. He had moved his father out of the city while sister Irene was off finding a husband.[39] Irene was already 19 and possibly at some boarding school for young ladies when her brother first moved their father to St. Louis. Col. Sanford had become insolvent, to his family's embarrassment. Once involved in steel manufacturing in the Shenandoah Valley of western Virginia, and once appointed as sutler at a Maryland fort, his debts overcame him.[40]

John F. A. Sanford, the oldest son, had sought his own fortune in the west and assumed the role as the family's provider. He was proud that he had paid for his sisters' and brother's educations.[41] The driven and ambitious young Sanford had hooked up with Gen. William Clark during Clark's post-exploration, Indian super-intendent days in St. Louis. After establishing himself in the city, Sanford had brought his father to St. Louis and set him up in the grocery business with one of his wife's wealthy relations. Col. Sanford didn't seem to take to the business though, so he quit after a while. Then his son bought the large farm for him in the country.

In the spring of 1840, when Irene Emerson came to live at the farm, most of her siblings were elsewhere. Eldest brother John and sister Mrs. Mary Sanford Bain-bridge, through whom she had met her husband, were enjoying a fashionable tour up the Mississippi with some prominent St. Louisans from the fur trade. Brother John also had pressing fur company business there. Younger brother Joseph had recently joined the navy, and her other two sisters lived with their officer husbands in other states.[42]

At the Missouri farm, old Col. Sanford lived with his second wife, a woman almost 20 years younger than he was.[43] This wife might have been Irene's mother, but she was definitely not the mother of John, the influential eldest brother.[44] The old man's second wife was not as socially adept as her stepchildren, and John viewed her with disdain. Since she was not fashionable or mannered in the genteel ways of ladies like his sisters, John, an aspiring social climber, had no use for her.[45]

On the farm to work the land, raise the horses, and serve the family's domestic needs were six slaves.[46] Old Col. Sanford had bought most of them with his son's money before moving west.[47] The farm even had a separate slave quarters,[48] and no doubt the Scotts were expected to live there. They had never been denied their privacy so rudely during their three years of marriage. Within these primitive slave quarters, Harriet had to find a place to cushion her toddler, Eliza. As adults, she and Dred could fend for themselves, but her child's very survival depended on her watchful eyes. The first-time mother probably devised novel ways to keep the two-year-old from harm while own daily attention and energies were demanded for work.[49] But the fireplace, boil-ing kettles, hot coals, and the sharp wood ax were only a few of the hazards her toddler could encounter. Now Harriet had to protect Eliza from the cruelties of race slavery as well. Harriet could content herself with the knowledge that their situation was temporary. They were only there while the doctor was away at war. Once he returned, they would leave again.

Simple mistakes had violent repercussions for slaves here. On Missouri farms, most slaves went to the fields in the early morning hours. Usually, a woman at the slave quarters cooked for the field hands, who were summoned to work every morning at four o'clock. The overseer blew the horn, which was the signal to begin working.[50] Missouri slave William Wells Brown wrote, "Everyone who was not ready to work…received ten lashes from the negro-whip, which the overseer always carried with him."[51] The grisly weapon was designed to inflict pain.[52] At Fort Snelling, the Scotts witnessed more whippings of soldiers than anyone else. Agent Taliaferro, who had been the primary lawgiver in the area, had rejected the idea of whipping Indians for the theft of settlers' cattle. This was both because the law didn't authorize it and because of the possibility of chastising the wrong person.[53] Soldiers' punishments occurred only after trial and only for very serious infractions. Here a slave could be whipped on the spot simply for being late getting to the field.

The circumstances of a house servant were usually better than those of a field hand,[54] and having been domestics before, the Scotts probably resumed those roles at the Sanford farm. Neither of them was adept at heavy field work, and as Dr. Emerson's servants, there was no justification to work them as field slaves. Dred was smaller and older than most active field slaves. He may have tended to the doctor's horses or other livestock. But although he enjoyed attending the races, the farm's racehorses were a select breed,[55] more valuable perhaps than he was, so they may not have been entrusted to his care. House servants were usually better fed and better clothed than field servants, and not obliged to rise as early.[56] But even house servants could hear the whip crack and the screams of field slaves. And at night all the tired workers, both field hands and domestics, came to sleep on the same common rag mattress on the slave quarter's dirt floor.[57] A person joining the household at the slightly elevated status of house servant was likely to cause resentment among the others who shared the slave quarters and labored in the fields. Comparisons were inevitable. To come in as a house servant was to take a position of slight privilege, though, for the Scotts, it was greatly diminished from their situations at the northern fort.

If anything, work was easier where they were spared the extreme winter cold. The material substances of life were also easier to come by, given the nearby town. With access to the city, the household could afford to be a little less prudent with its material goods. There were ready replacements in the markets for anything broken or used up. A broken cartwheel wasn't the catastrophe here that it had been at the Indian agency with winter approaching. The pantry did not need to stock a half-year supply of food, and rations did not need to be measured one by one with the same degree of care needed at the Indian agency.

Firewood was not required in nearly the quantities of wood consumed for heat in a single northern winter's day. The area had also been settled long enough that the more permanent conveniences of wells, pumps, and cisterns were established. The gardens harvested a greater variety of vegetables at this latitude, and there were even fruit orchards. To prepare dinners at the main house, one didn't rely on wild game and fish brought by the hunters and Indians. Frying a chicken meant only a trip to the henhouse.

Although winter visited St. Louis, it was mild compared the winters of endurance at the Mississippi's headwaters. Thus, the main houses could afford to be more decorous than solid in construction, and less effort was necessary each autumn to secure them against the cold. Despite freezing temperatures and sometimes snow, the harder winter aspects—bone-chilling, mind-deadening cold, fierce winds; blowing and drifting snow; and even snow blindness—never troubled this latitude.

CHAPTER 20

The House of Chouteau

T HE RURAL FARM and the company of her stepmother would not long hold the interest of the young doctor's wife, particularly after she had spent two years in the social isolation of a remote army post. Mistress Irene must have turned her attention to the dazzling St. Louis social life. In the same way that her brother had introduced his sisters into society,[1] the Sanford name now opened doors, and Mistress Irene could take advantage of this connection during her sojourn without her husband. (Indeed, her husband would later use these social connections to try to keep his job.) Brother John was extremely prominent in the city, and Irene was now respectably married. Among women of her class, visiting, gossiping, and entertaining were the order of the day.[2] Among those she would visit were her brother's in-laws, the Chouteaus, who knew her before her marriage.[3]

Dred probably drove her in the buggy to the Chouteaus' grand home in town. It made a good impression to use a driver, especially if he was neatly attired.[4] Dred had no reason to know the house personally, although the Chouteau mansion was renowned throughout the city. Dred had been brought west by Virginia immigrants and the French aristocrats were a separate society. This was probably his first approach to the door of the fine house of Chouteau but, given the way things turned out, one that he would surely remember.

Driving through the city's dirt streets, Dred could observe more closely how the city had changed during his seven years in the North. There were still quaint, wooden houses that resembled shabby, French colony architecture, but the downtown street names were no longer French; the streets had been renamed for numbers and trees.[5] Mass was still said in French because the Chouteaus liked it that way, and they underwrote the debt on the large new cathedral—although the new Catholic immigrants were German, Irish, and Italian and did not understand French.[6]

The Chouteaus had built a new mansion at the corner of Seventh and Market. While Mistress Irene visited, Dred would have had some free time as he waited with the horses. A high wall surrounded the family garden along Seventh Street, but above the wall, one could see the broad second-story porch and greenhouse.[7] Although Dred was gregarious, he'd learn little from the Chouteau slaves, who were expected to speak only French at their master's house.

The custom was to drink dark-roast chicory coffee with the hostess, Madame, and her adult daughter, Julia. Guests of the Chouteaus marveled at the mansion's richness, which featured every luxury money could buy.[8] Twenty-four-year-old Julia was interested in an army surgeon who was posted at the nearby barracks south of town, though she had not yet been permitted to marry. She had taken a motherly interest in her sister's son after Emily Chouteau Sanford had died.[9] The family pampered the slightly overweight boy.

Madame Chouteau, a Parisian grande dame, was her rich American-born husband's own first cousin. The Chouteaus maintained close contact with relatives in France and had a penchant for marrying their own. It was said in St. Louis that if one wished to make a name or a fortune there, it was best to be born a Chouteau and to marry another.[10] Their intermarriages solidified business alliances and produced a tight core of social and business eminence. That Sanford had won the hand of Chouteau's daughter had made his early reputation in the city.

Sanford called Madame Chouteau "mother," and he preferred her to his own father's second wife. Madame was Parisian, cultured, energetic, and devoted to the family. Sanford described her affectionately. "Mother is now occupied in arranging her new carpets—all bustle and if it was not that, it would be something else equally pressing. Occupation. Occupation. Action! Action! I cannot imagine what would become of her without it."[11]

The master of the household, Pierre Chouteau Jr., was the city's richest man and undisputed head of his extended family and the city's French-Creole community. His ancestors had founded the city three generations earlier. This was the man whom John F. A. Sanford, the Scotts' eventual legal opponent always sought to impress. Pierre Chouteau Jr. looked and acted the aristocrat as he dominated the lives of the extended family as well as his business partners. He was tall, handsome, and wore his thick, wavy, black hair parted on the side. John F. A. Sanford worshiped him. He was gracious, easy, and affable with everyone as well as resolute and politely ruthless. He was a man to be feared by those who opposed him. He had assumed his central role as patriarch of his family, and to some extent of the French of the city, by force of his personality, even though his aged father and his elder brother still lived.[12]

The family influence was more pervasive in commerce and real estate than in politics.[13] Once the Chouteaus had literally owned the entire county,[14] and their many cousins still made good livings selling off pieces of their inheritance. They had even provided the ground on which the courthouse stood. Buying and selling furs to New York, destined ultimately for the European market, had made the family fabulously wealthy. By 1840, Pierre Jr. had an immense fortune; by 1860, he was worth almost half a million dollars.[15]

Pierre Chouteau Jr. was more than lucky. "He had mastered the art of cutthroat competition, and the rules that he observed were simple, almost Machiavellian. Chouteau defeated rivals with price wars and moved quickly to take over a rival company's posts, its men, its territories and trade of rivals. Political influence would be fully exploited, and liquor shamelessly sold to the Indians when necessary... and [the trad-ers'] territories would be carefully divided."[16] Chouteau had also mastered the tech-nique of making money on both sides of the fur trade equation. As the primary buyer of furs, the frontier's basic product at the time, the American Fur Company deter-mined the prices that would be paid; as the leading mercantile wholesaler and outfitter, they could determine prices they charged. Supplying their fur traders, the military, and anyone else on the frontier needing commodities allowed them to profit on the entire range of household items. Even Agent Taliaferro had ordered from them. Anything needed on the frontier could be ordered from Chouteau & Co. in St. Louis and deliv-ered on a Chouteau-owned steamboat.

Though the fur trade was declining worldwide, the Chouteaus retained their posi-tion of wealth and influence in the town that was the gateway to the West. With the active participation of John F. A. Sanford, they were poised to diversify their holdings in other major investment directions. For them, the fur trade was simply a means to the end of enormous wealth. Their sizable fortune, amassed over a half century, was re-invested in more lucrative businesses: government contracting and transportation—first with steamboats and still later railroads. Through ownership of steamboats, the Chouteaus controlled travel into the American interior to a degree matched only superficially by the licensing capacity of Indian agents. While the Indian agency had the official authority over those entering Indian territory, Chouteau and his compa-nies owned the means of travel. Most travelers and even adventurers took Chouteau steamboats to their farthest destinations. Famed explorers Nicollet and Catlin, both of whom Harriet had served during their extended stays with the Taliaferros, had also enjoyed the French family's patronage to support their travels.[17] The Chouteaus had lieutenants stationed at virtually every known outpost.

In 1840, after their fashionable tour up the Mississippi, John F.A. Sanford and his mentor father-in-law were far up the Missouri River rallying the Indi-ans. To ensure their trading preeminence, they staged an Indian council to reestablish the company's dominant position. The idea was to drum up loy-alty within the tribes by orchestrating a public feast. The company practice explained Sibley's annual gatherings at Mendota as well. After the feast, and probably with the benefit of alcohol,[18] the company men encouraged the Indi-ans to sign a petition, much as they had scrambled to secure written advances during the treaty-making time.[19]

AS DRED WAITED with the horses to drive the mistress home, he would have had occasion to regard how the family treated their slaves. The Chouteaus had always held slaves, and they considered slave-holding to be a matter of privilege and right. The Chouteau extended family owned more than 100 enslaved persons,[20] many of them the children of earlier generations of Chouteau slaves.[21] Chouteau's company occasionally sold slaves to fur traders in the Northwest Territory when the oppor-tunity arose,[22] but, for the most part, the Chouteaus didn't emancipate them.[23]

The Chouteaus zealously litigated against any of their slaves who sought free-dom, and they pursued slaves who tried to run away.[24] No other single family pursued slave-holding litigation quite as persistently as the Chouteaus' extended family did.[25] Because the family had long and extensive operations in the Northwest Territory, several of their slaves had resided at fur trade posts in the free northwest. When a slave claimed freedom as a result, the family resisted, pressing the courts to the full extent to secure their advantage.[26] One woman named Marguerite spent 15 years in court, facing Chouteau opposition for her freedom.[27] She won at every turn. But even after Pierre Chouteau Sr. had lost all state appeals, he tried to appeal to the United States Supreme Court—although the appeal lacked any legal foundation and was promptly rejected.[28] During the next decade, their slave Pierre, and his brothers and sister, would pursue their freedom in the courts against the Chouteaus as well.

Sanford's father-in-law, Pierre Jr., did not necessarily orchestrate these legal actions; he saw more to gain on the bottom line from other business opportunities. But slave-holding was a family prerogative, and the Chouteaus were closely knit. As head of the family, Pierre Jr. certainly knew of the litigation and, given his influence, undoubtedly was consulted about the lawsuits of his father, brothers, uncles, and cousins. It was Sanford whom Pierre Jr. loved like a son who would become involved in the most notorious slave freedom suit of all time. According to Mrs. Emerson, Sanford fought the Scotts' lengthy lawsuit to its ultimate end in order to please the Chouteaus.[29]

When Sanford married Pierre Jr.'s eldest daughter in the cathedral built by the family, Sanford was accepted as if he were their oldest son. Over the years the bond grew even stronger. Sanford was older than Chouteau's own son, who wasn't yet ready to take up the family business.[30] Accordingly, Sanford, whose own father had embarrassed the family financially, sought to become the favored business partner of the richest man in St. Louis. Chouteau's other business partners—Sarpy, Papin, and Berthold—were French (or Francophones) and all related by blood and marriage, but Sanford was the most trusted, the most loyal, and perhaps the most driven. He was Pierre Jr.'s chosen one. This was the man to whom he had given his precious daughter. Likewise, Sanford regarded his father-in-law's success with an admiration he did not feel for his own debt-ridden father.[31]

Remarkably, Sanford had bound himself to this wealthy French family much as wilderness fur traders did to their local tribes: by marrying the chief's daughter and having children. During their short marriage, Emilie bore Sanford a son, further solidifying the family tie. And then, she died suddenly. Sanford surrendered the raising of his motherless son to the Chouteaus. This freed him to travel the fur-trading empire and to continue his frequent lobbying trips to New York and Washington on behalf of the family's interests. With his son well cared for, Sanford did not maintain a household of his own in St. Louis. The firm's business office was his address.[32] When the company opened a new office in New York in the early 1840s, its management was turned over to Sanford.

Dred could have little inkling, as he drove the buggy home from the Chouteau mansion,[33] that this was the powerful clan that he and Harriet would eventually take on in litigating their freedom. In the contest of their lives, they would be pitted against John F. A. Sanford, the son-in-law scion of the Chouteau fortune, financial power broker of the gateway to the west, New York financier, and Washington lobbyist.

Dred probably drove Mistress Irene to pay social calls on several other St. Louis ladies as well. Visiting was what ladies of her social status did. Mrs. Emerson and her sisters had social ties to many fashionable young ladies, including the Lane sisters, the Berry sisters,[34] and Fanny Wash. Fanny, a fabled beauty who had married a wealthy lawyer named George Goode (who would later represent Mrs. Emerson), lived just down the road.[35] But it was the house of Chouteau, and their son-in-law John F. A. Sanford in particular, with whom the Scotts would need to contend. Given how it all turned out, Dred surely had reason in his later years to recall his first visit to the house of Chouteau as Mrs. Emerson's driver.

CHAPTER 21

Black Social Life of St. Louis

ALTHOUGH IT'S FAIR to assume that the Scotts initially stayed at the Sanford farm, they weren't necessarily well suited to the life there, and the farm did not need them. There were already six slaves and possibly an overseer on the place,[1] and Mistress Irene's added presence did not justify the efforts of two more adult slaves. As historian Eugene Genovese has noted, "slavery require[d] all hands to be occupied at all times. In a labor system based on compulsion rather than wages, idle workers are at once dangerous and uneconomical."[2]

It was Dred whose labor was least needed at the Sanford farm. Other than being his mistress's driver and a passable cook,[3] there was little that a former valet was well suited for in the countryside, and at his age he was less adaptable than a younger slave.[4] He had spent the previous decade in the light work of keeping his officer-master's uniform brushed and boots blackened, chopping firewood, and helping out in the hospital, so he was neither accustomed to nor fit for the heavy demands of farm labor. Unless the household needed a butler, and his command over other servants was accepted (even more unlikely), it would have been difficult for him to become integrated into the farm's working life. Nor would he expect to be. He was not a Sanford family slave. Everyone knew that he belonged to the absent Dr. Emerson, that he was there only temporarily—and that as soon as the doctor returned, he and Harriet would depart again. Still, Dred was an agreeable fellow, given to talk and conviviality, so he probably got on better with the other slaves than did the more reticent Harriet.[5]

As the doctor's months away dragged on into years, it's likely that plans were made for the couple to be hired out. Rented out, singly or together, they could generate cash by working in St. Louis. St. Louis slave owners often made hiring arrangements for slave labor that they had no immediate need for, sometimes sending their slaves to find their own work and negotiate their own terms.[6] As an amiable fellow who knew his way around town, Dred, in particular, might have found his own position—though Harriet's services, particularly as a laundress, were more in demand. In some of these hiring-out arrangements, bound servants paid their masters a set sum each month and could keep a slim profit.[7] Since the Scotts had already received some wages working at the Minnesota fort, they would naturally be inclined to such an arrangement, if allowed.

Slaves were hired out in more formal ways, too. The most significant was the annual New Year's Day auction, when slaves were auctioned for year-long leases on the courthouse steps. One historian has noted that "many hiring transactions began, by custom, on New Year's Day. Across the South, that day was 'hiring day' on countless town squares, courthouse steps, and rural roads."[8] The same fate could have befallen the Scotts, but as they arrived in May, the timing was not right. It is unlikely that they were auctioned off.[9] Slaves could also be placed through advertising in the local papers, but making informal arrangements through friends and acquaintances was easier.[10] Mrs. Emerson and her father, Col. Sanford, later leased them out this way.

Since Harriet had never before lived in Missouri, she had no one to turn to in a crisis. There was no established household where she could seek the charity customarily expected of past patrimony. The city was new to her—except for that summer two years earlier when she had been pregnant and drifted with Dred from pillar to post in the streets of the city, before eventually returning by the *Gypsey* to the North

The town was the place to seek wages. One was more likely to find a position as a domestic among the new St. Louis merchants and industrialists than among the older French families, who preferred French-speaking slaves. The new businessmen emulated the luxurious life of the Chouteaus by building mansions and renting slaves. The new industrialists were New Englanders and Virginians for the most part, and the Virginians brought their own slavery traditions with them. By custom and institution, Virginian slave-holding differed from the old French ways.[11] It could be more coldly cruel or more callously commercial, but it was less permanently familial, for better or worse. When a Virginian had a problem with a slave, he simply sold the person away.[12] By contrast, the Chouteaus sent their slaves to another relative in town or in New Orleans. Virginians, more than the French, were predisposed to renting and leasing slaves as they needed them.[13]

The resettled Virginians were a separate community and posed something of a rival group to the old French Creoles dominated by the Chouteaus. The Virginians had emigrated from a collapsing agricultural economy. Many were second or third sons of failing planter patriarchs. But the Virginians were never as tightly connected nor as determined to consolidate their familial influence by close marriages as the Chouteaus. There was little new land in Virginia to bring into production, and lands in cultivation had been so run down by intensive tobacco farming that there was small chance for a younger son to make a good living there. Virginia's declining agricultural potential meant fewer slaves were needed. The slave surplus meant that younger sons took their inheritance in slaves to wherever there was a labor shortage.[14] They then sold their slaves or put them to work for cash wages.

A great many of the new generation of businessmen opened profitable mercantile houses selling groceries, drugs, furniture, and stoves. Initially these items were imported by steamboat from the East, but eventually, new factories of all kinds sprang up to manufacture goods locally. There was even a new yard for building steamboats.[15] Despite the burst of new enterprise, slave-holding was still a substantial part of the municipal tax base. Local taxes were based on land, live-stock, watches, pleasure carriages, polls, and slaves.[16]

Working in town, rented slaves like Harriet and Dred directly encountered the unique brand of racial segregation that the French and the Virginians, meet-ing at the steamboat depot on the frontier, had forged together. The Scotts inevi-tably learned from others that a little side money could be earned at the docks. Men earned money by carrying luggage, running errands at the docks and hotels, or even selling small items to steamboat passengers, and women earned by the tedious but necessary work of washing clothes for the city's inhabitants and new arrivals.

In "working out" arrangements, owners were often more lax in keeping daily tabs on their slaves, especially when slaves slept away from their masters' homes.[17] The prac-tice of allowing slaves to find their own work was illegal in St. Louis during the 1840s,[18] but it was tolerated with some grumbling. One public meeting denounced the practice as a great evil.[19] Owners were occasionally fined if their slaves appeared too conspicu-ously independent in negotiating their own arrangements. However, the practice was too economically useful for the slave-poor Virginians who continued to arrive in the city, and too economically convenient as a source of casual labor to be suppressed for long. People such as Mistress Irene, who temporarily had more slaves' time on her hands than needed, could generate additional income and save the costs of feeding and clothing their slaves by hiring them out.[20]

If the Scotts worked in town during the three years that Mistress Irene waited for the doctor to return, Harriet most likely did laundry. Most free black women earned their livings that way; servant women were hired for that purpose. The arduous, time-consuming work was in great demand. Everyone needed clothing laundered from time to time, and the task was so oppressive that wash day Mon-days were called Blue Mondays. Even those who were not particularly wealthy paid others to do their washing.[21] Economically, clothing was so costly and so valuable that even the dirty laundry had to be guarded against theft while in the laun-dresses' possession. Many a poor person was jailed for stealing a single article of clothing.[22] Clothing was so valuable that some persons' estates, fully probated, consisted of only their wardrobes.[23] Laundresses had to make sure that every item in their bundles was properly returned to its owner by the following Saturday. Socially, clean clothing was an important marker that separated those who were perceived as belonging in the town from unkempt vagrants who might be harassed by the patrols.[24] Once the laundry that Harriet washed had separated the settle-ment people from the Indians; here clean laundry separated the classes of respect-able people from the vagabond riff-raff.

Under the Sabbath law, even slaves were excused from all work, except chores on Sundays.[25] For washerwomen, work ended when the week's clean laundry had been delivered. The African Church held more Sunday services than most white churches in order to accommodate the different times that slaves completed their chores.[26] The town offered other social activities on Saturday evenings, when work broke off. Then one could find men bowling ten-pins in the alley, visiting barbershops to spruce up for courting or for church, going off drinking illegally, or going dancing at licensed all-black parties called "negro balls."[27] Some underground locales had gambling, and though it was illegal to sell liquor to people of color, there were grogshops where alcohol was available.[28] In the evenings, the patrol imposed a 9 P.M. curfew on all blacks. There were no street lights yet, and the watchmen carried lanterns and called the time on the hour throughout the night. One needed a pass to be on the streets at night. One contemporary slave wrote: "If we were out after that hour without a permit from the master, we would be locked up by the watch. Sometimes the watchman would take us home to our master. If he was a mean man, he would refuse to receive us and we would be locked up in the calaboose. If he failed to come down in the morning and pay a certain sum to get us out, we would be hit thirty lashes and sent home."[29] As a mother with a young child, Harriet may not have had the energy or inclination to go out dancing, and as a churchgoing woman, she'd avoid the bad places.

Without a municipal water system in the early 1840s,[30] most laundry was done at the river or at Chouteau's pond, a small shallow slough from which a stream trickled into the river. Otherwise, it might be done in the back alleys, wherever water could be found. Chouteau's pond had once run a grain mill, but now it was simply a pond of stagnant water that the city threatened to drain from time to time.[31]

The laundresses assembled in the early mornings to draw water, build fires, and set up tubs of water to boil. The city had designated a depot where driftwood was collected, north of the docks.[32] From the shore, gleaners could be seen walking up and down the levee with bags and baskets to pick up any scattered pieces that had fallen out of the steamboat shipments.[33] The muddy Mississippi River water was not suitable for laundering clothing, but experienced laundresses knew the secret: the water could be cleansed by giving it time to settle. If left to sit for an hour, the silt sank to the bottom and the clear washing water could be skimmed off the top.[34]

Since laundry was often done collectively, the river was a place to meet the sisterhood of other black laundresses in town.[35] There, the women were free to talk and gossip and even sing as washing women had done since ancient times. The St. Louis laundry women were few enough in number[36] and their routines sufficiently regular that they could easily know each other by name. Several washerwomen had established their freedom through the courts.[37] Sixty-year-old Winny, one of the first mothers to win freedom for herself and her seven children, was still alive and working as a washerwoman in the 1840s.[38] Winny's daughters, Jenny, Nancy, Lydia, Sarah, Hannah, and Malinda, who were now adults, had all successfully sued for their freedom as well.[39] Between 1840 and 1846, when Harriet and Dred filed suit, several more enslaved women—Alsey, Diana Cephas, Polly Wash, and Lucy Berry—would be freed by lawsuit. Polly Wash and her daughter, Lucy, had lives and aspirations for freedom much like Harriet's own. Although it cannot be established definitively that Harriet knew them, their lives intersected in so many ways, in the small circles in which they traveled, that there is every reason to believe that she must have. Harriet certainly followed the same path taken by Polly and Lucy.

Their masters' families were definitely well acquainted. Lucy's master, D. D. Mitchell, and his prospective bride actually traveled together aboard the steamboat *Malta* with Mistress Irene's brother and sister on the pleasure cruise up the river during the summer that the Scotts arrived in Missouri.[40] D. D. Mitchell and John F.A. Sanford had been friends since their bachelor days as Indian agents among the Mandans, and they had caroused together with tribal women.[41] Mitchell had recently been promoted to superintendent of Indian Affairs in the West, an extremely important position, previously held by William Clark. Mitchell's appointment was probably helped by John F. A. Sanford's lobbying in Washington. Sanford could now count on his old friend not to meddle in the lucrative treaty matters that most interested the company. When Dr. Emerson needed help later, in his attempt to remain in the Army Surgical Corps, he drew on the Sanford family name to seek help from Lucy's master, D. D. Mitchell.

Harriet and Polly and her daughter, Lucy, lived parallel lives—in their trade as laundresses, as members of the African church, and, most important, in bringing similar freedom suits based on residence on free soil in the St. Louis Circuit court during the 1840s. Both mothers, Harriet and Polly, sought freedom for themselves and their daughters in cases filed by the same lawyer. Polly and her daughter won their individual cases shortly before Harriet filed suit. Because Lucy, Harriet's contemporary, wrote her autobiography, we know the most about her circumstances, and reading Lucy's case file and Polly's case file together with the Scotts' gives greater insight into the social circumstances of black laundresses and freedom suits.[42]

Lucy was brought to D. D. Mitchell's household by his bride as part of her inheritance. (Quite possibly, some of the Sanford siblings attended the wedding.)

Young Lucy and her mother Polly had different last names, but unlike Harriet, neither held the last name of a husband. Their assumed last names reflected instead the households of their origin. Among white folk, slaves were not generally known as having last names. Instead, they were referred to by their owners' names: as the Berry's Lucy and the Wash's Polly; but black folks inverted the names and resisted taking the possessive form of the name of a subsequent owner: Lucy Berry and Polly Wash. Asserting a last name signified independence, even though that name also belonged to the master. Frequently, enslaved individuals kept the entire string of their owners' names. Lucy's last name was Berry because Lucy was born while her mother had lived in the Berry family; her mother's name was Wash. (Polly lived in the Wash household during the time together with her husband.) These names expressed their personal family origins better than any other names at their disposal.[43]

Dred had assumed the name "Etheldred," presumably the family name taken in faraway Virginia from a Blow family marriage two owners back.[44] Yet this was a way to recognize kin from a past forcibly stripped away. It's interesting to note that Dred was never referred to in any of the paymaster's records by the last name of Scott. (The earliest entry of a "Dred Scott" was in the 1836 Wisconsin Territorial census, and there is some doubt about whether that was the same person.)[45] After their marriage, Harriet Robinson, presumably obtained by Taliaferro from the Robinson farm in King George County, Virginia, took the last name "Etheldred" or "Dread."[46] She was not identified by last name when she sued for freedom—instead her case named her as "Harriet, of Color," whereas Dred's case was styled "Dred Scott" from the beginning.

Each laundress had a life story to recount as she washed the city's laundry, and the stories often had a point.[47] Sometimes the stories came with a message such as "Never leave the city." More important, telling the right story in a court case was necessary to achieving freedom. Polly's story was that she had been passed through a series of masters in Illinois before being sold to the Berrys in Missouri. She remained there without asserting a claim for freedom, because that's where she found a husband to love, though it's not clear that they were legally married. Missouri masters sometimes encouraged marriage in an attempt to placate their slaves. A man with a wife was less likely to try to escape.[48]

When their master died, her husband was sold and sent downriver—an event that haunted the slave family. Polly remained with the Berrys, clinging to the belief (or promise) that she would be freed when her old mistress died.[49] But when the mistress died without freeing Polly, Polly ran. According to Lucy's autobiography, her mother, Polly, hid, crossed the great river to Illinois, and made it as far as Chicago before she was tracked down, beaten, and brought back to St. Louis in irons. The case files indicate instead that Polly worked on steamboats plying the Illinois waters.[50]

Then Polly turned to the St. Louis court. There she proved that she was no longer a slave, having previously lived where slavery was banned by virtue of the Northwest Territorial Ordinance and the Illinois State Constitution. When Polly succeeded in establishing her freedom in 1841, it must have been the talk of the black community. Polly's legally declared freedom paved the way for winning Lucy's freedom. Under the principle of matrilinearity, children of a free mother were entitled to free status as well.[51]

That very summer, a dispute over laundry triggered daughter Lucy's suit for freedom as well. Each of her master's daughters had inherited one of Polly's daughters, but Polly had always told her daughters that they were entitled to their freedom—and that sooner or later, their freedom would be established. It was a question of timing and perseverance. Suing for freedom was not something that one did lightly, because it could generate the master's retaliation, and the time that a lawsuit required was fraught with hidden dangers. The timing of Lucy's case was triggered by the prospect that she too would be shipped south for sale as her father had been.

When Lucy came to the Mitchell's residence, she was unprepared to maintain a household for the new bride, who was a pampered debutante rather than trained as a homemaker. When Lucy was ordered to do the laundry, she didn't know the secret of clearing water. Thus, when she dumped the clothing in a tub of Mississippi River water and boiled it, the clothing became dirtier than it was before. Seeking help, she got another experienced laundress, a friend of her mother's, to try to get the clothes clean before the white people arose. But even the experienced laundress couldn't get the mud-stained laundry clean again.[52]

Lucy's mistake drew her mistress's displeasure, but Lucy resisted all of her mistress's attempts to harangue and to beat her. When eventually she was told to prepare to travel south because she had been sold, she fled, and her mother, as her guardian ad litem, filed suit for her freedom. Polly had warned her daughter never to leave the city because the countryside was a place of greater danger and fewer opportunities for escape.

Polly's residence in free territory established the basis of Lucy's free status.[53] There were a few other ways to argue freedom, but residence in free territory was the fixed North Star in the legal constellation on which most litigating slaves could pin their hopes. Most freedom litigants described their respective position with reference to residence in the Northwest Territory or, more westerly, the Missouri Compromise free territory—those lands north of the parallel. The Scotts had resided in free territory, but when their case came to the Supreme Court, the constellations would shift and the earth would move.

CHAPTER 22

The Doctor Returns

IN FLORIDA, THE war against the Seminoles was going well.[1] News reached
St. Louis that Col. William S. Harney, one of the city's own officers, had captured 40 Indian "savages" and hanged 10 of them on the spot. The newspaper
applauded the swift executions as more effective than the government policy, which,
they said, coddled the Indians and their runaway slave allies.[2] Although in war Col.
Harney's brutality made him a hero, he was already infamous among the black
population of St. Louis for having beaten a slave woman to death on the street for
disobedience.[3]

In early 1842, after almost two years, much of the time sick and serving in various makeshift swamp hospitals, Dr. Emerson was finally granted a leave. Surgeons
were required to accompany large troop movements, and so Emerson was assigned
to accompany a group destined for New Orleans. Even more to his liking, he was
permitted to take a leave of absence for 30 days once he reached New Orleans. By
Valentine's Day 1842, the tall, bespectacled, romantic husband was moving upriver
to St. Louis for a month with his wife.

At month's end, when the doctor reported to the Gulf for duty, Irene probably
accompanied him.[4] He later mentioned making arrangements for her.[5] His return
posting lay just off Pensacola—an area safe from where the fighting continued and
a suitable place for military wives to join their husbands. It's not certain whether
either of the Scotts accompanied the Emersons to Florida. If they were rented out,
there was no reason to disrupt a wage-earning arrangement. The doctor had previously arranged slaves' services in Florida. Even if Dred went along, there was no
reason to bring Harriet and their child.

Seeing St. Louis again only seemed to increase Emerson's desire to return permanently. By April, the homesick Dr. Emerson wrote his superiors, requesting
again to be stationed near St. Louis.[6] The doctor was edgy at Fort Pickens. He
feared a return to the miserable swamps, and he got into disputes again with the
local quartermaster there. They quarreled over worn-out hospital materials that

Emerson had discarded as trash.[7] He even antagonized the post's other surgeon.[8] When Emerson heard that two doctors junior to him had been given desirable postings to the nation's capital, he fired off an angry letter of protest.[9] On June 4, 1842, he was dispatched to the battle area again, at which point, Mistress Irene surely returned up the Mississippi to the comforts of St. Louis.

In Florida, events were being set in motion that would shift the Scotts to the service of other masters. The area commander in Florida received word from the president to stand down the forces and bring the Seminole War to an end.[10] Days later, as the jungle war neared its end, Dr. Emerson received the shock of his life. Without warning, he was discharged from the Army Medical Corps. Washington policy makers decided that with the war over, the army no longer needed so many officers, so dozens received discharge notices.[11] Only those well protected by both rank and the allegiance of others were able to keep their posts. Emerson, the perennial complainer, was not so lucky.

The tall, myopic doctor headed back to St. Louis, glad to leave Florida but in despair about being discharged from the army. He had expected greater things once the war ended. He had expected to sit for promotion to the rank of surgeon or at least to be assigned to a post of his choosing. He didn't expect to be cashiered when the miserable war finally concluded. Having served his time in the dismal swamps expecting reward, he now felt cheated. He found himself without a job— and without the promise of future possibilities.[12]

Upon his return to St. Louis, the doctor purchased a place of his own for himself and his wife. He couldn't expect to move in with his father-in-law. To do so was as unseemly as his discharge itself. He bought a small plot of land, just 19 acres, above Chouteau's Pond, three miles from the city limits, on the Manchester Road. The acreage was tiny compared to the 380-acre Sanford farm about eight miles to the north.[13] Not large enough to raise cash crops, the acreage was just enough for a house, a stable, and a small pasture.[14]

The disappointed doctor still hoped to return to the surgeon's corps. He mobilized a group of eminent gentlemen of the city to write to the army on his behalf. Emerson clearly hoped that the Sanford family's social connections would help him win back his position. Hat in hand, sloshing through the mud of the St. Louis streets, he paid a series of social calls to various St. Louis notables, probably having Dred drive him by carriage since a black servant added to one's appearance. Dred may have even received a new set of clothes for the visits.[15] As the contemporary Mark Twain said, "Clothes make the man."[16]

Most St. Louis notables whom Emerson visited were friends of the Sanford family. The Sanford sisters were friends of the Lane sisters, whose father, an eminent physician and politician, wrote a letter on Emerson's behalf. Emerson also paid a visit to Lucy's master, D. D. Mitchell, the newly appointed Indian superintendent. (Lucy remained in jail awaiting trial when Emerson called at the house.) The letters written on Emerson's behalf seem only weakly supportive of his qualifications. Rather than extolling his virtues, these important men of St. Louis stressed their affection for his wife's family. One writer did him the favor of describing him as measurably unfit and unprepared for other business, given his long attachment to the army. The assessment was probably true, but not helpful.[17] The Emersons might have received sympathy from their military in-laws for his misfortune, but his brothers-in-law did not write letters for him.[18] The fact that they retained their army positions probably exacerbated the doctor's embarrassment. Through December, the doctor wrote several letters himself. He stressed his neediness, his loyalty, and his brush with heroism. (He had been with a unit that had captured a large number of Seminole Indians.) "I have a family depending on me for support and hope and trust you will not turn a deaf ear to my application," he added.[19]

As Emerson continued to press for readmission to the surgeon's corps, a friend of his, the army paymaster, told him that his personnel file contained an obstacle to his reappointment. Unbeknown to Emerson, the doctor succeeding him in Minnesota had registered a complaint against him two years earlier. He was accused of giving away the army's pork to the Indians, a serious charge. Misuse of army stores was one of the worst infractions in the code book. (The quartermaster at Fort Crawford had been court-martialed for giving away empty barrels.)

The doctor reacted to this news by writing still more letters. "I have been thrown on the world in a manner which has cast great doubts over me so as to deprive me of the means of supporting myself and family. If there is any charge against me, may I beg of you to inform me and give me a chance to clear all things against me to your satisfaction."[20] In his characteristically effusive manner, John Emerson wrote expansively, attempting to explain every aspect of his handling of army rations. "As to the charge of my giving the hospital pork to Indians," he wrote, "I never directly or indirectly gave an ounce to an Indian out of hospital provisions that I had not accounted for in a proper manner." One possible implication of his statement is that he gave more pork to the Indians, probably through Taliaferro's intermediation, but that the barrels were *accounted for*. In any case, Emerson poured out the anguish of his predicament in long letters of over-explanation. The context of the complaint seemed to implicate his servants, Dred and Harriet. Dr. Emerson continued: "Sometimes during the winter a poor hungry Indian would come to the hospital and beg for something to eat. I would purchase a loaf of bread at the bakehouse and would request of the cook in the kitchen if there was any cold meat to give him a small piece to appease his hunger, which never amounted to more than an ounce or two and which I returned to the hospital tenfold. All given away did not amount to more than five or six pounds and which was given by me through the purest motives."[21]

Harriet was most likely to have been directly implicated in any incident concerning food and the Indians, since she was the person most likely to have carried out his directives. She certainly knew the Indians as individuals better than anyone inside the fort. Even if the doctor or the matron was responsible for the hospital food stores, Harriet was more likely to be expected to deal with the begging Indians, given her status. She must have known a few words of Dakota. Certainly she had heard the begging words many times. The instinct of her former master, Agent Taliaferro, had been to provide them food whenever possible, and she had been trained in his household. Whatever the truth about the missing pork, Harriet and Dred had been there, and probably in the midst of the transaction.

Now that these dealings had brought about bad fortune, the Emersons may have sought to distance themselves from Harriet. Her former master, Taliaferro, had often implored others with surplus to donate food to the Dakota. (Taliaferro's diary attests to his repeated efforts to persuade everyone he knew with access to food stores to use a part of them to ease the Indians' desperate need.) If the Emersons regretted yielding to his appeals, Harriet was the last remaining person representing that connection. Often slaves were seen as extensions of their former masters and punished for association with misfortune in a transference of feelings.[22] Emerson's anguish and stress over his predicament was palpable in his letters, and it would be surprising if it didn't spill over onto Harriet.[23] This sort of transference of feelings of frustration was unfair, but a privilege that masters sometimes allowed themselves, by virtue of their position. By spring, Dred and Harriet were sent away to serve an in-law, and the unemployed doctor had three fewer mouths to feed. Given his untimely death, they probably never saw him again.

"This trifling circumstance has been magnified...and used to my disadvantage....In the presence of God, I never directly or indirectly gave away or squandered to the amount of one cent the public property. Ask Col. Davenport,"[24] Emerson protested in his letters.

Emerson's situation was a bureaucratic bind. Only officers actively serving the army could request an inquiry. Because he had been discharged by a reduction in force, he had no way to clear his name. Because an allegation besmirched his reputation within the corps, he couldn't be reappointed. He could only clear his name if he was reappointed—but on the damaging, but unchallengeable record, he could not be heard.[25] There was no way back into the surgeons' corps that had ejected him.

Without a regular income, Emerson could be expected to do what most cash-strapped Louisians did: rent out his slaves for money, if he could, or, if not, turn them loose to find their own sources of hire and support. After all, his military paycheck had once given him a salary plus a stipend for a servant. Now he received neither. Selling the Scotts in St. Louis was not an option unless he was prepared to ship them south. St. Louis buyers were wary of slaves known to have lived in the North because they were entitled to be set free by law, if they sued. Rachael's case had set this precedent for Fort Snelling slaves years before.[26] Thus, sellers could not warrant title for such bondsmen.[27]

Far easier than trying to sell the Scotts was simply letting them "work out"—letting them fend for themselves for a while until the situation changed; perhaps they bought back some of their own time. They would remain his slaves legally, but as slaves without assured sources of food, clothing, and lodging.[28] Over the winter of Emerson's great disappointment, it's possible that the Scotts stayed on the 19-acre homestead on Manchester Road—but it is more likely that they were sent out.

In the months after his discharge, Emerson did not seem able to establish himself in medical practice in St. Louis. With his many social contacts, one would have thought he'd have found a place there. But he never did. The circumstances of his discharge, advertised no doubt by the very men he had approached in St. Louis to aid him, probably further damaged his reputation, and there was no shortage of doctors in the city—just a shortage of clients who could pay.

Dr. Emerson decided to move back to the place where his military career began, near the decommissioned Fort Armstrong, midway between St. Louis and Fort Snelling. He still had property claims there on the river's Iowa shore, and development was finally starting west of the river. One new town was named for his friend Davenport and the other for his friend LeClaire. These towns offered Emerson fresh opportunities to establish himself as a doctor and perhaps to make his fortune. By spring 1843, Dr. Emerson ran advertisements in the local Iowa newspaper offering his services as a physician. He took rooms at the grand hotel that his friends had recently built. No longer entitled to wear the army surgeon's uniform, he hired a local tailor to make him a distinguished new coat suitable for civilian life.[29] What is more, by April, it was clear that Irene was pregnant again. As further evidence of his blossoming prospects, Emerson began construction of a new house in Davenport—not just an ordinary house, but a grand house by local standards, built by the best local craftsmen. By July 1, when the army fully rejected his final application, Dr. John Emerson, civilian, had begun a new life in the newly founded river town. During 1843 the year he established himself there the Scotts remained in St. Louis in service to a new master.[30] Mistress Irene stayed in St. Louis, too, waiting for the new house to be completed and for a new baby to be born.

Soon another Sanford sister, Henriette Clarke, and her children arrived in St. Louis from a frontier fort. Henriette was pregnant again, and she moved in with the Emersons. Her officer husband was supposed to be at Fort Leavenworth with his troops, but he was often sick and regularly returned to St. Louis on sick leave.[31] Henriette and the children settled in with her sister on the Manchester Road, waiting to be delivered of her next child.[32]

CHAPTER 23

1843 Interlude: Jefferson Barracks between Wars of National Expansion

T HAT SPRING, A third Sanford sister, Mary, and her officer husband, Capt. Bainbridge, arrived in St. Louis from Florida under circumstances much more favorable than the doctor's. The Bainbridges had introduced Dr. Emerson to his wife, when Irene visited them in Louisiana in search of a husband. Since then Capt. Bainbridge had enjoyed a plum assignment recruiting in New York but he had reached Florida just in time to see some action and the end of the war.[1] Soon after he rejoined his unit, the third infantry, it was feted in Tallahassee as the war's heroes.[2] What fortunate timing! Now Capt. Bainbridge's unit returned from the war in high spirits,[3] and it was assigned to Jefferson Barracks, south of St. Louis—exactly where Dr. Emerson had long desired to be.

The Bainbridges needed servants at the barracks, and they took on Dred and his family. Thus, the Scotts left the city and went to live again at an army post—this time the largest and best maintained facility in the west. Jefferson Barracks was located on the Mississippi River, 11 miles south of the city.[4] Dred would stay in the captain's service for the next three years.

In their work lives, servants like Harriet and Dred had to accommodate the new personalities, preferences, agendas, and needs of their succession of masters and mistresses.[5] At Jefferson Barracks, the couple's primary tasks were keeping house for a master and mistress who were a very popular couple in the military social set and entertained often.

Capt. Henry Bainbridge was 40, and his pretty wife, Mary, was just 25. Bainbridge was a military blueblood, though his family was mostly navy. (He also carried a famous name. Commodore Bainbridge, a relative of his, was credited with winning the American war against the Barbary pirates.) The middle-aged captain, educated at West Point, had acquired a taste for the finer things that his education and birth had offered him. Although he was considered a fine officer, he was settled in his comforts, as Dred would later learn.[6] He had a liberal turn of mind and read widely, particularly esoteric new works. He enjoyed socializing with other officers in erudite conversation and evening salons, along with his charming wife. Bainbridge seems to have been a reasonably good master to the Scotts, and Dred later described him as "a good man."[7]

The lucky captain was indeed well placed at Jefferson Barracks. He got along wonderfully well with his commanding officer, who had been his West Point roommate. Major E. A. Hitchcock was the more ambitious of the two men, and he had risen very rapidly in the military ranks to take charge of the third infantry. Bainbridge showed him no jealousy; instead, he linked himself to Hitchcock's rising star. Bainbridge was sufficiently comfortable. After all, he had been able to remain in the army (unlike his unlucky brother-in-law) when the war ended.

Mary Sanford Bainbridge, Mistress Irene's younger sister, was a young, lively, and attractive feminine complement to her husband. She was considered one of the brightest stars among the officers' ladies.[8] Her company was sufficiently prized that she was often seated beside the distinguished visiting male guest at official dinners and social occasions. Though married more than a decade, the Bainbridges were not burdened with children, as, for example, were the Kearneys with their 11.[9] Parties, dinners, conversations, visiting ladies, the officers' society, and, from time to time, matchmaking were Mrs. Bainbridge's primary interests. She filled her life with the active social engagement calendar of a pretty and popular military wife.

Mistress Mary often accompanied her husband from posting to posting—not to endure the hardships with him but to enliven them. In the marrying manner of all the Sanford sisters, she had met the captain at a fort in Arkansas when she was just a teenager, visiting her older married sister. She followed Capt. Bainbridge to Natchitoches and to New York, and she was with him in Florida, living comfortably in Tallahassee, for the conclusion of the war. The concluding days of the Seminole War were particularly dazzling as the state capital celebrated victory. Mistress Mary had occupied a glittering role in the limelight there. The Florida governor, a widower, had designated her his hostess for some celebrations.[10] Even her husband's superior, Maj. Hitchcock, described her as the cleverest lady on the scene.[11]

In the clubby Bainbridge household, the Scotts fulfilled the basic chores and assisted their new masters' social lives, grooming them to look their best and serving when they entertained guests. With Dred as valet and a reasonably good cook[12] and Harriet's training in Mrs. Taliaferro's secrets of an innkeeper's daughter, the Scotts supported their new master and mistress in a headier social scene than they had seen in some time. As Dred cared for the captain's horse, his uniform, and his boots, Harriet undoubtedly served as Mistress Mary's dresser for the parties, helping her style her hair and lacing her into the tight bodices of her flowing gowns. Dred was no longer listed on other officers' pay slips, and Harriet was not listed at all.[13] Persons of Capt. Bainbridge's rank were entitled to receive support for only one servant, but they were more likely to have exclusive arrangements with their servants rather than sharing them with others, like lieutenants did.[14] Ranking as a captain, Bainbridge was entitled to a desirable choice of rooms in the red brick officers' quarters. By tradition, officers of the same rank were grouped together, so the Bainbridges' neighbors were other captains in the third infantry,[15] although, socially, they seemed to see Maj. Hitchcock most often.[16] Surrounded by friends and allied closely with the chain of command, the Third Infantry set at Jefferson Barracks was a very congenial group, and the couple Harriet and Dred served was at its center.

In this household of socially active adults, it was important that five-year-old Eliza not make noise that might upset a master and mistress unaccustomed to children and seeking the refined company of adults.[17] Children were usually expected to be quiet and keep out of sight, and servants' children were even less likely to be indulged. The five-year-old girl was old enough to be left to her own devices and even to help in the kitchen, though she must have had playmates among the other families.

The social life was very active at the barracks that year.[18] Most of the third infantry was there, joining the fourth infantry. More than 30 officers returning from war were joined by their wives, children, and servants. Those officers without wives were actively thinking of marrying during this time of peace, and Mistress Mary was willing to oblige them by making introductions. This was military life at its best. No wonder Dr. Emerson had sought so often to be stationed here. In gallant fashion, the gentlemen of the fourth infantry threw a party for the ladies of the third.[19] As "the cleverest lady" of the third, Mistress Mary must have been the evening's favored guest. If things ever grew dull at the barracks, the city of St. Louis was just a carriage ride away, an especially desirable attraction for officers accustomed to the deprivation of either isolated western frontier posts or the swamp camps of the Florida war. This lucky community of officers had survived the war, been given credit for winning it, and escaped the reduction in force that felled many of their colleagues. Now they enjoyed the good life at the most sought after post in the west. The military community embraced the peace with exuberance. They reveled in their good fortune and each other's good company.

Everything about the place was pleasant and in moderation. Though the troops drilled daily on the parade grounds, military duties seemed to weigh less heavily here on everyone. The climate at this midpoint of the Mississippi River was moderate. Jefferson Barracks seemed more like a college campus than a fortified installation. It sat high on a sloped hill, overlooking the river and the Illinois bottomland. Red brick buildings occupied three sides of a square that opened toward the river. Surrounded by rolling green posture and lined with trees and gardens, it was scene of well-run military order within a setting of pastoral domestic tranquility. The post housed everything that the troops passing through would need: a hospital, dispensary, mess hall, storerooms, and sufficient officers' quarters for an entire village of their families.[20] Morale was high and discipline easy.[21] Even whiskey consumption was down.[22] Moreover, extreme and harsh penalties for infractions and desertions were no longer needed. Men who disobeyed regulations were generally sent to march the green grass of the parade ground peacefully from one end to the other, from dawn to dusk, to pay their penance.

As western headquarters for more than a decade, Jefferson Barracks served as the staging area for every U.S. military engagement on the national horizon. From here, troops were sent to the Blackhawk War in the mid 1830s, to the second war against the Seminoles most recently, and within two years, Capt. Bainbridge's unit would be sent to the Mexican War. Wherever troops were needed on the nation's expanding frontier, the army outfitted and prepared them at Jefferson Barracks. As the staging area for troop deployments, this western headquarters also served as a clearinghouse for the many slaves held by army officers in the west as they transferred in and out.[23] Army officers dispatched to the wilderness frontier would require slaves as household help, and those slaves could be acquired while at Jefferson Barracks.[24]

Only a single incident disturbed the summer's tranquility,[25] but it placed the Scotts' master in the center of a national maelstrom. In keeping with Capt. Bainbridge's temperament, the incident was one of official leniency. Capt. Bainbridge commanded F Company with the help of two junior officers,[26] one of whom was Brevet 2nd Lt. D. C. Buell, a short, stocky young man from West Point with no sense of humor.[27] Buell was arrested for striking one of his men with a sword and cutting off part of the man's ear.[28] Similar actions of over reaction had ruined other young officers' careers. The entire officer corps was familiar with the case of junior officer, Lt. E. K. Kirby, the man who had risen from the dead—court-martialed, discharged, reinstated with family influence, though his reputation was always tarnished—and Harriet and Dred knew Lt. Kirby personally from a winter spent at Fort Snelling.

Army rules required that Buell be tried by court-martial. No doubt Dred and Harriet prepared the captain's dress uniform, as they had Dr. Emerson's when the doctor was called upon to defend those accused. This junior officer's trouble also reflected badly on Bainbridge. The tribunal, including the captain, acquitted the impulsive young lieutenant on the grounds of self-defense: his blows were no greater than necessary.[29] The judges were content to let the matter rest. Life was good; live and let live. There was no reason to impose a harsh penalty or to upset things, and so they adjourned.[30]

The higher-ups reviewing the sentence were dissatisfied, however, that impetuous young Buell had gotten off so lightly, and they started a series of appeals and countermeasures. Gen. Winfield Scott, known as a stickler for detail and an "enemy" of Commander Hitchcock,[31] took the unusual action of ordering the military court to be revived to explain their decision. The panel members took this as an affront. They were not obligated to give reasons, according to the rules, and they felt their integrity was impugned. They protested rather than comply. In a letter to Washington, they accused the general of acting outside his authority.[32] The series of appeals from the military tribunal to Washington that summer presaged the several contested stages in the Scotts' own lawsuit, begun three years later. As servants attending to a master in the hot seat, it was a lesson for the Scotts in the stress of prolonged disputes, hierarchical rules, allegiances, and the national notoriety that can come from appeals. Every dispute couched in rules rather than facts eventually got appealed to Washington. Jurisdictional rules contests became the most protracted. The dispute pitted the local officer corps against the Washington military establishment. The stakes rose the higher the protest went. Both sides dug in. The Scotts' lawsuit later evolved in much the same way. The Buell affair went public when the secretary of war sided with Gen. Scott, accusing Bainbridge, among others, of failing in his duty to convict Buell. The panel members reacted by writing Missouri senator Thomas Hart Benton, prompting a congressional investigation.[33] The case became less about 2nd Lt. Buell than about the turf battles of the army's elite, just as the Scotts' cases would become less about them than about sectional tensions, states rights, and federal jurisdiction. Nonetheless, the actors' fates were at its core and hence they were most vulnerable.

The usually complacent Master Bainbridge was beside himself. The 40-year-old captain worried that his career was on the line. He sought out Commander Hitchcock in whom to confide about his anxiety. Hitchcock promised to back his friend, telling Bainbridge if it went badly, it would go badly for all of them. The commander reassured Bainbridge that they could prevail together.[34]

The Scotts must have worried about how this highly publicized dispute might affect them. Each turn of the rising stakes of the contest was probably felt viscerally in the Bainbridges' quarters when the anxious master was at home. Although the captain didn't own the Scotts, their stability depended upon his position in the army. They had closely observed the career traumas of two masters: Dr. Emerson, who experienced near nervous collapse at his involuntary discharge, and Taliaferro, who spun into an angry, manic frenzy even as he voluntarily resigned. If the captain lost his job, would they end up with another master as good as he was? Would they be on the street again, sold, or in some worse situation?

The president of the United States finally stepped in to call a halt. The matter was dropped. (Master Taliaferro had always placed his faith in the president to sustain him.[35]) Capt. Bainbridge was relieved. At home in the army, he'd have been no more fit for civilian life than Dr. Emerson. He'd dodged a bullet. The good life went on as before.

On a July Sunday, the Bainbridges attended the Unitarian Church in town with Commander Hitchcock, the pregnant Mrs. Emerson, and other friends. Dred probably drove them into town. Along the way, they picked up Dr. Beaumont's daughter, Sarah.[36] There was talk among the friends that day that the youngest Sanford brother, a navy officer, might propose marriage to the much-sought-after Miss Beaumont. Both Mistress Mary and Mistress Irene were keen to see their younger brother well married, and the Beaumonts were very prominent people.[37]

The bachelor Commander Hitchcock was also interested in Sarah's hand, although he was a family friend more than twice her age. Perhaps the talk that she might marry another set him off because Hitchcock noted the conversation in his journal. Then, sitting quietly in church that day, he became so ill that he had to leave. Doctor Beaumont insisted that the sick commander stay with them rather than return to the Barracks that night.[38] Most likely, the Bainbridges returned home that evening in the buggy driven by Dred, talking between themselves about the commander's sudden affliction. It was something for Mistress Mary, the matchmaker, to ponder.

As the Third Infantry officers had defended their integrity in their handling of Buell's court-martial, the Fourth Infantry officers located in another block of the officers' barracks began fighting over gentlemanly integrity in a case involving a young black servant woman. The incident created enough of a stir at the barracks to call for a court-martial, so it could not have escaped Harriet and Dred's notice. When the young servant woman, Amanda, was found absent from her sleeping quarters for several nights, her master, Major Staniford, investigated. Staniford told others that he would strip her down to the skin and beat her until she told him where she had gone. Whether he did or not, Amanda disclosed that Lt. Prince had paid her three dollars to sleep with him four times. Staniford's other servant, Charley, corroborated the story. Still others had seen Lt. Prince wink at the servant girl when she entered a room to serve water.[39]

The flap that resulted revealed what actions were considered "conduct befitting a gentleman and an officer," and what was kept quiet. Staniford mentioned his servant girl's claim to several other officers, while they were standing outdoors near open windows of the officer's block where the Fourth Infantry families had their parlors. For this act of communicating the unmentionable, Major Staniford found *himself* called to court-martial, rather than Lt. Prince.[40]

One of the officers told Staniford immediately that such things should not be mentioned, warning him that he would endanger himself.[41] Another officer relayed the information to Lt. Prince, who flatly denied the claim, "on his honor," though not necessarily under oath. Through a series of go-betweens, Lt. Prince challenged Staniford to retract the statement, which Staniford agreed to do if Prince would state that Amanda, the servant girl, had lied. Lt. Prince claimed that he need not stoop so low as to further deny the claims of servants. At this point, Lt. Prince brought charges against Staniford, claiming that the loud embarrassing statement made before the officers' parlor windows was conduct unbecoming an officer. The charges proceeded to court-martial.[42]

The court-martial accounts demonstrate the attempts of all officers involved to avoid delving into the truth of the matter by focusing instead on Staniford's manner of speech. Did he speak too loudly? Did he intend to communicate the lewd circumstances to ladies who might have been in the front parlors?[43] Struck from the deliberation was the central issue of whether Amanda's claim was true. Amanda was at the center of the commotion, but she could not be heard for one significant reason: black servants were not permitted to be witnesses by the tribunal.[44] Neither Amanda, nor the servant Charley, who had seen her enter Prince's quarters, could say what they knew or what they had said. Staniford conceded that he could not prove the truth of his statement (presumably, without her testimony.) In the end, Major Staniford was reprimanded by the court martial for uttering the "exceptionable" words.[45] By the conclusion of the proceedings most of the participants who could speak took turns insulting Amanda. Major Staniford apologized to Lt. Prince, saying that he was wrong to believe a servant who he had once valued, now making the concession that he believed Prince's denial. The court-martial officially lamented that an officer's reputation was besmirched by "a dissolute and abandoned wench."[46] The officers closed ranks by blaming the legally silenced Amanda for the incident. It is not known what became of Amanda.

IN LATE SUMMER, the pregnant Mrs. Emerson left the city to join her husband upriver in Davenport, Iowa. In November, she gave birth to a daughter at their friend's new hotel, where they stayed while waiting for their own house to be finished.[47] Within a month, however, their fortunes changed dramatically and, accordingly, so too did the fortunes of the Scotts.

Just after Christmas, it became clear that the doctor was dying. He quickly drafted a will, leaving his estate to his wife and infant daughter—without mentioning the Scotts. On December 29, 1843, Dr. John Emerson died in the hotel at the age of 40. The big new house they were building for their new life in Iowa was not yet completed. Their baby daughter was 32 days old.

Emerson's rapid death seems to have caught Mistress Irene by surprise. She asked the hotel manager to advance her some cash for expenses.[48] On the last day of the year in 1843, the tall doctor was buried, probably in the new suit of clothes he had commissioned for his civilian life. His was one of the first graves dug in the new Catholic cemetery on the Iowa bottomland west of the Mississippi. His funeral was conducted by the same young priest who had accompanied Bishop Loras during the summer of the Sioux Ojibwa war.[49]

At his death, John Emerson was not necessarily wealthy, but he was certainly a man of prospects. On the threshold of success, he had staked land claims in two states and owned part interest in a steamboat,[50] and he had a line of credit from Sanford, his wealthy brother-in-law, the kind of financial backing that many men lacked.[51] The records for the months leading up to his death show his involvement in numerous land transfers.[52] His two business partners, both successful former fur trade men, were prominent in the area. Emerson had no steady income, however, and his estate was tied up with debts from the expensive new house construction.

Mrs. Emerson exchanged the expansive clothing she had worn during the confinement phase of her pregnancy for black widow's weeds. Relying on her husband's partners to settle his financial affairs there, she and her infant returned to St. Louis. (The great river didn't freeze in solidly at Rock Island, Illinois, so they could take a steamboat back to St. Louis after the funeral.) Irene returned to her father's roof[53] rather than the Manchester Road property owned by her husband. By custom, black crepe hung in the doorway signified a house in mourning. The doctor's wife, at age 30, was now Widow Emerson, the first Sanford sister to lose her husband.

Irene's father, Col. Alexander Sanford, was named executor in probating the doctor's Missouri holdings.[54] The inventory suggests that the house on Manchester Road[55] was scantily furnished by St. Louis standards. The entire inventory consisted of beds and tables.[56] Absent from the inventory was the silver set given to the couple when they married and the silver child's cup. Had it been sold to finance the move to Iowa? Most important, the Missouri probate did not list the Scotts in the inventory at all.[57] They were neither freed nor claimed; they were simply neglected.

It was customary for even slaves to pay condolence calls when masters died.[58] Dred probably drove the Bainbridges in from Jefferson Barracks to pay their respects to Mistress Irene when she returned. Harriet might have ridden along out of simple Christian charity. It was the proper thing to do. If the Scotts were apprehensive about their future, they might have left Eliza behind so Mistress Irene didn't see that the little girl was growing. On the other hand, in their current circumstances, anything could happen.

Dred had spent many years with Dr. Emerson.[59] Emerson had spoken up to secure a stove for them in winter and permitted Dred to earn money of his own. Most important, he often left them alone. To be left alone was to be allowed the luxury of developing one's own family life in privacy.

But now the Scotts had to be uneasily aware of the more basic fact of their existence. If Dred was not free, someone else now owned him, and Dred may very well have been the last person to find out who that was.[60] When a master died, all property interest passed to the heirs and everything about the slaves' lives could change. They could be sold to pay the decedent's debts. The death could dissolve even those slave family ties that had been respected by the master, once the heirs became involved. Dred had experienced this kind of separation from his first wife. The Scotts had no way to know what the doctor's will said. The last they knew the doctor had been in financial straits when he returned from Florida and sent them to the Bainbridges.

The Scotts would want to see for themselves what the widow's intentions for them might be. They were doubtless too vulnerable to ask directly, but they would want to see her face. Although the custom of slavery forbade them from looking directly into her eyes, they would want to watch how she regarded them. Did she cut her eyes when she saw them? Did she inquire after their daughter or pay them any special attention? They would want to read, if they could, her intentions for their family's future.

The Scotts may have contemplated seeking their independence even at this point, though there had been little need for them to act, or react, until now. The doctor had respected their marriage and permitted them to stay together. During his life, remaining in the doctor's service supported their growing family's stability. By now, Harriet may have known that she was pregnant again. In the five years since Eliza's birth, she must have borne at least one son, who had died—a common experience of motherhood in those times.[61] Now she was bringing another child into the world, with greater awareness of its fragility.

While Dr. Emerson lived—as a nominal master, if an absent one—his existence maintained their security. A slave family's options were necessarily constricted by the alternatives available. Choosing to remain with him, if it could be called a choice, represented, for the Scotts, the subordination to one coercive institution—slavery—in exchange for the protected privilege of maintaining their family unity. Their actions were like those of other slaves, who remained where they were even though they already gained the legal grounds to bring a freedom suit.[62] Within the protectorate of the doctor's ownership, the Scotts were able to carve out a sphere of familial independence. Though certainly not free, they were able to remain together, a family stability prized by many slaves. Moreover, having an absent master, who was not unfavorably disposed to them, was a useful cover: it prevented anyone else from bothering them or interfering more malevolently in their lives. No white man would dare to steal their children or bother them as long as they could be said to belong to some respectable white man somewhere. Now, however, with Emerson's death the legal regime of his patrimony no longer gave them cover; instead, remaining in the status as former slaves of a cash-strapped, dead master threatened to separate them.

Although the doctor's frequent absences often left Dred unsupervised, he never took that opportunity to escape. To run away meant permanent exile from loved ones left behind. Fugitives could never return.[63] With one child and another on the way, remaining at Jefferson Barracks wasn't a bad option, considering the alternatives.

Mistress Irene was probably still in shock at her husband's death. He often complained of ailments,[64] but his activity in his last months and the manner in which he seemed to have thrown himself into building a new life in no way indicated impending death. The new grand house, never finished but now no longer needed, and her new baby without a father gave the young widow enough to occupy her thoughts. She probably gave little thought to the servant family and paid them little notice. She had to pack away her own vanished dreams and return to dependence upon her father and elder brother for her material needs, and the sympathy of her several sisters.

FOR THE SCOTTS, January of a new year rolled out amid the uncertainties of their situation. But the sameness of the pattern of their lives at the barracks must have lulled them into tranquility again. Mrs. Emerson had done nothing surprising. They were not asked to pack up, to get ready for sale, or to relocate. They were still needed by the Bainbridges, and so, for the time being, things continued as before. A new baby would soon fill their lives with the immediacy of its physical needs and the intense feeling of regeneration.

At the Bainbridges, social wheels continued to whirl. The officers' dating games became a light farce. New West Point graduates arrived in the spring. Young 2nd Lt. U. S. Grant arrived and began courting his West Point roommate's sister, who lived at a farm a few miles away.[65] The dozen young, unmarried officers at the barracks were the most promising young bachelors in the entire city.[66] Julia Dent, who would become engaged to Ulysses S. Grant, described the excitement when a bevy of new officers arrived at the barracks, "looking so handsome in their brilliant uniforms with epaulettes and aiguillettes, and chapeaux in their hands."[67] Young women of good families fished for invitations to visit the married ladies at the barracks, and Mistress Mary was an accommodating hostess and an effective matchmaker, just as she had been in finding Dr. Emerson for sister Irene. Commander Hitchcock's niece was visiting the city from Nashville, and the astute Mrs. Bainbridge invited her to visit them at the barracks. Caroline Hitchcock, eligible to marry, was on an extended visit from home. She stayed with the Bainbridges for some weeks during both the spring and fall of the year.[68]

An unmarried lady guest needed another as company to make it more discreet and less awkward for several young officers to come calling. There was propriety in numbers. To keep the commandant's niece company, Mistress Mary invited Sarah Beaumont to stay with them as well. Here was Mary Bainbridge's social genius.

Not only was Caroline the commandant's niece (so Hitchcock was grateful for the gesture), but by now, everyone suspected that Sarah was the aging bachelor's secret love. Despite their age difference, the two did have a special relationship, corresponding earnestly and frequently.[69] Bringing both his niece and his secret love to her household was an act designed to put the commander at ease. He could respectably pay calls on his niece and thereby spend more private time with Miss Beaumont. Since returning from Florida, the middle-aged commander had indicated his readiness to marry by dropping broad hints, confiding in several officers' ladies that he believed he really was the marrying type.[70]

For Harriet and Dred, guests meant more housework and certainly fancier dinners. Harriet now had three ladies to assist with their primping, their dresses, and their ironing, as all three sought to look their best. As servants, the Scotts were in a position to overhear the Bainbridges' views as well as their guests' reactions. Masters never bothered to hide their feelings from servants. Instead, it was often prudent to let them in on the social agenda so they knew who was likely to be at home for whom when a gentleman came calling. Thus, the servant couple was probably enlisted in their mistress's designs.

One would expect that they were also drawn in as knowing go-betweens between the ladies and their beaux. Without other means of communication, slaves could be customarily relied upon to carry messages.[71] Their comings and goings went unnoticed, and so they could discreetly transport billets. Sarah Beaumont was accustomed to sending notes to officers.[72] A note passed confidentially to Harriet as she made up the lady's chamber or helped her brush out her hair could be quietly given to Dred, who, in turn, was at liberty to enter any gentleman's quarters in the barracks and deliver the note to the officer whose heart was in question. In the intimate sport of courtship, a young lady's eyes, ears, and confidante was often her maid. Dred could report how the officer had responded. Mary Bainbridge too may have questioned Harriet and Dred about what they knew, what they saw, or what the other servants said. Slaves were sometimes even asked to comment about what they thought of particular gentlemen callers, as if they had a particularly attuned sense of character.[73] They could be trusted to ensure the young ladies' privacy and their reputations, and they might even receive a penny for their efforts. The courting display of visiting bachelors must have provided the Scotts with a source of amusement. In what other setting is body language both so apparent and yet so circumspect in the formalities of propriety? For the Scotts, there was nothing at stake in this charming, harmless theater.

Despite her youth, Sarah Beaumont had already declined several handsome marriage proposals.[74] The rumors were that Sarah declined because she was spoken for by Hitchcock. The commander was well aware of these rumors, but as a stalwart family friend, he protested, albeit weakly. As her father's friend, perhaps his best friend, he had watched Sarah grow up from the time that he and Dr. Beaumont were posted together at Fort Crawford. The eminent Dr. Beaumont, resigned from the army, now had a successful practice in St. Louis and enjoyed worldwide fame for his studies of the stomach.[75]

The farce continued until Sarah sent the commander a message, telling him that she had a secret to tell him. The commander recorded receiving her note in his diary with considerable anticipation.[76] He had been expecting some modest expression of affection from her for some time. He recognized their age difference, but other men his age had proposed to her. He had even jested to her father, to avoid putting the matter too pointedly, that he too might not be out of the running for her hand. The remark was perhaps too coy. The brilliant commander of the army's third infantry, who was able to stand up to the generals and the secretary of war, was acting like an infatuated schoolboy.

When the commander met Sarah at the appointed rendezvous, he was stunned to learn that her secret didn't involve him. More shocking, she told him that she had accepted a marriage proposal from another officer. She had consented to marry Lt. Irwin, a younger man of lesser rank, a subordinate in Hitchcock's own command. Hitchcock was blind-sided. The commander, so adept in plotting strategy, even skilled in winning at military in-fighting, had not seen this coming.[77] The couple had courted so discreetly at the Bainbridges'—under his very nose—that he was unaware that any feeling existed between them, all while he had waited to make his move. He wrote in his diary that as a man of honor, he would do all he could to support the marriage of this fine young couple.[78] His words, however, conveyed a sense of disciplined self-resolve in the context of raw, emotional ambivalence. This, he wrote wistfully in his journal, would at least put an end to the rumors that he had intentions regarding Miss Beaumont.[79]

What caught the commandant by surprise must have been perfectly apparent to Harriet and Dred, who would have known exactly who visited their houseguest. They probably observed how she received him. The social antennae of slaves were attuned to anticipating occurrences, and they had to be observant because of their vulnerability. The body language and emotional registers of all who were their superiors within the household were the necessary details of their existence. Observing a mistress's signal—though perhaps not directly watching—might help a slave anticipate a later emotional outburst (one that could ricochet on them). The Scotts were in an excellent position to anticipate the infantry commandant's surprise and observe his subsequent confusion.

With the announcement of the couple's engagement, the wedding plans could commence. Mrs. Bainbridge had scored another matchmaking success. Commander Hitchcock began to find some of the other officers' sisters very interesting.[80]

That year, the winter evenings in the Bainbridges' quarters were spent entertaining with salons devoted to the supernatural which were referred to as "animal magnetism." Hypnotism, called "magnetic sleep," and communicating with the dead were parlor games of great popularity at the barracks. A medium was in town giving performances, and he and his young female protégée were invited to the barracks to amaze the officers with their supernatural powers of unspoken communication. Hitchcock recounted these evenings, as well as the Bainbridges' presence there.[81] Mary Bainbridge was more likely to be hostess than the bachelor commandant, so these evenings probably occurred in the Bainbridges' parlor, where Dred served the drinks and Harriet prepared a cold buffet.

Sometime that year, Harriet's second daughter, Lizzie, was born. Harriet may have felt more apprehensive about this impending birth than her first.[82] Like her sister, baby Lizzie was probably named for a Taliaferro slave. The name is also on Taliaferro's list.[83] Although born in a slave state, the baby's status drew from her mother's. If Harriet was free, then this baby too inherited the free status, regardless of her place of birth.[84] The laundresses' stories brought hope.

Through the winter, plans were under way for Sarah's wedding. The following spring, Mistress Mary went to the Beaumonts' country home a few days before the wedding to help prepare for the happy event that was the culmination of her matchmaking.[85] It was customary for ladies like Mrs. Bainbridge to take along a maidservant of their own when visiting, especially with all the work to be done for a wedding. Harriet may have accompanied her. The wedding had fewer than a dozen guests in attendance.[86] Commander Hitchcock attended, as a friend of the family.[87] The couple was married at the same Unitarian Church the friends had attended together with the hopeful, pregnant Mrs. Emerson just the previous summer—before so much had changed. (Newly widowed, Mrs. Emerson did not attend.)[88]

The bride was an accomplished pianist who performed regularly for family and friends, and she may have done so to entertain the assembled guests. Dr. Beaumont, who was deaf to most tones by this time, had an unusual way of appreciating her music. While she played, he sat very close to the piano, resting his top teeth on the vibrating sounding board. In this way, he felt the music's vibrations, rather than hearing them, through his teeth.[89] It took a doctor to have invented this means of compensating for deafness. Harriet certainly had never seen such a thing before. It was indeed a curious world of blindfolded psychics who sensed what people held in their hand, doctors who examined the contents of wounded men's stomachs, and deaf men who heard music through their teeth.

ONE MONTH AFTER the wedding, the pleasant interlude at Jefferson Barracks was broken by national politics. American expansion fever now focused on Texas. The country planned to annex territory that Mexico still claimed. Texas had already declared its independence from Mexico, but Mexico refused to acknowledge it. Efforts were under way in Washington to add Texas to the United States. American troops were needed in the southwest, should Mexico decide to try to retain control of the territory.

Hitchcock conveyed the deployment orders to Captain Bainbridge and the other officers at breakfast on April 20, 1844.[90] The regiment was ordered to move downriver to Louisiana and remain alert until needed. The news lit the barracks with excitement. The military objective was to concentrate a force on American soil, near the borders of Texas. The orders indicated haste. The whole infantry was supposed to be ready as soon as a steamboat could be chartered to transport them. All extra belongings—horses, household furniture, everything that could not be taken along—were hurriedly sold or disposed of. Last-minute farewell dinners were given, and officers' families paid up their debts to local merchants and made final courtesy calls. Someone sponsored an impromptu dance, a final fling, and some young officers used the occasion to propose marriage to their sweethearts.

The army expected to go to war, and so families were not necessarily welcome on this deployment. A military campaign meant living in tents, which was not exactly appropriate for officers' ladies. No military barracks existed in the Louisiana piney woods where the men were ordered, and few suitable rooms were available in the nearby towns. It is unlikely that many, if any, officers' wives accompanied the ship.[91]

That Mary Bainbridge did not accompany her husband seems evident from pay slip records, which authorized the St. Louis-based paymaster to disburse the captain's May 1845 salary to his wife, instead of to him at his encampment.[92] The paymaster, A. D. Steuart, maintained his office in St. Louis and traveled the Mississippi River to pay the troops. Mrs. Bainbridge may have been anywhere on his route, but in all likelihood she was in St. Louis, quite probably at her father's farm. The succeeding pay slip, also out of place in the usual numerical ranking, was a payment to her brother-in-law, the sickly Captain John B. Clarke, who was usually recuperating in St. Louis.[93]

It appears that Harriet and her children stayed behind in Missouri, too.[94] Slave women were less useful if the officer's family was not in transit. Slave babies and small children were particularly unwelcome to an army on the move. The officer's pay records demonstrate that most officers who had hired women servants at Jefferson Barracks replaced them with men when the infantries moved out.[95]

On April 27, 1844, Bainbridge, the white officer and Dred, the black bondsman set out aboard an enormous steamship with the entire Third Infantry. Some 350 men, comprising eight companies of infantrymen, were bound for Louisiana.[96] At the last minute, Commander Hitchcock invited the traveling spiritual medium team to accompany them aboard the transport ship. They, too, were bound south for public engagements in New Orleans and would go their own way when they reached port. On the voyage, the team entertained with more parlor tricks in the officers' stateroom.[97]

The skies were drizzling rain when the ship set off. At the pier stood hundreds of ladies, waving their white handkerchiefs in farewell. Harriet was probably there, clutching her infant daughter in the sling with one arm and holding little Eliza's with the other. She must have exchanged prayers and wishes with her husband for his safe return. More important even than saying goodbye, the married servants had to devise a plan about how to find each other again after the war. A servant woman with an insecure position could not necessarily remain independently at any one place for the time her husband spent away with the army. Harriet really didn't belong anywhere in St. Louis. She had no fixed ownership nor kinfolk where she would be welcome to stay. Simply finding each other again would not be easy, when—or if—Dred did return. Although a few servants were simply left at the barracks, they were not assured food there.[98] Dred could perhaps ask after her at Col. Sanford's farm or at the African Church when he came back. But who could tell for sure that they would ever find each other again?[99] Her husband's departure surely bound Harriet to Widow Emerson and the Sanford family as the easiest means of maintaining a tie to him. Although no one might have had a true legal claim to Harriet, the person with the strongest hold on her husband was the young widow. Captain Bainbridge's pay slips give some indication that the family still viewed Dred as their slave. At least one listed him as "Eldred Slave."[100] To maintain her tie to Dred in these circumstances, Harriet had to stay close to the owner who claimed him. She couldn't afford to anger her mistress. She had to go where she was sent. To be separated was hard, but to be lost to each other forever would be worse.

And then they were gone. Shortly after the Third Infantry departed, the Fourth Infantry also was ordered to Louisiana. Jefferson Barracks was practically empty now, cleared out to send American troops to a new war, to conquer a new territory, and to expand the nation. Mary Bainbridge probably remained with Irene to keep her company and to help her with the baby, an ironic setting for the pretty woman who had no children of her own and enjoyed most being the toast of the military circuit. But the party was over. A war was about to begin.

It appears that Harriet was put to work earning wages in town at the home of the Russells instead of returning to the Sanford farm. Colonel Sanford drove Harriet and her babies in a wagon to the Russell house. Mistress Irene made the arrangement with Mrs. Russell, whom she'd known for several years and who also attended the Unitarian Church, like the Beaumonts. The men saw to the financial side of things. Mr. Russell paid Harriet's wages to Col. Sanford, on Irene's behalf.

Did Dred even know exactly where Harriet was? Perhaps he'd had time to ride along with the buggy that delivered her and the children to the Russells, so he would know where they were taken. Separation was a state of enormous uncertainty for servant families, who couldn't determine their own movements or even decide to remain in a single place. Sometimes freedom is the ability to move on; sometimes it is simply the ability to stay put. For the duration, Harriet had neither freedom.

Like many slave mothers, Harriet was on her own with her girls. If she needed Dred, she couldn't get word to him, and he was too far away to help anyway. Still, it was necessary to stay where she was sent in order to be found again. For the two intervening years, Harriet had no way to know whether her husband was alive or dead.

CHAPTER 24

Dred with the Army of Observation and Harriet with the Children in St. Louis

THE STEAMBOAT TRIP to Louisiana took a week. Along the lower Mississippi, Dred could see slaves at work in the sugar and cotton fields. It took little imagination to understand the hard lives they lived. He had once lived that life, as a young man, working an Alabama cotton plantation for the Blow family before being brought to St. Louis.

The large military expedition arrived at the mouth of the Red River, but the Mississippi steamboat was too large for its tributary. All aboard transferred to the smaller steamer and two days later, the troops disembarked and were trucked through the woods with horse teams to break a new camp, 25 miles southwest of Fort Jesup. By May 10, the regiment had established headquarters at a place named in honor of the same war secretary who had feuded with Hitchcock.[1] All that was behind them now. The army was unified in preparing for war.

In mid-June, General Zachary Taylor, who had once commanded Ft. Snelling, arrived to take command of the forces which he named the "Army of Observation." But there was little for the army to observe yet. The troops remained at the temporary camps, hidden in backwoods Louisiana, waiting for the president, or else the upcoming presidential election, to give them a signal. The stay at the temporary camp in Louisiana dragged on for well over a year. The officers fully expected to move nearer to Mexico before winter fell, but out of precaution, they built huts against the colder weather. That turned out to be a wise decision since they remained at that location through the winter.[2] Bainbridge and Hitchcock were close companions during these months of waiting,[3] riding horses together and sharing books. Hitchcock brought along his entire library, which included more than 700 books. The captain read the Book of Mormon, which had caused such excitement in Missouri and the West. Hitchcock meditated on the works of Marcus Aurelius Antoninus, who had been a Roman emperor and had also encamped for a winter with his army, awaiting the time to advance.[4]

In late November, word came that Polk had been elected president. Polk had called for war. The officers received limited word from St. Louis, though Stephen Kearney, the commander of the Western Division, wrote Hitchcock once stressing that the subject of slavery was part of the political deliberation of when and whether to invade Texas:

"There is a very strong feeling in the members from the free States in opposition to the annexation unless upon the expressed understanding...that an equal number of free and Slave states shall be made out of the Country. We shall know the result before long." He added a personal note: " Leiut Irwn of your regt is still at Dr. Beaumont's—I see but little of him. Mrs. I continues well, and has not yet, to my knowledge, increased the number of her family."[5]

Once Polk was inaugurated in March, the signal finally came. The third infantry was ordered to move into Texas along the Gulf coast.[6] As soon as General Taylor heard that Texas voted to join the United States, he was to lead his whole command to the extreme western border of Texas and defend the banks of the Rio Grande. Any armed Mexican troops attempting to cross the river into Texas were to be met with force.[7] When Texas voted as anticipated, the waiting infantries moved out of the Louisiana backwoods to the white sands of the Texas beach. Dred was again in the midst of an army on the move.[8] The third infantry left central Louisiana on July 7, 1845, bound for Texas by way of New Orleans. At New Orleans, the swell of forces overwhelmed the city's barracks. Two weeks later, at 11:00 P.M., the third infantry formed into a line in the street, wheeled into column and, to the inspiring air of their regimental quick-step, played by fife and drum, marched through the late-night streets to their transport. Trailing behind the soldiers, in charge of the officers' gear, were Dred and the other manservants.[9] The moon was just rising as they marched out, gilding the domes and the housetops. As the bayonets glistened in the mellow light, the third infantry left the New Orleans dock at 3 A.M., onboard the steamship *Alabama*,[10] to conquer new territory.

After two days, the ship reached St. Joseph's Island, Texas.[11] In a show of territoriality, a lieutenant raised a pole on the top of the highest sand hill and unfurled the star-spangled banner to cheers and applause from the troops.[12] Dred's unit stayed on the island for several days, finding good water and even fresh oysters for the officers' breakfasts. Because their large ship could not navigate the shallower waters to reach the mainland shore, the companies and their horses had to be shuttled to a smaller steamer and then to even smaller rowboats to land at the beach of Corpus Christi.

One evening in the first week of August, it came time for Capt. Bainbridge to take his men to shore. The shuttle ship arrived quite late.[13] Given the lateness of the hour, the captain opted to remain aboard the larger ship, the *Undine,* for the night. On shore, Commander Hitchcock was expecting Bainbridge, and he sent the landing boat to meet the *Undine* about 10 P.M. The captain sent part of his company with the message that he wished to remain onboard till morning—"to sleep!" The disappointed Hitchcock sent the small boat back, insisting that Bainbridge come ashore, but Capt. Bainbridge returned the messenger again with the note: "As before." Now clearly miffed, Col. Hitchcock ordered Bainbridge ashore.

At 1:00 A.M. the direct order brought Bainbridge to land, with Dred undoubt-edly scrambling to pitch his master's tent and set up his master's cot. Thus, in Capt. Bainbridge's service, Dred was not asked to suffer great deprivation for his master's heroism. Dred's job was to temper the roughness of the encampment for his middle-aged master, a man who appreciated maximum comfort in the circumstances.

Every day more men and tents arrived creating the spectacle of the largest body of men assembled as an American army since the Revolutionary War.[14] All along the white beaches of the Texas coastline, rows of canvas tents, neatly ordered, housed different companies of the army of observation. The rows of light-colored canvas tents and campfires extended all along the sandy white beach for more than a mile. The naval fleet waiting in the Gulf of Mexico regularly restocked the amass-ing troops with stores brought from New Orleans.

Few incidents during those months were memorable enough to be recounted. One morning in late summer, a terrific thunderstorm swept through the beach-side camps with lightning and torrents of rain. The tent city was the only shelter anywhere on the exposed beach for the entire army. The officers' servants were assigned to stay outside to ensure that the tent posts held. In the thick of the storm, a palpable crash and shudder was felt throughout the camp, and a smell of sulfur went through the air. Lightning had struck two of the black servants obediently standing in the rain to hold their masters' tents. One was killed instantly while the other was badly injured.[15] It could have been Dred. There, but for the grace of God...

In January, word finally came to engage the enemy. President Polk ordered the army to advance again, this time beyond the Rio Grande. Since the massive numbers could not be mobilized overnight, it was March before General Taylor signaled the move to Matamoras, 150 miles south, to establish the next camp.

During this time of mobilization, Dred was sent home. When the army of observation finally broke camp to march south, Dred was not with it.[16] Dred said that once the fighting broke out, the captain sent him back to St. Louis.[17] The beach at Corpus Christi was perfectly deserted. The bright waters of the bay looked as sweet as ever. The army, encamped there for seven months and 11 days, was march-ing into war, but Dred was already aboard a vessel bound for home without see-ing combat. He had served the advancing American army in Texas as part of the largest military gathering in American history and he returned now to his family in the slave state of Missouri. The route back went through New Orleans, aboard the large ships shuttling supplies to the area of war. Other steamboats relayed per-sonnel and material up the Mississippi to St. Louis. Dred may have traveled with other servants sent out of the range of fire. As the nation's troops advanced into Mexico and mobilized for battle, Dred Scott made his way in the opposite direc-tion, steaming against the current to St. Louis, back to his wife and family.[18]

We don't know exactly how Harried managed during Dred's absence. What was announced as an urgent military campaign stretched on for almost two years. Left behind, her primary task these years was ensuring her children's survival. If she didn't watch out for them, no one would. With one child still nursing at her breast and a six-year-old to feed, clothe, and care for, the conscientious mother did whatever was necessary. There was more than enough work to see to the children's changing needs.[19]

Harriet probably lived where she worked, at the home of a wealthy grocery merchant on 4th Street. Mrs. Russell[20] later testified that the Scotts came to work for her from Capt. Bainbridge's employ about two years before the lawsuit began, which corresponds to the time Capt. Bainbridge departed with Dred. There is some ambiguity about the timing because Mrs. Russell's deposition wasn't taken until the second trial and she described both Scotts being brought to her home in a wagon by Col Sanford. The greatest uncertainty in the available facts is whether Harriet spent these two years at the Russells or somewhere else in St. Louis, but the Russells are the persons whom both Scotts claimed enslaved them. When Col. Sanford brought Harriet to the Russells, they lived in a house on 4th Street, just two blocks from the courthouse. She was probably still waiting there when her husband came back two years later. During these two years, Harriet became familiar with living in town.

Again her masters' agendas, social life, and personalities determined the rhythm, tenor, and atmosphere of her new life. Master Russell and his partner, William Bennett, were in the retail grocery business like dozens of other merchants in town. Old Col. Sanford was in the same line of business briefly,[21] and the families had once been neighbors.[22] Russell and Bennett owned a warehouse on the wharf, filled with basic and specialty goods from around the globe.[23] The Russells' store advertised coffee from Rio and Havana, Sumatra peppers and other exotic spices, bottles and casks of Holland gin, Muscat, Claret, Tenerife, and Madeira wines and brandies.[24]

The Russell household was unlike any in which Harriet had lived and served before.[25] Whereas the army barracks was a world dominated and run by men, with ladies only socializing in the parlours of the predominantly masculine terrain,[26] the Russells' extended family household was a ladies' world of pampered merchants' wives and dreamy preadolescent girls. The extended Russell-Bennett-Dubois family occupied three adjacent houses on 4th Street, tied together by three sisters and the merchant husbands they had married. Mr. Russell and Mr. Bennett had gone into business together in Ohio and "each had married a beautiful Creole girl"—one of the Dubois sisters.[27] The extended family had moved west to St. Louis, where they were very successful. The adjacent households may have functioned as a family compound.[28] One visitor noted that the families lived in "splendid houses set in park like grounds,"[29] and they had the means to live very well.[30] They depended neither on military shipments, nor hunting, nor raising their own food. The best of everything was available to them through their own store. But though the Russells were people of considerable means, they were not fabulously wealthy like the Chouteaus, so for them it was even more important to display their wealth to their neighbors. They furnished their home with carpets from Brussels, bronze and marble statues, and many, many pieces of marble-topped mahogany and rosewood furniture.[31]

Mrs. Russell, Harriet's new mistress, was the middle sister of three, all of whom were reputed to be extremely vain about their appearances.[32] Sister Cate Bennett was considered the most beautiful woman in St. Louis at the time, and she and Sister Josephine had daughters as well. Among sisters and their several daughters, the subjects of dressing, courtship, and marrying well were surely their most important concerns, as they generally were for women of their class. For Mistress Russell, preparing her pretty, blonde Almira for a fine marriage was particularly important because her younger sister Josephine had married badly at first.[33] Josephine's marriage to a wealthy local Frenchman was annulled within a year, and she suffered the indignity of returning to her parents' home. It was important that Almira not make such a mistake. A few years later when Almira did marry it would be in a fancy society wedding to a very promising young military officer.[34] The Russells moved in the city's best circles, and the girl cousins probably attended one of the city's schools of instruction for young ladies.[35] Almira not only played piano, she also learned to play the organ.[36]

With the Russells' two children already school-age and some slaves of their own, Harriet was undoubtedly hired to do the brute work of laundry. St. Louis ladies often hired an additional servant just for laundry.[37] As a hireling, Harriet's relationship to Mistress Russell would likely be distant.[38] Where once Harriet may have shared her lonely mistress's confidences, when both were marooned by snow drifts at an isolated house for days on end, or participated in her matchmaker mistress's agenda at the barracks, it was unlikely that she had any personal relationship with Mrs. Russell at all. Mistresses preferred to favor their own slaves with the more trusted role of chambermaid.[39]

The number of household servants not only increased the social distance between Harriet and her mistress, in turn, it provided her with greater contact with the servant group. There were seven slaves among the three houses, living in the alley behind and below the red brick houses and probably more in the alley behind the adjacent houses.[40] As the hireling bondswoman, Harriet was unlikely to be treated as well as the household's own slaves, who by custom had first claim to the families' clothing castoffs.

From the Russells' front door on 4th Street, one could see and hear slaves being sold on the courthouse steps, just two blocks away. The auctioneer raised a loud voice to draw a crowd near to see the bodies of people for sale that day. Sometimes the huckster was a private entrepreneur who dealt in human property in the city; sometimes it was the sheriff himself.[41] One group of 26 slaves, brought from Mississippi, were regularly sold on the courthouse steps. They had been promised freedom in their master's will. They sued to enforce their promise of freedom under the will of their former owner, Milton Duty. But for several years, until the lawyers, the executor, and the heirs could sort things out, they were auctioned every July—to earn their keep as well as to generate money for the estate. All around town, one came upon different persons who were Milton Duty's slaves, leased to temporary masters, just as Harriet herself was now.[42]

Around the corner from the Russells was a familiar face: Catherine from Fort Snelling, once Lt. Thompson's wife, then expelled from Fort Snelling when she was found under the bed of another officer. Catherine was now Catherine Anderson, married to an Englishman who distilled liquors, and she had four more children.[43] Who knows how she had parted with Lt. Tappan and married William Anderson.

The summer that Dred left, the rivers were rising upstream,[44] and June brought the greatest flooding that St. Louis had ever experienced.[45] All along the shore, the great river swelled up and became a sea covering the Illinois bottomlands and the city's many dockside warehouses and homes. Flooding drove the animals dwelling on the littoral lands to higher ground, so that snakes and rats overran the basements in advance of the river's waters and remained nested in low-lying areas when the waters receded. All along its length the great river reclaimed the bottomlands. The inundation soaked out the roots of trees, toppling them where they stood and sweeping even massive trunks along in the current. The foundations of houses swayed loose and the river carried large objects and debris along its path heading south. Even the dead, buried in graveyards along the river bottomland, were loosened from their resting places and coffins were sent floating downstream in a grim spectacle. Dr. Emerson was buried upstream in a new cemetery on low-lying bottomland, which was sufficiently ruined by the flood to eventually be relocated to higher ground. The swollen river uprooted even the buried past.

The Russells' home, standing four streets back from the river, sat safely along the same gradient as the courthouse, and the waters stopped just before they reached this higher ground. But the slaves, living on lower ground behind 4th Street, may have found their quarters inundated. By mid-July, when the waters subsided and the slime remained caked to the walls, citizens were advised to use disinfectants to purify those living areas inundated, due to the sharp increase in the number of deaths in town.[46]

Little is known of specific events in the Russells' household, but the laundry schedule in stable households like theirs was a set routine. Monday was wash day, the heaviest and hardest day of the week. It was followed by days of starching, ironing, and mending that also entailed sewing freshly laundered collars on each of the master's shirts.[47] Six-year-old Eliza could watch the baby or help as a fire tender for the washing.[48] On Sundays, Harriet probably found her way with the city's other African Americans to the African Church, located just three blocks away in the opposite direction from the courthouse.[49]

At the center of the congregation was the Reverend Meachum, a remarkable but complex man who was financially successful and committed to raising up the black community. He had founded the Black Baptist Church in St. Louis more than a decade earlier.[50] At some point Harriet joined the Baptist Church, though Dred was never listed as a member.[51]

The Reverend Meachum was roughly Dred's age, 51, but larger in stature and stronger.[52] Meachum had pulled himself out of slavery by luck and hard work and then gone on to buy several other family members from enslavement.[53] The industrious Meachum, together with his sons, had found a profitable niche making barrels for the western markets, since barrels were necessary for all kinds of steamboat shipments departing St. Louis. (The salt pork and flour arriving at the Indian agency may have been packed in Meachum's barrels.) From his profits he financed the purchase of still other slaves, with the understanding that they would work off their payment to him. But Meachum did not advocate abolition, insurrection or legal reform. Advocating abolition was illegal in Missouri.[54] Meachum required the slaves he purchased to pay off their purchase price by monthly payments. If they didn't work to repay him, he had them tied up in his house.[55] Although he had freed half a dozen slaves over the previous decade through this "working off" method, three of his slaves sued him for their freedom, insisting that they were free by operation of the Northwest Ordinance. Surprisingly, but unsuccessfully, he actively resisted their freedom claims in court.[56] By 1840, he was the head of a household responsible for 13 free black people, and he enjoyed a large following among African Americans in the city.[57]

The Baptist minister advocated independence through hard work. He preached and wrote out his specific vision for improving the condition of the people.[58] His philosophy was simple: each able-bodied person should raise himself up by industry, save money to buy his freedom, and then, in turn, save to buy the freedom of others.[59] He mixed his message of hard work and self-reliance with an inspirational message of the possibilities of collective action. The Reverend Meachum spoke to his congregation of industry and idleness, which he called "King Cure-all" and "Mr. Pull-down-all."

"Providence has placed us all on the shores of America.... Industry and education should be your concern about this young race,"[60] Meachum wrote. "Come friends...you are not getting much by sitting looking into that little fire you have." "Let us attend to the things that are calculated to elevate the colored citizens of America," he preached. "Who owns all the fine houses? Do the colored citizens? No, with few exceptions, you are too idle or too wasteful. With industry you may have as good a farm as your neighbors. You are to be a nation in time to come, let us be an industrious people."

The Reverend Meachum advocated members of the community becoming farmers, which he claimed was the most independent life open to them.[61] One can assume that Harriet knew better than her minister that working a stake of land, as the Coldwater squatters had, meant nothing if the government soldiers could burn you out. It also wasn't as easy for a black person to stake a claim on lands open for settlement. Little did Reverend Meachum realize that states like Illinois were preparing legislative measures to close their doors to new black immigrants. Although the federal homestead laws permitted blacks to cultivate a claim on lands that the government opened for settlement, the state laws did not necessarily permit them to enter unless they had documented freedom papers *and* were able to post a substantial bond upon entering.[62]

The Reverend Meachum also focused his parishioners' attention on the younger generation, advising parents to plan well their children's futures. He urged mothers in particular to "wake up on this matter."[63] Of daughters, he wrote: "the dear little damsels, so near and dear to the mother. Touch one of them, and you touch her heart string at once. Then, dear mother, if you love your daughter, show it in doing all you can.... Teach her the right way to live in this world that she may be happy in the world to come.... Let them know that there is one right way. Industry is right, then make them industrious. You are accountable to God for the raising of the child."[64]

These messages weren't lost on Harriet. They resonated well with the themes she had heard so often from Taliaferro about labor being the path that the Dakota needed to follow to achieve independence. Diligent work was the means to self-sufficiency and independence. The message conveyed the hope that the future was in the hands of the industrious. The Reverend Meachum had in mind that Easter Monday be set aside as a national day of recognition for black families.[65] It would be Easter week when Harriet and Dred eventually filed for freedom.

The African Church provided social networks as well as spiritual inspiration. Singing out provided both slaves and freedmen with an exultant release. Occasionally, the singing brought complaints from the surrounding white communities, but generally whites tolerated the African church as a better alternative to having their slaves hanging around in the streets and getting into mischief on the Sabbath. At the church there were sermons, prayer sessions, and even a school to teach reading and writing.[66] Both free and enslaved Americans of African descent sought out the church for sustenance and support. "The church, in its prayer meetings, classes...and services, provided opportunities for slave women belonging to different owners to meet."[67] At church, slaves developed networks that could also transmit valuable information about survival, self-help, literacy, freedom, and the law.[68] And, of course, one could always catch up on the gossip. Several church members had successfully established their freedom by filing suit and a lawyer named Murdoch was bringing suit for several others in the community.[69]

On those days that she washed at the river,[70] standing on the shore with tubs full of the Russells' weekly laundry, Harriet could see the green bank of the free state of Illinois on the far side, just a mile away. Probably at her side, playing on the muddy shore, were six-year-old Eliza and baby Lizzie, just learning to crawl. The Mississippi was too vast and had a current too powerful to swim across. Though there were other ways to cross. There were people in town who could aid in escape. A year after Dred left, one party of escaping slaves was caught not far upstream.[71] Three men were seen pushing off in a skiff under cover of darkness. An ordinary citizen stopped them before they could get off into the current. Two more people, hiding on the shore awaiting their turn, ran before they were caught. No doubt, the captured runaways were whipped, and the courts dealt with the men who tried to help runaways.[72] To escape was to be hunted down with dogs. Once caught, the hapless person was beaten and dragged back to jail.[73] Runaways, regularly listed in the newspaper, were caught more often than not.[74] Those who tried and failed were whipped severely.

Harriet's attachment to her children must have made escape impossible for her.[75] How could she contemplate fleeing alone when her two small children depended on her? The physical strains placed on her body over the previous eight years, from bearing children and nursing two through infancy, would likely make escape unthinkable. How could she leave her babies? What would become of them? A responsible mother needed to make sure they were nurtured, fed, sheltered, and protected from abuse.[76] Some bondswomen did abandon their children. The Bates's Nancy had run away, leaving her four children behind to everyone's surprise.[77] But most mothers did not.[78] It was too overwhelming to muster the will and the physical strength necessary to break away. When Lucy's mother attempted to run away, she first promised her child she would return to purchase her, but fearing that her master might wreak vengeance the children, she returned.[79] In her autobiography, Lucy reflected upon this sentiment in explaining the dilemmas preventing mothers from escaping to freedom: "And so the mothers... have been ever slain through their deepest affections" for their children.[80]

Some slaves contemplating escape turned to fortunetellers for advice. An old slave named Frank told fortunes for those considering a break for free territory.[81] Harriet probably turned to her minister for counsel instead. The Reverend Meachum knew what awaited there on the far side of the river—and that runaways were not necessarily welcome. He knew that legal papers were necessary, and he would advise saving money to buy freedom.[82] But Harriet's family had lived in free territory. Under the law, that entitled them to freedom. It should have been as simple as that. As Harriet stirred a boiling pot of wet clothing, she probably contemplated the options swirling around her and began to make a plan. Still, for the time being, it was best to stay where she was in order to be found again. Dred was still far away with the army, and she was lucky to be able to remain in town.

IN EARLY MARCH 1846, Dred arrived at the dock by steamboat. He had accumulated some money during his two years with the "Army of Observation,"[83] intending to buy his freedom.[84] He returned to his wife and family triumphant. Dred was alive and back from the war unharmed. Reunited, they could resume plans of their own. His return catalyzed their action.

Soon thereafter, Dred asked Mrs. Emerson whether he could purchase his freedom. Both Dred and Mrs. Emerson recalled the conversation, but it would have been up to Dred to raise the topic.[85] Neither account mentions Harriet or the children. That omission might have been intentional.[86] Perhaps the Scotts did not believe that Harriet needed to buy her freedom from the Emersons, particularly if she never believed that they owned her.[87]

Dred had some money, and he told Mrs. Emerson that he knew a man who would financially vouch for him.[88] "An army officer and St. Louis gentleman," he said, promised to pledge the bond to assure that he paid off the debt. Among the St. Louis officers, Paymaster A. D. Steuart fits the description best for several reasons.[89] He was likely the only army officer still regularly in town now that the war was on. He traveled the river, shuttling between his St. Louis office and the army's encampment with the payroll. The paymaster controlled sufficient cash to make good on such a pledge. Dred had known him for years as the doctor's good friend. (He was actually the army insider who had tipped off Dr. Emerson to the letter in his personnel file.) He may have been aboard the ship that Dred returned on and pledged support to Dred en route. Further evidence linking him to the Scotts' freedom quest is that he and his clerks were summoned as witnesses in the later lawsuit.[90]

But Dred's mistress refused. It is the nature of property that all the financial security that a slave could post did no good if the owner was unwilling to sell. A slave could not demand that his master be reasonable. Selling was a matter of the master's prerogative. Mrs. Emerson said she waved him off, telling him that he was practically free anyway and that was sufficient. All she asked of him, she said, "was that he take care of his wife and family."[91] Deftly, she explained her refusal to release him formally with the counter-request, but she refused to give him the legal papers that would allow him the full legal and financial capacity to do so.

Why didn't she let them go? Simply letting them go was not enough to free them; in Missouri, African Americans needed papers. The practice of setting elderly slaves adrift led to public concern that slaves "abandoned" in this way—without a home plantation on which to stay—would drift to the cities and become paupers, thieves, or beggars.[92] To prevent owners from simply ducking their obligation to provide for dependent slaves, Missouri, like several slave states, raised further legal barriers to manumission of the elderly.[93] The Missouri statute required that an owner emancipating a slave be held to their continued support if they were elderly or very young.[94]

Why didn't Mrs. Emerson accept Dred's offer? If the reason was simply money, the officer's backing guaranteed the purchase price. Yet, Dred was in that awkward situation where his labor was barely as valuable as the cost of his keep. In the slave market, slaves of age 50 commanded no higher a price than eight-year-old children.[95] The market was for young, strong, brawny men who could move the nation's heavy loads in transportation and agriculture.[96] Sellers sometimes tried to conceal an old slave's age, but there was no way to disguise the spareness of Dred's frame.[97] Masters saw older slaves as liabilities rather than assets and often simply cut them loose to fend for themselves,[98] as indeed, Mrs. Emerson now appeared to loosen her own obligation to feed and clothe him.[99] At 51 years of age, Dred was considered elderly. He had attained the full normal life expectancy of an enslaved man.[100] Throughout the South, those slaves lucky enough to survive to old age expected to live out the remainder of their lives with few chores. The antebellum social code permitted the surviving elderly slaves to rest.[101] Even Capt. Bainbridge had sent Dred home rather than take him with the army on the march.[102]

But the bound family's economic value was not Dred,[103] who was worth little more than eight-year old Eliza and less on the market every year. Their economic value as "human property" lay in Harriet and her daughters.[104] If Mistress Irene let Dred buy his freedom, her tenuous claim to Harriet and the children would be still weaker. Perhaps the financially strapped widow had come to rely on Harriet's monthly earnings, or perhaps she imagined her own daughter someday laying claim to Harriet's daughters. Under the custom followed in St. Louis society marriages, slave children were given to the master's white children when they married. (This was how Lucy was assigned to Mrs. D. D. Mitchell.) Eliza and Lizzie's entire productive lives lay before them. To maintain a claim of control over the Scotts' children, Mrs. Emerson had to keep control of Harriet, who did not seem to be part of Dred's purchase offer.

It's also possible that the ultimate decision rested with Mistress Irene's father. White women could not emancipate slaves without two white men to give oaths.[105] Irene Emerson lived with her father and continued to depend on him and her brother financially. Old Col. Sanford regularly collected the Scotts' wages from the Russells, and so he was clearly a factor in their enslavement. His influence was apparent even to them—at one point they sought to name him as a defendant for impeding their freedom. Legally, the old man was merely the executor of the doctor's estate, a probate that he never followed through to completion, and the inventory did not include the Scotts. He treated them as though they were subject to his control, nonetheless.[106] But Col. Sanford was more invested than simply as executor; he was also ideologically opposed to the very idea of manumission and politically active in proslavery causes. He opposed the idea of African Americans being their own men and women. Letting Dred go without formally freeing him was the easier option for Irene. But only legal papers could unravel him legally from the bondage of her control. Papers provided the security of not worrying about the night patrols. Increasingly, black persons needed to be able to prove their status on the streets of St. Louis. The mistress refused Dred the papers that would have placed his family beyond the reach of jail and sent them back to the Russells.

The anxiety of raising the touchy topic with the master's widow only to be refused brought the Scotts no closer to establishing their independence or preventing their separation by sale. They found themselves rented out indefinitely to the service of a different mistress and master on terms other than their own. So the Scotts took their fates in their own hands. Instead of waiting for the possibility that they might be sold on its steps, they entered the courthouse voluntarily as litigants. Harriet and Dred filed suit for their freedom.

Why they chose to file suit at this point in their lives has always been one of the great mysteries of this famous lawsuit.[107] After all, the Scotts returned to slave territory twice, and by the time they sued, Harriet had resided continuously in the slave state of Missouri for six years. Emerson claimed that one of his slaves had threatened to file suit for freedom in 1838.[108] What finally convinced them both to do so in 1846? The Scotts had ample opportunities to escape at times, particularly when away from Dr. Emerson, and like most St. Louis slaves, they could even move about the city during the day unescorted. Most historians have focused on Dred as a single actor, as if he were the lawsuit's only protagonist.[109] But viewing the case solely as Dred's endeavor misses the point of Harriet's agency and participation.

We have tended to regard slavery and freedom as such clearly opposite poles that it becomes impossible for us to contemplate why slaves would have ever remained in their situation for one minute longer than compelled to be. However, what is important to understand is that there were gradations of liberty, security, and autonomy and a person's optimal choice may have required trading off some liberties for others he or she considered most important. Having a nominal master who left one alone may have, in certain circumstances, been more secure than being declared free and subject to the random persecutions to which free blacks were sometimes exposed.[110] How else does one explain Polly choosing her timing: to sue first for her own freedom and then for her daughter's? Or others not filing for freedom until someone threatened to take them south by steamboat?[111] Considering that remaining in slavery may have, at times, provided certain stability or even security goes some distance in explaining otherwise anomalous choices in the timing of suits filed by oppressed and enslaved persons. The timing of such assertions of freedom depended upon the relationship between the particularized impulses to freedom and the individual specific circumstances of human bondage. Within the social contexts of human life, persons often make relative, rather than absolute choices, and they assess their choices within the sequence of their situated perspectives. The constraints holding the Scotts in slavery were not physical curtailments, like chains, jails, or leg irons; the ties that bound them were their desire to remain together and raise their children as a family. In Lucy's words, most mothers did not try to escape to freedom alone—they were "slain by their deepest affections," of wanting to do the best for their children.[112]

The social realities defining what was possible for Harriet and for keeping a family together under slavery were the most intractable constraints in preventing their escape.[113] Escaping as a family was virtually impossible. Even if the Scott family could simply slip across the river border to Illinois, they were likely to be followed. The children would slow their escape, and eventually the dogs of some bounty hunter would find them. How could they move quickly when their youngest daughter was too big to carry and both girls were too small to run fast enough by themselves?

Escaping to Canada may have held no appeal for the Scotts. They knew the hard existence of the far north from their years in Minnesota. The Canada they knew about was no refuge for struggling families. Almost no one from St. Peter's ever headed out for Canada, unless it was a drover with cattle to sell. The Canadian families whom they knew fled from the Red River Colony. Across long expanses of prairie, exhausted refugees had hauled oxcarts with their own muscular arms and with half-domesticated buffalos. They subsisted on dried buffalo fat and left Canada because there wasn't enough to eat to stay alive. Unless one was extremely wilderness hardy, and the Scotts were not, Canada would not seem to them a viable option for survival.

The children's ages must have affected the suit's timing as well. In 1846, when the Scotts sued, Eliza was eight, which meant that she was old enough to be hired out or sold away.[114] Eliza was at the age that slave children often first discovered the cruelties of their existence and that they *were* slaves.[115] Further, Eliza's value was bound to increase. As her separate market value rose, she was increasingly at risk of being sold away from the family.[116]

In Widow Emerson's precarious financial situation, she might sell off just one family member for ready cash, as Mrs. Mitchell had tried to sell Lucy.[117] Moreover, if Mrs. Emerson incurred debts, and her creditors thought that she owned Eliza, Eliza could be seized for sale to cover her debts. Owners often mortgaged the enslaved to borrow money, and in St. Louis, creditors often foreclosed on them with or occasionally without official mortgages.[118] With Dred worth little and Harriet still caring for two-year-old Lizzie, the Scotts' shy, eight-year-old girl was most susceptible. Eliza's growing vulnerability to sale must have gnawed on the Scotts' consciousness, suggesting to them that now was the time to act.[119]

As slaves, their daughters faced not only the indignity of bearing children for other masters but also casual predation or the sustained sexual oppression accepted as normal in the local culture,[120] but "unmentionable" in white society as Amanda's experience with Lt. Prince demonstrated. Any mother would be keenly aware of the particular sexual threat posed to her daughters. Bound girls sold in slave markets were priced not only for their work but also for their childbearing potential. Advertisements listed adolescent girls as "likely," meaning "likely to bear offspring."[121] A likely slave woman could increase her master's holdings. Even 28-year-old Harriet, four times a mother, would have her reproductive capability increase the price on her head.[122]

The Scotts deliberated only days before acting. Given the alacrity with which they filed suit, Harriet must have prepared for this moment even before Dred returned. Although Dred had been absent for two years, the Scotts found their way to court within a month. From Lucy's experience, the laundresses knew that filing suit legally prevented sale. Although Lucy was jailed while she awaited trial, she could not be removed from the city by her hostile master once she filed suit.[123]

As between Mr. and Mrs. Scott, the circumstantial evidence suggests that Harriet favored suing more than Dred. With no written account of how she felt, the only evidence is circumstantial. Throughout the litigation, Dred appeared ambivalent about the case, declaring the lawsuit as "a heap of trouble" when it was over. The statement might have been masking or expressing his true feeling.[124] Those who observed them together described Dred as agreeable but Harriet as the family's driving force. "Dred's real master was his wife," wrote the journalist who observed them together.[125]

Moreover, Harriet fit the profile of freedom litigants better than did Dred, since most freedom suits filed in the St. Louis courts were initiated by women. Men could run. They could take the risk of depending on their own wits, physical stamina, and speed. Men's chances of successfully escaping were better, particularly if they traveled alone. Running with children was doomed to fail.[126] Moreover, most of the women, like Harriet, were mothers with children.[127] Women frequently invoked as their reason for suit that a sale threatened to separate them from their children.[128] Filing suit preserved the maternal tie during its proceedings.

Harriet also had more reasons to believe herself free than Dred did. Her former master, Taliaferro, had expressed his intention to free his slave Eliza a decade before he brought Harriet to the wilderness.[129] Her publicly recognized marriage, her residence first in Pennsylvania and then in the northern Indian territories, and the things Taliaferro had said about her marriage to Dred gave her reason to believe she was free. There was nothing more that she could have done in free territory to establish her liberty. There had been no means to establish a guarantee of freedom back in Minnesota, and no point in trying. Official papers were simply not available because the territory lacked the requisite legal infrastructure to produce them. With no courthouse and barely a whiskey-selling magistrate in the area by the time the Scotts had left, even the paper on which to write letters was rationed.[130] Legal formalities in the wilderness frontier were accomplished by public displays rather than written papers. By performing the public act of marrying Harriet and Dred, Taliaferro had done as much in advancing their status as free persons as the limited capacities of his office could offer. Returning from

Indian territory, back in the United States, the Scotts should have been able to get the freedom papers they needed, without needing to rush things. However, there was no reason to insist immediately on a hypothetically greater sphere of freedom for herself while she experienced the protection marriage to Dred offered under his absent master. As early as the Scotts' 1838 trip together to St. Louis, the pregnant Harriet might have learned that a child born farther north had a greater chance of being free, and taken the steamboat north again with the Emersons?[131]

The most likely scenario is that it was Harriet, acting out of a mother's desire to keep her family intact and to protect her young daughters, who initiated their suits. As the Reverend Meachum recognized, "Then, dear mother, if you love your daughter, show it in doing all you can do for those so near to your bosom."[132] For her daughters to live in freedom, Harriet had to establish her own. Under the principle of matrilinearity, Dred's status had no effect on their children's status.[133]

We can never know the exact combination of reasons, emotions, counsel, readiness, or intuition that motivated them that particular day. But by paying attention to the dimensions and contours of their circumstances, it appears that freedom in the abstract was not their objective. Their imperative was probably much more situational and pragmatic, sustaining the thread of their family life so that it did not break. At the point that continued enslavement became significantly more intolerable, in their perception, they made their move.

This couple, who persevered for 11 years to the highest court of the land, was also demographically distinctive from the dozens of others who filed for freedom: they sued simultaneously as a married couple. Members of the same family often brought tandem legal actions, but Harriet and Dred were rare in that they were the only married couple to do so in a half century of freedom suits.[134] This momentous endeavor was possible, in part, because of their mutual support, and it was necessary in order to maintain that continuity and their mutual bond.

CHAPTER 25

The Courthouse and the Jail

T SOME POINT, Harriet must have called upon the attorney, Mr. Murdoch, who took more than his share of freedom suits. He had filed Lucy's initial papers.[1] Murdoch had been centrally involved in the legal fall-out of the incident that shaped the region's racial consciousness. As Alton's city attorney during the Lovejoy shoot-out, it was his task to prosecute both sides of the mob violence that resulted in Lovejoy's murder, the pro-slavery and the abolitionist combatants. Several men bragged about killing the abolitionist, though the jury refused to convict them. Failing to get a conviction, Murdoch left Alton in the aftermath of the riots and crossed the river to settle in St. Louis—not as a broken man, but as someone now willing to represent slaves in freedom suits.[2]

When Harriet told her story to Murdoch (where she came from, that she was once the slave of Lawrence Taliaferro), he must have recognized her former master's name because he even spelled it correctly in the complaint. This was the Lawrence Taliaferro of Bedford Falls, Pennsylvania, where Murdoch himself had read law as a young man. He must have known Harriet's former master personally, since the two men were about the same age and belonged to the same Presbyterian Church in the tiny town. As peers, and with so much in common, they were quite likely acquainted. By reading law in Pennsylvania, Murdoch certainly knew that as Taliaferro's slave, under that state's law Harriet would become free at age 28.[3] By reckoning from the time of her publicly recognized marriage, she had reached that age in 1846, the year she filed the suit. Murdoch could conceivably have pled Pennsylvania law to free Harriet,[4] but the choice of law was complicated when applied to a slave such as Harriet, who had lived in different jurisdictions, with different laws regarding slavery. It was easiest to plead Missouri law in the St. Louis courts because it entitled the Scotts to freedom simply and directly, given their residence in free territory.

An important part of the complaint was the slave's personal affidavit, yet it is difficult to know just how literally to believe the allegations in the couple's legal papers.[5] They state that, on a specific day, Saturday, April 4, 1846, Mrs. Emerson illegally detained the Scotts for 12 hours, depriving them of their liberty and imprisoning them. Attorney Murdoch used identical language in several other petitions, thus, the words were a pro-forma recitation that was required in all emancipation pleadings under Missouri law.[6] The law used plenty of legal fictions in pleading: something that had to be stated to raise the issues of the case but was only metaphorically true. The Scotts' claim of imprisonment by Mrs. Emerson on that day may have been simply a legal fiction—or it may have been true. Any owner could lock a slave in or confine him or her to the calaboose until the slave was more tractable. If the patrol were asked to arrest the Scotts that Saturday evening, they would not even know who ordered it done. The case file shows that the Scotts had considerable difficulty identifying just who had "assaulted" them to prove up the case. Any one of their several masters or mistresses—and almost any white stranger—had the power to send for someone to arrest them.

Enslavement was a shell game, especially when the presumption was enslavement rather than liberty.[7] Who was the real enslaver in a system so pervasive and so seamless? What particular constraints held them enslaved? A specific allegation of assault upon a slave's freedom was a necessary element of the lawsuit.[8] But, ironically, slaves' liberty was routinely curtailed every day of every year of their lives, except Sundays, by the discipline of their work orders. To establish a legal case for freedom, they were required to allege a specific incident. At whom could the Scotts point a finger? Whom would they sue? Who *exactly* held them in slavery, when they were presumed to be slaves by their race and the entire society was seamlessly structured to restrict their freedom, merely by default based on their race? Most likely they were detained by the Russells or Col. Sanford in the name of the widow's ownership. It was the old man who dropped them off in the wagon and regularly came around for the money. During the procedural maneuvering, the Scotts attempted to sue all three, searching for the legally proper party against whom to establish their freedom. It was the one person who restrained them who was supposed to be named in the petition to the court. Many freedom suits were filed first against one defendant, and subsequently against other defendants in order to make the case succeed.[9]

The specific date designated, Saturday, April 4, may have been a legal fiction as well, or it may suggest that something more significant occurred that day, something that impelled them to act. Most freedom claimants cited a specific incident, and many of the affidavits detail exactly "who did what"—a claimant was locked in a cell, or they were informed that they'd be sold, a suspicious man had appeared and ordered them to accompany him, they were sent away from their family, and so on. Often the incident that a claimant alleged for legal purposes actually was the event that triggered them to file suit—but not always.[10]

If that Saturday's confinement did trigger their resolve, the Scotts may have been on their way to do something special, something that confinement prevented them from doing. What was unique about Saturday, April 4, 1846, was that it was the Sabbath break before Palm Sunday, when most slaves left off work after chores.[11] Palm Sunday, celebrated as the day Jesus Christ rode triumphantly through the streets of Jerusalem to adoring crowds waving palm branches, was an important holiday in the Christian calendar and Baptist theology. Traditionally, this day of celebration started off the more solemn events of the rest of Easter week. Easter week had been designated by the Reverend Meachum as a time of special significance for black families.[12] If the Scotts were confined that day, they were prevented from joining the celebration and the baptisms that were usually performed at Chouteau's Pond.[13] That Palm Sunday was the first after Eliza turned seven and passed into the next stage of maturity. It may have been planned as her baptismal day, and for the reunited family to miss the event would have been a major disappointment.[14] By the Monday following Palm Sunday, the Scotts were able to reach their lawyer. Although married, Harriet, now 28, and Dred, 51, instituted separate suits.[15] "Harriet, of Color" and "Dred Scott" filed two claims against the doctor's widow: the more important one was to establish their freedom, while the lesser one charged that they had been confined against their will.[16]

Their attorney filed their papers in the brick courthouse, which was being renovated on land donated by the Chouteaus. As Murdoch approached the courthouse that Monday, a crowd had gathered on the steps to hear Henry Clay, architect of the Missouri Compromise (which was one of the very premises of the Scotts' lawsuit). "Harry of the West," as he was called, was a staunch supporter of the American Colonization Society, which urged that slaves should be repatriated back to Africa.[17] That day he stood on the courthouse steps facing the river, lecturing to an audience composed of the "citizens of St. Louis"—most of them white. The lawsuit would eventually test whether the Scotts were *citizens* at all. But at this juncture, the Scotts did not have their sights set on such a lofty proposition. Under the law of the time, they didn't need to be citizens to be freed under Missouri law; they only needed to establish that they had resided in free territory and now were denied their freedom.

AND THEN THE DEED was done. There was no turning back. Celebrating Easter that year, the Scotts probably harbored hopes that everything would be over by fall. Instead, the litigation lasted 11 years.[18]

By suing, the Scotts had staked out a defiant position that subjected them to possible retaliation. Just signing papers was an act of resistance. Slaves could be beaten for the insubordination of merely talking back. The personal costs of taking such a stand hostile to the slaveholder's interest were high, even if they won eventually. In order to sever their master's hold on them, slave litigants were required to allege publicly that in mistreating them, their owner acted illegally. They could expect ill will. And if the suit failed, they could expect retribution. For subservient persons such as the Scotts, especially vulnerable because they were responsible for young children, taking that fateful step risked all. It meant they could not easily turn back. There was nowhere left to retreat. They had put their children and their personal well-being on the line in order to gain the freedom to fully enjoy these very aspects of their existence. So well recognized was the risk of retaliation that the judge issued the standard court order that the Scotts should have "liberty to attend [their] counsel and the court," and should not be removed from the jurisdiction, nor subject "to any severity on account of" petitioning for freedom."[19]

Years later, when Mrs. Emerson attempted to explain the notorious lawsuit, she claimed the Scotts had met a young lawyer who was interested only in getting a share of their back wages.[20] But contrary to her claim, the initial lawsuit never even requested back wages—only $10 in damages based on their past enslavement.[21] Their lawyer, Murdoch, was no longer young, and he had to have had stronger reasons of principle and personal vindication for filing the lawsuit. Murdoch could not have expected money, because the Scotts' wages were paltry compared to the litigation costs. Rather than a financial bonanza, the lawsuit had virtually no way to pay for itself, and, in predictable succession, each of the several lawyers who attempted to help the Scotts eventually dropped out as the case dragged on.[22]

However personally significant the act of filing freedom papers was for the Scotts, their action went unnoticed locally. The local newspapers never reported emancipation filings—just slaves' more sensational criminal conduct. This lawsuit, which was to shake the nation, began as a simple, private matter. Other events overshadowed it at the time. Locally, Henry Clay's visit dominated the headlines, and nationally, the war with Mexico was the significant issue that month. Large territorial battles were at stake. The troops Dred had left in Texas were pushing past the Rio Grande into battle in Mexico. For the time being, St. Louis thrived on the patriotic jingoism of national expansion. The lawsuit of a pair of slaves was of no importance in this fever over national destiny. False reports reaching the city claimed that Gen. Taylor was surrounded. Volunteers quickly formed a militia, and businessmen contributed financially.[23] The volunteers encamped outside of town until they could be disciplined, drilled, and each outfitted with a blanket. Even D. D. Mitchell, from whom Lucy by now had won her freedom, took a leave of absence from the Indian agency to lead a company of volunteers into war. St. Louis was focused on backing the war. National expansion was good business for the city of shopkeepers to the west.

So insignificant did the Scotts' lawsuit seem at first that it went unnoticed even by the two men who later would be conventionally presented to history as the primary antagonists in the case. At the time, Irene's brother, John F. A. Sanford, was far too busy managing the fur company's interests to notice this minor lawsuit against his sister. (In fact, he didn't seem to take any note of it for the first two years—not until after his father died and he had to step in to settle the estate.[24]) The Scotts sued only Irene Emerson at this juncture. Henry T. Blow, the white man often credited as helping the Scotts and the man whose father had once owned Dred, appears to have had no connection at all to the early proceedings. He was occupied with expanding his factory and upholding his civic obligations, including procuring supplies for the volunteers headed for Mexico.[25]

The servant couple was not backed by money, power, or influence as they undertook the task of pursuing the legal case for freedom. They acted alone, presumably with the encouragement of a network of friends from the African church—and certainly with the assistance of a lawyer who probably knew Harriet's former master.

Only as their case dragged on, with each excruciatingly slow turn of the grinding legal machinery, did it rise—unresolved, unsettled, and yet unabandoned—in the courts and in significance. But for the first several years there was no inkling of the national attention and prominence it would later hold. The Scotts neither ran nor retreated from the legal conflict. They stood and held fast to their claim of freedom. As they held fast, the case attracted the attention of other contending forces, playing out other agendas. What the Scotts did, which was extraordinary for individuals so vulnerable and so multiply subjugated by the pervasive legal and social systems, was simply to not let go. In turn, they were in for the roughest ride of their lives, which brought them into the national limelight. It is indeed remarkable what can occur when individuals believe they are entitled to justice and entitled to be free.

ONCE THE DEED was done, the Scott family probably gravitated to the docks and shoreline seeking work. The litigating parents had to find some immediate way to feed and shelter their children. The streets were full of stray dogs, and hogs within the city had only recently been ordered confined.[26] They had to find somewhere safe off the streets for their young daughters to sleep. Whom could they turn to?

The Scotts could have been jailed initially, but since they did not face imminent shipment out of state by Mrs. Emerson, they were probably let go on their own recognizance. Early on, freedom claimants were routinely returned to their purported masters pending trial.[27] As a result, some were beaten, were found dead, or mysteriously disappeared.[28] By the 1840s, the court orders that the litigants not be abused for filing suit had become standard.[29] That left the question, however, of where the litigant should spend the time awaiting trial of his or her claim. In suing for freedom, Harriet and Dred could fully expect to be jailed until the lawsuit was resolved. Attorney Murdoch was aware of this and likely warned them. His client Lucy had been shut in for 18 months. The jail thus went hand in hand with the court of justice. There had been a jail in the city just as long as there had been a courthouse, and both were authorized originally by the same act of state. The jail held the bodies of convicted criminals, the accused, and some of the slaves suing for freedom.[30]

This was the paradox of seeking freedom through the courts. If urban slaves enjoyed any range of freedom before filing suit—to move about in the open streets, to negotiate their own hire, to sleep where they chose—then they had to be prepared to surrender these privileges sometimes for the duration of the suit and subject themselves to the direction of the sheriff and the jailor. In New Orleans, freedom seeking slaves were routinely held in jail.[31] To file suit was to enter a dark tunnel of even further curtailment of their liberties, though that was necessary in order to establish freedom. The paradox then was that the path to freeing oneself from bondage required a willingness to submit to still greater constraints, more severe limitations on privacy, and far less freedom of movement for an uncertain duration. And justice was usually delayed in the St. Louis courts.

Even locking up the freedom litigant for safekeeping incurred costs. After Lucy won her freedom, her jailer sought his recompense against the losing party, her former master, for housing and feeding her for 18 months. But the

St. Louis Jail, pictured on this carte de visite from a later time, appears very similar to the contemporaneous descriptions made of the jail. The cells of the three-story jail are at the rear of the building, the jailor's office is in the foreground, and the courtyard lies in between. *Photographs and Prints Collection, Missouri History Museum.*

court dismissed her boarding fees, surely to the jailer's disappointment.[32] Charles Dickens noted the irony on his visit to America of slaves being sold to pay the jail fees.[33] By the time of the Scotts' lawsuit, the circuit court seems to have fallen into an informal pattern of locking some litigants up, letting others slide by on their own recognizance, or hiring out still others to temporary masters.

Due to the expense of incarcerating freedom litigants during their suits, the court often required slaves to find someone willing to post a bond, promising to pay the court costs if the slave lost the suit. In other instances, when slaves were released on their own recognizance, the court might also require a bond equal to the slaves' value should they escape during the litigation. The court records show that although bond was posted to cover the Scotts' court costs, no bond was posted to secure their liberty,[34] suggesting perhaps that no one thought that bond was necessary, either because they were jailed or because they were not viewed as a flight risk. In all likelihood, no one insisted that they be jailed. And the Scotts probably just drifted to some place where they could find shelter. Surely the litigating servants were no longer welcome at the Russells', the Sanfords' farm, or Mrs. Emerson's place on Manchester Road. The Scotts would not wish to return to the Russells, given that they had filed suit to resist assignment there.[35]

They had no money to stay at a boarding house. Better to save their money for the children's food and clothing. Even a few cents a night could deplete whatever savings they had. Housing was still very crowded in the city. Staying at the home of a black freedperson could stretch that shelter to the limit. There were more than a dozen people living at the Reverend Meachum's, and he did not really encourage people to sue for their freedom.[36] Eventually the Scotts would need the patronage of a white man, just to be allowed to stay in his back alley. Eventually they'd turn to Dred's former owners, the Blows; there were no Taliaferros in St. Louis.

Harriet could find ready work as a laundress—provided she had a washboard and kettles and could find firewood and the materials to make soap.[37] She could exchange work for food and a place in a basement or a shed, where her family could sleep undisturbed. Several witnesses called at trial were probably her laundry customers, called as character witnesses to Harriet's ability to support the family, since they seemed to have had little to do with the basic elements of the lawsuit and no tie to the Scotts' previous lives.[38]

For Dred, the logical move was to seek work at the docks or around the outdoor markets. Runners were always needed to deliver messages around town and to carry things from place to place.[39] Dozens of boats docked in St. Louis each week, and the wharf was always crowded. Although no longer young or strong, Dred could run errands—though he'd have to compete with boys a fraction of his age for the jobs. But he could not use a handcart to carry valises or trunks because, by summer of 1846, the city council regulated public porters. If Dred wanted to use a wheelbarrow, he needed a license and a patch to show he was licensed.[40] Slaves weren't issued licenses, even if they believed themselves free and were in litigation to prove it. All manner of liberties and privileges required freedom papers, by custom, if not by law.

He might have found work at one of the city's four markets, which were open two shifts: from dawn until 10 in the morning and again from four until dark.[41] The bell rang each day to announce the closing time. There he could sweep out the market stalls or unload and pack up produce. He might even cadge some rotten potatoes or cabbage to take home. It took a fair amount of enterprise just to make do in the Scotts' circumstances.

Widow Emerson promptly moved to dismiss the suit, a quick indication that she intended to resist the claim and that she did not regard the lawsuit as amicable.[42] She was represented by George Goode, another former Virginian who owned a farm in the county near the Sanford estate.[43] Then nothing more was done until summer. The legal proceedings took an inordinate amount of time.

At some point the Scotts must have entered the courtroom for the first time. Curiosity must have drawn them to see the judge for themselves, even if the initial papers of the lawsuit could be processed by the lawyers without their presence. While political crowds gathered at the door, men were at work on the foundations. Every day, dozens of workmen, free and slave, arrived at the courthouse site to lay the bricks and stone for the new temple of justice. St. Louis had outgrown its old square, two-story courthouse, and a new cornerstone for an enlarged building had been laid. The cupola was to be replaced by a sweeping grand rotunda, rising to the height

St. Louis Courthouse, in the middle of renovation, showing portions of the old and of the new construction. *Photographs and Prints Collection, Missouri History Museum.*

of 130 feet. Three floors of galleries were planned, surmounted by a heavy 60-foot dome. But at the time the Scotts' attorney entered the courthouse to file the papers, there was only the ceremonious cornerstone and scaffolding. The old internal structure still housed the courts. Neither western law nor western courthouses were stable edifices. Both the common law and courthouses were works in progress.

Litigating slaves and their family members often hung around the courthouse, waiting to hear their cases called.[44] Inside the courtroom, walking gingerly on the red brick floor and not knowing whether they were permitted to enter, to sit, or to stand, the Scotts would have seen three white men on the dais: the trinity of justice. Judge Krum, in black robes, sat behind the raised bench in the highest position. Below and in front of him, on his left and right hand, sat the sheriff and the clerk. The court clerk organized the paperwork and kept records of everything that occurred in the courtroom. Looking down and scribbling over his papers, the old man, occupied with the ink and the quills, rarely looked up to see who entered the chamber.[45] The sheriff watched the door to see who entered, and to keep order in the courtroom. Litigating slaves like the Scotts had most contact with the sheriff over the ensuing years. County sheriffs were elected, and when the case was first filed, the sheriff was Samuel Conway. He took people into custody and turned them over to the jailer. With his handful of deputies, he also ushered people from jail to court during the day and back again at night and he saw that summons were delivered to everyone officially called to the room. The Scotts would learn to recognize him on sight. The sheriff enforced the judge's decrees, and as such, he also auctioned off bondspeople on the courthouse steps.

When the Scotts filed suit, there were fewer than half a dozen freedom suits under way, though dozens of black St. Louis residents had achieved freedom through lawsuits.[46] Most cases, like that of the Scotts,' were based on residence in free territory—either that the petitioners themselves had once lived in free territory or, under the principle of matrilinearity, that they were the child of a mother who had lived in free territory. A few suits involved cases of mistaken identity, when a free person of color was mistaken for a slave or the person's freedom papers were missing. These litigants, who had free status could be indignant, if mistaken as a slave, while litigants like the Scotts—first-time freedom seekers—were likely to be more apprehensive and hopeful. At the time the Scotts filed suit, Carolyn Bascom, a young, free black woman from Maryland, awaited trial after being scheduled for sale on the courthouse steps as part of her master's probate on the mistaken assumption that, as his house servant, she was his slave.[47]

Not surprisingly, freedom suits were unpopular with the white community, but they were an established fixture of Missouri law that had existed for as long as St. Louis had had a court.[48] Remarkably, indigent slaves claiming a legal right to freedom were aided by court-appointed attorneys.[49] While the court appointed lawyers for indigent slaves, it did not pay them, so the quality of representation varied considerably. Law partnerships frequently assigned these pro bono cases to the most junior lawyer in the firm.[50]

By dint of considerable legal precedent, the Scotts should have won their freedom, and relatively easily. Attorney Murdoch could reassure them of that. As long as they could produce witnesses to their residence in free territory, they met the requirements to establish their freedom. Freedom litigants usually prevailed in court, even though trials took a long time.[51] It wasn't necessary to have spent years in free territory as the Scotts had; simply being sent across the Mississippi river to Illinois to make hay for a single harvest season was usually sufficient.[52] Dozens of litigants had won their freedom by going to court.[53] But with a recalcitrant slave owner, and a strikingly inefficient court system, the process could drag on for months, and the delay was painful.

Under Rachael's case, the closest precedent, the Scotts' lawyer needed only to establish that they had lived at Fort Snelling and that after returning to St. Louis they were deprived of their liberty by someone, some person against whom they sought to establish their freedom.[54] Finding the appropriate person to sue was the sticky part in their trial.

As an initial legal matter, the Scotts had to help their attorney find witnesses in St. Louis who had seen them living in free territory. Getting testimony from Minnesota was difficult, although sometimes conscientious attorneys did travel to neighboring Illinois to get appropriate depositions.[55] Most of the army officers who knew the Scotts from their time upriver were now in Mexico, but Murdoch managed to get an affidavit from one soldier shortly before he, too, left for the Mexican War.[56]

Second, the Scotts had to establish their claim against some "enslaver" by demonstrating that that person had assaulted their liberty, either actually or figuratively.[57] Ironically, to establish their freedom, they had to prove they were deprived of freedom by someone, and the burden of proof was on them. One could not establish one's freedom against the world—as, for example, in an *in rem* action— freedom could only be established by bringing an action against a defendant who had acted to deprive them of it.

While the Scotts awaited trial, slave auctions continued to take place on the courthouse front steps. The despair of those waiting to be auctioned off contrasted with the lively circus of white camaraderie, which was often accompanied by music.[58] The Scotts encountered others, similarly awaiting trial and lingering in the courthouse hallways, in the jail, or even locked in the same jail cell.[59] These people were their compatriots in apprehension, and the Scotts watched as each took his or her turn in court. Not only would developments in their own case cause their spirits to soar or to crash, but they must have also been aware of the fortunes of other freedom litigants, who were subject to the same slow-turning legal machinery. On the streets, if they were hired out to work, they'd hear news of others sounding the waters for the route to freedom. In their condition of heightened vulnerability, with their lives staked on the suit, they were likely to interpret any small bit of legal news as some sign for victory or defeat in their own case. Who knew what to expect?

During the decade that the Scotts' fate remained undecided, there were early indications that the Missouri Supreme Court and the state legislature were tightening things up from above. The state high court handed down new legal precedents that the local judges were obligated to follow. The legislature had passed a law requiring that free blacks be licensed.[60] From the Missouri Supreme Court, Justice Napton in particular editorialized against privileges for African Americans whenever he got the chance.[61] And in one decision, the court sanctioned a steamboat captain who unknowingly transported a slave man carrying forged papers. One successful escape, the court wrote, "will stimulate others to try."[62] The court expressed outright anxiety about Missouri's geographic position as a border slave state, the border of the national compromise. The court wrote, "Our eastern frontier, being only separated by a navigable stream, from a non-slaveholding State, inhabited by many who are anxious, and leaving no stone unturned to deprive us of our slaves; render it necessary that the strictest diligence should be exacted from all those navigating steamboats on our waters, in order to prevent the escape of our slaves."[63] The ruling bred further suspicion of black persons legitimately traveling the rivers or even the back roads since any black traveler could be an escaping slave. A good Samaritan offering a black pedestrian a wagon ride might find himself sued for loss of the slave. But most of these rulings didn't directly affect the Scotts' situation since they didn't flee or forge documents. By setting themselves squarely on the prescribed legal pathway, however, they languished in the limbo of an uncertain status between slavery and freedom. With each new ruling, the 11-year trial must have taken them on an emotional roller coaster, with their freedom and family ties at risk. The protracted litigation governed everything about their present and their future.[64] No wonder Dred claimed that the legal proceedings were "a heap of trouble."[65]

By spring, attorney Murdoch was no longer on the case.[66] The Scotts' suit was the last freedom case that he ever filed in St. Louis.[67] That year, his creditors foreclosed on his mortgage and sold his property at a sheriff's sale.[68] The foreclosing creditor was former Judge Bryan Mullanphy, who had had a running battle with Murdoch's law partner. The foreclosure may have been personal.[69] Murdoch disappeared from the city, taking his wife and several children back to a brother in Michigan and leaving behind only a school-age daughter in the care of his father-in-law. He also left the Scotts with a viable lawsuit, but no lawyer.[70] Although Murdoch was successful in winning freedom for several of his slave clients, he had also annoyed members of both the old French Creole and the new Virginia society. In one case, he had even found it necessary to seek an injunction against a group of leading citizens to keep them from interfering with his client.[71] He may have felt that his personal usefulness had run out and the limits of the community's tolerance exceeded. On the other hand, Murdoch was peripatetic, and he moved every few years, ultimately settling in California.[72]

Both of the Scotts' cases were assigned to Judge Krum. Murdoch knew Krum only too well since they had both been involved in the Lovejoy debacle at Alton, when Krum was Alton's mayor and Murdoch was the town's prosecutor. Having served as Alton's mayor, Krum,[73] too, knew the risks of being thought soft on slavery. Years later, as the editor of a free labor newspaper in California, Murdoch wrote about the famous Dred Scott case without acknowledging that he had represented them. He did write tellingly of the profound frustration of representing slaves in court, stating, "The advocate who pleads against slavery wastes his voice in its vaulted roof, and upon ears stuffed sixty years with cotton. His case is judged before it's argued, and his client condemned before he is heard."[74]

CHAPTER 26

Other Matters at the Courthouse

WHILE THE SCOTTS waited, Judge Krum had a pressing case on the docket. Authorities had arrested Charles Lyons, a free mulatto man,[1] for the crime of being a free black residing in Missouri without a license, which Missouri law required.[2] The sheriff was expected to apprehend and jail any unlicensed black person. Only certain classes of free persons of color—those with good reputations who could support themselves—were even eligible to be licensed to remain in the state.[3] Under the statute, the court had little discretion; it was obligated first to fine them, if they could pay, or have them whipped if they couldn't, and then expel them from the state.[4] Since more free blacks lived in St. Louis than anywhere else in Missouri, the statute especially burdened the city's black population. White persons, on the other hand, were never required to obtain licenses simply to reside in the state. Unless they were vagrants, they were usually simply left alone.

Lyons challenged his arrest and the statute as unconstitutional,[5] so before Judge Krum could get to the Scotts' lawsuit, he had to rule on Lyons's liberty claim. There was no doubt that Lyons was free. Born in Kentucky, the son of a free black man and a Seneca Indian woman, he had moved to St. Louis from New York.[6] None of his forebears had ever been held in servitude. Like other free persons, he came west seeking opportunity, which he found working on riverboats.[7] The issue was the scope of his freedom under Missouri law. Did the state have the authority to restrict his freedom by subjecting him to licensing merely because he was black? How could freedom require licensing?

Lyons insisted that, as a free man, he was entitled to the protections of the U.S. Constitution and, accordingly, could not be deprived of his liberty by the Missouri statute. It was not until the Scotts' case reached the U.S. Supreme Court that this federal constitutional claim would be definitively resolved. Lyons argued that having been born free in Kentucky, he was fully entitled to all privileges and immunities of being a citizen. He was arrested without a warrant and neither charged with, nor guilty of, any crime. Lyons also argued that the licensing legislation was repugnant to the fundamental condition on which Missouri was admitted to the Union, which was to respect the privileges and immunities of other states' citizens. In essence, Lyons argued exactly what the Scotts would argue much later: that continued deprivation of their liberty by the state of Missouri violated the Missouri Compromise.

As the Scotts looked to the courthouse for their relief, a large group of white men with a very different agenda began holding large public meetings in the rotunda at night. The group, which called itself "the Committee of 100," feared that abolitionists were threatening to seize slave property in various parts of the nation.[8] Not surprisingly, most men in attendance were slaveholders, but many of them also were being sued in freedom suits.[9] Col. Sanford was among the group, likely spurred on by the Scotts' recent suit against his daughter. The group elected Col. Sanford to their select committee of governance. Although many members, like Sanford, came from the rural townships where most slaves were held, the committee focused primarily on limiting the liberties that free blacks enjoyed in town.[10] They not only backed strict enforcement of the licensing statute, but their agenda went further in curtailing the customary privileges and civil liberties of both slaves and free blacks. They proposed establishing a nighttime curfew for all black city residents. They also resolved that "all 'Negro preaching' and 'teaching' be deemed dangerous to the happiness, quiet, and safety of our slave population."[11] In October of 1846, the committee offered a constitution for their proslavery society.[12] Their efforts produced legislative results within the year. The Missouri legislature soon outlawed teaching blacks to read and write.[13] Slave owners feared that an educated black population would become too independent minded and perhaps even rebellious.

Judge Krum, still deliberating Charles Lyons's case, must have been aware of these evening gatherings in his courthouse. Krum was more a politician than a judge. It wasn't that the politically savvy Krum was ignorant of law books, one lawyer wrote, but that he did not seem to know "the principle for the use of them."[14] Large public meetings signaled more violent rumblings, and Judge Krum was well aware of how unpopular black causes were, having lived through the Lovejoy massacre in a position of political authority.

In mid-November, Mrs. Emerson's attorney entered her plea of not guilty to the claim of assault on the Scotts' liberty. In George Goode, Col. Sanford had found an attorney who was ideologically well aligned with the Committee of 100. Goode had "strong prejudices, and [was] most uncompromising in his adherence to slavery."[15] It was said that Goode viewed everyone who did not concur with him as an abolitionist and necessarily inimical to the South.[16] The Southern lawyer, who was fond of fox hunting, had left Virginia after participating in a duel.[17] He dabbled in law, usually taking property claims: reclaiming land, reclaiming horses, or reclaiming slaves.[18] In the small world of transplanted Virginia elite, this lawyer's extended family had also been sued by slaves in freedom suits. Goode's in-laws were the same family from whom Polly and her daughters had successfully wrested their freedom.[19] Lines already drawn in race and status were becoming reinforced by the circumstances of families' former slaves successfully attaining freedom.

Nothing more happened in the Scotts' lawsuit all winter as the case waited its turn. Judge Krum finally ruled against Charles Lyons, upholding licensing restrictions on free blacks. The decision was well received in the city. The proslavery group was so delighted that they reprinted the text of the decision for sale.[20]

It was Lyons's race that precluded him from citizenship, Judge Krum concluded in an opinion that presaged the eventual result in the Scotts' case. Because Lyons was a man of color, of mixed racial parentage, he could not be a citizen of Kentucky under Kentucky law, and hence was not entitled to protection under the U.S. Constitution. Freedom and bondage may be mutable statuses, Krum reasoned, but race was not.

> The free Negroes in the United States are for the most part the descendants of the same race, formerly held in servitude. It is quite immaterial how they became discharged from service.... They are Africans, and descendants of Africans, still. The fact that they are not held to service ... does not entrust to them the exercise of any function of the Government under which they live.... The petitioner is not a citizen of the State of Kentucky by reason of his birth there and nothing else establishes his citizenship.[21]

Bondage, not freedom, according to Judge Krum, was the predominant classification of Americans of African heritage, and without citizenship, Lyons had no claim to privileges and immunities against licensing under the Constitution. Judge Krum did not trouble to note that—important for constitutional purposes—Lyons's mother was actually Native American rather than African. Had Lyons emphasized his Native American heritage, he might have evaded prosecution.[22] But he challenged the statute head on, and he did not appeal; he paid his fine and registered for a license.[23] Within a month after the decision, more than 100 people of color visited the courthouse to apply for licenses after finding someone with money to pledge their bonds and attest to their character and their ability to earn their livelihood.[24] Among those seeking licenses was one freedman backed by Paymaster Steuart, who presumably had promised to back Dred's initiative to buy his own freedom.[25] But fewer than a tenth of the free blacks living in the city registered, and there was no way for Sheriff Conway to arrest them all. Moreover, St. Louis continued to be the western steamboat terminus and stopover for free blacks looking for better opportunities in the West. Now all free black travelers stopping over in St. Louis were subject to arrest. Over the next decade, intermittent enforcement of this licensing restriction would occur whenever the city's political sentiment favored clamping down on free black activity.

Thanksgiving came,[26] and another slave's case came to trial. Sarah, who shared the black women's cell, was called to trial. She had been taken from the Prosser plantation in Virginia along the same river highway that brought Harriet west. Although slaves were not required to appear for their trials, they were permitted to attend by judicial order, and it was one of the few acceptable ways for inmates to spend time away from the jail,[27] and they certainly were interested in the proceedings that determined their fates.

Sarah's "ownership" was as complicated as Harriet's own. Her opponent was a local man to whom she had been most recently hired out by the Prosser family. Sarah, too, had been handed off as needed among family members in the extended Prosser family after her master's death. Working first in Kentucky for one of the daughters, she was then taken to Illinois, where her master's widow had resettled. The widow was aware that Illinois was a free state, but she had no intention of registering or releasing Sarah. Instead, worried that the local abolitionists would steal Sarah away, her mistress sent her to work for a man in St. Louis. Sarah's time in Illinois was particularly tragic. Her teething baby, sick with dysentery, was the reason she remained through the winter there. Once the weather subsided, mother and baby were shipped to slave St. Louis, where the baby eventually died. The grieving mother continued working where she was assigned until a stranger appeared, seeking to take her south by steamboat. Then she petitioned the court for freedom. Now, after two years' wait, her case was finally called.[28]

For two consecutive days, Sarah left the jail cell with the deputy sheriff to walk the block to the courthouse in the morning and return at night to recount what had happened in court. The jury of 12 white men empaneled to decide her fate declared her free the following day. From the dais, Judge Krum gave the order that all the freedom litigants waited to hear: "Therefore it is considered by the Court that the plaintiff be liberated and entirely set free from the defendant and all persons claiming under him."[29] Sarah left a free person. Apprehension turned to joy! This was encouraging news. The Scotts bided their time until their turn.

Christmas came, then New Year's. For white folks, New Year's was a day of visiting; for black folks, New Year's brought the annual spectacle of the slave-leasing auction on the courthouse steps. The courthouse was only a block from the jail, so even those in the prison yard could hear both the revelry of celebrants shooting off guns and the harangue of the auctioneer's call. In mid-February, without having advanced the Scotts' case much at all, Judge Krum announced he was stepping down from the bench. Local lawyers viewed his resignation with quiet satisfaction.[30] With public approval of his ruling in the Lyons case, Judge Krum went on to run for mayor before long.[31] But for the Scotts, his resignation further delayed the court docket. In March 1847, a spring snowstorm blanketed the city.[32] At the Planters' House, across the street from the courthouse, the Whigs held their annual convention, marking the occasion with a good flow of bourbon. It was also the ball season of pre-Lenten festivities; and the different fraternal and military orders and even the French dancing school held lavish events to honor Washington's birthday.

Two months slipped by with no judge for the circuit court. There was considerable speculation over whom the governor would appoint.[33] Alexander H. Hamilton Jr., a Pennsylvania-trained lawyer, was finally selected to take over the circuit court and its long docket of pending lawsuits.[34] The middle-aged jurist, with the famous name but no known connection to the founding father, would prove to be surprisingly attuned to claims of personal liberties and sympathetic to the Scotts.[35]

Depositions weren't scheduled in the Scotts' suit until May of 1847. When Murdoch left, it appears that the Scotts sought help from the Blow family because the next person appearing as their lawyer was a Blow family in-law and another family member pledged court costs.[36] Various members of the extended family participated supportively in the suit from that point on. Like all indigent slaves, the Scotts were entitled to a court-appointed lawyer, but their suit was stalled in the court's backlog. Having initiated the lawsuit on their own, they needed someone to move it along. They needed the help of a well-established white family like the Blows.

The collective patronage of this extended family does not appear to have been accidental. The Blow family's efforts on the Scotts' behalf appear to have been coordinated by Taylor Blow and older sister, Charlotte Blow Charless.[37] Charlotte had become the heart of her family by the same set of circumstances that prompted Dred's sale. When both Blow parents died in rapid succession, leaving seven orphaned children, Charlotte and her husband, Joseph Charless, took charge of the family, Joseph probated the estate, and they sold one slave to pay Charlotte's father's funeral expenses.[38]

Perhaps Charlotte now saw herself as owing Dred something. Dred later credited the younger Blow brothers as supporting the case.[39] Taylor Blow, a younger brother who worked for Joseph Charless, married Charless's cousin, Eliza Wahrendorf,[40] and he remained in town during the protracted litigation whereas his sister and Charless were often away from the city—sometimes for months at a time.[41] Mistress Charlotte wasn't even in St. Louis when the suit began.[42] But once the Blow family became involved, subtle indications suggest that sister Charlotte and brother Taylor provided some of the support that the Scotts needed.

Joseph Charless had once represented freedom litigants like the Scotts,[43] though he didn't stay with the law;[44] he and his father were partners in a drug and apothecary business. Charlotte saw that her husband brought each of her younger brothers—Henry, Taylor, and William—into his manufacturing business of making medicines and lead for white paint and gunpowder (both of which were in demand on the expanding frontier).[45] Throughout her siblings' adult lives, Charlotte Blow Charless continued to wield moral influence as the family matriarch. Unlike Mrs. Russell and her sisters, Charlotte Charless prided herself in knowing how to run a household with simplicity and modesty rather than extravagance.[46] Unlike the Russells, however, the Charlesses had no fixed address. They followed the custom of some middle-class Louisians of "going into" and out of "housekeeping." Sometimes they rented a house and furnished it, going into housekeeping, and sometimes they moved in with relatives or took rented rooms.[47] Thus, during the course of the Scotts' litigation, even Joseph and Charlotte Charless could not have offered the Scotts the stability of any permanent situation or alleyway home.

Perhaps Charlotte felt obliged to assist Dred now in securing his freedom claim. Charlotte wrote with pride that no hungry person left her household without food and that no one was turned away.[48] Dred knew he could always come around for an old article of clothing or a bite to eat, in keeping with the custom of old Virginia patrimony in slaveholding. Now he must have sought legal help from them. The tie of obligation to former slaves survived even after their sale.[49] The elderly slave man had served his dead master faithfully in free territory, so there was no reason not to support his freedom suit since he was legally entitled to freedom under the law. The old slave had even chosen to bear the family name of Etheldred. Part of the Virginia social code was to look out for the household's dependents, especially when they couldn't care for themselves. Charlotte Charless's name doesn't appear on any of the legal papers—but then it could not have. Even free, white, well-to-do married women could not act in their own right in legal matters. She couldn't sell or free her own slave or file the papers or sign bonds without her husband's participation. She couldn't testify in open court without raising eyebrows. A white woman had to act indirectly if she acted at all by enlisting those men on whom she could prevail to act for her. "The moral authority white women were granted by their society could really only be expressed through influence," wrote one historian.[50] So it seems to have been with the Scotts' lawsuit. Holding her place at the heart of a close-knit family for two decades, Charlotte could request favors and allegiance from her several brothers and brothers-in-law.

Why Taylor Blow's name is not more prominent in the court proceedings may have been because as the younger brother and his brother-in-law's junior partner he was more deferential to the Charlesses taking the lead. He was just a boy when Dred had been sold away 15 years earlier, and he continued to work for Joseph Charless during the entire decade of the trial. Taylor Blow appears much more often than other Blow family members as a helper of several other slaves in establishing their freedom.[51] Dred credited him and youngest brother William as being his principal benefactors.[52] Taylor Blow later freed the Scotts after the devastating United States Supreme Court decision.[53]

In one of the many ironies of mixed allegiance and turnabout of fates, Charlotte, Taylor, and William Blow—those family members most benevolent in assisting the Scotts in the lawsuit—sided with the Confederacy in the Civil War, while brother Henry sided with the Union and was later rewarded with an ambassadorship by President Lincoln.[54] Thus, Henry was accorded the credit for the family's participation in the notorious lawsuit once slavery was defeated, and historians have conventionally credited him for assisting the Scotts.[55] Some of the confusion of credit is perhaps due to the fact that Henry's middle name was Taylor.[56] Unlike brother Taylor, however, the circuit court record books do not show that Henry assisted the freeing of any slave.[57] During the decade of the lawsuit, Henry too was often out of town, but on one occasion, he publicly and indignantly protested being linked to the people he called the "Black Republicans," as the Thomas Hart Benton party was then pejoratively called.[58]

Although Joseph Charless posted bond for the court costs in the event that the Scotts lost,[59] his only connection to the Scotts was through his wife and his business partner, Taylor Blow. At other times Taylor processed papers. Henry appeared at the trials as a witness, testifying to the simple fact that Dred was once owned by his father.[60] The Blows' late sister Martha had married attorney Charles Drake, who represented the Scotts for a few months before leaving the state.[61]

If anyone could work the family network, it was probably Charlotte, who often assumed the caretaking role with dependents and who had once taken care of all her younger siblings.[62] During the lengthy litigation, Charlotte further demonstrated her charitable propensity for helping elderly servants by founding a retirement home to aid elderly impoverished white servants. She became known throughout the city as the primary organizer for this charitable cause.[63] Most civic institutions providing relief for the poor were organized by prominent men. Mrs. Charless organized her lady friends to help her with the retirement home for house servants, which she tenderly named the "Home for the Friendless."[64] Charlotte was not an abolitionist but a public-spirited caretaker, known to be particularly concerned about providing for servants when they grew old, but not necessarily challenging the institution of class or servitude.[65] Like her siblings, she continued to own other slaves years after her family finally emancipated the Scotts.[66]

The letters between Henry Blow and his wife and a memoir of Joseph Charless, written by Charlotte, are the only direct evidence that remains of the Blow family's internal dynamics. Henry never inquired about the Scotts' lawsuit in his letters, and Charlotte does not mention the lawsuit in the memoir of her husband. Among Henry's correspondence, there is only a single possible reference to their case—in a letter from his wife mentioning a string of other family news. We can't know for certain that it refers to Dred Scott, but it does seem to refer to someone who was not one of their household slaves because the person is not referred to by name, as their household slaves are customarily identified in the letters. Mrs. Blow wrote her husband simply: "The Negro did not die"—as it seems, he was expected to.[67] What distinguishes this passage is that its subject is just "the Negro," and presumably not someone she knew by name.

It fits the slaveholding culture that, as domestic servants, the Scotts' well-being would be a woman's concern. But it is ironic that the lawsuit that later evolved prominently into the challenge of contested abstract principles of federalism, freedom, enslavement, and national expansion was sustained, when it almost faltered, as a matter of helping an elderly household servant. This case, which would emerge in the national consciousness as the prototype of all American slavery, was instigated by a family of urban house servants and helped along by a mistress as part of her domestic concern.[68]

If the Blow family was not ideologically committed to the lawsuit, as apparently they were not, why didn't they simply buy Dred, emancipate him, and be done with it? Of course, Mrs. Emerson's refusal would be an obstacle, but it would have been more difficult for her to refuse an offer of purchase for Dred from her social peers, who had owned him previously. In all likelihood, the Blows never made an offer. Negotiating a price to settle a lawsuit was not the sort of thing a white St. Louis lady was likely to do. Women traded in family favors rather than money.[69] Under coverture, married women did not deal with finances. Even when Mrs. Charless launched her charitable project, she didn't finance it herself; she prevailed upon gentlemen to do so because men managed money in antebellum St. Louis.[70] Working through men, Charlotte's involvement may even have extended to finding the Scotts' lawyer for the U.S. Supreme Court. Long after the trial, after Mistress Charlotte was widowed, she was to be found living at the St. Louis home of Frank Blair, brother of the lawyer who argued the case before the Supreme Court and one of the Black Republicans that brother Henry publicly disassociated from.[71]

Although the Scotts surely hoped their cases would soon be resolved with the opening of the May term of 1847, another significant freedom case, *Pierre v. Gabriel Chouteau*, was, at long last, ready for retrial after five years of litigation and one successful jury verdict. During the intervening years, Pierre had spent a lot of time in jail, and prolonged confinement was taking its toll on him.

The delays in Pierre's case were typical of the obstacles that litigants faced. Although he had begun his case in 1840 as a freedom suit against his mistress, Pierre had to file a new suit against her son and heir when his mistress died.[72] The son, Gabriel Chouteau, owner of the grain mill at Chouteau's pond and a brother of Sanford's father-in-law Pierre Chouteau, Jr., appealed when Pierre won a jury verdict.[73] The enslaved Pierre and his siblings, who were born and had lived their entire lives in slave St. Louis, based their freedom claim upon their mother's residence in free territory. Their mother Rose had lived at the Prairie du Chien fort before it came under American control. Under the Northwest Ordinance of 1787, anyone living in the region was free—and, by the principle of matrilinearity, so were the children of these free mothers. On appeal, Chouteau raised an ingenious argument, maintaining that when Rose lived at Prairie du Chien, the area was in British hands and so the Northwest Ordinance did not apply until after the War of 1812. Britain did not abolish slavery until later, and by 1812, Rose had been taken to St. Louis. Thus, Chouteau argued, Rose never really resided in free territory. The Missouri Supreme Court bought the argument.[74] Political geography really did determine destiny. (The courts called it sovereignty.) The high court countermanded Pierre's victory and ordered the case to be tried again. Like trailing barges tied to the lead steamboat, the lawsuits of Pierre's sister Mary Charlotte and then his two brothers followed the same fate.[75] By now Mary Charlotte had four children and the fate of all of them rode on the outcome of the suit.[76]

Pierre was represented by an energetic young New England lawyer named David N. Hall, a Yale college graduate, who responded to Pierre's defeat by taking the extraordinary step of researching Canadian law and sending to Montreal for depositions.[77] This young lawyer would later represent the Scotts as well. Although Hall was resourceful in pursuing the research, he wasn't confident of his trial skills, so he asked Edward Bates, an eminent St. Louis lawyer, to assist him. Hall's own senior partner, A. P. Field, was out of town, as he often was.

Edward Bates documented his view of the trial in his journal. Observing the new Judge Hamilton, Bates remarked that "being in his first official week, [he] was particularly green, in giving and refusing instructions."[78] After three days of trial, Pierre's case went to the jury. After three more days, the jury members returned to say they could not reach a decision—they were hopelessly, irreconcilably split on the matter. The novice judge, conducting his first jury trial, didn't quite know how to respond. So he dismissed them and ordered Pierre back to the sheriff's custody to be hired out. A week later a second freedom suit misfired under Judge

Hamilton's direction when a second jury deadlocked as well. Clearly, the new judge did not know how to bring the jury to the legal conclusion consonant with his instructions.[79]

Charles Drake, the Blow family brother-in-law who picked up the Scotts' case, made only a cameo appearance in the litigation and handed the depositions over to his junior assistant.[80] Time and again, the Scotts' litigation was passed down to the junior partner in a law firm.[81] Even as the depositions were taken by Drake's junior associate, Drake prepared to leave the state, and Lackland, his junior associate, did not step up to take over the case after Drake left.[82] The legal community gave Drake a grand send-off dinner at the deluxe Planter's House across from the courthouse before he closed his practice and left.[83] When the dogwood and the red bud were blooming again along the river, process was finally served on the Scotts' witnesses. Catherine Anderson, former wife of a Fort Snelling officer, gave her deposition at her home, just around the corner from the Russells.[84] She stated that she and others had hired Harriet while Dr. Emerson was away from the fort.[85] Inch by inch, the cases moved forward as Harriet and Dred waited in uncertainty—but victory should have been straightforward.

With depositions gathered by Drake's junior partner, yet a third attorney, Samuel Bay, handled the trial phase of the case.[86] Samuel Bay had recently arrived in the city from a successful career in the state's interior, selling five of his own slaves to finance his move to St. Louis.[87] It's not apparent how he came to represent the Scotts, whether by court appointment or as a lawyer new to town, taking over the remaining cases of a departing one. Bay was certainly an experienced lawyer, but stepping into the case just before trial, he failed to prepare sufficiently and made a crucial mistake.

The deputy delivered the summonses a week before trial. Five people were called to testify for the Scotts: the wealthy grocer Samuel Russell; the steamboat captain who had taken them north on the *Gypsey* when Eliza was born; Henry Blow; the army paymaster; and merchant Thomas O'Flaherty, who seems to have had no connection to the case except perhaps as a character witness.[88] There were depositions from Catherine Anderson and from a soldier who knew Dred at Fort Armstrong. When the paymaster could not be found in town, the Scotts summoned his clerks instead.[89] Paymaster A. D. Steuart might have been called to attest to the Scotts' residence in free territory, but that evidence was already adequately covered in the depositions of others. Instead, he may have been called to testify to Dred's reliability, particularly if he had pledged to back Dred's purchase of freedom.

Severe thunderstorms with torrential rains moved through the area.[90] Other than the storms, the city was quiet. Most of the town's prominent men had gone to Chicago for a convention to improve river transportation.[91] On June 30, 1847, well over a year after staking their fate with the courts, the Scotts' claims finally came to trial. Harriet and Dred were probably present in the second-story courtroom.[92] Escorted by the sheriff's deputy, they probably had high hopes that their case would turn out like Sarah's, and that, shortly, they too would be released once and for all. They had waited for their day in court for 18 months just as long as Sarah had.[93] A freedom suit actually involved two combined issues. First, the litigant had to demonstrate residence in free territory or another basis for claiming freedom, such as by will or by contract. But that alone was insufficient for a judge to declare an enslaved person free. The second issue was that litigants had to demonstrate that someone committed the physical act of confining or assaulting them—that is, a trespass on their liberty. Litigants could only prove their entitlement to freedom by showing that they had been illegally deprived of it.[94]

The difficult issue in this case was to show the trespass: that Mrs. Emerson was guilty of illegally imprisoning the Scotts; they did not claim that she assaulted them. This was the less important claim, but it was embedded in the freedom action. Since that day before Palm Sunday, two Easters had come and gone. No wonder the decision to sue was so daunting and the decision taken so seriously. In reality, one pursued freedom by spending much of the duration of the process in and out of jail.

As the lawyers argued in a courtroom in the second story of the courthouse (now partially brick and partially limestone), the workmen continued to build new walls, columns, and porticos around them. Attorney Samuel Bay's reserved and dignified appearance made him appear haughty and overbearing to people who didn't know him,[95] as the Scotts surely did not. He was reputed to be concise, though not eloquent.[96] The opposing counsel, George Goode, was passionate: certain in his mind that blacks should not be free, he grew irritable when anyone suggested otherwise.[97] In court, he was articulate and vehement. Judge Hamilton was slightly more experienced than weeks earlier when he'd presided over the debacle of two hung juries. In this third freedom trial, he should have been apprehensive about how the proceedings would go.

Somewhere between one lawyer's preparation and another's presentation of the evidence, there was a slip. Like the courtroom drama that it truly was, Master Russell's testimony caught attorney Samuel Bay off guard. The wealthy grocer stated that he never actually hired Dred from Mrs. Emerson, against whom the suit was being brought. Although the evidence showed that the Scotts had worked for the Russells, the lawyer lacked evidence to establish the legal connection between Russell and Mrs. Emerson.[98] Thus, there was no evidence proving that *Mrs. Emerson* had deprived them of their liberty or that the Russells were her agents, so the case fell apart. The links in the hiring chain of enslavement were too tenuous. Who was the real enslaver? the person responsible for keeping the Scotts enslaved? One could not establish freedom against the world with the proof of residence in free territory alone. When Bay failed to tie Samuel Russell to Mrs. Emerson, the named defendant, the case fell apart.[99]

In the midst of the July heat and the gritty dust of limestone construction, 12 white men retired to a jury room and decided against the Scotts, finding that the widow was not guilty of trespass upon their freedom.[100] The Scotts heard the jury foreman, an elderly well-to-do farmer from Kentucky,[101] stand and pronounce the decision on their fates. Bay's haughty demeanor surely did not help, and he probably took little time to explain the loss to the Scotts. He was surprised, to be sure, at losing, but he did not choose to represent many slaves, so he was probably more ruffled at his loss of face than at his clients' loss of liberty. He scrambled to save the situation by simultaneously requesting a new trial and appealing the case, alleging that he was surprised by Master Russell's testimony.[102] George Goode moved that court costs, which Joseph Charless had bound himself to pay, be assigned against the losing party.[103] Judge Hamilton granted the Scotts' motion for a new trial.

The Scotts were truly in a quandary about whom to name as defendant in the suit. Who was the proper party? As the doctor's heir, Mrs. Emerson seemed to be the proper party, but her father, Col. Sanford, had delivered them to the Russells and collected the money. It was Master Russell who paid the old man for their services, but it was Mrs. Russell who gave them orders. Like a nineteenth-century version of the game of Clue, they had to identify the correct assailant in order to win. In the customary division by gender, the ladies had dealt with each other about assigning the servants; the men dealt with each other about the money. The case was all the harder to bring because, as domestics, the Scotts were under the ladies' control. Yet ladies were usually insulated, distanced from the provable legal instrumentalities of making contracts and financial payments, as well as the physical instrumentalities of ensuring enslavement by violence. If Mrs. Emerson had been observed striking them with a broom, the claim would have been easier to prove. But the St. Louis custom was for the husbands to perform the disciplinary violence. Even when Lucy had disobeyed, her mistress asked her husband to do the beating.[104] The nature of mistresses was that though they directed household servants, they often didn't participate in the conventional obvious acts of violence needed to prove a legal case against them.[105] The Scotts had to prove some incident of deprivation or assault to establish their freedom.

In the face of this unraveling lawsuit, the attorney tried the logical next move. He sued all three defendants: Mrs. Emerson, Col. Sanford, and Samuel Russell. Such a move had been successful in previous freedom suits,[106] but Judge Hamilton, still new to the bench and with cases backing up due to the two hung juries, ordered them to choose one defendant. Because enslavement in St. Louis was socially pervasive, it was sustained by interlocking customs. The judge required the proof against their enslaver to be precise. This was probably a bad legal ruling on his part,[107] but he may have shied away from handling the more unwieldy freedom case against three separate defendants. Nearing the end of the spring term, he gave them the summer to think about it.

Not surprisingly, faced with a case that was going to require additional legal work due to his disastrous trial mistake, Samuel Bay quietly left the Scott's representation as soon as he was appointed to represent the state bank, which gave him a lucrative practice.[108]

In mid-July, the 26 former slaves of Milton Duty were auctioned again on the courthouse steps to new temporary masters while they awaited a court ruling on the validity of their master's will.[109] The heirs had successfully cast doubt on the legality of Milton Duty's will because it was drawn up out of state, under the technicalities of Mississippi law rather than Missouri law.[110] The freedom claims of the

26 Milton Duty slaves wove through the docket book, along with Dred and Harriet's claims, through the next decade.

Lawyers came and left the Scotts through their whole lengthy ordeal. The case was simply not sufficiently important for any single attorney to pursue it, and there was no other lawyer on the scene as devoted to helping slaves as Francis B. Murdoch had been. The firm of Field and Hall, which had represented Pierre in his last deadlocked trial, took over the Scott suits—their fourth set of lawyers within two years.[111] There is no reason to believe that Alexander P. Field took anything but a nominal representational role in the Scotts' case. Most of their case filings were signed by David N. Hall, the firm's junior partner from New England.[112]

Alexander P. Field was truly an unusual choice to be representing plaintiffs in freedom suits, even nominally.[113] A. P. Field seemed to seek out controversy, but his position on slavery was simply incoherent. Two decades earlier, he had led the partisan forces attempting to make Illinois a slave state, despite the Northwest Ordinance.[114] But he had also become a personal friend of lawyer Abraham Lincoln, and when Field relocated to New Orleans, he helped to buy a slave's freedom for his friend, Lincoln.[115] Field had more recently been accused of actually kidnapping five members of a free black family in Illinois and bringing them to St. Louis for sale—at the behest of their former master's heir, who disputed that his father had ever freed them.[116] On the other hand, Field was credited with defending an Illinois interracial couple who had married, contrary to Illinois law.[117] He was an embattled Illinois attorney general (the governor tried to throw him out of office) and former secretary of the Wisconsin Territory. The larger than life A. P. Field seemed to be based in St. Louis, where his wife and children lived with his in-laws—but he was not often in town.[118] A. P. Field would go on to serve as Louisiana attorney general and get in a huge row in Washington when Congress wouldn't seat him as congressman from Louisiana. He had no reason to think the Scotts' case would become controversial. Otherwise, given his penchant for controversy, he might have become more involved.[119]

Again, like most law partnerships assigned freedom suits, the work of the case fell to David Hall, the young Massachusetts lawyer, to take the Scotts' case further.[120] The depth of David Hall's participation in the case has never been noted by previous historians.[121] In fact, David Hall acted as the Scotts' benefactor for more than a year before his death, and he assumed entire representation of the Scotts' case when Field left St. Louis permanently. (Had David Hall lived, he might have become the devoted lawyer for slave litigants that St. Louis now lacked with Murdoch's departure.) Hall had conscientiously represented Pierre, in sending to Canada for testimony and attending trial, and he personally paid for the hire of Dred and of several of the Milton Duty slaves, presumably to keep them out of jail.[122]

The summer of 1847 was as hot in St. Louis as usual. Over the summer that the court was adjourned, a pitiful incident occurred nearby that must have reinforced Harriet's resolve to protect her daughters. When eight-year-old Sarah, a little slave girl no older than Eliza, was sent by her owners to work at the Tanners' household, she cried, threw tantrums, and rebelled. As a result, the Tanners beat her—ultimately to her death.[123] It wasn't clear who was responsible, since Sarah had been severely mistreated by several persons in the household. Some neighbors accused Mrs. Tanner, who was said to have a temper. They said that she tied the girl to a tree when she disobeyed and whipped her with a stick, not giving the girl anything to eat or drink in the heat.[124] Neighbors heard the child's wails and passersby saw her tied to the tree. Others said the Tanners' son struck her with sticks, driving her into the creek when she went for water. Still others accused another slave woman in the household, Cornelia, for her death, saying that she had tried to drown Sarah in the creek—but that the "little devil had gotten out."[125] With so many witnesses to so many incidents of violence, it wasn't clear exactly who was responsible for her murder.[126]

But worse, after weeks of abuse, the Tanners had tried to return the girl to her owners when she contracted the whooping cough. Sarah's owners didn't want the sick child back, so they advised the Tanners to tie her up in an outhouse instead. Eventually the Tanners sent her home anyway, with a note that they could do nothing with her. The note ended with the self-serving justification that she not be allowed near white children. "I have sent her home as she has completely worn me out."[127] The little girl was so emaciated and covered with sores that her owners barely recognized her,[128] and she died within days. No wonder enslaved mothers warned their children, "Never go out of the city."[129] Harriet may have needed only to hear the tale told in the streets to recommit herself.[130] "Touch one of them," the minister had said, "and you touch her mother's heartstring."[131] Sarah's brief, tragic life reinforced the lesson that slaves should not provoke their masters. But who would avenge this child's torture and death? Striking an Indian child or even cutting his hair would have sparked retaliation at St. Peter's.[132] In St. Louis, the incident was handled by an inquest, albeit with finger pointing in so many directions it was difficult to produce a specific indictment. Both Mistress Tanner and her slave Cornelia were indicted for the murder, but only Cornelia was jailed—probably in the cell reserved for black women inmates. Mistress Tanner was acquitted in a single day in October.[133] The slave Cornelia was held longer in the hopes of finding enough evidence to press charges, but she too was eventually released. There was no justice for Sarah.[134]

CHAPTER 27

Filing Suit Again

F ROM BOTH TOWN and county, slaves continued to take chances to run away. The newspapers announced the departures with tiny inked emblems of men carrying hobo packs and women carrying tied handkerchiefs, marching across the columns of the want ads: "$400 reward. Ranaway THREE NEGROES: one woman about 35 years old named Matilda: one mulatto boy and a small girl named Puss—black."[1] The ad identified Matilda as the mother and, ominously, indicated that all of her front teeth were knocked out. Bounty hunters pursued the runaways and many were caught and returned—first to the jail and then to their masters as provided by statute.[2] Matilda, running with children, was probably recaptured. The web of enslavement did not require each slave to be continually locked down.

The circuit court did not resume again until late November.[3] Expectant litigants often hung around the courthouse because, if they were absent when the case was called, their suit could be dismissed.[4] The freedom litigants watched as more fortunate slaves came to court to be freed voluntarily by their masters. Judge Hamilton handled manumission matters at the beginning or the end of the day, accommodating the slaves' working hours.[5] More than a hundred persons had been voluntarily manumitted by their masters in the two years since the Scotts filed suit. Some had purchased their own freedom, as Dred tried to.[6] Some parents had saved money to buy their children's freedom.[7] Everyone needed court papers documenting their masters' willingness to emancipate them, and white male witnesses to attest to this fact. No woman, black or white, could attest to a slave's manumission.[8] If a free black person stood to emancipate a relative or friend, two additional white men were needed to give oaths. The docket entries were often couched in physical description, and few persons had last names to give. Jacob (age 40; five feet, eight inches tall) is described as "spare made, quite black, white eyes, a knot on the right wrist, and a cooper by trade." Many descriptions identified the enslaved person by their scars: "scar on forehead over left eye." One entire family (parents and four children)[9] were freed together. Upon release from bondage, some took their places in the community of free black people in St. Louis; some left town as soon as possible, never to be heard from again.[10] Though these fortunate slaves now owned their own time, they were subject to licensing if they remained. Further, if they didn't earn enough to maintain their independence, they could find themselves confined to the workhouse on grounds of poverty.[11] The city kept a check on the casual workforce that was so useful by the selective enforcement of licensing and vagrancy laws.

When the fall term recommenced, the Scotts elected to sue Widow Emerson again, despite losing against her the last time. As the doctor's heir, she had the clearest claim of ownership—of Dred at least. Whether she formally hired them to the Russells or not, she directed them there and received their wages. This time they had to clarify the series of relationships that kept them in bondage and demonstrate the links in that chain to the jury. They needed Mistress Russell's testimony.[12] At no time did Irene Emerson testify.[13] Mrs. Emerson probably never appeared in the courtroom, since ladies usually gave their testimony by deposition in the privacy of their own homes or lawyers' offices. It was unseemly for respectable women to testify in open court with the white male jury staring at them.[14] But although Mrs. Emerson was the principal party in both claims, she was a silent ghost in the proceedings. She was a passive participant in this lawsuit, insulated by her gender from direct inquiry and shielded by her father and her lawyers from confrontation by the couple whom she continued to hold in slavery.

That particular fall, the St. Louis Circuit Court heard none of the pending freedom cases. The court was being audited, and so the docket was delayed further.[15] During the audit, Judge Hamilton noticed that during the spring term he'd neglected Harriet's case—in the fiasco of deadlocked juries and mismanaged cases, only Dred's claim was formally submitted to the jury. Now that the error was discovered, he patched up the problem by an explanatory entry in the docket book, indicating that he had intended to try Harriet's case along with Dred's. For correction, he simply recopied the entries of Dred's case in Harriet's name, down to the names of the jurors, as if her case had been placed before them six months before.[16] From the judge's viewpoint, overlooking Harriet was a harmless error as long as he granted her a new trial too. It seems that Harriet had been denied even this initial day in court—probably denied even this moment of the jury's attention. As Dred's wife, she was treated as just an appendage to her husband, much as history would treat her, swept along for the ride.

Still awaiting trial, now for a third time was Pierre, who, of all the pending litigants, had waited the longest.[17] Pierre was still confined, and, though his siblings were rented out to other private masters, no one wanted to hire him. His long confinement and the litigation setbacks had taken a terrible toll on his spirit. He, too, had been hired out for a while but he acted so strangely that his employer no longer wanted responsibility for him. So, Pierre's employer returned him to the sheriff, offering to pay his board in jail rather than be responsible for having the rattled man in his household.[18]

Among the other freedom claimants was a handsome, part Indian and part African American woman named Nancy, whom the Scotts may have known from Jefferson Barracks, where Nancy too had lived. She had grown up as a "wild" little girl who hung around the 4th Infantry camps when the unit was stationed in the Creek nation.[19] She was brought along when the troops transferred to Jefferson Barracks because she helped the soldiers' wives with laundry.[20] She was left behind, however, when the troops departed for Texas. Someone took charge of her, assuming she was the slave of an absent officer. To free herself, Nancy sued and won by establishing that she was Native American. (Charles Lyons would probably have been similarly successful in evading licensing if he had stressed that his mother was Seneca, rather than African American.)[21] The court awarded her only one penny in damages for her enslavement.[22]

One night that fall, a supernatural light flooded the sky to the east. Gaslight lanterns brightened the dark streets for the very first time, and people were struck with the unusual brilliance of night lighting.[23] Omnibuses drawn by horses bumped noisily along the uneven streets, their nighttime passage enabled by the new invention. Louisians had only just become accustomed to the brilliance of nighttime gaslight when another new invention caught their attention: the telegraph. They marveled at the speed with which the telegraph carried the president's address to Congress, transmitting it from Washington to the telegraph office in Vincennes, Illinois. The St. Louis newspapers, receiving the message from Vincennes via fast horse, printed it within three days of its delivery to Congress half a continent away. "Truly, Man is created omnipotent over matter," one observer praised. No longer did the local newspapers need to depend on riverboat pilots to bring news.[24] The great river still posed a natural barrier to reaching the city, but eventually all the eastern news could be retrieved by ferry and packet boat from the Illinois shore.

Christmas Day 1847 was very cold and cloudy, with a slight sprinkle of powdery snow, but the last days of 1847 were warm for the season.[25] One civic-minded observer wrote, "There has not yet been a call for the public charity in the city this winter.... The poor are employed and paid and consequently, all are independent."[26] All, that is, except those enslaved, those hired out by others, or those litigating their freedom.

If the Scotts were jailed during this time, they probably found some way to place their daughters with someone outside. If they were lucky, the sheriff might have allowed them to be released upon their guarantee to earn their keep elsewhere. Missouri slaves expected to receive their Christmas boxes—the treasured gift of new clothes that would get them through the coming year.[27] Without a master to provide them with these necessities, however, the Scotts depended on what they could beg as well as what they could earn.[28] William Blow's wife regarded the Scotts as something of a nuisance whenever they came around.[29] "Quarters, half-dollars, and old clothes were the least of his demands," she is quoted as saying of Dred.[30] The Scotts may have tried Christmas calling, a custom in St. Louis as well as St. Peter's. The Scotts too had hungry children to feed and clothe. At St. Peter's, the Dakota begged by offering to shake hands: "*Hirharha nampetchiyuza.*" Only the proud, ascerbic Ojibwa Chief Flatmouth had expressed the position: "we beg for justice, not charity."[31]

Obtaining adequate clothing was a problem for most city slaves, but hired-out slaves and freedom litigants had the most difficulty and looked the shabbiest of all.[32] Harriet and the girls probably hadn't had new clothing since working for the Bainbridges. Normally the hiring arrangement obliged the new master to furnish the slave's necessary clothing, but masters who temporarily hired slaves were notably reluctant to provide durable clothing because of expense. One slave remarked that even the dogs knew how to distinguish the well-dressed and barked more aggressively at those shabbily clothed.[33] One man suing for his freedom had to petition the court to receive permission to set aside enough money from his wages to cover his decency, since his pants had worn out.[34] In litigation almost two years now, the Scotts' children had probably worn out and outgrown their clothes.

Eighteen forty-eight was an election year, and on Washington's Birthday, 4,000 men thronged to the courthouse rotunda to nominate Zachary Taylor for president.[35] Judge Krum announced his candidacy for mayor. Despite the popularity of his ruling upholding mandatory licensing of free blacks, the local newspapers now criticized him for being too soft on abolitionists during his time as mayor in Alton, for allowing Lovejoy to set up a press in the first place.[36] There always seemed to be someone in St. Louis espousing an even more extreme position than any racially restrictive position taken.

In February 1848, the old man who seemed to stand in primary opposition to the Scotts died. Col. Alexander Sanford, in his late sixties, died at his farm in the county. The newspaper announced that a cortege of carriages had been organized to follow the body to the graveyard. Sanford family friends, and particularly friends of the wealthy Pierre Chouteau Jr., were invited to meet at the courthouse steps, where mourning carriages waited to convey them to the residence of the deceased to pay the family condolences. They would then proceed to the Episcopal burying ground. The funeral cortege was paid for by Sanford's father-in-law and the city's wealthiest man, Pierre Chouteau Jr.[37] Such a grand funeral procession for a man who had once been insolvent demonstrates how successfully the eldest son had refurbished his father's respectability.[38]

If Harriet and Dred were on their own recognizance then, they might have watched as the black carriage drivers, on that rainy day, held umbrellas for the white guests as they stepped into the black-draped carriages at the courthouse steps. The old man's slaves, who had served him since before the Scotts' arrival at the farm years earlier, now could expect to be sold—and soon they were.[39] The Scotts' situation was relatively better than that; at least they couldn't be sold while their case was pending, and their residence in free territory might still be their passport to freedom.

The Scotts would not mourn this master's demise. Col. Sanford had resisted their freedom efforts at every turn and had worked actively to further the proslavery agenda. With his death, it seemed that the Scotts had survived their primary antagonist. Mistress Irene did not appear to be that involved in the lawsuit.[40]

But shortly after the funeral, Widow Emerson appeared personally at the courthouse to attend to some of her own business. She signed papers to sell her Iowa land for a goodly sum of cash.[41] Col. Sanford's death must have placed new financial pressure on her because a week later, her lawyer petitioned the court to compel that the Scotts be hired out to work. This particular request does not appear to have been made earlier in the litigation. Because this sort of request was not uncommon in freedom cases, the court ordered that the sheriff take them into custody and hire them out to best advantage in order to generate money, pending resolution of the case.[42] Now an additional type of bond was necessary, to be posted by whoever hired the Scotts as a promise to pay their wages to Mrs. Emerson, should she prevail in the litigation.[43] The implication of this action is that either the Scotts had been out on their own recognizance previously keeping their own wages or that they had sat idly in the jail. At any rate, it seems that until this time the Scotts were not accumulating wages for disbursal by the court to the lawsuit's eventual winner.

Why hire them out now? Why at this juncture in the proceedings? Col. Sanford's death may have been the impetus. No document exists to identify who hired the Scotts with this initial order in 1848.[44] As of one year later, on March 17, 1849, Dred (and Dred only) was hired out to David N. Hall, the Scott's young lawyer from Massachusetts.[45] Hall had hired Dred for the duration of the lawsuit, but that hire lasted only two years and 23 days thereafter—until Hall's death.[46] Again, Harriet was unaccounted for, for better or worse.

This motion must have struck the Scotts as especially hypocritical, given the widow's refusal to allow Dred to buy his freedom: explaining that he was practically free anyway and should support his family.[47] They were hardly free to support themselves with their earnings; now she wanted those wages paid into the court to accumulate potentially for her eventual profit, wages that would be beyond their reach for the duration of the lawsuit. Even more disingenuously, she later attempted to explain that the whole lawsuit was prompted by a greedy lawyer and the Scotts' wish to claim back wages from her.[48] She would later collect these accumulated moneys when the case concluded.[49]

The work order, filed a month after Col. Sanford's death, suggests that Sanford was not the only one tightening the screws on the Scotts. A bill showing up later in John F. A. Sanford's estate suggests that the local person pressing advantage, while John Sanford was absent in New York, was a Virginian named Benami S. Garland.[50] B. S. Garland seemed to be in the debt collection business.[51] He left a record in the St. Louis courts of pursuing debts for creditors, sometimes even in circumstances that he had not been asked to—although always claiming payment therefor.[52] B. S. Garland is best known to history for actively pursuing his runaway slave man, Joshua Glover, to Wisconsin and litigating an unpopular case there under the Fugitive Slave Law—an event that triggered an antislavery uprising and an attempt by the state of Wisconsin to nullify the federal Fugitive Slave Law.[53] For the most part, historians have not previously noted that B. S. Garland was simultaneously involved in the Scotts' suit.

As early as June 30, 1847, he was summoned as the only witness for the defense. His testimony was never taken though.[54] He had been involved in Dr. Emerson's probate, assessing the value of the Manchester Road property for the estate.[55] It may have been in that capacity that he was called as a witness for Mrs. Emerson. But seeing a sum to be collected, Garland had a tendency to dig in and go after it. After Col. Sanford died, son John asked B. S. Garland to sell the farm, its stock, and its slaves.[56] Almost a decade later, after the conclusion of the litigation and after John F. A. Sanford's death, B. S. Garland requested compensation from the estate "for 10 years services attending to Dred Scotts' case. Suing for freedom of self and family employing counsel, attending to hires, and collecting same at the request of Mr. Sanford from Nov 1846 to Jany, 1858."[57]

What exactly Garland did in this respect is unclear, but he wanted to be paid for his services. B.S. Garland seems to have been the person riding shotgun on the Scotts' trial, and in all likelihood, the man insisting that they be hired out for wages at this juncture in the litigation.

The court order probably landed the Scotts in jail, at least temporarily until the sheriff could hire them out. They must have known that freedom litigants could not escape spending some time imprisoned.[58] Most were jailed when they were not hired out as well as between hirings—though, by now, there was also a workhouse where long-term inmates and vagrants were sent to work for their keep.[59] During the Scotts' incarceration, it's likely that Eliza, now nine, and Lizzie, three or four years old, accompanied them to jail at least temporarily, since small children were imprisoned with their slave parents.[60]

As the city had outgrown its old courthouse, so too had it outgrown its old jail. A new one had been built next to the old jail where Lucy had been held.[61] The old jail was also the place from which a mob had seized McIntosh and taken him to a tree to be tied up and burned alive.[62]

The Scotts entered the new jail complex through a low entrance on 6th Street that led first to the small one-story building that housed the jailer's office.[63] The jailer, a young white man named Lewis Martin, lived there with his wife. He held the keys to the Scotts' confinement off and on over the next several years. As freedom litigants, the Scotts were there under the sheriff's authority and the judge's orders. As once the quality of their lives was determined by the nature of their masters' households and agendas, their lives were now governed by the bureaucratic trinity of the courts, the sheriff, and, most closely, the jailer. Whenever they were not hired out by the sheriff, they could expect to be housed in jail.

Going through the jailer's office to the back, the Scotts entered a small outdoor yard with high side walls. In this yard, free blacks who were found to be unlicensed were whipped.[64] The new jail stood three stories high at the far end of the yard. Thirty-six separate cells were arranged 12 to a floor on opposite sides of a central atrium extending from the ground to the roof's sealed skylights. A noisy clamor filled the place, and through their barred cell doors, the inmates could watch what happened in the central space and talk to one another. With its three-story galleries, the new jail was a grisly echo of the courthouse central rotunda and galleries. Pairs of stairs flanked the central atrium. The Scotts took their places in separate cells designated for blacks, on the ground floor. It seems that, throughout their lives, the Scotts were lodged in basements. Black inmates were kept separately from whites, and the men apart from the women.[65] Pierre had become almost a permanent resident of the cell reserved for African American men.[66]

The jail, which housed 15 to 20 inmates at a time, saw a lot of turnover. During 1847, more than 250 persons spent time in one of the cells.[67] Dred, who was the more talkative of the couple, probably struck up conversations with newly arriving strangers. Harriet, more reserved than her husband, probably listened and watched. The air was bad inside the poorly ventilated building. Each eight-foot-square cell held a couple of inmates on a stone floor and had a high ceiling that dwarfed human proportion. Dim light trickled in through a narrow window slit in the thick stone wall. There was water, drawn from a common bucket set out in the hall that the jailer refilled from time to time. The inmates got two meals a day: meat soup, vegetables, and bread, ladled onto tin plates. The plan had been to heat the building by a furnace (particularly on wet days, the thick stone walls held in the damp and cold),[68] but the defective mechanical construction never worked, so there was never enough heat, especially in winter. Instead, two stoves were set up in the halls. So miserable were the conditions in winter that once, when the jailer extinguished the stove's fire, an inmate attempted suicide rather than endure the cold.[69]

For warmth, each cell had only a dirty buffalo robe, which lay on the stone floor.[70] It was on this musky fur bed that Harriet must have put her daughters to sleep if they were confined with her. Ironically, Harriet, the washerwoman who laundered others' fine linens, was left to warm herself and her children against the cold with a filthy buffalo hide. She might tell her daughters stories of how she had seen the Indians bring hides like this one to the fort to trade—anything to erase the fear from their dreams of freedom. All night long, Dred and Harriet were locked in their separate cells. Certainly, things were worse here than at the Minnesota fort, where, although the Scotts were deemed slaves, they were able to sleep next to each other—Dr. Emerson had even gotten them their own stove.

Despite their confinement, many prisoners spent the time knitting socks.[71] Inmates were not completely sealed off from those outside; visitors were allowed in. Dorothea Dix, the nationally known prison reformer, was a notable visitor to the jail in 1846 and 1847, while traveling from the East.[72] The Scotts, whose lives had already crisscrossed those of so many prominent people of the decade, probably paid little attention to the prim New England woman as she inspected the new jail. Given Dix's interests and report, she most certainly overlooked them. In choosing to help the poor and insane, she specifically disavowed any interest in reforming slavery. Even this angel of mercy knew that antislavery talk was off limits. Southerners appreciated this and so welcomed her to inspect their jails.[73]

The Scotts' fellow inmates included convicted felons, suspected murderers, petty thieves, notorious burglars, and insane men and women whose misfortunes had reduced them to helplessness. Because the city had no hospital for the insane, anyone locked up for reasons of insanity resided in the jail. In addition, the jail often served as the lockup place for slaves picked up by the night patrols or for free blacks discovered to be without a license. Sorted for incarceration by color and gender rather than by crime or condition, these individuals ended up as the Scotts' cellmates. Other slaves were dropped off with the jailer for safekeeping. Many slaves were held there when their masters died, until they could be auctioned on the courthouse steps. The owners simply paid the jailer the daily fee as if kenneling a dog.[74] The jailer charged 25 cents per person per day for custodial care and board.

Thus, because the jailer charged the sheriff for the keep of slaves (just as did he did masters whose slaves might be picked up by the night patrols), the sheriff had an incentive to hire out slaves in his custody. The county didn't have to pay the jailer if the freedom litigant was hired out.

Prisoners did escape from time to time. A couple of white convicts made a daring escape from the third floor of the jail by scratching out the mortar around a stone and dislodging it from the wall. The hole was only a foot wide and 18 inches long, and it was three stories up—but the men were able to squeeze through. Using strips of buffalo robe tied together to make a rope, they lowered themselves to the ground and escaped.[75] Those who were recaptured forfeited their time already spent. So dismal was the prospect of return that one apprehended escapee told the court he'd rather die than be sent back.[76]

News came to the Sanford family of another officer husband's death. Sister Henrietta's husband, the sickly Captain Clarke, was killed in Mexico, and the army sent his body back to St. Louis for burial that spring.[77] Henrietta's circle of friends surrounded her with emotional support and expressed pity that reflected on her sister, Mrs. Emerson's, living situation. "What will become of her?" one friend wrote.[78] "I do hope Sanford will behave kindly to Mrs. Clarke, but from the way Mrs. Emerson has been left, I have small hopes of it."[79] The letters implied that the sisters' wealthy older brother, John, had not done right by Irene. Widow Emerson may have been insulated by her male relatives from direct participation in the Scotts' lawsuit, but her peers did not envy her standard of living.

With his father's death, John F. A. Sanford reclaimed the value of everything that he had bought for his father during the past decade.[80] There was no will providing for the other siblings and no distribution to them. With the sale of the Sanford farm, Mrs. Emerson and the now widowed Mrs. Clarke made plans to move with their children to Springfield, Massachusetts, to live near their more fortunate and wealthy sister, Mrs. Barnes.[81] Their widowed stepmother accompanied them.[82]

The idea of living "at the North," as it was called, was irksome to St. Louis ladies like the Sanford women. Louisians found the servants less dependable and surlier there. One typical letter described a northern friend as "being without a servant which you will think terrible."[83] Another wrote that during her sojourn there, she had to both sew and keep house herself. "We have a girl, but such a dirty creature that I have to watch that we are not poisoned. Save me from living in a free state."[84] There was no thought of taking along the slaves. The court proceedings froze the Scotts in place in St. Louis, and slaves could not easily be taken to increasingly abolitionist Massachusetts.[85] Leaving Missouri, Mrs. Emerson appears to have been content to leave the lawsuit behind but not sufficiently disinterested to abandon her interest. Dred and Harriet never saw her again, although her claim of ownership continued to rule their lives for eight more years.

The Scott family's fate was now entirely in the judge's hands. The sheriff, equipped with a court order requiring them to earn wages, was a regular constraint in their lives. David N. Hall was the only person assigned to look out for their interests.[86] Their whereabouts during the winter of 1848–49 remain a mystery. Like hundreds of other slaves, they simply slipped from recorded view.[87]

As rented-out slaves[88] they could expect to be used more harshly than an owner's own slaves. Being hired out took a toll on freedom litigants, as did sitting in jail. The Duty slaves, who numbered 26 when they first sued for their freedom, had seen many of their members die in the interim while hired out. True, additional children were born to the slave women in the group, but many died, and Duty slaves seemed to be abused, to be ill-treated, and to die prematurely while hired out to an even greater extent than other slaves in the city. By 1852, only seven remained of the original 26, although two men sent to work on steamboats successfully escaped.[89] By 1850, Milton Duty's heirs wrote the court that the years of being hired out had so damaged the Duty slaves that they had become worthless, and that they wished to have them sold for whatever money could be gotten for them.[90] Perhaps out of pity, David N. Hall hired some of those remaining.[91]

As usual, the court closed down for the summer months, when Judge Hamilton left the city. For those free to walk about, summer meant visits to Lamoalfa's ice cream saloon, opposite the Planter's House.[92] In the heat, others turned to stronger drink, and the calaboose was often full of drunks on warm summer nights.[93] Summer days in St. Louis alternated between stormy spells and bright sizzling hot days. There were "Flying thunder clouds…in all directions and occasional slight shower, with gleams of hot sunshine between."[94] Late summer turned dry as the heat of the sun baked the streets to dust. By July came the hottest day, and by August, Louisians were complaining that grasshoppers had destroyed their gardens.[95]

In November, when the telegraph[96] brought the news that Zachary Taylor had been elected president, an immense crowd spontaneously celebrated with a torchlight parade.[97] Their general, commander of three successful territorial expansions (the Mexican, the Seminole, and the Blackhawk Wars), had risen to the country's highest post. To most Americans, the new president was a hero.[98] But unique among Americans, both Scotts had been in a position to have actually observed the general in person. As servants at army posts under his command, they probably knew his personal manner and habits, which gave rise to his nickname "Rough and Ready."[99] There were only two dozen officers at the forts in the Upper Mississippi valley during the Scotts' time there, and Zachary Taylor had been in command, as he had the larger army of Observation in Texas. They probably heard about Taylor in the manner that the servants of one master learned of the traits of others. At table, Harriet may have come to know how he cut his meat or buttered his bread. Attending the surgeons, Dred may have heard about the commander's medical history or whether he snored at night. In the nature of domestic service, it was common for the details of a master's person to be known to slaves other than his own. Still, Harriet Scott and her husband would have been ciphers to him. If he could place them at all, it would be only by identification to their masters.

Harriet probably knew better than to view the general's election as a good omen. The new president had an entire plantation of slaves of his own. What difference did it make that a couple so lowly had known the next president of the United States? In the succeeding decade, all Americans would hear about the lawsuit and recognize the name Dred Scott—although even prominent men such as

Zachary Taylor, who had come into the Scott family's close contact, would never remember the details of their existence. Slaves whose troubles would shake the nation were invisible even when close by.

The court didn't start its new term until late November.[100] This time, Louis T. LaBeaume, a corpulent man, sat as sheriff at the judge's right hand. Luckily for the Scotts, as a shirttail relative and family friend of the Blows, LaBeaume could keep an eye on the progress in their cases.[101]

That fall another enslaved man named Scott filed suit.[102] He was not related to Dred, but he had much in common with him. Tom Scott and Dred had both been to the Southwest during the American expansion; by coincidence, they had both taken the same last name, and they had parallel freedom suits before Judge Hamilton at the same time. Tom's legal problem, however, was that though he'd traveled far into the frontier to Santa Fe, none of his travels had taken him into free territory. He'd been neither north of the latitude under the Missouri Compromise nor north into the states of the old Northwest Territory. Those territorial dimensions defined the slave's holy grail.[103] By law, the frontier was only free north and west of the Ohio River and north of the Missouri Compromise line—though events in Kansas would change even that compromise.[104] Tom Scott's lawyers soon discontinued his case because he had no chance of winning. It was not enough to travel to the wild frontier and back.[105]

Pierre still sat in the black men's cell in jail, running up a bill for his keep but without prospect of being hired out. The former sheriff petitioned the court to be relieved of his care and custody. The new sheriff was reluctant to take custody of him.[106] Judge Hamilton tried to find him a home at the county farm. The jailer's affidavit stated that he believed Pierre was of unsound mind and that he had been insane for at least the past 10 months that he'd spent in jail.[107] Since the jail also held the insane, it is where Pierre remained.

During December, Judge Hamilton was occupied in his own jurisdictional contretemps with the judge from the criminal court. The dispute was over the liberty of a man who had been accused of a crime and held in jail without trial for a long time. The criminal court simply kept delaying his trial with continuances. Judge Hamilton released the jailed man on habeas corpus, only to find that the criminal court judge reissued orders to have him arrested again.[108] The feuding judges of the civil and criminal benches alternately ordered the man released and rearrested. As the stubborn judges continued their jurisdictional wrangling over the defendant's liberty, Sheriff LaBeaume faithfully rearrested the man when ordered to do so. But when the jailer released him by order of Judge Hamilton's writ of habeas corpus, the criminal court judge charged the jailer with contempt.[109]

The local lawyers were not impressed by the judges' shenanigans. "They are both wrong. One is an ass and the other a mule.... it can lead to nothing but an endless round of capture and discharge."[110] It is significantly revealing about Judge Hamilton's character, however, that his sensibilities were decidedly on the side of releasing the accused from prolonged incarceration without trial. Judge Hamilton eventually prevailed in the dispute when the criminal court judge was replaced.[111]

CHAPTER 28

1849: Trial by Pestilence, Trial by Fire

O N NEW YEAR'S DAY, 1849, the city engaged in the usual holiday entertainments, and a traveling circus company, driven from New Orleans by a cholera panic, came to town to add to the festivities.[1] The circus was in town, but the cholera was trailing not far behind.

It was not until early 1849 that a buyer was found for Sanford's farm.[2] The farm, together with three slaves, was sold to one of the city's richest former Virginians.[3] On the first of March, the livestock, carriages, and household furniture from the Sanford estate were auctioned off.[4] With his primary residence at the company's New York office, Sanford liquidated almost all his Missouri assets with B. S. Garland's help, giving Garland one of his father's carriages as partial payment for his services.[5]

Mrs. Emerson also sold her small acreage on Manchester Road, marking her permanent departure from Missouri.[6] Irene, by now widowed for five years, had not remarried, but she had a child to raise and no independent means of support. She lived on the charity of relatives. In a letter to John Darby, the lawyer closing out his father's estate, John Sanford added a postscript.[7] He had seen some mention of a proceeding of some slaves against his sister. Did Darby think it could be reopened? In the context of liquidating his holdings, the question posed was strictly a financial one: was there any money for his sister in the lawsuit? If there was money to be had, Sanford knew the man to collect it. After all, he now had two widowed sisters and a widowed stepmother, and five or six fatherless nieces and nephews who depended upon him. The word around town was that he had done little to provide for poor Irene.[8] This note, occurring two years after the Scotts filed suit, marks Sanford's first direct involvement in the case that would bear his name for posterity.[9] Half a century later, Mrs. Emerson remembered that her brother had paid all the costs for the lawsuit and that she had lost track of and interest in it.[10] Her father's death seems to be the point at which John F. A. Sanford took over.

At the end of February, the sheriff again delivered a round of summonses for the Scott trial.[11] But almost no business was done at the courthouse that year.

On March 17, 1849, the Scotts' attorneys, Hall and Field, signed a bond to release Dred from jail, but there was no similar bond in the file for Harriet.[12] Twenty-eight-year-old David Hall had been recently married in Connecticut, to the daughter of an esteemed clergyman and well-known naturalist. Mrs. Hall assisted her talented father by producing detailed specimen drawings. Hall's wife of a little more than a year was expecting their first child in January of 1849. Sad to say, both she and the child perished in childbirth.[13] Since Hall and Field signed the hiring papers for Dred two months after her death, it's unlikely that Dred was expected to work for Hall directly. Although Hall owned a house on Pine Street,[14] he lived with Field, his law partner's in-laws. This family had slaves of their own. It seems that A. P. Field, his flamboyant senior partner, had already made plans to leave St. Louis for New Orleans.[15]

When Judge Hamilton opened the spring term as usual on the third Monday of April, it was difficult to find county people willing to come into town to serve on juries because the cholera was afoot. Judge Hamilton was never in the habit of advancing the court's business very much during the spring term anyway,[16] often binding trials over with continuances until fall. This year the bar association members convened in the courthouse law library and agreed to dispense with court until the cholera abated. The judge promptly left the city as he did every summer. By now, the Scotts' trial was stalled in a backlog of more than 300 cases.[17]

That spring, the river was uncommonly high for the season, and it was still rising.[18] High water could lead to flooding, but it was good for steamboat traffic. Fully 50 boats were reported to be docked at the wharf. South of town, the triumphant 3rd Infantry returned to Jefferson Barracks from winning the territorial war with Mexico, though with heavy losses. The city hosted a parade for the returning heroes. Dred may have found a way to be there to see and cheer on the passing faces of the men with whom he had spent two years. Like many Mexican war veterans, Capt. Bainbridge was severely wounded in the battles. Mistress Mary rejoined him at Jefferson Barracks.[19]

That year, Harriet and her family, in the twilight status of being half free, half slave, were legally confined in St. Louis while a pair of plagues descended on the city. The cataclysmic events of 1849 slowed all life in St. Louis. Living on the streets and rented out to temporary masters, the Scotts must have encountered it directly. The cholera started in small numbers, although the initial announcement caused a small panic. Each week the city's inhabitants hoped it had ended, but the disease lingered and spread, killing still more. It reached major proportions; in a city of 30,000 people, more than 10 percent died during the spring and summer.[20] Hundreds fled the city, moving to outlying villages and farms in hopes of avoiding the disease.[21] The newspapers blamed the town's many foreign immigrants for the scourge. As word spread, steamboats attempted to bypass St. Louis, and the city quarantined arrivals on an island in the river.[22] There was no fleeing by river to escape the epidemic. Cholera had contaminated steamboats, so they were stripped of their carpets and scrubbed down.

The plague affected people in every station in life: the richest of men, the poorest of women, whites and blacks, free and slave, new immigrants, and old prominent families—both Virginians and French. It took its toll by weakening the victim's body with spasmodic cramps, vomiting, and diarrhea. Dazed, weakened, stumbling to their beds or to alley outhouses, victims often died of dehydration within a matter of hours. No one knew what precautions to take against the disease, but the demand for servants and laundresses surely increased. The paper told the city's readers that "[c]lean clothing is a certain sequence of daily bathing. No [one] can tolerate, for a moment, any other than clean wearing apparel."[23] Wherever she was assigned within the city, Harriet's workload surely increased. But what no one yet knew was that cholera was carried by water itself—that the very water the citizens were encouraged to bathe in, the very water Harriet used to launder clothes, sometimes spread the disease.

Dred and Harriet were required to remain, by legal order, within the city limits under the sheriff's supervision. Doorways on every street were swathed in the black shroud of mourning. Servants carried bodies on stretchers to the dozen graveyards of each religious denomination. The poor, often without religious affiliation, went to the city cemetery.

As the epidemic mounted day by day, another pestilence hit. On the evening of May 17, 1849, a fire broke out on one of the steamboats moored on the levee. The fire on the steamboat *White Cloud* quickly spread to the damaged *S. B. Edward Bates*, which was also moored at the levee. Someone cut the damaged, burning boat loose and thrust it out into the river to drift away. However, the current was strong from the northeast, so instead of drifting away, the boat floated along, bumping down the line of boats like a large floating torch igniting a quarter of a mile of moored boats. Within minutes, more than 20 wooden boats were in flames. The intense heat and sparks from the long line of blazing boats set the docks and dockside warehouses afire. The winds stoked the conflagration out of control.[24]

The fire grew larger and hotter from the tinder of wooden warehouses and barrels of dry goods until it engulfed the town's Main Street. People ran everywhere. Normally, in case of fire, people would run toward the river, both for water and to avoid the rising smoke and flames. But the entire line of docks was a burning firewall. In the resulting chaos, some fled, while some turned back to save precious belongings. Some braved the heat to rescue items from the buildings caught up in flames. Some 57 individuals were arrested that night for looting.[25]

It was a terrible night. Ordered to remain in the city and possibly confined to jail whenever they weren't working, the Scotts' captivity was complete. The smoke from the hellstorm blew from the east, over the jail and its inmates. Locked in just two blocks from the fire's edge, the prisoners in their cells smelled the smoke and clamored for release as it drew nearer. With the noise, the fumes, the smoke, and the heat, wherever they were that evening, Harriet's children must have clung to her in fear.

Late at night, the flames stopped at 3rd Street, and eventually the blaze was put out. The buildings on the 4th Street ridge, including the courthouse, the Russells' home, and the African Church, were spared. But fire destroyed Henry

Blow's house, which was closer to the river. Fortunately he, like others, had already moved his family out of the city to avoid the cholera.

When the sun rose and the smoke cleared, one could see the enormity of the fire. It had devastated the entire city center, creating a hole some 15 blocks in size from the river through the city's commercial area, warehouses, and hotels. All the brick and wood-frame buildings within three blocks of the river—from Walnut Street on the north to Locust on the south—were destroyed.[26] The fire's swath contained few houses—with the exception of one block that housed 26 blacks in wooden structures, tucked away in the alley.[27]

It took two weeks for the embers to cool enough for ash and rubble to be cleared.[28] There was no place along the damaged wharf for arriving steamboats to dock, given the massive obstructions caused by the sunken remains of so many burned steamboats. One prominent citizen wrote, "It will be several weeks before anything like system or order can be restored."[29] People crowded the local markets to stock up on food. The city fathers commandeered more than 500 workers to remove the rubble. As day laborers, Harriet and Dred were probably assigned to fill baskets with stones to be carried away by stronger men and women. The city's needs surely took precedence over private work, and the Scotts were part of the work crew that Sheriff Labeaume could commandeer.

On the small rise above the river, the empty courthouse, on which the Scotts had pinned their hopes of freedom, loomed over the burn zone, partially in scaffolding but unscathed by the fire. Like the Scotts' lawsuit, work on the building was suspended indefinitely.

But the great fire neither purified the area nor quelled the deadly epidemic. On into the summer months, people continued to die each day in the ravaged city surrounding the pit of rubble and ashes. The city seemed emptied out, though a few doctors, like the deaf Dr. Beaumont, feeling an obligation to attend to the sick, actually moved back into town for the duration. Even the learned Dr. Beaumont was baffled. He wrote, "Doctors stand aghast in mute astonishment and mortification at the resistless rapidity of a disease so little understood and over which their most profound skill and judgment and professional efforts can have no salutary . . . effect. . . . May God avert the fell disease from your community, and spare you all."[30] A more cynical observer wrote: "No two [doctors] agree with each other. And no one agrees with himself two weeks at a time. They run off into speculative theories and each one of them kills off his patients in strict accordance with his scientific theory for that week! Sometimes physicians advised their patients not to eat fresh fruits and vegetables, sometimes they thought that the dirtiest places were the safest, other times they speculated that the dirtiest places were the most dangerous."[31] The usual treatment for cholera was large doses of calomel, so laced with mercury that survivors of cholera might succumb to mercury poisoning. (Dred may have been familiar with the mercury treatment; Doctor Emerson had often medicated himself this way.) The medical guideline was to give patients enough of the toxic substance to make their gums bleed.[32]

From the records, it appears that Harriet and Dred worked for a pair of doctors on Greene Street during the epidemic, though Hall continued to pay for Dred's hiring. These men, first Dr. S. F. Watts and later Dr. R. M. Jennings, were first summoned as witnesses for the couple the next time the court docket was called. Both were to be found at approximately the same address.[33] That neither was called earlier suggests that they only made the Scott's acquaintance between the trials.[34] Their offices, just opposite the city's New Market, were near Clabber Alley, a neighborhood of black washerwomen and their families.[35] The neighborhood had a high concentration of deaths—40 in one night.[36] The Scotts probably assisted the doctors attending to the sick and preparing the dead for burial. Little is known about the doctors' practices that year, except for doctor's bills found in the estate of Miles H. Clark, the witness for the Scotts, who died that year of cholera on his return to the city. Dr. Jennings billed Miles Clark's estate for vaccinating an "Indian girl" and a "Negro boy," that year, as well as attending upon Clark himself at hospital on the day he died. Other doctors submitted bills for cupping and leeching treatments on Clark.[37]

From his long service to Dr. Emerson, Dred may have been able to undertake some of the basic tasks of cupping and leeching.[38] Known to have served a doctor, Dred may have even been sought out for advice. Members of the African American community expected that a servant was knowledgeable in matters pertaining to his master's profession and sought their opinions on those matters.[39]

Dred could also bury the dead. It was difficult to find enough grave diggers. During the epidemic's height, people were dying so rapidly that bodies were taken to mass graves in the several cemeteries around town. To prevent the spread of diseases, the bodies were sprinkled with lime, a substance Dred later used to earn a living as a whitewasher. Harriet could wash the disease-infected clothing and bedding. It is remarkable that they survived the epidemic, given their likely exposure. At the river, where she once had washed Mistress Russell's fine silk and satin dresses, Harriet must have now burned and boiled the cast-offs that others wouldn't touch. There was a temptation to keep the clothes of the deceased, given that clothing itself was so valuable—but those who did sometimes perished of the disease.[40]

The surreal days of that summer drifted by, punctuated by funerals and thunderstorms. Funeral processions filled the streets every day. In mid-June, several thunderstorms stunned the living in the city.[41] Reaction had turned from panic into the resignation of a prolonged epidemic. With the future so uncertain, many were unwilling to work. Some young people who remained in the city turned to excessive drinking as a way to cope. There were bouts of public drunkenness and rowdiness, and the jail filled nightly with those who had disturbed the peace. In the recorder's court, one of those arrested slyly claimed that he had simply drunk a little too much cholera medicine.[42]

In times of epidemic, the usual institutions of city government slow to a standstill. Cities attempt brave new reform projects, but sometimes even the systems in place cannot be maintained. With none of the measures having any perceptible effect, the public turned against the officials for their ineptitude. The domed courthouse rotunda, though just a hollow shell, was still the site of impromptu public meetings urging officials to do something about the cholera. At one of these courthouse meetings, A. P. Field, the Scotts' gadabout lawyer, took the floor to make an impassioned speech.[43] Some called for the mayor and city council to resign. The officials called their critics' bluff. They offered to resign and deputize in their place the group calling for their resignations, but no one was willing to step forward to accept office, because no one had any better idea of how to stop the epidemic.[44]

With workers in short supply, the price of day labor rose to 25 cents a day, if contractors could find workers willing to work. Although the epidemic generated more work than usual, there were fewer disciplined people healthy enough to do the work. Morse's telegraph service publicly apologized for the long suspension of service, explaining that it was because of "the death of all my managers upon this line, save one."[45] The healthy wisely shied away from contact with others, closing their doors, latching their shutters, and locking themselves in. Dred and Harriet had no choice but to stay in the city and do whatever they were assigned, whether moving stones and brick from the rubble, attending the sick, burying the dead, or laundering. They probably performed the most dangerous and emotionally draining of tasks. Quite likely they were part of the small legion of city conscripts put to work tending the poor and burying those who had died of the cholera, and who had no family.

The cholera came in waves, raging with increased malignancy at the end of June. "The deaths have mounted to the fearful height of 60–80 a day....Hearses may be seen moving to the different graveyards at every hour of the day and even in the night," wrote one resident.[46] But with so many funerals, the grieving could hardly draw comfort from the company of other mourners. "Funerals are so common that few attend them and much of the accustomed solemnity is dropped. No time must be wasted. The hired carriages are wanted for other funerals, and so the hearse with its diminished train, moves at a trot."[47] Slaves and freedmen looking for convenient places to sleep sometimes unwittingly spread the cholera from one household to another. One observer noted, "The dissolute, the poor, the ignorant new emigrants...died without physicians or friends about them, and were carted off, sometimes three or four to a load to unknown graves, wherever it was most convenient to put them out of sight."[48] In some boardinghouses, black servants were ordered to bring the bodies down the stairs in such haste that the bodies thumped down every step.[49] By the end of June, the epidemic's deaths numbered about 100 a day. Several churches appointed a day for fasting and prayer.[50] An enterprising householder advertised what he called the "Hotel for Invalids," where, it was said, "there were always doctors to be found."[51] The city tried various public measures, including intentionally fumigating the air with smoke and burning coal tar and sulfur at all the street intersections in a desperate attempt to stop the dying in July.[52]

In July the number of deaths reached 125 a day.[53] Among the victims was the Scotts' second lawyer, Samuel Bay (who had fumbled their first trial), and the aged patriarch of the wealthy Chouteau family.[54] The traditional Independence Day celebrations were cancelled, but not the public beatings of those who had violated the licensing law. Despite the epidemic, two free black men were flogged—given the more severe amount of 20 lashes—for failing to have licenses on July 4.[55]

The monstrosity of the scourge spawned morbid imagination, and rumors flew around the city. By one rumor, five coffins were found floating in Chouteau's pond, where washerwomen did laundry.[56] People engaged in idle speculation about where the deaths were most concentrated and the propensity of various groups to succumb. "Some people wonder that there are fewer deaths…among the Presbyterians."[57] Weeks earlier, it had been thought that a particularly disorderly poor area was healthier than other places. "Can it be that the rank exhalations from that rot-pit are a sort of natural medicine? A counteracting influence to the cholera principle?"[58] By July, the situation had reversed, and the cholera was said to have hit that particular area even harder. "No theory is certain. No system is safe, as regards Cholera."[59]

The commonplace funeral scenes sometimes unexpectedly struck even the most stoic observers. One wrote, "This is to me a melancholy day. The first since the pestilence raged among us is that my buoyant spirits have been at all depressed. The scene in our church was awful and touching. There in the midst of a large assembly, all in tears, lay the three coffined bodies.…I lost my equanimity melting down like a child in spite of my best efforts. I had to yield to the softening torrent."[60]

By fall the epidemic had run its course. The normal patterns of life resumed. At the courthouse building, lawsuits began again. The jailor, Lewis Martin, was one of the unluckiest of public officials that year. Not only did he have to house those arrested in the time of cholera but he was also saddled with the cost of maintaining slaves, including Chouteau's Pierre, and caught in the jurisdictional crossfire between the two feuding city judges. Once the cholera epidemic subsided, he found himself taken to task for his running of the jail.[61] A. P. Fields, the Scotts' flamboyant lawyer, came to his defense.[62] The jailor's attempts to clear his name were not entirely successful, and Martin was replaced.

As the winter months approached, those still confined to the jail attempted to keep warm with only the heat from the two stoves. But one night the stovepipe set the jail's roof ablaze. The firemen extinguished the fire while the prisoners clamored to be released.[63] Dred was still hired out to D. N. Hall or to the doctors. One can hope that on this night Harriet too was permitted to sleep elsewhere.

By the time that the Scotts' long-awaited trial finally appeared on the docket in December 1849, attention was fixed on a sensational murder committed by a deranged, visiting French gentleman at a local hotel.[64] The murder caused such excitement that a mob threatened to storm the jail and seize the Frenchman for hanging—until authorities smuggled him out into hiding. By now, Judge Hamilton was under increasing public criticism to move his 350-case backlog along.[65] Still, the Scotts' trial was knotted up through the end of the year. Summonses were reissued as the trial date was repeatedly postponed a few days at a time.[66] A heavy snowfall covered the ground, and the atmosphere was uncomfortably damp and raw.[67]

The entire complement of witnesses had been summoned for trial several times before. Significant in this round of summonses were the two doctors added to the witness list. The Scotts knew that the Plymptons were back in the area, for Maj. Plympton, whom Harriet had served in free territory at Fort Snelling, was actually sought out at Jefferson Barracks as a witness. However, he could not be found there on the day the sheriff's deputy called. The Scotts did not attempt to summon Bainbridge.[68]

Mrs. Emerson's original attorney, George Goode, had left the case, having landed a new real estate case that would net him such a tremendous fee that he later retired from practicing law. Attorney Goode became famous locally, not for his participation in opposing the Scotts' lawsuit but for earning the most exorbitant attorney's fee anyone in Missouri had ever heard of.[69]

When Goode resigned, B. S. Garland probably arranged for Mrs. Emerson's new attorney: Garland's cousin, Hugh.[70] Hugh Garland had recently moved to St. Louis, after losing his patronage job in Washington. He came to St. Louis slave poor, his large family supported by the wages of the 10 slaves inherited from his wife's family.[71] Hugh Garland was an unlikely person to be defending the absentee slave owner in the most notorious slave case of the nineteenth century. This man of letters was happiest being a clerk and teaching classical Greek.[72] He had actually written several learned tracts on public issues.[73] During his patronage job as clerk of the House of Representatives, he was so taken with the eminence of his predecessor that he wrote that clerk's biography,[74] a task that seemed to capture more of his attention than his law practice.

Ironically, his junior partner, Lyman Norris, though from the North, was more stridently proslavery than Hugh Garland.[75] Although Norris was from Michigan and he'd recently graduated from Yale,[76] he became so immersed in Democratic, anti-Benton politics that he referred to himself as a southerner.[77] The young bachelor had more drive than the aging Garland and fewer dependents. He not only practiced law but he also ambitiously took over as editor of a Democratic Party newspaper.[78] "I have become an incognita editor and something of a politician and I am working like a slave..." Norris wrote his mother.[79]

Norris's involvement may very well have been more significant than Hugh Garland's, who sometimes signed himself as "of Counsel," suggesting a lesser professional involvement.[80] Norris's explanation of how he inherited the case bears this out. "The defense had passed through several lawyers and finally was turned over to me, as a hopeless case by the older lawyers for 50 cents as a retainer."[81]

Shortly before Christmas, the lawyers finally took Mrs. Russell's affidavit,[82] providing the critical link between the Scotts' service in her household and Widow Emerson. She maintained, "I did not know Dr. Emerson; I was acquainted with Mrs. Emerson. I have known her 8–12 years. I know the plaintiffs...they were in my service for two years....I have known them some four or five years. They were under the control of Mrs. Emerson, but they were delivered to me by Mr. Sanford, her father. I think it has been between two and three years since they left my house. At the time I hired these Negroes they were in the service of Col. Bainbridge."[83]

Although both Samuel Russell and Henry Blow appeared to testify,[84] each was probably distracted—one by good fortune, the other by bad. Master Russell's daughter was soon to be married in a lavish society wedding,[85] and Henry Blow had recently suffered a financial loss when his paint factory burned in a second large city fire.[86] Neither probably stayed around for the verdict.

On January 12, 1850, the Scotts' won their freedom suit. They probably sat listening to the trial as they had two-and-a-half years before, when their hopes unraveled in Samuel Bay's hands. David N. Hall argued their case, almost exactly a year to the day after the death of his wife and child.[87] This time the jury found the defendant, Mrs. Emerson, guilty of impinging upon the Scotts' freedom.[88] After four years of waiting, including a year enduring a hellish existence of plagues, the Scotts were vindicated. There was cause for jubilation! God was merciful. At long last, it had come to an end, or so it seemed.

CHAPTER 29

Declared Free

Although the Scotts were declared free, there was a good chance that the widow's attorneys would appeal. So, pending a possible appeal, they remained in custody. As long as D. N. Hall, their lawyer continued to hire Dred, he could avoid jail. Harriet remains unaccounted for. The Scotts were probably at greater liberty to organize their own work under this arrangement. The two girls, now reaching early adolescence, were never mentioned in these hiring contracts, nor in the state court papers.[1]

Ten days after the verdict, the Russells' house, where it seems that Harriet had patiently waited for Dred, was mobbed by a crowd waiting to catch a glimpse of the debutante wedding and social spectacle of the year—as one historian described it, "the union of wealth and military prestige."[2] The Russells' golden-haired Almira married a very promising West Point lieutenant, W. S. Hancock, who would eventually run for president with the nickname "Hancock the Superb." Almira had made a very good catch.[3]

Lieutenant Buell, the stocky young man who had once been court-martialed as Capt. Bainbridge's subordinate, was best man.[4] Given Mary Bainbridge's talent for social maneuvering, the Bainbridges were probably there also.[5] Jefferson Barracks had again become the home of "a very lively garrison" with frequent parties and balls.[6] The Russells went over the top in terms of finery for the wedding. Almira's wedding dress was adorned with glass beads fashioned by immigrant German craftsmen. In the streets a rumor had circulated that the bride's dress was made of glass, and a large crowd gathered around the house to see. The weather turned stormy, but the crowds stayed to glimpse the bride, despite the rain and lightning.

The bridal pair was also feted at the neighbors' home. That the Harneys hosted a reception was a social compliment for the couple, since the wealthy heiress Mrs. Harney did not associate with "low people."[7] Col. Harney was famous for taking a tough line in executing the Seminoles in war as well as being the army officer who had beaten a slave woman to death, a crime for which he'd been charged but never convicted.[8] His wife often said that if the colonel "was not waited on as he liked he thought nothing of taking a chair and knocking a waiter down."[9]

Two other weddings took place in the Sanford family in 1850, and those events, together with the Scott's victory in the trial court, could have brought a happy conclusion to the Scotts' litigation—had Mrs. Emerson not appealed. Both Irene Emerson and John F. A. Sanford married new spouses that year. In Massachusetts, Irene, who had resided with her sisters in Springfield, married Dr. Calvin C. Chaffee, a widower with two children.[10] Chaffee was sufficiently well established and able to provide for her and her daughter that Mrs. Emerson no longer needed any of the Scotts' wages for support. In New York City, John F. A. Sanford, who had remained single for more than a decade and had long since left the raising of his son, Ben, to his Chouteau in-laws, married Isabelle Davis, a woman 20 years younger than he. In keeping with his practice of marrying the daughters of the wealthiest families, his second wife was the daughter of one of New York City's richest men. Through their further partnerships, both Sanford and Thomas E. Davis, his new father-in-law, would become still richer over the next decade.[11] Sanford, who was usually referred to as "Maj. Sanford," moved into his wealthy father-in-law's household—and that could have ended the story.

But Mrs. Emerson did appeal[12]—a decision that must have been made in Missouri by B. S. Garland, who still managed the case in St. Louis for Sanford. When she appealed,[13] both sides agreed to a seemingly technical stipulation: that inasmuch as the legal issues in Harriet and Dred's separate cases were similar, only Dred's case would be advanced. The couple's individual cases were consolidated into a single appeal. It was agreed that the resolution in her husband's case would apply to Harriet's suit as well.[14] Conventional attitudes that prioritized men's interests over those of women, as well as the Blows' patronage, tended to steer the decision to advance Dred's case at the expense of Harriet's.

With what seemed to be merely a technicality, the lawyers submerged Harriet's case for the sake of expediency. The claims were not identical. Hers was the messier case. It was clearer who, if anyone, could be identified as "owning" or at least "claiming" Dred; it was not at all clear that anyone owned Harriet, yet a freedom case needed a defendant. She had to establish her freedom against someone. Here was the irony of a default rule that presumed that persons of color were slaves,[15] but a free status that could only be established by demonstrating "illegal enslavement" by an appropriate defendant.[16] One could not establish one's freedom against the world, only against an appropriate defendant.

Another freedom petitioner experienced a similar difficulty in finding the appropriate defendant.[17] Elsa Hicks's owners, who had brought her to St. Louis from Illinois to hire her out, evaded her attempts to sue them for her freedom by leaving the jurisdiction whenever the sheriff came to deliver a summons upon them. Elsa attempted to solve the problem by finding a cooperative defendant, who was willing to accept service and suit. This tack brought her owners back to the jurisdiction, complaining that she could not establish her freedom by a set-up case against a stranger.[18] In Harriet's case, there was no deed or proof of sale conveying her from Taliaferro to Dr. Emerson. Moreover, the sale of a slave in free territory should not have been valid anywhere. And yet, since the enslaved petitioner had the burden of proving all the elements in the case, technically, Harriet had to prove the negative in order to establish her freedom.[19] The one attorney attuned to the legal relevance of the factual differences in her claim, Francis B. Murdoch (who also knew Taliaferro), had long since left the city. All of the Scotts' subsequent attorneys were amateurs in freedom suits.[20]

In truth, their present lawyer, David N. Hall, may have acted with confidence in consolidating the suits, since he had just won a favorable verdict. He was justified in expecting that both of his clients would win their freedom without relying on the factual distinctions in their personal circumstances. Legal precedent supported the Scotts, and they had reason to be hopeful. Still, strategically, in retrospect, the decision to consolidate the suits into Dred's case was probably an error. Not only did Harriet's factual claim stand on a stronger legal base than Dred's, but her claim was central to determining their daughters' status. Due to the principle of matrilinearity, Dred's freedom had no legal relevance to their daughters' fate. Consolidating the claims, however, expunged her personal biography from the case and subsumed the children's chance at freedom within Dred's case. Her distinctively different life circumstances—as a former slave whose last master lived in Pennsylvania; was sold, if at all, in free territory; and married in that free territory to a slave—may have made a legal difference in her case. But these details were erased from the court record by the stipulation. Her claim, now subsumed as the slave litigant's wife, was wagered on the strength of Rachel's precedent—which had been the law of Missouri for half a century.[21] That mountain of precedent would crumble when the Scotts' case reached the Missouri Supreme Court again.

Under David N. Hall's hire at this time,[22] it's likely that the Scotts now settled in one of the networks of alleys north of town where most free blacks lived. At this time, the alleys located between the streets on the northwest side of town were home to the largest concentration of free black inhabitants in the city.[23] The various alleys had nicknames; for example, "Clabber Alley" was the location of a dairy making sour milk clabber, or curds.[24] The Scotts were listed in the city directories as living in this general neighborhood of alleyways from the 1850s onward.[25]

Their everyday life was probably much as it had been: Harriet taking in washing and Dred sweeping up the lawyer's office and whitewashing walls. The larger national events were remote and had little effect on their daily existence, but their fate was riding on several unstable political currents over which they had no control. In the meantime, the fur company manager Henry Sibley had been elected to Congress from Minnesota. Traveling from the frontier periphery to the nation's capital he found remarkable the "exciting scenes in the House, principally connected with the slavery question...it is evident that there exists between the surface the elements of violent and deep seated feeling, which will soon manifest themselves."[26] Sibley even received a letter from the New York headquarters of the American Fur Company, principally about the quality of some cigars that he had ordered, but carrying a message about the importance of slavery to the union's stability. The clerk opined the view that slavery was best abolished by degrees, but if it couldn't be done, the status quo should be maintained.[27] The clerk's letter concluded with greetings from Chouteau and Sanford.

Those political currents would eventually determine the Scotts' fate. For the time being, their lives were more directly affected by the conditions in their immediate locale, by the elements, the weather, making a living, and their neighbors in the same crowded alleys. The winter was dark and murky "with light snow and drizzling rain, and consequently [more] sloppy streets, than I remember ever to have witnessed," one observer wrote.[28] But by late March 1850, it was snowing hard, which made laundering difficult.[29]

By the last court ruling, Harriet and Dred now occupied the status of free blacks, a status of increasingly precariousness in the city in the 1850s. Local newspapers termed the rising status of free blacks "the Negro problem." "[T]his question which…continues to excite ill feeling…is not in slavery, but rather in the existence among us of another and different race with which there can be no amalgamation, without further degrading the white man."[30] The more downtrodden condition of slaves, so long as that status remained subordinate, was not viewed as the social problem. Missouri law now banned free blacks from migrating into the state.[31] The local newspapers peppered dozens of articles with messages that were unwelcoming to free blacks. Enforcement of the licensing requirement was sporadic, but in 1850, what had been simply a licensing and fining arrangement became the justification for more frequent public displays of violence directed against free blacks discovered to be lacking a license. Increasing numbers of persons were subjected to the standard sentence of 10 lashes on a bare back.[32] One reporter, comparing the recent census to the numbers of licenses, complained that the law was underenforced: 684 free blacks were in violation of law.[33] Thereafter, the paper regularly noted individual prosecutions.[34] The newspapers took up the rallying cry that free blacks comply or be punished.[35] "It is notorious that the [licensing laws and the ban on] slaves being permitted to hire their own time, are not duly and properly enforced; and as a consequence slave property is now more unsafe than any other kind."[36]

The solution to the "Negro problem," as the local papers deemed it, was to remove blacks to Africa. The newspapers obsessed over the issue and banged the drum to rid the country of all its black inhabitants. The front-page news stories alternated between topics of colonization efforts, fugitive slave prosecutions in the North, and local police crackdowns on free blacks without licenses.[37] One of Missouri's white ministers spearheaded the local efforts of the Colonization Society. When the Missouri chapter held its meeting nearly every protestant minister in St. Louis was named a vice president.[38] Reverend Shumate announced the first exodus of eight former slaves to Liberia. All eight came from the state's rural counties, where slavery was much more prevalent than in the city. Still, the newspapers trumpeted the success of the minister's efforts as they paraded the eight model travelers' itinerary across their columns.[39] The paper boasted that the president, Zachary Taylor himself, had attended the Colonization Society's national annual meeting.

Though neither of the Scotts could read, the urban population in which they resided was barraged with tabloid style messages of sensationalized language aimed at the barely literate.[40] The Scotts didn't need to be able to read to sense the increasing hostility to their newly declared status.

Some articles advocated the end of emancipation altogether.[41] One claimed that the very presence of "this unfortunate class of people" universally tended to encourage evil among the slaves. Hope was a dangerous encouragement. Although the writer conceded that forcibly removing all free blacks from the state was unjust, he proposed an extensive legal measure to prevent their numbers from increasing.[42] The writer proposed an elaborate and ingeniously perverse scheme, creating an official "superintendent of free Negroes," who would also act as agent for removing slaves to Africa. Under the plan, manumission would be permitted only on condition of leaving the United States, and all blacks would be required to pay an annual fee for a license, the proceeds of which would fund the costs of sending the manumitted to Africa. Thus, the government would tax those who remained to finance the deportations.

> This plan, if properly carried out, would remove from our midst a floating and improvident population and secure a greater decree of safety in slave property, and [it] would not be oppressive or burthensome to those entitled to reside here under the existing laws.... The slave would be better satisfied, and more contented.... [T]he gradual and prospective removal of the whole race from this continent back to the land of their forefathers... is the only remedy for an evil, which has threatened the stability of our glorious union.[43]

The newspaper was so pleased with the proposal's cleverness that it printed the lengthy proposal twice.

Attorney Edward Bates, who had aided David N. Hall in Pierre's freedom trial and who would eventually become Lincoln's attorney general, accepted the honorary presidency of the state's colonization society. He promised one of his own slaves freedom, if he served him a few more years and agreed to leave for Liberia. Still, the "Negro question" as he called it troubled him:

> There must be something in the... question that my mind is incapable of appreciating... [B]oth the Negro factions—the lovers of free Negroes in the north, and the lovers of slave Negroes in the south—are alike stupid tricked. The one would destroy the constitution and thereby destroy the world's only hope of civil liberty, because it permits slavery to exist, anywhere under its jurisdiction; and the other would dissolve the union, tear the nation into pieces and consign its bleeding frequently to imbecility and anarchy... Why, it is the very madness of the moon![44]

The speed and immediacy of telegraphed communication now brought St. Louis many reports that some states of the nation saw the "Negro question" differently. Before the telegraph, Louisians were lulled into the comfort of their regional isolation by their distance from national politics—distanced by the many days of steamboat travel required to bring news of eastern developments. Now, the city was brought up to date daily with alarming news of the North's contrasting responses to the "Negro question." This sense of urgency intensified the local rhetoric leveled against blacks.[45]

The composition of the servant population in St. Louis had also changed, with the massive influx of new European immigrants from the tumultuous, failed European revolutions of 1848.[46] In the decade that Harriet had lived in St. Louis, the black population had doubled, but the numbers of European immigrants, mostly German and Irish, had tripled. Thus, blacks were a smaller proportion of the city's population than before.[47] Even in those alleyways that housed the working poor, free blacks were now the minority. In the middle of a city block containing 200 or more middle-class, white residents (with front doors properly opening onto city streets), one generally found three to five households of free blacks and 10 to 12 European immigrant families living in the back alleys.[48]

A free soil editorial exhorted visitors not to bring their slaves west. "If you propose to come to Missouri to live, my advice is to sell your slaves before coming." The large foreign immigration, it was reported, drastically affected the value of slave labor, and many owners were selling their slaves because they weren't profitable. One problem with black servants, the writer explained, was that "[s]ervants hired out in this way soon become worthless and discontented. For this reason, and for others that I need not mention," the anonymous author hinted broadly, "a preference is given more and more every year, to white servants, even at higher wages. In fact, our citizens are more than half from free States, and not knowing how to manage Blacks, never employ them."[49] St. Louis bourgeois families including the Russells, the Blows, the Charlesses, and the Bateses now hired Irish servants as well as keeping slaves.[50]

German observers, by contrast, explaining the attraction of Missouri for immigrants, compared Missouri slavery to the conditions of domestic servants in Germany. "Slaves are treated well in Missouri…better treated than the German 'Dienstbooten.'

> They are fed well, they are given medicine if sick. Slaves live in separate quarters; spouse of male slave looks after the [slave] household and children. Slaves get hours off at noon when they return to their houses and spouses to rest. Slaves are given time off Saturday afternoon and all of Sunday. They can take a horse on Saturday afternoon to visit their families. The horse does not need to be returned until Monday morning. Children of slaves play with white children.[51]

Although many nativists resented the European immigrants,[52] they were generally seen as a positive, amalgamating influence in the American population. One observer wrote, "[t]he old French are lost in the map—their children and grandchildren have become American. The population is mixed up of all the varieties of Europe.... Some people are afraid of them, as foreigners.... For my heart... let them be Dutch and Irish, as much as they please, but they can't, for the life of them, beget foreign children."[53] The children of Europeans became Americans. It was not that America was a melting pot; it was a roiling laundry kettle that seemed to wash ethnicity from white immigrants by the second generation, rendering them "Americans."

Yet, the Scotts, for all of their lifelong residence, their distinctively American, frontier experience, and their work contributions to the community, were denied this privilege of contributing their progeny to the American people. Eliza and Lizzie were still regarded as members of a separate class, as subject to a heritable status that kept them apart from the citizenry and made them, presumptively, slaves. Free blacks, according to Judge Krum's ruling, were not American citizens. With the Colonization Society's efforts, even their remaining in America was coming into question.

With the influx of European immigrants seeking work, free black women had a tougher time finding work as servants in households. Prompted by numerous newspaper reports of servants' deception, slaveholders showed increased anxiety that their black servants might try to poison them or their children: One St. Louis woman inquiring after another's slave wrote: "Have you Anney yet? I hope Anney has made no more attempts upon Sarah's life."[54] When two slave women were prosecuted for attempting to poison a local white family, the reading community followed the trial with intense interest.[55] Even slave women who had been long-time domestics were viewed with increased suspicion.[56] White families sometimes expressed ambivalence at a runaway's escape. When it became clear that one runaway would not return, the family consoled themselves with the thought, "you would never have felt comfortable if anything had happened to [your children]."[57] On a household-by-household basis, white mistresses were replacing black hirelings and their own slaves with European immigrants. As the supply of immigrants seeking work as domestics increased, the market for urban slaves declined. One sister wrote another describing similar circumstances. "I am to get next week a German girl. She does not speak one word of English.... Papa has sold Melinda [out of the city]. She was anxious to go up and live near her husband. So now I hope she will be satisfied."[58] It did not occur to the writer that Melinda might have desired freedom as well as the chance to live near her husband. The predominant belief among St. Louis's white population was that servants were better off enslaved than free and struggling for their livelihood.

Language and culture presented some problems in hiring immigrant help. Not only was communication with the German-speaking servants a problem but the different cultural work expectations of European immigrants also made some situations difficult. Masters saw the immigrants as insufficiently deferential. German or Irish servant woman might take up with a man and leave their service. Masters could bring seduction actions against someone enticing away their servant girl.[59] Most male immigrants had worked for men on farms in Europe, not women in households. Many immigrants were hired as couples, following the prior pattern of retaining both a slave man and slave woman, and expecting their cohabitation to provide stability.[60] Male immigrant workers expected to be treated as men—and did not expect to take orders from mistresses. When an Irish couple quit service, their master commented that the husband "has some very Irish quirky oddities that make him unwilling to obey the orders of a woman. And so, as no one shall stay on my place, who does not know that my wife is Mistress and Queen, the word, the law, and the household, I dismissed him."[61] The well-run St. Louis household almost always had the mistress in charge. Slave men were far more tractable in taking orders from the mistress. Slaves could be depended upon to obey; they were never allowed to question or to talk back to the mistress. Male gender trumped class among the immigrants' work culture values.

Moreover, immigrants did not need to remain where there were difficulties. Unlike slaves, they could quit and move on. Thus, households accustomed to being in total control of their staffing complained about the frequent turnover of the new class of domestics.[62] Each new couple required a settling-in period and training into the household, but unlike slaves, they could leave for better conditions, for better pay, or to move farther west—and sometimes did.

However the Scotts got by that year, there were dim rumblings that the legal situation for African Americans was worsening. In the autumn of 1850, Congress passed the Fugitive Slave Act, requiring free states to aid in the capture and return of runaways. The passage of the new law sparked another spontaneous public meeting in the courthouse rotunda to rejoice over this magnificent compromise. It was supposed this would hold the line against slavery's erosion and finally settle all disputes on the subject.[63]

Meanwhile, the Scotts had little reason for concern about Mrs. Emerson's appeal, since freedom litigants eventually won on appeal.[64] But as early as October that year, rumors circulated among the members of the bar that the state high court was contemplating reversing its own precedent.[65] Edward Bates was told "that the majority of the Court...were about soon to give an opinion overruling all former decisions...declaring Negro slavery emancipated by a residence northwest of Ohio, in virtue of the Ordinance of 1787."[66] This rumor circulated several months before the Scotts' case was heard. The tack was to declare that Congress had no power to legislate on the subject of slavery in the territories, and "consequently, all the enactments on that subject are merely void!"[67] Judge Ryland, one of the three sitting justices of the Missouri Supreme Court, opposed the reversal and was expected to write a dissent, if it came to that.[68]

But although the state court justices were canvassing the bar and each other about overruling precedent,[69] they heard no case that term. That term of court was aborted because of low water on the Missouri River. Steamboats could not travel between Jefferson City, the state capital, and St. Louis. The low water detained two of the judges from reaching the city, and one went home early by stagecoach.[70] Meanwhile, the state prepared to elect its supreme court judges for the first time. By the time the state supreme court convened again to consider Mrs. Emerson's appeal, a different panel would be in place.

The appeals were handled by the two young Yale graduates representing the opposing parties. Thirty-year-old David N. Hall, the Scotts' attorney, wrote a straightforward brief that relied on the 17 cases of precedent.[71] Twenty-six-year-old Lyman Norris's opposing brief was three times as long in argumentation. At this time, Hall also suffered from some mysterious ailment. The doctor who had attended his wife during her confinement and before her death now visited him every day, from mid-1850 through the beginning of 1851. From January of 1851 on, David N. Hall bought opium from the apothecary three or four times a week, until his death on March 7, 1851.[72] There was no reply brief to Norris's tirade, and when the Missouri Supreme Court later decided the appeal, the Scotts no longer had a lawyer.

Dred had been hired out to Hall and his law partner Field until the conclusion of the litigation, according to the note of obligation. But with Field's departure from the state and the death of Hall the term of employment was cut short, to April 9, 1851—the date that the bill was submitted to Hall's estate. David Hall's other client, Pierre, who had been confined since the mistrial in 1848, was also left without a lawyer.[73] The Scotts now needed a new sponsor to hire them out as a nominal master, or the sheriff would auction them for hire on the courthouse steps. The Scotts didn't necessarily work directly for their sponsors.[74] Their hirers probably permitted them to find their own work situations and pay their wages into the escrow fund.[75] Later newspaper reports confirm this sort of arrangement.[76] For the year 1851 to 1852, it is not clear who their sponsor was. The corpulent LaBeaume was no longer the sheriff. He was replaced by Henry Belt, who had been a member of the proslavery Committee of 100 agitating for more repressive racial measures.[77] Still, if the sheriff didn't rent them out, he'd be violating the court order and incurring a charge at the jail, so he probably accepted something similar to their previous arrangement. A year later, a combination of Taylor Blow's brothers and brothers-in-law stood as security for their release, paying $6 per month for Dred and $4 per month for Harriet.[78]

Taking in laundry on her own, Harriet could no longer depend on a head of a household to supply her with the soap, firewood, washboard, and iron kettles that were the necessary tools of her trade. It's also not clear that she even had a secure yard in which to wash and hang the clothes, so she would have to be more vigilant against their theft. One observer of St. Louis washerwomen wrote that black washerwomen returned to their homes on Mondays, "toting a week's dirty laundry from two or three white families." Another laundress remembered carrying "ten to twelve sheets…twenty to thirty towels, twenty-four pillowcases, three and four tablecloths, and no end of shirts and other clothes and things" from each family. The work, all done by hand in wooden washtubs and iron pots of boiling water, was "steamy, strenuous and laborious. Wet sheets and tablecloths doubled in weight. Lye soap irritated hands and arms."[79]

The scrubbing work required the most physical exertion: rubbing with one's hands so vigorously that perspiration poured down a washerwoman's face.[80] Most washerwomen had young helpers to stoke the fires,[81] so the girls probably assisted Harriet when they could, and Dred may have delivered the clean piles of laundry to her customers.[82] As a semi-independent washerwoman, responsible to earn her family's keep, she now made her own soap from lye, drained from ashes that she bought from the ashman's wagon or gathered wherever she could. Then she needed fat drippings. The washerwomen sometimes approached the steamboats at the dock to beg the cooks for their sludge to make soap.[83] Rural washerwomen took pride in the soaps that they made. St. Louis washerwoman may have done the same. To turn ashes and drippings into soap, Harriet would have poured hot water over the ashes and drained it into a big iron kettle. Then, she needed to drip the lye solution slowly through a trough called an ash hopper. Keeping the water hot through the ash hopper was often the job of the young assistant.[84] When the noxious concentration was strong enough "to dissolve a turkey feather," grease cracklings and any kind of fat that wasn't good enough to eat were stirred into the lye solution. The smelly soap solution was boiled down until it clung to itself. When it sank to the bottom, the mass was ready to cool, be cut into chunks, and placed on boards to dry as hard soap the following day.[85]

From handmade bricks of soap, Harriet built her path to independence. In the sustained heat of the many processes, and the aches that came with routinely lifting heavy loads of wet clothing, Harriet must often have felt fatigued at the endless work that determined her existence, year in and year out. But she took pride that she could take care of herself and her family by earning her own living.[86] In the philosophy of Master Taliaferro, who had released her, she deserved her independence.[87]

By now half a dozen agents in town were buying and selling people as a primary business. Lynch's holding pen on Locust Street offered to pay the highest prices in cash and to board "Negroes in comfortable quarters and secure fastenings," where "Negroes were for sale at all times." O'Gorman operated a sales room from the cellar of the fashionable Planter's House, opposite the courthouse.[88] The slave traders frequented a particular eating house near the courthouse, and although many people avoided them in social settings,[89] business was good. The Planter's House was a popular residence for visiting southern families, who availed themselves of the opportunity to buy from the St. Louis market and take slaves with them when they returned home.[90] Slave dealers often simply sent their coffled-together human inventory south for sale, although traders tried to assuage the consciences of the households that sold their family slaves by promising to "take good care in placing favorite household servants."[91] Traders played on their owners' sentiments that they were simply helping to find placements for their unnecessary dependents. Within a few years, though, public sentiment induced the St. Louis slave traders to change their method of driving slaves through the streets. Fearing that they might be mobbed some day, they moved slaves to the boats between four and five o'clock Sunday morning, when nobody was stirring.[92]

One slave trader named Reuben Bartlett operated at the very edge of legal boundaries as a repossession man. He coordinated with several owners to participate in surprise seizures of their slaves. They simply took the slaves from sites where the servants were living or working when the time came for sale. Bartlett had a reputation as being unscrupulous even as slave traders went, and he was accused of kidnapping free blacks and selling them downriver as slaves.[93] Bartlett had an office in town, but no slave pen; he apparently used the county jail as his holding tank.

Twice a year, in March and October, the state high court visited St. Louis to hear the bulk of the appeals, which were generated from the city's many courts.[94] This term, 1851, the court refused to recognize a marriage between a free woman of color and her slave husband, a pattern that paralleled Harriet's own. "Marriage is a civil contract, which can exist only between persons who are free, and capable of contracting. A slave cannot contract."[95] The mixed status couple had no right to the marital privileges that free persons did. Ironically, had the court considered the full consequences of its ruling, it would have had to declare many other Missouri marriages invalid as well. Many girls married under the age when they could not legally contract, and hence their marriages would be invalid as well.

Strand by strand, political forces were at work in Missouri to strip away legal privileges from free people of color and to unravel even the slight legal protections they enjoyed by virtue of long-standing custom.[96] A new panel of judges opened the Missouri Supreme Court term in October 1851,[97] but the composition of the bench did not seem to portend the radical ruling that would occur. Ryland, the only justice remaining from the previous court, was seen as the moderate in that company and rumored to dissent if the court proposed to change the rules in free-dom cases. The new judges included a St. Louis attorney, Hamilton Gamble,[98] who was unlikely to take any extreme position, and an upstate lawyer, coincidentally named William Scott. Justice William Scott was a wild card, since upstate judges tended to be more proslavery, reflecting the prevailing sentiments of the coun-tryside.[99] Justice Napton, said to be the architect of the proposed reversal was not reelected.[100] This appeared to be a favorable omen, since two votes were necessary to reverse precedent.

In the fall of 1851, an unprecedented amount of activity in the free states north of Missouri seemed aimed at discouraging free blacks from entering. Like Missouri, state after state—Iowa, Illinois, Indiana, and Ohio—enacted barriers to free blacks entering their borders.[101] Free blacks mounted some resistance, often calling for national conventions, including one in Cincinnati. The call went out: "See to it colored men—you who are taxed, yet denied a representation, and made aliens in the land of your birth, that you are largely represented in said convention. The time has come when you must act or perish."[102]

That winter was long and hard. Ice froze thick on all the ponds around town; even the river, which usually remained open all winter, ceased to be navigable and horse drawn sleighs could cross the frozen river.[103] When the cold let up, rain drizzled on muddy roads and unpaved alleys throughout the city. The wealthy of the city, and the Chouteaus in particular, still lived well. After New Year's, the Chouteaus gave a grand ball at the well-lit Planter's House opposite the court-house.[104] Sanford's father-in-law sent out 500 invitations and paid nearly $10,000 for the gala. Everyone in town was talking about it.[105] The Chouteaus had consoli-dated family power and influence again by marrying Pierre's only son to his first cousin, and now the newlyweds made a splash when they returned to St. Louis to set up household. "Madame Charles is in her new house and it is magnificently furnished. The glasses are said to be something much more grand than ever seen here."[106] The bride's father, retired army general Gratiot, had served the family's interests as a lobbyist in Washington. Sanford coordinated with him, collecting debts owed to the family by the government.[107] The Chouteau-Sanford-Gratiots were still deeply involved in the government contracts of military procurements and sutlerships in forts farther west on the Missouri River.

The tiny number of black St. Louis families with great wealth held fancy balls of their own, from which working black families and the newly emancipated were excluded.[108] The mark of class status was the number of generations the family had lived in freedom. Second-generation free blacks did not necessarily approve of their children socializing with or marrying the newly emancipated. One extremely wealthy black family opened a luxurious bathing saloon to expand their barbershop, located across from the Planter's House. Fitted with marble columns and chandeliers, the Clamorgans offered wealthy steamboat travelers the refreshment of Italian baths and the finest perfumes from around the world.[109] Inheriting extensive land holdings from their white forefather had allowed the Clamorgan family to transcend the racial barrier. At the top of the black social register, they were not even listed as "colored" in some city directories.[110]

In late January, an earthquake in the city seemed to forecast things to come.[111] There were major fault lines in the Missouri bedrock. Louisians watched the first prosecutions of fugitive slaves in free states under the new national statute with close attention. The new Fugitive Slave Law required northern courts to capture and return runaways. Each day the papers carried some new account.[112]

The Fugitive Slave Law did not seem to quell the incidence of runaways reported in the St. Louis newspapers—if anything the reported occurrences increased measurably. The papers now carried regular columns advertising for runaway slaves, still dotted with the silhouette figures of slave men and women, walking across the newspaper columns as if on the roads of letters. It was a field day for bounty hunters.[113] And for the first time, the newspapers noted the new phenomenon of slaves running away in groups. They initially referred to these departures as "slave stampedes," as if the escapees were witless horses.[114] This sort of group exodus suggests some prior planning and outside assistance to avoid detection. The phrase "underground railroad" eventually surfaced in the newspapers to denote an organized escape route.[115]

CHAPTER 30

Missouri Changes Its Course

In MARCH OF 1852, a year after David Hall's death, the Missouri Supreme Court
decided the case and revoked the Scotts' freedom, reversing its own precedent,
which had endured almost half a century. The Scotts had believed themselves
free for more than two years, relying on that longstanding precedent. Now the
state high court changed the rules. It would no longer honor the Missouri Compromise in its courts, to recognize residence in free territory as grounds for freedom in Missouri.

The three judges split their decision two to one. Only Justice Gamble, from
St. Louis, dissented. Justice Ryland, who had previously pledged to dissent, if it
came to it, changed his mind and cast the critical vote to reverse precedent. The
third justice, William Scott, from the rural counties, wrote the opinion, couch-
ing it in terms of the dignity of the states as entities rather than the dignity of
peoples or individuals. A slave state's dignity as a sovereign was impaired when
other law transgressed its boundaries, the court reasoned. If a slave state was
required to recognize those slaves who had entered free states as having attained
freedom, the slave state's sovereignty was violated. The majority cast the issue as
maintaining state integrity against external forces of confiscation: "It is a humili-
ating spectacle, to see the courts of a State confiscating the property of her own
citizens by the command of a foreign law."[1] By labeling the law of other states as
"foreign," the Missouri Supreme Court blatantly ignored the principles of judicial comity: that states respect each others' laws and recognize their judgments.
"If Scott is freed, by what means will it be effected, but by the Constitution of
the State of Illinois, or the territorial laws of the United States? . . . Are not those
governments capable of enforcing their own laws; and if they are not, are we
concerned that such laws should be enforced, and that, too, at the cost of our
own citizens?"[2]

The court viewed a law that could transform a slave's status as harmful to the
interests of Missouri citizens as property holders, despite the fact that with Mrs.

Emerson remarried and living in Springfield, Massachusetts, she was no longer a Missouri citizen, nor was there any Missouri citizen who claimed Dred as property. Moreover, this perspective only made sense if applied to the case of a slave returning to Missouri. It made no sense at all as applied to Harriet, who was a former Virginia slave brought to Minnesota by a Pennsylvania resident.

Missouri's geography heightened the state's awareness that its neighboring states' positions as free states threatened its peculiar institution:

> The prohibition in the Missouri Compromise is absolute [prevailing] along our entire western boundary.... If a slave passes our western boundary by the order of his master ... does he thereby become free? Most of the courts of this Union would say that he does.... Some of our old cases say, that a hiring for two days [violates the Illinois constitution] and entitle[s] the slave to his freedom.... Now are we prepared to say, that we shall suffer these laws to be enforced in our courts?[3]

The transforming miracle of prior residence in free territory was what most litigating slaves placed their hopes upon.

And then the opinion played a typical lawyer's trick of slippery slopes:

> If two days [hiring of a slave in a free state would free that slave], why not one? Is there any difference in principle or morality between holding a slave in a free territory two days more than one day? and if one day, why not six hours? ... If not go the entire length, why go at all? ... Slavery is introduced by a continuance in [free] territory for six hours as well as for twelve months, and so far as our laws are concerned, the offense is as great in the one case as the other.[4]

The opinion also presupposed that the doctor's mind-set in taking Dred to Illinois was incidental to his relocation rather than purposeful. The two-judge majority supposed Emerson never would have assented to free Dred thereby. Instead the court posited that the doctor simply couldn't protect himself against being ordered to report to a free state and therefore had to take his property with him. In reality, their sympathy was ill-placed—given that John Emerson had earnestly sought to get into the army surgeon's corps and that he had purchased Dred expressly for the purpose of serving him in free territory, always collecting the subsidy the military paid for a servant. Dred's master had specifically acquired him as property in order to serve him in Indian territory, where servants were hard to come by and slavery was illegal. But based on its mis-supposition of Dr. Emerson's sacrifice in being called to free territory, the court interpreted his acts instead as lacking assent to the consequence of freeing the slave: "To construe this into an assent to his slave's freedom would be doing violence to his acts."[5]

Moreover, Dr. Emerson probably knew the consequences since Dred's situation was customary of most military slaves who were taken north, having been purchased in a slave state and imported into free territory. Justice Gamble certainly knew the custom, having represented William Walker, the notorious slave trader in *Rachael v. Walker*, before the Missouri Supreme Court. The rest of the court would know this from reading the facts of *Rachael v. Walker*, the state's leading precedent. The court now absolved the doctor of knowing the law, and doubted that he had voluntarily introduced slavery into Illinois or the Missouri Compromise lands. His estate was allowed to keep Dred as its human chattel.

The emergent rule was that a former slave's return to slave territory meant return to the status of enslavement. Since he hadn't been formally manumitted in the free state, Dred, once a slave, resumed his status of enslavement upon return to Missouri. The court ignored the impossibility of getting a court decree where courts did not exist. The opinion declared that slavery be preserved in the wilderness frontier, where, of course, a slave would be unable to get a judicial declaration of freedom because courts had not yet been established there.

> In States and kingdoms in which slavery is the least countenanced, and where there is a constant struggle against its existence, it is admitted law, that if a slave accompanies his master to a country in which slavery is prohibited, and remains there a length of time, if during his continuance in such country there is no act of manumission decreed by its courts, and he afterwards returns to his master's domicil [*sic*], where slavery prevails, he has no right to maintain a suit founded upon a claim of permanent freedom.[6]

This statement of the law contradicted not only Missouri's own precedent but falsely represented the precedent of most states. Under the new rule, upon returning to Missouri—without finalizing his manumission in the free state—Dred, once a slave, resumed his status as a slave.

The opinion rendered its ruling using only a single set of facts—Dred's. The contrasting facts of Harriet's independent existence were submerged far too deeply in the litigation to be seen. The lawyers' stipulation had accomplished that. The ruling did not fit her life circumstances at all. Harriet never had been a Missouri slave before her arrival in 1840. Taliaferro was a civilian government agent rather than an officer under military orders, so he was not under the same obligation to take his slaves to free territory with him that the state supreme court posited for Dr. Emerson. Taliaferro had affirmatively expressed an intention to free some of his slaves while in Minnesota, and he had acted accordingly by relinquishing his claim to Harriet and giving her away in marriage. None of these facts were raised because of the lawyers' stipulation to resolve her claim according to Dred's outcome.

The majority carefully avoided using the word "abolition" in their ruling. (Professing abolition was still illegal in Missouri.) Instead, the opinion described the sentiment as an "insurrectionist" political movement. (In a rhetorical tirade, Mrs. Emerson's attorney had argued they were "Black vomit.")[7] The court acknowledged Missouri's changed perception of the national sentiment.

Times now are not as they were when the former decisions on this sub-ject were made. Since then not only individuals but States have been pos-sessed with a dark and fell spirit in relation to slavery, whose gratification is sought in the pursuit of measures, whose inevitable consequence must be the overthrow and destruction of our government.[8]

Under such circumstances, the court continued, "it does not behoove the State of Missouri to show the least countenance to any measure which might gratify this spirit."[9]

Deflecting sentiments that enslavement itself was cruel, violent, and inhu-mane, the opinion invoked sympathy for the long-suffering slave master instead, stating that the slavery's consequences "are much more hurtful to the master than the slave."[10] American slaves were lucky to be in a far better condition than "their miserable race in Africa."[11] The court majority congratulated themselves at the prospect that

when [blacks'] civilization, intelligence and instruction in religious truths are considered, and the means now employed to restore them to [Africa], bearing with them the blessings of civilized life, we are almost persuaded, that the introduction of slavery amongst us was, in the providence of God...a means of placing that unhappy race within the pale of civilized nations.[12]

Within the pale, indeed! To the state supreme court, that the slave labored for his master was the least he could do for the many blessings showered on him. The opinion reflected the contemporary belief in the peculiar institution's benevolence—and now, the recolonization effort's further benevolence: that a slave returning to the country of his ancestors was lucky to have learned civili-zation from his slave masters. According to this belief, release from enslavement was linked to recolonization to Africa but not the freedom to remain in the United States.[13]

Justice Gamble's tepid dissent was the Scotts' only favorable vote. By compari-son to the fervor of the majority decision, Justice Gamble simply favored preserv-ing precedent once established.[14] He didn't necessarily criticize the institution of slavery.[15] Gamble spoke in the neutral, disimpassioned tone of one following the rules laid down. He knew the military custom all too well, as these were the same grounds on which he had lost in *Rachael v. Walker*.[16] Though losing the case that established the precedent, he chose to follow precedent.

The March 1852 decision flatly revoked the freedom that the Scotts had won two years earlier, but it's uncertain how they got the news. They no longer had a lawyer. A. P. Field had left the state well before David Hall's death, and no one had been assigned to represent them since his death. Did someone explain the opinion to them? The person most likely to have told them the outcome was the St. Louis circuit judge Alexander Hamilton. Did he simply tell them the result? Or did he read out to them the convoluted sentences, the tortured words, and the factual errors that reclaimed them as slaves? Did he try to explain to them the majesty of the law and the majesty of state sovereignty? The decision supermanded everything that one might assume the Scotts had come to believe was law, and its premises contradicted the facts of their own life experience. The Scotts had endured the contest over their freedom for six difficult years, only to discover that now the Missouri Supreme Court changed the rules to hold them in slavery. It is difficult to imagine a decision that could have been worse for them. Adding insult to grave injury, the court etched a theory of state sovereignty that pitied slave states rather than slaves. The court's assessment of slavery considered that the misery in their lives was an "act of Providence," and implied that they had had the good fortune to be enslaved. With this decision, they could reasonably expect incarceration, sale, or being turned over to some slave trader, since their putative "masters" were no longer even in the state. Their daughters now had no hope of freedom, whether Eliza, by virtue of being born in free territory,[17] or Lizzie, by matrilinearity. And they had no lawyer to even counsel them.

With the March 1852 Missouri Supreme Court ruling, the Scotts were techni-cally no longer under Judge Hamilton's protective authority, though they remained in the city within his jurisdiction. Judge Hamilton had little left to do in the case but the ministerial act of entering the final judgment. There were no remaining issues to decide in either the trespass or the freedom suit. Still, he seemed to have taken an interest in their case, and, somewhat extralegally, he issued a stay of the judgment against them until they had exhausted their federal remedies.[18] Judge Hamilton simply failed to inscribe the final judgment, and thereby maintained continuing jurisdiction over them.[19] He may have also found them their next law-yer, Roswell Field, who was a friend of his.

Mrs. Emerson's lawyer must have been in contact with the Scotts, too. In the month that the decision was handed down, Lyman Norris wrote his mother sev-eral times about the momentous case that he had just won.[20] In his own words, he stated, "The defense had passed through several lawyers and finally was turned over to me, as a hopeless case by the older lawyers for 50 cents as a retainer....I argued it before the old bench of justices...and won it," he crowed.[21] The letter provides no evidence of a political impetus behind the litigation or that Norris was "recruited to a cause."[22] Norris's contemporaneous letter repeated the posi-tion stated in his brief that slavery represents "the workings of the providence of God for the Black."[23] Norris also described St. Louis abolitionists as "ignorant" and "quacks."[24] Norris told his mother to "put away all the balderdash, raw hand and bloody bones of flogging, chains, scars, stripes, etc."[25] Though Norris articulated strong, proslavery sentiments, he wrote his mother that he had also offered to help Dred, if Dred would work for him for several years.

> I told Dred Scott...that I should buy him and his family for 400$ of his
> master—...and then Dred must make an agreement to pay me 100$ a year
> and take care of my room etc....until it was paid and then he would be
> free—but he was certain of winning...and now he is a slave for life—hard

is it not? I thought [it was hard] too[,] but my sympathies were all thrown away.... I had my own duty, as a sworn attorney.[26]

Norris also tried to explain the outcome, to his mother, as beneficial to Dred and his family.

[Dred Scott] is in a low state of existence, but *that is not his fault or his master's—there he must remain*, and how much better is it for him to remain a happy and contented slave, than a poor squalid and destitute free negro. Before the decision Dred and his wife had to work day and night to live. He wore old cloths and always had a thin anxious [illeg.] look that belongs to a poor free negro. I hardly ever remember him to laugh ... The moment the matter was settled and his master took charge of him again, gave him a house, clothed him up, warmed and fed him—he was another man, his face shines with fat and contentment, you can hear his loud guffaw a mile, and nothing does him more good than to sit on a box in the sun and abuse "poor white folks.[27]

It's hard to know what to make of this report of the Scotts' condition when made by the man who had argued against their freedom. It seems unlikely that B. S. Garland or John F. A. Sanford had provided Dred with a house or new clothing after the decision. The statement might have been simply a way for the young attorney to assuage his mother's concerns.

The state supreme court ruling had resounding consequences for the black St. Louis community in which the Scotts lived. On its most concrete level, it dealt a body blow to all the freedom litigants patiently waiting in line for their turn at trial.[28] The Scotts had lost not only for themselves but also for everyone waiting their turn. Their case turned the whole tide of the law against others seeking their freedom through the courts. The other freedom litigants must have been familiar to Harriet and Dred;[29] they were people with whom they had spent time, sitting together for empty hours and days in the St. Louis Jail, sleeping on the same musty buffalo robe of a bed in the cells designated for persons of color, and fed the same two meals a day—or sometimes similarly released to be hired out by the sheriff to work for impounded wages.

That spark of hope nourished through several generations was extinguished with this decision in the Scotts' case.[30] Since Winny's victory, freeing herself and seven of her children, more than 100 others had won their freedom through the courts; the Scotts were perched on a shaky bridge to freedom that had collapsed upon them, two years after being declared free. The realization must have been the death of hope, although they did not give up.

Bad judicial decisions sometimes bespoke violent outcomes for those who could not defend themselves. The opinion seemed to invite retaliation against those still seeking their freedom. With David N. Hall's death, Pierre continued to languish in jail, his sanity sorely stretched by a decade of incarceration. The jailer did not want him, nor did the county hospital.[31] There was some thought to return him to the very man from whom he sought his freedom, in order to provide for his food, clothing, and shelter. One night thereafter, the slave trader Reuben Bartlett joined Gabriel Chouteau, Pierre's putative master, in a covert raid on the jail to capture Pierre. While he was locked in his jail cell, the two white men jumped him and whipped him violently, but they were unable to remove him that night. The beating was likely retaliation unleashed for the aggravation that resulted from his lengthy freedom claim. Pierre was so badly hurt in the attack in the dark that he couldn't tell the sheriff exactly who had whipped him, whether it was his jailer or his former master. He'd lain suffering in a daze in the cell all weekend only to be found beaten and confused on Monday morning.[32] Although Pierre's whipping came to light, somehow Bartlett and Gabriel Chouteau were eventually allowed to remove him from jail and conceal him in the city.[33] When Pierre's newly assigned attorney went to see him that Tuesday, the jailer feigned to deny him admittance, knowing that Pierre was gone. Pierre's lawyer sought the court's assistance to find his client by petitioning that the beaten man be delivered to the court.[34]

After the Scotts' adverse court ruling, another freedom litigant, Laura, was decoyed from where she was working by being told she was being taken to see her lawyer. Then she was kidnapped and placed on a steamboat heading south. Judge Hamilton did what he could. He issued sharp contempt penalties against the kidnappers, but he couldn't bring Laura back once she was removed from the jurisdiction.[35] He had no authority beyond the jurisdiction of his court, and the new sheriff, who had been a member of the Committee of 100,[36] was no friend of freedom seekers. The Fugitive Slave Act only worked in the one direction: returning persons to slavery, not returning them to their legal claims of freedom when kidnapped.

But though the decision defeated the Scotts, somehow they must have maintained a faltering belief that the decision was wrong, for they did not give up. They had been defeated before, and the ruling had turned around. They had to believe in the courts, to think that they could win again; otherwise they had nothing.

The Missouri high court had taunted the free states to enforce their own laws on their own territory, knowing that slaves such as the Scotts could not invoke the jurisdiction of another state while confined in a slave state.[37] Now that the Missouri Court had thrown down the gauntlet to its sister states, the only legal redress open to the Scotts was to sue in federal court.[38] Once the summer of 1852 passed, the Scotts challenged the ruling by filing a new suit in federal court.

It's not clear how their next lawyer, Roswell Field (no relation to A.P Field), came into the case.[39] (Roswell Field had no known connection to the Blow family, but he was a friend of Judge Hamilton.) Thus far, their first lawyer had moved to California, their second lawyer moved to Ohio, their third had died of cholera, their fourth lawyer moved to New Orleans, and their fifth lawyer had died young. Roswell Field was a tall, commanding figure who strode around the courtroom, his arms crossed behind him as he made his case. His style was conversational; he was neither a stirring orator nor stiff like Samuel Bay. This man, who sometimes sat on his front steps and played the flute for street children,[40] did not seek to inspire or to exhort; he simply reasoned closely and logically to the conclusion.[41]

This time the Scotts sued Mrs. Emerson's brother, John F. A. Sanford. It's not clear why they chose to sue him. Sanford had more of a presence in town than did Mrs. Emerson. Perhaps the attorneys could not find her under her new married name; she now went by "Mrs. Chaffee." Perhaps they couldn't serve process on her since she no longer had an address in the state. Many a slave's suit was dismissed if the sheriff couldn't find the defendant.[42] One element stipulated in suits brought in federal court was "diversity" of state citizenship between the parties—in this case, meaning that one of the parties had to reside outside the state of Missouri.[43] A suit against Mrs. Emerson, now a Massachusetts resident, would have satisfied the diversity requirement just as well as a suit against Sanford, a New York resident. Sanford was certainly well known as the son-in-law of the city's richest man, and he was easy to find, although he was rarely in the state. Perhaps the Scotts saw the widow's defense team as reporting to him since Mrs. Emerson had been out of the state and out of the picture for so long—and since Sanford appeared to be financing the suit.[44]

Although Dred was the central plaintiff in the federal suit, the family (this time even Dred's daughters) were represented in various claims. The suit included claims for Harriet's loss of familial services through her husband and for the children's loss of a father by virtue of his enslavement. Yet, as before, the petition's several allegations seem more symbolic than actual. The papers allege that on January 1, 1853, in St. Louis, John F. A. Sanford, with force and arms, assaulted all four family members, and that all were threatened with beatings and confined for six hours and put in great fear.[45] In all likelihood John F. A. Sanford wasn't even in Missouri on that New Year's Day. Yet these allegations were legal fictions sufficient to invoke a lawsuit.

John F. A. Sanford was actually in St. Louis when he was served with process.[46] The marshal's order says that he read the summons to Sanford,[47] probably having found him at the Chouteau family home. Sanford did not refuse service of process. By nature, the feisty Sanford was not opposed to litigating. By the time he became a direct defendant in the case, he'd lived in New York City for almost a decade, and he had little contact with the St. Louis men of the Committee of 100, who were his late father's friends. Although he had remarried into a very wealthy New York family, he still considered Pierre Chouteau Jr. to be his closest mentor and confidant. His financial interests revolved far more around the company's investments, particularly the Illinois Central Railroad, and obtaining lucrative government contracts for supplies to the West than in owning slaves, whether domestic servants or agricultural laborers.[48] Sanford still owned two slaves in Missouri[49] (probably left in the Chouteaus' charge), but they were a tiny fraction of his vast holdings, which were primarily composed of modern forms of wealth such as stocks and bonds. As Harriet and her husband had been eking out their living waiting for what they thought would be the final appeal to the Missouri Supreme Court, Sanford had spent the years amassing a singular fortune.

Sanford could easily have ducked the lawsuit, claiming (as we now know to be true) that he simply didn't own the Scotts.[50] Yet he defended and eventually won. The most plausible explanation of why he defended is that he was still very much under the influence of Pierre Chouteau Jr.—and if this man, who was the successful father Sanford always wanted to have, favored the lawsuit, then pursue the suit he would. Mrs. Emerson said that Sanford pursued it for the Chouteaus.[51] The Missouri Supreme Court's reversal was a tremendous windfall for the Chouteau family, who had devoted several generations to litigating against the effect of the Northwest Ordinance on their family's slave-holdings. Why not defend the federal suit?[52]

From Sanford's correspondence it seems that the lawsuit, in which he was to become the most notorious defendant of the century, was really the least of his concerns. From his New York offices at the American Fur Company, Sanford had taken over much of the responsibility for the firm from the company's major partner, Ramsey Crooks. A significant amount of Sanford's work now centered upon coordinating information and managing the correspondence with his European partners over fur sales. He had become the nerve center of the company's extensive worldwide dealings. From time to time, he traveled to Europe, visiting Paris, where the Chouteaus still had family, and the London and Leipzig fur markets to contact buyers and agents.[53] His letters to the London buyers and to the St. Louis supply firm of Chouteau and Co. suggest that he was quite expert not only in managing a diverse portfolio of investments, deals, shipments, and treaties, but also at manipulating the market to the greatest financial advantage and optimal yield. His letters consider in detail the sale price of each type of skin: "Mink is only safe article on list to buy. Otter was dullest article." He was meticulous and shrewd, plotting clandestine measures to control the market supply in order to raise the price. "Our holding back skins must be a closely guarded secret," he wrote. "We have cause to be well pleased with sale."[54] In other letters he wrote about his longer term strategies for conquering the competition psychologically, materially, and legally through select legal battles. "Every third or fourth year," Sanford's London partner advised him, "a certain amount of money must be spent in opposing others with a view to a safe and good business subsequently."[55] He saw litigation and the use of courts as a possible preemptive strike in framing the rules for business. Sanford was a player.

By 1850, it was clear the fur trade business had almost played out. The company's London partner informed Sanford that "[b]usiness has been spoiled beyond the possibility of resuscitation and I advise you to continue sales on your side whenever you can do so at fair rate."[56] Still, Sanford, who had been fully aware of the slide in demand for furs for some time, strategized to capture the remaining profits in the endgame. Sanford calculated how to seize on whatever short-term profits could be squeezed out of the remaining trade. For future investment, the company planned to further diversify in government contracts and other industries and capital markets as it had for some time. Chouteau and Sanford now moved into the business of banking and finance.[57]

Although Sanford had ascended to the central position in running the company, he still sought continual reassurance and guidance from Pierre Chouteau

Jr. Sanford consulted him regarding every significant plan for restructuring the company. Sanford urged him to join him in New York: "Your presence is needed here more than ever. I need your counsel."[58]

Even from Minnesota, lucrative business opportunities flowed into Sanford's hands through the regular, longtime business network established by the fur company. Henry Sibley, now a congressman, contacted John F. A. Sanford in 1852 with a business proposition. Sibley and Franklin Steele, who had replaced H. N. Dillon as sutler at the fort and was now Sibley's brother-in-law, had managed to seize the land claim for the area's most important water power resource. Maintaining hold on that most valuable natural resource had not been easy for Steele because it was a likely prize for claim jumpers at a time when land title could not yet be established. This was the very water power site that so many had coveted during the Scotts' time at the fort. First, Stambaugh had attempted to take possession of the mill site when he was sutler. Then Dr. Emerson and Dr. Wolcott fought each other for their positions at Fort Snelling in the hope of eventually claiming land near the site. Capt. Plympton had similarly schemed for the prize by setting the boundaries of the federal reservation land in such a way so as to enhance his opportunity.[59] Steele had beaten out Col. Plympton and Capt. Martin Scott to stake the land while Emerson was finding a bride,[60] but now Steele needed more financing for its development. The prize of all of these intrigues was now offered to John F. A. Sanford, on the princely terms of part ownership and 10 percent interest on moneys lent. Sanford not only took the offer, but he brought in his new father-in-law, Thomas E. Davis, and his new brother-in-law as well.[61]

By summer of 1852, Sanford succeeded in getting Pierre Chouteau Jr. to come to New York for an extended visit. Chouteau wrote home that they had celebrated the French holiday of Bastille Day at Sanford's home and with his new wife and child, who he was pleased to learn spoke French.[62] As one of the first in the West to invest in steamboats, Chouteau now invested in railroad stock. Sanford's Massachusetts brother-in-law, James Barnes, had made a fortune in Eastern railroads and had even traveled to Russia as a railroad consultant. By 1853, Sanford was working primarily on the Chouteau interests in the Illinois Central Railroad, soon to be constructed.[63] By 1853 and 1854, most of the company's communications focused on its railroad investment and securing the railroad franchise in Illinois.

But Sanford was not about to give up on the company's continued interest in lucrative government contracts for territorial expansion. In Washington, at midyear, Zachary Taylor died in office,[64] and Vice President Fillmore was sworn in. When the 32nd Congress convened for its winter session, J. F. A. Sanford traveled to Washington to ensure that the company's interests were secured in congressional approval of Indian treaties made in the field. He reported to Chouteau, "[t]rip to Washington resulted in nothing positive. Treaties will pass but with much opposition."[65] Sanford was experienced in counting the votes and watching the opportunities to lobby for government payouts in treaties, as well as for the occasion to appoint his friends to influential positions. When the 34th Congress opened its winter session at the end of 1855, Sanford again traveled to Washington and was able to report proudly that he had made a decent settlement of $36,500 for the company's interests in Fort Pierce. Sanford usually dealt in large five- and six-figure numbers, not the small scale of the values of a pair of St. Louis slaves.[66]

Sanford, already accustomed to trading favors and indebting Washington politicians to him, took greatest advantage of most situations. He even leveraged a debt owed to the company by Daniel Webster.[67] By 1855, Sanford was joined in Washington by Dr. Chaffee, Irene's new husband, who had just been elected congressman. Ironically, Dr. Chaffee was elected to Congress from Springfield, Massachusetts, representing the Free Soil Party.[68] With Sanford's keen interest in maintaining political connections, and with the central role he had always played as his sisters' patron, he was sure to contact Irene and her congressman husband if it might be helpful to the company. In a later account of his life, Dr. Chaffee reported modestly that he hadn't really intended to run for election, and having been elected, he decided to turn up in Washington simply on a lark, expecting to resign after the first week.[69] But Chaffee and his wife stayed on, and he even ran for reelection. There is no doubt that Irene was indebted to her brother, for financing her education and the years she lived at the farm that he owned. Sanford would surely encourage a brother-in-law lucky enough to be elected to stay in Congress. Even Sibley's election to Congress had been met with gushing wishes of congratulations from the then company director, Ramsey Crooks.[70] Whether Congressman Chaffee performed favors for Sanford is unclear, but he did lobby on behalf of his sisters-in-law. He introduced two separate private bills, one for Mrs. Bainbridge and one for Mrs. Clark, ensuring that they received special widows' pensions for their husbands' military service.[71]

Back in St. Louis, holding the reins on the Scotts' enslavement was B. S. Garland. Just weeks after the Missouri Supreme Court decided against the Scotts, one of Garland's own slaves escaped.[72] Garland advertised in the *Missouri Republican* that a man named Joshua had run away from his farm four miles west of the city.[73] We cannot know whether Joshua planned his escape before or after the *Dred Scott* case failed (when his master's attention was perhaps otherwise occupied), but his timing was excellent, and his whereabouts went unknown for the next year. B. S. Garland learned that his runaway slave Joshua Glover, was working at a sawmill near Racine, in the free state of Wisconsin, a year after his escape.[74] How he received this word is not clear,[75] but B.S. Garland quickly sought a writ from the St. Louis court for Joshua and left for Wisconsin to execute the writ under the Fugitive Slave Law.[76] A month later, at night, Garland, accompanied by U.S. marshals obligated by federal law to return fugitives, surprised Glover in his cabin, where he was playing cards with friends. Though Glover attempted to bolt the door, one of his "friends"—a black man later suspected of informing on Glover— let the men in, and Glover was captured.[77] Glover was taken by wagon to jail to await extradition to Missouri.

It was at this point that events in Wisconsin took an unexpected turn; the people of Racine, Wisconsin, stormed the jail in order to free Glover. In Wisconsin, where the Republican Party would be born and free soil, antislavery sentiment was strong,[78] the mob forced Glover's release by breaking down the jail's door with pickaxes and a battering ram. Glover was of an age to have remembered McIntosh's forced removal from the St. Louis jail before he was tied to a tree and burned alive, so he must have been extremely apprehensive when the mob came for him. Doubtless surprised at the turn of events, when learning that the mob wanted to free him, Glover is said to have tipped his cap to the crowd, crying "Glory, Hallelujah!" before a waiting buggy spirited him away to hiding places and eventually across the waters to Canada.[79]

B. S. Garland was not a man to accept this sort of setback and loss of his slave, so he pursued every legal means available to prosecute those aiding Glover's escape. These efforts eventually lead to a constitutional crisis in Wisconsin.[80] Garland sued the abolitionist newspaperman, who had stirred up antislavery sentiment in Racine. For his efforts, however, Garland himself was jailed for a day, for disturbing the peace.[81] In a series of legal engagements, Garland pursued damages against abolitionist newspaper editor Sherman Booth, eventually winning judgment and levying against Booth's printing press.[82] During Garland's actions against Booth that May, another of his slaves managed to escape from his St. Louis farm.[83] The slave, James, appears never to have resurfaced. While Garland was not a poor man, neither was he wealthy, and the extended litigation of the Glover case may have required outside financing. Is it possible that the Chouteaus or Sanford underwrote the suit?

WHILE THE SCOTTS worked at whatever low-skilled jobs they could get, the children grew into adolescence and went into hiding.[84] Their parents knew where they were and presumably could contact them surreptitiously,[85] but it was safer for them to be out of reach of the law. One often hides that which one values most.

Because most St. Louis city blocks, like those in many southern cities,[86] had no alleyways, there were only two neighborhoods with large concentrations of free black families. One such area was Almond Street, south of the courthouse and in the second ward (not far from the Russells' house), which, at that time, was a wharfside district of bawdy houses, drinking, and gambling.[87] The Almond Street neighborhood, where the original African church was located and where many washerwomen had once lived, had acquired an unsavory reputation and was subject to increased police surveillance and arrests. River men and soldiers on leave from the fort frequented the area to drink and play cards at coffeehouses and taverns like the Robbers' Roost. The police periodically raided the area and arrested ladies of the night.[88] As a result, many working-class free black families, like the Scotts, migrated to the alleyways north of town. The network of alleyways in the blocks between Franklin and Morgan and Wash and Green Streets was now home to dozens of free people of color.[89] There were also incidents of riots, knifings, and roughhousing in that vicinity, particularly when white laboring men got into fights or took to the streets in collective action.[90]

The tenor of the reporting in the town's major newspaper, the *Missouri Republican,* had become quite patronizing of the dignity of free blacks. The newspaper began referring to them mockingly as "colored pussons."[91] The sting of this mockery was still felt years later when a woman who had survived slavery commented, "I think the press is inclined to treat the colored people unfairly. When it mentions

them it is generally in a spirit of ridicule. It appears to take keen delight in repro-
ducing their awkward speech."[92]

The Scotts lived in an alley off Wash Street between 10th and 11th Streets that
year. Wash Street was named for man who had once been the custodial owner of
Polly Wash, her daughters, and a half a dozen other slaves.[93] Wash Street was also
aptly named, as Harriet took in washing and, according to the city directory, Dred
did whitewashing.[94] Whitewashing was a useful purifying skill, considering where
the Scotts had had to live these past years, and since it didn't require swiftness or
strength, it was considered an appropriate trade for older black men.[95]

Tensions and divisions appear to have been rising within the black community. In July, a group of young black men decided to take action by physically
attacking other blacks who were suspected of reporting on those who were in the
state without a license.[96]

The free black community was a God-fearing one, and there was a prolifera-
tion of churches within the neighborhoods, which caused further divisions.[97] Now
that most of the black population had abandoned the Almond Street neighborhood, where the Reverend Meachum's church was located, church members had
founded a second Colored Baptist church in a hall located next to a fire station,
near the Scotts' residence.[98] This is the church where Harriet was registered as a
member.[99] The split caused some dissatisfaction with members loyal to the original church,[100] but more divisions were to come within the free black community,
which now included several black clergymen.[101]

There were now three major Christian denominations serving the black community: the Catholic Church, the African Baptist Church and the African Methodist Episcopal (AME) Church. African Americans who had been slaves of the city's
French Creole Catholic residents, like their owners, were Catholic and formed a
separate society from the free black Protestants. African American Catholics did
not organize their own churches, as they were permitted to attend mass in the
cathedral.[102]

Both black Protestant denominations sent itinerant ministers from their
churches in the East to found churches among African Americans in the West.
Missouri was identified as a key mission site.[103] All the traveling preachers naturally stopped in St. Louis, the transportation hub, for a time.[104] Within the alleyway neighborhoods of St. Louis's northwest side—Franklin and Morgan Streets
extending from 6th to 11th Street—black Baptists seemed to live side by side with
AME church members, although by the early 1850s, five different chapels were
located within the neighborhood network of alleyways.[105] One can assume that
slavery conditions and freedom were debated in these denominations, just as these
issues were being debated in many of the nation's religious institutions. There
likely were splits over what responses to slavery, recolonization, emancipation,
and manumission were prudent or progressive among the communities in these
local churches as there were among the national decision-making bodies of the
Black Baptist and the AME Churches.[106] The Reverend Meachum, who had never
preached abolition or even achieving freedom through litigation, had waning
influence on the community these years, as parishioners left his Almond Street

Church. On Sunday, February 19, 1854, the Reverend Meachum announced his Bible text,[107] and died suddenly at the pulpit. The community attended his funeral in great numbers. But within a year, his widow was accused of assisting the escape of slaves through the underground railroad.[108]

In October 1854, a disturbance took place in another church in the northside neighborhood in which the Scotts lived, pitting black neighbors against each other. The subject of the dispute was not revealed, but the disturbance lead to the temporary closing of the AME church. Among the itinerant preachers from the AME Church who traveled west was Hiram Revels from Ohio. (Hiram R. Revels would later become the first African American congressman after Reconstruction.)[109]

One Wednesday evening while the Reverend Revels was preaching at a prayer meeting in the Green Street community, his remarks provoked some of the parishioners.[110] The newspaper reported that Revels "had made himself very unpopular with a portion of his congregation by abusing them in his sermons—using vile epithets, etc." But that "another portion sustain[ed his choice of words].... Notwithstanding the dissatisfaction..., the minister still persisted [and some members] determined to either stop such language or run the preacher out." When the Reverend Revels drew attention to the apparent dissatisfaction in the audience, the congregation grew increasingly uneasy until someone spoke out and a shouting match ensued. Some suggested that those who were dissatisfied leave the church, while others wanted the minister to leave. It was reported that in the melee, the minister fell from the pulpit onto one of the ladies sitting nearby, and hastily left.[111] Unlike the neighborhood's white immigrant population, which frequently took their disputes to the streets,[112] members of the black congregation were sufficiently afraid of the police that they tried to avoid any skirmish outside the church.[113] The church was quickly vacated, and the disputants retired to their nearby homes without damaging either person or property.

Still, the police were called in. The next morning some indignant parishioners gave the police the names and addresses of others who had disturbed the peace. The police immediately arrested the persons designated, who then in turn informed on their informers. In all, police arrested more than 20 otherwise law-abiding church members.[114] Harriet belonged to the Baptist church rather than the AME Church, but this incident occurring in her neighborhood and concerning her neighbors must have occupied her family's attention as well. After the fracas, the mayor ordered the AME church closed, and local church leaders contacted the AME bishop in Ohio requesting that he come to St. Louis to persuade the mayor to allow it to be reopened.[115]

Since the Reverend Revels, who had no license to be in the state, he was arrested and charged on those grounds. The internal parish dispute also brought the critical attention of the dominant white population onto the Green Street community. The paper reported: "The police... are going to make a general clean out, [of unlicensed Free Black Persons] unless they take themselves away before they are caught."[116] The arrested were locked up in the calaboose, but most of them found bail for their appearance before the recorder the following morning. A month later the long line of persons charged in the church riot was still winding its way through the recorder's court.[117] In the Reverend Revels's trial, a question of his color came up. It was claimed that the law distinguished in favor of those who were less than one-fourth black. Revels was so light-skinned that he argued that he didn't need a license. To settle the issue, the counsel called upon several people who were simply bystanders in court to give their opinion as to the quantity of the minister's blood, the issue being whether the largest preponderance was white or black.[118] The newspaper reported that "Rev. Mr. Revel's privileges to the immunities of a guard room are yet in abeyance."[119] It's not clear from the newspaper accounts how the trial was concluded, but Revels was probably released because he was arraigned again on the same charge before the justice of the peace—though he was soon discharged on the ground that he couldn't be punished twice for the same offense.[120]

When the AME Bishop Payne arrived in St. Louis to try to reopen the church, he blamed Hiram Revels for the turmoil. "This internal riot of our Church in St. Louis...grew out of a difficulty between the Church officers and [Reverend Revels] himself."[121] The bishop punished the leaders of the contending parties by suspending them for a time. Bishop Payne tried to remove the Reverend Revels from St. Louis by appointing him to a church in Columbus, Ohio. But Revels remained in the city after, according to Bishop Payne, "misleading followers advised him to remain in St. Louis and establish a Presbyterian Church."[122] In his later account of the incident Revels stated simply that he was jailed "for preaching the gospel to Negroes."[123]

When the Second Colored Baptist Church, where Harriet attended, celebrated clearing its debt on its new church, the dominant white community now saw the church members as model blacks, though not as citizens. "Our colored congregations, in this city...ask no foreign aid. Their churches are neat; their observance of religious duties more devout, than that of the 'Freedom shriekers' of the North. 'Come to Missouri, Brother Beecher,'" the newspaper taunted the New York abolitionist preacher, "'and learn from your colored brethren.'"[124]

IN SPRING 1854, the Scotts' case went to trial for the third time—this time in federal court before federal Judge Robert W. Wells.[125] The construction work continued on the St. Louis Courthouse, but there was no longer room in the building for federal trials. One after another of the architects were fired or resigned in disagreements with the court over the design, the financing, and the lack of progress.[126] By the early 1850s, all that could be said for sure was that the old brick structure had been completely demolished. The city had grown accustomed to its courthouse being in a continual state of renovation. When some of the surrounding scaffolds were removed to allow the public to see the building's dubious progress, the papers wrote wiggishly "we are at last made acquainted with the style of the Court House.... 'grand, gothic and peculiar.'" One editorial reported, "We fondly hope that it will be consummated before this century is out."[127] With no building of its own, the federal court held trial in a rented room on the second floor of the

Papin Building (a building named for the Chouteaus' cousins), which had been built in the burned out pyre of the city center.

This third trial was very streamlined, without witnesses or testimony; Roswell Field, the Scotts' new lawyer, simply submitted a written statement of the facts and argument.[128] Hugh Garland signed the stipulation of facts. The mature federal judge instructed the jury with his customary, shrill, effeminate voice and awkward hand gestures.[129] Like much of the Missouri bar, Judge Wells was from Virginia and a slaveholder, though he was said to believe that the institution of slavery stood in the way of the state's development. When the jury returned, the foreman announced the verdict for Sanford, concluding that Dred, Harriet, and the girls were his property by law.[130] The Scotts had lost before, but their spirits must have sunk again to hear the foreman declare that the jury had sided against them. Given the verdict, Harriet and Dred probably sought, at this time, to change the girls' hiding place before someone moved in to seize them. Presented with this unfavorable federal court verdict, their attorney sought to appeal to the U.S. Supreme Court. (There was no U.S. Court of Appeals at the time, so all appeals from federal trial courts went directly to the United States Supreme Court.)

In May of that same year, 1854, after a bitter debate, Congress approved the Kansas-Nebraska Act, which repealed the Missouri Compromise of 1820 to the extent that it had allowed the two territories to decide for themselves whether they wished to adopt slavery. Thereafter, defenders of slavery and Free Soil men flooded the western counties of the state, resulting in multiple violent clashes. "Bleeding Kansas" became a national battle cry for organizing abolitionists' efforts.[131]

One afternoon the following month, lightning struck near the Scotts' alleyway home, hitting a local church steeple and sending slivers flying for several blocks.[132] Dred had experienced the same sensation of proximity to a lightning bolt before, when lightning fatally struck his fellow servants on the broad flat beach in Texas.[133] He probably winced more than most at the crack of nearby the thunder and lightning flash.

That fall, Sanford's lawyer, Hugh Garland, died. His young partner, Lyman Norris, who had delivered the extraordinarily stinging tirade against abolitionism before the Missouri Supreme Court, returned to Michigan, all but dissolving the partnership practice.[134]

Hugh Garland's estate was almost entirely composed of books.[135] No slaves show up in the probate because all 10 of the Garland slaves were the property of his wife.[136] Upon Hugh Garland's death, one of his wife's slave women, Elizabeth Keckley, who was a very talented dressmaker, renewed previous and repeated requests to be allowed to buy her freedom. Elizabeth Keckley would become First Lady Mary Todd Lincoln's extraordinary dressmaker.[137] Eventually, the executor agreed. Elizabeth Keckley was permitted to buy her own freedom and that of her son, but it would be four years before she was able to work off her debt and receive her license.[138] It appears that the arrangement was finally accepted after Hugh Garland's death—either because Garland had opposed freeing her or because she earned good money for the Garlands.

The words Hugh Garland wrote in his biography of John Randolph of Roanoke, Virginia, the book that he considered the greatest contribution of his life, portray a more complicated man. In it, Garland described how Randolph advocated gradual emancipation when the subject was debated in the Virginia legislature during 1831 and 1832 (a period during which Hugh Garland himself was also in the Virginia legislature).[139] In the two-volume book, Garland called the Missouri Compromise, banning slavery north of the latitudinal line, "obnoxious."[140] But he ended the biography with a touchingly dramatic depiction of Randolph freeing all of his slaves and providing support for them upon his death.[141] Hugh Garland's book and his Virginia past suggests that the stinging ideological diatribe presented to the Missouri Supreme Court was Lyman Norris's thought and words.

CHAPTER 31

Before the High Court

A FTER HUGH GARLAND'S death, a much more prominent St. Louis lawyer, Henry S. Geyer, took over representing Sanford in the appeal. (His services too were probably arranged by Benami Garland.)[1] Sanford himself was planning another trip to Europe at the time.[2] Geyer appears to have been more of an ideological choice than Garland's cousin, Hugh. Henry Geyer had represented the state in defending mandatory licensing of free blacks challenged by Charles Lyons by arguing that Lyons had no privileges and immunities that were impinged by the law because he was not a citizen of Kentucky where he was born free.[3] Geyer would similarly claim in the high court that the Scotts were not citizens. Geyer had recently defeated Missouri senator Thomas Hart Benton for his Senate seat in the 1850 election. He agreed to argue the case without compensation,[4] an incongruous gesture since his client was one of New York's richest men. Former attorney general Reverdy Johnson was enlisted for Sanford as oral advocate before the nation's high court. Reverdy Johnson had not only been U.S. attorney general in Taylor's cabinet, but he had also represented the Chouteau family previously in land claims before the Supreme Court.[5]

Montgomery Blair, a former St. Louis judge who had resettled in Washington, D.C., was asked to represent the Scotts.[6] Blair and Geyer stood on opposite sides of Missouri's political factions, which had polarized since Geyer defeated Benton for the Senate.[7] Blair did not appear willing to take the case initially. One person seeking to enlist him was Roswell Field, who had lost the Scotts' case in federal court.[8] But Roswell Field may not have been the only person urging Blair to become involved on the Scotts' behalf. The Blair brothers were also friends of the Charlesses.[9] In late 1855, at Roswell Field's persistent urging, Blair agreed to represent the Scotts.[10] It's unlikely that Blair ever met his clients, or even encountered them, except perhaps in passing in the halls of the courthouse years earlier when he was a judge in the St. Louis Court of Common Pleas and, like Judge Hamilton, had heard other freedom cases.

Back in St. Louis, the city jailer, the man who regularly furnished the water bucket for the inmates under his care, died of typhoid at the jail.[11] Rather than causing a panic, news of the jailer's death prompted several people to compete for the vacant position. When a new jailer was appointed, the newspapers lamented that the jail—brand-new when the Scotts had begun their lawsuit—was now inadequate to hold the many people routinely kept there. Much of the jail's overcrowding was related to slavery and race-related legal offenses, rather than the usual crimes of a frontier town. Of the 80 people jailed at the time many were free blacks arrested without licenses, captured runaways, slaves awaiting sale, and occasionally someone charged with attempting to steal a slave away.[12] It seemed unlikely that a new jail would be built, however, while the courthouse was still incomplete.

There were rumblings in the newspaper about a new law that would make it more difficult to voluntarily emancipate slaves. As a result, several owners who had been planning to eventually emancipate their slaves went to court promptly to do so. More slaves were emancipated during November and December 1855 than during any previous term of court.[13] Among this group, Charlotte Charless and Taylor Blow, together with their spouses, freed one slave woman, following the terms of Charless's mother's will.[14] Usually, emancipating any slave required a white man's bond[15] but remarkably, several slave women married to free black men were freed without a bond, since they could be expected to be their free husbands' dependents under coverture law. Some of the newly emancipated apparently left the city as soon as they were released,[16] but where could they go? Laws in Iowa, Illinois, Indiana, and even Oregon prohibited their entry. Their successes in receiving their cherished freedom papers were not necessarily matched by finding a place where they were welcome. The best one could reasonably hope for was to find a place where the laws on the books were simply not enforced.

For an entire week in February 1856, the U.S. Supreme Court heard the lawyers' arguments in Dred Scott's case. Irene and her husband, Massachusetts Congressman Chaffee, seemingly oblivious to the suit that would soon cast them into the national limelight, continued to live in Washington while Congress was in session, and in Springfield, Massachusetts, otherwise.[17]

A decision in the Scotts' case was expected by the end of the Court's term, but no decision came. Instead, the Court ordered re-argument the next year and adjourned for the summer. Some say the justices retreated to visit the luxurious mountain resort of Bedford Springs that summer to escape the Washington heat.[18] Some say that the justices wanted to see the results of the presidential election before deciding the case.[19] On May 22, 1856, Massachusetts senator Charles Sumner was brutally caned by Congressman Preston Brooks as Sumner sat at his Senate desk. Brooks acted to avenge his uncle, Senator Andrew Butler of South Carolina. Sumner had insulted Butler repeatedly for his support of slavery two days earlier in an impassioned Senate speech entitled "The Crime against Kansas." Dr. Chaffee, Irene's husband and Sumner's Massachusetts colleague, visited Sumner immediately after the attack. It took Sumner four years to recover sufficiently to return to the Senate, but his beating inspired John Brown's attacks on proslavery southerners in Osawatomie, Kansas, on the night of May 24.[20] Public meetings in the Chaffees' home town of Springfield, Massachusetts, raised money to send to John Brown's aid.[21]

Dred became very sick during the winter of 1856 and was expected to die. He suffered from tuberculosis. From years with Dr. Emerson, Dred must have known how to apply warm cups to his own body to draw out the unhealthy vapors, though Harriet probably tended to him.[22] Dred survived through March, and Minerva Blow wrote to her husband, noting that Joseph Charless had reported that "the Negro did not die."[23] Dred's death would have rendered the Supreme Court case moot. By fall of 1856, Dred was well enough to work again, sweeping up the law offices of Roswell Field and his new junior partner.[24]

In the summer of 1856, Henry Blow protested a newspaper article that had associated him with the Benton party: "I have been opposed to Col. Benton for the last 18 years and... [I] will still be found acting as heretofore—fully and fairly with those in this State who feel it alike a duty to crush Black Republicanism, and keep Col. Benton, Mr. Blair's brother, and other agitators, from place and power."[25] Clearly, Henry Blow declared himself as decidedly unsympathetic to Republican antislavery sentiments and not at all aligned with the Blair brothers, one of whom was arguing the Scotts' case before the nation's highest court.

In November the city braced itself for the sort of campaign shenanigans that usually accompanied elections. The mayor issued an order to close up all the coffeehouses and drinking houses and keep them closed "until the heat of the election is over. All boys are also to be kept at home, or if caught in the streets are liable to be sent to the calaboose."[26] In a three-party race, the nation elected James Buchanan over Millard Fillmore and Senator Benton's son-in-law, John C. Fremont, who had once surveyed the upper Mississippi River as Nicollet's apprentice.[27] Missouri voted for Buchanan.[28]

In New York City, Chouteau and Sanford made further investment plans for the Illinois Central Railroad. Chouteau wrote home, "Sanford leaves (N.Y.) tomorrow for Chicago."[29] There was no mention of the impending case or Sanford visiting St. Louis. Whether Sanford made the trip cannot be determined; a few weeks later, Chouteau wrote: "I am very busy as Sanford rarely comes to the office."[30] By this time, Sanford had famously attained immense wealth, lived in New York City's most fashionable Fifth Avenue neighborhood, and was listed in a publication on the very rich called "Wealth of the World Displayed."[31]

In December of 1856, just as the Court was scheduled to hear re-argument in the case, Sanford suffered a nervous breakdown. What happened to Sanford? The Chouteau family didn't know. He was transferred from his high class residence at 138 Fifth Avenue in New York City to a sanitarium. Did he finally sense the role he would be remembered for in history? His name was featured in the storm that was gathering about the Scotts' Supreme Court case, even though it was routinely misspelled in the court papers. Still it could be recognized where Sanford was well known: in New York social circles and Boston financial centers, where slavery was not necessarily popular. If Sanford received criticism from his social milieu, there is nothing in any of his extant papers to evidence it. Did he break down because he was simply overextended? Pierre Chouteau Jr., his mentor, thought so. Even the shrewd Chouteau, master of the game, felt that Sanford's myriad business dealings had overwhelmed him.[32]

Sanford probably had no sense of the turmoil he had put the Scotts through, even in his new weakened state. Sanford had cultivated his class-appropriate tastes as he climbed the social ladder, but he was not a man of deep human sensibility or reflective conscientiousness. There was no expression of sympathy for the financial depredation that the fur trade wreaked on the independence of successive Indian peoples in his papers.[33] He did not comment on the young Mandan Indian woman who had been his lover when her people were completely wiped out by smallpox. Unlike Agent Taliaferro, Sanford did not leave a legacy of letters or actions suggesting that he viewed the Indians as deserving of fairness or charity though he too had been an Indian agent. Rather, he seems to have regarded their dependency as a business opportunity.

Mrs. Chouteau, whom he called "mother," visited Sanford at the hospital in January. She said that she found him *"Comme par le passé. Qu'il était impossible de s'appercevoir de ce qui s'était passé. Il est vieulles reconduire a quelques Mille & a retourné avec son domestique.... Il y a donne tout espoir qu'il reviendra avant long-temps. Il connait parfaitement sa situation."* [As he was in the past. It was impossible to perceive how this happened. He is journeying out some distance and has returned with his maidservant. There is hope that he will recover after a long time. He knew his situation perfectly.] By February, Sanford seemed to have rallied temporarily, sufficiently that the family reported: "Sanford is perfectly well and leaves soon for Europe."[34] However, he never made the trip,[35] and he may never have left the sanitarium, where he died later that year.

IN THE FINAL DAYS before the decision, the St. Louis newspapers followed the Scotts' Supreme Court case, daily reporting the arguments made by the four distinguished attorneys.[36] Dred's name now appeared regularly on the front pages.[37] He had become famous in the city in which he was captive.

At the nation's high court, out east in Washington City, Sanford's lawyer, Mr. Geyer, argued the broad principle that an African descendant was incapable of becoming a citizen. He pointed out that when the Constitution was adopted, every state left open the African slave trade for 20 years, and so, he was quoted as saying, "it was not the framers' intention to *import* material for citizenship."[38] On December 15, 1856, while the Supreme Court was hearing argument in the Scotts' case, another heated dispute broke out in the House of Representatives over a proposed ban on the reintroduction of the slave trade.[39] The *Missouri Republican* reported the slave trade's potential profits: the sale of 450 slaves aboard ship (estimating coldly that 50 people would die at sea) at the price of $600 each would net $270,000.[40] Another newsworthy tragedy temporarily delayed court business. On January 3, 1857, Justice Daniels's wife suffered the fate of burning to death when her dressing gown caught fire from a candle.[41] The Court adjourned until after the funeral.

By the end of the first week of January 1857, the newspapers were already reporting that the slave Dred Scott would lose.[42] At their first conference of the new year, it was agreed that Chief Justice Taney would prepare the opinion pronouncing the

Missouri Compromise of 1820 unconstitutional.[43] By January 20, the votes were confirmed in what would become one of the Supreme Court's most notorious opinions.

The Missouri papers applauded the outcome, even though, of course, no one had yet seen the opinion's text or rationale.[44] One article trumpeted: "The Democrats…have been right from the beginning.…The executive, legislative and judicial tribunals of the United States have united in the removal of the Missouri Compromise from the statute book, as unconstitutional, null and void; and the people of the Union have confirmed that decision by their own votes last November."[45] The Missouri Compromise was dead, according to the United States Supreme Court, and the St. Louis newspapers celebrated victory. Slavery lived, particularly in the frontier west, and its gateway city.

It was not until March 6, 1857, that the Court issued its written decision in the case. All seven justices now felt moved to explain their votes, with seven separate opinions rendering the decision 130 pages long.[46]

In the majority opinion, written by Chief Justice Taney, the Court blocked the Scotts' avenues to sue for freedom in three different ways—and by three different extraordinary rulings. The most significant blow for Harriet and Dred, and the one having greatest consequence for Americans of African descent, was the highly racialized ruling that they could never be citizens of the United States, and were hence denied access to the federal courts to assert their freedom or anything else. The United States Supreme Court bought the very argument that Henry Geyer had crafted 11 years earlier in Charles Lyons's licensing case: people of African descent could never be citizens.[47] But Geyer was not the only person contributing this idea. Chief Justice Taney's argument that blacks could never be citizens, comprising almost half of his 55-page opinion, paralleled a memo that he himself had written years earlier as President Jackson's attorney general. The language that African Americans were a "degraded class"[48] appears to be something that Taney was persuaded of even before the case was heard. Historian Don E. Fehrenbacher contended that "Taney found that he could use the Dred Scott case to vindicate his extreme views at length and graft them authoritatively onto American constitutional law."[49]

Taney's motives, however, are less relevant to Harriet's situation than his words, the ruling, and its legal consequences. The United States Supreme Court was their final appeal. By its threefold ruling the Court closed every door to freedom litigants like the Scotts. As outsiders to the court's machinations, Harriet and Dred's perception of the decision would have stemmed from what they heard in the streets, through reports in St. Louis newspapers or what their local attorneys told them. There is little likelihood that Washington-based Montgomery Blair communicated with his clients on strategy, political ramifications, or anything else.

Taney's decision, conventionally regarded as the majority decision, reflected upon not just two, but three races in the struggle for survival and dominance on the frontier and participation in the life of the nation. He identified each of the three peoples—black, white, and Native American—as separate and distinct races, each accorded different sets of entitlements and privileges rather than as different races merged into one people—that is, "Americans." In this respect,

Taney's opinion is distinctive. The opinion provides a three-race formula for legal rights and privileges through a series of three dyads, with the white race central to the ordering.[50] The two "lesser" races, individuals of African origin and Native Americans, were assigned separate packages of rights based in their social relationship to the white racial norm. Persons of African origin were accorded virtually no privileges in the schema. Taney went further to declare that they were entitled to no rights that white men were deemed to respect.[51] In his earlier memo as attorney general, he expressed a very similar view:

> The privileges they are allowed to enjoy, are accorded to them as a matter of kindness and benevolence rather than of right...And where they are nominally admitted by law to the privileges of citizenship, they have no effectual power to defend them, and are permitted to be citizens by the sufferance of the white population and hold what rights they enjoy at their mercy.[52]

In the opinion, which would come to be called "the Dred Scott decision" Taney bluntly stated three premises of exclusion that he said existed when the Constitution was adopted, implying that nothing had changed. First, when the Constitution was adopted people of African origin were

> regarded as beings of an inferior order, and altogether unfit to associate with the white race, either in social or political relations; and [second,] so far inferior, that they had no rights which the white man was bound to respect; and [third,] that the negro might justly and lawfully be reduced to slavery for his benefit.[53]

Justice Daniel chimed in support, stating, "the African negro race never have been acknowledged as belonging to the family of nations."[54]

Although dozens of principles of legal belonging had shifted in the 80 years since the nation's founding as the frontier expanded and new states and populations were added, Chief Justice Taney wrote as if the status of African Americans was frozen in time by virtue of the moment of the constitution's founding and these individuals' seizure by the slave trade. By applying his pronouncement to all persons of African origin, he imprinted this diminished status upon the group, regardless of whether the person had had enslaved ancestors.

The opinion emphasized that in rendering the decision, it spoke "of that class only [of] persons who are the descendants of Africans who were imported into this country, and sold as slaves."[55] (The importation language seems to have been taken from attorney Henry Geyer's argument.)[56] "This population's situation was "altogether unlike that of the Indian race,"[57] Taney wrote. The Africans' descendants were in a class by themselves, sui generis, discrete, and peculiar, like the institution of American slavery itself.

National Indian policy was at stake in the Dred Scott decision as well as black slavery. Chief Justice Taney, who had never visited the frontier, even on one of the "fashionable" steamboat tours popular among wealthy Easterners, wrote broadly and often mistakenly of proclivities, loyalties, and capacities that he only imagined to be true on the nation's developing frontier, but matters that Harriet and Dred must have known from experience were otherwise. Through the lens of their lived experience, Taney's rationale must have seemed as foolishly cavalier as it was disappointing in outcome.

Regarding Native Americans, it could hardly be maintained that indigenous peoples did not belong on the continent. By 1857, it could also not be expected that they could always be removed farther west, especially after the 1849 California boom. Although, manifest destiny had taken hold,[58] there was no "farther west" to continue to export Native Americans to, and of course, there was no other continent suitable for their removal, as the Colonization Society maintained that there was in the case of Americans of African descent. Consequently, room had to be accorded to Native Americans and their rights within the legal system had to be distinguished from those of African Americans. Thus, national Indian policy recommended that Native Americans be assimilated as yeoman farmers in the white settlement pattern—a pattern that Harriet had seen fail from watching Agent Taliaferro's diligent efforts. The assimilation policy had failed at St. Peter's Agency, in part because the Dakota wanted others to do the work of farming for them to ensure their parity with settlement leaders who had servants to till the soil for them. The chiefs had only experimented in ploughing and tribeswomen were expected to plant corn and do the heavy work for their people.[59]

In Taney's logic of separate legal categories, racially distinct peoples were necessary to keep the system of legal privileges distinct. The most difficult problem in his categorization system concerned the children of two races: the Métis, the mulatto, or families like the Bongas, who were descendants of both Ojibwa and African Americans, or Joseph and Margaret Bonga Fahlstrom's children, who were descendants of three. Taney addressed the legal circumstances of persons of mixed heritage only by reference to colonial laws that prevented intermarriage between blacks and whites.[60]

Taney declined to recognize Métis existence by writing that the Indian people "never amalgamated with" the colonial communities "in social connections or in government."[61] This claim was probably not true even of the colonial situation,[62] but it was completely antithetical to then contemporary U.S.-Indian relations in the Mississippi valley[63] and it completely contradicted what the Scotts themselves had witnessed on the northern frontier during the previous two decades. Planned and intentional "amalgamation" and "marriage" into the Indian tribes was exactly the means by which white fur traders established their positions in Indian territory,[64] and the progeny of these many amalgamations had become a critical political factor in the frontier regions. As fur traders, settlement men "married" chiefs' daughters in order to establish advantageous fur trade positions with the tribe, until the furs ran out and the fur trader pushed farther into the wilderness, leaving children behind like Pahkahskah and her brother and seeking new alliances with other tribes by taking another chief's daughter as a wife.[65] The kinship relationship offered advantages to the tribe as well, which is why chiefs had offered Sibley their daughters as wives.[66]

Moreover, Métis people had been central to almost every decisional fairness issue of the upper Mississippi community, from the circumstances of Scott Campbell—would the Metis interpreter be entitled to a land allotment under the treaty?— to Joseph Renville—a full-blood Indian who successfully passed as Métis for a time, though Taliaferro lost trust in him for doing so. Métis issues influenced Chewaygecum's acquittal—was it a dispute between two Indians over a woman or the murder of a white man's son? In very directly material ways, Métis issues affected who received what under the treaties ceding land. Petitions had been written seeking to deny "quarter-bloods" the annuity status of "half-bloods."[67] Insisting as Justice Taney did that the salient historical fact was that there was no "amalgamation" between Indians and whites at the time of constitutional founding was simply foolish and demonstrated profound ignorance of the actual conditions in the expanding West. Yet Taney's claim was rhetorically useful and necessary to the viability of the sharp racial categorical structures that he sought to impose on the fluid, complex, multifaceted American social reality. Acknowledging the actual melting pot of American family relations would have complicated his simple categorization with unsolvable problems and evolving circumstances, unless he was prepared to treat all alike.

Although Native Americans were "uncivilized," Justice Taney wrote, "they were yet a free and independent people, associated together in nations or tribes, and governed by their own laws."[68] From years serving Indian Agent Taliaferro, Harriet must have known how to distinguish the Dakota, whom her master was authorized to provision, from the Ojibwa, whom he could not. Four years on the northern frontier would have convinced her that regardless of whether they were considered legally "free and independent," neither Indian nation was materially independent any longer. It was material independence that would determine their chances of survival. If Indian nations were dependent upon shipments from the U.S. government, then, by the Court's algorithm, they should have been less entitled to their freedom than she and other self-sufficient working black persons. Even the *Missouri Republican* noted that the members of Harriet's church sought no foreign aid.[69]

Taney used the fact that the U.S. negotiated treaties with Indian tribes to demonstrate that Indian nations' freedom had always been acknowledged.[70] (Ironically, this very legal mandate to make treaties with the Indian nations before taking away their land was explicitly expressed in the Northwest Ordinance that Taney was in the act of declaring unconstitutional.)[71] Harriet had been at the scene of one such treaty and had witnessed the circumstances of treaty making more closely than most Americans. Government acknowledgment of tribal independence, freedom, and dignity in treaty making was one concept in Justice Taney's understanding and something quite different for persons like Harriet and Dred, who had seen it in operation. For example, when the Ojibwa insisted that their grandchildren be entitled to renegotiate the terms on which they relinquished the Wisconsin forests to the American government, Governor Dodge simply refused their request.[72] When the Ojibwa wished that the treaty provide lands to their Métis children, often left with their Indian mothers, Governor Dodge told them to take it as cash out of the Indian nations' share.[73] When Hole-in-the-Day and other Ojibwa chiefs complained that the treaty was not being enforced as they had understood its terms in even its first year, they were sent packing to La Pointe and denied the opportunity to negotiate with the great father again.[74] This treatment belied the representation that the Indian nations' independence was always acknowledged, since the tribes had not been in a position to refuse or shape the deal that they were offered.

According to Taney's opinion, subsequent events had brought the Indian tribes "under subjection to the white race."

> It has been found necessary, for their sake as well as our own, to regard them as in a state of pupilage, and to legislate to a certain extent over them and the territory they occupy.[75]

According to Taney, Indian peoples, like "the subjects of any other foreign Government," had the capacity to be naturalized and "if an individual should leave his nation or tribe, and take up his abode among the white population, he would be entitled to all the rights and privileges [belonging] to an emigrant from any other foreign people."[76] Since Taney did not recognize that Indians and whites had children in common, he did not perceive the harder, more important, contemporary question of whether the large population of Métis people were citizens from birth or had to be naturalized to enjoy these rights and privileges.

That assimilation, as Taney imagined it, entitled Native Americans to all the rights and privileges of a foreign immigrant must have seemed naive to persons who had seen Indians' reception in western towns like St. Louis. Harriet knew an Indian woman named Nancy who was forced to sue to maintain her freedom after "taking up her abode among the white population,"[77] lest she be mistaken as an African American.

"The question before us is, whether the class of persons, to which [the Scotts belong,] compose a portion of this people, and are constituent members of this sovereignty?"[78] Taney declared that the Scotts did not belong. They were not constituent members of the country. An African slave who was fully culturally assimilated could never become entitled even to the privileges and immunities of foreign immigrants. "The unhappy black race were separated from the white by indelible marks, and laws...and were never thought of or spoken of except as property, and when the claims of the owner or the profit of the trader were supposed to need protection."[79]

"We think they are not, and...were not intended to be included, under the word 'citizens' in the Constitution, and can therefore claim none of the rights and privileges which that instrument provides for and secures to citizens of the United States."[80] Regardless of the national expansion initiatives, peaceful or militaristic, which African Americans had helped to advance, they were not even citizens for the purposes of bringing suit in federal courts. Roman slaves could win their freedom by individual acts of heroism or service in the expansion of empire,[81] but American slaves could not. Taney did not focus on the particular people who Harriet and Dred were, nor the specific acts they had performed on the frontier in further constituting American sovereignty there. There was no theory of merit or just desert in the designation of freedom or enslavement, and no possibility of changing status for persons immutably classified as the descendants of African slaves. The law did not make note of their skills, their unique experiences as human beings, their distinctive contributions to social survival, and the richness of their observations and memories. Harriet had fed the treaty commissioners and, apparently run for help to save her former master's life. Dred had inoculated the Dakota against smallpox and accompanied the U.S. army into Texas to the brink of war with Mexico. The Scotts, as persons, were simply the factual preamble to the categorical decision that the Court proceeded to impose as the governing rule. In this regard, they were treated as dismissively as the Missouri Supreme Court had treated them, when it sought to reverse its precedent on the Missouri Compromise.

Justice Taney's opinion was very unlike the ad hoc, lay judgments that Taliaferro had dispensed on the frontier. Taliaferro was called "Four hearts" by the Indians for his equanimity in judging different peoples. Taliaferro invented a resolution to fit the circumstances and suit the disputants' abilities to continue to live side-by-side. Taney's decision was neither even-handed nor individually tailored justice, nor did it seek to see the Scotts for who they were. The fact stipulation compounded that difficulty.[82] Because the opinion was not fact-sensitive at all, it may not have mattered if Harriet's actual circumstances had been before the Court. The nature of appellate review and the Scotts absence and distance from the courtroom exacerbated Taney's blindness to them. Justice Taney demonstrated little interest in the particulars—either the unique human characteristics or the living reality of experience. He made no recognition of the thinking, working, sentient human beings, the family whose entire lives had been as much a part of the fabric of American society as his. Taney's rule was a cold statement of sharply bounded categories into which judges were to file their litigants, and it appears that it was irrelevant to the outcome whether the categories fit the circumstances of the petitioners before them or not. This was the man whose high rank placed him in the position to judge their fates without knowing their lives. The quality of Supreme Court law was so very different from the justice that Agent Taliaferro used to satisfactorily resolve disputes on the frontier. This appellate decision was the institutionalized rule of law at its worst.

Taney described the framers of the Constitution, as "great men—high in literary acquirements—high in their sense of honor." These men "knew that it would not in any part of the civilized world be supposed to embrace the negro race, which, by common consent, had been excluded from civilized governments and the family of nations, and doomed to slavery." Taney also maintained that "[i]t was regarded as an axiom...which no one thought...open to dispute; and men in every grade and position in society...acted upon it in their private pursuits, as well as in matters of public concern, without doubting for a moment the correctness of this opinion."[83] "On the contrary," Taney made clear, people like Harriet and Dred were "considered as a subordinate and inferior class of beings" when the Constitution was adopted.[84] Nothing that had happened since the Constitution was adopted, no change in the circumstances of national advancement, and nothing that the Scotts had achieved or contributed since mattered. They were part of a class of beings "who had been subjugated by the dominant race, and, whether emancipated or not, yet remained subject to their authority, and had no rights or privileges, but such as those who held the power and the Government might choose to grant them."[85] Taney's opinion made race matter even more than before.

By this ruling, Harriet and Dred were not only denied the possibility of ever becoming American citizens but they were simultaneously declared to be citizens of no country, neither the United States nor anywhere else. The Constitution did not reserve diversity jurisdiction in the federal courts exclusively for American citizens; citizens of foreign states could invoke diversity jurisdiction to utilize the U.S. courts just as U.S. citizens could. By allowing foreign state's citizens as well as U.S. citizens to invoke federal court jurisdiction, the framers' plan to provide federal court jurisdiction to protect against state favoritism of their own citizens, covered almost all residents of the United States. It is not clear that the constitutional framers contemplated that any American resident would be stateless. The only class of individuals without access to U.S. courts were individuals who had no citizenship anywhere, such as those stripped of citizenship because of treason. To grant the Scotts access to the U.S. courts they only needed to determine that they were within the group of outsiders appropriate to having their cases argued or "citizens" for the purpose of utilizing the federal courts. Such a ruling would have done little damage to constitutional theory, but the argument did not prevail.[86]

But since their ancestors had been "imported as slaves," Harriet and Dred were simultaneously deemed to be stripped of any citizenship that might have been attached to them and hence they were deemed to be persons without a country. Harriet was a domestic alien and an alien domestic. She could be deported, or presumably "recolonized," but she could never be naturalized; hers was an immutable condition of status. She was in the thrall of a government to whom she owed loyalty, and it owed her nothing.[87]

In the words of this decision, Harriet would have recognized the accented notes of distrust toward the British, against whom her former master had always railed, and toward the French, whom the master preferred but never completely trusted—but she would have been surprised by the language of distrust targeted at the Indians. Taney explained that Congress never considered the naturalization of Indians at the time of constitutional formation because of "the atrocities they had...committed, when they were the allies of Great Britain in the Revolutionary war."[88] From Taliaferro, she would never have heard distrust of the Indians, whom he referred to as "his children." In fact, Taliaferro's approach to the Indians was closer to that of the language in the Northwest Ordinance:

> The utmost good faith shall always be observed towards the Indians, their lands and property shall never be taken from them without their consent; and in their property, rights and liberty, they never shall be invaded or disturbed, unless in just and lawful wars authorized by Congress; but laws

founded in justice and humanity shall from time to time be made, for preventing wrongs being done to them, and for preserving peace and friendship with them.[89]

The categorical distinction that Taney painted between African Americans,
as permanent outsiders, and Native Americans, as indigenous teachable insid-
ers, was practically the inverse of the views held by the settlement community on
the frontier near St. Peter's Agency. African Americans were viewed as belonging,
as members of the settlement community as defined by a shared culture. They
could give testimony in court, as John Bonga had done in Che-weyes-ga-cum's
trial;[90] they could be licensed to trade with the Indians as George Bonga was;[91] they
could establish credit at the sutler's store as Dred had; they could marry Indian
women as James Thompson had or white men as Margaret Bonga had married
Jacob Fahlstrom,[92] or each other, as Harriet had married Dred. The cultural distinction on the frontier loomed larger than the racial distinction in determining
belonging.

Taney presented the Indians as holders of their own sovereignty and trainable
to citizenship, though in a savage state. Frontier slaveholders brought black servants to the frontier because they were regarded as better able to assimilate to the
Western traditions than were Indians. Still, according to the court, their laboring
efforts and their cultural assimilation did not permit their apprenticing to citizenship. Even the degree to which blacks fully participated in furthering settlement
practices in the national interest did not fit them for citizenship, from Taney's
viewpoint. African Americans had learned to do the laundry, cook favorite recipes,
and wash floors in the ways of better households in order to make frontier states-
men and their wives comfortable in their remote stations. African Americans had
run the steamboats, inoculated Indians against smallpox, and kept the fastidious
military uniforms spotless and polished for inspection, but for all of their mastery
of settlement customs, they themselves could never, even if free-born or formally
emancipated, be considered eligible for the lower order privileges of citizenship,
such as using the federal courts. Harriet's household, organized under the auspices
of the federal government's Indian Agency, had been devoted to holding together
the strands of disparate cultural communities in order to forge a peace through
a set of just results. The mission of the Taliaferro household fostered the federal
government's end. Dred had been taken to the frontier by a military doctor and his
support had been paid directly from the U.S. treasury.

Where Taney's opinion touched upon family law, it ignored the reality of the
marriage of the very parties in the case before him. His opinion spiraled off on
the irrelevant threat of miscegenation. Did Taney really suspect that black citizenship would increase miscegenation rather than decrease it? He cited, primarily,
anti-miscegenation statutes to demonstrate the unfitness of blacks for citizenship.
While the several statutes that Taney cited indicated the popularity of ill-chosen
legal policies enacted against interracial marriage, those laws had nothing to do
with Mr. and Mrs. Dred Scott's circumstance.[93] Laws discouraging interracial
marriage did not apply to the Scotts, who were regarded as of the same race.[94]

Moreover, if an amalgamated racial population was the worst thing to be feared in emancipating the enslaved black population, how could the court turn a blind eye to the fact that most mixed-race children were the product of white men's advances toward slave women, advances the black women were unable to legally resist or have publicly acknowledged? Without legal or customary recourse, black slave women had no rights against their white masters.[95] (One mulatto man in St. Louis, then a free black entrepreneur who knew Dred Scott, claimed that Justice Catron, one of the members of the Taney Court, was his father.)[96]

The Scotts conformed to all the appropriate cultural expectations of a self-supporting family, keeping a household of their own. They were, in fact, a model married couple, working hard, obeying the rules, and taking responsibility for their children. They had been married by the man who was the highest civil authority on the frontier, just like several other couples, in order to demonstrate and symbolize the importance of monogamous relationships in "acculturating" the frontier to settlement norms and mores. They had kept that faith; they had stayed together and worked hard to achieve their independence. They had earned their own money, and they had attempted to be responsible in supporting themselves, a task more difficult with their wages impounded by the court during the litigation. Dred and Harriet had been married, just as half a dozen Métis couples were, to set an example for the Indians. Marriage served different state purposes in different state settings. Minnesota marriages were not about the cooptation of subservient persons to their status of servitude as some slave marriages in slave states were.[97] Instead, they were a symbol of yeoman independence, where the primary racial and cultural divide was between indigenous and transplanted settlement peoples. Marriage was utilized as an instrument to culturally domesticate the Métis and Native Americans to the yeoman's family model. The incompatibility of marriage with slavery forced even Taney to examine the circumstances of the combination of the competing structures. Taney wrote the infamous lines that were dicta in the case, but certainly indelible: "this stigma, of the deepest degradation, was fixed upon the whole race."[98] In the case that would always be associated with his name, Taney utilized a category constructed starkly in black and white.

The Court did not stop with the determination that Dred was not a citizen and thus, could not invoke the jurisdiction of the U.S. courts, a ruling that many legal scholars have recognized would have been sufficient to resolve the case.[99] The Court went further to declare two acts of Congress, the Missouri Compromise of 1820 and the Northwest Territorial Ordinance of 1789, unconstitutional. Declaring just one congressional enactment to be unconstitutional would have been a rare event in U.S. Supreme Court jurisprudence.[100] To declare two congressional enactments unconstitutional in the same opinion was virtually unprecedented. Yet since Dred had lived on free soil in Illinois, which was part of the Northwest Territory, and Fort Snelling, which was free by virtue of the Missouri Compromise, the Court took the opportunity to declare unconstitutional both of the congressional enactments by which those lands were deemed free soil.

The rulings on congressional authority, however, had little importance to the Scotts, once they had been declared stateless. What did it matter how the balance of federal and state powers was altered or maintained by the Court's ruling if you were by designation eternally and inalterably disenfranchised from legal rights or privileges, or even access to federal courts.[101] In the Scott family's context, the stipulation bound Harriet to Dred's fate, but it did not necessarily bind daughter Eliza, who was born aboard the steamboat *Gipsey*, on the Mississippi River north of the Missouri compromise line. As an African American, even without "state or federal" citizenship, Eliza could have sought federal jurisdiction to argue the emancipating effect of either the Missouri Compromise or the Northwest Ordinance on the basis of comity—that the state courts were bound to consider federal law. That was an independent basis of federal jurisdiction because it was a federal question concerning the interpretation of federal law or a slave state's obligation to respect comity in the federal system.[102] By ruling those bases of emancipation unconstitutional, Justice Taney blocked those potential avenues of recourse as well.

Deciding the unconstitutionality of two congressional enactments—the Missouri Compromise and the Northwest Ordinance destroyed other freedom litigants' potential arguments. The court's declaration that the emancipating provisions of those two congressional acts were null and void (because the acts themselves were unconstitutional) precluded a freedom litigant from ever being able to bring that case in U.S. courts based upon residence on free soil. The State of Missouri had seen fit to no longer give emancipating effect to a slave's residence in those territories in its courts, but with the U.S. Supreme Court opinion declaring those enactments unconstitutional, no other free state could use those discredited bases in the future either. Taney's ruling declaring both congressional actions unconstitutional meant that there was no longer a federal comity issue at all. It also meant that slaves who found themselves in territories with as scant a judiciary as a territorial justice of the peace could not establish their freedom before returning to places where courts did exist, because the emancipating basis no longer existed. Now, no freedom suit based on residence in the former Northwest Territory or lands north of the Missouri Compromise line had a basis in law, in federal courts, in Missouri, or otherwise.

The two dissenters, Justice Mclean and Justice Curtis, made arguments quite unlike that of the majority. The dissenters read out their opinions from the bench, a recitation that took four hours. Justice Mclean and Justice Curtis each disaggregated the complexities of the question along other axes. McLean and Curtis did briefly join issue with Taney's racial categories. Justice McClean suggested that Taney's rationale did not go back far enough into history. "If we are to turn our attention to the dark ages of the world, why confine our view to colored slavery? On the same principles, white men were [once] made slaves. All slavery has its origin in power, and is against Right."[103] True, Taney had focused upon the enactment of the Articles of Confederation and the Constitution, but he did not recognize that at that time white persons too could be held in slave-like circumstances of involuntary servitude—for example, as redemptioners. Justice McClean noted also the flip side—that free black persons in New York and Louisiana were recognized as citizens, just as American Indians were—enactments that contradicted Taney's presumptions of incapacity.[104]

Justice Curtis disaggregated the notions of privileges and immunities entailed by the denomination of citizenship and further split the elective franchise from other civil rights.[105] The idea that some privileges and immunities did not attach to certain persons did not mean that those people were not citizens. For example, Justice Curtis reasoned, a naturalized citizen does not immediately enjoy all the privileges and immunities of all citizens, since he cannot be elected president or hold some offices within a certain amount of time from his naturalization. "But whether native-born women, or persons under age, or under guardianship because insane or spendthrifts, be excluded from voting or holding office, or allowed to do so...no one will deny that they are citizens of the U.S."[106]

If Harriet had heard the words with incredulity and dismay, they were applauded by the St. Louis newspapers. It's unlikely that anyone read Taney's 55-page opinion aloud to Harriet. But in claiming to be a rule of law opinion, the decision failed one of the basic premises expected of all just decisions: it did not really address the losing party's actual situation at all. Nor was there anything in the opinion to give the losing parties any faith in the integrity or justice of the constitutional system. As litigants Harriet and Dred could rightly feel that they had been cheated and betrayed by the legal system, more than once. The Scotts asked only to have those few rules which benefited them enforced to their advantage—not changed—when they knocked on the courthouse door. Before both the Missouri Supreme Court and the highest court in the country, the Court had reversed the rules when they knocked, and the high court's chief justice declared that they had no rights that white men were required to respect.

ℰ

CHAPTER 32

Aftermath and Epilogue

IKE THE COMET that lit the skies of the Northern hemisphere that month,[1] the decision riveted the nation's attention. The *Dred Scott* case was the headline story in newspapers across the country, with reaction to it splitting the North and the South.[2] But from the Scotts' vantage point the St. Louis newspapers' coverage of the story affected them most directly. The family's newfound notoriety made them the subject of a public curiosity that they could have never imagined. A series of articles in the *Missouri Republican* asked the same perplexing question, "Who owned Dred Scott?"[3] From Massachusetts, the extremely embarrassed Congressman Chaffee disclaimed having any knowledge of the matter. Even Dred wondered who his master was after the ruling.[4] *Frank Leslie's Illustrated* stated, "He is anxious to know who owns him, being ignorant whether he is the property of Mrs. Chaffee or Mr. Sanford."[5]

In the city where the Scotts continued to live, the spotlight was almost exclusively on Dred. The news articles rendered Harriet's husband a celebrity in the streets. One news article pointed him out to the reading public as someone who could "frequently be seen passing along Third Street."[6] No longer did Dred's race give him cover to walk about the streets unnoticed; he was now in the words of one newspaper, "the best known colored person in the world."[7] So singular was the focus of the decision upon Dred that even the courts used his first name in citation, defying the conventional custom of legal documentation. That very nomenclature encouraged the notion that Dred was the only petitioner. The nation was probably not aware that the suit involved the fate of a family, and that by law, the key to Eliza and Lizzie's fate was the case's co-litigant, their mother. In a sense, the continued focus on Dred spared Harriet and their daughters publicity.

According to some articles, Dred did not appear "discouraged" by the celebrated case.[8] He is said to have laughed heartily at all the fuss made about him, but stated that he would not have done it again if he'd known what it would entail. "He seems tired of running about with no one to look after him, while at the same time he is a slave."[9] "He talked about the affair with the ease of a veteran litigant,... and he was evidently hugely tickled at the idea of finding himself a person of such vast importance. He does not take on airs, however." Dred divulged the basic facts of his family life, having been married twice, with his first wife sold away from him, and having two daughters—but he did not divulge their whereabouts. The newspapers interpreted this as: "His daughters, Eliza and Lizzy, less conscious about the matter took advantage of the absence of restraint on their movements a year or two since, to disappear, and their whereabouts remain a mystery."[10]

People encouraged Dred to make a tour of the North.[11] "He says grinningly that he could make thousands of dollars, if allowed, by traveling over the country and telling who he is."[12] People wanted to see him. Although one man offered Dred $1,000 dollars to do so, he declined. According to the journalists who visited the house, Harriet was most predisposed against the publicity.[13] She had seen what playing to crowds did to Indians who performed begging dances for the curiosity of tourists. She had to have known Indians taken on a tour of the country who returned with new clothes and broken promises. The circus producer P.T. Barnum had brought Tom Thumb to town to draw the crowds.[14]

Some articles recognizing Dred's celebrity were respectful: "Dred, although illiterate, is not ignorant. He has traveled considerably, and has improved his stock of strong common sense by much information picked up in his journeyings."[15] Others were not. A correspondent from Rochester, New York, who traveled to St. Louis to see the famous Dred Scott, wrote diminishingly, "Dred, who is a slender, very ill-looking and very black negro, came into an office where I was sitting, and I was formally presented to this great embodiment of Constitutional Law; this Ebony point on which the Union turns.... I looked upon Dred Scott with more amazement than I did upon the Mississippi river. Parties must be hard up for issues, when they are built up around such a poor specimen of humanity as this very common darkey."[16]

Several local newspaper articles mention that the Scott girls were in hiding. One article revealed that, empowered by the decision, "the agents of Mrs. Chaffee dispatched a policeman to hunt [them] down."[17] That pursuing agent was likely B. S. Garland, who claimed he managed these matters.[18] The newspapers often got the girls' names wrong: "Daughter Eliza and Jane [sic] having achieved their freedom by their heels. Their whereabouts has been kept a secret."[19]

Meanwhile, the embarrassment regarding the decision fell on Congressmen Chaffee, who had stood for Congress from Massachusetts as a free soil man and befriended Massachusetts Senator Charles Sumner.[20] Chaffee moved as quickly as possible to transfer ownership of the Scotts to someone in Missouri who would free them.[21] The Scotts, resident in Missouri, could only be manumitted by a Missouri resident.[22] Taylor Blow took care of the paperwork. Chaffee publicly announced that he did not and had never wished to profit from the case. What went unnoticed, however, was that Mrs. Chaffee's attorney appeared in court to collect the wages that the Scotts had earned during the long trial.[23] In the end, it seems all the wages earned by the Scotts for the trial's duration were paid over to Chaffee's attorney,[24] and probably transferred to Irene Emerson Chaffee through the Chouteaus. From New York, Pierre Chouteau Jr., still the patriarch of the wealthy family, wrote the family in St. Louis: *"Me domiant une apperçue des sommes reçue par Mr. Sanford pour Mad. Emerson; Sur nos livres nous ne trouvons que la precision somme mille piastres à son credit. Nous ne trouvons rien à son debit pour Mad. Emerson. Veuillez voir sur vos livres s'il est charge de quelques sommes payé à cette dame."* [Regarding the sum received by Mr. Sanford for Mrs. Emerson, on our books we find only the sum of 1,000 piastres [probably dollars] as his credit. We find nothing of his debt for Madame Emerson. Look at your books to see if there is a charge of some amount to pay this lady.][25]

Almost anticlimactically, Taylor Blow then filed the $1,000 freedom bond necessary to emancipate each of the Scotts, as he had done for several others before.[26] Dred and Harriet each signed their freedom papers with the same shaky "x" that they had used in filing their lawsuit. With the freedom papers finally secured,[27] the girls came out of hiding. "Their father knew where they were and could bring them back at any moment, he will doubtless recall them now."[28] Eliza was now 19 and Lizzie was 14 years old, though they appeared younger, perhaps by years of malnourishment.[29] Their parents had been shouldering the emotional and physical burden of the litigation for the better part of the girls' childhood and adolescence. They had grown up in hiding.

Ultimately, Dred, Harriet, Eliza, and Lizzie were freed not by declaration of law in any of the state or federal courts where they had pursued their freedom. They were declared free as a consequence of the fact that their loss publicly embarrassed the Massachusetts congressman to whom their ownership had devolved. The chances of that avenue ever freeing anyone else held in bondage were nil. Instead the United States Supreme Court by constitutional interpretation had cut off access to the courts in diversity cases for anyone of African heritage and by substantive legal basis for any slave who claimed freedom as a result of residing in the Northwest Territory or north of the Missouri Compromise line.

As the Missouri Supreme Court's reversal of precedent in 1852 had foreclosed most freedom litigants' cases in the St. Louis Courts, so too the U.S. Supreme Court's decision in 1857 fell on an even broader class of people. All African Americans, whether free or enslaved, were no longer eligible to use the U.S. courts or to enjoy the privileges commonly identified with citizenship, including obtaining U.S. passports. To test the ruling, Massachusetts senator Henry Wilson, who would become a major architect of the Thirteenth Amendment, attempted to aid one of his free black friends in publicly applying for an American passport.[30] The state department refused to issue the passport to the free black Boston resident who was now deemed not to have American citizenship.

Two months after the infamous decision was handed down in the case that would make his name famous, John F. A. Sanford died in an asylum for the insane in New York.[31] The Missouri press treated Sanford graciously; he was reputed to be the humble servant of Congressman Chaffee and his sister.[32] John F. A. Sanford's wealthy, young widow moved to France with the children and stayed for the duration of the Civil War, inheriting not only Sanford's vast fortune but also one that he had helped build for her father.[33] She later saw their daughter well married to a prominent French count.[34]

In his newfound celebrity, Dred Scott was offered work as a doorman at Barnum's Hotel, downtown near the wharf.[35] Theron Barnum was a superb promoter of his business, and cousin of P. T. Barnum, the traveling circus producer.[36] Barnum figured that hotel guests coming to St. Louis would be interested in meeting the famous Dred Scott.[37] Now well past being able to lift or carry heavy trunks, Dred was hired simply as a celebrity to greet the hotel guests. After all, two decades earlier, tourists had journeyed to see the charred locust tree where the black riverman had been burned alive. Dred attracted considerable attention from strangers as he moved through the St. Louis streets and he sometimes received a gratuity.[38] He knew enough to comport himself in a humble fashion. He busied himself in delivering the clean clothes that Harriet washed.

Harriet seemed satisfied with obscurity and repose. She simply wanted to be left alone, to care for her aging husband and finally enjoy her daughters' company in peace and security. Observers perceived her as neat, industrious, and devotedly attached to her husband and children, an acceptable member of the Baptist Church. She took in laundry.

AT THE ST. LOUIS fair grounds one spring day, Dred was beckoned by a prominent local gentleman. The men asked him if he would sit for a portrait. Would he not go to Fitzgibbon's gallery and have a daguerreotype taken? The local gentleman explained that it was proper for him to have his likeness in the nation's "great illustrated paper." Dred was wary, which the journalists attributed to superstition. He did not show up for the photograph.

When the men tracked him down again at home, a place that was hard to find, Harriet saw them coming while she and her daughters ironed. "Is this where Dred Scott lives?" She answered cautiously, "Yes." The men read from the tone of her remarks that she was Dred's wife and described her as his watchful guardian.

"Is he at home?" "What is the white man after that Negro for?—Why doesn't the white man tend to his own business, and let that Negro alone?" she replied. From behind a duplicate ironing table in the back of the room Dred emerged from a noonday nap, telling her, "It is all right." He'd seen the men before.

Harriet remarked that she knew that there were white men who were trying to entice Dred away, telling him that the people wanted to see him. But she added that she'd always been able to earn her own living, thank God, and earn an honest one, and she didn't want money got in that way; she didn't believe any good would come of it. Harriet was most predisposed against the publicity as she had seen a good deal of human evil in her life.

The next day the family presented themselves at Mr. Fitzgibbon's, dressed in their finest clothes, and everyone sat for the camera. The newsmen didn't ask Harriet her story, nor did she offer it. The journalists wrote that Dred's name "for a century to come, will be... repeated in the political struggles which will agitate the country." And so it was.

DRED LIVED LESS THAN two years after the lawsuit ended. In September 1858, the local newspaper reported his death.[39] Taylor Blow, who had freed him, also paid for his burial in the middle grave of three plots. Harriet could never have hoped to join him at his final resting place, as the extra grave plots were left open to separate the famous black man's grave from the adjoining plots for white people.

In the coming Civil War, everyone was required to take sides. But when the Emancipation Proclamation was issued in the midst of war, it did not free the slaves of Missouri because Missouri did not join the Confederacy. Missouri itself split, with Judge Hamilton Gamble becoming provisional governor of a state that was half in secession and half with the union. Harriet remained in the torn city through the war.

The Blow brothers split, with Henry taking the Union side and Taylor and William favoring the Confederacy. Joseph Charless, Charlotte's husband, was murdered by a man against whom he testified in court. She retreated to live first at the home of Frank Blair and later with her daughter, who had married a man from New Orleans. Major Taliaferro became an army officer again in the Union's cause. Eliza, the enslaved woman who shared Harriet's early life at St. Peter's Agency, continued to live with the Taliaferros in Bedford with her Minnesota-born daughter, Susan.[40]

The interpreter Scott Campbell's wife left him. He died alone, drunk, his body found half frozen by a roadside. Campbell's son Antoine accompanied another delegation to Washington, led this time by the former whiskey seller turned magistrate, now turned politician and Indian agent, Joseph Brown. Antoine Campbell continued to petition the government for the land grant that had been promised to his father but which had been stricken by the Fur Company's lobbying before Congress ratified the treaty.[41] Henry Sibley eventually became governor of Minnesota. In the midst of the Civil War in 1862, members of the Mdewakaton Sioux attempted an uprising for their independence. In one of the most violent and controversial chapters in Minnesota history, Governor Sibley suppressed the uprising and hanged one of Scott Campbell's sons, who had joined forces with the uprising.[42] Knowledge of the uprising and subsequent crackdown were overshadowed by the Civil War battles.

Henry Bainbridge never saw the war. On May 31, 1857, he died in the burning of a steamer off the coast of Galveston, not far from the place he had refused to disembark to spend the night.[43] The widowed Mary Bainbridge remained with her sisters in Massachusetts.

Harriet enjoyed another 20 years in freedom, earning her way as a washerwoman.[44] She lived to see one daughter married and her grandchildren born to freedom. Eliza, the older daughter, never married. The city directories continued to list Harriet's address and denoted her race, with a small "c" in brackets to indicate her difference. They even gave her notoriety as "Dred's widow,"[45] Mrs. Dred Scott.

Harriet Robinson Scott died on June 17, 1876, in alleyway housing located between 7th and 8th Streets and Locust and Olive Streets—less than five blocks from the courthouse.[46] It is amazing what can happen when an individual comports herself as if she is indeed entitled to justice and holds fast to the possibility.

APPENDIX

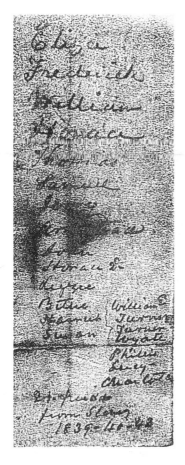

Lawrence Taliaferro's list of slaves that he says he owned and freed in the years 1839–41. The list is scribbled on the back of a form that shows his membership in the Franklin Society. *Lawrence Taliaferro Letters, Minnesota Historical Society.*

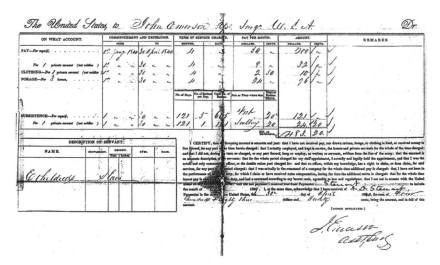

One of Dr. John Emerson's pay slips from the Settled Accounts of the Army Paymaster file, showing Dr. Emerson claiming moneys for the support of his servant Etheldred, who is declared to be a "slave" at Fort Snelling, signed by J. Emerson and by Army paymaster A.D. Steuart. The original is in the National Archives.

ACKNOWLEDGMENTS

They say ev'rything can be replaced,
Yet ev'ry distance is not near.
So I remember ev'ry face
of ev'ry man who put me here.
　　　　　　—Bob Dylan*

Thank you,

Research Assistants: Sandya Subramanian, Bethany Berger, Susan Brehm, Chad Warren, Kris Matsumoto, Alison Harvey, Steve Wieland, Jim Sheets, Katie Rector Steffen, Mark Andre Timinsky, Jennifer Baugh, Brad Geier, Karissa Hostrup-Windsor, Casey Jarchow, Tiana Gierke, Craig Regens, Matthew Volk, Jocelyn Cornbleet, Stephanie Fisher, Ethan Domke, Angela Johnson, Todd Johnston, David Loetz, Kenneth Price, William Ripley, and Christina Welling, Joel Brown, George Tyler Coulson, Cindy Lane, Xiaowei Li, Kristen Stoll, Thad Wilson, Jake Sadovsky.

Historians: David Konig, Mary Dudziak, William Wiecek, Leslie Schwalm, Ken Winn, Lucy Eldersveld Murphy, Father F. Paul Prucha, Kris Zapalac, Louis Gerteis, Michael Les Benedict, Austin Allen, Fred Fausz, Linda Kerber, Art McEvoy, Wayne Fields, Paul Finkelman, Bob Gordon, Mac Rohrbaugh, Sarah Hanley.

Legal Scholars and Colleagues: Peg Brinig, Akhil Amar, Len Sandler, Jerry Wetlaufer, Randy Bezanson, John Whiston, Sandy Levinson, Laura Cooper, Barbara Babcock, Peggy Cooper Davis, Adrien Wing, Mark Tushnet, Martha Mahoney, Jack Balkin, Pat Bauer, Carol Sanger.

The University of Iowa Law Library's splendid Librarians: John Bergstrom, Mary Ann Nelson, Ted Potter, and Arthur Bonfield.

Fellow searchers of the upper Mississippi Valley Heritage: Walter "Mac" MacDonald, Walter Bachman, Mary De Julio, Regina Schantz, Scott Wolfe, Judge Mike Kirchman.

Park Rangers: Mark Kollbaum, Thomas Shaw, Bob Moore.

Venues and Hosts: Matt Pinsker, Dickinson College, Harvard University, Charles Ogletree, Washington University, St. Louis, Minnesota Federal Courts, Steven Rau, Missouri Supreme Court and the

Missouri Supreme Court Historical Society, Wisconsin Supreme Court Sesquicentennial Commission, Michal O'Hear, Marquette Law School.

Guardians of Treasures: Alan Woolworth, Debbie Miller, Lynne Morrow, Mike Everman, Marie Ceselski, Dennis Northcott, Mario Favazza, Mary Freymiller and James Hansen, Carolyn and Rhoda Gillman, Karen Needles, Duane Sneddeker, Bill Glankler.

Justice Michael Wolf, Judge Michael J. Davis, Justice Stephen Limbaugh, Judge Michael McConnell, Justice Shirley Abrahamson, Justice Ray Price.

Mel Conley, Kenneth Kaufmann, wherever you are.

Sustaining Friends: Gerda Suppanz Shebeck, Richard Kuhns, Maggie Conroy, Regina Austin, Judith Wegner, Chuck and Maleah Grover-McKay, Randee Fieselman, Beth Auerbach, Joe Knight and Susan Mask, John A. Madison, Jr., Lynne M. Jackson, M. R. Ottoson, Marta Little, Marylynn Robinson, Nikolaus Benke, Elizabeth Holzleitner, Kailash Satyarthi, Bhurian, Pryanka.

Deloris VanderVelde, Lori VanderVelde, and Johannes Ledolter, who followed each turn of the path.

Mary Sleichter, who typed everything over and over again. Diana Dewalle, Eric Andersen, Jon Carlson, Willard "Sandy" Boyd.

People who know how to make a good book: David McBride, Angela Chnapko, Joellyn Ausanka, Michael O'Malley.

NOTES

Abbreviations

CCHRP	Circuit Court Historical Records Project (St. Louis circuit court records from the nineteenth century). Available at http://stlcourtrecords.westl.edu/resources.php
LT Journals	Journals of Lawrence Taliaferro, Minnesota Historical Society Manuscript Collection
Minn HS	Minnesota Historical Society, St. Paul
Mo HS	Missouri Historical Society, St. Louis
NA	National Archives, Washington, DC
PCDP	St. Louis Probate Court Digitization Project, 1802–1900. Available at www.sos.mo.gov/archives/mojudicial/stl_history.as
S Accts RG 217, E 516	Settled Accounts of the Army Paymaster, Research Group 217, Entry 516, National Archives

Introduction

1. 60 U.S. 393 (1857).
2. These facets of Dred Scott have been explored in sources such as: Paul Finkelman, *An Imperfect Union: Slavery, Federalism, and Comity* (1981); Stanley I. Kutler, ed., *The Dred Scott Decision* (1967); Walter Ehrlich, *They Have No Rights: Dred Scott's Struggle for Freedom* (1979); Don E. Fehrenbacher, *The Dred Scott Case: Its Significance in American Law and Politics* (1978); Dianne Lewis Heafer, *A Historiographical Study of the Taney Court and the Dred Scott Decision* (1985); Vincent C. Hopkins, *Dred Scott's Case* (1951); Joel Parker, *Personal Liberty Laws, and Slavery in the Territories* (1861); Theodore Clarke Smith, *Parties and Slavery, 1850–1859* (1906).
3. The Dred Scott decision played a major role in the Lincoln-Douglas debates of 1858. In the speeches leading up to the debates, Senator Stephen Douglas argued that the right to bring slaves into formerly free territory was meaningless if the local legislature and law enforcement did not enforce it. Abraham Lincoln blamed Douglas's Kansas-Nebraska Act of 1854 for demonstrating a moral indifference that would eventually lead to a totally slave-holding United States. In the debates themselves, Douglas accused Lincoln of supporting full racial equality while Lincoln claimed that while he did not believe in full equality, he did profess that blacks had the right to earn their own living as whites did. David Brion Davis, *Inhuman Bondage: The Rise and Fall of Slavery in the New World* (New York: Oxford University Press, 2006), 288–90.

4. Fehrenbacher, *The Dred Scott Case,* 240.

5. Johnson, *Soul by Soul*; Martin, *Divided Mastery*; Glymph, *Out of the House of Bondage: The Transformation of the Plantation Household.*

6. Schafer, *Becoming Free*; Berlin, *Generations of Captivity*; Kennedy, *Braided Relations, Entwined Lives.*

7. See, e.g., opinion of Justice Campbell emphasizing that the stipulated facts suggested that Dred Scott had been living for years under the dominion of Missouri's slave laws before he filed suit. He later reiterated the point misstating his belief that Dred had been in Missouri 15 years when the suit was brought. Justice McLean mistakenly assumes that Harriet was purchased in Missouri, positing a lack of evidence that the Scotts returned to the slave state voluntarily.

8. See Wood, *Black Majority*; Gallay, *The Indian Slave Trade*; and Usner, *Indians, Settlers, and Slaves.*

9. See, for example, Lucie E. White, "Subordination, Rhetorical Survival Skills and Sunday Shoes: Notes on the Hearing of Mrs. G," 38 *Buffalo Law Review* 1 (1990); Notes, The Plaintiff as Person: Cause Lawyering, Human Subject Research, and the Secret Agent Problem, 119 *Harvard Law Review* 1510 (2006). See also Marshall and Barclay, "In Their Own Words" ("A wave of scholarship about legal consciousness has demonstrated how law shapes the everyday lives of ordinary people"). For a theoretical examination of whether this can ever truly be known at all, see Gayatri Chakravorty Spivak, "Can the Subaltern Speak?"

10. The issue of whether Harriet ever traveled to Louisiana is one of those instances where the evidence is contradictory. See discussion in Chapter 13.

11. Don Fehrenbacher's Pulitzer Prize–winning account, *The Dred Scott Case,* was drawn primarily from Professor Walter Ehrlich's factual research, and Walter Ehrlich told me that he never looked deeply into Harriet's background, nor did he find the Taliaferro diary (Ehrlich, *They Have No Rights*; conversation with Walter Ehrlich).

12. For example, Mrs. Taliaferro's black and white china was noted in the shipment of furnishings home from the frontier. Shipping manifest included in the Lawrence Taliaferro Papers, Minn HS.

13. Ehrlich, *They Have No Rights,* 9–30.

14. In this regard, the work should be compared to and distinguished from other well-known accounts of slave women's lives such as Jacobs, *Incidents in the Life of a Slave Girl.*

15. We can presume that Harriet conformed to expected norms of behavior and did not actively resist her frontier servitude because she wouldn't have survived such a departure from expectations. We can assume that she did not attempt to flee to a free state because that conduct would have found its way into the papers that were left of the time and place, as others' attempts were.

16. See, e.g., McLaurin, *Celia, a Slave.*

17. See Chapter 1.

18. Newspaper article, *Los Angeles Times,* March 18, 2003.

19. http://stlcourtrecords.wustl.edu/index.php.

Chapter 1

1. *Frank Leslie's Illustrated Newspaper,* June 27, 1857.

2. See, for example, instances of kidnapping of free black persons from Illinois and St. Louis in the freedom cases: *John Singleton v. Alexander Scott and Robert Lewis* (kidnapped from Illinois, 1827); *Laura v. Henry Belt* (1852), CCHRP.

3. Ibid.

4. Ibid.

5. One historian notes that freedwomen's idea of freedom must accommodate "Virginia Newman's idea of freedom: (a blue guinea with yaler spots.) This was Newman's first 'bought dress,' and it represented, for her, control over her 'whole life' and concomitantly, the diminished control white people had over it." Glymph, *Out of the House of Bondage,* 10.

Chapter 2

1. Lawrence Taliaferro's diary documents that he traveled north from St. Louis on the steamboat *Warrior* each spring after 1834. LT Journals, 1834.
2. Men paddling keelboats up the Mississippi are described in one of the early women's narratives (Adams, *Early Days,* 16).
3. The term "Dakota" is the word by which the Dakota people refer to themselves. The term "Sioux" was used interchangeably with Dakota in the English-speaking community of St. Peter's Indian Agency at the time. I have continued to use the terms interchangeably in this book because it is the linguistic perspective from which Harriet would have encountered the Dakota people. Agent Taliaferro used the term more frequently in his Journal, and presumably in his household.
4. Lawrence Taliaferro was reappointed by President Jackson on April 14, 1835 (Lawrence Taliaferro Papers, Minn HS); Taliaferro, "Autobiography," 190–97.
5. "The Tate House: A Period Piece," *Pioneer* 3 (4): 1 (describing what came to be known as the Taliaferro-Tate House in Bedford, Pennsylvania), April 1978.
6. As early as 1832, near the completion of an earlier term, Taliaferro had told the Indians that perhaps he would be leaving them forever. LT Journals, June 28, 1832.
7. As a slave girl living in the northern frontier, her circumstances do not conform fully to those of a slave in the antebellum South; she was not chained, beaten, or compelled to labor for the production of some good for sale in the market by her owner. Nor were her circumstances exactly those of a servant girl, or even an indentured servant girl. Her master, Lawrence Taliaferro, never referred to any of the several black former slaves that he brought to the frontier as "slaves," rather as "servants" in his diary. For example, Eliza and William are referred to as his servants. LT Journals, March 31, 1826 ("my bound boy, William"); February 1, 1831 ("all my servants"); February 13, 1831 ("servant girl Eliza"). Thus, I use the terms *slave* and *servant* virtually interchangeably when referring to her status on the frontier. In truth Taliaferro's servants experienced some indicia of enslavement or servitude and some of freedom, as the story will show.
8. A handwritten list on the back of a membership in a charitable organization is among Taliaferro's papers in the Minnesota Historical Society Collections, roll 1, document 3. Taliaferro lists by name all 21 slaves that he owned and states that they were all "freed from slavery 1839–40–42."
9. Taliaferro's journal lists the stages of his return journey from St. Peter's to Bedford. LT Journals (July 14–August 12, 1832).
10. Petersen, *Steamboating,* 176–76, 252–53.
11. Merrick, *Old Times on the Upper Mississippi,* 34.
12. George Davenport was Indian Agent Lawrence Taliaferro's counterpart at Fort Armstrong, Rock Island, Illinois. Charlotte, indenture papers registered in Galena, Jo Daviess County, Illinois by George Davenport, Deed Record Book A. Nov. 2, 1824, recorded July 9, 1831. Charlotte's indenture was for seven years, so she may have been released by spring of 1835 by the time Harriet came through.
13. There would have been no real reason for Taliaferro to meet the new post doctor, and his diary suggests that they did not meet until two years later when Dr. Emerson was reassigned to Fort Snelling. Emerson reported for duty at Fort Armstrong, Rock Island Illinois on December 1, 1833. According to the U.S. Army paymaster's records, Dred was with him (SP Accts RG 217, E 516, Post returns for Fort Armstrong).
14. Their regular correspondence suggests a familiarity and frequent entreaties that Taliaferro and his lady should extend their stay with his family. Joseph Montfort Street Correspondence, 1827–1840, Iowa Historical Society, Des Moines, Iowa.
15. Smith, *The History of Wisconsin,* vol. 1, p. 283.
16. Ibid.
17. Rayman, "Confrontation at Fever River," 278; Rayman, "Establishing the Sac and Fox Indian Agency," 261.

18. Whiskey or, in some interpretations, brandy, was referred to as "eau de vie," water of life, and sometimes described as "firewater" in French-Indian communication. McDermott, *A Glossary of Mississippi Valley French, 1673–1850*.

19. There are numerous sources documenting slave anxiety about impending events over which the enslaved individuals had no control. These many sources belie the myth of the happy-go-lucky slave. For example, Jonathan Martin describes how pending New Year's Day sales ruined the happiness of the Christmas holiday. Martin, *Divided Mastery*, 45.

20. Blassingame, *Slave Testimony*, 160 (detailing slaves' nighttime socializing).

21. The first steam whistle did not appear on the upper Mississippi until about 1848 (Petersen, *Steamboating*, 109).

22. Smith, *The History of Wisconsin*, 282–83.

23. Lawrence Taliaferro described the policy of recruiting Dakota warriors to attack the Sac and Fox as impolitic. LT Journals, June 19, 1832.

24. The Pond brothers report that Wabasha was "held in high esteem by both the whites and Indians for his good sense and upright conduct" (Pond, *The Dakota or Sioux in Minnesota*, 7–8).

25. Richter, *Facing East from Indian Country*, 176 (describing the stability of the greeting rituals across various Indian Tribes).

26. See, generally, Prucha, *Indian Peace Medals*, 99.

27. Treaty with the Sioux, August 19, 1825.

28. White, "A Skilled Game of Exchange," 229–40.

29. Anderson, *Little Crow*, 17.

30. LT Journals, June 10, 1834.

31. Travel journals and letters often described this moment. See Bray, *Journals of Joseph N. Nicollet*, 10, and Marryatt, *Diary in America*, vol. 2, ch. 28. Jarvis letter (June 1, 1833) Minn HS.

32. Bliss, *Reminiscences of Fort Snelling*, 340–41. Jarvis Letter (June 1, 1833), Minn HS. "[Steamboat arrivals] excite considerable stir in this...isolated spot. Our Boat being the first this season was greeted on her passage up by the shouting of the Indians in their villages along the river and occasionally the firing of their rifles."

33. Catlin, *George Catlin's Letters and Notes*, 142. Iron cutter was a clever name for the man who gave orders to the blacksmith for cutting iron. It was also almost a direct translation of the Italian meaning of his name, talia-ferro.

34. The region around the agency was the traditional land of one particular tribe of Dakota, the Mdewakanton, a word meaning "spirit lake." Four of the local villages of the Spirit Lake Dakota Indians were Black Dog's, the Sixes, Cloudman's, and Big Thunder's villages. Several bands of Dakota, traveling in from the plains farther west, had arrived and set up their lodges in one area of the plateau. The tepees were made of buffalo hides stretched taut on long poles. The four local Dakota bands didn't necessarily need to move to the plateau to visit the Agency; their traditional summer village sites were within walking distance along the river.

35. Pond, *The Dakota or Sioux in Minnesota*, 43.

36. Minnesota, Wisconsin, Iowa, North and South Dakota.

Chapter 3

1. Jarvis letter (February 28, 1835), Minn HS.

2. Mrs. Taliaferro must have brought up a piano on this or an earlier trip, as she is known to have played her piano with Nicollet in a later winter, without having made a trip south in the intervening time.

3. This routine of cleaning out living quarters at a northern fort is described in Eastman, *Aunt Phillis's Cabin*. Nancy Eastman lived at Fort Snelling as an officer's wife a few years later.

4. The house was described as "a five bay" measuring 36 by 42 feet in size. This description and these measurements are taken from a loose map in the collection of papers. Lawrence Taliaferro Papers, 1813–1868, Minn HS.

5. Lawrence Taliaferro Papers, 1813–1868, Minn HS.

6. LT Journals, August 12–14, 1830.

7. Pond, *The Dakota or Sioux in Minnesota*, 25. For a description of Campbell's lineage, marriage, and connection to Taliaferro, see Wozniak, *Contact, Negotiation and Conflict*, 40–41.

8. Later that autumn the agent proposed to construct a replacement building with a house for smith, shop, and coal house under the same roof (Rhodes, "The Fort Snelling Area in 1835," 22).

9. Once when Taliaferro returned from spending the winter away, he found that his fence had been salvaged for wood. LT Journals, May 28, 1832.

10. LT Journals, June 23, 1839. Taliaferro remarked in his diary, "In twenty years no harm has come to my animals" on the occasion that one of them was injured by an Indian.

11. This was the common design of kitchens in houses at that time.

12. Nacy, *Members of the Regiment*, 56, 58, 61, 63, 93.

13. *Rachael v. Walker*, 4 Mo. R. 351 (1836) (slave woman purchased when officer married); Bliss, *Reminiscences of Fort Snelling*, 340 (slaves purchased when officer's wife and child moved north to Fort Snelling).

14. Coen, "Eliza Dillon Taliaferro," 146–53.

15. Featherstonhaugh, *A Canoe Voyage up the Minnay Sotor*, 278.

16. Glymph, *Out of the House of Bondage*, 000.

17. Coen, *Eliza Dillon Taliaferro*, 146. Etiquette books advised that the hair papers cannot be removed on rising because the hair would not keep in a curl till evening. Instead, the hair papers were supposed to be concealed under a lace cap a "bandeau of lace" (Thornwell, *The Lady's Guide to Perfect Gentility*, 119).

18. Nacy, *Members of the Regiment*, 55 (documenting class distinction between officers' wives as ladies and soldiers' wives).

19. *Army and Navy Chronicle*, August 20, 1835.

20. Thornwell, *The Lady's Guide to Perfect Gentility*, 151. Only among their most intimate friends could they refer to "my husband." Only very young ladies, like 15-year-old Miss Loomis, were permitted such lapses as referring to their husbands by their Christian names.

21. Bliss, *Reminiscences of Fort Snelling*, 340 (detailing with significance the arrival of Mrs. Taliaferro and Mrs. Miree). Most officers' ladies seemed to express a similar feeling of desperate loneliness at their husband's postings on the frontier. Robert Clouston Journals, 1846, 1850, Minn HS.
    "Our fashions came from the east.... But some lady, either a citizen or of the army, would arrive from the east, and she would be kind enough to lend her dress to some friend to make one by. That friend would lend to her friend, and so on until we all were served." Baird, *O De Jit Wa Win Ning*, 88.

22. Bliss, *Reminiscences of Fort Snelling*, 336.

23. Ibid.

24. Hole-in-the-Day was not a chief's son. He and his brother, Strong Ground, had found favor in the household of the prior chief of the Sandy Lake Ojibwa, first becoming the childless chief's favored pipe bearers and then virtually his adopted sons. The relationship to the band was cemented when Hole-in-the-Day took one of the Chief's daughters as an additional wife (Diedrich, "The Chiefs Hole-in-the-Day of the Mississippi Chippewa," 378–409).

25. LT Journals, June 4, 1835.

26. Ibid.

27. His people killed one in return. Ibid.

28. Ibid.

29. Ibid.

30. Anderson, *Little Crow*, 41.

31. Ibid.

32. LT Journals, June 3, 1835.

33. Ibid.

34. Treaty with the Sioux, August 19, 1825.
35. LT Journals, June 4, 1835.
36. LT Journals, June 19, 1839 ("I am compelled to ask favors in order to carry on friendly intercourse [with the Indians]"). In 1819 Calhoun had sent Taliaferro a detailed letter explaining his duties, which in essence meant that Taliaferro had to be many agents: to the local fur traders; to the representatives of the American Fur Company in the area; to the military commander of the Fort; to the District Superintendent of the Indian Office; to the Indian Office in Washington; to the whites, including settlers, missionaries and sightseers; and to the Dakota Indians. Wozniak, *Contact, Negotiation and Conflict*, 40; Prucha, *Documents of U.S. Indian Policy*, 14, 17, 30, 64.
37. Ibid.
38. Taliaferro, "Autobiography," 249. Taliaferro identifies the four peoples as "French, Scotch, Sioux, American," though Ojibwa and Sioux were better represented by 1835.
39. Although the government provided traps to the Indians through the agency blacksmith, after the suspension of the factory system, the government no longer bought furs from the Indians. So the government-provided traps actually subsidized the Company's business (Whelan, "Dakota Indian Economics," 246–76).
40. Blegen, "The Unfinished Autobiography," 329; Gilman, "How Henry Sibley Took the Road to New Hope," 220–29; Sibley, "Reminiscences, Historical and Personal," 457–70. An additional biography is West, *The Ancestry, Life, and Times of Hon. Henry Hastings Sibley*.
41. Bliss, *Reminiscences of Fort Snelling*, 347 (description of Sibley as a young man).
42. Blegen, "The Unfinished Autobiography," 348 (Sibley's account of Crook's soliciting him for the position).
43. Nute, "Calendar of Papers," calendar entry 40, from Hercules Dousman, Prairie du Chien, October 14, 1834, "Bailley will not sell his outfit"; Nute, "Calendar of Papers," calendar entry 54, November 1, 1834, from Henry H. Sibley gives reasons for Bailly's agreeing to sell out his interest to Sibley, Dousman, and Roulette.
44. There are not as many recently published secondary sources about the American Fur Company on the Upper Mississippi as a reader may want. Listed in the bibliography are several excellent older and current works on the fur trade in the far West, on the Missouri River, and in Canada. Lavender and Wishart, *The Fist in the Wilderness*; Sunder, *The Fur Trade on the Upper Missouri, 1840–1865*; Chittenden, *The American Fur Trade of the Far West*; Christian, *Before Lewis and Clark*.
45. Throughout Sibley's long stay in Minnesota, he wrote the New York office regularly, particularly if lobbying needed to be done in Washington (Blegen, "The Unfinished Autobiography," 39–75).
46. John Jacob Astor sold out to Crooks in 1834 (Christian, *Before Lewis and Clark*, 378).
47. In this position, Henry Sibley had been tutored by Lawrence Taliaferro's primary rival, Henry Schoolcraft. Sibley had taken over the business of Schoolcraft's father-in-law. Henry H. Sibley Papers (1815–1930), Minn HS.
48. Bliss, *Reminiscences of Fort Snelling*, 349.
49. LT Journals, June 9, 1835.
50. Ibid.
51. Letter of Benjamin Clapp to Sibley, January 1846: Henry H. Sibley Papers (1815–1930), Minn HS. "We are therefore induced to make inquiry of you whether a suitable person can be found in your part of the country who would undertake to transport say five or six hundred gallons of Alcohol to be sent from this place" (for the purpose of providing the Blackfoot Indians with liquor and to avoid drawing the Company's name into the smuggling operation).

Chapter 4

1. Ad regarding Horatio Dillon's Inn in *Bedford Gazette*, April 14, 1837.
2. LT Journals, June 6, 1835.
3. Ibid., 1833.

4. Nacy, *Members of the Regiment*, 4.
5. The Reverend Williamson had been a doctor in Ohio before deciding to become a missionary. His medical training was useful in tending to accidents and illness and even outbreaks of epidemic, since the post's surgeon was the only diplomaed doctor within several hundred miles. Riggs, "In Memory of Rev. Thos. S. Williamson, M.D.," 372.
6. The Second Great Awakening (1790s–1850s) was a religious backlash against the perceived Enlightenment elitism of the Deist founders and the established "high" churches. Methodists and Baptists experienced explosive growth and brought evangelical fervor to the antislavery cause, among other moral causes they pursued. Slaves ardently joined in the "liberating message" of the religious revival as a means of achieving personal dignity and justice. On the frontier, itinerant preachers spent more energy on organizing effective administration of frontier circuits and revivals than they did on biblical exegesis. Wills, *Head and Heart*, 287–89; Howe, *What Hath God Wrought*, 178–79, 184–85.
7. Samuel was called Red Eagle, *Wam-dee-Doota*, while his more robust brother, Gideon, took the name, Grizzly Bear, *or Mato-Ho-tah* (Pond, *Two Volunteer Missionaries*, 23, 59; see also Pond, *The Dakota or Sioux in Minnesota*, and Pond, *Dakota Life*).
8. Nathan Jarvis letter, July 2, 1834. Minn HS.
9. Ivey, *Ancestry and Posterity* (page number not available).
10. LT Journals, August 25, 1838.
11. LT Journals, June 14, 1835. "70 Indians appeared requested council."
12. LT Journals, July 12, 1835.
13. Ponds, *Two Volunteer Missionaries*, 63, claimed that the original church was founded with 22 persons of "European extraction" through Methodist revivals or the African Methodist Episcopal church.
14. The Reverend Williamson was opposed to slaveholding. His father had moved from South Carolina to Ohio to fulfill his grandfather's testamentary wish to free his slaves. Riggs, "In Memory of Rev. Thos. S. Williamson, M.D.," 372. On the other hand, slaveholding as a practice was not financially subsidized for the missionaries as it was by the Army for its officers.
15. The Stevenses followed this pattern.
16. Riggs, *A Small Bit of Bread and Butter*, 111–12; Riggs, *Mary and I*, 65.
17. Riggs, *Mary and I*, 65.
18. LT Journals, June 9, 1835.
19. LT Journals, June 14, 1835. In 1821, Taliaferro had complained that "not one solitary soul [was present] to assist [him] in the manual labor of the department." LT Journals, September 13, 1821.
20. No one knows exactly what the basement of the agency house looked like, but the commandant's house at the fort had a similar external structure, and it is quite likely that the houses were built the same way inside. Like the other houses within the fort, the kitchen probably had an earth-banked enclosure burrowed into the foundation as a pantry that could be kept cool.
21. "So far as I can, some have been furnished with fish hooks and lines, fish spears, and a small amount of powder, lead, and flints" (LT Journals, June 24, 1835).
22. The buffalo dance was only danced by the Sioux. Bray, *Journals of Joseph N. Nicollet*, 260; LT Journals, June 11, 1835; July 13, 1835.
23. Ibid.
24. LT Journals, September 17, 1829 ("An Indian woman deranged who has a young child, her whole state seems to be to the want of human flesh.") LT Journals, September 19, 1829 ("The Indian woman entered the fort last night and frightened Capt. Jouett's family. She wished a piece of her servant to eat as she was very fat.")
25. Blegen, "Unfinished Autobiography of Henry Hastings Sibley," 361–62.
26. See description of his exchange with commissioners on the subject of his daughter. LT Journals, summer 1838, Chapter 14. Gary Clayton Anderson claims in his book that Taliaferro's relationship with the young Sioux woman was an "affine" relationship, or one deriving from blood ties, that gave Taliaferro important

leverage with the Little Crow band at the same time that it placed pressure on Taliaferro to assist his new kinsmen (Anderson, *Little Crow*, 24).

27. The other children were the children of Capt. Lamont, Capt. Williams, and Capt. Ortley (LT Journals and letter, March 2, 1836).

28. Ibid.

29. The surveyors set out on June 18 with Lt. William Storer and Philander Prescott (Fort Snelling Post returns, June 1835).

30. Ladies sporting umbrellas on arriving steamboats were so iconic that they were even painted on the symbolic picture of the first steamboat arriving at Fort Snelling. In private collection, copy on file with author.

31. LT Journals, June 24, 1835.

32. LT Journals, June 25, 1835.

33. He assigned each his amount of the annuities in turn and then, to demonstrate what he regarded as his patrimony toward them, he usually gave each of the principal men some additional small gifts.

34. Peterson, *Steamboating*, 152.

35. Dana and Dana, *A Fashionable Tour*.

36. The leading books about George Catlin are Dippie, *Catlin and His Contemporaries;* Catlin, Gurney, Dippie, and Renwick Gallery, *George Catlin and His Indian Gallery;* Catlin, *George Catlin's Letters and Notes*. Catlin endeavored to reach all of the tribes of North America to deliver faithful renderings and descriptions of them to the American public (Catlin, *Letters and Notes*, 21–22).

37. Catlin, *Letters and Notes*, vol 1, 137–38.

38. Dippie, *Catlin and His Contemporaries*, 37.

39. Marryatt, *Diary in America*, vol. 2, ch. 28. "Here for the first time, I consider that I have seen the Indians in their primitive state."

40. The Sac and Fox had been expelled from their lands in Illinois. Near Prairie du Chien, the Winnebago and Menominee tribes were said to be in a disgraceful state of desperation and drunkenness.

41. Patricia Limerick has wisely noted that the closing of the frontier occurs with the expansion of tourism (Limerick, *The Legacy of Conquest*, 25).

42. LT Journals, June 26, 1835.

43. So he subtitled the picture *The Dandy* by George Catlin (ibid.).

44. George Catlin, *Letters and Notes*, vol. 2, 137–38.

45. Ibid., 132–34 (with several sketches.)

46. Ibid., 131, 139.

47. Note list of Nathan Jarvis acquisitions at the Brooklyn museum (Feder, *Art of the Eastern Plains Indians*).

48. Jarvis, "Letters of Nathan Jarvis," July 2, 1834, Minn HS.

49. LT Journals, August 10, 1839. Late in his journal, when reflecting on his several decades, Taliaferro noted that the Sioux always live in the short-term. "The present moment with them is as far as their short-sighted vision is capable of comprehending." Ibid.

50. Truettner, *The Natural Man Observed*.

51. "Negro cloth" was a tough worsted, woven in bolt lengths especially to outfit servants and slaves.

52. Catlin, *Letters and Notes*, vol. 2, 135.

53. LT Journals, July 3, 1835. It was a noteworthy sign of respect that the pairs approached Agent Taliaferro rather than the recently arrived Presbyterian minister, who had married Miss Loomis and her lieutenant.

54. Letters between Street and Taliaferro on their authority as Indian agents to conduct a legal marriage. September 1, 1831, letter of Joseph Street to Lawrence Taliaferro. Lawrence Taliaferro papers, 1813–1868, Minn HS.

55. Other meanings for Waukon were "holy" or "divinely spiritual."

56. LT Journals, July 4, 1835; Pond, *Dakota Life in the Upper Midwest*, 113–16.

57. Catlin, *Letters and Notes*, 135. According to Joseph Nicollet, in this wartime dance, the Sioux excluded children and "perform[ed] before strangers that have come to their country, when they wish to draw attention to themselves. They use the dance to express themselves in harsh statements" (Nicollet, *The Journals*, 258).
58. Catlin, *Letters and Notes*, vol. 2, 136.
59. Ibid., 137.
60. Not all settlement people were as receptive to the Dakotas' begging dog dance. The Pond brothers disapproved. As Gideon Pond wrote in his diary, "[W]e considered it to be our duty to grievously offend them by disregarding them" (Pond, *Two Volunteer Missionaries*, 94).
61. Catlin, *Letters and Notes*, 140 (sketch of Ojibwa encampment).
62. LT Journals, July 16, 1835.
63. Nicollet, *The Journals of Joseph N. Nicollet*, 258.
64. Toasts given at social gatherings and their respective musical flourishes were frequently printed in newspapers.
65. Essence of lemon was a common purchase in the sutler's store. Sutler's accounts, Henry H. Sibley Collection, Minnesota Historical Manuscripts Collection. The commandant's wife had served ice cream and strawberries at a party the previous July. LT Journals, July 4, 1838, Manuscript Collection. Strawberries show up in various memoirs in the area (Riggs, *A Small Bit of Bread and Butter*, 36; Bliss, *Reminiscences*, 340).
66. Petersen, *Steamboating*, 176–77 (detailing Throckmorton's participation in using the Steamboat *Warrior* against the Indians in the Blackhawk War).
67. LT Journals, July 18, 1835.
68. Catlin, *Letters and Notes*, 167n.
69. This is the current prevailing wisdom according to the Pipestone National Monument Website, www.nps.gov/pipe/.
70. Ibid.
71. Loyd Haberly, *Pursuit of the Horizon*, 95.
72. Pond, *The Dakota or Sioux*, 138–39.
73. The portraits Catlin painted were: 1. *Wa-nah-de-tunk-ah*; 2. *Toh-to-wah-kon-da-pee*, Blue Medicine, medicine man; 3. *Ah-no-je-nahge*; 4. *We-chush-ta-doo-ta*; 5. *Ki-ah-kis-gaw*, "Indians pursuing a stag in the waters of the Minnesota." There were also sketches of several of the dances and tableaux that he would later make full-size paintings: the Eastern Sioux Dog Dance at Fort Snelling; one each of the Eastern Sioux and of the Ojibwa performing the Brave's Dance; the Ojibwa performing the Snowshoe Dance, at the first snowfall; the Ojibwa gathering wild rice near the source of St. Peter's River and making portage around the Falls of St Anthony; and an Ojibwa village and dog feast at the falls. Catlin, *Letters and Notes*, vol. 2, 132–41.
74. Densmore, *Chippewa Customs*, 34.
75. Dippie, *Catlin and His Contemporaries*, 37–38.

Chapter 5

1. Adams, *Early Days at Red River Settlement*, 77–83.
2. Williams, *The Story of the City of Saint Paul*, 66.
3. Even in the hardest times, the refugees from Selkirk community celebrated nuptials with much gaiety and a party to do honor to the occasion (Adams, *Early Days at Red River Settlement*, 84).
4. Taliaterro recorded 114 refugees on that trip, bringing the number to a total of almost 500 refugees that had passed through since 1821. These trekkers were on their way to Vevay, a Swiss settlement in Indiana (LT Journals, July 28, 1835).
5. Adams, *Early Days at Red River Settlement*, 84.
6. LT Journals, July 29, 1835.
7. LT Journals, August 4, 1835.

8. Sibley's letter to his mother. August 1, 1835. Henry H. Sibley Papers (1815–1930), Minn HS.

9. Blegen, "The Unfinished Autobiography," 358. The man was named Joe Robinson.

10. Ponds, *Two Volunteer Missionaries,* 132.

11. Ibid., 66–67.

12. From September to October 1835, Jarvis had a man named Plumb working for him at Fort Snelling. Plumb must have been a servant sent to him by his family back east. S Accts RG 217, E 516. But in November 1835, Plumb was replaced by blue-eyed Morton (ibid.). Dr. Jarvis refers to sending Plumb back to his brother and sister in New York because he no longer needs him. Nathan Jarvis letter, July 4, 1833, Minn HS.

13. During the previous winter of 1834–35, some of the young officers, including Lt. Ogden, created a long list of Dakota words with their English meanings with the aid of Scott Campbell. Campbell dictated in Dakota as the officers went down through the English dictionary and recorded their definitions. These word lists became the basis for versions expanded and used by the missionaries (Pond, *Two Volunteer Missionaries,* 53).

14. *Minnay Sotor* means turbid waters (Featherstonhaugh, *A Canoe Voyage Up the Minnay Sotor,* 286).

15. Berkeley and Berkeley, *George William Featherstonhaugh,* 71).

16. Ibid., 157–58.

17. Bray, *Joseph Nicollet and His Map,* 161, quoting a letter of Troost sent to Nicollet on the subject of Mr. Featherstonhaugh. With his air of superiority, the geologist irritated Henry Sibley as well (Sibley, "Reminiscences, Historical and Personal," vol. 1, 481.

18. There are numerous slighting accounts of Henry Schoolcraft throughout Taliaferro's diary. See, e.g., LT Journals, June 22, 1839 (blaming Schoolcraft for profligate distribution of Indian medals).

19. LT Journals, September 16, 1835.

20. Ibid.

21. Featherstonhaugh, *A Canoe Voyage Up the Minnay Sotor,* 278–79.

22. Ibid.

23. Bliss had requested his second-in-command, Loomis, to see to the visitor's accommodations (ibid).

24. LT Journals, October 10, 1835.

25. LT Journals, October 19, 1835.

26. Joseph Rolette had long operated an extensive trading empire there similar to one Sibley was setting up at Mendota (Murphy, "To Live among Us," in *Contact Points,* by Cayton and Teute, 275–76, describing hierarchically ordered Creole communities).

27. The fact that Taliaferro's journal refers to "Lt. Storer & family" indicates that there was more to Storer's entourage than just him and his bride. In his journal noting the comings and goings in Indian territory, Taliaferro distinguished between officers traveling with their "ladies" and those officers accompanied by a larger entourage. Lt. Storer's pay slips list "Betsy" as his new servant (LT Journals, September 27, 1835).

28. Taliaferro usually sent a servant with a rifle to guard the corn. Once a young slave boy, William, given a rifle to shoot a hawk accidentally injured another curious child, an officer's son (LT Journals, March 29, 1826).

29. Pond, *The Dakota or Sioux in Minnesota,* 27.

30. Ibid.

31. Nacy, *Members of the Regiment,* 76–78.

32. "Dr. N.S. Jarvis: wrote a note to him for an Indian woman whose case of labor was doubtful. The Doctor declined having any hand in this matter" (LT Journals, October 27, 1835). "I addressed to Dr. Jarvis a note, but he says that he has no instruments—so that the caesarian operation cannot be performed and that the woman must die" (LT Journals, October 27, 1835).

33. Dakota Indians routinely placed bodies on scaffolds or in trees to decay (Pond, *The Dakota or Sioux in Minnesota*, 162; Keyser and Klassen, *Plains Indians Rock Art*, 62).

34. "I built an ice house this day with my servant & one man" (LT Journals, September 12, 1835).

35. LT Journals, July 6, 1835.

36. The blacksmith that winter was Antoine Papin and the striker was Joseph Reasch (LT Journals, financial records, September 19, 1835).

37. The man retained as the treaty blacksmith couldn't buy food for his family with the money he earned (LT Journals, September 19 and 21, 1835).

38. Peter Garrioch Diaries, 1837, 1843–1847, Minn HS (describing mudding a house). Kinzie, *Wau-bun*, 83 (Mrs. Kinzie describes doing the process herself). On page 89, Mrs. Kinzie describes Mrs. Twiggs as fortunate enough to have well-trained servants to do for her that which she had to do herself because her "little dark handmaid" could not.)

39. LT Journals, September 23, 1835.

40. LT Journals, October 12, 1835.

41. Pond, *The Dakota or Sioux in Minnesota*, 28–29. Mary Riggs noted that summer strawberries and gooseberries and fall cranberries were the only local fruits in the area (Riggs, *A Small Bit of Bread and Butter*, 36).

42. Riggs, *A Small Bit of Bread and Butter*, 59.

43. Sibley letter to his mother (August 1, 1835). Henry H. Sibley Papers, Minn HS.

44. He owed some $2,500 (Gilman, "Days of the Mississippi Fur Trade,"128). Goodman and Goodman, *Brown, Adventurer on the Minnesota Frontier*, 122).

45. Sibley, "Reminiscences," 466–70.

46. LT Journals, September 17, 1835.

47. Featherstonhaugh, *A Canoe Voyage*, 311.

48. Ibid.

49. If Harriet had no fixed understanding of her parentage, as many slaves in her situation did not, she may have wondered if this Pah-kah-Skah was, in fact, kin to her. The world was wide, and there were many Robinsons, but to an adolescent servant girl, the coincidence of hearing her last name so far from where she came from could seem more significant to her than perhaps it was. Like many slaves, Harriet may have believed herself to have a white father.

50. Featherstonhaugh, *A Canoe Voyage*, 312.

51. Ibid., 312 (description of Mrs. Taliaferro).

52. Ibid.

53. He wrote much later in his memoirs that he thought of her often (ibid.).

54. *Army and Navy Chronicle*, December 10, 1835.

55. Bliss, *Reminiscences*, 351.

56. LT Journals, November 17, 1835.

57. $58.50 in all (LT Journals, November 16, 1835).

58. This method of debt collection was known as "distress."

Chapter 6

1. LT Journals, November 23, 1835.

2. Jarvis Letter, November 30, 1835, Minn HS.

3. Bray, *The Journals of Joseph N. Nicollet*, 264.

4. "The sutler … was a civilian peddler who offered comestibles and small wares to men under arms…for a price" (Delo, *Peddlers and Post Traders*, 1, 47–60). A sutler was a civilian trader appointed and given the exclusive right to sell to the corps. The army guaranteed the sutler a moderate but certain profit (ibid., 50).

5. Each night wolves were heard in the distance that particular November.

6. LT Journals, December 9, 1835. "Stambaugh and several gentlemen of the fort dine at the Agency."

7. Nute, "Calendar of Papers," entry 99.
8. Nationally, the Company was at work lobbying Congress to forbid sutlers from competing with them in the Indian trade. "Exclude the sutlers by law from having anything to do with the Indian trade" (Nute, "Calendar of Papers," entry 397, April 18, 1835, from Ramsey Crooks to H. H. Sibley).
9. Letter from Hercules Dousman, November 29, 1835, asks to get goods cheap in order to undersell small traders. He has offered Stambaugh to join in suttling of Fort Snelling (Nute, "Calendar of Papers," entry 1047). Letter from Hercules Dousman, January 12, 1836; Sibley has agreed with Stambaugh for sutling of Fort Snelling (Nute, "Calendar of Papers," entry 1183).
10. Jarvis letter, November 30, 1835, Minn HS.
11. The agency used the 90 cords of wood that winter (LT Journals, December 28, 1835). Flint and steel were used to get a spark at this time before matches were readily available (Riggs, *A Small Bit of Bread and Butter*, 75).
12. Johnnycake, cornpone, and dodger are described in Murphy and Venet, *Midwestern Women*, 186; Hardeman, *Shucks, Shocks, and Hominy Blocks*, 145.
13. LT Journals, December 1, 1835.
14. LT Journals, December 2, 1835.
15. The slavery literature is replete with mention of the custom of masters giving slaves presents, often of clothing items at Christmas. Franklin, *From Slavery to Freedom: A History of Negro Americans*, 150; Genovese, *Roll, Jordan, Roll: The World the Slaves Made*, 574; Parsons and Stowe, *Inside View of Slavery: Or, A Tour Among the Planters*, 41; William Wells Brown, *From Fugitive Slave to Free Man*, 82; King, *A Northern Woman in the Plantation South*, 94.
16. *History of Bedford, Somerset, and Fulton Counties, Pennsylvania*, page not available. *Pennsylvania Magazine of History and Biography*, 1915, Authored and published by the Historical Society of Pennsylvania Philadelphia, 29.
17. The custom of providing gingerbread for Indians who came calling on Christmas and New Year's Day was described by Charles E. Flandreau, "Reminiscences of Minnesota During the Territorial Period," in Stevens, *The History of the Bench and Bar of Minnesota*, 218.
18. LT Journals, December 31, 1835.
19. Anderson, *Little Crow*, 13 (description of tepee construction).
20. Riggs, *Mary and I*, 65; Pond, *The Dakota or Sioux in Minnesota*, 154–55 (describing the Sioux as bathing in their clothing).
21. Murphy, *To Live among Us*, 280–81 (describing the significance of milking routines in pioneer acculturation).
22. Technically, "hivernauts," sometimes spelled "hivernants," were distinguished from "*Mangeurs a pork*," eaters of pork, but by 1835 most of the area's French-speaking descendants and Métis ate pork along with their winter game, though all suffered the endurance test of hivernauts.
23. Lucy Eldersveld Murphy, "Gender in the Western Greats Region," in Cayton and Teute, *Contact Points* (detailing the difficulty of baking anything like bread without a proper oven).

Chapter 7

1. LT Journals, October 7, 1835, and February 26, 1836.
2. Jarvis letter, October 10, 1833, Minn HS. See also Adams, *Early Days*, 98 (describing how cards and drinking were the principal ways to kill time at the fort).
3. LT Journals, February 13, 1836. He subscribed to several papers. From St. Louis, he received the *Globe*; the *Bedford Gazette* came from Pennsylvania; and the *Northwestern Gazette and Galena Advertiser* from Illinois. His journal entry of February 18, 1836, discusses receipt of papers once a month and criticizes the demanding nature of residents of St. Louis.

4. Unrau, *The Rise and Fall of Indian Country* (detailing Indian Country as a separate place than the United States).

5. One article that Taliaferro probably didn't discuss with the chiefs that day was entitled "Abolition" (*Galena Advertiser*, February 27, 1836). He did not favor abolition at the time. The *Galena Advertiser* (January 30, 1839) also carried notices promising rewards for capturing runaway slaves.

6. LT Journals, March 11, 1836.

7. Taliaferro recorded that with regard to "Removal of squatters near this agency," the Indians responded, "Have the people near us done any mischief that is necessary to send all off and who are to be sent away in the spring?" (LT Journals, February 24, 1836).

8. LT Journals, February 24, 1836.

9. In addition to being mentioned in the Lawrence Taliaferro Journals, this phenomenon is noted in Stratton, *Pioneer Women*, 79–80, 85–88.

10. Stratton, *Pioneer Women*, 85–88.

11. Bliss, *Reminiscences of Fort Snelling*, 340; Jarvis letter, July 1833, Minn HS; Robert Clouston diary, Minn HS; Kinzie, *Wau-bun*, 68.

12. Kinzie, *Wau-bun*, 89.

13. Kinzie, *Wau-Bun*, 68, 237. This is quite a different pattern from the one in the plantation South, where there was a sufficient degree of contact between white ladies to constitute a social cohort which in turn supported stricter distinctions between women of different classes and women of the master class and their servant women of the slave class in particular. Glymph, *Out of the House of Bondage;* Kennedy, *Braided Relations, Entwined Lives;* Edwards, *Scarlett Doesn't Live Here Any More.*

14. LT Journals, February 9, 1836. According to John S. Wozniak, Madeliene was the daughter of Duncan Campbell and hence the niece of Scott Campbell, but in any case, she was married at the council house, suggesting that she was living with the Campbells whether as daughter or niece (Wozniak, *Contact Negotiation and Conflict*, 86).

15. Strand, *A History of the Swedish Americans of Minnesota*, 129–33.

16. Pond, *The Dakota or Sioux in Minnesota,* 140–42; Marryat, *Diary in America*, vol. 2, ch. 30.

17. The slave man, James Thompson, took a Dakota wife. Folwell, *A History of Minnesota*, vol. 1, 204–5.

18. A mulatto woman, Maria Fasnacht of Prairie du Chien, had married several white husbands in Prairie du Chien. At the even more remote Red River colony, Barbara Adams reported that there was a sharp competition for wives (Adams, *Early Days*, 83).

19. Harriet was a popular name at the time; Commander Leavenworth's wife had been named Harriet and bestowed the name on Lake Harriet.

20. Samuel Pond, *The Dakota or Sioux in Minnesota*, 93–96. On special occasions, to temper themselves to the harsh winter climate, the Dakota built little sweat lodges (Bray, *The Journals of Joseph N. Nicollet*, 195–99).

21. The agent picked up on the distinction by denominating some of his visitors as "respectable" families, hence, members of the tribes' elite. Dr. Jarvis analogized the social differences in Indian society to the Free Masons. He wrote, "like their white brethren, they have signs by which they know each other." Nathan Jarvis letter, August 3, 1834, Minn HS.

22. Bray, *The Journals*, 195–22 and 209–11. See also Nicollet, *Joseph N. Nicollet on the Plains and Prairies*, 258; Eastman, *The Soul of an Indian*, 65–66.

23. LT Journals, February 8–9, 1836.

24. Taliaferro's idea of an Indian school was not the first. There was an Indian school in Kentucky and one in Prairie du Chien. General Street wrote a letter to the editor about the Indian school. There was an editorial against Street's project (*Galena Advertiser*, May 28, 1836).

25. LT Journals, March 2, 1836. "Letter to H. K. Ortley and D. L. Lamont, St. Louis, relative to their children in Indian country."

26. Featherstonhaugh, *A Canoe Voyage,* 415.
27. Perhaps bringing the child, unable to speak English, into their home was more of an act of Christian charity than the mistress could muster. On the other hand, Taliaferro had reasons to oppose the idea if raising his Métis daughter disturbed the delicate balance he tried to maintain with the various tribes. He did not wish to be seen as the son-in-law of one tribal chief rather than the Great White father to them all. The girl was very attached to her mother and was probably disinclined to stay in a strange house with strange customs.
28. On March 3, 1836, Taliaferro wrote that the Reverend J. D. Stevens called at the office in reference to the Indian schools and certain children (LT Journals, March 3, 1836).
29. Gilman, *Henry Hastings Sibley: Divided Heart,* 51.
30. Sibley seemed to have gotten on better with Horatio Dillon, Taliaferro's young brother-in-law, who was closer to his own age. The two took a hunting trip together on horseback to the Cannon River in the fall, but young Dillon wasn't listed on the gambling tab at Sibley's. Taliaferro may have stood in the way of their developing a real friendship, because in a few years when Dillon returned, Sibley would move in to crush Dillon's business. See Chapter 18.
31. Blegen, "The Unfinished Autobiography," 354.
32. Ibid. Lts. Gardenier and Wood were transferred away leaving only one lieutenant and Sibley from the original gang (Fort Snelling Post returns; LT Journals, February 23, March 26, 1836).
33. Blegen, "The Unfinished Autobiography," 354. "The Creole towns were hierarchical systems with a handful of elite fur traders at the top, generally Euramerican and métis men and their métis and Indian wives and children. These elites employed "retainers"—contract workers and tenant farm families—and owned a few Indian slaves. In the middle were a few moderately successful traders and small farmers and the occasional artisan or professional. . . . Creole towns coexisted with Indian villages nearby" (Murphy, "To Live among Us," 275–76).
34. Blegen, "The Unfinished Autobiography," 362.
35. Wozniak, *Contact, Negotiation and Conflict,* 43, detailing white Indian alliance networks as serial monogamy.
36. Goodwin and Goodwin, *Brown: Adventurer on the Minnesota Frontier,* 128.
37. LT Journals, February 22, 1836.
38. LT Journals, February 15, 1836; Pond, *The Dakota or Sioux in Minnesota,* 31.
39. LT Journals, February 19, 1836.
40. Jarvis letter, March 17, 1836, Minn HS.
41. Ibid.
42. Bray and Bray, *Joseph N. Nicollet, On the Plains and Prairies,* 263.
43. LT Journals, March 20, 1836.
44. LT Journals, March 16, 1836.
45. LT Journals, March 24, 1836. "One of my old cows has fed them a day or two."
46. Ibid.
47. At the end of March, Sgt. Eveleth and his aide returned to the fort painfully snow blind (LT Journals, March 27 and 29, 1836).
48. On March 5, Taliaferro's mother died in Fredericksburg, Virginia, at the age of 63.
49. Prucha, *Broadax and Bayonet* 29, 126.
50. Sugaring was more an Ojibwa tradition than a Sioux one. The most grueling part of the month-long sugaring effort was standing all day in the melting slush stirring the collected sap as it was boiled down into sugar. The season extended from March through April (LT Journals, March 19, 1836) (that people went sugaring); Murphy, *To Live among Us,* 276–79 (describing maple sugaring as women's work).
51. Strasser, *Never Done,* 52–54, describing the burdens of laundering as the work of black women even after emancipation.
52. LT Journals, March 22, 1836.
53. "Servant girl Eliza delivered of a female child this morning after 1:00 a.m." (LT Journals, February 23, 1831).

54. LT Journals, February 23, 1836.
55. Riggs, Mary, *A Small Bit of Bread*, 43.
56. If Eliza named the boy Jarvis because the doctor was his father, it would be a matter of delicacy for Taliaferro not to record the event by name in his daybook. On the other hand, Eliza may have named the child after the doctor simply because he was a respected man, which one would think Taliaferro would have recorded.

Chapter 8

1. LT Journals, March 26, 1836.
2. Ibid.
3. LT Journals, April 19, 1836 ("More snow prevents early farming").
4. LT Journals, April 28, 1836.
5. The tuber was called "pinsinchincha" (Pond, *The Dakota or Sioux in Minnesota*, 28–29).
6. Lt Journals, May 1, 1836.
7. LT Journals, May 2, 1836.
8. He wrote: "I have held on to Mr. R—through good and through evil reports— because he could do much good, and more harm with his position—color, and influence. His being an Indian—wearing the garb of a white man, and insisting on being of mixed blood—enjoying a license under the government for many years and with a numerous family and connection—all conspire to cause a feeling of leniency, unless indeed his case be proven of too bare-faced a nature" (LT Journals, May 14, 1836).
9. LT Journals, April 23, 1836.
10. LT Journals, April 23, 1836.
11. Catlin portrait of Chief Black Dog in Catlin's Indian Gallery at the Smithsonian Institution.
12. Prucha, *The Great Father*, 000.
13. Northwest Territorial Ordinance of 1787, Article 4.
14. Northwest Territorial Ordinance of 1787, Article 5.
15. Sibley, "Reminiscences of Early Days of Minnesota," 265.
16. Only one dissenting justice in the Scotts' case noted this nuance. See decision of Justice at Dred Scott v. Sandford, 60 U.S. 619–20 (Justice McLean, dissenting).
17. Blegen, "The Unfinished Autobiography," 265.
18. This form of address is utilized in the Wisconsin Territorial Papers collection.
19. In October, the first territorial legislature was convened at Belmont, east of the Mississippi a horse ride from Prairie du Chien. The State was composed of only four counties: Crawford, Iowa, Milwaukee, and Brown counties. Based on the census returns, a decision could be made as to whether it was timely to petition Congress for statehood (Bloom, *Papers of the Wisconsin Territory*, vol. 27, 51).
20. Ibid. Letter of Commissioner of Indian Affairs, February 20, 1837 (Bloom, *Papers of the Wisconsin Territory*, vol. 27, 738–39).
21. This provision was part of the Northwest Territorial Ordinance, Section 14, Article 3.
    "The utmost good faith shall always be observed towards the Indians; their lands and property shall never be taken from them without their consent; and in their property, rights, and liberty, they shall never be invaded or disturbed, unless in just and lawful wars authorized by Congress; but laws founded in justice and humanity, shall from time to time be made for preventing wrongs being done to them, and for preserving peace and friendship with them."
    See, generally, Satz, "Chippewa Treaty Rights," 4.
22. Ibid.
23. This phrase is used repeatedly in Taliaferro's journals.
24. LT Journals, December 27, 1835.
25. Bloom, *Papers of the Wisconsin Territory*, vol. 27, 56–57, 634, 760–61.

26. Taliaferro waited for someone to arrive and take up the position from the end of September 1835 through the first part of 1837. James B. Dallam was appointed September 11, 1835 (ibid., 57). Letter of Commissioner Elbert Herring to William Sinn, May 26, 1836 (ibid., 56–57). Letter of reprimand, August 4, 1836 (ibid., 634). Daniel P. Bushnell was appointed on November 1, 1836, but prevented from traveling up to his post because navigation had closed. On April 13, 1837, he was still at Detroit trying to find funds for supplies (ibid., 760–61).

27. Bloom, *Papers of the Wisconsin Territory*, vol. 27, 34.

28. Letter of Alexis Bailley to Delegate Jones, April 15, 1836 (ibid., 38).

29. Ibid. Brunson letter, February 10, 1836; Bailley letter, April 15, 1836; and letters in index concerning "land," 1346–47.

30. He wrote, "Junior officers have generally had more to say upon Indian affairs than was once called by their peculiar connection with the government" (LT Journals, Apr. 20, 1836).

31. Wozniak, *Contact, Negotiation, and Conflict*, 88.

32. LT Journals, April 22, 1836.

33. "Where there are whites...within range of Indian tribes occasional disputes will occur...growing out of their trade, property in horses or cattle, and from personal insults. In my civil capacity, I experience, however, no more trouble from the petitioners as from those actually in the Indian trade." On April 14, Taliaferro wrote members of Congress; he wrote again on April 22, 1836. LT Journals of the same dates.

34. LT Journals, April 22, 1836.

35. Jarvis letter, February 2, 1834, Minn HS. Jarvis describes his rooms as looking "something like a Museum hung around with pipes, tomahawks, war clubs, etc."

36. Bruce White, "A Skilled Game of Exchange," 229.

37. Ibid.; Anderson, *Little Crow*, 17.

38. Jarvis letter, July 2, 1834, Minn HS.

39. Jarvis's collection now residing at the Brooklyn Museum of Art is detailed and documented in Feder, *Art of the Eastern Plains Indians*.

40. Ibid.

41. Sibley's shipment invoice that spring numbered a total of 293,288 animal furs, skins, and buffalo robes shipped downriver (July 20, 1836, Invoice). Henry H. Sibley Papers (1815–1930), Minn HS. Philander Prescott brought his furs to independent trader, B. F. Baker.

42. Letter of Henry Sibley to Ramsey Crooks, December 24, 1836, reporting incidents of the spring of 1836. Blegen, "The Unfinished Autobiography," 59–61.

43. These were a slave man, Wilson, who served Lt. Mitchell; Lucy, who served the Lt. Gwynnes; and Julius and Nancy, who served the commander and his wife. Only one lieutenant, Plummer, had no slave of his own and seemed to take whatever domestic serving arrangement presented itself (SP Accts, RG 217, E 516).

44. Letter of Dr. Emerson, April 1, 1835. Dr. John Emerson Personnel File, NA.

45. Fehrenbacher claimed that Emerson was a Pennsylvanian (Fehrenbacher, *The Dred Scott Case*, 242). However, locating his brother Dr. Edward P. Emerson in Pennsylvania established that his brother was born in Ireland and then settled in Pennsylvania. It is possible that John Emerson was born in Pennsylvania but more likely that like his brother he was born in Ireland and came to Philadelphia to study medicine.

46. Although Dr. Emerson graduated from the medical school in Pennsylvania in 1824, he did not appear as working at Jefferson Barracks until about September of 1832 (Jefferson Barracks and St. Louis Armory Post returns). He may have apprenticed with his brother Dr. Edward P. Emerson in western Pennsylvania.

47. In those days, the doctors were assigned to forts rather than attached to individual infantry units (Field, *Forts of the American Frontier*, 40). By the time of his appointment, John Emerson had been nominated by none other than Thomas Hart Benton, senator from Missouri. From the senator's vague letter of recommendation,

it's not clear that he even knew Emerson, but the senator's recommendation worked and Emerson was appointed as assistant surgeon. Recommenders described him as a strong Jackson man (Letter of A. Buckner Sept 12, 1832. John Emerson Letters and Reports, 1833–1843, Medical Officers File, RG 94, Old Military Records Division, NA). Thomas H. Benton claimed that Dr. Emerson was from North Carolina. No other document corroborates that association (Letter of Recommendation of Thomas H. Benton July 12, 1833). Dr. John Emerson Personnel File, NA.

48. Ehrlich suggests that Emerson also had a slave named Norman, but I have not found an original source for this claim. Emerson may have been involved in helping a friend in St. Louis maintain his slave, because a man named John Emmerson was sued in 1832, Tenor Washington v. Henry Scott and John Emmerson, (November 18, 1832) which corresponds with the doctor's residence there (St. Louis Circuit Court cases).

49. Ehrlich, *They Have No Rights*, 11–15.

50. Fehrenbacher maintains that Emerson built a log cabin with Dred doing most of the work (Fehrenbacher, *The Dred Scott Case*, 244). But it is more likely that Emerson financed another couple to build the cabin and live on the claim. The couple lived on his claim when he left and he wrote many letters soliciting their well-being. Dr. John Emerson letters in Antoine Le Claire collection, Putnam Museum, Davenport, Iowa.

  Emerson also chipped in to hire a person other than himself, in this case Philander Prescott, to build a cabin when he staked lands in the Minnesota area. See Chapter 18. Dred is not known to have performed any heavy work like cabin building in any of the records.

51. Both Lts. Shaw and William Price arrived with Dred and Dr. Emerson and stayed from October 1835 to April 1836. Lt. John Beach became engaged to one of Agent Street's daughters and later received one of Patsey's children as a servant. The third lieutenant whom Etheldred had served was reassigned to Fort Crawford rather than Fort Snelling (SP Accts, RG 217, E516).

52. The price of a male slave in St. Louis was less than $500 according to most probate inventories at the time. See generally, inventories in St. Louis probates, PDCP.

53. The army paid $2.50 per month for a servant's clothing allowance and $6 per month for a servant's pay, and 20 cents per day for his rations (an additional $6 per month).

54. Col. William Davenport shared a last name but does not appear to have been related to Emerson's business partner, the trader, George Davenport, at Rock Island.

55. Bliss, *Reminiscences*, 336. "Col. Stambaugh's lady remains" (LT Journals, May 9, 1836).

56. Lt. Wood, who was also moving out, was served at Fort Snelling by a slave man named Frederick, quite possibly one of Taliaferro's own slaves. (Frederick is one of the names listed near the top of the later registry Taliaferro made of his slaves.) Frederick did not show up as Lt. Wood's servant when he reached his next post. With the lieutenant's transfer, Frederick may have returned to the agency household and attended to the spring chores. In July of that year, however, the census reports Taliaferro as having only two female servants and only one male servant in the region.

57. James Thompson's wife was also a daughter of the local chief Cloudman, as was the mother of Taliaferro's daughter.

58. LT Journals, June 10, 1835.

59. Jarvis letter, May 29, 1836, Minn HS.

60. The officer temporarily commanding the post had ordered the doctor thrown into the brig over the matter, an even more distressing affront that he immediately protested to the surgeon general and was promptly released (Dr. John Emerson Personnel file, date not available, NA).

61. Letter from Dr. Emerson, date not available (Dr. John Emerson Personnel file, NA)

62. LT Journals.

63. Ibid.

64. Pay slip for Dr. Emerson, listed forage paid for 2 horses June–October (1836). SP Accts, R G 217, E 516, N.A. The hospital also owned three cows.

65. Jarvis letter, July 1833 (Minn HS).

66. LT Journals, May 14, 1836.

67. LT Journals, May 18, 1836.

68. "We cannot forget your turning over two Sioux to the [Chiefs] Flat mouth and Strong Ground in 1827 for killing two of our people and wounding many others before our door." LT Journals, May 18, 1836.

69. This portrait may have been by Catlin but there were also portrait painters in Washington, D.C., such as Charles King, who painted individuals who came with delegations.

70. LT Journals, May 18, 1836.

71. Ibid.

72. Taliaferro continued to pressure the Sioux to surrender the men who had murdered the Ojibwa. He also talked to them of the government's interest in their lands east of the Mississippi. He began to consider the package of terms that would set the framework for later treaty negotiation. "I have counseled the Upper Medawakanton Sioux relative to a cession of all their land east of the Mississippi to the U.S. and with some opposition the following sum would procure $1,400,000 worth of land for below Lake Pepin. $500 annually for education of children. $5,000 annuity for 15 years on June 1. $800 for Agricultural implements. $1000 for a blacksmith, iron, and steel. $800 for mechanics. Ten reservations of 320 acres each to male and female half-bloods." LT Journals, May 19, 1836.

73. LT Journals, May 29, 1836. Lawrence Taliaferro subscribed to the *Globe*, *Galenian*, *Bedford Gazette*, and the *Commercial Bulletin* (LT Journal). "Burned by Mob" and "Burning of the Negro" appeared in the *Galena Advertiser* May 7 and May 14, 1836.

74. When Baker returned to St. Peter's on the *Frontier*, he told his own eyewitness account of the McIntosh murder. A letter from Dr. Jarvis described how the mob kept the fire burning under their victim so that McIntosh suffered for over an hour. Jarvis letter, May 29, 1836 (Minn HS).

75. Buchanan, *Black Life on the Mississippi*, 44.

76. Scharf, *History of Saint Louis and Missouri*, vol. 1, 123–24.

77. Grimsted, *American Mobbing, 1828–1861*, 104.

78. *The Missouri Republican*, edited by Joseph Charless, condemned the actions. Joseph Charless's wife had sold Etheldred to Dr. Emerson in closing her father's estate. (Estate of Peter Blow, PDCP).

79. Lovejoy's famous electrifying editorial was published in the *St. Louis Observer*, (May 5, 1836. Gerteis, *Civil War St. Louis*, 340, n. 7.

80. Lovejoy had winced at the inhumanity of McIntosh's murder. That sensitivity, couched in the minister's religious conscience, led to his own martyrdom. When the mob turned on the minister, a lawyer was appalled at the injustice of it.

81. LT Journals, June 2, 1836.

82. LT Journals, June 1, 1836. Bill of lading and goods from Chouteau & Company.

83. LT Journals, May 23, 1836.

84. LT Journals, June 3, 1836. The Sioux had murdered the Chippewa on July 9, 1835.

85. Ibid.

86. LT Journals, June 4, 1836.

87. LT Journals, June 6, 1836.

88. Ibid.

89. Ibid.

90. LT Journals, June 8, 1836.

91. "Weather unpleasant. . . .130 Sioux arrive expecting annuities. June 11, Tobacco rotten and calicos of very bad quality. 514 Sioux present" (LT Journals, June 10, 1836).

92. The tribes expected included the Yankton, Sussiton, and Wahpeton Sioux from Lac Traverse, Big Stone, and the Lac qui Parle.
93. LT Journals, June 12, 1836.
94. Ibid.
95. Settlers sometimes reported that Indians disliked pork even though they were described as eating just about everything that walks or crawls on the earth. Their aversion could have come from eating bad pork. Dr. Jarvis and the Ponds made this claim about the Indians' ability to eat anything (Jarvis letter, July 2, 1834, Minn HS; LT Journals, June 15, 1836).
96. LT Journals, June 15, 1836.
97. LT Journals, May 22, 1836.
98. LT Journals, June 23, 1836.
99. Dr. Emerson claimed payment for vaccinating the 300 Indians between June 10 and June 18 (LT Journals, September 22, 1836).
100. Pond, *The Sioux or Dakota in Minnesota*, 166, 168.
101. His daughter had arrived from Wabasha's village just two weeks before with the symptoms.
102. LT Journals, June 19, 1836.
103. Taliaferro also gave him a small mill for grinding corn.
104. LT Journals, June 19, 1836.
105. 1838 Annuities list of Lawrence Taliaferro lists 54 households in the Good Road's band for a total of 182 people. Lawrence Taliaferro Papers, 1813–1868, Minn HS.
106. LT Journals, June 24, 1836.
107. Taliaferro's first reference to Dr. Emerson is in a letter to Col. Davenport relative to "my interpreter being stopped in the discharge of his official duties by the Sergeant of the guard within the Fort. He being there on business with the Surgeon Doct. Emerson . . . " (LT Journals, June 25, 1836).
108. Taliaferro wrote: "in addition to the passengers named yesterday, I perceived also a Doctor Emerson, . . . and several others with whom I had no acquaintance" (LT Journals, July 3, 1836).

Chapter 9

1. LT Journals, July 3, 1836.
2. Taliaferro, "Autobiography of Lawrence Taliaferro," 242.
3. LT Journal, July 2, 1836.
4. Nevins, *Fremont*, 30.
5. A tribute to his charm was that when he later set off for a short exploring expedition, two officers asked the commandant for permission to accompany him at least as far as a day's ride. Bray, *Joseph Nicollet and His Map*, 168.
6. Fremont, *Memoirs of My Life*, 56. John Fremont assisted Nicollet in surveying the upper Mississippi.
7. Nicollet, *Report Intended to Illustrate a Map* (Topographical Engineers), 67–68.
8. Nicollet, *Report Intended to Illustrate a Map* (Topographical Engineers).
9. Fremont, *Memoirs of My Life*, 59.
10. Nicollet, *Report Intended to Illustrate a Map*, 68.
11. Ibid., 169
12. This description is borrowed from Henry James, *The Ambassadors* (New York: Harper, 1903), 8.
13. LT Journals, July 27, 1836; Bray, *Joseph Nicollet and His Map*, 179. Schoolcraft coined the name from the central letters of "veritas caput," meaning "true head" or "headwaters of truth."
14. Fully six officers from Fort Snelling, including the commandant, went down to Fort Crawford for the trial. Fort Crawford courts martial files, Old Army Files, Judge Adjutant General (JAG), RG 153, 1836, NA.

With so many officers departing, many of the officers' wives took the occasion to accompany them in order to renew their acquaintances with the ladies at the next post. Traveling ladies, of course, required servants to assist them, so the entire entourage must have consisted of several dozen people.

15. This official documentation could attest to some independence of Mr. Scott in maintaining his own household. Unexplainably, he is listed as a head of a household of several people as if he were the head of the household (U.S. Census for 1836 Dubuque County in the Wisconsin Territory, 1836).

Mr Taliaferro 1   -   1   2   = 4.

Lawrence Taliaferro's census entry lists only one man in the household, together with two girls and a boy. Perhaps the child is the baby boy born to Eliza around April 1. The child was noted as five and one-half months old at the time of his death later in the fall.

16. *The St. Louis Observer,* date not available.
17. LT Journals, July 17, 1836.
18. Letter of Dr. John Emerson, August 22, 1836. Dr. John Emerson Personnel File, NA.
19. Fort Crawford Courts Martial files, Old Army Files, JAG, RG 153, 1836, NA.
20. Dippie, *Catlin and His Contemporaries,* 41–42.
21. August 9, 1836 from Prairie du Chien, Dousman writes to Sibley that Catlin is on his way to St. Peter's. Henry H Sibley Papers, Minn HS.
22. Catlin needed a passport to enter Indian territory. The fort commander signed the permit, rather than Agent Taliaferro this time (Fort Snelling Post Returns, August 1836, NA).
23. Catlin, *George Catlin's Letters and Notes,* 167.
24. LT Journals, August 20, 1836.
25. LT Journals, August 27, 1836.
26. LT Journals, September 5, 1836.
27. Catlin, *George Catlin's Letters and Notes,* 166.
28. Ibid. "[W]e felt disposed to pity, rather than resent, though their unpardonable stubbornness excited us almost to desperation."
29. "We have started to go and see it; and we cannot think of being stopped" (Catlin, *George Catlin's Letters and Notes,* 166–67).
30. Nevins, *Fremont,* 35.
31. Catlin, *George Catlin's Letters and Notes,* 190, unnumbered note.
32. LT Journals, October 22, 1836. Catlin brought one message along himself of Indian talks and messages of trespass and the agent dutifully placed it on file. Dr. Emerson—a letter from him requesting compensation for 300 Sioux forwarded to the commissioner of Indian affairs.
33. LT Journals, September 5–6, 1836.
34. LT Journals, September 6, 1836.
35. Dippie, *Catlin and His Contemporaries,* 42.
36. LT Journals, June 30, 1836.
37. Pond, *The Dakota or Sioux in Minnesota,* 7, 68; Wozniak, *Contact, Negotiation and Conflict,* 87.
38. Wozniak, *Contact, Negotiation and Conflict,* 87.
39. Ibid., 86.
40. LT Journals, June 27, 1836.
41. LT Journals, June 27, 1836 and June 30, 1836. "Milk cow of mine came home this day badly wounded with an arrow" (LT Journals, June 23, 1836 and June 29, 1836). In the course of the summer. Jacob Falstrom, J. B. Raymond, and others were accused of stealing the wood (LT Journals, September 13, 1836).
42. According to the 1860 census for Bedford, Pennsylvania, the servant Eliza's daughter, Susan, also born on the Minnesota frontier, would have been only two or three years old in 1835, though she does not appear to have been listed as present in the Minnesota census for the Taliaferro household (United States Census Record, 1836).

43. See, for example, LT Journals, Sept 16, 1836. " I am heartily tired of and disgusted with the...conduct of the Indian Dept."

44. LT Journals, September 4 and October 30, 1836.

45. "However troublesome it is, to store for safekeeping thousands of articles for the Indians, yet though it be out of the line of my duty, I have promptly done so and the Indians are grateful" (LT Journals, September 3, 1836).

46. LT Journals, September 14, 1836.

47. "Strength of Case" on p. 1, *Galena Advertiser*, October 1, 1836.

48. It was said that "while young, [he] took to his bed a negress, made her the mother of a family of mulattoes and finally, upon her death, took a second daughter of Africa, and by whom he became the parent of a second edition of mulattoes" (ibid.).

49. *Galena Advertiser,* November 5, 1836.

50. *Galena Advertiser,* October 7. The *Galena Advertiser* also featured articles titled "Revolt of negroes at Port au Platt" (LT Journals, September 10, 1836) and "$200 reward offered by Governor Duncan for escaped negro murderer" (LT Journals, September 24, 1836).

51. LT Journals, September 27, 1836 (letter from Nicollet arrived at Taliaferro's announcing his return).

52. Flatmouth had sent two men to plant the American and British flags before Nicollet's tent, an invitation to the Frenchman to attend a council with him. Nicollet, the diplomat, refused to speak under the British flag as he was traveling under United States auspices and did not have a "forked tongue" (Bray, *Joseph Nicollet and His Map,* 177).

    Flatmouth (Esh-ke-bug-e-coshe) was the Chief of the Ojibway Pillagers from roughly 1805 to his death around 1860. Flatmouth's father became chief through skillful use of poisons rather than heredity, and his siblings were murdered by the Dakota. As chief of the Pillagers, Flatmouth took revenge on the Dakota for his nephew's murder, just as his father had taken revenge on them for the murders of Flatmouth's siblings. However, the younger chief declined to fight in the War of 1812 on the side of the British, saying that he would not meddle in the quarrels of white men. This laid the foundation for a later relationship with the Americans, just as much as the adoption of the American Lt. Zebulon Pike into the Pillagers. Flatmouth lived to be at least 78 and had grandchildren (Warren, *History of the Ojibway People,* 17, 178, 269, 324, 349–350, 352, 359–363, 369).

53. Even Nicollet's work as an ethnologist of Indian culture has received praise over time. Bray, *The Journals of Joseph N. Nicollet,* 30.

54. LT Journals, September 29, 1836.

55. Bray, *The Journals of Joseph N. Nicollet,* 114.

56. He might have been referring to Major Bliss's form of punishment, which was to keep prisoners in a black hole or dark cellar. Bliss, *Reminiscences,* 336.

57. "When the harangue ended, Flat Mouth proceeded with the presentation of the gifts.... First, the pipe and the stem: they represent his life and soul with which he is entrusting me. The wood is that which cradled him as a baby, that which guided him at the councils and at war, that which never left him. It is the instrument that drove away the bad thoughts his head has sometimes entertained. He told me that each time I gaze at this stem, with the numerous ornaments decorating it, I must recall him, Flat Mouth and the things he has told me today" (Bray, *The Journals of Joseph N. Nicollet,* 112–18).

58. LT Journals, September 15, 1836.

59. Ibid.

60. LT Journals, September 17, 1836.

61. LT Journals, September 14, 1836.

62. LT Journals, September 16, 1836.

63. LT Journals, September 17, 1836.

64. LT Journals, October 25, 26, 1836.

65. Nicollet to Gabriel Paul and Jules de Mun, November 1, 1836 Jules de Mun Papers (Birdsall Collection), Mo HS, quoted in Bray, *The Journals of Joseph N. Nicollet*, 23.

66. To Nicollet, if Native Americans "were not noble, they were at least more honest and more natural than civilized man" because of their harmonious lifestyle. Thus, scholars translate Nicollet's use of the word *sauvage* to the more neutral term *Indian* (Bray and Coleman, *Joseph N. Nicollet on the Plains and Prairies*, app. III, 252).

67. Ibid., 252–53. From Nicollet's, *Notes Geographiques Sur les Noms Anciens et Modernes des Lieux et des Nations Indiennes de L'Amerique du Nord*, 5, 6.

68. Bray, *The Journals of Joseph N. Nicollet*, 24.

69. Ibid., 25.

70. LT Journals, November 8, 1836.

71. Taliaferro paid the considerable sum of $140 for wood to be cut and hauled in from the nearest site, some four and sometimes six miles away (LT Journals, October 25, 26, 1836).

72. LT Journals, November 16, 17, and 20, 1836.

73. "Auction of damaged pork very bad." Nine barrels were sold to the poor people at $16 on an average, some went as high as $20.50 a barrel. The government contract price was set at $11.50, an advance of $9 on rotten pork (LT Journals, November 9, 1836).

74. LT Journals, November 14, 1836.

75. LT Journals, November 16, 1836.

76. "We are all of one mind, and when you are ready to advise us on the subject, we will be ready to listen and to do as you may say best for the interest of our people. Our people wish to know when you have any news from below. We shall not be far off and can hear soon. I think something might be taken off of the smiths and charged into presents," Taliaferro recommended. LT Journals, November 16, 1836.

77. LT Journals, November 21, 1836.

78. Adams, *Early Days*, 101. Adams commented upon one couple drummed out of the service and set adrift in a canoe. "I have often wondered at the fate of those persons. There was not a human habitation between Fort Snelling and Prairie du Chien, and I have thought they may have perished from hunger and exposure."

79. LT Journals, November 14, 1836.

80. LT Journals, December 25, 1836.

81. Ibid.

82. LT Journals, December 28, 1836.

83. LT Journals, December 26, 27, 1836.

84. Pond, *Two Volunteer Missionaries*, 64–65.

85. Letter of J. H. [Joseph H.] Lamotte, Prairie du Chien, to William Beaumont, St. Louis, regarding Dr. Emerson. September 2, 1836. William Beaumont Collection, Washington University School of Medicine Library, St. Louis: Mo.: "Dr. Emerson is courting Miss Stevens at St. Peters.—Should he fail there, he is to court Miss Meeks, an antiquated sister of Mrs. Loomis, almost as large and almost as interesting!" (underlining in original). Mrs. Loomis' elder sister was actually Miss Mix.

86. LT Journals, December 31, 1836.

Chapter 10

1. Some wood shipped from Pittsburgh had been lumbered even farther away in the interior of New York state (Van Antwerp, "Reminiscences from Iowa"; Livingston, "Biographical Sketch of Verplanck Van Antwerp").

2. Northwest Territorial Ordinance of 1787.

3. The American Fur Company's communications are indexed in Grace Nute, "Calendar of Papers of the American Fur Trade." *American Historical Review* 32 (1945): 1926–27 and the indices reference extensive communications regarding the treaties and even John F. A. Sanford's involvement in their ratification by Congress.

4. Sanford also worked with another Chouteau in-law, Gen. Gratiot, who had formerly been a high-ranking military officer (chief of engineering), but his present duties were to watch out for the Company's interests by providing the government selective military advice about the frontier.

5. LT Journals, date not available.

6. Flatmouth speech to Nicollet. Bray, *The Journals of Joseph N. Nicollet*, 113–18.

7. LT Journals, date not available.

8. As a legal matter, giving the traders first priority for the Indian debts in the land exchange gave them a privileged position as first creditors.

9. LT Journals, August 11, 1836.

10. November 23, 1836, Letter of Governor Henry Dodge to Commissioner Herring (Bloom, *Territorial Papers*, 673).

11. Ibid.

12. Anderson, *Kinsmen of Another Kind*, 151, quoting fur trade letters.

13. Governor Henry Dodge wrote: "I have ascertained that a company is formed for the erection of sawmills in the Chippewa country," composed of three Company men, two from Prairie du Chien, Sibley, and the Fort Snelling sutler, Mr. Stambaugh and Judge Lockwood and Jean Brunet. (November 23, 1836, Letter of Governor Henry Dodge to Commissioner Herring, in Bloom, *Territorial Papers*, 673–74). "The amount which should be paid to the Chippewa for each sawmill of one saw, I would estimate at $500 per annum, payable in corn, blankets, ammunition, an equal amount of each—the articles to be at Cost, adding the expense of transportation." Ibid.

14. Ibid.

15. According to Davenport the cronies that Stambaugh hoped to contact were Governor Cass, who was on the eve of going to France and Gen. Jesup who had left for Georgia. Davenport letter to Maj. Cross, Bloom, *Territorial Papers*, 794.

16. Letter of Col. Davenport to Adjutant General Jones, May 27, 1837 (Bloom, *Territorial Papers*, 792–94).

17. January 30, 1837, letter from Taliaferro to Governor Dodge. Dodge sends it on to Commissioner Harris, February 20, 1837 (Bloom, *Territorial Papers*, 739).

18. The spoils system that allowed Mr. Stambaugh to ascend to the office of sutler was a product of President Andrew Jackson's belief that long terms in office produced more harm than retaining the benefits of experience. He vigorously defended himself from charges of corruption by protesting that he never made appointments but for the good of the nation, even though many new appointees were prominent Jackson supporters like Stambaugh, and many of the replaced were supporters of Jackson's defeated opponent, President John Quincy Adams. Objectively speaking, the excess turnover as the result of Jackson's firings was probably comparable to the number of firings after Thomas Jefferson's Democratic-Republicans defeated the Federalists in 1800 (Brands, *Andrew Jackson*, 417–20).

19. Letter from Taliaferro to Governor Dodge, November 30, 1836 (Bloom, *Territorial Papers*, 678).

20. LT Journals, December 25, 1836.

21. Blegin, "The Unfinished Autobiography," 59–60.

22. Ibid.

23. Letter of Ramsey Crooks pursuant to Sioux treaty of 1837, letters received by Congress, NA.

24. LT Journals, December 27, 1836.

25. Once when a hired man at Mendota fell ill, the doctor sent him a box of pills with the instruction to take a small dose daily. A little while later, the doctor sent a second messenger to look in on him. The second messenger reported that the man had not only swallowed all the pills but was chewing up the box as well. Simple-hearted, honest fellow named Sinclair was the man who took the pills. He was visited by N. W. Kittson (story attributed to Hansen in Williams, *The Story of the City of Saint Paul*, 123).

26. Emerson letter to Surgeon General, May 12, 1837 (Dr. John Emerson Personnel File, NA).

27. Ibid.

28. Based on the record of charges in the account books, the store does not appear to have been open every day, only four to five times a week. Fort Snelling Sutler's Account Books, 1836–39, Henry Sibley Papers, Minn HS.

29. The other servants were Silas Hallowell, Etheldred, Caroline St. L., Lucy, a black, Wilson, Laura Denison, and James or J. Emmitt (SP Accts, R G 217, E 516 NA). There was a black woman named Lucy working for the Gwynns; Wilson, owned by Lt. Mitchell; and a mulatto woman named Laura Denison who served both the Loomises and the Ogdens.

30. Kinzie, *Wau-Bun,* 89–90.

31. Dec. 18, 1836, Emerson buys ½ gal apples & gal peaches; Jan 4, 1837, gal apples, currants; Feb. 21, 1837, Sutler's store, currants and Tin kettle (December 18, 1836, Post sutler records). Mendota Trading post and Fort Snelling Sutler's Account Books, 1836–39, Henry Sibley Papers, Minn HS. Emerson's liberal ingestion of the metallic toxin explains his frequent cravings for fruits and sweets.

32. February 1, 1837, Sutler's store tickets to the upcoming ball to McClure, Plummer. Fort Snelling Sutler's Account Books, 1836–39, Henry Sibley Papers, Minn HS.

33. May 10, two companies of the 5th infantry were ordered to proceed from Fort Howard to Fort Winnebago (*Army-Navy Chronicle,* May 11, 1837).

34. LT Journals, May 19, year.

35. Brunson, *A Western Pioneer,* 63–64.

36. During his absence some of his children must have perished. He later stated that seven of their children died before coming of age, some probably during this time of his absence. His wife, daughter of Chief Cloudman, lived at the Lake Calhoun settlement. The slave's wife and Taliaferro's lover were sisters, making their children cousins. James Thompson's wife had also taken the name Mary. The couple was married around 1830 (Roll of Mixed-Blood Claimants, 1856. Affidavit no. 68 of James Thompson).

37. Newson, *Pen Pictures of St. Paul,* vol. 1, 11–12.

38. 1837, June 20, 15, Mary and Stephen Riggs, "One of the Methodist missionaries, Mr. King, & a colored man & members of this church from the Fort & mission completed our band of 15" (Riggs, *A Small Bit of Bread and Butter,* 37). The "colored man" would have been the freedman James Thompson, who was then a translator for Mr. King.

39. Account Books. Henry H. Sibley Papers Minn HS.

40. Folwell, *History of Minnesota,* vol. 1, 205.

41. Brunson's strongly pro-settlement views on the frontier were often made public. Letter of Alfred Brunson to Delegate George Wallace Jones (Bloom, *Territorial Papers,* vol. 27, 14).

42. "Your own knowledge of Indian character," he wrote, indicates that "money does not do them the fourth part of the benefit that goods and labor would.... If the Agents would employ the missionary to cultivate their soil, the poor natives would not be exposed to the vices of the whites, which they too often learn from those who first mingle with them. The missionary, by thus mingling instruction in letters, morality and religion with that of the domestic arts, would be more likely to succeed in their renovation. I wish you would use your best efforts to have their annuities thus paid hereafter. I view it as all important to the salvation of that afflicted race of our species" (ibid.).

Chapter 11

1. The active government policy of treaty making with the northern tribes was sponsoring numerous Indian delegations to meet the president. The *Irene* also

conveyed Maj. Street and the Sac and Fox delegation to Pittsburgh on their way to Washington City. "$45 each, amounting to $1,080 for Indians, myself, interpreters and medical assistant from Rock Island to Pittsburgh" (letter from Joseph Street to Governor Dodge, August 27, 1837, in Bloom, *Territorial Papers,* 841–44).

2. Leopold, *A Sand County Almanac,* 27.
3. *Iowa News* (Dubuque) July 1, 1837, 15, 22; August 5, 1837, 12.
4. General William R. Smith of Pennsylvania was chosen to be the third commissioner. President Van Buren had intended to pair him with another man, but the man was unexplainably delayed and unable to arrive in time for the treaty making.
5. "I have not consequently had any official intercourse with them" (letter from Daniel P. Bushnell to Governor Dodge, June 19, 1837 in Bloom, *Territorial Papers,* 799). On July 15, 1837, the orders arrived. The letter sent on June 19 did not reach Governor Dodge's office until July 18, 1837, a few days before the treaty making was set to begin (letter from Daniel P. Bushnell to Governor Dodge, June 19, 1837 in Bloom, *Territorial Papers,* 799).
6. "June 26, 1837, Order Asst. Surg. E. B. Wolcott to accompany troops from Ft Crawford to Ft. Snelling, and there remain on duty" (*Army-Navy Chronicle,* June 29, 1837).
   "Movements of Troops—Six companies of the First infantry, from Ft. Crawford, arrived at Jefferson Barracks on the 21st, ult. and four companies of the same regiment from Ft. Snelling on the 19th, so that the whole regiment is now concentrated at Jefferson Barracks" (*Army-Navy Chronicle,* August 17, 1837).
7. "A, E, F, I only 6 in company A, 2, in company E, 5 in company F, 6 in company I; 1 in arrest; 19 privates " (Post Returns, U.S. Army, Fort Snelling, July 15, 1837–August 20, 1837, NA).
8. The captain knew that his command was temporary. The next commandant had already been appointed but awaited deployment and transport with his troops.
9. Rayman, "Confrontation at the Fever River Lead Mining District." Dodge's career is described on 282–83.
10. "When I look at you I am struck with awe. I cannot sufficiently understand your importance, and it confuses me. I have seen a great many Americans, but never one whose appearance struck me as yours does" ("Proceedings of a Council with the Chippewa Indians," 414).
11. Bloom, *Territorial Papers,* 63–67.
12. Toby had been in his service since he was nine. Captain of the Dragoons Dodge had listed Toby on his pay slip for monthly support amounts. SP Accts RG 217, E 516, Henry Dodge accounts. Verplank's account mentioned that Dodge's man cooked for them on the float trip downstream. Van Antwerp, "Reminiscences from Iowa," 346.
13. Livingston, "Biographical Sketch of Verplanck Van Antwerp."
14. LT Journals, July, 1837.
15. LT Journals, December 25, 1836.
16. Letter of Henry H. Sibley to Ramsay Crooks, June 27, 1837. Henry H. Sibley Papers (1815–1930), Minn HS.
17. LT Journals, July 13, 1837.
18. "Proceedings of a Council with the Chippewa Indians," 409. There are several accounts of the treaty: Van Antwerp's as secretary, Lawrence Taliaferro's simultaneously recorded journal and his "Autobiography," which differ slightly, Lyman Warren's account (Warren, *History of the Ojibway People*), and Henry Sibley's account. For this biography of Harriet, I have adopted Taliaferro's account where accounts differed (Taliaferro, "Autobiography," 214–19; Satz, "Chippewa Treaty Rights").
19. Satz, "Chippewa Treaty Rights," 411.
20. Harmen Van Antwerp.
21. A Sioux chief expressed his confidence in the gathering and stated that he and his men "will set far off and listen" (LT Journals, date).

22. "Proceedings of a Council with the Chippewa Indians," 411.
23. Ibid., 413.
24. Letter from Maj. Taliaferro to Governor Dodge, July 24, 1837. Enclosed by Dodge to Commissioner Harris, August 15, 1837 (Bloom, *Territorial Papers,* 828–30).
25. This government monopoly on trading furs with the Indians was called the "factory system."
26. "[It] was discontinued through the influence of this company. As various as the plans under the laws enacted have been for the better security of the Indian in all that might be considered material to his advancement in Civilization, and the ordinary comforts of a naturally laborious life—all has failed as yet to be productive of any permanent advantage to him. The Factory system ought to be revived under the sound and wholesome regulations and directed by persons of mercantile experience and sound integrity" (letter from Maj. Taliaferro to Governor Dodge, July 24, 1837, enclosed by Dodge to Commissioner Harris, August 15, 1837; in Bloom, *Territorial Papers,* 828–30).
27. Ibid.
28. "Proceedings of a Council with the Chippewa Indians," 414–19. This parallels John Wozniak's categorical distinctions of ascribed and achieved status in their social identities (Wozniak, *Contact, Negotiation and Conflict,* 97).
29. "Proceedings of a Council with the Chippewa Indians," 414–19.
30. Ibid.
31. Flatmouth described himself as a self-made man. "My ancestors were chiefs of the tribes, I do not, however, hold my title from them, but have obtained it by my own acts and merits" (ibid.).
32. Ibid.
33. Ibid., 420.
34. Ibid., 414.
35. Ibid., 420.
36. Ibid.
37. Taliaferro, "Autobiography," 216.
38. Ibid.
39. Ibid.
40. LT Journals, date.
41. "Proceedings of a Council with the Chippewa Indians," 424.
42. From the gesture it is not clear whether the Ojibwa wished to retain just the maple, from which they traditionally gathered sugar each spring; the oak, from which they survived on acorns in times of desperate hunger; or all broadleaf trees in the territory.
43. Quotations that follow all from "Proceedings of a Council with the Chippewa Indians," 425–28.
44. Ibid. Flatmouth probably referred to Miles Vineyard, then assisting Taliaferro as subagent to the Sioux, as the second "father." Subagent Bushnell probably didn't know what to make of it. He had no experience in estimating land values or the Indians' needs. He'd never yet even dispensed annuities under the old treaties.
45. Ibid.
46. "Proceedings of a Council with the Chippewa Indians," 430.
47. Ibid.
48. Ibid., 431.
49. Ibid., 432. The presence of scalps used in costume was a continued source of tribal antipathy between the Ojibwa and Sioux recurring in Taliaferro's journals during his time as Indian agent.
50. Kappler, "Treaty with the Chippewa."
51. This bonus was "much to the chagrin of the sensible thinking Indians and the surprise of intelligent lookers-on, a sufficient sum having already been set apart for the payment of all just debts of the tribe to their traders."
52. $800,000.
53. Fort Snelling Sutler's Account Books, 1836–39, Henry Sibley Papers, Minn HS.
54. Gilman, "Last Days of the Upper Mississippi Fur Trade," 139.

55. Diary of Peter Garrioch, July 29, 1837. The investor group consisted now of Sibley, Dousman, Stambaugh, and two smaller local traders: Lyman Warren, who had bullied his way into the treaty making to the tune of an additional $20,000, and Aitken, father of the murdered man.

56. Leopold, *Sand County Almanac*, 114–15.

57. He described himself in the third person when he wrote: "The agent had first to get clear of some 1,200 Chippewas without bloodshed,…though there were but a few men for duty…and many Sioux present." Taliaferro, "Autobiography," 217.

58. Ibid.

59. Taliaferro, "Autobiography," 204.

60. She remained through the time of the treaty making to continue to act as hostess to the commission and to maintain a fine table. However, it had been several months since she had seen her family in Bedford. The Taliaferros were not planning to spend the winter at the Fort, and so she returned east.

61. The subagent, Miles Vineyard, stayed on briefly, probably to close up the agency house before he too left.

Chapter 12

1. Pond and Pond, *Two Volunteer Missionaries*, 115. On June 24, the white trader Philander Prescott married an Indian woman with whom he had lived for 15 years (Riggs, *A Small Bit of Bread and Butter*, 19; Taliaferro, "Autobiography," 234).

2. The date of their marriage is not recorded, as there are no existing Taliaferro Journal entries for this momentous year. Taliaferro wrote in his autobiography that he had pleased Dred considerably by giving him the hand of Harriet in marriage (Taliaferro, "Autobiography," 234).

3. Taliaferro, "Autobiography," 235. Among the many marriages Taliaferro mentions at which he officiated, Taliaferro identifies four marriages by bride and groom and uses the phrase "closing with the union of Dred Scott with Harriet Robinson my servant girl, which I gave him." Ibid. Other marriages are recorded in his daily journal. By chronology, the listed marriage of Alpheus R. French and Mary Henry occurred on November 29, 1836. LT Journal, November 29, 1836.

4. We have no information about slave marriages on the frontier. This is the only wedding of former slaves noted as taking place in the Fort Snelling materials.

5. Taliaferro, "Autobiography," 235.

6. Dred himself is the source of the claim that he had been married before. *Frank Leslie's Illustrated Newspaper*, June 27, 1857.

7. Although some slave owners sought and maintained long-term, genuinely affectionate relationships with enslaved women, many others forced enslaved women to offer their sexual favors "willingly" to avoid the beatings that would otherwise follow (see Blassingame, *The Slave Community*, 154–55). Henry Bibb's master forced one slave girl to be his son's concubine; M. F. Jamison's overseer raped a pretty slave girl; and Solomon Northrup's owner forced one slave, Patsey, to be his sexual partner (see also Fox-Genovese, *Within the Plantation Household*, 325–50, describing slaveholders' efforts to exploit enslaved women sexually and enslaved women's acts of resistance). For additional descriptions of white masters' sexual predation, see William Wells Brown, *From Fugitive Slave to Free Man*; Jacobs, *Incidents in the Life of a Slave Girl*; McLaurin, *Celia, A Slave*.

8. The Northwest Ordinance of 1787, Section 14, Art. 6.

9. See, generally, Bray, *Joseph Nicollet and His Map*.

10. Sibley wrote that he had been a citizen of Michigan, Wisconsin, Iowa, and the Minnesota Territories without ever changing his place of residence at Mendota west of the Mississippi River. Sibley, "Reminiscences of Early Days of Minnesota," 265. Second Wisconsin Territorial Legislature met in Burlington, Iowa, west of the river. Bloom, *Territorial Papers*, vol. 27 [131].

11. Rachael v. Walker, 4 Mo. 350, 354 (1836) (holding that if a military officer chooses to bring a slave to free territory, the slave is entitled to freedom even if the officer is ordered to travel there). Rachael had also lived at Fort Snelling.
12. Ibid.
13. The Northwest Ordinance of 1787, section 14, Art. 2. "The inhabitants of the said territory shall always be entitled to the benefits of . . . judicial proceedings according to the course of the common law."
14. William Blackstone outlined the basic prerogatives that a master was authorized to exercise over a servant woman, Blackstone, *Commentaries*, vol. 1, 142, n. 30; VanderVelde, "The Legal Ways of Seduction" (explaining the legal privileges of mastery that the employers continued to hold over their servant girls in America under the common law in the nineteenth century).
15. When, for example, Mr. Baker left the community to go south to buy supplies in the spring, he had lent Taliaferro his horse (LT Journals, March 26, 1836). The arrangement gave the borrower the use of the animal and assured the lender that the animal would be cared for.
16. In November 1838, "H. Etheldred," identified only as a black person, 5 7″ tall with white eyes and black hair, was also listed as serving Lt. Samuel Whitehorne. Lt. Plympton later lists "Har. Etheldred" as his servant. SP Accts, RG 217, E516 NA.
17. What determines positive law in the wilderness of a diaspora, where no state appears to have jurisdiction?
18. Sutler's account book, August 20, 1838. Sibley collection, Minn HS.
19. For example, Julia Dent echoed the norm, when she was offered her first proposal by the young U. S. Grant. She replied simply, "Mamma would not approve of my accepting a gift from a gentleman." Coffmann, *The Old Army*, 112.
20. Slaves counted on receiving new clothing annually, usually at Christmas. Brown, *From Fugitive Slave to Free Man*, 82.
21. Master Taliaferro had left two days before this purchase was recorded.
22. Jarvis letter (July 1833), Minn HS. "The uniformity of a garrison life is like clockwork," Jarvis wrote, describing the times of activities at Fort Snelling.
23. Lt. Gwynne's slave, Lucy; Julius and Nancy, slaves of Col. Davenport and Laura Denison; Thomas Barker's slave, Caroline. The Fifth Infantry officers had brought no new slave women to the post perhaps because they arrived directly from other northern Wisconsin forts without the opportunity to visit the St. Louis slave market.
24. Brunson, *A Western Pioneer*, 81, 97, 100, 131.
    There was also another mulatto man in the area named Joseph Robinson who worked as a cook for Henry Sibley at Mendota (Blegen, "Unfinished Autobiography,"358). Sibley's autobiography doesn't identify exactly when Joseph Robinson worked for Sibley, but multiple entries in the accounts books of the New Hope store from August 19 to September 30, 1837, suggest that Robinson started with Sibley in 1837. Sibley recorded in his daybook: "Jos. Robinson commenced this morning labouring with the other men until Mr. Dousman's arrival when he will be there disposed of as Mr. D may think proper. Delivered him his rations for the week. Worked only 4 days."
25. In November, an H. Etheldred, identified only as a black person, 5 7″ tall with white eyes and black hair, was also listed as serving Lt. Samuel Whitehorne.
26. Catherine testified that Harriet worked for her for two or three months around September 14, 1837. The official paymaster's reports tell a slightly different story. The official reports never show Harriet hired out to the Thompsons at all. Instead, they show Lt. Thompson collecting money from the army for a white woman servant named, coincidentally, Catherine, his wife's name. The fact that Harriet is not recorded as working for the Thompsons does not imply, of course, that she did not do so. Lt. Thompson may simply pocketed the full amount of money.
27. SP Accts, RG 217, E516, NA. The Thompsons purchased an entire pantry of kitchen utensils on their arrival, which seems to indicate that the lieutenant had not

supported a household kitchen of his own at his prior posting (July 17, Sutler's Account, Sibley Papers [1815–1930], Minn HS). They purchased a tin gridiron, a long-handled frying pan, four tin pans, a wooden tub, a bucket, two jars of jelly, one nine-inch loaf of sugar, a jar of pearl ash for cleaning, one brass kettle for boiling water, and a coffee mill. On August 3, Lt. Thompson was charged for one pair of child's shoes and one pair of ladies prunelle shoes.

28. 1850 Census listing for James L. Thompson, Greenfield Township, Wayne County, Michigan. The entry includes father and son, James L. Thompson, Jr. 17 years old and two women servants.

29. December 19, 1837, New Hope accounts book, Henry H. Sibley Papers (1815–1930), Minn HS.

30. Elizabeth T. Baird, *O-De-Jit-Wa-Win-Ning*, 70–74.

31. Louisa Edmonia Plympton was born November 30, 1837 (Reynolds, *Genealogical and Family History of Southern New York*), 1312.

32. Chase, *A Genealogy of the Family of Plimpton*, 103.

33. LT Journals, August 8, 1838. See also LT Journal, August 3, 1838 (Major Plympton quoted as saying "it is unnecessary to talk much").

34. Portraits of black servants are among the Livingston family paintings.

35. "R. Perry," listed in the records (SP Accts, RG 217, E 516) is presumably Rose Ann Perry, the third daughter of the Perrys who would later marry J. R. Clewett in 1839. Clewett would become a spokesperson for the squatter settlement.

36. The Plymptons' children born on the frontier were baptized in the Dutch Reformed Church in New York City, Mrs. Plympton's family church. Capt. Plympton was not a church member but was said to be "a Christian of the purest sort."

37. LT Journals, May 29, 1826.

38. Harriet is listed as serving Plympton from November 1837 to February 1838 (SP Accts, RG 217, E 516, NA).

39. Survey dated October 19, 1837. Bloom, *Territorial Papers,* vol. 28, p. 53, n. 35 and p. 343, n. 5.

40. Ibid.

41. Records of the sutler's store for August 20, 1837 included "Lt. Thompson 3 pr children hose." Sibley Papers (1815–1930, Minn HS).

   According to the paymaster's records, Plympton had Thomas Williams and R. Perry working for him since he arrived on August 20, 1837. Emerson listed Dred; Capt. M. Scott listed Jack; Lt. J. C. Reid listed Bill Johnston described simply as "Negro."

   There were other servant arrangements that did not seem to involve African Americans: Lt. E. K. Smith listed Sarah West (there is an Irish man named West in the 5th infantry and Sarah may have been his wife). Lt. A. H. Tappan listed David Barry, described as "light," and Lt. D McPhail listed Mr. Langridge as light and 5' 2'. Lt. Samuel Whitehorne first listed "G. Cripps" and then listed "Harriet Etheldred" as working for him in November.

   Dred was listed as working both for Dr. Emerson and Assistant Surgeon Wolcott. SPAccts, RG 217, E 516, NA. Dred could not have worked for both doctors, stationed so far apart, simultaneously. According to the Post Returns, Dr. Emerson's orders were:

   Aug. 19, Special order, Asst. Surg. J.J.B Wright to Ft. Snelling to relieve Asst. Surg. Emerson, who will repair to Jefferson Barracks and await further orders. Fort Snelling Post Returns RG 94, NA, Records of the Adjutant General's Office. Sept. 22, Emerson ordered assigned to Ft. Jesup. Jefferson Barracks Post Returns.

42. Indictment September Term, 3rd day. PDC. *U.S. v. Che-ga-weye-cum.* Court docket book, found in the basement of the county courthouse in Prairie du Chien.

43. Secretary of Indian Affairs Joel Poinsett signed the treaty for the United States. September 29, 1837. The site was described as Dr. Laurie's church.

44. Sibley letter to Ramsey Crooks, September 29, 1837, Blegen, "Unfinished Autobiography," 66.

45. Ibid.

46. "It caused much labor and inconvenience to the garrison to obtain the necessary fuel—and should the post be needed for the next 20 years the difficulty would be increased." Plympton letter, documented in Kane, *The Falls of St. Anthony*, 11–14.

47. Letter of John N. Macomb to Plympton, November 17, 1837, in Bloom, *Territorial Papers*, 875 (acknowledging receipt of map).

48. Plympton letter, documented in Kane, *The Falls of St. Anthony*, 11–14.

49. Letter of Dr. Emerson. Selected letters received SGO RG 112, NA. The Fort Snelling Post returns for November 1837 list "Transferred J. Emerson by order of August 19. Left post on Oct 20." Records of Adjutant General's Office, RG 94.

50. List of doctor bills paid by Henry H. Sibley to Emerson for himself, for dressing the wound of John the mason and extracting teeth for Dupuis and "Joe" (Henry H. Sibley papers, Minn HS).

51. SP Accts, RG 217, E516, NA.

52. Sutler's account book for January 22, 1838. Sibley Papers (1815–1930), Minn HS.

53. Long after he could have incurred the debt, the quartermaster entered an order that Dr. Emerson be charged for bread from the company bake house. "Jan. 25, 1838, Dr. Emerson bake house charge per order of Lt. McPhail. Feb 7, charging Dr. Emerson for order to bake house per order of Lt. McPhail. $2.25/ mo." Sutler's account book, Sibley Papers (1815–1930), Minn HS.

54. All entries are from the sutler's account books, which can be found in the Henry Sibley papers of the Minnesota Historical Society Manuscripts Collection. In November and December, Plympton bought a substantial number of consumer goods: Bacon, butter, a padlock. 2 yds ticking, 2 yds ribbon, 1 bot cologne. 1 tin cup, 1 teapot, 1 loaf sugar, doz. 1 lb. crackers, 2 yds ribbon, 2 sk silk. 1 bot oil, 1 doz segars, 2 pr gaters. 3 qts molasses, 2 yd silk, 2 India rubbers, 1 lb peaches. Ginger, 1/2 gal molasses, 1 broom. 1 bonnet board, 2 bots brandy. 4 bots mustard. 1 box blacking.1 qt oil, 2 doz buttons, 1 Iron buckle.(belt) 1 pr children's shoes, 1 bot cayenne pepper, Loaf sugar. 1 pr Kid gloves, 1 bucksaw. 1 loaf salt. 10 lb lard, 1 p. Pins. 1 gal Madeira; ½ t. Cinnamon, 2 nutmeg; 2 bots wine 1 gal wine.

55. Chase, *A Genealogy of the Family of Plimpton*, 101.

56. Taliaferro's presence on this date is noted by his letter; letter in Lawrence Taliaferro's letterbook sent from St. Peter's, November 11, 1837, renominating Scott Campbell as interpreter. Taliaferro letters, Minn HS.

57. Dr. Emerson and Taliaferro must have crossed paths on the Mississippi, Dr. Emerson traveling by canoe on his way down to St. Louis, Maj. Taliaferro on the *Rolla* steaming up river. The *Rolla* left St. Louis on November 1 for St. Peter's (*Army-Navy Chronicle*, November 23, 1837).

58. Taliaferro, "Autobiography," 220.

59. The fact that Taliaferro knew exactly the day that the ice made, however, suggests that he was there to witness it and left with the mail carrier in a Mackinac boat.

60. The doctor was Erastus B. Wolcott, born in New York, appointed New York assistant surgeon January 1, 1836. He resigned April 15, 1839. Frank, *Medical History of Milwaukee*, 5–6.

61. We don't know why Dred didn't work for Dr. Wright, who, after all, arrived earlier and could easily have assumed his services immediately. Dr. Wright instead asked a soldier's wife, Mrs. Langridge, to serve him. She also worked for Lt. McPhail. Mrs. Langridge was probably the wife of Sgt. Alfred Langridge, who was in Capt. Scott's company with another year to complete his tour of duty, having enlisted at Fort Howard on June 23, 1835, for a term of three years.

62. *Army-Navy Chronicle*, November 23, 1837.

63. Joseph J. B. Wright was also from Pennsylvania. His first commission as assistant surgeon was October 25, 1833.

64. There were two doctors for only 67 men in the garrison. Only one or two persons were sick each month, and the doctors had the assistance of a hospital matron, steward, and two servants.

65. The identity of the author of the poem "A Visit from Saint Nicholas" or " 'Twas the Night before Christmas" is subject to some dispute. Some claim that the author was Henry Livingston, Mrs. Plympton's cousin, but others maintain that it was Clement Clarke Moore. Livingston proponents claim that Livingston wrote it some 15 years before Moore claimed authorship, and that Livingston was dead by the time that his heirs discovered Moore's claim.

66. Harriet's first child was born in October of that year. Brunson, *A Western Pioneer*, 125.

67. Smith, Thompson, Reid, and the commander.

68. Martin Scott was born January 17, 1788, in Bennington, Vermont, son of Phineas Scott and Thankful Kinsley of Sunderland, Franklin County, Massachusetts.

69. Sutler's account books show coffee purchases made by Captain Scott. February 1, March 6, 1838. Sibley Papers (1815–1930), Minn HS.

70. Baird, *O-De-Jit-Wa-Win-Ning*, 91–92. "Captain Scott had a colored boy by the name of Jack, of whom he made a great pet. Jack seemed to be a lad of-all-work. He not only waited upon the master but attended to the dogs. In fact, the Captain required his whole household to be attentive to his dogs. It was less matter about the affairs of his house, and many who wanted a favor of the Captain took care to be very devoted to the dogs. Jack was a faithful servant and was constantly with his master over whom he gained great control, unknown to the Captain." Ibid.

71. Others also regarded Captain Scott as a bit "parsimonious" until it was discovered that he surreptitiously sent the bulk of his pay home to support his widowed mother and disabled sister (Van Cleve, "*Three Score Years and Ten*," 28–29).

72. E. K. Smith Personnel File, NA.

73. Edmund Kirby-Smith Papers, Southern Historical Collection, Manuscripts Department, Wilson Library, University of North Carolina at Chapel Hill. One of the confusions in this family is that the Kirby Smiths named both of their sons "E. K. Smith." The family papers are under Edmund's name.

74. Prescott must have been very cold when he arrived since he immediately brought some warm clothes. The first entry for him in the sutler's account book is a charge for a flannel shirt, a pair of Indian rubbers, and two pairs of flannel drawers (Sutler's account book, March 8, 1838, Sibley Papers, Minn HS).

75. Pond and Pond, *Two Volunteer Missionaries*, 100–101; Riggs, *Mary and I*, 70.

76. Pond, *The Dakota or Sioux*, 30 (indicating that dog flesh was eaten only on great occasions).

    "They cut up our women in a horrid manner," said one of the Sioux (words of Marc pee ah snee to Taliaferro, on June 23, 1838). Round Wind said: "I was one who assisted to bury their bodies. We felt disposed to go to war—but decided first to report all to you what had taken place. It is our wish that you do us justice try, and give us four of this people—put them in our hands for the satisfaction of those of our people who have lost their relations and then everything will go on as usual." "The Chippewas after being feasted on the best we had got up in the night and cut up our people in pieces" (LT Journals, May 30, 1838).

77. Letter of Frederick Ayer to President Van Buren, September 30, 1837 (Bloom, *Territorial Papers*, 856–57).

78. LT Journals, June 7, 1838, reporting account given by Big Thunder.

79. "I felt much mortified and hurt at such expressions. I did not expect such a reception. I did not sell my land for a medal." When Taliaferro was told the following summer he reassured the chief. "It was not necessary to think of what had passed between [you two]. Had Mr. Dousman possessed a Sioux heart, he would have talked and acted differently, therefore let it pass" (LT Journals, June 1838).

80. Words of Esetakenbah (LT Journals, June 21, 1838). The Indians complained that their game was nearly gone and what they were able to kill their traders wouldn't take. "We know not what to do in the coming winter. These things give some of our people hard feelings and they often behave amiss in consequence."

81. Letter from Lawrence Taliaferro, February 21, 1838, Bedford, to Scott Campbell. Lawrence Taliaferro Papers, 1813–1868, Minn HS.

Chapter 13

1. On November 16, 1837, Dr. Emerson reported his arrival at New Orleans, a month after his departure from St. Peter's. In the evening of November 22, Emerson finally reported to Fort Jesup, Louisiana, still listing Dred in his service during Emerson's time in Louisiana. Dred was listed as simultaneously in the service of assistant surgeon Dr. Wolcott at Fort Snelling, some thousand miles upstream. SP Accts, RG 217, E 516, NA.

2. Dr. Emerson letter to the surgeon general from Fort Jesup, Louisiana, December 9, 1837. Dr. John Emerson Personnel File, NA.

3. Dr. John Emerson Personnel File, NA.

4. Letter of J. F. A. Sanford to Pierre Chouteau Jr. (February 5,1838): "Irene is to marry Dr. Emerson." Sanford-Chouteau Letter file.

5. There are no records to be found of the event through the usual research paths.

6. "To have a slave in the house who could perform menial tasks at the bidding of a white woman was a Southern ideal" (Martin, *Divided Mastery,* 114).

7. SP Accts, RG 217, E 516. NA.

8. Harriet was replaced in Col. Plympton's household by Nancy; a later record refers to his servant as "N. Jacobs." (Nancy was also the name of the Davenports' slave, but the Davenports had left, presumably taking their Nancy with them.) Their other servant, Thomas Williams, was replaced by Peter Conant, a private in the 5th infantry, who had enlisted in March 16, 1833, served out his five years, and chosen not to reenlist (ibid.).

9. Catherine Anderson testified that the Scotts left for the South—Fort Gibson, she thought—in April 1838. Since Dr. Emerson had made a trip accompanying troops to Fort Gibson, he may have posted a letter from there requesting that Dred and Harriet join him. A month after his wedding, the doctor was ordered to accompany some recruits sent to a fort in Arkansas, a trip taking six weeks (Testimony of Catherine Anderson, May 7, 1847). (Dred Scott Case Collection, CCHRP).

10. The entry in the sutler's account books suggests that Col. Plympton paid Dr. Emerson for her services rather than paying Harriet herself. Harriet and Dred were probably replaced in the service of their respective masters because the doctor sent for them.

11. The Reverend Brunson states that the Scotts' baby was born aboard the *Gypsey* as they traveled upstream from Missouri to Fort Snelling that fall (Brunson, *A Western Pioneer,* 125).

12. Fehrenbacher claims that it seems fairly certain that Dred and Harriet made the long journey to Louisiana (Fehrenbacher, *The Dred Scott Case,* 245). However, there is at least as much evidence to suggest that they did not.

    The strongest evidence that Harriet traveled as far as Louisiana is contained in the allegation by Harriet that she did so, which may have been a legal fiction, necessary to indicate that Emerson had exerted some control over her, while he lived. Most allegations tying Harriet to Emerson cannot be corroborated by independent sources, but some such allegations were necessary to make the case that Emerson's widow would be the appropriate person for Harriet to sue in order to establish her freedom.

13. April 23, 1838, Emerson letter to the surgeon general. Dr. John Emerson Personnel File, NA.

14. Confusing the situation still further, Dr. Emerson continued to list Dred by name on his pay slip in order to draw servant's support money for the entire four months he was in Louisiana, although all reliable accounts place Dred at Fort Snelling during this time. Dr. E. B. Wolcott also listed Dred as serving him at Fort Snelling during the identical four-month period. Between the two, it seems more likely that Dr. Emerson rather than Dr. Wolcott was misrepresenting Dred's service. In other correspondence, Dr. Emerson complained that he had had to leave all his possessions behind when he hurriedly departed the upper reaches of the Mississippi by canoe before the waters froze (SP Accts, RG 217, E 516, NA.).

15. The *Burlington* arrived May 25. Although steamboat passage could be paid by entries in the sutler's book, there is no entry for passage for either Dred or Harriet.

Passage was entered in the sutler's book dated April 24, 1838, indicating that Capt. Martin Scott provided $15 for transport "to Crawford." Dred and Harriet could have been entrusted to the care of Capt. Throckmorton for transport downriver as well. Other slaves, such as Mariah, who had attempted murder, and Fanny, who was too much the favorite with the men of the post, had been turned over to Capt. Throckmorton's custody for transport to St. Louis and the slave markets there.

16. The season's first steamboat, the *Burlington*, arrived at Fort Snelling's dock on May 25 with stores of goods for all the traders and the post sutler.

17. Buchanan, *Black Life on the Mississippi*, 19–54.

18. Letter to the editor titled "Messrs. Editers [*sic*]," *Missouri Republican*, July 4, 1838.

19. "The few references to the treatment of Negro passengers indicate that, as might be expected, there was no place for them in the cabin except as servants of passengers" (Hunter, *Steamboats on the Western Rivers*, 391, n. 3).

20. Harney, *Adm'r of Duty, v. Dutcher & Dutcher*, 15 Mo. 89, 55 (1851).

21. See, generally, Buchanan, *Black Life on the Mississippi*.

22. Ibid., 101–7.

23. *Missouri Republican*, April 30, 1838.

24. Petersen, *Steamboating on the Upper Mississippi*, 363–67.

25. *Missouri Republican*, February 8, 1838, September 20, 1838. In the largest steamboat explosion, 184 persons of the 280 aboard were killed near Cincinnati when the *Moselle* exploded on the Ohio River (*Missouri Republican*, May 1, 1838).

26. Lucy, the slave who served Lt. Hooe's family, was probably from the same area in King George County, Virginia, as Harriet. The Hooes and the Taliaferros were closely intermarried and occupied the same expanse of Virginia tobacco plantations of Harriet's childhood. If Lucy was from Alexander Hooe's family in Virginia, then the two young women would have known each other as children.

27. Patsey's son, Henry, worked for the Street daughter who married John Beach. Dred had worked for Lt. John Beach at Fort Armstrong (SP Accts, RG 217, E 516, NA.).

28. Since few slaves knew their actual ages or dates of birth (Blassingame, *Slave Testimony*, 388), promising to release a slave at a specific age placed trust in the master. Suppose the slave's new master refused to let him go when he came of age; would he have to sue for his freedom or run away? Was he free automatically on his birthday or did he require release papers from his master? Who even recorded his birthday to determine when he reached 21? The servant woman Eliza had been promised her freedom and yet she still remained with the Taliaferros. Was she a captive or a dependent?

29. Tom, about 70 years of age; Lear, about 52; Jim, about 50; and Joe and Toby, both about age 34. Manumission Papers of Henry Dodge's five slaves, April 14, 1838, Circuit Court (Iowa County): Clerk of Court Papers, 1809–1868, Box 1, no. 20–22, Wisconsin Historical Society, Madison.

30. Toby's Manumission Paper, April 14, 1838, ibid.

31. Johnson, *Soul by Soul*, 42.

32. Toby's Manumission Paper. April 14, 1838, Circuit Court (Iowa County): Clerk of Court Papers, 1809–1868, Box 1, no. 20–22, Wisconsin Historical Society, Madison.

33. Court records, Prairie du Chien Courthouse, Prairie du Chien, Wisconsin. May 24–25 term, 1838.

34. Warren, *History of the Ojibway People*, 484–85. John Bonga, the free black-Ojibwa man who probably lived with his sister, Mrs. Falstrom, at Coldwater Spring, was a witness in the court proceedings.

35. "To have a little quelquechose" was how the Prairie du Chien community described the drinking practices of juries (Kinzie, *Wau-Bun*, 40).

36. The accused had spent two full years in fort stockades, one winter at Fort Snelling awaiting transport south and the other at Fort Crawford as the trial was delayed by the treaty land rush.

37. "The half-breeds who live among the Chippewa are . . . very dissatisfied with the acquittal. . . . They feel that they are not protected by the laws. . . ." Bushnell's report in President's message to Congress 1838, 25th Congress, 3rd session, S. Doc 1.

38. "The Indian has been unfortunately cleared—a horrid example our civil tribunals are too uncertain for Indian justice—we must continue to receive with impunity such repeated insults" (LT Journals, June 8, 1838).

    At St. Peter's a similar murder awaited resolution. Another white trader's half-blood son, too, had been murdered by a full-blood Indian a few months earlier. Provencal, the trader, sought out Taliaferro to decide what to do. Taliaferro remarked, "All that could be done with the Indian, who killed your son last winter, was to put him in the guard house 'feed and fatten him on bread and pork' send him for trial to Prairie du Chien, and, of course, without satisfactory testimony of the fact, have the additional pain of witnessing his being set at liberty by the jury." The trader professed this was "very true and heart-rending" to a parent (ibid.).

39. July 3, 1838, *Missouri Republican.*

40. January 16, 1838, in Alton, Ilinois. Gerteis, *Civil War St. Louis*, 19.

41. Even the *Missouri Republican* criticized the man and his cause. "Some philanthropic abolitionist has published a life of the Rev. E.P. Lovejoy, who fell at Alton, *nobly*... defending his press. Truly this is the age of humbugs" (*Missouri Republican,* April 3, 1838).

42. Murdoch had been living in St. Louis for some time anyway. On May 10, 1838, Francis Murdoch married Mary Johnson, daughter of Col. John Johnson in a St. Louis wedding performed by the Reverend Lutz and recorded in the Alton newspaper, Alton, Illinois. Francis Murdoch continued to practice law now in St. Louis, joining with two lawyers, Ferdinand Risque and Gustavus Bird.

43. Buchanan, *Black Life on the Mississippi,* 136 (account of Leah at whose home the gang boarded).

44. This expectation would be consistent with social conventions. See Edward Bates's account of his mother's former slave coming to spend the night with his own slaves. Charless, *A Biographical Sketch of the Life of Joseph Charless,* 106, 133 (offering the charity of a place to sleep and being charitable generally).

45. Charless, *A Biographical Sketch of the Life of Joseph Charless,* 133. Letters to Charless's grandchildren outline the family history, noting the Etheldred name. Ibid., 31.

46. Slaves: An act concerning slaves. Art. IV. Concerning Runaway Slaves, approved March 19th, 1835. Missouri Statute.

47. Ibid., 15.

48. *Missouri Republican,* September 25, 1838.

49. *Missouri Republican,* July 4, 1838 (or possibly July 7, 1838).

50. Even Leah, who ran the boarding house and later became involved in a notorious robbery, was a church member (Buchanan, *Black Life on the Mississippi,* 136).

51. Brown, *From Fugitive Slave to Free Man,* 34.

52. Anonymous Letter of a Traveler to St. Louis, Mo HS. Collection to come.

53. See Brown, *From Fugitive Slave to Free Man,* 8. "No part of our slave-holding country is more noted for the barbarity of its inhabitants than St. Louis."

54. Colonel Harney, an army officer at Jefferson Barracks, whipped his slave woman, Hannah, to death believing that she would reveal the location of some misplaced keys. A mob chased him out of town, but he returned and was acquitted for the crime of murder (Frazier, *Slavery and Crime in Missouri,* 135–39).

55. One man also recounted a barbaric practice that former Virginians brought with them to Missouri called "Virginia play." To punish a servant, the master tied him up in the smokehouse, whipped him, started a fire from tobacco stems, and smoked him until he was more compliant (ibid., 5).

56. Ibid.

57. Ibid., 14.

58. William Wells Brown feared that he would be sold in the South when he was transported there despite his owner's denials (Brown, *From Fugitive Slave to Free Man,* 41).

59. Don Fehrenbacher took the view that Dred and Harriet did travel to Louisiana, a view supported by the allegations in the case. Fehrenbacher did not have available

to him the pay slips listing both Dred and Harriet at Fort Snelling (SP Accts, RG 217, E 516, NA). If Dr. Emerson's claim is correct that one of "his negros" was contemplating suing him for freedom, who was it? Would that person willingly get on a steamboat heading south if he or she contemplated suing for freedom? It may be that alleging that Harriet traveled to Louisiana was simply necessary to show Dr. Emerson exercising some control over her, whether the claim was fictitious or true.

60. See Petition to Sue for Freedom, Harriet Scott, *Scott v. Emerson,* http://library.wustl .edu/vlib/dredscott/transcripts/scott_02.html (Dred Scott Case Collection, Circuit Court of St. Louis Historical Records Project). However, in the U.S. Supreme Court opinion, both parties stipulated that the Scotts had remained in Missouri since 1838, when Dr. Emerson moved them down from Ft. Snelling (Opinion, *Scott v. Sanford,* 60 U.S. 393, 398 [1856]).

61. Emerson letter, July 10, 1838, Fort Jesup, Dr. John Emerson Personnel File, NA.

   It is possible that Dr. Emerson is referring to some other slave, although there is no evidence of his owning anyone but Dred. He made a point of saying that he traveled downstream by canoe alone leaving everything at Fort Snelling. There would have been no reason for him to buy a slave in St. Louis and leave the person there. He received decent transport by steamboat south to Louisiana from St. Louis. This corroborates an arrival date of Dred and Harriet in St. Louis in early June. In order to communicate this resistance to Louisiana, Dred and Harriet must have arrived in St. Louis by early June.

62. The court case, which is based on several erroneous statements of facts as part of the streamlined stipulation, states that Harriet did travel down to Louisiana. Given her pregnant condition and her more tenuous relationship to the doctor it would be surprising if she traveled on to an unfamiliar locale if her husband stayed behind in St. Louis. On the other hand, so many statements about Harriet's life were simplified or stylized for the purpose of bringing an easier case that it is possible the case file contains this error purposely to establish that Dr Emerson exercised some dominion over her, a fact necessary for her to establish her freedom from his control (see Petition to Sue for Freedom, Harriet Scott, *Scott v. Emerson,* http://library.wustl.edu/vlib/dredscott/transcripts/scott_02. html (Dred Scott Case Collection, Circuit Court of St. Louis Historical Records Project).

63. He asserted, "Three medical officers are not needed" (Emerson letter, June 27, 1838, Dr. John Emerson Personnel File, NA).

64. Ibid.

65. "Let me again entreat you to have me ordered to [one of the northern posts]. I left Ft. S. last October I had to come down the river 300 miles in a canoe and was consequently compelled to leave everything after me at that fort. I am even without my books and other things necessary" (Emerson letter, July 10, 1838, Dr. John Emerson Personnel File, NA).

66. The date is listed as August 8 in the *Army and Navy Chronicle,* August 16, 1838.

67. "The lands in Iowa, commonly called Black Hawk's purchase, will be offered for sale, it is expected in about two months" (*Missouri Republican,* September 1, 1838).

68. *Missouri Republican,* April 24, 1838.

69. LeCompt, "John F. A. Sanford," 40.

70. Ramsey Crooks was the person writing letters to see that Scott Campbell's land allotment in the treaty was set aside. John F. A. Sanford was credited with lobbying the Winnebago treaty through Congress (Letters received by Congress, NA).

71. May 19, 1838 entry in Mary Riggs diary: "and that 11 of the 14 who went on board, died. From these [men] it spread far and wide, often making whole lodges its prey" (Riggs, *A Small Bit of Bread and Butter,* 72).

72. No report actually laid blame upon the Chouteau firm that controlled transport upriver.

73. See Chapter 13, note 41.

74. Catlin article on the "Extinction of the Mandan," reprinted in Catlin, *Letters and Notes*, Appendix A, 257.

75. William Clark's will names at least 11 different slaves and by inference of unnamed children suggests ownership of at least 14 (William Clark Probate, 1839, PCDP.)

76. VanderVelde, "The Role of Captives in the Rule of Capture," 667–68.

77. *Missouri Republican*, September 18, 1838.

78. On September 8, an entire family, consisting of a man and woman and their five children ranging from ages 4 to 14, stood on the steps facing the river to be sold. They were advertised as available to be sold separately or together as suited the purchaser (*Missouri Republican*, September 5, 1838).

79. It is not clear what boat the Emersons took from New Orleans to St. Louis. The *Governor Dodge* left New Orleans on September 8 and arrived in St. Louis on September 18. The *Clyde* was a regular steam packet ship that shuttled without extra stops between St. Louis and New Orleans. The *Little Red*, the *Pawnee*, and the *Wilmington* made it to St. Louis and left for New Orleans again on September 30.

80. Alexis Bailley based his claim to his contraband whiskey on this basis. The Reverend Meachum is reputed to have organized a school on the river to escape the state statute against teaching African Americans to read.

81. *Missouri Republican*, May 14, 1838; a different issue of the paper reported that "the *Gipsy* left port on Wednesday, Sept 25th at 10:00 a.m."

82. Brunson, *A Western Pioneer*, 125.

83. *Missouri Republican*, September 1, 1838, reporting on the *Burlington*'s arrival from Galena.

84. The stovepipe of the ladies' cabin caught fire on the ship's downriver voyage (LT Journals, November 5, 1838). The boat's only advantage was that its shallow draft allowed it go where other boats could not. Brunson, *A Western Pioneer*, 125.

85. Donovan, *River Boats of America*, 127–28 (quoting Capt. Marryat, *Diary in America*, vol. 2, ch. 3).

86. Fehrenbacher, *The Dred Scott Case*, 246; Ehrlich, *They Have No Rights*, 25.

87. Mrs. Taliaferro was sometimes referred to as "dear cousin Eliza" by Taliaferro's correspondents (Lawrence Taliaferro papers, letter of Joseph Street, January 2, 1829). Taliaferro's journal of Wednesday, February 23, 1831, states: "note servant give [*sic*] Eliza delivered of a female child this morning after 1:00 a.m." Harriet was probably in Taliaferro's household at this time and may have attended at the birth. Still later, Taliaferro's journals mention the death of Eliza's five-and-a-half-month old son, Jarvis (LT Journals, September 9, 1836). Eliza's name is also the first name on the list of slaves Taliaferro says that he freed (see Taliaferro's list of slave names on page 325, Appendix of this volume). Another name on Taliaferro's list of slaves he had owned was Lizzie, the name of the Scotts' other daughter.

88. G. C. R. Mitchell was one of the first lawyers of Davenport, Iowa. Letter of Dr. Emerson to surgeon general of July 10, 1838, says that three years earlier he had entered a claim on a farm in Galena. Someone had filed suit against him in chancery, and his agent had sold his valuable farm at half the price. Dr. John Emerson Personnel File, NA.

89. Letter from Governor Dodge to Commissioner Harris from Prairie du Chien, October 9, 1838. "The Steamboat *Ariel* arrived here from St. Peters last evening. Aboard was the dispensing agent sent by Major Hitchcock. Determined that Chippewa should not be paid until spring 'in interests of justice' so all can be informed to go to La Pointe" (Bloom, *Papers of the Wisconsin Territory*, vol. 27, 1074–75).

90. LT Journals, October 20, 1838.

91. LT Journals, October 18, 1838. "Steamer *Gipsey* brought with Chippewa goods $4750.00" (LT Journal, October 21, 1838).

Chapter 14

1. LT Journals, October 21, 1838.
2. Jim Thompson had even taken a job building a house downriver for a couple of former soldiers, who wanted to stay on in the territory to make their fortunes. The one named Phelan and his partner, Hays, were an odd couple in some ways, but they had united in the project of hiring Jim Thompson to build a house for them (Spangler, *The Negro in Minnesota*, 20).
3. Daughter Sarah was listed in Affidavit 68 of the Mixed Blood's claimant's files. Sarah was listed as "age 18 last October" on 1856 files and in the 1860 Census as 21 years. Miscellaneous Reserve Papers: Sioux Affidavits, Roll of Mixed-Blood Claimants, 1856, Relinquishment by Lake Pepin Half-breed Sioux. RG 75, NA.
4. LT Journals, October 21, 1838.
5. Letter of John F. A. Sanford, Washington, to Ramsey Crooks, Esqr, New York (entry 5544, Manuscript Department, New-York Historical Society).
6. Welter, "The Cult of True Womanhood," 151–74.
7. "Mrs. Plympton and family leave for the East aboard the *Ariel*" (LT Journals, October 5, 1838).
8. Elizabeth T. Baird, *O-De-Jit-Wa-Win-Ning*, 74. Details of the expulsion are found in Lt. Tappan's Personnel file, NA.
9. Ibid.
10. James L. Thompson filed for divorce from Catherine Thompson, June 14, 1838.
11. See, e.g., LT Journals, October 29, 1838.
12. LT Journals, October 2, 1838, and again, July 25, 1839.
13. "While absent on duty with my Delegation at Washington, the officers of the 5th regiment stationed at Ft. Snelling laid their hands upon [the tracts at the mouth of the St. Croix—at the Falls of St. Anthony west—by citizens and foreigners."] (LT Journals, July 21, 1838).
14. To offset the loss of the slaughter of two of the Perrys' cattle, Taliaferro ordered the Indians to relinquish 10 barrels of flour from their treaty allocation (LT Journals, October 18, 1838).
15. LT Journals, July 12, 1838.
16. "It was unofficially reported that the Sioux had killed several head of livestock belonging to the residents on the Reserve at this post." Maj. Taliafierro wrote, "It would be sound policy to keep the whites and Indians as far apart as the local condition of things in this country will permit" (LT Journals, June 1, 1838).

    Message of Big Thunder. "I desire to let you know that there are two men, Peter Perrant and Old Man Perry near us on the River. They have cattle and other property. Would it not be best to order them off—or until we hear from our treaty—tell them to be careful not to insult our young men.... Our young men might do them some harm or kill their cattle" (LT Journals, June 9, 1838).

    "Proposed a meeting of the citizens for two days hence for the purpose of hiring a guard to attend the herding of all cattle of citizens—to prevent loss by Indian depredations through the summer. July 12 I proposed to the citizens of this post to hire one man as a guard to herd their cattle for the summer months. of the residents cattle" (LT Journals, July 10, 1838).
17. LT Journals, July 14, 1838.
18. When half of the treaty goods promised to the Indians arrived, they were of such a poor quality and ill-fitting to the needs of the starving Sioux that Taliaferro thought about urging the Sioux to reject them, but he knew that these were the only items they would have before winter fell (LT Journals, October 11, 1838.
19. LT Journals, October 25, 1838.
20. "On October 29, 1838, *Gipsey* left for Prairie once more" (LT Journals, October 29, 1838).
21. "The Plympton family left on October 5th on the Ariel" (LT Journals, Oct 5, 1838).
22. Lt. Darling, Capt. Scott, (still served by his man, Jack), and the young Lt. McPhail were all single men.

23. Jack was the only black servant other than Dred listed in the Paymaster's accounts for Fort Snelling for that winter. SP Accts RG 217, E 516.
24. The sutler recorded identical purchases for hank thread and skeins of embroidery silk, and baking ingredients. The Thompsons favored molasses with concoctions of nutmeg, cloves, allspice, cinnamon, mace, and brandy, while the Emersons used the more expensive ingredients of almonds and raisins. The preceding year Lt. Thompson had bought these ingredients in the same season of the year (December 8, 1837, and December 11, 1837, New Hope accounts, Sibley papers, Minn HS).
25. McPhail and Whitehorne, December 19, 1838. Sutler's accounts, Sibley papers, Minn HS.
26. Both men bought several packs of cards over the winter. Sutler's accounts, Sibley papers, Minn HS. Dr. Jarvis had mentioned that this was a common vice among officers at remote posts like Fort Snelling. Jarvis letter (October 10, 1833) Minn HS.
27. A fireplace would be necessary for the installation of a stove for them, which Doctor Emerson later insisted upon.
28. Dred is listed on Lt. Darling's payslip for August 1838–December 1838 and into January 1839. SP Accts, RG 217, E 516.
29. Although a few soldiers had been stonecutters, most identified themselves simply as "laborers." Fort Snelling muster rolls, in SP Accts, RG 217, E 516. 1838.
30. Some had been signed up by the doctor's new brother-in-law, Capt. Henry Bainbridge, on recruiting duty in New York where he was reassigned after Louisiana. His name continued to appear on the pay rosters of these recruits, linking their pay with his enlistment efforts (Paymaster's roster for Fort Snelling soldiers, SP Accts, RG 217, E 516).
31. The records usually list him as coming from Pennsylvania, where he attended medical school and where his older brother lived. On one occasion Ireland was suggested to be his birthplace. Letter of complaining Quartermaster, date not available, Dr. John Emerson Personnel File, NA (complaining about Emerson asking pointedly how an Irishman had ended up in the U.S. Army surgical corps).
32. Dr. John Emerson's brother was Dr. Edward P. Emerson, Blairsville, Pennsylvania, born in Ireland (1850 Census).
33. November 2, 1838.
34. There are no other earlier records of his name in the register.
35. Fort Snelling Post returns for 1838 show no one in confinement. By February, there were three privates in the brig on charges. By March, there were six, and by April, nine (Fort Snelling Post Returns, Records of AGO, RG 94. NA).
36. At the first court-martial, on December 19, 1838, Pvt. George W. Couch's defense was purely technical—that he had never legally enlisted because he never accepted the enlistment payment. The records supported his claim, but he was convicted nonetheless. Fort Snelling courts-martial files, Old Army Files, JAG, RG 1838, NA.
37. Lt. Thompson bought more than most officers from the sutler's store that Christmas: a length of calico, a padlock, two books, three tumblers, a tin cup, a set of cups and saucers, and a pair of gloves (Sutler's books, December 25, 1838, Sibley Papers, Minn HS).
38. Sutler's account books, Sibley Papers, Minn HS.
39. Bray and Coleman, *Joseph N. Nicollet on the Plains*, 263.
40. Newly promoted to officer from the ranks, Darling had never enjoyed the privilege of having a subsidized servant of his own before.
41. February 23, 1839, Emerson letter regarding Lt. Darling. Lt. William Darling Personnel File, NA.
42. March 3, 1839, Sutler's account books, Sibley Papers, Minn HS.
43. The syntax suggests that Dred got the money himself.
44. Sometime during 1839 an entry for Dred occurred on B. F. Baker's account books: "Dread Dr. Emerson's slave, $6.84——debt."
     The exact arrangements of the debt are unclear. But the entry is recorded differently from the way the regular debts of masters incurred by servants were recorded. If a servant incurred a debt on the master's account, it was recorded

as "master, per servant" and the amount. In this record only Dred's name is mentioned; he is still identified as a slave, but that the entry is in his own name rather than on Dr. Emerson's account, "per Dred, his slave" (B. F. Baker's Account Books, undated, B. F. Baker's estate, Kenneth McKenzie Papers, Mo HS).

45. On February 23, 1839, Emerson wrote to Antoine LeClaire about Lindsey land (Letter of Dr. John Emerson, February 23, 1839, Antoine Le Claire collection, Putnam Museum, Davenport, Iowa).

46. Letter, date not available, in Dr. John Emerson Personnel File, NA.

47. Over the winter of 1837–38, Philander Prescott got Samuel Pond to inhabit his home for a month while he braved the cold to seek treatment from the fort hospital (Prescott, *The Recollections of Philander Prescott,* 166–67).

48. From Brown docket February 16, 1840, *Prescott v. Foote.* Joseph R. and Samuel J. Brown Family Papers, Minn HS.

49. "It was my intention to take up a small tract at the mouth of the St. Croix—& went upon it for this purpose—but while absent on duty with my delegation at Washington—The Officers of the 5th Regt stationed at Ft. Snelling laid their hands upon in—also the falls of St. Anthony west—by citizens & foreigners. So old Residents have been thus defeated in a place—after passing the prime of their lives in Indian Country" (LT Journals, July 21, 1838).

50. Kane, "The Falls of St. Anthony," 12–13.

51. Ibid., 11.

52. Joseph Plympton letter, reprinted in Williams, *A History of the City of Saint Paul to 1875,* 77–79.

53. Williams, *A History of the City of Saint Paul,* 79.

54. Kane, "The Falls of St. Anthony," 12–13.

55. Joseph Plympton letter, reprinted in Williams, *A History of the City of Saint Paul,* 77–79.

56. Stambaugh letter to the Secretary of War, reprinted in Williams, *A History of the City of Saint Paul,* 61.

57. Clewitt letters, in Bloom, *Territorial Papers,* vol. 28, 87–89, 259–61.

Chapter 15

1. Capt. Hooe brought his family up from Prairie du Chien to join him for the summer April 21, 1839. Hooe's family was composed of his French Métis wife, four children, and the slave, Lucy, who may have been company for Harriet, or even her kinfolk. The slaves of cousins were likely to have been cousins themselves, extended family if not related by blood. Lucy had served the Hooe family in the Northwest territory about as long as Harriet had been at St. Peter's.

2. According to Dr. Emerson's weather log the steamboat *Ariel* arrived on April 19, 1839 (Minn HS). St. Martin, *One Hundred Eighty Years of Weather: Ft. Snelling.*

3. Slave Register, Bedford County Recorder of Deeds, Bedford, Pennsylvania: June 1, 1822, Betsy daughter of Eliza Diggs, registered to Humphry Dillon until age 28. Dec, 6, 1823, Louisa, daughter of Eliza Diggs, registered to Humphry Dillon until age 28. Jan 1, 1828, Charles, son of Eliza Diggs a female negro servant of Humphry Dillon, registered to Humphry Dillon until age 28. Slave Register, Bedford, Pennsylvania Pioneer Historical Society, Bedford, Pennsylvania.

4. *Bedford Gazette,* April 14, 1837: "Washington Hotel and General State Office. Formerly known as Humphrey Dillon's Hotel, daily Mail Stage lines stop at Hotel.... The Larder will offer choicest viands serving Invalid and Epicure... Joseph Ottinger, Horatio N. Dillon."

5. The earliest indication of this arrangement is a business entry on May 15, 1839, in a bill from H. N. Dillon as a trustee of Baker. Baker planned to become sutler after the first of May: April 27, 1839, bill for goods shipped on Steamboat *Fayette* for B. F. Baker from Campbell and Chilton, Louisiana.

6. LT Journals, April 14, 1839: This was the first entry in Taliaferro's diary after an interval of several months, indicating his return to St. Peter's Agency, since Taliaferro did not record a journal during his stays in Pennsylvania.

7. This was how the Reverend Brunson regarded James Thompson's manumission. Brunson, *A Western Pioneer,* 63–64.

8. Dred may have helped out at the agency as well. The same steamboat that brought Agent Taliaferro in took the ailing Lt. Darling away on permanent medical leave (*Darling away with leave by virtue of April 19 order of Asst Surgeon,* Fort Snelling Post Returns, April 1839, NA).

9. Early in April, the burly Gideon Pond moved his wife and child from Lac qui Parle to Lake Harriet again. The government paid Indian farmers $600 per year.

10. Pond and Pond, *Two Volunteer Missionaries,* 134.

11. There is no discussion in any of the primary texts of Indian women being taught to shoulder the plow (Anderson, *Kinsmen of Another Kind*).

12. LT Journals, June 16, 1839.

13. "The Good Road Chief asked if a Farmer had been assigned to his village.. Told it was Peter Quinn, he said, no, no. I want Alexander Faribault to be our Farmer. The Little Crow wanted him, but I have prevented him from going to his village. I replied: Mr. Faribault has never asked for a place…and it would now be too late as all the nominations had been made of Farmers and forwarded by mail" (LT Journals, June 13, 1839).

14. Anderson, *Little Crow,* 33.

15. Pond and Pond, *Two Volunteer Missionaries,* 134. Accounts of influential traders, like Jean Brunet, noted that he never did manual labor himself. Bartlett, "Jean Brunet, Chippewa Valley Pioneer," 39.

16. A strong slave man could cost anywhere from $350 to $500 in the St. Louis market at this time according to slave inventories in the St. Louis Probate files. A domestic servant would be valued at $150 to $200 (see, for example, inventory of slaves of Milton Duty probate, PCDP).

17. LT Journals, August 4, 1838 (statement of Kokomoko).

18. LT Journals, date not available.

19. Taliaferro had recommended the falls of the St. Croix as the distribution site in a letter to Governor Dodge, July 16, 1838 (LT Journals, July 16, 1838).

20. LT Journals, June 18, 1839.

21. Charles E. Flandrau, "Reminiscences of Minnesota," 199; Brunson, *A Western Pioneer,* 120.

22. LT Journals, June 21, 1839.

23. Entry for Stephen Bonga in Sibley's store at New Hope, June 18, 1839.

24. It cannot be claimed that Sibley knew of the mission, but Sibley astutely absented himself later when Taliaferro looked to him for help with the situation (see note 25).

25. LT Journals, June 10, 1839.

26. LT Journals, June 19, 1839.

27. Nacy, *Members of the Regiment,* 57 (describing the general view that quartermasters were stingy with material).

28. Dr. Emerson's practice in drawing provisions became the subject of criticism by Dr. Turner who succeeded Emerson at Fort Snelling. Emerson explained his own practice in a series of letters to the Surgeon General, attempting to be reinstated in the surgical corps after being discharged in a reduction in force. See Chapter 22.

29. Ibid.

30. Dr. Emerson's letters attempting to be reinstated in the surgical corps after being discharged (Dr. John Emerson Personnel File, NA.)

31. LT Journals, June 20, 1839.

32. LT Journals, June 21, 1839.

33. One of the chiefs remarked upon the presence of settlement children among the gathering (LT Journals, June 21, 1839).

34. Ibid. The chief was indicating the presence of women and children in the audience.

35. LT Journals, June 21, 1839.

36. Ibid.
37. Ibid.
38. LT Journals, June 29, 1839.
39. LT Journals, June 21, 1839.
40. Anderson, *Little Crow,* 25; LT Journals, June 22, 1839.
41. "The Astor Medals are in high vogue at this date, and are taking precedence of those of the President of the United States to offer rewards to Indians to prevent competition by any one out of the pale of their own Company" (letter of Maj. Taliaferro to Governor Dodge dated July 24, 1837, forwarded by Dodge to Commissioner Harris, August 15, 1837, in Bloom, *Territorial Papers,* 828–30).
42. "When even the boys got medals, the dirty fellows noticed and the fort medals were brought into disrepute" (LT Journals, June 22, 1839).

Chapter 16

1. LT Journals, June 21, 24, 1839.
2. LT Journals, June 23, 1839.
3. LT Journals, June 21, 24, 1839.
4. Within two weeks of his arrival, Horatio Dillon was authorized by B. F. Baker to commence business in the sutler's store at Fort Snelling with an interest in the business (LT Journals, July 11, 1839).
5. LT Journals, June 25, 1839.
6. Adams, *Early Days* 87–88 (detailing the hard living conditions of the Red River community).
7. LT Journals, June 27, 1839.
8. LT Journals, June 26, 1839.
9. Ibid.
10. Ibid.
11. LT Journals, June 30, 1839.
12. LT Journals, July 1, 1839.
13. "Chief Hole-in-the-Day claimed that Mr. Aitken had blackguarded him and spoke disrespectfully of me" (LT Journals, June 30, 1839). As a preventive measure against the Ojibwa returning again next year, the agent wrote a letter immediately, requesting that the Ojibwa be allowed to receive payment closer to their new grounds.
14. LT Journals, July 1, 1839.
15. LT Journals, July 2, 1839.
16. Father Pelamorgues, the priest who would later perform Dr. Emerson's funeral, was the bishop's assistant.
17. DeCailly, *Memoirs of Bishop Loras,* 79.
18. LT Journals, July 1, 1839.
19. Rupa-co-ka-Maza. The assailants were members of the Pillager band of Leech Lake. The boy's name was Marc-pee. Pond and Pond, *Two Volunteer Missionaries,* 139.
20. Ibid.
21. LT Journals, July 2, 1839.
22. A small detachment was dispatched under Sgt. Mason (LT Journals, July 2, 1839).
23. The Pond brothers describe these incidents as without parallel (Pond and Pond, *Two Volunteer Missionaries,* 139).
24. The Pond brothers claimed that the battle at Rum River was the revenge for Hole-in-the-Day's treachery in attacking his hosts two years earlier. "In the heart of a Dakota an act like this is never forgiven" (Pond and Pond, *Two Volunteer Missionaries,* 102).
25. LT Journals, July 3, 1839.
26. Evan Jones, *Citadel in the Wilderness,* 222.
27. LT Journals, July 4, 1839.

28. It was always an issue of protocol whether the Indians could enter the fort's gates to reach the hospital.
29. Gilman, *Henry Hastings Sibley*, at 77.
30. LT Journals, July 4, 1839.
31. Pond and Pond, *Two Volunteer Missionaries*, 136.
32. The detachment was also sweeping the area for soldiers who had used the opportunity of this excitement to desert, including Pvt. Richard Thomas, who was later court-martialed for desertion. Fort Snelling courts-martial files, Old Army Files, JAG, RG 153, July 20, 1839, NA.
33. LT Journals, July 5, 1839.
34. Capt. Hooe's Métis wife was Catholic, however, and participated as godparent for several more baptized that day. Hoffman, "New Light on Old St. Peters and Early St. Paul," 8 *Minnesota History* 49 (1927).
35. Abbe Pelamorgues, who accompanied the Bishop, would bury Dr. Emerson at Davenport, Iowa, four years later. Mrs. Emerson's family must have been Protestant, since her father was buried in Christ Church Cemetery. Alexander Sanford Probate, PCDP.
36. LT Journals, July 7, 1839.
37. Taliaferro, "Autobiography," 225.
38. Fort Snelling Post Returns for August '39 detailing Martin Scott in hospital, Records of AGO, RG 94, NA; LT Journals, July 8, 1839.
39. LT Journals, August 24, 1839.
40. Sibley, "Reminiscences of the Early Days of Minnesota," 265.
41. LT Journals, July 10, 1839.
42. Dr. Emerson had requested a 21-day leave for the fall. Emerson letter to Antoine LeClaire (July 14, 1839). Le Claire Collection, Putnam Museum, Davenport, Iowa.
43. Letter book entry for July 15, 1839, to the Honorable T. H. Crawford (Taliaferro Papers, Minn HS).
44. LT Journals, July 1839.
45. Ibid.
46. LT Journals, June 11, 1839.
47. LT Journals, July 17, 1839.
48. LT Journals, July 23, 1839.
49. Dr. Emerson's weather log for July 24 through 29 shows temperatures in the 90s. Dr. John Emerson's weather log for Fort Snelling, NA.
50. Post Returns of Fort Snelling, July 1839, NA.
51. Court-martial adjourned to July 22, as Lt. Whitehorne had previously appointed a sale of public provisions at this time. Fort Snelling courts martial files, Old Army Files, JAG, RG 153, July 22, 1839, NA.
52. LT Journals, July 31, 1839.
53. LT Journals, July 21, 1839.
54. "Threat: Hee-pee, an Indian a dirty fellow, from the Sixes village, has sworn to murder the agent" (LT Journals, July 20, 1839.)

Chapter 17

1. "Col. S. C. Stambaugh left with certificates countersigned as trustee for certain orphan children. The Comm. L.D. Pease and W.L.D. Ewing were much incensed at my refusal to prevent the half-breed to be defrauded out of their money but none seemed so violent or incensed in this matter as Wm. L.D. Ewing of Illinois who RASCALITY" (LT Journals, July 25, 1839).
2. "My valuable dog Nero, a most beautiful black Newfoundland and half spaniel, was in the possession of one of the lumber men at St. Croix" (LT Journals, August 2, 1839).
3. Ibid.

4. LT Journals, July 29, 1839.

5. Joseph Massee is listed in LT Journal notes on June 18, 1839.

6. LT Journals, July 29,1839.

7. LT Journals, August 4, 1839.

8. Ibid.

9. Ibid.

10. Ibid.

11. LT Journals, October 1, 1839.

12. LT Journals, August 11, 1839.

13. "Idle speculation on resignation" (LT Journals, August 18, 1839).

14. LT Journals, August 7, 1838. Why Taliaferro came to this conclusion is unclear. His journal does report a number of meetings that he deems "secret" (see, e.g., LT Journals, September 27, 1838). Perhaps these sources informed him that the Métis had aggravated the peace between the Sioux and the Ojibwa. The agent wrote his resolve: "I have come to the determination to start off all the half-breed connections, both Sioux and Chippewa of a certain description, from the U.S. Reservation near this agency and fort, if seconded by the commanding officer" (LT Journals, August 7, 1838). Major Plympton had his own reasons to support such an agenda.

15. LT Journals, September 1, 1839.

16. LT Journals, August 26, 1839.

17. August 26, 1839, letter of Lawrence Taliaferro to Samuel Pond. Pond Family Papers, Minn HS.

18. LT Journals, September 6, 1839.

19. "I had thought that when it was known that I had no interest in sutling,…my lukewarm friends would let their ill-judged objections and opposition cease. But not so, things do not suit some gentlemen yet" (LT Journals, September 28, 29, 1839).

20. "Some hints from Samuel Findley, while drunk today, develops some strange views and hidden intentions of…officers in the fort…to oppose Mr. Dillon," in his partnership in the sutler business. Some officers were urging their men only to do justice to half the amount of their pay—hoping that their remarks and retraction would affect the sutling establishment generally (LT Journals, September 28, 1839).

21. LT Journals, September 21, 1839.

22. "I felt amused at this as the case was that some of the Sioux went over last evening and scared him out of his house, when he would give them no more whiskey. The house was not injured. A small opening in one corner of a loose roof to scare him out which seemed easily affected and they entered and helped themselves to a few gallons of whiskey" (LT Journals, September 22, 1839).

23. LT Journals, September 8, 1839.

24. "Bad Hail" (LT Journals, September 23, 1839).

25. LT Journals, September 26, 1839.

26. LT Journals, September 27, 1839.

27. Newson, *Pen Pictures of St. Paul*, vol. 1, 11.

28. LT Journals, September 28, 1839.

29. Henry C. Menck is listed as a single man between 30 and 40 years old, living among several residents of Coldwater who had been displaced in the 1840 U.S. Census, St. Croix, Western Division.

30. LT Journals, October 5, 1839. The agent later recorded, "This foreign deputy sheriff kept me in custody for nine hours without producing a bond. Though security was proffered and refused. I am falsely imprisoned for the acts of drunken Indians & the whole process is unfounded & illegal in the procedure against me." (LT Journals, October 5, 1839; Taliaferro, "Autobiography," 226–28).

31. He referred to settlers that he hired from the area as "hired men." For example, when he built an ice house he described that it was accomplished with the help of a servant and a hired man (LT Journals, September 12, 1835).

32. Settled Paymaster's accounts for "servants" for 1839. SP Accts RG 217, E 516 (filed under A. D. Steuart, Paymaster, Ft. Snelling, 1839–40).

33. Taliaferro's journals imply that he had no other servants that year. There was no one to help him with the carrying of stores. There was no one else to open the door when the Indians knocked on it in the early morning of July 1. His autobiography describes his being accosted in a sick room, but not necessarily the hospital because he speaks of "sending a note to the Fort," implying that he was not in the fort. Taliaferro, "Autobiography," 227.
34. "Refused Dr. Emerson, a free holding in Iowa" (LT Journals, October 5, 1839).
35. He had been describing them in his journal as his "lukewarm friends" for weeks (LT Journals, September 28, 1839).
36. October 6, 1839, last entry of LT's journals.
37. Philander Prescott named a son after him. U.S. Census 1850, Dakota County, Minnesota 70, lists Lawrence T. Prescott age 12 in the family of Philander Prescott.
38. Babcock, "Major Lawrence Taliaferro, Indian Agent," 375; Dippie, *Catlin and his Contemporaries*, 184–85.
39. There were no records indicating any law suit brought by Menck in the magistrate's order books.
40. Babcock, "Major Lawrence Taliaferro, Indian Agent," *Mississippi Valley Historical Review*, Vol. 11 (December 1924): 365. Babcock documents Bailley filing suit twice, but speculates that the suits must have been dropped. I did find a judgment entry of Bailley against Taliaferro in the 1840s in a court log book in the courthouse safe in Prairie du Chien, Wisconsin.

Chapter 18

1. Pond, *Two Volunteer Missionaries Among the Dakotas*, 147. Mary Riggs, the missionary's wife, knew about Mary, and she wrote that she was surprised that it was "so exceedingly common for officers in the army to have two wives or more—but one, of course, legally so." That year, she wrote "[t]here were but 2 officers not known to have an Indian woman and Indian children." Riggs, *A Small Bit of Bread*, 43 (July 31, 1837).
2. Hansen attributes the end of the Kaposia mission to the war-like character of the tribe and its general hostility to missionaries. Hansen, *Old Fort Snelling, 1819–1858*, 155; Folwell, *A History of Minnesota*, 205.
3. The day before Baker died in St. Louis, he signed a power of attorney over to another St. Louis financial partner, Mackenzie, who assisted Sibley. All partnerships would cease with Baker's death anyway. Mackenzie wrote Sibley of the matter. "We apprize Mr. Dillon of what has occurred. Some conversation with Major Taliaferro when last here on his way east, he will be a candidate for the sutling at your place, in the belief he entertained that Mr. Baker could not live." Letter from MacKenzie to Sibley, Henry H. Sibley Papers (1815–1930), Minn HS.
4. He cited the amount now owing Chouteau and MacKenzie as "a trifle more than $21,000" (ibid.).
5. Folsom, *Fifty Years in the Northwest*, 755–56. The early winter stove incident must have taken place in the fall of 1839 because that is the first time that McPhail served as quartermaster. Corroborating that date, Lt. Whithall, also mentioned in the account, only arrived that year (Fort Snelling Post Returns for the year 1839, Records of AGO, RG 94, NA).
6. Folsom, *Fifty Years in the Northwest*, 755–56.
   This description is based on Lt. McPhail's portrait in the National Portrait Gallery, Washington, D.C., serial no. MD140880.
7. That other officer was identified as Lt. Whithall. Folsom, *Fifty Years in the Northwest*, 755–56.
8. Sutler accounts for 1840, January 9, 1840, Henry H. Sibley Papers, Minn HS, St. Paul, Minn.
9. He had also been arrested at his previous posting in a jurisdictional dispute with an officer over a man temporarily assigned to him as hospital steward. Dr. Emerson

had complained bitterly at the injustice of it all, and gotten something of a formal endorsement from the Surgeon General (Dr. John Emerson Personnel File, letter, January 6, 1836, NA).

10. During the winter of 1839–40 new ladies were added to the company: Mrs. Gear, the chaplain's wife; Mrs. Margaret Wright Lynde; and Mrs. Eliza Livingston Plympton. Identifying the presence of officer's ladies at a fort is often a matter of inference from the presence of the officers there themselves, and their wives' proclivities for joining their husbands on the frontier, purchases identified as particularly ladies' items, such as shoes or perfume from the sutler's store, or in some case, later genealogical sources attesting to the birth of an officer's child at a frontier location.

11. The quartermaster accused the doctor of forcing the other patient, a white man and a sergeant, to give up his sickbed to make room for the doctor's own slave (Dr. John Emerson Personnel File, letter, date not available, NA.

12. Eventually the surgeon general supported his position. "There is no special regulation in the medical dept. authorizing slaves, private servants of officers, to be admitted into a military hospital, nor is it customary to put slaves or black men into the same wards with the soldiers. Should a hospital, however, have several wards, and one of these be unoccupied by the soldiers, there can be no impropriety in giving a place to the servant of an officer who is sick and cannot be properly accommodated in the officer's quarters or the kitchen." In response to Lt. Wyse's possible complaint that Dr. Emerson was born in Ireland, the surgeon general denied any knowledge of the matter or the ability to investigate into army records to which he did not have access (October 4, 1841, letter of surgeon general addressed to both Dr. Emerson and Lt. Wyse at Ft. Lauderdale. Dr. John Emerson Personnel File, NA).

13. By the end of 1839, nine new cabins had been built south of the reserve, an area that would become the city of St. Paul. Some of these nine, including the house of Phelan and the murdered Hays, were built by the freedman Jim Thompson. Williams, *History of the City of St. Paul*, 98.

14. The act of March 3, 1807, entitled An Act to prevent settlements being made on lands ceded to the U.S. until authorized by law: "The interests of the Service requiring that the intruders on the land recently reserved for military purposes opposite to that post east of the Mississippi river be removed therefrom, the President of the U.S. directs that, when required by the Commanding Officer of the Post, you proceed there and remove them under the provisions of the law." The orders stated: "Should you be obliged unfortunately to use force in order to accomplish the object, you are authorized to call for such as you may deem necessary, on the commanding officer at Fort Snelling." Bloom, *Territorial Papers*, vol. 28, 53.

15. Saturday, November 16, 1839, meeting of citizens of the Cave district held at the house of Mr. Abram Perret. On motion, J. R. Clewett, Esq. was called to the chair. Bloom, *Territorial Papers*, vol. 28, 87.

16. Bloom, *Territorial Papers*, vol. 28, 103–4.

17. November 1, 1839, Brown Docket, re: Phalen for murder of Hays. Dr. Emerson testified that Hays had been murdered (Joseph R. Brown and Samuel J. Brown family papers, Minn HS). The murder of Hays by Phelan is recounted in Williams, *History of the City of St. Paul*, 90–93

18. Catlin, *Letters and Notes*, vol. 2, 137.

19. On November 26, 1839, the court-martial convened. Fort Snelling courts martial files, Old Army Files, JAG, RG 153, November 26, 1839, NA.

20. Court adjourned. Court reconvened November 29, 1839. Pennington court martial, Fort Snelling courts-martial files, Old Army Files, JAG, RG 153, November 29, 1839, NA.

21. Letter of E. P. Gaines. "Dissolve the court and rescind the order." April 6, 1840, Sentencing order of Court martial revoked. Fort Snelling courts-martial files, Old Army Files, JAG, RG 15, April 6, 1840, NA.

22. Ibid.

23. This letter of Sibley's requesting a gift for Emerson's little one is the only mention made of a child born to the Emersons in the early years of their marriage. Letter of Henry Sibley, December 21, 1839, in Blegen, "Unfinished Autobiography," 71.

24. January 29, 1839, from Washington, J. F. A. Sanford writes Ramsey Crooks, taking responsibility for the silverware for Dr. Emerson. Sanford-Chouteau letters on file with author. In early December 1838, Emerson bought a dozen corset laces from the sutler, together with a half yard muslin, probably used to make a discreet ladies' undergarment for Irene. This garment may have been for Irene's figure before the birth or postpartum. Also purchased was a bottle of wine (December 6, 1838, sutler's account). Henry H. Sibley Papers, Minn HS.

25. Letter of Henry Sibley, December 21, 1839, in Blegen, "Unfinished Autobiography," 71.

26. Since the gender is unspecified, the child may not yet have been born (ibid.).

27. Henriette Emerson, born five years later, was the only child of the Emersons known to survive her father's early death. Henriette is listed in her mother's obituary ("Death of Mrs. C. C. Chaffee," *Springfield Republican,* February 12, 1903).

28. Dr. Emerson's medical condition could also have affected the child's health. Dr. Emerson took large doses of a strong toxin, mercury, for his syphilitic condition, which could have caused a fatal birth defect in his child.

29. See Chapter 7, describing the death of Mrs. Storer's newborn and Eliza's baby son, Jarvis.

30. Fort Snelling post muster roles, NA.

31. Dr. Emerson letter to surgeon general, February 18, 1840 (Dr. John Emerson Personnel File, NA).

32. Sibley's daughter, born August 28, 1841, at Mendota was later named Helen Hastings. Gilman, *Divided Heart,* 76.

33. February 1840, Ft. Snelling Post Returns.

34. April 1840, Reduction in force: total 108, aggregate 114, down from 342 last month; 48 privates only; 1 drummer. No fifers. No buglers. Only company E left. 8 sick. 5 from company E. 1 left from company A. 2 left from company I. 6 privates under arrest. All from company E. Only J. Plympton, D.H. McPhail, and H. Little left. Lt. Whithall out on detail procuring Public Lumber. "J. Emerson With Leave: Asst surg. Post order of April 27 1840." Fort Snelling Post Returns for April 1840, NA.

35. 1840 Brown Docket, Sunday, February 16, *Prescott v. Foote.* Brown, Joseph R. and Samuel J. Family Papers, 1826–1956, Minn HS. The 1850 census for Grand Chute, Brown County, Wisconsin, lists "Edward Foote age 29 a Farmer."

36. Prescott, *The Recollections,* 170.

37. Ibid.

38. February 19, 1840 (Bloom, *Territorial Papers,* vol. 28, 87, n. 98).

39. Emerson letters to LeClaire (February 27, June 6, July 14, September 17, October 8, and November 4, 1839, March 12 and May 7, 1840), Antoine Le Claire Collection, Putnam Museum, Davenport, Iowa.

40. Now another of Emerson's old friends, former Lt. John Beach, was head of the land office in Dubuque. Emerson letter to Le Claire, March 12, 1840. Antoine Le Claire Papers, Putnam Museum, Davenport, Iowa.

41. J. Emerson leaves, according to Post Order No. 42, of April 27, 1840. Fort Snelling Post Returns for April 1840, NA.

42. The doctor may have temporarily accompanied the troops downstream on April 27 as well. Army orders usually required a doctor to accompany movements of troops and there were more troops departing than remaining at the post. He is noted in the April post returns as with leave by order of April 27, 1840, and no surgeon is marked on the end of the month post return. Fort Snelling Post Returns for 1840, NA.

43. Hansen, *Old Fort Snelling, 1819–1858,* 194–95; Williams, *History of the City of St. Paul,* 94–96; Folsom, *Fifty Years in the Northwest,* 27.

44. Sibley claimed the soldiers fell on the settlers without warning, and that they were rude, insulted the women, wantonly broke furniture, and fired upon and killed cattle. Deputy Brunson denied everything, maintaining that the soldiers were supervised and civil in the face of squatter resistance. Folsom noted that the eviction of these western Acadians never aroused the sympathies of the poet. Folsom, *Fifty Years in the Northwest*, 28. One of the best compilations of these events is found on a website: Ferguson, *The Eviction of the Squatters from Fort Snelling*, www.celticfringe.net/history/eviction.htm.

45. The heads of household of the principal families were Abraham Perry, Joseph Rondo, the Gervais Brothers, and Joseph Turpin. Ibid.

46. Dr. Emerson had returned from escorting the troops downstream. Ft. Snelling Post Returns, April, 1840.

      For the fur trade people owing the doctor, J. B. Faribault paid Dr. Emerson $27 for the account of Joseph Robinson, $25 for the account of Mrs. Bailley, and $15 for his own account, for a total of $67. $1. Charge to Joseph Robinson, a mulatto man, who had worked as a cook for Sibley previously, seems to be receiving treatment on Faribault's account. The others listed are Louis Saramme, Augustin Rock, Duncan Campbell Jr, P. Felix, A. Robertson for A. M Anderson, A. Faribault, D. Faribault, and O. Faribault; each had a small account with the doctor ranging from $1.50 to $25. The last entry on the New Hope books is an entry of August 1, to the amount of Emerson's account at Prairie du Chien for sundries. ["Paid men $10. And 4 yds Indian Rubber Cloth $6."] Altogether Emerson collected various amounts of money for a hefty total of $131.50. Sutler's account books and New Hope account books, Henry H. Sibley Papers, Minn HS.

47. Dr. Emerson's weather and temperature journals end on this date.

48. Fort Snelling Post Returns, NA, and Dr. Emerson's weather log, Minn HS; St. Martin, *One Hundred Eighty Years of Weather*.

49. The 1840 U.S. Census showed only 96 inhabitants at Fort Snelling. The only other black man remaining at the fort worked for Franklin Steele, the new sutler.

50. The Pond families occupied half the house; the Reverend Gavin and Mr. Denton and their families lived in other half. Pond, *Two Volunteer Missionaries Among the Dakotas*, 148.

51. These steamboats were listed in what appears to be Emerson's last entry in the surgeon's weather journal, May 27, 1840. Dr. John Emerson, Fort Snelling Weather Journal, Minnesota Historical Society microfilms collection, Records of the Weather Bureau, RG 27, NA; St. Martin, *One Hundred Eighty Years of Weather*.

52. Traveling north to St. Peter's on a pleasure cruise aboard the *Malta* that May was John F. A. Sanford and his sister Mrs. Bainbridge, among a traveling group of St. Louisians (Kennerly, *Persimmon Hill*, 103).

Chapter 19

1. One of the few African American pioneers who was able to make it settling in Illinois was Free Frank (Walker, *Free Frank*). The only employer taking on workers in the north woods were the lumbering companies, but lumber companies were hiring strong sturdy men, who for the most part lived in bunkhouses, not as families with wives and children.

2. The Second Seminole War (1835–42) resulted from white slaveholder resentment of the Seminoles' tendency to harbor runaway slaves and also from their independence. These were the same issues that had motivated the First Seminole War. The Seminoles also added to their fighting strength by recruiting slaves from plantations. A little over half of these black Seminoles were granted the freedom to be removed to Oklahoma alongside their defeated Indian comrades, but the rest were reenslaved (Howe, *What Hath God Wrought*, 516–17).

3. June 27, 1840, Dr. Emerson arrived at Cedar Keys, west Florida, with instructions to proceed that evening for Tampa Bay (Emerson Personnel File, June 30, 1840, NA).

4. Pay slips for January 1841 through March 1841, October 1841 through February 1842, and July 1842 through December 1842 all show "William" listed as a slave for whom Dr. John Emerson is receiving the servant allowance payment (SP Accts RG 217, E 516).

5. William is listed as a slave on Dr. Emerson's pay slip in Florida as of January 1841 and for several months thereafter (ibid.). There was little reason to incur the expense of bringing Dred to Florida only to send him back a month later (see, for example, Dibble, "Slave Rentals to the Military," 101–13, detailing rentals of slaves for military tasks and service as personal servants).

6. The phrase "the world and its family" is from Primm, *Lion of the Valley*, 142.

7. Delo, *Peddlers and Post Traders*, 34–35, 41.

8. "If a tenth part of the immense throng now pouring into this city stay, our population will be augmented several thousands this season" ("Immigration," *Missouri Republican*, March 28, 1840).

9. During the 1840s, the business district began a gradual westward expansion (Scharf, *History of St. Louis*, vol. 1, 157–58).

10. The city center ran along Main Street between Walnut Street and Washington Avenue. The Planter's House was built in 1841 (Scharf, *History of St. Louis*, vol. 2, 1442).

11. A report about St. Louis in a Philadelphia paper described the wonderful progress of the city in the last few years ("St. Louis," *Missouri Republican*, January 27, 1840, reprinted from the *Philadelphia Enquirer*).

12. See Chapter 12.

13. The "Henderson Gang," was sentenced to death for killing two countinghouse clerks and setting the building on fire. Constables procured their "confessions" by threatening them with the prospect of being burned alive by the people of St. Louis (Buchanan, *Black Life on the Mississippi*, 140–44).

14. Johnson, *Soul by Soul*, 122–23. The awful spectacle of the St. Louis Slave Auction took place for the last time in 1860 (Kargau, *St. Louis in Frueheren Jahren*, 142).

15. Johnson, *Soul by Soul*, 144–49; Blassingame, *Slave Testimony*, 503, 507–8.

16. Johnson, *Soul by Soul*, 119.

17. Ibid., 1; Blassingame, *Slave Testimony*, 508.

18. One recent book describing slave coffles as transport in detail is Deyle, *Carry Me Back: The Domestic Slave Trade in American Life* (New York: Oxford University Press, 2005).

19. Ehrlich, *They Have No Rights*, 12; Keckley, *Behind the Scenes*, 44–45.

20. Ehrlich, *They Have No Rights*, 12.

21. Slave traders included Corbin and Thompson on 6th between Pine and Chestnut, B. Lynch on Locust, and one establishment located at the corner of Elm and Fifth. There were several slave auction rooms on Main Street engaged in the public auctioning and the private sale of human beings: Patterson and Dogherty, No. 73 Main Street (*Missouri Republican*, January 16, 1840); Johnstone, Dreyer and Trowbridge, 68 Main Street (*Missouri Republican*, January 16, 1840; January 18, 1840; January 22, 1840; and April 3, 1840); and J. S. Pease and Co. on Main St. (Hurt, *Agriculture and Slavery in Missouri's Little Dixie*, 225).

    By 1844, C. Lewis, Agent, was advertising, "The highest prices in cash, will, at all times be paid for Negroes at No. 55 Olive street, two doors west of the Theater, between Third and Fourth Streets" (*Missouri Republican*, July 2, 1844; Primm, *Lion of the Valley*, 187).

22. William Walker's financial troubles appear to have been mixed up with Brant's position as quartermaster at Jefferson Barracks, because his name is prominently mentioned in Brant's court-martial proceedings (Joshua Brant's court martial, Old Army Records, JAG, RG 153, 1839–40, NA, reprinted Rep. No. 996, August 15, 1842).

23. "M'Affee" was so notorious that he was even mentioned by name in *A Child's Anti-Slavery Book* as a St. Louis slave trader (Thompson, "Mark and Hasty," in *The Child's Anti-Slavery Book*, 26).

24. In 1840, the U.S. Census estimated that there were 1,529 slaves and 531 free blacks out of a total population of 16,469 people in the city of St. Louis. There were 4,616 slaves in St. Louis County (United States Census Records, 1840, 88–90; Primm, *Lion of the Valley*, 186–87).

25. Wade, *Slavery in the Cities*, 79. In Washington, D.C., for instance, the majority of alley inhabitants were black. It was customary for slaveholders to house their slaves on their property in small alley houses (Borchert, *Alley Life in Washington*, 19–25).

26. Harris, "South of Haunted Dreams," in *Family Travel*, 280–82; Primm, *Lion of the Valley*, 187–88.

27. Mo. "Freedom" Stat. sec. 12 (1835); Cobb, *An Inquiry into the Law of Negro Slavery*, 67. "Typically all southern blacks were presumed to be slaves, subject to arbitrary 'seizures' of their 'persons'" (Amar, *The Bill of Rights*, 161).

28. Closer to the farm, on the southern bank of the Missouri, sat a very old French settlement called Owen's Station, which was later renamed Bridgeton (Scharf, *History of St. Louis*, vol. 2, 1895).

29. Patricia Morton reports that: "many urban slave women lived in households where they were expected to perform a vast variety of domestic chores. Certainly, in the middle-class households of New Orleans, slave women performed all of the chores necessary for the operation of the household. They cleaned, cooked, nursed, washed, sewed, marketed, and gardened. It appears that slaveholders did as little of the work as possible" (Morton, *Discovering the Women in Slavery*, 188). St. Louis women fashioned themselves, both in dress and manners, like the French culture-influenced, women of New Orleans.

    Moreover, wealthy white women certainly did not do heavy field work. Even when poor women worked in the field, "it was considered temporary, irregular, or extraordinary" (White, *Ar'n't I a Woman?* 120).

30. An Act for the Gradual Abolition of Slavery, March 1, 1780, Laws of the Commonwealth of Pennsylvania, cited in Finkelman, *An Imperfect Union*, 242–43.

31. George Bonga, a prominent Minnesota trader, "recognized only two kinds of people, Indians and white men, and he frequently spoke of himself and a white trader, John Banfil, as the first whites who came to the fur country of Minnesota." People who knew Bonga described him as one of the blackest men they had ever seen (Savage, *Blacks in the West*, 70).

32. *Missouri Republican*, June 30, 1841.

33. Specifically, whites viewed blacks as motivated only by base desires and fleeting urges, especially sex, so much so that Thomas Jefferson referred to them as "a libidinal race" (Lyons, *Sex among the Rabble*, 230).

34. Gross, *Double Character*, 87.

35. Indeed, the *Missouri Republican* later began imitating what they assumed was black speech; see notes 91–92, chapter 30.

36. Mo. "Abolition" Stat. sec. 1 (1837) in Missouri Laws (1836) printed in (1840); ABOLITION. *AN ACT to prohibit the publication, circulation or promulgation of the abolition doctrines*. Feb. 1, 1837.

37. Letter to the editor, George K. Budd, *Missouri Republican*, March 16, 1840, and March 25, 1840. In describing the defeat of a candidate because of the "mad-dog hue-and-cry" of having been accused of being an abolitionist, Darby writes: "At that time, no man in this then community of slave-holders who was suspected of being an Abolitionist could possibly be elected by the popular vote" (Darby, *Personal Recollections of Many Prominent People*, 289).

38. The most detailed description of the Sanford farm comes from its sale advertisement in the local newspaper at the time of Alexander Sanford's death (*Missouri Republican*, January 1, 1849).

39. Deed between Leanna Quarles and John F. A. Sanford, July 14, 1837 (B2/178, St. Louis Registry of Deeds, St. Louis Registrar's office, St. Louis, Mo. Wetmore, *Gazetteer of the State of Missouri*, 178).

In his letter to John Darby, July 31, 1848, John F. A. Sanford details his efforts in bringing his father to Missouri in 1834, first setting him up in business with Berthold, a cousin of the Chouteaus, and then buying him the farm. Sanford-Chouteau letter file.

40. Alexander Sanford's trade and location Winchester, Virginia, were mentioned in Irene Sanford Emerson Chaffee's obituary ("Death of Mrs. C. C. Chaffee," *Springfield Republican,* February 12, 1903).

41. John F. A. Sanford had five younger sisters and one brother, Joseph Perry Sanford, who attended the Naval Academy (letter of John F. A. Sanford to Darby, July 31, 1848, Sanford-Chouteau letter file).

42. The 1840 U.S. census lists Alexander Sanford in St. Ferdinand Township, Town of Florissant. His household comprises "3 white males 30–39; 1 white male 60–69; 1 white female 10–15; 1 white female 40–49; and 5 slaves: 2 females 10–24; 1 male 24–36; 2 males 10–24." All five slaves are said to be employed in agriculture. According to a letter of John F. A. Sanford to John Darby regarding the estate of Alexander Sanford, four of the slaves, three men and one woman, were purchased by Alexander Sanford with John F. A. Sanford's money, and the other slave woman was claimed by Alexander Sanford's new wife (letter of Sanford to John Darby, July 31, 1848, Sanford-Chouteau letter file).

43. She appears in the Springfield, Massachusetts, 1850 census as "Mary Sanford" age 58, living in the household of Henrietta Clark, one of the Sanford sisters.

44. A letter from John F. A. Sanford to John Darby refers to his "stepmother" (July 31, 1848). Sanford-Chouteau letter file. There is even more question about the identity of the "1 white female, 10–15." This person might have been Virginia Sanford, the youngest of the sisters, born 1825 in Maryland. Mrs. Irene Emerson, born in 1815, would have been 25. The three white males are also a mystery. Youngest son, Joseph P. Sanford, had left for the Naval Academy in 1832.

45. J. F. A. Sanford, letter to Darby, referring to his stepmother (July 31, 1848). Sanford-Chouteau Letter file.

46. 1840 U.S. Census entry for Alexander Sanford, St. Ferdinand Township, St. Louis County, Missouri.

47. Letter from John F. A. Sanford to John Darby (July 31, 1848). Sanford-Chouteau letter file.

48. Advertisement describing the farm (*Missouri Republican*, January 1, 1849).

49. Missouri slave Mattie wrote that her mother had to keep her brother in a box so he would not interfere with her work (Jackson, *The Story of Mattie J. Jackson,* 9).

50. The Sanfords may have had an overseer. The 1840 Census lists a white man younger than Alexander Sanford in the household and lists a poorer family immediately after the entry of Sanford's household.

51. Brown, *From Fugitive Slave to Free Man,* 27–28.

52. Ibid.

53. LT Journals, July 22, 1838.

54. Brown, *From Fugitive Slave to Free Man,* 28.

55. Wetmore, *Gazetteer of the State of Missouri,* 178.

56. Ibid.

57. It was a common practice for slaves to sleep in a heap of rags (Johnson, *Antebellum North Carolina,* 525).

Chapter 20

1. For visiting as a significant social activity for upper class antebellum women, see Kennedy, *Braided Relations, Entwined Lives,* 163–66. The protocol of visiting ladies and paying visits upon ladies is reported in E.A. Hitchcock Journal, April 26, 1844. John F. A. Sanford had just invited his sister Mary Bainbridge along

with the prominent St. Louisians touring the upper Mississippi (Kennerly, *Persimmon Hill*, 103–4). William Clark's letters describe how John F. A. Sanford had brought his sister Henrietta to town and made the acquaintances that resulted in her marriage to an army officer (see letters of William Clark, William Clark Collection, Mo HS).

2. John F. A. Sanford's acquaintance included practically everyone of any importance in town. His old friend D. D. Mitchell had married Martha Eliza Berry, daughter of Maj. James Berry, in the year Mrs. Emerson resettled in St. Louis.

3. Letter of J. F. A. Sanford to Pierre Chouteau Jr. concerning Irene's marriage, February 5, 1838 (Sanford-Chouteau letter file, on file with author).

4. Brown, *From Fugitive Slave to Free Man*, 67 (describing how Brown had been purchased to be a driver for a St. Louis lady who always kept her servants very well dressed).

5. Scharf, *History of St. Louis*, vol. 1, 132. Missouri and the surrounding territories had previously been French, then Spanish colonies before France ceded it to the United States. That St. Louis was a bustling port was a testament to its explosive growth. A 1770 Spanish census recorded only 51 people in the township (Frazier, *Runaway and Freed Missouri Slaves*, 42).

6. Foley and Rice, *The First Chouteaus*, 200.

7. Kargan, *The German Element in St. Louis*, 118.

8. Christian, *Before Lewis and Clark*, 5.

9. In her correspondence about family matters she referred to him often: "Ben had measles but is now better" (letter of Julie Chouteau, June 2, 1841, in Chouteau Family Papers, Mo HS).

10. Hafen and Carter, *Mountain Men and Fur Traders of the Far West*, 24.

11. Sanford wrote to his brother-in-law Charles when he was away at school (ibid., 95).

12. For work on the Chouteaus, see LeCompt, "Pierre Chouteau, Junior,"; Chouteau Family Papers, Mo HS, St. Louis; *The Book of St. Louisans*; Christian, *Before Lewis and Clark*; Finkelburg, *Under Three Flags*; Foley and Rice, *The First Chouteaus*; Scharf, *History of Saint Louis*, vols. 1 and 2.

13. The Chouteaus did not appear to run for elected office.

14. Scharf, *History of St. Louis*, vol. 1, 183–84.

15. The 1860 census lists him as worth more than $450,000 (Scharf, *History of St. Louis*, vol. 1, 183–84).

16. Hafen and Carter, *Mountain Men*, 32.

17. The Chouteaus also supported the travel of J. J. Audubon in 1843 (Christian, *Before Lewis and Clark*, 387–88).

18. Indian rendezvous were fabled as giving the Indians generous amounts of liquor. Sibley was once asked by a Chouteau clerk if he could find a reliable man to smuggle alcohol in from Canada to the Missouri River because the Blackfeet would not sign with the American Fur Company without liquor, which was being embargoed in U.S. waters. Letter to H. H. Sibley on behalf of Chouteau and Co., H. H. Sibley papers, Minn HS.

19. D. D. Mitchell, from the St. Louis office of the Indian Agency was with them. Chouteau and Sanford invited the Indian agency representative. D. D. Mitchell was an old friend of Sanford's. Also in attendance were the company's agents from Rock Island, who were also Dr. Emerson's old friends, who looked after his Iowa property claims in his absence (Berthrong, "John Beach and the Removal of the Sauk and Fox," 319).

20. Six slaves served at the large, comfortable home and another dozen worked at the country place where Pierre's father lived. There were no free colored people in the Chouteau household (U.S. Census, 1840 and 1850, St. Louis).

21. They rarely brought new slaves. His father's household listed 13 slaves and two free black men to serve the five principal Chouteau family members who lived there. Julie bought slave women from time to time (sales receipts of Julia Chouteau Maffitt. February 12, and October 13, 1848), Chouteau Family Papers, Mo HS,

St. Louis. Sanford bought Virginia slaves, who were skilled cooks when he returned east (September 7, 1837, St. Louis, letter from Pratt, Chouteau. Sanford-Chouteau letter file, on file with author, also listed in Nute, *Calendar,* entry 3098). Cabanne requested Sanford to purchase three slaves for him, one cook and two housemaids. Ibid.

22. Joseph Rolette letter to Pierre Chouteau refusing slave offered for sale to him by Chouteau (letter on file with author), date not available, Illinois Territorial papers.

23. Only Pierre Jr.'s brother, Paul Liguest Chouteau, appears to have been willing to emancipate his slaves on occasion. (Free Negro Bonds of the City of St. Louis, Slavery Collection, Mo HS, St. Louis.).

24. See, for example, *Missouri Republican,* December 4, 1853; January 17, 1854.

25. *Chouteau v. Marguerite,* 12 Pete 507 (Missouri 1838); *Chouteau v. Pierre,* 9 Mo. 3 (1845).

26. In another suit, a Chouteau relation, cousin Gabriel, pursued the chase when a man slave sued for his freedom. The man's mother, Rose, was born in Montreal and taken from there to Prairie du Chien, in the Northwest Territory of the United States before coming to St. Louis. Chouteau's lawyers argued that at the time Rose resided there, before 1789, the Northwest Ordinance was not yet in effect, the land was still in British hands, so Rose never resided in a free state, and hence, her son could not be free (*Chouteau v. Pierre,* 9 Mo. 3 [1845]).

27. *Chouteau v. Marguerite,* 12 Pete 507 (1838).

28. The Court could not grant his petition for review for failure to state a federal claim (*Lagrange v. Chouteau,* 29 U.S. 287, 290 [1830]).

29. "Famous Dred Scott Case: Mrs. Chaffee, owner of old slave, still living in Springfield," *New York Times,* December 22, 1895.

30. The only son, Charles, was sent to New York to school at the recommendation of an American Fur Company major partner, Ramsey Crooks, whose own children attended there. He later took over his father's interests in one specific firm in St. Louis.

31. Letter of Sanford to Darby (July 31, 1848.).Sanford-Chouteau letter file, on file with author.

32. 172 Market Street, St. Louis City Directory (1860) Mo HS.

33. Portrait of Pierre Chouteau Jr. (Foley and Rice, *The First Chouteaus,* 46). See also "The Old Chouteau Mansion," engraving in Richard Edwards and M. Hopewell, *Edward's Great West and Her Commercial Metropolis, Embracing a General View of the West, and a Complete History of St. Louis* (St. Louis, MO: Edwards's Monthly, 1860).

34. Miss Berry, her sister Mrs. Coxe, Sanford, and his sister Mrs. Mary Bainbridge are listed as passengers on a pleasure-going steamboat trip on the *Malta* in 1840 (James Kennerly diary, Kennerly family papers, Mo HS).

35. The letters of Ann Carr Lane, daughter of Dr. William Carr Lane, refer to Mrs. Emerson and her sister, Henrietta Clark, from time to time. See, generally, Letter from Anne Lane, New Orleans, to Sarah Glasgow, St. Louis, Mar 2, 1844. Letter from Anne Lane, New Orleans to Sarah Glasgow, St. Louis, February 29, 1844, Letter from Anne Lane, Allegheny, to Sarah Glasgow, St. Louis, September 21, 1847 *The Lane Collection, William Carr Lane.* Papers and Collections, Mo HS.

Chapter 21

1. 1840 Census entry of Alexander Sanford in the St. Louis County.

2. Martin, *Divided Mastery,* 18–20. See also Trexler, *Slavery in Missouri,* 28.

3. "Famous Dred Scott Case: Mrs. Chaffee, owner of old slave, still living in Springfield," *New York Times,* December 22, 1895.

4. Reflecting on Dred Scott personally, Kennerly expressed the view that he had been sold to Dr. Emerson initially as a body servant because it was the only work for which he was fit (Kennerly, *Persimmon Hill,* 237).

5. *Frank Leslie's Illustrated Newspaper,* June 27, 1857.

6. Brown, *From Fugitive Slave to Free Man,* 55–56; Kirsten E. Wood, *Masterful Women,* 40.

7. "Some were 'self-hired' slaves, sent out to live on their own and find their own work, who turned over wages to their owners" (Martin, *Divided Mastery,* 1–2).

8. Ibid.

9. Trexler, *Slavery in Missouri,* 28–35 (describing slave hiring practices in Missouri).
  For a person contemplating independence, the experience of being auctioned often triggered action, and the Scotts didn't file suit for several years. Many slaves attempted to leave their new masters shortly after sale (Johnson, *Soul by Soul,* 194–95).

10. Mrs. Emerson arranged for Col. Sanford to deliver Dred and Harriet to Adeline Russell to work for them (deposition of Adeline Russell, Scott v. Emerson, No. 1 [Mo. Cir. Ct. 1847], available at http://library.wustl.edu/vlib/dredscott/transcripts/scott_49.html).

11. Brown, *From Fugitive Slave to Free Man,* 31–33.

12. See, e.g., Delaney, "From Darkness Cometh the Light," 21–22.

13. Consider, for example, Peter Blow, who originally owned Dred Scott along with a number of other slaves and brought him from Virginia to Alabama, then ultimately to St. Louis to be sold.

14. Primm, *Lion of the Valley,* 185–86, 190. This was considered part of the solution to the resolution of the Virginia debate over abolishing slavery in 1832. The solution was to send surplus slaves west.

15. There were "two foundries,...; 20 cabinet and chair factories; 3 factories making lead-pipe;...; 11 coopers and 9 hatters; 6 grist-mills, 6 breweries;...a sugar-refinery; a chemical and fancy-soap manufactory; a pottery and stoneware manufactory" (Scharf, *History of St. Louis,* vol. 1, 00). There were several newspapers, but no library. The city had three markets, a workhouse, two colleges—one Catholic, one Episcopal—and a female seminary under the charge of the nuns. There were 12 churches including two African churches. Ibid.

16. Scharf, *History of St. Louis,* vol. 1, 193.

17. Trexler, *Slavery in Missouri,* 35–37; Wade, *Urban Frontier,* 126–27, 221–23; Buchanan, *Black Life on the Mississippi,* 22–23. The Reverend Meachum had earned the money for his freedom this way and he preached the practice. Stevens, *History of the Central Baptist Church,* 7.

18. Mo. "Slaves" Stat., Art. 1, section 7 (1835); An Act Concerning Slaves (March 19th, 1835), *Laws of Missouri* (1836). Trexler, *Slavery in Missouri,* 35–37.

19. A local editor in 1824 called the custom "one principal source of the irregularity and crimes of slaves in this place" (Trexler, *Slavery in Missouri,* 36). Another writer agreed, contending that "the prime source" of their "bad habits is the liberty,...of hiring themselves out." "While they remain *slaves,*" he counseled, "they must, for their own good, as well as for the public benefit, be held under very rigid constraint" (Wade, *Slavery in the City,* 50). Nine years later, the city, finding that law unequal to the task, added its own ordinance because, as the *Missouri Republican* put it, "the evil is a very serious one" (Wade, *Urban Frontier,* 222–23).

20. "Mrs. Le Rue, on breaking up housekeeping, allowed Hasty to hire her time for two dollars a week, on condition that at the end of each month the required sum was to be forthcoming, and in the event of failure, the revocation of the permission was to be the inevitable consequence" (Thompson, "Mark and Hasty," in *The Child's Anti-Slavery Book,* 36).

21. Strasser, *Never Done,* 104–11.

22. "A free colored woman named Priscilla Mason was arrested and put in the Calaboose yesterday, charged with having stolen sundry articles of clothing" (*Missouri Republican,* January 13, 1847); Buchanan, *Black Life on the Mississippi,* 29 (describing the New Orleans calaboose as the destination for steamboat slaves guilty of local misdemeanors and for free blacks arrested by levee police).

23. Probate of Silver Crevassall, 1841. PCDP.

24. A St. Louis city ordinance in 1839 created "deputy marshal" officers with the power to seize "all night-walkers, malefactors, rogues, vagabonds, and all disorderly persons" (Scharf, *History of St. Louis,* vol. 1, 738).

25. Trexler, *Slavery in Missouri,* 27 (describing Sabbath Law).

26. Kennedy's St. Louis Directory (1860).

27. Clamorgan, *The Colored Aristocracy of St. Louis,* 60; *Missouri Republican,* August 22, 1845 (describing a fight at a "negro ball").

28. Buchanan, *Black Life on the Mississippi,* 42–43, 76.

29. "There were at that time seven or eight 'nigger pens,' as they were called, where negroes were locked up and held for sale" (Blassingame, *Slave Testimony,* 503).

30. Scharf, *History of St. Louis,* vol. 1, 782.

31. Ibid. Gabriel Chouteau owned the pond and millstream.

32. Article VI, Woodmaster's code, sec. 5 and 13. No one was allowed to stop driftwood in the Mississippi between North Market and Hazel St. (Sec. 12 of Article V, Harbor Dept. April 1, 1850). Krum, St. Louis Ordinances.

33. The practice was considered some kind of racket (*Missouri Republican,* November 12, 1849).

34. Delaney, "From the Darkness Cometh the Light," 24–26.

35. There are only five or six washerwomen in the 1840 city directory who are not identified as "colored," and even among this small number, some women, like Julia Essex, who did not have the designation "colored" beside their name, in fact were recognized as people of color, as evidenced by their registering for a "free negro license." Julia Essex, washerwoman, registered for a license in May 1842 (Free Negro Bonds, Mo HS).

36. The 1840 St. Louis City Directory lists fewer than 100 washerwomen. Of this group, the majority are identified as "colored". St. Louis City Directories Collection, Mo HS.

37. Those washerwomen who established their freedom by suit can best be identified through the St. Louis Free Negro Bonds. They include Winny, bond 1842, 60 years old; Ramsey, Delphine, bond 1835; Aspisa, Bond 1842; Polly Wash, bond 1843; Turner, Lucy A., bond 1846; Levina Titus, bond 1835; Charlotte Whitesides, bond 1843; Matilda, bond 1842; Alsey, bond 1843; Celeste, bond 1842; Judy LeCompte, bond 1835 (Free Negro Bonds, Slavery Collection, Mo HS, St. Louis). There are doubtless a dozen others, but making one-to-one identifications is difficult because the Milly and the Matilda who sued and won their freedom are likely among the several women listed by that first name. Winny's daughters' names are also represented in the first names of several washerwomen in the list, but identifying them specifically is more difficult to do.

38. Winny Free Negro Bond 60 years old 1842 (Winny v. Whitesides, 1 Mo. 472 [Mo. 1824]); Winny v. Whitesides, no. 190 [1821], CCHRP). The 1840 city directory (St. Louis City Directories, Mo HS, St. Louis) lists "Minney Whitesides" as a colored washerwoman living at the corner of 2nd and Hazel Street. This inscription may have been a error in spelling but the woman was surely one of Winny's daughters who sued for freedom with their mother, if not Winny herself.

39. Jenny v. Robert Musick, no. 194, Nancy v. Isaac Voteau, no. 193, Lydia v. John Butler, no. 192, Sarah v. Michael Hatton, no. 191, Hannah v. Phebe Whitesides, no. 197, Malinda v. Phebe Whitesides, no. 198. Winny's sons Jerry and Daniel won their freedom by lawsuit as well, no. 195 and 196, CCHRP.

40. James Kennerly Diary for May 26, 1840, Kennerly Family Papers, Mo HS.

41. Thomas and Ronnefeldt, *People of the First Man,* 8. "Mckenzie, Sanford, and Mitchell stayed behind at the fort, the prince commenting wryly in his journal that "they seemed yet unwilling for a separation from their Indian beauties."

42. Delaney, "From the Darkness Cometh the Light," 39–49.

43. This practice was probably easier because many slaves received only first names (Sweet, *Bodies Politic,* 69; Blassingame, *Slave Testimony,* 373–74, 485, 581, 585, 639).

44. Charlotte Taylor Blow Charless's letters to her grandchildren outline the family history, noting the Etheldred name, though giving no mention of Dred Scott or the lawsuit (Charless, *A Biographical Sketch of the Life and Character of Joseph Charless*).

45. In my article with Sandhya Subramanian, we reproduced the page of the Wisconsin territorial census to allow the readers to consider whether this entry was as it seems to be written, "Dred Scott" (VanderVelde and Subramanian, "Mrs. Dred Scott," 1122). Upon further investigation, I must say that I am less sure, since I cannot account for the many individuals listed in the household, nor can I identify the names listed near the name "Dred Scott" as persons who could be expected to be listed near where he resided.

46. Pay slip for Joseph Plympton at Fort Snelling listing "Har. Dread" and sometimes "H. Dread" as his household servant, November 1837 to February 1838. Pay slip for S. Whitehorne identifies "H. Etheldred" as his servant for November 1837 (SP Accts, RG 217, E 516).

47. Clerk's office records: Suit filed November 1839. Polly Wash sued to recover her wages on September 22, 1843. Free negro license issued to Polly Wash, September 1843 (Free Negro Bonds, Slavery Collection, Mo HS).

48. Brown, *From Fugitive Slave to Free Man*, 67–68 (describing his white mistress's attempt to interest him first in one woman slave and then in another, a move that he regarded as a trap by her to keep him from attempting escape).

49. Delaney, "From the Darkness Cometh the Light," 14.

50. Ibid., 22–23

51. The principle of matrilinearity provided that the status of the child followed the status of the mother. Stroud, *A Sketch of the Laws Relating to Slavery*, 3.

52. Delancy, "From the Darkness Cometh the Light," 22–23.

53. Ibid., 41–42. Not surprisingly, the story Lucy told of her mother in the slave community differed slightly from the legal record later told in the courts, but both Lucy and the legal record told stories for slightly different purposes, for moral and legal claims, on the state of freedom. The truth lay in between.

Chapter 22

1. For a brief description of the Seminole War, see note 00, ch. 00.

2. Letter from "St. Augustine," reprinted in *Missouri Republican,* January 19, 1841.

3. Brown, *From Fugitive Slave to Free Man*, 34.

4. Emerson orders papers dated February 28, 1842, St. Louis. Letter of Dr. Emerson, March 23, 1842, Fort Pickens, reporting for duty (Dr. John Emerson Personnel File, NA).

5. One of the doctor's letters to headquarters indicates that if he was to be reassigned to the jungle, he wished to be informed in order to make arrangements to make *his family* comfortable (Dr. John Emerson, letter from Fort Pickens, March 23, 1842; Emerson Personnel File, NA).

6. Letter of Dr. Emerson, April 7, 1842, Emerson Personnel File, NA.

7. Letter of Dr. Emerson, Fort Pickens, May 18, 1842, Emerson Personnel File, NA.

8. The other surgeon was Dr. Satterlee.

9. Dr. Emerson protested the assignment because two assistant surgeons who were his juniors, were ordered to report to Washington (letter of Dr. Emerson, Cedar Key, Eastern Florida, August 18, 1842, in Emerson Personnel File, NA).

10. The Second Seminole War continued until the middle of August, 1842.

11. The order in the *Army and Navy Chronicle* listed 13 as disbanded as of the same date, September 23, 1842.

12. Mrs. Emerson's recollections published in the *New York Times* in December 22, 1895, are not at all corroborated by Emerson's personnel file. She omits entirely their return to Fort Snelling in 1838 and Dr. Emerson's service in Florida. The account, which may have been a newspaperman's attempt to mix her account with the published facts of the opinion, suggest that Dr. Emerson left the service from Fort Snelling in 1838. To this she appears to add a fabrication that burnishes her first

husband's reputation. "In 1838 there was a reduction in the number of staff officers in the army, and those at Fort Snelling drawing lots to see who would remain in the service, Dr. Emerson got a blank and was compelled to leave" (ibid.).

13. He bought the Manchester Road property from one of the Chouteau's relatives, Gabriel Paul (March 8, 1849, St. Louis Registry of Deeds, St. Louis Registrar of Deeds, St. Louis, Mo.).

14. John Emerson Probate Missouri, 1844 PCDP; John Emerson Probate Iowa, April 1, 1844, Scott County, Iowa.

15. Brown, *From Fugitive Slave to Free Man*, 67 (describing being a driver for his owners and the importance to them of dressing their servants well).

16. Mark Twain quoted in Shapiro and Epstein, *The Yale Book of Quotations*, 782.

17. Dr. William Carr Lane described Dr. Emerson as an old friend, saying "a great intimacy has subsisted between some of the members of his wife's family and my own family" (William Lane Carr, letter November 27, 1842; see also D. D. Mitchell letter of December 3, 1842, and Silas Reed letter of November 28, 1842, all in Emerson Personnel File, NA).

18. Dr. Emerson's personnel file contains no letters from either Captain Henry Bainbridge or John B. Clarke on Emerson's behalf (Emerson's Personnel File, NA).

19. Letter from Dr. Emerson, St. Louis, to Secretary of War Spencer, December 8, 1842, St. Louis. Emerson forwarded a letter of the surveyor general (E. T. Langham) written on his behalf (Emerson to Spencer, December 8, 1842, in Emerson Personnel File, NA).

20. Letter of Dr. Emerson, St. Louis, December 14, 1842. Dr. John Emerson Personnel File, NA.

21. Emerson letter, February 8, 1843, St. Louis (Emerson Personnel File, NA).

22. Several slave narratives give accounts of receiving mistreatment when their masters experienced bad luck.

23. Outwardly, the doctor justified and defended his actions to his superiors, whom he could not seem to reach. Inwardly, the Emersons may have vented their frustration against the person near them who embodied the cause of their distress.

24. February 8, 1843, St. Louis, Emerson letter (Emerson Personnel File, NA).

25. "Laid it before my friend Maj. A. D. Stuart paymaster, who advised me to say that in case I should be reappointed I wish to demand a court of inquiry" (letter of Dr. Emerson, March 27, 1843, in Emerson Personnel File, NA).

26. In that case, the owner had a slave, Rachael, purchased for him in St. Louis; he brought Rachael with him to Fort Snelling to serve him while he was an army officer stationed there (*Rachael v. Walker*, 4 Mo. 350, 350–51 (Mo. 1836)).

27. Some buyers even rescinded contracts for slaves once they learned they had lived in the North. "Being informed that the Negro woman and children bid off by me at the Court House on Monday last claim that they are free, and that a suit has been instituted for the purpose of obtaining their freedom, I have to inform you that I decline to pay for, or receive them, because at the time of sale I understood that there was no dispute regarding the title to them as slaves" (letter signed K[enneth]. Mackenzie, St. Louis, to Gabriel S. Chouteau, May 3, 1843, Slaves and Slavery Collection, 1772–1950, Mo HS Archives).

28. For example, "Mariah Ritty, at ten or eleven years old, may have been hired out for food and clothing" (Larson, *Bound for the Promised Land*, 18).

29. "Dr. John Emerson offers his professional services to the citizens of Davenport and surrounding country" (*The Davenport Gazette*, May 4, 1843, Davenport, Iowa).

30. From March 1843 through March 1844, Dred is listed as serving Capt. Henry Bainbridge at Jefferson Barracks (Henry Bainbridge pay slip, SP Accts, RG 217, E 516). Harriet's presence there is inferred from her having given birth to Lizzie at Jefferson Barracks and Mrs. Russell's testimony that the Scotts were formerly in Capt. Bainbridge's service.

31. Letter of R. S. Jones explaining why Captain Clarke should be passed over for promotion (*A Compilation of the Messages and Papers of the Presidents*, 420). The

1850 census indicates that her son, Alexander S. Clarke, was born in Missouri that year. This is corroborated in Alexander S. Clarke's military biography in Cullum, *Biographical Register of the Officers.*

32. Letter from Anne Lane, New Orleans, to Sarah Glasgow, St. Louis, February 29, 1844, Mo HS. In Capt. Clarke's service was a different slave, Mary, who may have been attending to Mrs. Clarke and his family.. SP Accts, RG 217, E 516, Captain John B. Clarke, Sept 1842–March 1843, NA.

Chapter 23

1. Captain and Mrs. Bainbridge are first noted as arriving in Florida in E. A. Hitchcock's journal entry for February 19, 1843. E.A. Hitchcock Journal, in the William A. Croffut Papers, Manuscript Division, 813E, Library of Congress.

2. E. A. Hitchcock Journal (March 4, 1843), in the William A. Croffut Papers, Manuscript Division, 813E, Library of Congress. "Gov'r Call has sent me a very handsome letter of invitation to a party to be given by him on the 7th...in honor of the success of the late expedition....He directed the letter to me requesting me to invite the "gallant officers" who were with me and all others on this station."

3. More recently, the Bainbridges had been in Ft. Stansbury, New York, where Bainbridge had had the plum assignment of recruiting duty. Cullum, *Biographical Register of the Officers*, 273.

4. Dred is listed as their servant for the month of August and again for December 1843. "ELDRED" is listed in the pay records as the servant to Henry Bainbridge at Jefferson Barracks in February 1844 (SP Accts, RG 217, E 516).

   Dred's affidavit, Dred Scott Case files, April 1846, says that he was left at Jefferson Barracks instead of accompanying Emerson to Florida and that he was "left in the charge of one Capt. Bainbridge, to whom said Emerson hired petitioner."

   Harriet's affidavit says the following: "That afterwards said Emerson was ordered to Fort Jesup in Louisiana, and having married then, he had petitioner removed to that post from Fort Snelling. After remaining at Fort Jesup about six months, the said Emerson went back to Fort Snelling on the St. Peters River, in Iowa Territory and took petitioner with him, where she remained with him as a servant about a year longer, and from thence was brought to St. Louis County aforesaid where he left her in charge of his wife, while he proceeded to Florida" (Dred Scott v. Emerson case file).

5. Keckley, *Behind the Scenes*, 19–20, 30–31; see, generally, Jacobs, *Incidents in the Life of a Slave Girl.*

6. E. A. Hitchcock journal describing Bainbridge (August 5, 1845), William A. Croffut Papers, Manuscript Division, 813E, Library of Congress.

7. *St. Louis News*, April 8, 1857.

8. E. A. Hitchcock journal describing Mrs. Bainbridge (March 30, 1843), William A. Croffut Papers, Manuscript Division, 813E, Library of Congress.

9. More good fortune for the socially astute Mary Bainbridge. Stephen Kearney, the commander Western Division, his wife, and their many children occupied a grand home. The Sanford sisters knew Mrs. Kearney as a longtime girlhood friend, again through their brother. Mrs. Kearney had been William Clark's stepdaughter. William Clark's journal details Ms. Bullit, who married Kearney, spending time with Henrietta Sanford Clarke at his home (William Clark diary, William Clark Papers, Mo HS).

10. E. A. Hitchcock journal (March 30, 1843), William A. Croffut Papers, Manuscript Division, 813E, Library of Congress. In describing one party, Hitchcock stated that it was his office to attend upon the Florida Governor's daughter. "I assigned the Governor to the duty of escorting Mrs. Bainbridge, one of our cleverest married ladies." Hitchcock also mentions her en route to St. Louis on April 6, 1843 and April

12, 1843. "We have had merry dinners every day...The ladies even, Mrs. Bainbridge and Mrs. Henry being at table at most of the meals."

11. Ibid.

12. "Famous Dred Scott Case: Mrs. Chaffee, owner of old slave, still living in Springfield," *New York Times*, December 22, 1895.

13. I cannot make these claims conclusively because I have not checked every one of the thousands of pay slips for the three-year period, but I have checked several hundred of them and the pattern bears out (SP Accts, RG 217, E 516).

    By custom, junior officers were most likely to share the services of servants. At Jefferson Barracks, several junior officers shared the services of Fielding, Manuel, and Willis. (SP Accts, RG 217, E 516).

14. "Dread" or "Eldred" was the name exclusively to be found on Capt. Bainbridge's pay slip (SP Accts, RG 217, E 516).

15. Other Third Infantry captains stationed at Jefferson Barracks at the time were Otis Wheeler, John W. Cotton, and Henry Swartout.

16. This included his West Point classmate, Capt. Otis Wheeler, who was something of an alcoholic, Capt. John W. Cotton, Capt. J. Van Horne, and Capt. Henry Swartwout, who had a young family. Capt. Bainbridge commanded Company F of the Third Infantry with the assistance of his first and second lieutenants, Joseph Eaton and D. C. Buell. He was under the command of Maj. William Lear and Lt. Col. Ethan A. Hitchcock. Maj. Lear had as his men slaves John and Columbus. Hitchcock had his longtime slaves: Little John, Wiley or Miles (SP Accts, RG 217, E 515).

17. One of the slave narratives describes a similar curtailment of slave children kept in the kitchen (Jackson, *The Story of Mattie J. Jackson*, 9).

18. King, *The True Ulysses S. Grant*, 75. "The barracks were a famous resort for the beaux and belles of the neighborhood. Music and dancing, or riding and driving parties, filled up the leisure hours. Drills and duties except the daily dress parade were usually completed in the morning" (ibid.).

19. The former quartermaster had arranged for the purchase of the slave Rachael, just as he routinely provisioned the western forts with horses; afterward, this was where Rachael and others were sent to be sold. Although buying and selling slaves was not the quartermaster's official function, it was a favor to the officers (see, e.g., Rachael v. Walker, 4 Mo. 350, 350–51 [Mo. 1836]).

20. Jefferson Barracks Heritage Foundation, *Jefferson Barracks Heritage History*, www.jeffersonbarracks.org/JB_hist.html.

21. U. S. Grant, newly assigned to Jefferson Barracks during that period, wrote: "Every drill and roll-call had to be attended, but in the intervals officers were permitted to enjoy themselves, leaving the garrison, and going where they pleased, without making written application to state where they were going for how long, etc., so that they were back for their next duty" (Grant, *Personal Memoirs*, vol. 1, 45).

22. The infantry took pride in the fact that a court-martial had taken care of the last of its drunkards. Nearly 400 men and officers signed a temperance pledge at a revival meeting. Bainbridge's commander crowed, "We have not now a regular drinker left in the 3rd Infantry and but few who touch liquor at all" (E. A. Hitchcock Journal (October 14, 1843), William A. Croffut Papers, Manuscript Division, 813E, Library of Congress.

23. The best evidence of this is to be found in the army pay slips as a slave or servant serving one officer can be found to serve other officers at Jefferson Barracks.

24. Rachael v. Walker, 4 Mo. 350, 350–51 (Mo. 1836); Bliss, *Reminiscences of Fort Snelling*, 336.

25. Steamboats could dock at Jefferson Barracks. Troops and recruits traveled up and down the river through St. Louis and Jefferson Barracks. Different steamboats plied different stretches of river and Gulf waters, so the troops changed boats at St. Louis and then again at New Orleans (Petersen, *Steamboating on the Upper Mississippi*, 000.

26. Bainbridge's lieutenants, both West Point graduates, were Lt. Joseph Eaton and Lt. D. C. Buell (Jefferson Barracks Post Returns, NA).

27. Engle, *Don Carlos Buell*, 24.
28. Ibid.
29. In addition to Capt. Bainbridge, the court-martial was composed of Maj. W. W. Lear, president of the case; three captains; four first lieutenants; and four second lieutenants. Capt. H. Swartout was judge advocate. (Col. S. W. Kearney's order book in William Clark papers, Mo HS).
30. Ibid.
31. E. A. Hitchcock Memoirs (October 13, 1842), in the William A. Croffut Papers, Manuscript Division, 813E, Library of Congress ("...with Gen'l Scott I have made an implacable enemy..."); October 16, 1842 (anticipating General Scott to attempt to injure him).
32. No rule authorized him to demand reasons or revive an adjournment (Engle, *Don Carlos Buell*, 26).
33. Missouri Senator Thomas Hart Benton quite naturally sided with the local officers and proposed that the Senate investigate the Army's general. Ibid.
34. E. A. Hitchcock Journal, William A. Croffut Papers, Manuscript Division, 813E, Library of Congress.
35. "The President sustains me nobly" (LT Journals, June 8, 1836).
36. For biographies of Dr. William Beaumont, see Horsman, *Frontier Doctor*; Nelson, *Beaumont*.
37. July 9, 1843, Joseph P. Sanford, their brother, would later marry with the assistance of yet another younger sister, Virginia Sanford. Howard, *Materials for a Genealogy of the Sparhawk Family in New England*.
38. E. A. Hitchcock Journal (July 9, 1843), William A. Croffut Papers, Manuscript Division, 813E, Library of Congress.
39. Court-martial of Major Thomas Staniford, 16–17. Testimony of Lt. C. Hoskins. Jefferson Barracks courts-martial files, Old Army Files, RG–E–184–, NA.
40. Ibid.
41. Ibid., 12–13. Testimony of Lt. C. Hoskins.
42. Ibid.
43. Ibid.
44. Ibid.
45. The court words are described as "exceptionable," as in the words that Lt. Prince had taken exception to at ibid., 31.
46. Ibid. Order of Major S. Kearney approving reprimand of Major Staniford.
47. November 30, Emerson paid 10 days Board for wife & Child. Dec 4, weeks board for self & wife. No board paid for servants (Emerson's account at the LeClaire house, Antoine LeClaire Papers, Putnam Museum, Davenport, Iowa). According the local deed registry, Emerson buys land on December 28, 1843, and had it recorded next day (Scott Co., Iowa Registry of Deeds, Scott County Courthouse, Davenport Iowa). Henrietta Emerson Snyder's birthdate appears on her tombstone.
48. December 31, 1843, account books of the LeClaire house demonstrate money advanced to Mrs. Emerson. Antoine LeClaire papers, Putnam Museum, Davenport, Iowa.
49. Snyder, "John Emerson, Owner of Dred Scott," 440–61.
50. His Iowa property included the land that he had staked with the aid of stakeholders and the lot where he was building a new house. His property in Missouri consisted of 19 acres of land and a few articles of household furniture. He may have continued to own a stake in the partnership with officers in Minnesota, although I have found no probate for Emerson's interests there.
51. Entries in the Scott County, Iowa, Registrar of Deeds by John Emerson. See also Bureau of Land Management, Government Records Office, www.glorecords.blm.gov/
52. Mrs. Emerson later described the estate that she inherited from Dr. Emerson as substantial (*New York Times*, December 22, 1895).

53. *New York Times*, December 22, 1895 (stating that Mrs. Emerson and her daughter "went to the home of her father, who was then living in St. Louis, and lived there until his death, about five years after that of Dr. Emerson").

54. Alexander Sanford, to whom was committed the settlement of the St. Louis estate, filed a bond of $4,000 for the execution of the trust (1844 Emerson's will probated. George L. Davenport and John F. A. Sanford, executors). John Emerson's will appears in two separate probates, one in Iowa and one in Missouri. The Iowa probate file is at the Scott County Courthouse in Davenport Iowa. The Missouri probate file can be found at PCDP.

    In his hastily drawn up will, Dr. Emerson left his medical books to his brother, Edward P. Emerson. There are two Edward P. Emersons listed in the U.S. Census, but only one is a doctor, who would have been interested in medical books. Dr. Edward P. Emerson lived in Blairsville, Pennsylvania (1850 Census). According to Walkinshaw, Edward P. Emerson settled in Blairsville, Pennsylvania, in 1819. He was born in Ireland, practiced first at Ebensburg, and came to Campbell's Mills before Blairsville was laid out (Walkinshaw, *Annals of Southwestern Pennsylvania*, 178).

55. His holdings in St. Louis, included only the "19 acres of land situate about three miles west of the city of St. Louis, on Manchester Road, bought by John Emerson of St. Paul and wife," and its furnishings (John Emerson Probate, PCDP).

56. The annual settlement was filed December 1845 in the amount of sale of $32.26. The probate file suggests that Col. Sanford was slow in responding to probate court orders to move the proceedings along. Eventually, St. Louis city mayor, John F. Darby, worked on the probate (ibid.). The estate contained a high-post bedstead, a feather bed, a large mattress, two card tables, and a dining table.

57. Ibid.

58. Lucy describes her father's reaction at the death of his master as one of being torn between seeing his master safely laid in his grave and anxious about the future consequences for their family (Delaney, "From the Darkness Cometh the Light," 12).

59. Ironically, Mrs. Emerson Chaffee's later remembrances suggest that Dr. Emerson whipped Dred often because of his gambling (*New York Times*, December 22, 1895).

60. Dred expressed this concern in an interview several years later after the lawsuit's conclusion and the death of John F.A. Sanford. "He is anxious to know who owns him..." *Frank Leslie's Illustrated Newspaper*, June 27, 1857.

61. This describes Polly's situation in remaining with her husband, Apollo, in a state of enslavement, even though she had already lived in Illinois which would be the basis of her successful freedom suit (Delaney, "From the Darkness Cometh the Light," 11–14).

62. William Wells Brown recounted that although he thought well of a slave woman in whom his master and mistress tried to interest him, he resolved never to marry again because if he had a wife he would not be willing to leave her behind and bringing a wife along would make a successful escape unlikely (Brown, *From Fugitive Slave to Free Man*, 68).

63. Perhaps twice according to the interview in "The Original Dred Scott, a Resident of St. Louis—A Sketch of His History," *St. Louis News*, April 8, 1857. The article mentions two sons dying soon after birth. The usual timing of a woman's reproduction suggests pregnancies at two-year intervals, which would be the length of time that a mother's nursing of a toddler may have precluded her conception. The time span of seven years between Eliza and Lizzie's births suggests that one or both of these sons may have been born between the births of the Scotts' daughters, or they may have been born after Dred's return from Texas.

64. Fehrenbacher, *The Dred Scott Case*, 242.

65. Ulysses S. Grant arrived in the summer of 1844 (Grant, *Personal Memoirs of Ulysses S. Grant*, vol. 1, 51).

66. Jefferson Barracks seemed to be the site of many courtships by young officers (see, for example, DiNardo, Nofi, and Longstreet, *The Man, the Soldier, the Controversy*, 56).

67. Quoting Julia Dent (Tidball, *No Disgrace to My Country*, 69).
68. E. A. Hitchcock Journal (November 30, 1843), William A. Croffut Papers, Manuscript Division, 813E, Library of Congress. "My niece Caroline came here on a visit about a fortnight since & was at Mrs. Bainbridge's & Mrs. B. invited Sarah as she had on two former occasions to come down and pass some time with Caroline."
69. Horsman, *Frontier Doctor*, 257. E. A. Hitchcock Journal (April 27–28, 1843), William A. Croffut Papers, Manuscript Division, 813E, Library of Congress. Upon returning to St. Louis and visiting the Beaumont family again, Hitchcock is extraordinarily tender in describing Sarah. "It is impossible to describe the perfect at-homeness with which I am at the Doctor's. Sarah was not the least embarrassed thus giving evidence that her feelings were free and that is the only point on which I would have any solicitude."
70. E. A. Hitchcock Journal (December 29, 1842), William A. Croffut Papers, Manuscript Division, 813E, Library of Congress. After spending some time with Mrs. Dobbins, Hitchcock replied, "I ought to be a married man, there is no doubt & everybody tells me so."
71. Thomas, *From Tennessee Slave to St. Louis Entrepreneur*, 97.
72. E. A. Hitchcock Journal (October 11, 1842), William A. Croffut Papers, Manuscript Division, 813E, Library of Congress (recording "a playful friendly letter" from Sarah Beaumont). Sarah also sent notes to Robert E. Lee, also a family friend (Horsman, *Frontier Doctor*, 255).
73. Thomas, *From Tennessee Slave to St. Louis Entrepreneur*, 96, 70.
74. Horsman, *Frontier Doctor*, 255.
75. Dr. Beaumont's path-breaking research was performed on a soldier named Alexis St. Martin, who had been shot in the stomach and whose wound refused to heal. As a result, Beaumont could ask St. Martin to eat something and observe just how the gastrointestinal tract functioned. No one had ever had access to the inside of a functioning human stomach before. Beaumont published his observations of digestion, and they were translated into several languages. He continued to win awards for this work. Myer, *Life and Letters of Dr. William Beaumont*, 117, 293.
76. E. A. Hitchcock Journal (November 30, 1843), William A. Croffut Papers, Manuscript Division, 813E, Library of Congress.
77. King, *The True Ulysses S. Grant*, 74 (describing Hitchcock's reputation as a brilliant tactician among the officers at the time).
78. E. A. Hitchcock Journal (November 30, 1843), William A. Croffut Papers, Manuscript Division, 813E, Library of Congress.
79. Ibid.
80. E. A. Hitchcock Journal (December 2, 1843), William A. Croffut Papers, Manuscript Division, 813E, Library of Congress.
81. Capt. Bainbridge was drawn into the first demonstration. The blindfolded young hypnotized woman claimed to be able to recognize objects held in the hands of people in the audience. To demonstrate the feat, she was asked what the captain held in his hand. The parlor audience was amazed when she coughed as her sign of recognition of the pinch of tobacco he was holding. E. A. Hitchcock Journal (April 29, 1843), William A. Croffut Papers, Manuscript Division, 813E, Library of Congress.
82. Dred's account of two sons dying soon after birth ("The Original Dred Scott, a Resident of St. Louis—A Sketch of His History," *St. Louis News*, April 8, 1857).
83. On the other hand, both Eliza and Lizzie were popular names at the time. That exact name was on the list of 26 slaves that Taliaferro claimed he had freed, listed near Harriet's own. Taliaferro could not have known the name of Harriet's child born years later, so Lizzie must have referred to another slave woman. The list of 21 slaves that Lawrence Taliaferro claims to have freed appears to have been listed in some chronological order; the names "Eliza" and "Lizzie" precede Harriet's name. Taliaferro, Lawrence, Lawrence Taliaferro Papers, 1813–1868, Minn HS.
84. This would follow from the principle of matrilineality. See note 51, Chapter 21, for legal authority.

85. E. A. Hitchcock Journal (March 20, 1844), William A. Croffut Papers, Manuscript Division, 813E, Library of Congress.

86. E. A. Hitchcock Journal (March 20, 1844), William A. Croffut Papers, Manuscript Division, 813E, Library of Congress.

87. Myer, *Life and Letters of Dr. William Beaumont*, 268 (William Beaumont hearing vibrations through his teeth). E. A. Hitchcock Journal (March 20, 1844), William A. Croffut Papers, Manuscript Division, 813E, Library of Congress.

88. E. A. Hitchcock named all the wedding guests in his diary: Mrs. Bainbridge, Mrs. Craig, Captain Kingsbury, Mr. Edwards and Susan Glasgow. E. A. Hitchcock Journal (March 20, 1844), William A. Croffut Papers, Manuscript Division, 813E, Library of Congress.

89. William Beaumont Papers, Mo HS, St. Louis; Myer, *Life and Letters of Dr. William Beaumont*, 268.

90. E. A. Hitchcock Journal (April 20, 1844), William A. Croffut Papers, Manuscript Division, 813E, Library of Congress.

91. Major Hitchcock, who usually carefully noted the ladies' presence in his officers' company, failed to mention any accompanying lady on this particular voyage (E. A. Hitchcock Journal (April 28, 1844), William A. Croffut Papers, Manuscript Division, 813E, Library of Congress.

92. "The paymaster will please pay the within amount $115.30 over to Mrs. Henry Bainbridge." Signed Ft. Jesup, La., June 1, 1845, by Henry Bainbridge (SP Accts, RG 217, E 516, NA).

93. John B. Clarke pay slip from A. D. Steuart was numbered 92, whereas William Bainbridge's was numbered 91. Although the two captains were in the same infantry, normally their pay slips would not have been numbered consecutively unless they were in the same place or were paid at the same place. Capt. Clarke's pay slip was disallowed, which seems to indicate an additional irregularity. Their proximity in A. D. Steuart's numbered register when their presence was not proximate suggests that perhaps Steuart was attempting to do Mrs. Bainbridge and her sister Mrs. Clarke a favor by paying them both from their husband's funds while they were waiting in St. Louis (SP Accts, RG 217, E 516).

94. Most of the officers took their servants with them, and most of the accompanying servants were male (SP Accts, RG 217, E 516).

95. The Army Paymaster's records bear out this gender preference for male servants once the officers left Jefferson Barracks. Of those persons serving officers of the Third and Fourth Infantry at Jefferson Barracks in St. Louis in peacetime, the majority are men. Daphne, for example, who served Philip Barbour at St. Louis, was replaced by Anthony when the troops settled in camp in Louisiana. Paymaster's records for Philip Barbour, October to December 1843, February through March 1844, and October 44 through December 1844 (SP Accts, RG 217, E 516).

96. "The arrangement is for the *Maria* to take us all (about 350 and she is 1400 tons burthen." (E. A. Hitchcock Journal (April 25, 1844), William A. Croffut Papers, Manuscript Division, 813E, Library of Congress.

97. E. A. Hitchcock Journal (May 3, 1844), William A. Croffut Papers, Manuscript Division, 813E, Library of Congress.

98. Nancy who later sued for her freedom was one servant left behind (Nancy v. Enoch Stein, no. [1848], CCHRP).

99. Although it can be corroborated that Dred accompanied Capt. Bainbridge to Louisiana, it's unlikely that Harriet did, now that she had two babies to care for: Lizzie, born within the year at Jefferson Barracks, and Eliza, just five.

100. Most entries on the pay slips refer to him as "Eldred" or "Dread," rather than "Etheldred" as he was listed in Dr. Emerson's pay slips. See, for example, Capt. Bainbridge's pay slip for May, 1845 at Fort Jesup, Louisiana, and July 1843 pay slip in Jefferson Barracks. During this period, Capt. Bainbridge received $10.00 per months for the pay of a private servant, $2.50 for clothing of a private servant, and $6.20 for subsistence (20 cents per ration) for a total of $15.70 per month for the "keeping" of Dred (Bainbridge's August 1843 pay slip, SP Accts, RG 217, E 516).

Chapter 24

1. Camp Wilkins (Hitchcock, *Fifty Years*, 195).
2. Ibid.
3. New Year's Day 1845 found Capt. Bainbridge and the Army still at the makeshift camp (Hitchcock, *Fifty Years*, 189).
4. In the evening, the captain attended a fine dinner hosted by Lt. Stephen D. Dobbins for 15 guests (E. A. Hitchcock Journal [January 1, 1845], William A. Croffut Papers, Manuscript Division, 813E, Library of Congress). Such domesticity suggests that some officer's wives, such as Mrs. Dobbins, were in camp as well. He notes paying calls with Capt. Bainbridge upon all of the families of officers in both regiments, but he never mentioned Mrs. Bainbridge and he spoke regularly of spending time alone with the captain. For example, later that same evening of New Year's day, he describes taking a plate of soup together with the Captain at the 3rd infantry regular mess. Ibid.
5. Letter of Stephen Kearney to E. A. Hitchcock, Edward E. Ayer Manuscript Collection, Newberry Library, Chicago.
6. Anticipating a favorable vote by the people of Texas to annex to the United States, the army was ordered to proceed to a point along the Gulf coast. Orders came in June. Henry, *Campaign Sketches*, 9–10.
7. U.S. attempts to annex Texas seemed to the Mexicans an egregious provocation. Wheelan, *Invading Mexico*, 50–52, 86.
8. Hitchcock, *Fifty Years*, 195.
9. Other black servants accompanying the officers of the Third Infantry were Willis, Fielding, A. Johnson, and Emanuel (SP Accts, RG 217, E 516).
10. This took place on July 23 (Henry, *Campaign Sketches*, 12–13).
11. Ibid.
12. Ibid.
13. Company H arrived on August 6 (Hitchcock, *Fifty Years*, 195).
14. Henry, *Campaign Sketches*, 34.
15. The storm on August 24 killed Lt. Braxton Bragg's servant (ibid.). Bragg was in a different unit so his tent would not have been next to Bainbridge's, but certainly within the officers' compound of tents.
16. An army on the march comprised 177 officers and 2,111 men for an aggregate of 2,288 fighting men. By March, Capt. Bainbridge also was assigned to the frontline provocation of Matamoras, where he and his men would encounter the Mexican troops.
17. *St. Louis News*, April 8, 1857. *Frank Leslie's Illustrated Newspaper*, June 27, 1857.
18. Ibid. This account is corroborated by Capt. Bainbridge's pay records. After the army was ordered to invade Mexico, Capt. Bainbridge no longer lists Dred as his servant (SP Accts, RG 217, E 515).
19. Bay, "In Search of Sally Hemings," 407, 412, citing White, *Ar'n't I a Woman?* 70 (explaining that one reason women were underrepresented in the fugitive population was because of childrearing, which meant that the woman was either pregnant, nursing, or had at least one small child to care for).
20. Mrs. Russell deposition, *Dred Scott v. Emerson* case file.
21. Russell was also one of the 13 directors of the St. Louis Insurance Company. The insurance company sold life insurance and advertised that they would also "insure the lives of slaves whether working on shore or on boats navigating rivers" (St. Louis Insurance Company advertisement in the *Missouri Republican*, January 1, 1840).
22. Years earlier, Russell had taken rooms next door to Col. Sanford's family when he first arrived in St. Louis. The 1836–37 St. Louis City directory lists "Sanford A. r 181, n 5th" and "Russell Samuel, 179 n 5th" (Mo HS).
23. Two white employees lived upstairs from the store (Mersman, *The Whiskey Merchant's Diary*, 21, 89, describing Russell and Bennetts' store).

24. Russell and Bennett, ad in the *Missouri Republican*, July 2, 1844; July 31, 1844; September 12, 1845; March 3, 1846; May 9, 1846. Russell's store was well enough known that it was visited by Mersman who sought to make contact with the grocer (Mersman, *The Whiskey Merchant's Diary*, 154).

25. The Russells had only one residence in the 1840s at 31 S. 4th St., which they had bought on September 13, 1844. In 1855 the Russells bought an estate called Longwood, near Jefferson Barracks, nine miles south of town (St. Louis Registry of Deeds, St. Louis).

   Mrs. Russell's parents and sisters lived next door on the same block. Between the related families there were half a dozen household slaves. Given the severe shortage of housing in the city, it was customary for even established middle-class families to double up and live together. Living with the Russells was Mr. Russell's business partner.

26. See, generally, Nacy, *Members of the Regiment*.

27. Tucker, *Hancock, the Superb*, 45.

28. One sister had married William Bennett, who was Mr. Russell's business partner. They had children and slaves of their own. The Russell and Bennett families lived together before the Russells acquired the house next door. Farther down the street lived the mistress's parents, along with her third sister and her husband, James R. Sprigg. 1850 U.S. Census for St. Louis.

29. Tucker, *Hancock, the Superb*, 46.

30. Samuel Russell's wealth was estimated as $30,000 in the 1850 Census.

31. Samuel Russell Probate (1859), PCDP.

32. Winn, "Arsenic and Feminine Beauty." The fashionable Catherine Bennett died at the age of 37 after a brief illness as a result of whitening her face with arsenic.

33. Kennerly describes St. Louis families as being "naturally ambitious for [their] girls to make brilliant marriages…" (Kennerly, *Persimmon Hill*, 111). Josephine Dubois married Hubert S. Benoist, July 4, 1835, and later Sprigg. Catherine Dubois married William Bennett, March 14, 1835. Nicholas Dubois married Margaret Morelte, April 8, 1834. Missouri marriages, on line at Ancestry.com.

34. Almira Russell married Winfield Scott Hancock in January 1850. Tucker, *Hancock, the Superb*, 75.

35. One such school was the Mississippi Valley Female Seminary on Broadway, run by the Reverend J. C. Abbott of the Presbyterian Church (Advertisement, *Missouri Republican*, March 22, 1847).

36. Tucker, *Hancock, the Superb*, 61.

37. The *Missouri Republican* frequently advertised for women who were good washerwomen.

38. The 1840 St. Louis Census lists the Samuel Russell family has having two female slaves aged 10–24 before Harriet came to their employ. The 1850 Census lists a 40-year-old female and two boys. The 1850 census lists 16 slaves living in the alley behind the houses.

39. Wood, *Masterful Women*, 170.

40. 1840 Census, 1850 Census. Samuel Russell's probate in 1859 shows him owning three slaves: Andy age 40, Louis age 16, and Lucy age 17 (Samuel Russell probate, PCDP). Archibald Gamble also owned slaves who by custom would occupy the adjoining alleyway (Archibald Gamble entry, 1840 Census, 1850 Census). The probate also lists "a harp, piano and guitar, a pearl inlaid chess set, a dozen marble top tables, mahogany furniture, 3 or 4 Brussels carpets, rosewood bedsteads, a dozen rosewood chairs, two rosewood sofas, two rosewood armchairs, 10 mahogany dining chairs, 12 cane seat chairs, six pairs of silk damask curtains, cutglass bohemian vases and glassware, marble and bronze statuary, seven oil paintings including one of Windsor castle, at least 75 pieces of silver and additional silverware, two dozen champagne glasses. Worth $11,000. Two and a half story brick house with an alley behind, fronting on 4th St., a four story brick warehouse on second street, and a country home in Carondelet, other real estate and shares of stock" (Samuel Russell probate, PCDP).

41. Trexler, *Slavery in Missouri*, 51, 60, n. 12.
42. *Missouri Republican* advertisements. The executors of Duty's estate dealt with a number of slave suits after his death. See, for example, Nat v. Coons, 10 Mo. 543 (Mo. 1847); Bill, Preston v. Coons, no. 674, at ˙7–18 (Mo. Cir. Ct. 1841) (requesting an injunction to prevent the sale of numerous slaves formerly belonging to Milton Duty), available at http://stlcourtrecords.wustl.edu (St. Louis Circuit Court Historical Records Project); Jordan Duty v. Darby, no. 20, at ˙15 (Mo. Cir. Ct. 1850) (consolidating seven freedom suits by Milton Duty's former slaves; CCHRP).
43. St. Louis Directory, 1848: Anderson, William, rectifier, 19 Front, res 90 Myrtle. Summons sent to the dwelling house of William Anderson, 90 Myrtle Street.
44. *Missouri Republican*, June 10, 1844.
45. *Missouri Republican*, June 16 to June 24, 1844.
46. *Missouri Republican*, July 17, 1844.
47. See, for example, Brown, *From Fugitive Slave to Free Man*, 150–51 (describing the mistress's setting of the laundry schedule).
48. Ibid.
49. Listed as erected in 1842, First African Baptist Church, on Almond St. between 4th and 5th streets, in Kennedy's St. Louis Directory (1860). It was referred to as simply the African church in early directories, when it was the only African American church in the city.
50. In 1827. Other sources say the church was established in 1818. The first church building was erected in 1825 at Third and Almond streets (Stevens, *History of Central Baptist Church*, 7).
51. Ibid.
52. Born Goochland County, Virginia, May 3, 1789; in 1854, the Reverend Meachum bought his wife and his father and freed them. Meachum, *An Address to All the Colored Citizens*, 3.
53. The 1845 city census lists 12 people in his household, evenly split between men and women.
    "Colored males: 2 <10; 2 from 18–21, 2 from 21–45; 1 > 45
    Colored females: 1<10; 2 from 18–21; 1 from 21–45; 1 > 45."
    "This gentleman was very wealthy, and had at one time, two fine steamers plying on the Mississippi, all under the command and management of white men, to whom he trusted altogether. As late as 1836, he sent two sons to Oberlin Collegiate Institute, desiring that they might become educated, in order to be able to manage his business; who although he could read and write, was not sufficiently qualified and skilled in the arts of business to vie with the crafty whites of the Valley" (Delany, *The Condition of Colored People*, 138).
54. Brunetta Barnes v. Meachum, no. 121, at ˙1 (Mo. Cir. Ct. 1840), CCHRP.
55. Archibald Barnes v. Meachum, no. 120, at ˙1 (Mo. Cir. Ct. 1840), CCHRP.
56. See Meechum v. Judy, 4 Mo. 361 (1836); see also Brunetta Barnes v. Meachum, no. 121 (1840); Archibald Barnes v. Meachum, no. 120 (1840); Green Berry Logan v. Meachum, no. 22 (1836); Judy Logan v. Berry Meachum, no. 40 (1837); Archibald Barnes v. Berry Meachum, no. 41 (1840), CCHRP.
    By the early 1840s his business seemed to be foundering, and several of his suppliers were pursuing him to collect on his debts.
57. Kennerly papers, December 27, 1837. Reporting that B. Meachum preached at funeral of Betsey, Kennerly's slave, and a number of blacks attended.
58. Meachum, *An Address to All the Colored Citizens*.
59. Meachum's message in stressing hard work and industriousness differed from that of AME minister David Walker, who stressed education in a pamphlet entitled "An Appeal to the Colored Citizens of the World, But in Particular, and Very Expressly, to Those of the United States of America," published September 28, 1829 (Howe, *What Hath God Wrought*, 423–25). By 1846, when Meachum released his pamphlet, Missouri had passed a law prohibiting the expansion of black literacy.
60. Delany, *The Condition of Colored People*, 137–38.

61. "Let us sell some cattle and horses, and buy another farm for James or Nancy, as they are coming up in years and will soon be of age. Take notice, this is all come up from the earth. I would not recommend this people to settle on poor ground, like many of the free people in old Virginia and North Carolina, who settled on poor hills that will hardly bring blackberries" (Meachum, *An Address to All the Colored Citizens*, 25–26).

62. Walker, *Free Frank,* 67–68, 77.

63. He advocated literacy and training in the trades, "so that we may possess among our people all the arts and sciences that man is in possession of" (ibid.). He announced the gathering of a national convention of the colored citizens of America to be held in Pittsburgh in September 1847. He published a little book of his plans entitled *An Address to All the Colored Citizens of the United States.* The Reverend Meachum was working on a new idea to found an organization called the National Negro Convention. The visionary senior minister planned to send out a call for African Americans to unite across the nation.

64. Ibid.

65. General call to all colored citizens of America to attend the National Convention in Pittsburgh, on the first Monday in September 1847 (September 6, 1847). Ministers calling the convention from the July 1846 meeting of the convention of colored ministers in Philadelphia included John B. Meachum of St. Louis, Mo.

66. Stevens, *History of Central Baptist Church,* 7.

67. Lyerly, "Religion, Gender, and Identity," in Morton, *Discovering the Women in Slavery,* 213.

68. These religious services were unique among slave gatherings in the relative degree of approval they received from slaveowners (Wade, *Slavery in the Cities,* 145, 160). Yet, as Wade describes, whites tended to feel a residual distrust of slaves' churches:
    "They feared the independence which separate churches implied. Never certain of what went on inside, they became convinced that abolitionist literature was circulated clandestinely and that insurrection was nightly plotted. The churches were, as one Charlestonian put it, 'nurseries of self government' and hence dangerous. The slaves get 'excited by the privileges they enjoy, as a separate and to some extent independent society,' warned another [citation omitted]. The fear of white townspeople was in part justified, for in these churches the Negroes did in fact get some experience in managing their own affairs...In the life of these churches the first signs of traditional Negro leadership were visible in the cities even before the abolition of slavery" (Wade, *Slavery in the Cities,* 172). Discussing the connection between slave churches and violent resistance to slavery, Elizabeth Fox-Genovese argues that "the churches and secret religious networks undoubtedly provided the institutional links between acts of individual resistance and revolts in the name of collectivity" (Fox-Genovese, *Within the Plantation Household,* 425).

69. From 1844 to 1846, F. B. Murdoch filed more freedom petitions in St. Louis than any other lawyer. When Lovejoy died, Francis B. Murdoch, the St. Louis lawyer who filed the first complaints for Harriet and Dred, was Alton's city attorney, personally opposed to slavery, but responsible for prosecuting both antislavery and proslavery zealots charged with capital offenses tied to slavery.
    The Reverend John Anderson, a young man who would break off from the Reverend Meachum's church, had been a typesetter for Elijah P. Lovejoy's abolitionist press. There is some thought that he may have lead the Scotts to Murdoch. There is no direct evidence that Anderson and Murdoch knew each other, but they both had antislavery inclinations and came from the same small town in Illinois (Ehrlich, *They Have No Rights,* 37–38).

70. Almost all the African American women listed "laundress" when asked their occupation on censuses and freedom bonds (see, for example, Freedom Bonds, Slavery Collection, Mo HS).

71. *Missouri Republican,* October 25, 1845.

72. The slave trader was Mr. Curle (*Missouri Republican,* October 8, 1845).

73. Other escapes from Missouri are mentioned in slave narratives such as Brown, *From Fugitive Slave to Free Man*, 22–23; Delaney, "From the Darkness Cometh the Light," 22–23; Jackson, *The Story of Mattie J. Jackson*, 4, 7.

74. "Most slaves who ran away were caught in a short period of time" (Fraser, *A History of Hope*, 69).

75. White, *Ar'n't I a Woman?* 71–72; Bay, "In Search of Sally Hemings," 407–26.

76. Male runaways outnumbered female runaways in Virginia (Bay, "In Search of Sally Hemings," 413) as well as in the advertisements of the St. Louis newspapers).

77. Edward Bates letters, Bates Family Papers, Mo HS.

78. White, *Ar'n't I a Woman?* 71. White and Camp both emphasize that the combined circumstances of bondage and sexual fertility imposed severe restrictions in mobility on slave women (Bay, "In Search of Sally Hemings," 412).

79. Delaney, "From the Darkness Cometh the Light," 22–23.

80. Ibid.

81. Brown, *From Fugitive Slave to Free Man*, 70–71.

82. Meachum, *An Address to All the Colored Citizens*, 3.

83. Although Dr. Emerson was in financial straits when Dred began serving the captain, it is not clear that he charged his brother-in-law for the services.

84. *St. Louis News*, April 8, 1857. Similarly William Wells Brown describes obtaining little sums of money, while he was a slave, that he saved for "a rainy day" (Brown, *From Fugitive Slave to Free Man,* 70).

85. "Famous Dred Scott Case: Mrs. Chaffee, owner of old slave, still living in Springfield," *New York Times*, December 22, 1895 (Mrs. Emerson's recollection of Dred's request to buy his freedom). Dred was interviewed in the *St. Louis News*, April 8, 1857. "On his return from Mexico he applied to his mistress, Mrs. Emerson, then living near St. Louis, for the purchase of himself and his family, offering to pay part of the money down."

86. It is unclear whether Harriet was present at the time.

87. Offering to buy one's freedom is somewhat inconsistent with Dr. Emerson's earlier claim, made when Harriet and Dred were sent for, that one of his slaves was threatening to sue for freedom. See Chapter 13.

88. "The Original Dred Scott a Resident of St. Louis—A Sketch of His History," *St. Louis News,* April 8, 1857. Paymaster Maj. A. D. Stueart was later summoned as a witness in the lawsuit. Maj. Stueart did post bond for another free black man that year (Entry for Ralph Harrison, Adam D Steuart, December 30, 1846, Free Negro Bonds, Mo HS).

89. Adam D. Steuart, whose name was sometimes misspelled as "Stewart," was the primary paymaster in St. Louis through the Mexican War until 1854. Though born in Virginia, like many St. Louis gentlemen, he was appointed from Missouri and made his home there (Henry, *Military Record of Civilian Appointments*, vol. 1, 42).

90. Summons to A. D. Stueart and his clerks (Dred Scott case file).

91. "Death of Mrs. C. C. Chaffee," *Springfield Republican*, February 12, 1903.

92. "Some urban slaveholders solved the problem by sending their old slaves out to peddle or beg and thereby bring in some income as well as support themselves." Genovese, *Roll, Jordan, Roll*, 520.

93. In its 1795 Freedom Suit Act, Virginia set forth formalized procedures allowing slaves to sue for their freedom *in forma pauperis* and, incredibly enough, appointing counsel for indigent slave petitioners. However, despite the apparent liberality of some of the statute's provisions, its underlying intention clearly was not to facilitate suits for freedom but to free slaveholders from the harassment of frivolous habeas corpus suits. In effect, slaves had to obtain their masters' consent to be sued: slaveowners were required to provide the court with a deposit equal to the slave's worth or the court would hold the petitioner and charge the owner for its expenses in holding the slave. Furthermore, if the petitioner failed in his or her suit, anyone who had aided the suit was required to forfeit $100 to the slave's owner. Finally, a successful suit did not entitle the freed slave to monetary

damages or labor profits (Higginbotham and Higginbotham, "'Yearning to Breathe Free,'" 1247).

94. The statute continued, "*First*, Where the slave shall not be, in the judgment of the court, of sound mind and body; *Second*, Where the slave shall be above the age of 45 years; and, *Third*, Where the slave, being a male, shall be under the age of 21 years; or, being a female, shall be under the age of 18 years; and the circuit court of the county, where the person emancipating the slaves resides, may, upon application of any inhabitant of the county, order the sheriff to distrain and sell so much of the personal or real estate of such person, as shall be sufficient for that purpose" (Emancipation of Slaves, Laws of Missouri, 1846).

    To assure that the freed person did not become a vagrant, the courts levied a $1,000 bond against each master who freed an elderly slave. The obligation was secured by a bond. In order to emancipate someone who was aged, young or unable to work, the emancipating owner was required to post an additional bond of $1,000. Thus, the statute made it more expensive to legally emancipate anyone over 50 or under 10 than it was to keep them. It meant that for their mistress to give them all papers, three special bonds of $1,000 were required for each of them. The statute required the sheriff to "distrain and sell a sufficient amount of her property,... in order to continue to maintain" three of the four members of the Scott family. The statute also provided that if emancipated slaves were delinquent in paying taxes and their property was insufficient to cover the cost of the taxes, the person who had emancipated them would be responsible for paying the taxes.

    "When any slave, emancipated by virtue of this act, shall neglect or refuse to pay any taxes or levies imposed by law, and the collector shall not find property of such liberated slave out of which to make such tax or levy, it shall be the duty of such collector to distrain and sell, of the goods and chattels of the person who shall have liberated such slave, if he be in his county, as much as will be sufficient to pay such tax or levy, as if the same had been assessed to such person himself." Ibid.

95. Dred was replaced by a slave, "William," in Dr. Emerson's service a month after Emerson went to Florida. When Emerson died in Davenport, Iowa, it appears that neither Dred nor Harriet had not been in his direct service for some time. Emerson had been staying at the LeClaire House, a fancy hotel in Davenport as he and his wife were engaged in building a house The records for the probate of his estate show hotel charges for himself, sometimes for his wife and an infant, and even for keeping a horse. There are no charges listed for servants' lodging or meals.

96. Genovese, *Roll, Jordan, Roll*, 521 (contrasting "slaveholders' boast of tender care" of their aged slaves with abundant evidence of neglect, which often manifested itself in owners' manumission of old slaves to escape responsibility of them, as in Maryland); Johnson, *Soul by Soul*, 20; Hurt, *Agriculture and Slavery in Missouri's Little Dixie*, 270; Trexler, *Slavery in Missouri*, 38–39 (identifying values for "prime hands").

97. See Frazier, *Runaway and Freed Missouri Slaves*, 19 (discussing the William Wells Brown narrative).

98. Johnson, *Soul by Soul*, 42.

99. In the Deep South in a stricter social culture of slavery, only the peer pressure that other masters brought to bear kept masters of elderly slaves from turning them out (Genovese, *Roll, Jordan, Roll*, 521). One of the first things masters did at the time of emancipation was to cut their losses by setting their elderly slaves out.

100. Even the Missouri Code deemed a slave old at the age of 45 and required additional bonding support for emancipating a slave of this age (Laws of Missouri, "Slaves," art. 2, sec. 4, 1835).

101. Particularly within the Virginia slave culture in which he had been raised, slave men expected to live out the ends of their lives in relative peace.

102. Contemporary observers characterized Mr. Scott as "lazy and shiftless," a caricature that draws from recognizable racist biases (Hodder, "Some Phases of the Dred Scott Case," 3–22). Dred's so-called "laziness" invokes an epithet that white

slaveholders frequently flung at slaves (see Genovese, *Roll, Jordan, Roll*, 295–324, comparing accusation of "laziness" with alternate interpretations of work ethic, including slaves' conceptions of work). Nonetheless, his age and his weakness from tuberculosis may have slowed him down.

103. Kennerly described Dred as having been sold to Dr. Emerson as a body servant because that was the only work for which he was fit (Kennerly, *Persimmon Hill*, 237).

104. We can estimate the prices that the Scotts would have commanded at an auction by looking at comparable figures from that time period and region. For instance, in 1855, James Shannon asserted, "The average value of an ordinary lot of slaves is generally estimated at one-half the price of a prime field hand. Such a slave will now readily sell for 1,200 dollars" (Shannon, *An Address Delivered Before the Pro-Slavery Convention*, 7).

 A lower figure comes from an inventory of an 1838 St. Louis estate, whose greatest assets were land and slaves. Trexler, *Slavery in Missouri*, 31–32. From this estate, enslaved women were valued at $500 and $400 each, while enslaved children were valued at $350 each. Relying on these figures, we get an estimate of about $1,200 for Harriet, Eliza, and Lizzie; Dred, being near the end of his working days, could not have brought more than a few hundred dollars, so the family would have been valued at around $1,500 or $1,600.

105. Article II, Of the Emancipation of Slaves (March 19, 1835), Laws of Missouri (1836). Usually the person's master or a lawyer appeared and swore to attest to the emancipation deed. If the man was a stranger to the judge, he had to produce two witnesses to swear an oath attesting to his signature. Widow Emerson could never have secured the Scotts' freedom alone because she could not swear the oath.

106. Although Emerson did not list his only claimed slaves, he made a point of another specific bequest, bequeathing his medical books to his brother.

107. Ehrlich, *They Have No Rights*, 33–36; Fehrenbacher, *The Dred Scott Case*, 271; Kaufman, *Dred Scott's Advocate*, 137–43.

108. Emerson letter, July 10, 1838, Fort Jesup, Dr. John Emerson Personnel File, NA. The only St. Louis freedom suit involving a John Emerson or "John Emmerson," was a suit by Tenor Washington against Henry Scott in 1833. Tenor Washington, a woman of color, sued Henry Scott though she defaulted on the first suit. In a follow-up suit against Henry Scott, she also impleaded John Emmerson as participating in perpetrating an assault on her freedom, by beating her and locking her up, as stated in the pro forma language of freedom suits in general. Tenor was awarded her freedom, though little is known of the John Emmerson who was sued. Dred's master had arrived in St. Louis by the time of Tenor Washington's suit and he may have assisted a friend, Henry Scott, in attempting to restrain Henry Scott's claim. I have found no direct link between Dred's master and Henry Scott that would either establish or rule out the identity of this John Emerson.

 If this was Dred's master, it would have given him early notice of the nature of freedom suits based on residence in free territory, but it could not have been the lawsuit to which Emerson was referring in 1838, because this lawsuit was completed and Tenor Washington had achieved her freedom almost five years previously.

109. Hill, *Decisive Battles of the Law*, suggesting case was for monetary reasons; Fehrenbacher, *The Dred Scott Case*, 3–22.

110. Kaufman, *Dred Scott's Advocate*, 9. (A master was someone slaves could look to if they got in trouble or aroused suspicion.) As Kenneth Kaufman wrote: "neighborly respect for what belonged to others assured a degree of property protection..." but a Black man without papers "was a very likely target of abuse from every drunken rabble-rouser, irate shopkeeper, abusive petty official, or zealous policeman in the city."

111. See, e.g., Eliza Tyler v. Nelson Campbell, no. 35 (1835); Sarah v. William Waddingham, no. 81 (1845).
112. Delaney, "From the Darkness Cometh the Light," 23.
113. The value of family security to slaves is documented in Martin, *Divided Mastery*, 49. "What little power slaves could amass they deployed in the service of a stable family life."
114. Age seven features as a prominent age in slave narratives. John Anderson reported that when his mother had done something to offend his master, his mother was sold away from him when he was seven (*The Story of the Life of John Anderson*, 9).
115. Jacobs, *Incidents in the Life of a Slave Girl*.
116. Walter Johnson, *Soul by Soul*, 140 (describing patterns in the selling of children).
117. Delaney, "From the Darkness Cometh the Light," 28–29.
118. Several of the St. Louis freedom suits document instances when slaves were reassigned to cover owners' debts. See, for example, Alsey v. William and Randolph, William Sullivan (firm of Randolph & Tracy), no. 305 (1841); Samuel (aka Sam) v. John Howdeshell, no. 6 (1844); Louisa v. Francis B. Jameson and McCabe, no. 107 (1854). CCHRP.
119. If the entire family was sold, it was highly improbable that they would be able to stay together. More likely, they'd be split up, sold to different owners in different locations, and some sent downriver in which case they would never see each other again. The multitude of instances of separating families according to the dictates of the slave market bears witness to many slave owners' opportunism. John Blassingame, concluding that the forcible separation of families was "the most brutal aspect of slavery," nonetheless approached it exclusively from the perspective of disempowered male slaves, helpless to protect their wives and children from sale (Blassingame, *Slave Testimony*, 160, 522). In actuality, the narratives of female ex-slaves asserted a sense of rage and powerlessness that was just as vivid. See, for example, Griffiths, *Autobiography of a Female Slave*; Jacobs, *Incidents in the Life of a Slave Girl*, 70. Of course, apologists for slavery sought to deny that the splintering of families was a prominent feature of the slave trade. See, for example, Kennerly, *Persimmon Hill*, 100 (asserting contrary to advertisements in the *Missouri Republican* that in St. Louis only estate slaves were sold publicly); 8 De Bow's Review 122–23 (1850) (asserting that "an object of prime consideration with…slaveholders [is] to keep families together").
120. McLaurin, *Celia, A Slave*; Index to Jacobs, *Incidents in the Life of a Slave Girl*, 304 (listing more than a dozen instances of sexual predation). "Slavery had no horror then for me, as I played about the place.…As I carelessly played away the hours, mother's smiles would fade away, and her brow contract into a heavy frown. I wondered much thereat, but the time came—ah! Only too soon, when I learned the secret of her ever-changing face" (Delaney, "From the Darkness Cometh the Light," 13).
121. "The white man's pursuit of black women frequently destroyed any possibility that comely black girls could remain chaste for long. Few slave parents could protect their pretty daughters from the sexual advances of white men" (Blassingame, *The Slave Community*, 154). To fend off such predation, young enslaved women may have resorted to tactics similar to those that Harriet Jacobs's persona, Linda Brent, was forced to employ: forming a sexual liaison with one white man to ward off the advances of another, her master, whom she deeply feared and despised (Jacobs, *Incidents in the Life of a Slave Girl*, 81).
122. A "likely" woman was fertile and able to work. Enslaved women's reproductive capacity was crucial in determining their value. When William Law Olmstead investigated United States slavery, he received a report asserting, "In the states of Maryland, Virginia, North Carolina, Kentucky, Tennessee and Missouri, as much attention is paid to the breeding and growth of Negroes as to that of horses and mules. Further south, we raise them both for use and for market. Planters command their girls and women (married or unmarried) to have children; and I have known a great many Negro girls to be sold off because they did not have children. A breeding woman is worth from one-sixth to one-fourth more than one that does not breed" (McLaurin, *Celia, A Slave*, 18–19);

W. E. B. Du Bois, *Black Reconstruction*, 44. One planter "calculated that the moment a colored baby was born, it was worth to him $300" (ibid., 43).

123. Insight into Harriet's motivation can be gleaned from the circumstances under which Rachael sued. Rachael's initial owner brought her from Prairie du Chien, where she lived and worked as a slave, to St. Louis to be sold at the slave market soon after she had had a baby James Henry. (Petition for Leave to Sue for Freedom, Rachael v. Walker, no. 82, at ˙1 [Mo. Cir. Ct. 1834], CCHRP). What prompted her sale at that point is unknown, but it is clear that in order to sell the slave and child at much of a profit, the owner had to bring them as he did to the St. Louis market. At St. Louis, Rachael and James were first sold to one purchaser, then soon sold again to a slave dealer. Rachael v. Walker, 4 Mo. 350, 350–51 (Mo. 1836) (describing the facts of the case).

An affidavit by a man of color, identified only as John, explained that Rachael's suit was instigated because Walker was "about to remove said Rachael and her child from Missouri down the Mississippi for sale" (Affidavit of John, Rachael v. Walker, no. 82, at ˙2 [Mo. Cir. Ct. 1834], CCHRP). John did not sign his name but was duly sworn and attested with a cross (ibid.). The complaint went on to state that Walker "with force and arms...assaulted the said plaintiff and he then and there did beat and bruise and ill treat and strike and also then and there imprisoned the said plaintiff," claiming damages of $500 (Trespass for Freedom Issue Summons, ibid. at ˙5–6). The judge appointed an attorney to represent her as a poor person (Order Granting Leave to Sue for Freedom, ibid., ˙3).

These few facts establish four relevant circumstances: first, her wish to hold on to her baby, whose name is repeatedly mentioned in the transcript; second, her fear of being sold down river; third, the assistance in bringing suit that she received from John, a man of color, who attested that he had seen her at Prairie du Chien; and fourth, that she had to allege some physical brutality at the hands of William Walker.

The history of domicile of the enslaved Rachael in Rachael v. Walker matched Harriet's closely. Rachael's master, an officer of the United States Army, had held her in slavery first at Fort Snelling, had then taken her to Prairie du Chien, and had finally sold her in St. Louis. Moreover, because Rachael lived at Fort Snelling in 1830–31, it is likely that her suit became well known among the slaves living there.

124. "The Original Dred Scott a Resident of St. Louis—A Sketch of His History," *St. Louis News*, April 8, 1857.

125. *Frank Leslie's Illustrated Newspaper*, June 27, 1857.

126. Mattie describes the disastrous attempt of her mother to flee with children.

"Two years after my father's departure, my mother, with her two children, my sister and myself, attempted to make her escape. After traveling two days we reached Illinois. We slept in the woods at night. I believe my mother had food to supply us but fasted herself. But the advertisement had reached there before us, and loafers were already in search of us, and as soon as we were discovered on the brink of the river one of the spies made enquiries respecting her suspicious appearance. She was aware that she was arrested, consequently she gave a true account of herself—that she was in search of her husband. We were then destitute of any articles of clothing excepting our wearing apparel. Mother had become so weary that she was compelled to leave our package of clothing on the way. We were taken back to St. Louis and committed to prison and remained there one week, after which they put us in Linch's [*sic*] trader's yard, where we remained about four weeks" (Jackson, *The Story of Mattie J. Jackson*, 7).

127. VanderVelde, "Redemption Songs" (unpublished ms. on file with author, detailing the freedom suits in the St. Louis Courts); Kaufman, *Dred Scott's Advocate*, 139 - (reporting 60% were filed by women); Schafer, *Becoming Free*, 16, notes that all but one of the bondspersons suing for freedom in New Orleans were women but for quite a different reason. Most based their claim on having been taken to France, and women servants were more often taken along as personal servants for New Orleans residents traveling to France.

128. See, for example, suits by mothers as guardian ad litem for their children as well as suits by mothers for their own freedom (CCHRP).

129. Comment in Lawrence Taliaferro's journal that Lt. Plympton's wife could borrow Eliza but that he intended to give her her freedom (LT Journals, May 29, 1826).

130. Taliaferro used the back of his own *bona fides* of social standing, a statement of membership in a society of learning, as a note paper for other notes he made (Taliaferro Collection, Minn HS. Reprinted on page 325, this volume).

131. Of the couple, Harriet, who presumably spent the preceding two years in St. Louis, had the best opportunity to learn how to sue whether from the laundresses at the river or from the attorney Murdoch. She was more committed to the African Church. Dred's social resources included the pledge of a St. Louis gentleman to finance his freedom and the ability to call on the family that had once owned him. But initially, his former master's family, the Blows, weren't involved in the suit.

132. Meachum, *An Address to All the Colored Citizens*, 20–21.

133. The principle of matrilinearity was described as "partus sequitar rentrum," or the offspring of a slave mother must be a slave. O'Neal, *The Negro Law of South Carolina*, Ch. II, "Slaves, Their Civil Rights, Liabilities, and Disabilities" (1848); Stroud, *A Sketch of the Laws Relating to Slavery*, 3.

134. Only the very early case of Laban and Tempe involved a slave couple. See Laban v. Price, no. 182 (Mo. Cir. Ct. 1821), CCHRP.

Chapter 25

1. It does not appear that the court appointed him. See Scott v. Emerson, no. 1, at ˙2, 4 (1846) (Judge Krum's order permitting the freedom suit but not mentioning that the Scotts were suing as poor persons). Murdoch had represented plaintiffs in at least 16 other freedom suits. See Drusella v. Curle, no. 252 (1844); Ann v. Wilson, no. 39 (1844); Ann v. Jameson, no. 394 (1844); Jefferson v. Hopkins, no. 219 (1844); Celestine v. Dumont, no. 15 (1844); Britton v. Mitchell, no. 18 (1844); Smith v. Knox, no. 120 (1844); Hannah v. Pitcher, no. 28 (1843); Rebecca v. Black, no. 24 (1843); Charles v. Christy, no. 359 (1842); Gazen v. Sparr, no. 33 (1842); Alonzo v. Sparr, no. 32 (1842); Vica v. Hobart, no. 31 (1842); Alsey v. Randolph, no. 305 (1841); Jonathan v. Brotherton, no. 32 (1841); Cephas v. Scott, no. 254 (1840), CCHRP.

2. Murdoch's new wife was the daughter of a previous St. Louis mayor, John Johnston, and his one-time Indian lover. A year later, Murdoch became active in organizing a new religious group, the Swedenborgians, hosting occasional discussion meetings at his house. On Sunday, November 20, 1842, Francis B. Murdoch was listed as a member of the First New Jerusalem Society of St. Louis (Scharf, *History of St. Louis*, vol. 2, 1741).

3. The same minister had performed both their marriages a few weeks apart. For an excellent description of Pennsylvania law on gradual emancipation, see Finkelman, *An Imperfect Union*, 46–69.

4. For example, Pennsylvania had a six-month rule that protected the slave property of out-of-state visitors who stayed less than six months (ibid., 46). If Harriet had only spent six months in Pennsylvania between her acquisition in Virginia by Taliaferro and her move to the frontier, the duration of her residency in Bedford, Pennsylvania, might have been insufficient to emancipate her. On the other hand, Taliaferro was building a house in Bedford, so he might have been deemed domiciled there rather than an out-of-state visitor.

5. It is difficult to know how to assess the truth of the pleadings in the court documents. The documentary record is ambiguous. Harriet Scott's 1846 statement that Emerson had "bought" her from Taliaferro may have been necessary to stipulate as a legal matter to file for freedom against Emerson. There is no record in Taliaferro's journals of selling Harriet although there is reference to Taliaferro's sale of another slave, Horace (LT Journals, May 17, 1832). Taliaferro claimed in documents he wrote later to have freed Harriet, although he also claimed to have

freed Horace. List of Slaves Taliaferro claimed to have Freed, Taliaferro Papers, Minn HS.

6. Missouri Statute, Freedom: An act to enable persons held in slavery to sue for their freedom. January 27, 1835. § 9. "The action to be brought under the leave given, shall began action of trespass for false imprisonment, and shall be instituted in the name of the petitioner, against the person holding him in slavery or claiming him as a slave."

   Lucy's papers said the same thing, although in her own account of the events she denied ever being struck by Master Mitchell (Delaney, "From the Darkness Cometh the Light," 28–29).

7. See Max Weber, *General Economic History*, 128. Who was the real enslaver when the social control of slavery was ubiquitous?

8. Mo. "Freedom" Stat. sec. 1 (1835) § 2 of An Act to Enable Persons Held in Slavery to Sue for Their Freedom (enacted January 27, 1835), published in Laws of Missouri (1836).

9. Some examples were Ralph v. Coleman Duncan and James Duncan, no. 35 (1830) followed by Ralph v. Robert Duncan and James Duncan, no.99 (1833), Matilda v. Elijah Mitchell, no. 47, followed Matilda v. Henry G. Mitchell & H.C. Russell, no. 55, both filed in 1832; Celeste v. Laforce Papin, no. 41 (1837) followed by Celeste v. Alexander Papin, no. 335 (1839), all in CCHRP.

10. VanderVelde, *Redemption Songs* (unpublished ms. on file with author, detailing the freedom suits in the St. Louis Courts).

11. Missouri Statute establishing that slaves were free on Sundays. Mo. "Crimes and Punishments" Stat. art. 8, § 28 (1835).

12. Meachum, *An Address to all the Colored Citizens*, 33.

13. Stevens, *The History of the Central Baptist Church*, 10.

14. Baptism was a family ceremony of great significance in the 1830s and 1840s. Scott Campbell had declined even Taliaferro's urgent war-related errand on the day his family planned to baptize their children. Charlotte Blow Charless describes the adult baptism of her daughter as one of a parent's proudest moments (Charless, *A Biographical Sketch*, 39).

15. Dred Scott v. Irene Emerson was docketed as number one for the November term, 1846: Scott v. Emerson, no. 1 (Mo. Cir. Ct. 1846). Harriet Scott v. Irene Emerson was number two: Scott v. Emerson, no. 2 (Mo. Cir. Ct. 1846), all available at http://stlcourtrecords.wustl.edu (St. Louis Circuit Court Historical Records Project).

16. Although they filed suit simultaneously, what remains of the file contains a personal bond posted by Murdoch only in Harriet's suit and not in Dred's. Perhaps Dred's bond was lost or stolen from the file because of his fame. Perhaps there only was ever the one, posted by the attorney for the slave from Pennsylvania whose master he knew personally.

17. *The Story Of An Old Clerk*, at 1 (detailing Chouteau's donation of land on which Courthouse stood); Howe, *What Hath God Wrought*, 586.

18. Order of Judge John M. Krum, April 6, 1846. Dred Scott v. Emerson Case File.

19. In the court papers, Harriet claimed she was brought to Fort Snelling by Major Taliaferro from the state of Virginia about 11 years before; after serving Taliaferro for about three years, he sold her to Emerson.

20. *New York Times*, December 22, 1895. "The suit for Scott's freedom was accordingly brought in 1848 . . . with the money alleged to be due for wages for fourteen years, which would amount to some $1,700." A variation of this account is republished in news of Mrs. Chaffee's death ("Death of Mrs. C. C. Chaffee," *Springfield Republican*, February 12, 1903).

21. Petition, Scott v. Emerson, no. 1, at 5 (Mo. Cir. Ct. 1846), CCHRP.

22. The Scotts were represented by F. B. Murdoch, Charles Drake, Samuel Bay, A. P. Field, David N. Hall, and Roswell Field, and at the Supreme Court by Montgomery Blair and George Ticknor Curtis.

23. Scharf, *History of St. Louis*, vol. 1, 362–67; Primm, *Lion of the Valley*, 178–79.

24. Letter of J. F. A. Sanford to John Darby, July 31, 1848. Sanford-Chouteau letter file, on file with author.

25. The first involvement of the Blow family does not occur until more than a year later, when on July 2, 1847, Joseph Charless bound himself to pay all costs adjudged against plaintiffs should they lose. Dred Scott v. Emerson Case File.

26. St. Louis ordinances, no. 1183. Hogs. June 30, 1843. Original ordinance applied only to old limits of the city. An amendment in 1848 extended it to embrace the entire limits of the city. June 23, 1848. No. 2039 (Krum, Revised Ordinances City of St. Louis, 1850).

27. See Ralph v. Duncan, no. 99, at ʼ17 (Mo. Cir. Ct. 1833) (stating that Ralph, while suing for his freedom, was hired out during the litigation), CCHRP.

28. James Duncan succeeded in smuggling several of his slaves from place to place whenever they attempted to file suit for freedom. See, for example, Vincent v. James Duncan, no. 110 (1829). There were numerous unexplained disappearances of the slaves of Milton Duty from places where they were hired out and later Pierre was simply beaten up by his putative owner, Gabriel S. Chouteau. Pierre v. Chouteau, no. 125 (1842), CCHRP.

29. See, for example, Action of Trespass and False Imprisonment, Suzette v. Reynolds, no. 9, at ʼ4 (Mo. Cir. Ct. 1828); Petition for Freedom, Charlotte v. Chouteau, no. 13, at ʼ2 (Mo. Cir. Ct. 1843), CCHRP.

30. The 1850 St. Louis Census lists Pierre Chouteau in jail in the status of a freedom litigant.

31. Schafer, *Becoming Free, Remaining Free*, 24, although one woman petitioned the court to be allowed to "enjoy her freedom" during trial.

32. Britton v. Mitchell, no. 18 (Mo. Cir. Ct. 1844), CCHRP. Although the Mexicans had surrounded and captured a small unit of American dragoons on April 24, 1846, Gen. Taylor defeated the Mexicans at Palo Alto after a half-day engagement where they "were driven from the field with great loss." Taylor subsequently pursued the Mexican army to the western bank of the Rio Grande (Scharf, *History of St. Louis*, vol. 1, 362).

33. The citizens of St. Louis were in a patriotic fervor even before learning of the war's outbreak. Companies of new volunteers formed so fast that they could be seen drilling in the streets without any uniforms whatsoever (Scharf, *History of St. Louis*, vol. 1, 362–65).

34. See documents Dred Scott v. Emerson Case File.

35. It is possible that the Scotts returned to the Russells' given the ambiguity of Mrs. Russell's deposition, though it would seem inconsistent with their desire to assert their independence if they were not paid, or if the Russells continued to pay Mrs. Emerson.

36. There is no record of the Reverend John B. Meachum helping a slave litigant according to the Freedom cases on the Web, either as guardian ad litem or as witness. CCHRP.

37. Out of 299 licenses for free black women in St. Louis, the "List of Free Negroes, Licensed [in] ... St. Louis County" listed 229 "washers" (Frazier, *Runaway and Freed Missouri Slaves*, 67–68).

38. Throughout the series of summons issued for call to trial, O'Flaherty was repeatedly called though he had no known connection to any place that the Scotts might have lived in a free state or free territory. John Loring, a coffee house owner, and two doctors, S. F. Watts and R. M. Jennings, had no known connection to necessary evidence except perhaps as persons who had hired the Scotts and could attest to their good character and ability to support themselves without falling dependent upon the community charity.

39. Brown, *From Fugitive Slave to Free Man*, 35.

40. In order to use a wheelbarrow, public porters had to register with the mayor's office, pay $5, and post another large bond, $200 (No. 1696 Hackney Carriages, Drays, etc. Sections 11–14, July 22, 1846). Krum, "Revised Ordinances of the City of St. Louis." All licensed public porters had to wear badges conspicuously on their persons on which was painted their names and license numbers.

41. Article V. Markets Several Rules and Regulations Section 1. Krum, "Revised Ordinances of the City of St. Louis."

42. April 8, 1846, G. W. Goode, Attorney, files notice of motion to dismiss to be argued on April 9. Harriet received the notice from Sheriff William Milburn. See Defendant's Pleading, McCray v. Hopkins, no. 162, at ˙7 (Mo. Cir. Ct. 1845), CCHRP.

43. George E. Goode, born in Virginia in 1815, earned a reputation as a land lawyer for his work in a case involving a huge tract of land that netted him a $60,000 fee, which was enormous at the time. Contemporaries reported that he was "most uncompromising in his adherence to slavery," a position that lost him many friends throughout his life (Bay, *Reminiscences of the Bench and Bar,* 569–71).

44. Polly Berry did this for her daughter Lucy (Delaney, "From the Darkness Cometh the Light," 29–43).

45. "The Story Of An Old Clerk," originally in *St. Louis Weekly Reveille,* October 15, 1848, available at www.umsl.edu/virtualstl/phase2/1850/events/perspectives/oldclerk.html.

46. Still in the courts were the following freedom suits: Martha Ann v. Cordell, no. 9 (1849); Preston v. Coons, no. 674 (1846); Bascom v. Ferguson, no. 20 (1846) CCHRP.

47. Bascom v. Ferguson, no. 20 (Mo. Cir. Ct. 1846), CCHRP. According to Bob Moore's list of slaves scheduled for sale by the probate court, Caroline Bascom had been sold in private sales on December 19, 1845 before she sued. Sales of slaves by the St. Louis Probate Court, on file with author, to appear on the Jefferson Memorial Park St. Louis Courthouse website.

48. The first emancipation suit, the Billy Tarlton petition, was filed in 1813: William Tarleton v. Horine, no. 7 (1814), CCHRP.

49. Mo. "Freedom" Stat. Sec. 1 (1835) § 2 of An Act to Enable Persons Held in Slavery to Sue for Their Freedom (January 27, 1835), Laws of Missouri (1836). See, for example, Petition for Freedom, Hannah v. Pitcher, no. 28, at ˙2 (1843); Petition for Freedom, Rebecca v. Black, no. 24, at ˙3 (1843); Alsey v. Randolph, no. 305 (1841), CCHRP.

50. This seemed to be true in the Scotts' case, with James Lackland taking depositions for Drake and D. N. Hall representing Pierre against Gabriel Chouteau while his senior partner A. P. Field was out of town (see Chapter 26).

51. See, for example, Curd v. Barksdale, no. 1 (1850) (petitioner found to be free where the jury instructions required her to prove that she had resided in Ohio); Jury Verdict, Martha Ann v. Cordell, no. 9, at ˙59 (1844) (finding the plaintiff free because she had been taken to Galena, Illinois, for six months as a slave); see also Motion for New Trial, Rebecca v. Black, no. 24, at ˙21 (1843) (appealing a jury verdict in favor of the petitioner as she had been brought to Illinois).

    Often, defendant slaveholders would leave the county when faced with a freedom suit based on residence. See, for example, Petition and Order of the Judge, Milly v. Duncan, no. 63, at ˙2 (alleging that the petitioner's master brought her to Galena, Illinois, for several weeks, then to Dubuque, in present-day Iowa for several months of mining labor); Petition to Sue *in forma pauperis,* Celestine v. Papin, no. 42, at ˙2 (1837) (alleging that petitioner's slave mother had been taken to free areas in the Northwest Territories), CCHRP.

52. Daniel Wilson v. Edmund Melville, no. 10 (1835), CCHRP.

53. Dozens of litigants had already won their freedom. See, for example, Jackson v. Fraser, no. 103 (1842), CCHRP.

54. See Rachael v. Walker, 4 Mo. 350, 354 (1836) (holding that if a military officer chooses to bring a slave to free territory, the slave is entitled to freedom even if the officer is ordered to travel there).

55. Attorney Gustavus Bird traveled to Illinois and Kentucky to take depositions for his clients litigating their freedom. See Deposition of Edward Ridly, Ralph v. Duncan, at ˙15–21 (1830) (taken in Kentucky), CCHRP; Deposition of Lowry May, ibid. at ˙25 (taken in Illinois).

56. Affidavit of Miles H. Clark, Scott v. Emerson, no. 1, at ˙31–32 (Mo. Cir. Ct. 1846).

57. The related tort claim permitted the illegally enslaved person to sue for a small amount of damages for the tort. This was useful because damages were not available through the Missouri statutory freedom claim.

58. Johnson, *Soul by Soul*, 15–16, 130.

59. Slaves with pending freedom suits sometimes lingered near the courthouse waiting for their case to be called (Delaney, "From the Darkness Cometh the Light," 33–35).

60. In 1835, the Missouri Legislature passed the "Act Concerning Freed Negroes and Mulattoes," requiring free people of color to carry licenses at all times, followed by an 1837 law banning abolitionist speech (Frazier, *Runaway and Freed Missouri Slaves,* 8, 91).

61. In one freedom suit, Justice Napton cautioned against emancipating people of color from the state of servitude that the law imposed upon "the mass of their species," writing, "Neither sound policy nor enlightened philanthropy should encourage, in a slaveholding State, the multiplication of a race whose condition could be neither that of freemen nor of slaves, and whose existence and increase, in this anomalous character, without promoting their individual comforts or happiness, tend only to dissatisfy and corrupt those of their own race and color remaining in a state of servitude" (Charlotte v. Chouteau, 11 Mo. 193, 200–01 [1847]).

62. Eaton v. Vaughan, 9 Mo. 743, 748 (1846). Steamboat captains were now obliged to detect runaways at the peril of their own financial liability.

63. Ibid.

64. With the exception of Wade (*Slavery in the Cities*), there is a dearth of sources to describe slaves' lives in cities before the Civil War. For instance, the oral histories for the state of Missouri that the Federal Writers project of the Works Progress Administration recorded in the 1930s recount very little about antebellum slave life in cities. Most ex-slaves interviewed had lived in the Deep South or in the Missouri countryside before the war, arriving in cities only long after the war's end (see Rawick, Federal Writers' Project, Missouri, 11 The American Slave: A Composite Autobiography, Arkansas Narratives Part 7, and Missouri Narratives).

65. McGinty, "Dred Scott's Fight for Freedom," 34.

66. Since he filed petition papers for so many litigants, he may have seen his job as simply filing the initial papers for slaves seeking their freedom. Some cases that he filed, including Lucy's, were turned over to other attorneys for suit, although he had successfully pursued at least one other to the Missouri high court. See Randolph v. Alsey, 8 Mo. 656, 657 (1844) (overcoming the defendant slaveholder's motion for a new trial).

67. See St. Louis Circuit Court Historical Records Project, CCHRP.

68. St. Louis Register of Deeds office: "Lot of F. B. Murdoch mortgaged to Mullanphy auctioned to Gottlieb Conzelman for $2517. se. corner of 5th and Elm." Property first mentioned June 9.

69. Judge Mullanphy's fight with attorney Ferdinand Risque was first documented in the newspaper ("A Scene in the Circuit Court," *Missouri Republican,* December 14, 1841) and then made part of St. Louis legend in John Darby's memoirs (Darby, *Personal Recollections*, 305–6).

70. The next census, 1850, shows Murdoch and most of his family in Berrian County, Michigan, but Murdoch's daughter remained behind in St. Louis with his father-in-law (Francis B. Murdoch in Berrian, Div. 10, Michigan in August 13, 1850, Census). A child, Rosella Murdoch, was in the St. Louis household of her grandfather, John W. Johnston (1850 Census entry for St. Louis). A lawsuit concerning his estate identifies Rosella as the daughter of Francis B. Murdoch. Her grandfather, John Johnston, did not leave money to any of the other Murdochs (John Johnston probate, PCDP).

71. Francis B. Murdoch v. Reliesan alias Melanie Christy, John Christy, Samuel Wiggins, Elias Langham & Archibal Carr. in Chancery, Nov. Term 1843, CCHRP.

72. Francis B. Murdoch appears in the 1860 census as F. B. Murdoch, age 55. Born: Maryland; Home: San Jose, Santa Clara County, California. Birthplaces of children suggest that he moved from Michigan to California between 1851 and 1855.
73. Scharf, *History of Saint Louis City*, vol. 1, 678.
74. *San Jose Telegraph,* April 28, 1857, edited by Francis B. Murdoch.

Chapter 26

1. The 1850 census gives more demographical information for Charles Lyons. His widow, Mrs. Nancy Lyons, is included in Cyprian Clamorgan's *Colored Aristocracy,* 54 (first published in 1858). Clamorgan claims that Charles Lyons died in California, leaving Mrs. Lyons $25,000. There is no St. Louis probate listed for Lyons, however (PCDP). Harriet C. Frazier's *Runaway and Freed Missouri Slaves* (66) gives an account of Nancy Washinga Dore Lyons.

   Julie Winch, the editor of Clamorgan's reissued book, claims that barber R. J. Wilkinson sued in addition to Lyons and that they were noticed by the authorities as being in violation because of their wealth (7). This seems to be contradicted by the fact that R. J. Wilkinson had already been licensed in June of 1842.

2. An Act Concerning Free Negroes and Mulattoes (March 26, 1845), Laws of Missouri (1846). A licensing statute was also passed in 1843.
3. "Such license shall not be granted to any free negro or mulatto, except:

   First. Such as were residents of this State on the second day of January, 1840, and continue to be such residents at the time of application.

   Second. Such as have been emancipated or born free within this state.

   Third, such as have been, or shall be, bound as apprentices or servants, according to the laws of this State, and shall have faithfully served out their terms of apprenticeship.

   Fourth, the husband or wife of a slave held and owned within this State, the parties having been married before first day of December 1835, with the consent of the master or mistress of the slave.

   Fifth, The husband or wife of a slave lawfully brought into this State by the owner, the parties having been married, by consent of the owner of the slave, before such slave was brought into this State.

   Sixth. Free negroes or mulattoes who produce a certificate of citizenship from some one of the United States" (ibid.).

4. In the matter of Charles Lyons: Petition for Habeas Corpus. Circuit Court docket book, p. 382, November 26, 1846. The Missouri statutes of 1855 "in regard to free colored persons" were very severe: "No colored person could live in this State without a license, and these licenses were to be issued only to certain classes of them; moreover, bond, not exceeding a thousand dollars, had to be given in security for good behavior. The negro was not allowed to retain in his possession the license or other free papers, though he could obtain them in the event of his moving from one county to another, as they had to be filed with the clerk of the county court where he resided. No free negro or mulatto could emigrate into the State or enter the State unless in the service of a white man, or for the purpose of passing through. In either case the time that he could remain in the borders was limited. If he stayed longer he was liable to arrest, a fine of $10, and expulsion. If the fine was not paid he was further liable to not more than twenty lashes, and the court could either order that he immediately leave the State or else hire him out until the fine, costs and expenses of imprisonment had been paid for by his labor" (Conard, *Encyclopedia of the History of Missouri,* 604–5).

5. Attorney Uriel Wright represented Lyons though he did not take freedom suits (Circuit Court docket book, p. 382, November 26, 1846).

6. Charles Lyons worked on the steamboats according to the occupation that he later listed on his license, as "fireman," and his residence in the 1850 census in the 4th Ward, St. Louis, was among a group of free blacks who were boatmen.

7. Buchanan, *Black Life on the Mississippi*, 19–52.

8. Citing *St. Louis Daily Union*, November 15, 1846, in Merkel, *The Antislavery Controversy in Missouri 1819–1865*. The committee's stated mission was "to adopt measures 'for the protection of slave property against the evil designs of the abolitionists and others'" (Scharf, *History of St. Louis*, vol. 1, 585).

9. Frederick Norcom, for example, vice president of the organization, was later sued in Hester Williams, Ella Williams, & Priscilla Williams, by their next friend, Jordan W. Early v. McAffee, B. & Frederick Norcum, Granville C. Blakey, & William E. Moore, filed in 1853.

10. See Scharf, *History of St. Louis*, vol. 1, 586.

11. Ibid.

12. Henry B. Belt, who acted as secretary, would later become sheriff of St. Louis County and in charge of hiring Harriet and Dred out to labor.

13. In February 1847, the Missouri legislature prohibited anyone from teaching blacks or mulattoes to read or write or to hold religious services without supervision from a white government agent (An Act Respecting Slaves, Free Negroes and Mulattoes [February 16, 1847], Laws of Missouri [1848]).

14. Describing Judge Krum, attorney Edward Bates wrote, "His mind is too loaded down and confused with a multitude of odds and ends of cases, that it has not the faculty to grasp a principle, and will never find out that a thing is, because it ought to be" (Bates Journal, January 29, 1847, Bates Family Papers, Mo HS).

15. Profile of George W. Goode in Bay, *Reminiscences of the Bench and Bar*, 569–71.

16. Ibid.

17. Ibid. Dueling rendered him ineligible to practice law in Virginia.

18. Ibid. Goode's last case before the Missouri Supreme Court concerned the detinue of a black slave. In McDermott v. Doyle, 17 Mo. 362 (Mo. 1852), Goode represented the plaintiffs; he had worked as plaintiff's counsel in similar prior cases. See Moreland & Barnum v. McDermott, 10 Mo. 605 (Mo. 1847).

19. George Goode's wife, Fanny Wash, was a half-sister of Cox's wife and Mitchell's wife (Delaney, "From the Darkness Cometh the Light," 12).

20. Reprints of the decision offered for sale (*Missouri Republican*, January 9, 1847).

21. In the matter of Charles Lyons: Petition for Habeas Corpus, Dec. 9, 1846, St. Louis Circuit Court records (Record book p. 420).

22. The statute by its terms applied to "Negroes and Mulattoes"; however, persons whose mothers were Native Americans did not suffer the same presumption of servitude or subservience as persons whose mothers were black. See, for example, Nancy v. Steen, no. 4 (April 1848) and Perryman v. Philibert, no. 255 (November 1848), CCHRP. I have been unable to ascertain any person known to be of Native American ancestry other than Charles Lyons who was subjected to the registration requirement or who registered voluntarily.

23. Charles Lyons's Free Negro Bond was issued in December of 1846 (Free Negro Bonds, Slavery Collection, Mo HS).

24. One hundred and thirty four persons filed for free negro bonds in December of 1846 (Free Negro Bonds, Slavery Collection, Mo HS).

25. Free Negro bond of Ralph Harrison, Adam D. Steuart, December 30, 1846 (Free Negro Bonds, Slavery Collection, Mo HS). Dred described the willingness of a St. Louis army officer to back him in "The Original Dred Scott a Resident of St. Louis—A Sketch of His History," *St. Louis News*, April 8, 1857.

26. Bates Journal, December 3, 1846, Bates Family Papers, Mo HS.

27. Delaney, "From the Darkness Cometh the Light," 39.

28. The Circuit Court docket book states that her case went to trial on December 15, 1846, and was resolved in her favor the following day (Sarah v. William Waddingham, 434, 436, Circuit Court docket book).

29. Clerk of St. Louis Court record book, Wednesday, December 16, 1846, 436. The list for Free Negro licenses provides a "Prasser, Sarah, 27 years old, 5' 4 1/4'" supporting herself as a house servant, licensed in March 1847.

30. "I am heartily glad that he is about to resign, even if we have to draw straws for his successor" (Bates Journal, January 29, 1847, Bates Family Papers).

31. Krum became mayor of St. Louis in 1848 (Scharf, *History of St. Louis*, vol. 1, 678). Walsh, *The Story Of An Old Clerk*, 2 (describing Krum as mayor of Alton and St. Louis).

32. Bates Journal, March 11, 1847, Bates Family Papers.

33. *Missouri Republican* from January to April, 1847 (speculation on who would become next judge).

34. *Missouri Republican*, April 6, 1847.

35. Little is known about Judge Alexander Hamilton. William Bay's *Reminiscences of the Bench and Bar*, Scharf's *History of Saint Louis*, and the memoirs of John F. Darby, a lawyer and congressman from St. Louis, all make only passing references to him (see John F. Darby, *Personal Recollections*, 325). We do know that Hamilton was born in 1811 and was admitted to practice in Philadelphia in 1831 (Martin, *Martin's Bar and Bench of Philadelphia*, 274). Judge Hamilton received his appointment to the Circuit Court bench in 1846, where he served until 1857 (Thomas T. Gantt, *Judicial Nominations*, 6 S. L. Rev. 554, 560–61 [1881]).

36. Joseph Charless Jr. posted bonds for Dred and Harriet's court costs on July 2, 1847 (Bond for Cost, Dred Scott v. Emerson and Bond for Cost, Harriet Scott v. Emerson, Case File). Charles Drake appeared as counsel for the Scotts on May 7, 1847.

37. Menius and Blow, "Mother of the Kindergarten," 13. Charlotte is credited with holding the family together after their mother's death of cholera in 1831 followed soon after by their father's death (ibid).

38. Whether Dred was the slave sold to pay for the funeral cannot be definitely established, but he was sold to Emerson shortly before Peter Blow's death (or shortly afterward) because a financial transaction from Emerson appears in the probate (Peter Blow Probate, PCDP).

39. *Frank Leslie's Illustrated Newspaper*, June 27, 1857.

40. Taylor Blow's father-in-law Wahrenberg had participated in slaves' emancipations in St. Louis before. See Jonathan & Gilbert, free men of color v. Duncan, Edmund Tracy, and Charles Wahendorf, no. 304 (March 1831), CCHRP.

41. Charless, *A Biographical Sketch of the Life and Character of Joseph Charless*, 81, 86, 131.

42. When the suit was filed, she and brother Henry's wife were visiting relatives in Mobile, Alabama. A letter of March 6, 1847, from William Carr Lane, Mobile, to Ann Lane, St. Louis, reported seeing Mrs. Charless and Mrs. Minerva Blow in Mobile. Lane Family Collection, Mo HS.

43. Joseph Charless Jr. was born in Louisville, Kentucky, in 1804. A printer by trade, he later studied law and took over the Charless, Blow and Co. drug business in St. Louis. He also served in high posts in Missouri banks and railroad concerns. In 1859, a man against whom Charless had testified in an embezzlement case shot Charless to death on a public street in broad daylight ("The Charless Tragedy at St. Louis," *New York Times*, June 8, 1859). Charlotte Blow later wrote a biography of her late husband, *A Biographical Sketch of the Life and Character of Joseph Charless*. Before giving up the practice of law, Joseph Charless Jr. had represented at least seven slaves in freedom suits: Angelique v. Reynolds, no. 10 (1828); Edmund v. Reynolds, no. 11 (1828); Suzette v. Reynolds, no. 9 (1828); John v. Reynolds, no. 12 (1828); Rector v. Bivens, no. 26 (1827); Merry v. Tiffin, no. 18 (1826); Jefferson v. McCutcheon, no. 23 (1826), CCHRP.

44. Joseph Charless Jr. posted bonds for Dred and Harriet's court costs on July 2, 1847 (Bond for Cost, Dred Scott v. Emerson and Bond for Cost, Harriet Scott v. Emerson, Case file). Charles Drake appeared as counsel for the Scotts on May 7, 1847.

45. 1860 City Directory (http://rollanet.org/~bdoerr/1860cydir/1860cd.htm).

46. Charless, *A Biographical Sketch,* 24; description of wedding and its simplicity.
47. Ibid.
48. Charless, *A Biographical Sketch,* 133. Charlotte attributed this generosity to her deceased husband, but then again that was the point of her book written in his honor to her grandchildren who would never know him. Charlotte's own actions in fostering institutional help for former servants are documented in her founding of the Home for the Friendless (*Missouri Republican,* November 2, 1854).
49. From the slaveholder's point of view, selling a family slave did not necessarily sever the family tie. "The relationship of master and slave was like marriage," one contemporary slaveholder wrote—"pretty much 'for better or worse'" (Kennerly, *Persimmon Hill,* 100). Henry Blow's testimony suggests that his father sold him to Emerson. If this were true it would mean that Dred had been sold earlier than customarily believed.
50. Marli F. Weiner, "Mistresses, Morality, and the Dilemmas of Slaveholding," 285.
51. Taylor Blow participated in freeing Frankey Cuterfoot and Fanny Overton on February 7, 1847, Nicene Clark on April 28, 1854, and Ophelia (daughter of Silvia McCoy) by will of Sarah Charless (executors Joseph Charless, C. T. Charless, Taylor Blow and E. A. W. Blow), Dec. 4, 1855. (All emancipations in the Circuit Court docket books for those dates.) He had served as witness for the emancipation of Hester Reed by Frances E. Twitchell on June 10, 1854, and he had played some role in the support of Alexander Ball (T. Blow named on free negro bond as warranter, December 29, 1846; see Free Negro Bonds, Slavery Collection, Mo HS). Taylor Blow also sat on the jury in three freedom suits, Martha Ann v. Hiram Cordell, Hannah v. John Pitcher, Preston v. Coons, CCHRP.
52. *Frank Leslie's Illustrated Newspaper,* June 27, 1857.
53. See chapters 31 and 32.
54. Lincoln appointed Blow minister to Venezuela in 1860. He went on to serve in the U.S. House of Representatives and as minister to Brazil (Scharf, *History of St. Louis,* vol. 1, 608–9).
55. Hodder, "Some Phases of the Dred Scott Case," 3.
56. Henry Blow never freed any of his own slaves according to the St. Louis Emancipation list compiled from the docket books and one published listing (Mo HS). Peter Blow, the oldest brother, 33 at the time, did not appear in the case file at all.
57. Henry's father-in-law was notoriously proslavery and a member of the Committee of 100. Thornton Grimsley was also a member of the proslavery Committee of 100. He served the committee as chairman of the 2nd ward, where the Russells lived (Scharf, *History of St. Louis,* vol. 1, 585).
58. Henry T. Blow wrote to the newspaper about his objections to being identified with Benton and Blair (*Missouri Republican,* July 27, 1856).
59. No separate court cost bond seems to have been requested for Harriet's separate case.
60. *Missouri Republican,* July 27, 1856.
61. Charles Drake was born in Cincinnati in 1811. After brief service in the navy, he studied law and became a prominent lawyer in St. Louis. He went on to be elected a U.S. senator in 1867 and then the chief justice of the U.S. Court of Claims in 1871; he died in Washington, D.C., in 1892 (Lawson, *American State Trials,* 226). Another Blow brother, Peter, had married into the LaBeaume family and still another later served as St. Louis sheriff.
62. Charlotte's corresponding letter was not preserved. The family correspondence also shows Henry Blow's continued receptiveness to sister Charlotte's influence. One letter refers to a long letter he'd received from her, and that Henry tells his wife he is thinking it over. She must have been attempting to persuade him of something. Blow Family Papers, Mo HS.
63. *Missouri Republican,* November 2, 1854.

64. The newspapers credited her with single-handedly obtaining the charitable contributions necessary to maintain the institution. She led the civic campaign when she returned from her travels to discover that a servant woman she knew had died in poverty. The Home for the Friendless was a house for women, sparked by the death of a once-wealthy society woman who died without friends, down on her luck (The Home for the Friendless Centennial Report 1853–1953, 6, and *Missouri Republican*, November 2, 1854).

65. This apparent contradiction was in fact common to white slave-holding women according to Marli F. Weiner: "Those wealthy white women who sympathized with slaves and who were sensitive to the practical and moral responsibilities they represented did not want to abandon the institution of slavery. Most kept their discomfort to themselves or articulated it in contradictory and ambivalent terms to female correspondents; they did not develop a program to end slavery nor could they imagine a world without it.... In their view, the difficulties they faced were not the result of anything fundamentally wrong with the institution of slavery itself. Challenging slavery overtly was simply too dangerous a position for them to take: it smacked of the heresies of women's rights and abolitionism" (Weiner, "Mistresses, Morality, and the Dilemmas of Slaveholding," 290–94).

66. The 1860 slave schedule census for St. Louis lists one slave owned by Charlotte Charless and another owned by her brothers. She did participate with her husband and younger brother in signing emancipation papers for two other elderly slaves. Her mother-in-law had promised one of her elderly slaves freedom in her will. Her husband saw that the promise was kept. The pattern of her emancipating activity appears to be limited, however, to elderly family slaves. She never sought to free all slaves, nor even all slaves whom her family owned. Her most extensive writing, the memoir about her murdered husband, does not express any criticism of slavery. (See, generally, Charless, *A Biographical Sketch*.) She still is listed as a slaveholder in the 1860 St. Louis Census Slave Schedule.

67. Unlike her own slaves, whom she identified in her letters by name, this man was nameless to her (letter from Minerva Blow to Henry Blow, March 8, 1856. Blow Family Papers, Mo HS).

68. One historian writes that "white women's moral universe was supposed to include all needy recipients of care" (Weiner, "Mistresses, Morality, and the Dilemmas of Slaveholding," 280).

69. Women could sometimes blur gender distinctions when rendering favors, especially in the political arena where they could pull strings in support of male friends and family (Wood, *Masterful Women*, 111–12).

70. *Missouri Republican*, November 2, 1854.

71. "1860 Kennedy's St. Louis City Directory" entry: "Charless, Charlotte T., wid. Joseph, residence Carondelet, resides Frank Blair's house" (Ken Kaufman, *Dred Scott's Advocate*, 156–58) (suggesting that Charlotte Blow Charless was one of Dred's principal benefactors).

72. Pierre v. Therese Chouteau, no. 192 (November 1840); discontinued at death of Therese Chouteau; refiled in 1842 as Pierre v. Gabriel S. Chouteau, no. 125 (November 1842), CCHRP.

73. Pierre v. Chouteau, no. 125 (Nov. 1842), CCHRP.

74. Chouteau v. Pierre, 9 Mo. 3 (1845).

75. Louis v. Chouteau, no. 51 (April 1844); and Paul v. Paul, no. 151 (April 1844), CCHRP. Circuit Court record book, 378, states that the parties in Michel Paul v. Gabriel Paul agree to abide by the final judgment in the cause of Pierre v. Gabriel S. Chouteau, no. 125 (November 1842), and Charlotte v. Chouteau, no. 13, (November 1843). This suggests that Michel was a brother of Louis, Mary Charlotte, and Gabriel. (Mary Charlotte is sometimes simply referred to as Charlotte in the court papers.) Rose is known to have had several more children, though some may have died and others transferred away from St. Louis during the intervening years. These four are the only four children of Rose known to have filed suit.

76. Charlotte v. Chouteau, no. 13 (November 1843) document listing her four children.
77. Pierre v. Chouteau, no. 125 (November 1842), CCHRP. Dedimus to examine witnesses in Canada filed June 30, 1845 by Pierre's then lawyers, Field, Hall, and Hudson. David N. Hall (b. Mass. 1820, d. Missouri March 31, 1851).
78. "I appeared for the plaintiff at the trial to aid Mr. Hall, whose senior (Col. Field) was absent" (Bates Journal, May 1, 1847, Bates Family Papers).
79. Martha Ann v. Hiram Cordell, Case no. 9, CCHRP. Jury deadlocked May 13, 1847. The two juries were different groups of men, but notably Taylor Blow had been a member of this deadlocked jury (St. Louis Circuit Court record book).
80. Charles Drake had married Martha Blow. Despite her death, the bonds of family probably induced Drake to keep this case temporarily from failing for lack of a lawyer (Fehrenbacher, *The Dred Scott Case*, 569; Kaufman, *Dred Scott's Advocate*, 156).
81. Similarly, Alexander P. Field handed the case over to David N. Hall.
82. Bates Journal, March 1, 1849, Bates Family Papers. James R. Lackland, who was Drake's junior associate, married a daughter of Lawellin Brown about the time that Drake left the state and the firm dissolved, May 1, 1847.

    May 13, 1847, Miles H. Clark's deposition was taken at the office of Charles D. Drake, in the City of St. Louis. Miles Clark also stated that he was now a second lieutenant in Capt. McNair's Company of Volunteers known as the "Missouri Guards" raised for service in New Mexico, and probably some time next week the Company will leave for its destination.

    Although Drake would later play an antislavery role in the Civil War, he was not necessarily an abolitionist at this time. He had represented the free black Reverend Meachum at the Supreme Court, but he had urged the ironic argument on the black minister's behalf that free black men should not be permitted to testify in court. The Reverend Meachum sought to quash the testimony of a free black man who had testified against him (Meachum v. Judy, 4 Mo. 361, 363 [1836]).
83. Bates Journal, May 22, 1847, Bates Family Papers, Mo HS.
84. Catherine Anderson testified that the Scotts left for the south, Fort Gibson she thought, in April 1838. The summons is addressed to the dwelling house of William Anderson, 90 Myrtle Street. The St. Louis City directories list at least three different William Andersons, but the William Anderson who resided on Myrtle Street was a "rectifier," or distiller of alcohol (1848 city directory). From that identification, he can be matched to the William Anderson who founds "William Anderson & CO., rectifiers and commercial merchants." Catherine Anderson later resided at "ws 6th, bn Market and Chestnut," according to the 1852 city directory.
85. Missouri Secretary of State, *State Archives Dred Scott Case, 1846–1857,* www.sps.mo.gov/archives/resources/africanamerican/scott/scott.asp.
86. Samuel M. Bay, born in Hudson, New York, in 1810, studied at a private school under future U.S. Supreme Court Chief Justice Salmon P. Chase. His propensity for books and solitude made him seem "haughty and overbearing" to those who did not know him well. He was elected to the legislature in 1836 and quickly appointed attorney general of the state. In 1846 or 1847, he moved to St. Louis and received a lucrative post as an attorney for the state bank. Bay's brother wrote a posthumous account of him, describing him as "fluent, concise, and logical, but never eloquent." He died of cholera in the 1849 epidemic (Bay, *Reminiscences of the Bench and Bar of Missouri,* 165–71).
87. *Missouri Republican,* August 1, 1845, advertising sale by S. M. Bay of Jefferson City, of "FIVE LIKELY NEGROES," before the Court House door, in the city of Jefferson. *Missouri Republican,* July 29, 1847, reported S. M. Bay selling land in Osage, Miller, and Cole counties offered in exchange for St. Louis city property.
88. Summonses issued on June 24, 1847, and June 30, 1847. All found except M. H. Clark and A. D. Stuart
89. See Summons, Scott v. Emerson, no. 1, at ˙81, CCHRP.
90. Bates Journal, June 23, 1847, Bates Family Papers.

91. Bates Journal, July 1, 1847, Bates Family Papers.
92. The judge's anti-retaliation order gave them the liberty to attend the trial (Dred Scott Case File).
93. (Sarah v. William Waddingham, 434, 436, Circuit Court docket book).
94. A litigant could be awarded damages for showing assault or false imprisonment in court, even if the damages were trivial. The act to enable persons held in slavery for their freedom (January 27, 1835) did not permit plaintiffs to sue for damages, section 15, but a simple trespass action did.
95. Bay, *Reminiscences of the Bench and Bar of Missouri*, 165–71.
96. Ibid.
97. Ibid., 571.
98. Fehrenbacher makes a parallel point. "The decision produced the absurd effect of allowing Mrs. Emerson to keep her slaves simply because no one had proved that they were her slaves" (Fehrenbacher, *The Dred Scott Case*, 254). His point is not technically accurate in a legal sense because it was unnecessary to prove her "ownership" as much as to prove her agency in depriving the Scotts of their freedom. The Scotts' attorney could prove neither her ownership nor her agency with Samuel Russell's testimony because he had had no dealings with Mrs. Emerson.
99. July 24, 1847, affidavit alleging surprise. June 30, 1847, motion to set aside jury verdict and request for new trial.
100. July 23, 1847. The jury included John Sappington, Leonidas Willson, James Longworth, Benjamin Perry, John Rudder, Thomas Rudder, William Stanton, Richard Turnilty, Isaac Williams, John W. McLaughlin, Hugh Miller, and Mathew McKinstry.
101. John Sappington, 1850 Census entry.
102. Bay simultaneously appealed to the Missouri Supreme Court and moved for a new trial. See Motion to Set Aside Verdict, Scott v. Emerson, no. 1, at ˙45–53 (1846). Because a new trial was granted, the Missouri Supreme Court found appropriately that because there was no final judgment in the lower court yet a new trial had been granted, there was nothing to appeal. See Orders Granting New Trial, Scott v. Emerson, no. 1, at ˙55–58 (1846); Orders Dismissing Appeal, ibid. at ˙71–74.
103. After Bay moved for a new trial between June 30 and July 1, 1847, Goode moved to require a bond to hire the Scotts out and to require their hirer to hold a bond assigning costs to the loser and to surrender the Scotts should they lose their freedom suit. See Motions, Scott v. Emerson, no. 1, at ˙67–70, CCHRP. See Motion, Scott v. Emerson, no. 1, at ˙67–68 (1846); Motion, ibid. at ˙69–70. Charless bond for Dred Scott July 2, 1847. Scott v. Emerson Case File.
104. Delaney, "From Darkness Cometh the Light," 28. Even Charlotte Charless asked her husband to discipline the servants (Charless, *A Biographical Sketch*, 47).

 Historian Thavolia Glymph documents many instances of white mistresses engaging in violence against their slaves (Glymph, *Out of the House of Bondage*, chapters 1 and 2). Within the city of St. Louis masters' acts of beating slaves in public had been socially discouraged since Major Harney's incident of beating his slave woman, and mistresses' actions would have been regarded as even more socially unacceptable if known or observed in the city.
105. Wood, *Masterful Women*, 49–51.
106. See, for example, Winny sued 13 defendants. Winny, a free woman of color, versus Pettibone, Rufus; Charles B. and Sally Hatton; Owen and Sally Wingfield; Isaac Voteau; John and Betsy Butler; John Whitset (a/k/a Whitesides); Michel & Thursa Sanford; John Whitset, Jr., Lucinda Whitset, no. 12 (July 1825), CCHR.
107. The practice of suing multiple defendants was customary in similar cases before his time on the bench.
108. Bay, *Reminiscences of the Bench and Bar of Missouri*, 170.
109. *Missouri Republican*, July 1, 1847, announces the sale of 26 slaves to hire by Geo. W. Coons, Administrator of estate of Milton Duty, deceased. *Missouri Republican*,

July 14, 1847. John F. Darby ad: "ON the 15th of July at the east front door of the Courthouse, I will hire all the slaves consisting of men, women, and children belonging to estate of Milton Duty deceased to the highest bidder, on the usual credit. The parties hiring giving bond and security."

110. Nat (Of Color) v. G. W. Coons, 10 Mo. 543, 1847 WL 3736 (Mo.) March Term, 1847.

111. Nothing appears from the context to explain what brought these lawyers to them as early as November 18, 1847, except that recently they also had had responsibility for Pierre v. Chouteau. Field and Hall were listed as sharing the same office as early as the 1847 St. Louis Directory.

112. David Hall signed several court documents on behalf of the Scotts, including their original petitions (Dred Scott Case Collection).

113. Stevens, "Alexander Pope Field," *Journal of the Illinois State Historical Society* 14 (1911–1912): 7.

114. Fehrenbacher, *The Dred Scott Case*, 254–55.

115. Stevens, "Alexander Pope Field," *Journal of the Illinois State Historical Society* 14 (1911–1912): 7.

116. Matilda, Anson, Mary Ann, Michael, Sam, Nathan v. Field and Mitchell, May 22, 1832, no. 47, 48, 49, 50, CCHRP.

117. Alexander P. Field is credited with representing the Shearods in an April 1834 prosecution in Union County, Illinois. www.womacknet.net/familylines/iveys.htm.

118. Alexander P. Field, born in 1801, had married Eliza Owings on November 13, 1841. In 1850, Eliza Field continued to live with her father, Joshua Owings, in St. Louis, with the Fields' three children and David N. Hall, Field's law partner (1850 St. Louis Census). Field traveled the Mississippi River, arguing suits in different jurisdictions, but he ended up in New Orleans permanently within a matter of months of coming to the Scotts' representation. He later turned over the St. Louis law firm to his partner David Hall (David N. Hall Probate, PDCP).

119. Alexander Pope Field died in 1876 shortly after becoming Louisiana's attorney general.

120. David N. Hall was born in Massachusetts in 1820 and died March 31, 1851. He graduated from Yale College in 1839 and had just married in Connecticut, August 29, 1847, when he returned to take up the Scotts' case (Ancestry.com, Connecticut Town Marriage Records, Barbour Collection).

121. American State Trials, a source that attempted to provide biographies for all the key figures in the Dred Scott case, simply says that not much is known about him (Lawson, *American State Trials*, 227). Fehrenbacher, like most historians, presumed that Alexander Field was doing most of the legal work for the Scotts (Fehrenbacher, *The Dred Scott Case*, 254, 263). Since David N. Hall died in the midst of the litigation, some historians presumed that he was an older man and Field's senior partner.

122. Hall's probate notes that he paid for the hire of nine of Milton Duty's slaves in 1849 in addition to paying Dred's hire (David N. Hall probate, PDCP). Hall had no business or farm that could have employed these slave litigants, so the act seems more an act of charity than oppression.

123. Sarah's Inquest file and Coroner's Report, on file with author.

124. Sarah's mistreatment is also mentioned in William Wells Brown, *From Fugitive Slave to Free Man*, 92–93.

125. Ibid.

126. Ibid.

127. Ibid.

128. Ibid.

129. Delaney, "From the Darkness Cometh the Light," 29.

130. This story must have been well known in the St. Louis community at the time. William Wells Brown noted it in his autobiography (Brown, *From Fugitive Slave to Free Man*, Appendix, 92–93).

131. Meachum, *An Address to all the Colored Citizens.*

132. Marcy, *Thirty Years of Army Life on the Border*, 9–10. "The insult must be atoned for by blood. With other tribes, quarrels can often be settled by presents to the injured party; but with the prairie Indians, the law of equity is such that no reconciliation can take place until the reproach is wiped out with the blood of their enemy."

133. Brown, *From Fugitive Slave to Free Man*, 92–93 (citing the *Missouri Republican* and the *New York Herald*).

134. Resolutions of the prosecution of Mistress Tanner and the slave Cornelia for Sarah's death. Tanner and Cornelia, Criminal Case docket, on file with author.

Chapter 27

1. *Missouri Republican*, November 6, 1848, 3.

2. Virtually every runaway ad posted in the Missouri Republican contained a reward that differentiated between whether the runaway was found in state or had to be brought back from out of state. See, generally, Harriet C. Frazier, *Runaway and Freed Missouri Slaves and Those Who Helped Them, 1763–1865.*

3. November 15, 1847, entry, St. Louis Circuit Court record book.

4. One freedom suit was dismissed because neither the petitioner nor her attorney was present when the case was called the preceding spring (McCray v. Hopkins, no. 162 [1845], CCHRP). Judge Hamilton usually reinstated the case when the unsuspecting litigants showed up at court again wondering when their case was to be tried, but failing to appear cost the petitioners further delay (ibid.).

5. The court's daybook lists subjects in the order in which they were taken up and invariably the manumissions (like the naturalizations) are at the top of the day's events or at the end.

6. Citation to manumission index and St. Louis Circuit Court daybooks.

7. St. Louis Circuit Court record book; Blassingame, *Slave Testimony*, 508–9.

8. Article II, Of the Emancipation of Slaves (March 19, 1835), Laws of Missouri (1836). Usually the person's master or a lawyer appeared and swore to attest to the emancipation deed. If the man was a stranger to the judge, he had to produce two witnesses to swear an oath attesting to his signature.

9. Philip Curtis (age 29; mulatto); Mahala (age 27; mulatto) and children Eliza Jane (age 12), Lucy Ann (age eight), Benjamin (age five), Cornelia (age two months) (St. Louis Circuit Court daybook, November 27, 1848).

10. Searching for settlement patterns demonstrated that many of the emancipated slaves did not show up in the next city census.

11. See, for example, *Missouri Republican*, July 22, 1850, and August 27, 1850: "Escape from the Work House yesterday—The result of advocacy of the unconstitutionality of the Vagrant Law, by one of our City Papers"; "The Work House is filled to its utmost capacity with convicts for various offenses, but the most expert and abandoned are those sent there for vagrancy."

12. Mrs. Russell's deposition was not taken until December 20, 1849.

13. Mrs. Emerson was called to once and made appearance through her attorney, August 30, 1847. They are not among the 61 documents identified as the official court record. Colonel Sanford made a declaration on October 23, 1847.

     Perhaps in the intervening years the records were lost or stolen by curiosity seekers, or perhaps the trail was intentionally clouded. Both documents might provide a world of information; unfortunately, they have long been missing from the court file.

14. Unmarried women generally could not testify in open court (Wood, *Masterful Women*, 69). Adeline Russell delivered her deposition for the Scotts in law offices well outside of court. See Deposition of Adeline Russell, Scott v. Emerson, no. 1 (November 1847), CCHRP.

15. The docket was occupied with commercial matters, real estate partitions, and steamboat liens (St. Louis Circuit Court record book for 1849).

16. The clerk wrote: "It appearing to the court that certain proceedings heard in this cause on the second day of December 1847, were by mistake omitted.... It is ordered that the same be now entered as of that day" (St. Louis Circuit Court record book for 1849).

17. Mary Charlotte filed suit against Gabriel Chouteau in 1843, no. 13. Brother Louis similarly filed suit in 1844. See Chouteau v. Chouteau, no. 51 (April 1844), CCHRP.

18. March 6, 1847, Affidavit of D. H. Bishop, deputy sheriff under Samuel Conway, Sheriff. Pierre was surrendered to Sheriff Conway about April 5, 1848. Mr. Churchill said that on account of his strange conduct, he was unwilling longer to keep him any longer; he would prefer to pay his board in jail. About the same time that the sheriff took the Scotts into custody, Pierre was back in jail. Sheriff Conway looked for someone else to hire him, but no one wanted a slave who acted strangely.

19. Deposition of Bridget Padget, Nancy v. Steen, no. 4, at '11–14 (April 1848), CCHRP.

20. Ibid.

21. See also Peggy Perryman v. Philibert, no. 255 (November 1848), CCHRP.

22. Ibid.

23. Bates Journal, November 7, 1847, Bates Family Papers, Mo HS.

24. "Telegraph! A memorable day in the history of St. Louis, for this day at 12 o'clock, the operation of the telegraph being completed to the east bank of the Mississippi, opposite St. Louis, the first message was transmitted along the river; and so, the electric communication to the eastern cities is completed" (Bates Journal, December 20, 1847, Bates Family Papers, Mo HS). Just before Christmas, the telegraph line was extended to reach the far shore opposite St. Louis.

25. Bates Journal, December 31, 1847, Bates Family Papers, Mo HS.

26. Bates Journal, January 1, 1848, Bates Family Papers, Mo HS.

27. "The hands drew their share of clothing on Christmas day for the year" (Brown, *From Fugitive Slave to Free Man*, 182).

28. "Clothing for these children was scanty and inadequate. One former slave recalled: 'The clothes that I wore did not amount to much, just a one-piece dress or gown. In shape this was more like a gunnysack, with a hole cut in the bottom for me to stick my head thru, and the corners cut out for armholes. We never wore underclothes, not even in the winter... We never had more than one at a time, and when they had to be washed, we went naked until they had dried'" (Clinton, *Harriet Tubman*, 7).

29. The comment of William Blow's wife about the Scotts' begging from the Blow family is noted in Fehrenbacher, *The Dred Scott Case*, 571.

30. Bryan, "The Blow Family and Their Slave Dred Scott." Kennerly, *Persimmon Hill*, 179, describes the St. Louis custom of calling among peers.

31. Bray, *The Journals of Joseph N. Nicollet*, 112–18.

32. Squire Brown v. Charles Anderson, July term 1841, CCHRP. "Defendant has for some time past hired plaintiff out and collected his wages and refused to furnish plaintiff with a single article of clothing unless plaintiff consents to a dismissal of the suit and plaintiff is now confined in jail."

33. Thomas, *From Tennessee Slave to St. Louis Entrepreneur*, 97.

34. Thornton Kinney v. John F. Hatcher & Charles C. Bridges (1853).

35. Bates Journal, February 22, 1848, Bates Family Papers.

36. "Imbecility, want of decision, vacillation and total unfitness" were the charges against the former judge according to the local newspaper. The people of the area had often shown their opposition to the publication of such a paper (*Missouri Republican*, March 28, 1848).

37. *Missouri Republican,* February 13, 1848.

38. I use the term bankrupt here more descriptively than specifically. I have been unable to find an actual attempt by Alexander Sanford in the Maryland or Virginia area. That is because I have been unable to find bankruptcy records for that era in those states. I have found notices to his creditors as well as J. F. A. Sanford's assessment of his father's circumstances. This evidence points to the conclusion that he would have availed himself of bankruptcy proceedings had they been available.

39. February 1, 1849, J. F. A. Sanford of New York. Sale of certain negro slaves to James H. Lucas. Sum of $1850. Sanford-Chouteau Letter Collection, on file with author.

40. She indicated as much later in the article, "Famous Dred Scott Case: Mrs. Chaffee, owner of old slave, still living in Springfield," *New York Times*, December 22, 1895.

41. On March 3, 1848, Bettendorf land to Alfred Churchill, $2400. Copy of deed registered in Scott County Registry of Deeds, Scott County, Iowa.

42. March 14, 1848. Missouri Statutes, section 00.

43. Fehrenbacher, *The Dred Scott Case*, 256.

44. Ehrlich notes that some Dred Scott papers were destroyed and others badly damaged by fire (Ehrlich, *They have No Rights*, 187–88).

45. Case No. 03424, Microfilm Reel C 30872, 1851.

46. David N. Hall Probate, PCDP. This bill for Dred's services, not mentioning Harriet's services, is buried deeply in David Hall's probate and seems reliable evidence that Hall did not hire Harriet. She was either hired out to someone else or she was able to exist below the radar of the sheriff's monitoring.

47. See Chapter 24.

48. "Famous Dred Scott Case," *New York Times*, December 22, 1895.

49. See Chapter 32, 321–22.

50. B. S. Garland is best known for actively pursuing his slave man Joshua Glover to Wisconsin and litigating an unpopular case there under the Fugitive Slave Law (see, generally, Jackson and McDonald, *Finding Freedom*; Baker, *The Rescue of Joshua Glover*). Garland, who had once run for clerk of court, had attested to the probate of the Manchester road property (John Emerson probate, PCDP).

51. The Garland family history includes only two entries for him spanning 40 years, but both involve debt collection: February 23, 1832, B. S. Garland wrote a business letter to his cousins concerning a note that was being served. He was in Lovingston, Virginia, at the time (Robert Alonzo Brock Collection: Garland Family Papers, 1762–1907; mss BR 84), March 28, 1870, B. S. Garland was mentioned as living in Missouri and attempting to reclaim jewelry of his nephew (letters received by the Office of the Adjutant General, 1861–1870; M619, roll 812, frames 219–221).

52. Heisterhagen v. Garland, 10 Mo. 66 (1846); Garland v. Harrison, 17 Mo. 282 (1852).

53. In re Booth, 3 Wis. 157 (Wis. 1854).

54. His testimony was never taken, so it's unclear what he would have said—perhaps that Mrs. Emerson was the beneficiary of the will.

55. John Emerson Probate, PCDP.

56. Bill submitted by B. S. Garland to J. F. A. Sanford's estate (John F. A. Sanford probate, PCDP).

57. John F. A. Sanford Probate, PCDP.

58. Delaney, "From the Darkness Cometh the Light," 33–35.

59. Scharf, *History of St. Louis*, vol. 1, 670. For more on the early night patrols that evolved into St. Louis's police department, see ibid., 737–47; *Missouri Republican*, January 10, 1849; *Missouri Republican*, April 5, 1851. "We notice an unusually large number of beggars are overrunning our streets, the majority of whom are mendicants by profession and have not the shadow of a right to the charities of their fellow citizens.... A fortnight's sojourn at the workhouse would benefit them vastly more than the most liberal donation from well-meaning, but undiscriminating philanthropists." Ibid.

60. See, for example, Elsa Hicks and child v. Patrick T. McSherry, no. 121, CCHRP.

61. "In May 1846, I found here, 20 prisoners; in April, 1847, 15 were in the new jail, and two in the old prison." (D. L. Dix). *Missouri Republican*, April 13, 1847.

62. Ibid. James Seward described his St. Louis jail conditions while awaiting his murder trial in 1841. "I am in a Spanish cell, 8 feet underground. The cell is 8 by 12, no light but though a loophole in the iron door. I have heavy handcuffs on each hand fastened in the center. Heavy irons are on my feet and fastened to a ring in the floor by a chain three inches long. My fare is coarse bread and water. In this cell are six other persons. The heat is so intense that the prisoners are to strip

naked upon entering, and remain so while they stay" (Buchanan, *Black Life on the Mississippi,* 144).

63. *Missouri Republican,* April 30, 1847. See also Brown, *From Fugitive Slave to Free Man.*

64. *Missouri Republican,* June 13, 1852.

65. Brown, *From Fugitive Slave to Free Man,* 61 (describing how he and his mother were locked up in separate cells at the St. Louis jail).

66. He is listed there in the 1850 St. Louis census.

67. Report on the St. Louis County and City Jail, *Missouri Republican,* April 30, 1847. For more descriptions of Missouri jails, see Thompson, *Prison Life and Reflections.*

68. *Missouri Republican,* April 30, 1847: report of D. L. Dix on the St. Louis county and city jail.

69. *Missouri Republican,* January 25, 1855: "Suicide attempted by a Jail Prisoner."

70. *Missouri Republican,* April 30, 1847: report of D. L. Dix on the St. Louis county and city jail.

71. Thompson, *Prison Life and Reflections,* 242.

72. *Missouri Republican,* April 30, 1847.

73. Tiffany, *Life of Dorothea Lynde Dix,* 148–49.

74. William Wells Brown visited his sister in jail where she was kept before being sold south (Brown, *From Fugitive Slave to Free Man,* 64–65).

75. *Missouri Republican,* February 5, 1847. The sheriff caught two escapees and brought them back to jail (*Missouri Republican,* April 1, 1847).

76. *Missouri Republican,* date not available.

77. John B. Clark died August 23, 1847. His funeral was held on April 14, 1848, at the Episcopal Burial Ground in St. Louis.

78. "I saw the death of a Major Clark in Veracruz," one friend wrote. "I do hope it is not our friend's husband, poor thing." Letter from Anne E. Lane, Allegheny, to Sarah Glasgow, St. Louis, September 21, 1847 (Lane Family Papers, Mo HS). "Poor Mrs. Clark. How much I feel for her." "I would write to her if I thought that anything I could say would give her a moment's satisfaction." Letter from Anne Lane, Louisville, to Sarah Glasgow, St. Louis, October 14, 1847 (Lane Family Papers, Mo HS).

79. Anne E. Lane, Louisville, to Sarah Glasgow, St. Louis, October 14, 1847, concerning steamboat trip and visit with MacRee family (Lane Family Papers, Mo HS).

80. Alexander Sanford's probate, PCDP.

81. James P. Barnes was said to be the fourth wealthiest man in Springfield, Massachusetts, by virtue of his work in railroads (Green, *Springfield, 1636–1886,* 478).

82. 1850 Census, Springfield, Massachusetts.

83. September 4, 1851, Farmington, Anne Carr Lane letter (Lane Family Papers, Mo HS).

84. June 17, 1848, Anne E. Lane, Vincennes, to Sarah Glasgow, St. Louis; report on health of family (Lane Family papers, Mo HS).

85. Mrs. Emerson even acknowledged this in her old age in an article in the, "Famous Dred Scott Case: Mrs. Chaffee, owner of old slave, still living in Springfield," *New York Times,* December 22, 1895.

86. Hall, who grew up in Sutton, Massachusetts, graduated from Yale College before coming to St. Louis (Benedict and Tracy, *History of the Town of Sutton, Massachusetts,* 319). Obituary Record of Graduates of Yale University, presented at the meeting of the Alumni, June 26, 1894.

87. March 17, 1848. The terms required that whoever hired the Scotts had to pay the sheriff their wages, post a significant bond ($600), and promise, against forfeiture of bond, that the Scotts would not be removed from the jurisdiction. The sheriff could try to find work for them privately, or, if worst came to worst, he could auction their services on the courthouse steps as he annually auctioned out Milton Duty's slaves (*Missouri Republican,* July 14, 1847).

88. Martin, *Divided Mastery,* 18–20.

89. For example, Nat's escape was the subject of the suit (Harney, Administrator of Duty, v. Dutcher & Dutcher., 15 Mo. 89 [1851]).

90. Heirs ask that slaves be sold because having been hired out so long, they were worthless (Milton Duty Probate file, PCDP).

91. Only seven slaves join the suit for freedom (no. 17–24, April 1850 CCHRP; David N. Hall probate file, PCDP).

92. *Missouri Republican,* May 20, 1848.

93. "A Full House—Since Saturday evening, there have been twenty-six individuals lodged in the Calaboose, for offenses of various kinds, committed in violation of the city ordinances, principally for drunkenness and disturbing the peace" (*Missouri Republican,* August 15, 1848).

94. Bates Journal, June 3, 1848, Bates Family Papers, Mo HS.

95. Bates Journal, July 14, 1848, and August 5, 1848, Bates Family Papers, Mo HS.

96. On the last day of October 1848, another St. Louis military leader, Maj. Kearney, died; he had been convalescing at the home of William Clark's family. His death struck a sympathetic chord with the Sanford sisters, who had been close friends of Mrs. Kearney. Their lives were the well-entangled lives of the military sisterhood of military wives. They most certainly attended the funeral to console their friend, a widow, like themselves.

    Henrietta Clarke, recently widowed, had known Mrs. Kearney, for almost 20 years, since she had first visited the Clark household in St. Louis with her older brother, and she had been a guest there when she met and married her husband. Later, both women were with their officer husbands at Fort Towson. Mary Bainbridge had joined them and met her husband, Capt. Bainbridge there. As her husband lay dying, Mrs. Kearney had just borne her eleventh child.

97. Bates Journal, November 12, 1848, Bates Family Papers, Mo HS.

98. On March 5, 1849, Zachary Taylor officially became president of the United States.

99. During the several years Harriet served Taliaferro, Taylor had commanded the territory from his post at Prairie du Chien. Dred had known him since the years of his master, Emerson's, surgeonship.

100. Court began the third Monday in November—November 20, 1848 (St. Louis Circuit Court record book).

101. LaBeaume's sister had married Charlotte Blow Charless's brother, Peter, and the Blows and LaBeaumes had several common business interests. Over the next few years, Louis T. and Charles LaBeaume played minor roles in the Scotts' legal proceedings.

102. Thomas Scott v. James Harrison, no. 90 (1848), CCHRP.

103. Charlotte (of color) v. Chouteau, 11 Mo. 193 (1847).

104. The Kansas-Nebraska Act of 1854 made the introduction of slavery into the state a matter of local sovereignty (Goodrich, *War to the Knife*; Graber, *Dred Scott and the Problem of Constitutional Evil*).

105. The terms of Tom Scott's hiring shed light on Dred's circumstances. Tom Scott had accompanied a New Mexico trader to Santa Fe about the same time that Dred returned from Texas. Tom returned to St. Louis in mid-1847 but waited a year to file suit for his freedom. He had crossed the great American desert twice, and he had negotiated his own financing and earnings as a rented-out slave for several months. Tom's master hired him out to the trading merchant for the Santa Fe trip, an expedition that usually lasted a year. The trader paid the man's owner $130 for his services, but he allowed Tom to earn some wages of his own by working for others (Thomas Scott v. James Harrison, no. 90, 1848, CCHRP).

106. The former sheriff noted that on May 4, 1847, Pierre was hired out at small wages until about April 1, 1848, after which the sheriff was unable to hire him out any longer. Pierre was delivered over to the jailer of the County of St. Louis where he still remained, at the charge of the said former sheriff, the present sheriff having refused to take the charge and control of Pierre (December 1, 1848. Petition of Samuel Conway's [late sheriff] to be discharged from the custody of Pierre).

107. Pierre's jailers submitted an affidavit stating that they believed him to have been insane the whole time of his incarceration (affidavit of Lewis H. Martin and William H. Kerrick, Pierre v. Chouteau, no. 125, at '227 [1842], CCHRP).

108. "A sharp controversy is going on between the St. Louis Circuit Court (J. Hamilton) and the Criminal Court (J. Townson) as to a question of jurisdiction and dignity. One John Jackson was indicted for assault with intent to kill, this case was incited at Sept term of Criminal court, continued to the Nov. Term. The terms of that court being bi-monthly. At Nov term, still current, the case was continued to the next term January. Soon after last continued. He applied to the Circuit Court for a Habeas Corpus claiming his discharge under sect. 25 of Art 6 of the Law of Practice in Criminal cases. And was discharged.

      "This day Judge Hamilton discharged the prisoner after reading a long opinion, which seemed to me to be as defective in style, taste and temper, as it is absurdly erroneous in law" (Bates Journal, December 20, 1848, Bates Family Papers, Mo HS).
109. *Missouri Republican,* January 17 and 28, 1849.
110. Bates Journal, December 20, 1848, Bates Family Papers, Mo HS.
111. Bates Journal, January 1849, Bates Family Papers: "Mr. Townsend has been left out and...and Mr. Hamilton was nominated and confirmed."

Chapter 28

1. *Missouri Republican,* January 1, 1849.
2. After running an advertisement in the paper for several weeks, on January 26, 1849, J. F. A. Sanford executed a deed to J. H. Lucas regarding the St. Louis County property describes the North half of tract containing 358 acres for $14,734. St. Louis Registry of deeds.
3. Bill of sale, February 1, 1849, J. F. A. Sanford of New York. Sale of John, Isaac, and Mary to James H. Lucas. Sum of $1850. Alexander Sanford probate, PCDP.
4. *Missouri Republican,* February 17, 1849, announcing public sale to be held on March 1. John Sanford had once made news in the city by importing fine horses to improve the region's breeding stock in 1837 (Wetmore, "Gazetteer of the State of Missouri," 178).
5. B. S. Garland bill for services submitted in John F. A. Sanford probate file, PCDP.
6. On March 8, 1849, Irene Emerson sold the land to Alfred Vinton (Vol. Y4, p. 446; G6 306). St. Louis Register of Deeds volumes, St. Louis Registry of Deeds.
7. J. F. A. Sanford to John F. Darby, July 31, 1848.
8. Letter from Anne Lane, Louisville, to Sarah Glasgow, St. Louis, October 14, 1847. Carr Lane Family Collection, Mo HS.
9. J. F. A. Sanford Probate files, PCDP. If B. S. Garland's note is correct, Sanford would have been involved in the case since November of 1846, or if B. S. Garland had been working for Alexander Sanford for the time, he was now simply charging that bill to John F. A. Sanford's estate. The note filed 10 years later shows that the starting date has been modified. The date of Garland's first involvement may be wrong, perhaps inflated to justify his fee.
10. "Mr. Sandford, being a wealthy and generous man, paid, himself, all the costs of the suit in the lower courts, and so, naturally came to be written down as the owner of the slave" (*New York Times,* December 22, 1895).
11. Summonses to appear were issued to the same cast of witnesses on February 27, 1849, and again on April 28, 1849, with the addition of Col. Plympton at Jefferson Barracks. In May 1, 1849, two new witnesses added were Dr. Watts, north side of Green Street, below 3d and Mr. John Loring. Dred Scott Case File.
12. David N. Hall probate contains evidence of a bond that he signed and payment to the sheriff that he promised for Dred from March 17, 1849, until Hall's death on April 9, 1851, PCDP.
13. David N. Hall estate showing expenses for doctor's fees for her confinement and the purchase of a burial plot on the day that the daily fees ended (ibid.).
14. Ibid.

15. A. P. Field is no longer listed in his father-in-law's, Owings's, household in 1850, though his wife and children continue to be listed as living there (1850 St. Louis Census entry for Owings). David N. Hall, age 30, and now a widower, is listed (1850 St. Louis Census entry for Owings). Owings's street address in the 1853 City Directory is "sw cor Pine and Tenth."

16. According to the *Missouri Republican,* December 16, 1849, Judge Hamilton called the fall term the working term.

17. "Judge Hamilton will, over course, wish to go to the neighborhood of the Rapids of the Mississippi, or to some other cool and fashionable summer retreat" (*Missouri Republican,* December 16, 1849).

18. Bates Journal, March 8, 1849, Bates Family Papers: Sunday April 1, 1849, is Communion day.

19. Henry Bainbridge back at Jefferson Barracks, 1848–49.

20. 4,317 people (Scharf, *History of St. Louis,* vol. 2, 1574–83).

21. Mersman, *The Whiskey Merchant's Diary,* xix.

22. The island where new emigrants to the city were ordered confined was ill equipped to handle large numbers of people. Still, almost 4,000 emigrants were confined there, "sorely against their will." "Yesterday, I went with Dr. Barrett (superintending physician), the Mayor (Berry) to the quarantine Island. It is just the beginning there" (Bates Journal, July 11, 1849, Bates Family Papers, Mo HS).

23. *Missouri Republican,* January 14, 1849.

24. "a horrid night" (Bates Journal, May 18, 1849, Bates Family Papers, Mo HS).

25. *Missouri Republican,* May 23, 1849.

26. Blocks 8, 9, 10, 11, 34, 33, 32, 31, 30, 59, 60, 61, 62, 63.

27. These people were now homeless. The 1845 city census, p. 93, lists simply "Negroes" residing on Block 31. They are recorded under the column for slaves.

28. "Great preparations are making for clearing off and rebuilding the burnt district" (Bates Journal, May 30. 1849, Bates Family Papers, Mo HS).

29. *Missouri Republican,* May 23, 1849.

30. Dr. Beaumont letter in Myer, *Life and Letters of Dr. William Beaumont,* 293.

31. Bates Journal, June 21, 1814, Bates Family Papers, Mo HS.

32. "Treatment of Cholera," *Northwestern Gazette and Galena Advertiser,* August 8, 1835.

33. Dr. Watts was summoned for May 1849, Dr. Jennings was called for December 1849. Both men were identified as having addresses near the same intersection of Green and 3rd Street: Dr. Jennings, "just below corner of Green and 3rd Streets" and Dr. Watts, "on North side of Green St., below 3rd." (The summons itself appears to read "K. M. Jennings," but it is likely that the individual was really "R. M. Jennings.") Jennings, Robert M., was listed on p. 122 of the 1845 St. Louis City census. The 1848 City Directory lists "Jennings, Robert M., M.D., 69 Green, res Broadway nr Reservoir." The 1857 City Directory listed "Jennings Robert M. Dr. c. 7th & Locust." (This could be block 181, 180, 128, or 127. If it is block 181, it is the same block on which Harriet died.)On May 1, 1849, Dr. Watts and John Loring were summoned. The 1848 City Directory listed "S. F. Watts, M.D. 69 Green, resides Missouri Hotel," but he was not in the partial 1845 census. John Loring was listed in the 1852 City Directory as running a coffee house, on the west side of Main Street, between Carr and Biddle (1852 City Directory).

34. The 1849 cholera epidemic, the city's most significant medical emergency during the decade, had occurred since the case was last tried. Dred and Harriet probably worked for these doctors named as new witnesses in their case during that interim time. Neither doctor was known to have dealings in free territory, so they probably were character witnesses called to attest to the Scotts' good character and ability to support themselves.

35. Bundles, *On Her Own Ground,* 46; Rammelkamp, *Pulitzer's Post-dispatch,* 22.

36. Bates Journal, July 11, 1849, Bates Family Papers.

37. Miles H. Clark probate, PCDP.

38. A contemporary black man serving a doctor later became a leecher and a cupper, attending to the medical therapy of drawing blood by applying leeches and using

warm cups on the body to draw blood from one place to the other (Covey, *African American Slave Medicine,* 21–23, 127).

39. "It used to be supposed by the colored population that because a professional gentleman kept a servant...near his person, that the servant would naturally absorb some knowledge from the atmosphere surrounding his master. The servant would in many cases assume the right to be authority on certain points." For example, the servant of Daniel Webster, the statesman, became the "colored statesman." General Wood's man, having just returned from Mexico, was the "Military man" (Thomas, *Autobiography of James Thomas,* 122–23).

40. One person arriving in St. Louis and suspected of having the cholera "strictly charged a negro servant to burn all the woolen clothes which I had brought with me. This good intention his cupidity probably defeated, as I afterward accidentally learned he was one of the first victims of the visitation of the pestilence which soon followed us" (Cooke, *Scenes and Adventures in the Army,* 196).

41. On June 14, 1849.

42. *Missouri Republican,* May 16, 1849.

43. Bates Journal, June 25, 1849, Bates Family Papers.

44. "In response to the ineffectiveness of city efforts another meeting was called at the Rotunda....Very strong resolutions are reported by the g— and passed unanimously, calling upon the authority to act with more efficiency and promptness.

    "While the case was out Col. A. P. Field made an empassioned speech against the authority, chiefly Mayor Barry, and moved that they be requested to resign. This way altered on suggestion of Maj. Pruel and put hypothetically—if they doubt their power and will not carry out the sanitary recommendations of this meeting, they be requested to resign. This passed by acclamation....

    "The effect was soon....On the first meeting of the Council, the alderman passed an ordinance, proposed by W. Maguire, deputing all their powers to a course by name, being the same course which reported the resolutions in the meeting"(Primm, *Lion of the Valley,* 163; see also Scharf, *History of St. Louis*).

45. *Missouri Republican,* November 1, 1849. "Some of the Negroes who had been pressed into service during this time sought reinforcement from brandy for a hard task." Bornstein, *Memoirs of a Nobody,* 101.

46. Bates Journal, June 24, 1849, Bates Family Papers, Mo HS.

47. Bates Journal, June 21, 1849, Bates Family Papers, Mo HS.

48. Bates Journal, July 5, 1849, Bates Family Papers, Mo HS.

49. Bornstein, *Memoirs of a Nobody,* 101.

50. Bates Journal, June 25, 1849, Bates Family Papers, Mo HS; *Missouri Republican,* May 16, 1849.

51. *Missouri Republican,* July 4, 1849.

52. Bates Journal, June 30, 1849, Bates Family Papers, Mo HS.

53. *Missouri Republican,* July 6, 1849.

54. Samuel Bay died of cholera in July, 1849 (Bay, *The Bench and Bar of Missouri,* 170). Pierre Chouteau Sr., aged 91, died of cholera (Bates Journal, July 11, 1849, Bates Family Papers, Mo HS).

55. *Missouri Republican,* July 4, 1849. Some citizens sponsored an effort to build a house of corrections. The target population, viewed as in particular need of long terms of confinement, were free blacks without licenses, who were often kept locked up because they couldn't pay their fines. Judge Hamilton received a petition reporting that during the past nine months, during the time of cholera, more than $500 in unpaid fines and costs were imposed on free blacks who could not pay. Judge Hamilton heard arguments on the matter, considered it, and quietly seemed to let the initiative die of its own accord (*Missouri Republican,* October 23, 1849).

    The matter went no further. Though Judge Hamilton enforced the law as laid down, he consistently seemed to favor leniency in these matters of liberty. The issue of a house of corrections for free Blacks did not come up again.

56. Bates Journal, July 11, 1849, Bates Family Papers, Mo HS.
57. Bates Journal, July 15, 1849, Bates Family Papers, Mo HS.
58. Bates Journal, 1849, Bates Family Papers, Mo HS.
59. Bates Journal, July 23, 1849, Bates Family Papers, Mo HS.
60. Ibid.
61. *Missouri Republican,* October 2, 1849, published the report of the grand jury with respect to the condition of the jail. "Mr. Lewis H. Martin, on whom the report reflects quite seriously, as jailor, informed us yesterday, that he would reply to it soon…" Ibid.
62. *Missouri Republican,* October 3, 1849. Several members of the bar signed a testimonial in support of the jailor, including A. P. Field. Field represented Martin in Lewis C. Martin v. The State of Missouri (1849).
63. *Missouri Republican,* November 20, 1849.
64. "Such a feeling of excitement in the city that an unruly crowd circled the jail in an attempt to hang them" (*Missouri Republican*, November 1, 1849).
65. A news article publicly criticizing him complained about the inordinate delay in his court (*Missouri Republican,* December 16, 1849). "Complaint about St. Louis Circuit court… [N]ext summer Judge Hamilton will, over course, wish to go to the neighborhood of the Rapids of the Mississippi, or to some other cool and fashionable summer retreat. In fact, the Judge has always called the fall session, 'the working term,' in distinction from the April Term, which he regards as a mere parade."
66. December 8, 1849, summons delivered. On December 17, 1849, John F. Darby was summoned to appear on December 18, 1849. December 22, 1849: This time both Joseph Charless and Taylor Blow were summoned. On January 12, 1850, summonses were issued to Thomas Gray, Thomas O'Flaherty; Henry T. Blow could not be issued a summons since he could not be found December 21, 1849.
67. Bates Journal, Friday, December 14, 1849: Last Wednesday night.
68. U.S. Census, Jefferson Barracks August 18, 1850, lists Henry Bainbridge, 47 years old, born in New York; Mary, 31 (or 37), was born in Virginia. No children and no servants are listed as occupying their household. Joseph Plympton and the entire family are there too. A free black couple now served the Plymptons (Joseph Plympton pay slip at Jefferson Barracks, 1850. SP Accts, RG 217, E 516, NA).
69. Bay, *The Bench and Bar of Missouri,* 569–70.
70. Payment request of B. S. Garland in John F. A. Sanford's probate, PCDP. Garland genealogy shows that Benami S. Garland and Hugh Garland were first cousins, born in the same county, Amherst County, Virginia, four years apart: B. S. Garland was born in 1809 and Hugh Garland was born in 1805 (http://byrnefamily.net/news.php).

     Hugh Garland received his education at Hampden-Sydney College, serving as a professor of Greek at the University of Virginia. After serving as a Virginia state legislator, he moved to St. Louis in 1840 where he practiced law until his death in 1854 (Lawson, *American State Trials*, 227–28).
71. One of the Garlands' 10 slaves, Elizabeth Keckley, was a particularly talented woman. She was literate and earned excellent wages through her skill as a seamstress of fashionable ladies' clothing. (She would later make fine dresses for the fashion-conscious Mrs. Lincoln, as First Lady.) A talented seamstress who could copy the Eastern fashions was a prized find in the frontier city. Elizabeth had tried to persuade her master to let her buy her freedom and her son's. Her wealthy clients promised to advance her the money, but, like Widow Emerson, her master refused. She was one of the more profitable assets earning income for the Garlands. Thus, she had to turn over all her earnings to the lawyer, who picked up Mrs. Emerson's appeal against the Scotts.
72. George Goode appears to have dropped out of the case because he was preparing to argue a land claim case before the United States Supreme Court in Washington. That case had $1,000,000 at stake, and when he won it, he netted himself a fee of

$60,000, the largest contingent fee St. Louis had ever known (Bay, *The Bench and Bar of Missouri*, 569–70).

73. He delivered five lectures on Protestantism and Government in St. Louis in 1852, published in *Brownson's Quarterly Review* (Benjamin H. Greene, St. Louis, 1852), and he wrote another tract called *The Second War of Revolution* (1839) (about the Bank of the United States). He is listed as an attorney of the Albemarle County Bar as early as 1830 (Woods, *Albemarle County in Virginia*).

74. Garland, *Life of John Randolph of Roanoke*.

75. Lyman D. Norris was born in Michigan in 1824. The *Missouri Republican* October 23, 1849, reported that as of September 24, 1849, Hugh A. Garland and Lyman Norris were associated in a law practice partnership office at 80 Chestnut Street upstairs.

76. Lyman Norris graduated in 1845. D. N. Hall is also graduated from Yale College in 1839. Garland's other young partner, Charles Whittelsey, was also an 1841 Yale graduate (Obituary Record of Graduates of Yale University, presented at the meeting of the Alumni, June 26, 1894).

77. "I sympathize freely and fully so long as I am a Southern man, with the State rights party" (letter from Lyman Norris to his mother, Rocena, March 31, 1852) (Norris Family Papers, Bentley Library, University of Michigan).

78. Lyman Norris was the editor of the St. Louis Times newspaper. Dwight Goss, *History of Grand Rapids and Its Industries*, 800.

79. Letter from Lyman Norris to his mother, Rocena Norris, April 8, 1851 (Norris Family Papers, Bentley Library, University of Michigan).

80. Dred Scott appeal papers signed by Garland. Scott v. Emerson Case File.

81. Lyman Norris to Rocena, March 31, 1852 (Norris Family Papers, Bentley Library, University of Michigan).

82. December 20, 1849, James Russell was one of the Committee of 100, the group committed to opposing all forms of abolition. Scharf, *History of St. Louis*, vol. 1.

83. Mrs. Russell's deposition, Dred Scott Case File. Mrs. Russell's deposition leaves some question about when Dred worked for her. By strict calculation of her dates, it would seem that Dred would have worked for her at the same time he served Capt. Bainbridge in Louisiana and Texas.

84. Mr. Russell stated again that the Scotts had been hired out to him and that he had paid Col. Sanford the moneys for them. Henry Blow attested to the fact that his father had previously owned Dred as a slave.

85. Scott, *Forgotten Valor*, 131.

86. Another huge fire struck the Henry Blow paint factory, reducing the building to ruins at a loss of $100,000 (*Missouri Republican,* November 15, and 22, 1849).

87. Benedict, and Averill, *History of the Town of Sutton*, 317, noting the death of Sarah C. Hall on January 15, 1849; page 319 notes the death of Mr. Hall's only child. Doctors' bills for treatment of Sarah C. Hall mention her condition as one of "confinement" which is generally used in reference to the last term of pregnancy (Probate of David N. Hall, PCDP).

88. Original Dred Scott v. Emerson Case File.

Chapter 29

1. The case had been to the Missouri Supreme Court before when Samuel Bay had both appealed and requested a new trial. Because the new trial had been granted, the appeal was improvidently requested and the Missouri Supreme Court regarded it so. Emmerson v. Harriet (of color); Emmerson v. Dred Scott (of color), 11 Missouri 413 (1848).

2. Tucker, *Hancock, the Superb*, 46.

3. January 24, 1850, was the date of the wedding (Tucker, *Hancock, the Superb,* 75). Winfield Scott Hancock was adjutant of the 6th Regiment. He and his bride met after his unit returned to Jefferson Barracks in the summer of 1848. Don Carlos

Buell introduced them. The wedding was conducted by William Greenleaf Eliot, pastor of the Unitarian Church (Hamilton, "Winfield Scott Hancock at Jefferson Barracks," *The Jefferson Barracks Gazette* 6, no. 4 [October/December 1998]). Hancock's nickname is utilized in the title of his biography. Tucker, *Hancock, the Superb*. Almira Hancock wrote her own account of the wedding in Almira Hancock, *Reminiscences of Winfield Scott Hancock by His Wife*. (New York, 1887).

4. Tucker, *Hancock, the Superb*, 45–47.
5. The minister was William G. Eliot, the same popular Unitarian clergyman who had married Sarah Beaumont and Lt. Irwin and with whom the Bainbridges at one time had traveled to St. Louis from Jefferson Barracks.
6. Scott, *Forgotten Valor*, 130 (detailing life at Jefferson Barracks from December 1849 to May 1850).
7. Letter from Anne Lane to Sarah L. Glasgow, July 27 or 29, 1851 (The Lane Collection, William Carr Lane, Mo HS, St. Louis).
8. William Selby Harney was married to Mary Mullanphy, the daughter of Hon. John Mullanphy (William S. Harney Papers, Mo HS, AMC94–000866).
9. Anne Lane Carr wrote, "Mrs. H[arney] makes a great fuss about low people, no 'common people' is her word, but as long as they behave they do not incommode me I gave Mrs. H credit for more sense if she would think of her father and her husband I should think she would talk differently. Today she said if Gen Harney told her I should hate to be in his company." Anne Lane Carr to Sarah L. Glasgow, July 27 or 29, 1851 (The Lane Collection, William Carr Lane, Mo HS).
10. The marriage occurred in November 1850. Dr. Chaffee had lost his first wife just two years before, so the delay in their marriage seemed like an appropriate time of bereavement.
11. "Disposing of Two Millions [*sic*]: the Will of the Late Thomas E. Davis," *New York Times*, June 28, 1878.
12. The 1850 Census entry for the 18th ward of New York, September 11, 1850, listed "'Thomas A. Davis, 65, M, none (profession), b. England, his wife Ann, Age 45, b. Ireland, and seven unmarried children." Thereafter John F. A. Sanford was listed as "Major Sanford, 43 M Merchant $50,000" and following him, "Isabella Sanford, age 19, b. N.Y." The family also had a waiter, a coachman, and five servant women, three from Ireland and two from France.
13. The court denied the request for a new trial January 19, 1850. Bill of exceptions filed by defendants February 14, 1850. At the time, Mrs. Emerson was represented by Charles Whittlesey of the firm of Garland and Norris. A Yale graduate from Connecticut, Whittlesey had moved to Missouri in the winter of 1840–41. Lyman Decator Norris was the first graduate of the University of Michigan Law School and editor of the *St. Louis Daily Times* while he lived in St. Louis. Norris married Whittlesey's sister.
14. Stipulation agreed to on February 12, 1850 (Ehrlich, *They Have No Rights*, 43).
15. Missouri Statute, Freedom: An act to enable persons held in slavery to sue for their freedom. January 27, 1835. §12.
16. Amar, *The Bill of Rights*, 161.
17. Elsa Hicks v. S. Burrell and Louis Mitchell and Elsa Hicks v. McSherry, no. 55 (April 1845) and no.121 (November 1847), CCHRP.
18. Ibid.
19. The very manner in which the cases were styled suggests a slight difference in the couple's legal status. Dred's case was styled: "Dred Scott, slave vs. Irene Emerson." Harriet's reads: "Harriet of color vs. Irene Emerson." She was not identified as enslaved. Her case is styled no differently than the lawsuit of a free woman of color. Harriet was not given the respectability of a last name, but then again neither was she identified as "slave."
20. Ferdinand Risque and Gustavus Bird were other plaintiffs' lawyers, who like F. B. Murdoch, had handled multiple suits on behalf of slaves seeking their freedom, but Risque had left St. Louis and Bird was dead. After Murdoch, David N. Hall was the only lawyer who had appeared on the scene willing to vigorously press freedom

suits on behalf of slaves. When Hall died, it was some time before litigants like the Scotts and Pierre found new legal representation.

21. Rachael v. Walker, no. 82, CCHRP.

22. This fact was not known to prior historians of the case.

23. *Missouri Republican,* January 15, 1851. Population of St. Louis, Ward by Ward: Free blacks in 1st ward = 13. In 2nd ward = 352. In 3rd ward = 227. In 4th ward = 464. In 5th ward = 96. In 6th ward = 107. This pattern of alley living seems to have been prevalent in many antebellum cities. See, for example, Borchert, *Alley Life in Washington.*

24. Dacus and Buel, *A Tour of St. Louis,* 415–16 (detail of clabber alley in St. Louis neighborhoods).

25. Dred Scott was first listed as living there in the City Directory of 185–. "Scott, Dred. (c) white washer. al. b. 10th and 11th, n. of Wash, BLOCK 261. Scott, Harriet, wid. Dred, (col'd,) laundress, al. Near Carr b. 6th and 7th, block 110 or 145. 1860 Scott Harriet (col'd) wid. Dred, r. alley bet. Franklin av., Wash, 7th and 8th [block 253, 5th ward]; 1864 Scott, Harriet, (col'd) wid. R. al. B. 8th and 9th, Franklin Av. And Morgan "[block 168, 5th]; 1866 Scott Harriet, wid., r. al. Bet. 8th and 9th, Franklin Av. And Morgan [block 168, 5th ward]; 1869 Scott Harriet, Mrs. (col'd) r. rear 811 N. 8th.; 1874 #Scott Harriet, wid. Dred, r. al. Bet. Wash and Franklin av. 7th and 8th [block 253 again, 5th Ward]."

26. Washington, D.C., Letter of Henry Sibley to Martin MacLeod, Lac qui Parle, December 16, 1849 (Henry Sibley Papers).

27. Letter of G. Franchere, New York, January 22, 1850 to H. H. Sibley in Washington, D.C. (Henry Sibley papers).

28. Bates Journal, February 2, 1850, Bates Family Papers, Mo HS.

29. Bates Journal, March 24, 1850, Bates Family Papers, Mo HS.

30. Contributing to the public's suspicion was the press's penchant for publishing outlandish stories about black fertility. One newspaper reported on a 42-year-old woman's 41st birth; another reported on another slave woman's 24th child. As Frazier notes, whatever the truth inhering in these accounts, the papers never seemed to report on black infant mortality counteracting the perception of a soaring black birth rate (Frazier, *Runaway and Freed Missouri Slaves,* 15).

31. An Act Respecting Slaves, Free Negroes and Mulattoes (February 16, 1847), Laws of Missouri (1848) (Scharf, *History of St. Louis,* vol. 1, 166).

32. St. Louis County records of names and persons beaten for residing in the state without a license.

33. *Missouri Republican,* January 15, 1851.

34. The 1850 census lists a Harriet Scott residing in the home of "William Chavers, 27 boatman b. Ohio and Eliza Chavers 23." The link of Harriet and an Eliza in the same household seems strong, but Harriet is said to be age 49, older than Mrs. Dred Scott would be, and born in New York, rather than Virginia. "Gender: Female Race: Black St Louis Ward 5" (Missouri Page: 270 Roll: M432_417).

35. The recent census determined that 1,259 free negroes resided in the county, but "[i]t appears from the records of the county court that the whole number of free Negroes licensed to remain in this county from September 1841 to December 1850 amounts to 575—leaving 684 in the city and county without license and in violation of law," the newspaper complained (*Missouri Republican,* January 15, 1851, 2).

36. *Missouri Republican,* May 7, 1850. Eight free blacks were whipped.

37. *Missouri Republican,* January 15, 1851. Population of St. Louis. Ward by Ward: Free blacks in 1st ward = 13. In 2nd ward = 352. In 3rd ward = 227. In 4th ward = 464. In 5th ward = 96. In 6th ward = 107.

"The number of free negroes [is] 1,259. It appears from the records of the county court that the whole number of free negroes licensed to remain in this county from Sept. 1841 to Dec. 1850 amounts to 575—leaving 684 in the city and county without license in violation of law."

38. *Missouri Republican.* January 31, 1851. The annual meeting of the American Colonization Society in Washington. President of U.S. in attendance (*Missouri Republican,* March 19, 1851; see Howe, *What Hath God Wrought,* 260–66).

39. Letter from W. D. Shumate of the Missouri Colonization Society. Published in *Missouri Republican,* January 4, 1851.

40. Even when blacks died accidentally, the newspapers covered their deaths in a matter-of-fact manner, emphasizing the loss of the slave owner's property just as much as the loss of life (Frazier, *Runaway and Freed Missouri Slaves,* 13).

41. *Missouri Republican,* January 19, 1851. Long article on free Negroes from "a Democratic Free Soiler."

42. "The free Negroes would be kept up only from the increase within; and under these restrictions they would not increase" (ibid.).

43. Ibid.

44. Bates Journal, January 1850, Bates Family Papers, Mo HS.

45. It was reported that Calhoun favored dissolving the union over the Negro question. The local paper reported, "He would desecrate the names of our fathers, pull down and destroy all of goodness and glory that they have built up, and they falsify the world's last hope of freedom of the white man, because he is not allowed to have his own wayward will about Negro slaves!" (*Missouri Republican,* March 6, 1850).

46. Howe, *What Hath God Wrought,* 792–836.

47. In 1854, St. Louis had a population of 77,860, of whom 4,054 were African Americans. Of these 2,656 were slaves, while the remaining 1398 were free persons of color (Kaufman, *Dred Scott's Advocate,* 8).

48. See generally the 4th and 5th ward of the 1850 St. Louis census.

49. *Missouri Republican,* October 18, 1848.

50. The best evidence of this is the number of Irish servants listed as living in St. Louis households, 1850 Census for St. Louis. Trexler also noted this phenomenon (Trexler, *Slavery in Missouri,* 19).

51. Baudissen, *Graf Adelbert, Der Ansiedler im Missouri-Staate* (Julius Badeser 1854).

52. Howe, *What Hath God Wrought,* 826 (describing how the surge in immigration provoked dramatic nativist reaction).

53. Bates Journal, April 29, 1851, Bates Family Papers, Mo HS.

54. Letter from Anne E. Lane to Sarah L. Glasgow, 1851 (The Lane Collection, William Carr Lane. Mo HS).

55. *Missouri Republican,* November 13, 1852 (account of Fanny and Huldah charged with poisoning the Menkens family).

56. Letter from Anne E. Lane to Sarah L. Glasgow, 1851 (The Lane Collection, William Carr Lane, Mo HS, St. Louis). The Missouri Legislature had long had a law banning the sale of poisonous substances to free blacks and slaves. Trexler, *Slavery in Missouri,* 71 (describing an 1804 territorial statute).

57. September 4, 1851, Farmington, Ann E. Lane to Sarah Lane Glasgow (The Lane Collection, William Carr Lane, 1837, Mo HS).

58. February 4, 1852, Sarah L. Glasgow to Anne E. Lane (The Lane Collection, William Carr Lane, 1837. Mo HS).

59. VanderVelde, "The Legal Ways of Seduction," *Stanford Law Review* 488 (1996):17, 876.

60. Bates Journal, date not available, Bates Family Papers, Mo HS.

61. Ibid., July 9, 1851.

62. Ibid., July 12, 1851: "John Ryan and Ellen his wife…began service with us at the rate of $200 per an: wages." September 15, 1851: "John Ryan and his wife left our service, in consequence of the dissatisfaction of the wife having served us only two months and three days."

      September 22, 1851: "Bryan Neil (who pestered and married Julia, who had been in our service for some time), with his new wife, entered our service."

63. Bates Journal, September 18, 1850, September 25, 1850, Bates Family Papers.
64. Ralph v. Duncan, no. 35 (July 1830), CCHRP; Merry v. Tiffin, no. 18 (November 1826), CCHRP.
65. October 26, 1850.
66. Ibid.
67. Ibid.
68. "The Supreme Court sat this morning (having barely opened yesterday) and heard the first argument of the term" (Bates Journal, October 26, 1850, Bates Family Papers, Mo HS).
69. Judge Napton wrote in his diary once the federal case was decided: "It came up to the Supreme Court of this state while I was on the bench, and I made up my mind on it and communicated my views to Judge Ryland and Judge Birch then my colleagues. I had previously frequently canvassed with Judge Scott on the subject, and he and I had often declared our determination to overrule the old decisions of our court, upon which Gamble in his dissenting opinion relies. This I communicated to Ryland and Birch, the former hesitating—the latter declaring his readiness to go with me and to go father, and say exactly what the federal Supreme Court has since said, that the Missouri Compromise is unconstitutional" (Napton's diary for 1857, Mo HS, 223).
70. October 24, 1850, Bates Journal, Bates Family Papers. "The Supreme Court was to have met here last Monday: Judge Birch has been here nearly a week: The other two Judges are detained by low water in the Missouri River. We learn that the boat they are in has been aground, just below Bonhomme Island for 4 or 5 days. If they don't arrive by Saturday, the term will lapse.

    "As to the Supreme Court, Judge Birch is gone home, and it is understood that Judge Napton must leave at the end of this week. So the Court will probably adjourn, after a rather abortive session" (Bates Journal, November 27, Bates Family Papers).
71. D. N. Hall brief to the Missouri Supreme Court, Emerson v. Scott Case File.
72. He was described as a "scholar, a sound lawyer, and a worthy man" (Bates Journal, March 8, 1851, Bates Family Papers).
73. The case file of Pierre v. Gabriel Chouteau indicates that Pierre had been in jail since April 1, 1848, that D. N. Hall was now dead, and that A. P. Field had left the state (no. 125, CCHRP).
74. The 1848 City Directory for St. Louis lists four Labeaume brothers in town: Labeaume, C. Edmund, Atty.; Labeaume, Louis T., sheriff; Labeaume, Louis A.; and Labeaume, Theodore.
75. Henry T. Blow listed three slaves in his household in the 1857–58 Carondelet census.
76. "For two or three years past Dred has been at large, no one exercising ownership over him, or putting any restraint upon his movements" ("The Original Dred Scott a Resident of St. Louis—A Sketch of His History, "*St. Louis News*, April 8, 1857).
77. Scharf, *History of St. Louis*, vol. 1, 586.
78. March 23, 1852, notice of hearing was addressed to Louis A. LaBeaume, ex-sheriff of St. Louis County, to produce bonds for the hire of slaves, proceeds due with 6 percent allowed by law. Also Samuel Conway, ex-sheriff of St. Louis County; current Sheriff was Henry B. Belt; Deputy was John R. Braxman.

    On April 9, 1852, C. Edmund LaBeaume as principal and Henry T. Blow as security posted bond of $600 in the matter of Dred Scott. Two weeks later, they posted a similar bond for Harriet: April 26, 1852, Edmund LaBeaume as principal and Louis T. LaBeaume, $600 security for Harriet.

    In the second bail bonding, C. Edmund LaBeaume stood as principal and Louis T. LaBeaume, instead of Henry T. Blow, stood as security. On June 8, 1852, a motion for order on L. T. LaBeaume was filed in Harriet of color suit. A motion for order on Samuel Conway (Sheriff) as well as motion for order on L. T. LaBeaume was filed in the Dred Scott suit. On June 29, 1852, the court denied the defendant's motion for an order on LaBeaume to return the bonds taken by them.

Blow put up the money for Dred. Two of the La Beaume brothers put the money up for Harriet. Dred was again hired out of the term of a year at $5 a month, Harriet for $4 a month.

79. Bundles, *On Her Own Ground*, 46.

80. Stratton, *Pioneer Women*, 69–70; Brown, *From Fugitive Slave to Free Man*, 151 (describing washing the old way before washing machines).

81. WPA Slave Narratives: laundresses having helpers to stoke the fires.

82. Thomas, *From Tennessee Slave to St. Louis Entrepreneur*, 2 (describing how young James Thomas delivered laundry for his mother to save her time).

83. Ibid., 105.

84. Ibid., 32.

85. Slave Narratives of Marie Akin Simpson, of Missouri, Ancestry.com database 41069–41078 of 80836, March 27, 2002; Tratton, *Pioneer Women*, 70–71.

86. *Frank Leslie's Illustrated Newspaper,* June 27, 1857.

87. Taliaferro's most important message to the Dakota was that labor would make them self-sufficient, independent, and free.

88. *Missouri Republican,* January 3, 1851. The yard was previously owned by White and Tooley. Another pair of slave traders offered to visit any part of the state from their St. Louis office in order to arrange a purchase or a sale. They, too, boasted of having a good yard and jail for boarding.

89. Trexler, *Slavery in Missouri,* at 45.

90. Treacy, *The Grand Hotels of St. Louis,* 7.

91. Advertisement of B. M. Lynch in the *Missouri Republican,* June 26, 1857.

92. Blassingame, *Slave Testimony*, 504.

93. A free black Pennsylvania river man sued him for his freedom when Bartlett seized him and claimed him as a slave. Geo. Johnson v. Reuben Bartlett, November 1852 # 281, CCHRP.

94. St. Louis had a probate court, a land court, a court of common pleas, and a circuit court. "I went downtown today, to vote in the city election, then what business to be done in the county. The Supreme Court had adjourn over and the Federal Circuit Court did what was on the docket" (Bates Journal, April 7, 1851, Bates Family Papers).

95. Hannah Coleman v. The State, 14 Mo. 157 (1851).

96. Reeves treatise (Cobb, *An Inquiry into the Law of Negro Slavery*).

97. It is the first term since the amendment to the Constitution, by which the judges were made elective by the people. The newly elected judges are Hamilton R. Gamble, William Scott (formerly of the same bench, but left on by G. W. King), and John L. Ryland (the only one of the late judges re-chosen by the people) (Bates Journal, October 1851, Bates Family Papers, Mo HS).

98. Hamilton Rowan Gamble, born in Winchester County, Virginia, in 1798, studied at Hampden Sydney College, and then moved to Missouri in 1818 where he was a prosecutor, then secretary of state. He moved to St. Louis in 1826, becoming a member of the Missouri Legislature 20 years later, then a judge on the state supreme court in from 1851 to 1855. After being elected Missouri's governor in 1861, he served until 1864, the year he died in St. Louis (Lawson, *American State Trials*, 240). Gamble was from a family of distinguished lawyers; his brother, also a lawyer, lived next door to the Russells.

99. See, generally, Hurt, *Agriculture and Slavery in Missouri's Little Dixie* (describing the slavery practices in Missouri's interior).

100. Justice Napton, who had orchestrated a number of proslavery victories in swaying the direction of law at the margin, was not reelected. He had long been influential in swaying the direction of law legal interpretations. Trexler, *Slavery in Missouri*, 153 et seq. (detailing Napton's opposition to Benton over the slavery issue).

101. *Missouri Republican,* February 21, 1851: "Free negroes are no longer permitted to settle in the State of Iowa." *Missouri Republican,* August 20, 1851: "Constitution of Indiana—Negro Exclusion." *Missouri Republican,* October 31, 1851: "Free Negroes— This unfortunate class of our population begins to find themselves placed under more restrictions in the Free, than in the Slave States. Illinois has inserted in her

Constitution a provision against their migration to, or residence in, the State. Indiana has adopted a provision of a similar character, and the Free States begin to be aware of the burden of such a population. Ohio is likely to have to follow in the footsteps of Illinois and Indiana, if the insolence of this class of her citizens is checked. One of the last Cincinnati papers contains a call for a State Convention of colored citizens of Ohio, in that city...." The object of the convention is to recommend and adopt such measures as are best calculated to promote the interest of the colored people of the State." *Missouri Republican,* November 14, 1851: "Oregon...Negroes are prohibited by law from being brought into Oregon Territory."

102. *Missouri Republican,* October 31, 1851.
103. Bates Journal, January 7, 1852, Bates Family Papers, Mo HS; Kennerly, *Persimmon Hill,* 182–83.
104. "January 3, 1852, Pierre Chouteau and wife gave a Grand Ball at the Planters House on Thursday, 8th inst. Jan 2, 1852." Letter from William Carr Lane to Anne Lane, St. Louis, January 2, 1852 (The Lane Collection, William Carr Lane, Mo HS, St. Louis).
105. Ibid.
106. January 3, 1852, "Mr. P. Chouteau gives a party at the Planters tomorrow night." Letter from Sarah L. Glasgow to Anne E. Lane, January 3, 1852 (The Lane Collection, William Carr Lane, Mo HS).

    January 4, 1852, "I had a long letter from Mrs. (Henrietta Sanford) Clark. She was rejoicing in a visit from Mr. Palmer. Mary has gone west again. I am afraid poor thing she is not very well married; I have no fancy for those Hardings any how." Letter from Anne E. Lane to Sarah L. Glasgow, January 4, 1852 (The Lane Collection, William Carr Lane, Mo HS). November 7, 1845, in Washington, D.C., Pierre Chouteau's only son, Charles, married his own first cousin.
107. When Gratiot was dismissed from the army, Sanford attempted to help him (Senate Judiciary Report, 32nd Cong., 1st session, S. Rpt. 357, 12). Sanford's activity collecting moneys from the government date from as early as 1838 (U.S. Treasurer's Accounts, 26th Cong., 1st session, H. Doc. 29, 171).
108. For instance, one young woman "fell out of society" and was not invited to a subsequent first-class ball because she had attended a black ball "of the second class" (Clamorgan, *The Colored Aristocracy*, 60–61).
109. *Missouri Republican,* March 15, 1852.
110. St. Louis City Directory for year.
111. Bates Journal, January 23, 1852, recording the earthquake at 2 P.M.
112. The details of one New York prosecution occupied the public's attention for a while, but the many incidences of runaways close to home kept the focus local (*Missouri Republican,* January 3, 1851).
113. Nearly all ads for runaways estimated the age of the slaves within a five- or ten-year span. This was possibly due to the fact that illiterate slaves could not record the date of births for their children. While it may have hampered efforts to recover runaways, ignorance of slaves' ages could also be beneficial, since a slave ignorant of her age could not contradict her master when he told a possible buyer that she was younger than she really was (Frazier, *Runaway and Freed Missouri Slaves*, 14).
114. *Missouri Republican,* November 12, 1849, August 20, 1850, September 11, 1852, July 16, 1856.
115. *Missouri Republican,* May 23, 1854, August 30, 1854. For one recent account of the Blackburn family's experience on the underground railroad, see Frost, *I've Got a Home in Glory Land.*

Chapter 30

1. Scott v. Emerson, 15 Mo. 576, 584 (1852).
2. Ibid.
3. Scott v. Emerson, 15 Mo. 576, 584 (1852).
4. Ibid., 584–85.

5. "[Dr. Emerson] was ordered by superior authority to posts where his slave was detained in servitude, and in obedience to that authority he repaired to them with his servant." Ibid., 585.

6. Ibid., 585–86.

7. It is not completely clear whether this vile epithet is intended to describe black persons traveling in the West or the speech of Abolitionists.

8. The fact that the free state judges in those cases hadn't nailed down the consequence of returning former slaves to slave territory was the shred of authority that gave the Missouri court the leverage to pry open the possibility of a person's reenslavement on return.

9. Scott v. Emerson, 15 Mo. 576, 586 (1852).

10. Ibid., 587.

11. Ibid.

13. Ibid.

14. "In all ages, and in all countries in which slavery has existed, the slave has been regarded not merely as property, but also as a being capable of acquiring and holding certain rights, by the act of the master" (Scott v. Emerson, 15 Mo. 576, 587 [1852]).

15. "It is, undoubtedly, a matter to be deeply regretted, that men who have no concern with the institution of slavery, should have claimed the right to interfere with the domestic relations of their neighbors, and have insisted that their ideas of philanthropy and morality should be adopted by people who are certainly capable of deciding upon their own duties and obligations" (Scott v. Emerson, 15 Mo. 576, 589–90 [1852]).

16. Gamble also acknowledged the voluntariness inherent in a slave master's taking his slave into a free state: "Any citizen of Missouri, who removes with his slave to Illinois, a right to complain that the fundamental law of the State to which he removes, and in which he makes his residence, dissolves the relation between him and his slave. It is as much his own voluntary act, as if he had executed a deed of emancipation. Nor can any man pretend ignorance." Scott v. Emerson, 15 Mo. 576, 589 (1852).

17. Technically, under the Missouri Supreme Court ruling, Eliza Scott may still have had an argument that she was free based on her birth in free territory. Given the Missouri Supreme Court's leanings it is unlikely that she would have won, but by the time that issues in her parents' case were resolved by the United States Supreme Court, it is an issue that she could not have won. See Chapter 13, detailing her birth on the Steamboat *Gypsey*.

18. This response on his part was not necessarily legal, but it was interestingly consonant with the earlier appeal to the Missouri Supreme Court when Samuel Bay had botched the case. Then the court had found that the appeal was faulty because it lacked a final judgment (Harriet v. Emerson, Prior Missouri Supreme Court decision).

19. Judge Hamilton did not close out the case from his docket until five years later, a week after the United States Supreme Court had ruled against the Scotts (Kaufman, *Dred Scott's Advocate*, 224).

20. Letters from Lyman Norris to his mother, Rocena Norris, March 25, 27, 28, and 31, 1852, Norris Family Collection, Bentley Library, University of Michigan.

21. Letter of Lyman Norris to his mother, March 31, 1852. Norris Family Collection, Bentley Library, University of Michigan.

22. Brendan F. Hug, "Racing Dred Scott: Local Ideology and the Advocacy of Lyman Norris" (unpublished, on file with author).

23. Ibid. (citing Lyman Norris's letter to his mother, March 31, 1852).

24. As Lyman Norris wrote in 1852: "Slavery is a curse to Missouri, an eating cancer on her body politic, and if *it could* be banished from her borders forever tomorrow, she would be richer, greater, and more powerful than any other state…" but it "cannot be eradicated" because abolition would "destroy[] [Missouri's] existence as a state

and our well being as a people. [W]ill we submit to be bound hand and foot and thrown upon the dissecting table to have our diseased limbs lopped off by a set of ignorant abolition quacks that know as little of our disease as they do of decency or constitutional law and whose remedy for a lame dog would be to cut his tail off" (letter from Lyman Norris to his mother, Rocena Norris, March 31, 1852, Norris Family Collection, Bentley Library, University of Michigan). Other abolitionists criticized the U.S. Constitution for implicitly accommodating slavery. Referring to the three-fifths provision, William Lloyd Garrison exclaimed, "What a travesty on the mathematics of justice to announce excitedly that two and two make six, to argue a bit about it, and then to shake hands on the number five" (quoted in Frazier, *Runaway and Freed Slaves*, 39).

25. Ibid.
26. Ibid.
27. Ibid.
28. Few freedom suits were filed in 1849, the year of the cholera when the courts closed down, but in 1850 and 1851, Mary and her children, Samuel and Edward, sued Lancelot Calvert and Bernard Lynch, the slave trader. Laura, a woman of color, sued Henry Belt, the sheriff. In 1848, Alfred Taylor, a man of color, sued Cornelius Van Houten and Norman Carter, and Jane Cotton sued James A. Little.
29. Laura in Laura v. Henry Belt, no. 22 (1852), CCHRP; Mary, of color, and her children Samuel and Edward v. Calvert, no. 1 (1851), CCHRP; Davis, v. Evans, 18 Mo. 249 (1853).
30. Winny v. Whitesides; Rachael v. Walker; Randolph v. Alsey, a Colored Person, 8 Mo. 656 (1844), and thereafter Wash v. Randolph, 9 Mo. 142 (1845); Daniel Wilson v. Melvin, 4 Mo. 592 (1837); Anderson v. Brown, of Color, 9 Mo. 646 (1845).
31. Pierre v. Chouteau, no. 125 (1842), 241, CCHRP. It appears that Pierre was eventually released on October 22, 1852, still of unsound mind after having spent four years in the jail. Pierre v. Chouteau, no. 125, 242.
32. Friday, August 13, 1852.
33. October 22, 1852, affidavit of Charles H. Mercier.
34. Pierre v. Gabriel Chouteau no. 125, CCHRP. Habeas corpus petition. Related cases: Gabriel S. Chouteau v. Pierre, of Color, 9 Mo. 3 (1845); Charlotte v. Chouteau, 21 Mo. 590 (1855), 25 Mo. 465 (1857).
35. Laura v. Henry Belt, Sheriff of St. Louis, no. 22 (1852), CCHRP
36. Henry Belt had been one of the original members of the Committee of 100, which had urged more restraints on slaves and free blacks. Scharf, *History of St. Louis*, vol. 1, 586.
37. Scott v. Emerson, 15 Mo. 576, 584 (1852). Often, defendant slaveholders would leave the county when faced with a freedom suit based on residence. See, for example, Petition and Order of the Judge, Milly v. Duncan, no. 63, at 2 (alleging that the petitioner's master brought her to Galena, Illinois, for several weeks, then to Dubuque, in present-day Iowa for several months of mining labor); Petition to Sue *in forma pauperis*, Celestine v. Papin, no. 42, at 2 (1837), CCHRP.
38. Another mystery is why the Scotts brought a new case in a federal circuit court, the lowest federal court at the time, rather than appeal from the Missouri Supreme Court to the U.S. Supreme Court. Austin Allen cites an explanation by Roswell Field that the action, started as a diversity action against Sanford rather than as an appeal from the Missouri Supreme Court, was thought to avoid the case's dismissal under the unfavorable precedent of Strader v. Graham, 51 U.S. 82 (1851).
39. Kaufman, *Dred Scott's Advocate*, 181.
40. Ibid. See also Bay, *The Bench and Bar of Missouri*, 236–41.
41. Ibid., 241. Roswell Field too had a junior partner, Arba Crane, though Crane did not arrive until 1856 (Kaufman, *Dred Scott's Advocate*, 212). Arba Crane was the person recognized by Dred as his lawyer when the journalists came to the house as described in Chapter 1.
42. See, for example, Elsa Hicks's first case: Elsa Hicks v. S. Burrell and Louis Mitchell, no. 55 (April 1845), CCRP.

43. The federal court would have had independent jurisdiction over the federal question of the constitutionality of the Northwest Ordinance without diversity of citizenship. So presumably under the federal question basis, the Scotts could have chosen to sue Missouri resident B. S. Garland. John Sanford resisted the suit on jurisdictional grounds, alleging that the court could not have diversity jurisdiction over a black person. The federal circuit court found that it did have jurisdiction but ruled against the Scotts on the merits of their case anyway (Bogen, *Privileges and Immunities*, 32).

    Ultimately, the U.S. Supreme Court found it impossible for blacks to be American citizens of any state. The court therefore had no diversity jurisdiction over the Scotts in the first place because they could not reside in any state (see Fehrenbacher, *The Dred Scott Case*, 346). See, generally, Simson, "*Dred Scott v. Sandford:* Right Result, Wrong Reasons?"

44. Mrs. Emerson Chaffee corroborated this view in an interview decades later. "Even then, a time not specified, the case would have probably been compromised in some manner if it had not been for a peculiar occurrence, which happened to take place just before the suit was brought. This was the wholesale flight of all the negroes belonging to the Chouteau family, into which John Sandford [*sic*] had married. In all seventeen escaped in one night and got over into Illinois, and from there to Canada, and the family was so angry over the matter that its members persuaded Sandford [*sic*] to fight out the Scott case till the last. Accordingly, Sandford [*sic*] took up the matter on his own account...and carried it on" (*New York Times*, December 22, 1895).

45. The date identified was January 1, 1853. Instead, the date was probably arbitrarily selected ("Dred Scott, Life of the Famous Fugitive and Missouri Litigant," T. W. Chamberlin Collection, presumed to be written by William Vincent Biars).

    Why January 1? January 1 was the annual leasing day. However, the Scotts could not have been rounded up for the annual New Year's Day slave auction. The entire family, living more freely after the trial court declaration, were still leased out for the year until April, so unless LaBeaume surrendered them, which was unlikely, the New Year's Day date had no meaning at all.

46. Dred Scott v. Sanford Case Files.

47. Ibid.

48. Stover, *History of the Illinois Central Railroad*, 26.

49. Sanford's will and inventory list four persons as his slave property in Missouri in 1857: Fanny, aged about 20 with her child about four weeks old; Lucy, aged 18; Josephine, aged 16; and William aged 14 appraised together at $2,800 (PCDP).

50. "Famous Dred Scott Case," *New York Times*, December 22, 1895, p. 26; Austin Allen implicitly acknowledges this in Allen, *Origins of the Dred Scott Case*, 148.

51. "Famous Dred Scott Case," *New York Times*, December 22, 1895.

52. Chouteau and Sanford met and dined with other wealthy St. Louisians traveling through New York, November 29, 1853, Metropolitan Hotel (Anne E. Lane to Sarah L. Glasgow, The Lane Collection, William Carr Lane, 1837, Mo HS, St. Louis). "Pa got hold of the Chouteaus's yesterday and out of complacency eats a second dinner with Chouteau. This is the best Hotel I ever was at. Every thing is first rate. Charges included." Ibid.

    "I saw Messrs Chouteau and Sanford in New York but nothing of the ladies. Chouteau looks remarkably well and doings seem to agree with him" (Anne E. Lane to Sarah L. Glasgow, New York, 1853–4). The Lane Collection, William Carr Lane, Mo HS).

53. April 4, 1851, J. F. A. Sanford to unknown correspondent. "I was in Paris for four or five days." Sanford-Chouteau letter collection.

54. March 13, 1851, J. F. A. Sanford to P. Chouteau Jr. and Co. Sanford-Chouteau letter collection.

55. May 7, 1851, C. M. Lampson to J. F. A. Sanford. Sanford-Chouteau letter collection.

56. July 17, 1851, C. M. Lampson to J. F. A. Sanford. Sanford-Chouteau letter collection.

57. See, generally, Chouteau papers, Mo HS, letters of the 1850s.
58. Letter of John F. A. Sanford to Pierre Chouteau Jr. November 1, 1851. Sanford-Chouteau letter collection.
59. Kane, *The Falls of St. Anthony*, 12–13.
60. Ibid., 14.
61. Ibid., 25.
62. Chouteau letter to Julie Chouteau, July 1852. Sanford-Chouteau letter collection.
63. Sanford-Chouteau letter collection; see, generally, Stover, *History of the Illinois Central Railroad*.
64. July 9, 1850.
65. 32nd Congress, 1st session, December 1, 1851 to August 31, 1852. Letter of John F. A. Sanford to Pierre Chouteau, February 17, 1852. Sanford-Chouteau letter collection.
66. 34th Cong, 1st session, December 3, 1855 to August 18, 1856. Letter of February 9, 1852, Pierre Chouteau Jr., New York, to Sarpy. Sanford-Chouteau letter collection. "This is to inform you that after two weeks of debate about Ft. Pierce, Sanford has succeeded in obtaining us a price of $36,500 for it, and I am going to receive a warrant for that amount on the city of New York." As early as 1838, Sanford collected $24,307 From the U.S. Treasury for the 4th quarter of 1838, making him one of the largest claimants in the entries under millitary department. U.S. Treasurer's Accounts, 26th Cong., 1st session, H. Doc. 29, 171.
67. Letter of Chouteau January 12, 1839, informing New York that Sanford advises prosecution of Webster on his debt. Sanford-Chouteau letter collection.
68. September 20, 1854, C. C. Chaffee was elected on the American Party ticket to fill a resignation by Henry Morriss of Springfield (Green, *Springfield, 1636–1886*, 502).
69. William Henry Chaffee,*The Chaffee Genealogy*, 303.
70. Letter of Ramsey Crooks to H. H. Sibley, Sibley Papers, Minn HS.
71. House of Representatives, 35th Congress, 1st session, report no. 27. Mary Bainbridge, widow of Lt. Col. Henry Bainbridge, introduced January 21, 1858, by Mr. Chaffee. Report no. 82, Henrietta S. Clark, introduced February 4, 1858, by Mr. Chaffee.
72. "TWO HUNDRED DOLLAR REWARD RAN away from the subscriber, living 4 miles west of the city of St. Louis, on Saturday night last, a negro man by the name of Joshua, about 38 or 40 years of age, about 6 feet high, spare, with long legs and short body, full suit of hair, eyes inflamed and red, his color is an ashy black. Had on when he went away a pair of black satinet pantaloons, pair of heavy kip boots, an old-fashioned black dress coat, and [?] shirt. He took no clothes with him. The above reward will be paid for his apprehension if taken out of the State, and fifty dollars if taken in the State" (B. S. Garland *Missouri Republican*, May 17, 1852).
73. Ibid.
74. *Missouri Republican*, May 17, 1852.
75. Brown's hotel, December 11, 1853, Anne E. Lane to Sarah Lane Glasgow (The Lane Collection, William Carr Lane, 1837, Mo HS). "Mr. Garland from St. Louis is here."
76. Baker, *The Rescue of Joshua Glover*, 2–3; Jackson and McDonald, *Finding Freedom*.
77. Baker, *The Rescue of Joshua Glover*, 2–3; Jackson and McDonald, *Finding Freedom*.
78. Howe, *What Hath God Wrought*
79. Ibid., 22–23.
80. Ibid.
81. Ibid.
82. Ex parte Booth, 3 Wis 134 (1854); Garland v. Booth; United States v. Sherman M. Booth.
83. "James, 18 years old, spare made, rather small for his age, copper color, with freckles on his face, large full dark eyes, hair somewhat inclined to curl, a scar on the lower part of the breast" (*Missouri Republican*, May 29, 1854).
84. *Missouri Republican*, May 27, 1857.
85. Newspaper source to come.
86. Wade, *Slavery in the Cities*, 61.

87. *Missouri Republican*, April 30, 1851.
88. *Missouri Republican*, February 4, 1849, April 30, 1851, October 16, 1851. (each documenting criminal and police activity in the Almond street area).
89. Several of the St. Louis city directories identify the African Americans by a small c in parentheses. By the 1850 directories, persons identified this way as persons of color were listed as living in an alley in one of these adjoining blocks. As early as the 1820s, an open space between Main and 2nd Streets, and not far from Green Street, had provided a place where African Americans were "accustomed to assemble in the pleasant afternoons of the Sabbath and dance, drink, and fight, quite to the annoyance of all seriously disposed persons." Buchanan, *Black Life on the Mississippi*, 42.
90. *Missouri Republican*, July 26, 1854. A fight involving about 300 persons, "mostly Irish," took place on Morgan between 5th and 6th streets (*Missouri Republican*, September 10, 1854, recorded a fight near the corner of 7th and Green).
91. *Missouri Republican*, February 16, 1854, May 16, 1854.
92. Testimony of Mrs. Susan Wright, resident of St. Louis describing her life experiences there (Blassingame, *Slave Narratives*, 509).
93. Delaney, "From the Darkness Cometh the Light," 12–13.
94. Scott, Dred. (c) white washer. al. b. 10th and 11th, n. of Wash, BLOCK 261. 1854–55 Directory of Citizens and a Business Directory.
95. At least 12 other black men listed whitewashing as their occupation when filing for licenses to remain in the state (Free Negro Bonds, Slavery Collection, Mo HS).
96. Henry Deering, son of a prosperous St. Louis free black woman, was charged with disturbing the peace and fined $50 (*Missouri Republican*, July 28, 1854).
97. Members of the black community listing their occupation as preacher or minister on the Free Negro Bonds included Aaron M. Parker, George W. Johnson, John Turner, Hiram Revels, James Peck, Emmanuel [sic] Cartwright, Isaac Overall, Thomas Struther. Two additional men, John Berry Meachum and John Richard Anderson, who were also ministers of the Baptist church, listed their occupations as cooper and painter. Similarly Jordan Early, an AME minister, listed his occupation as "waiter" whereas in the 1845 City Directory he was identified as a "riverman."
98. On March 22, 1846, two church elders from the First African American Church, Richard Sneethen and John R. Anderson, began preaching in the hall next to Liberty Engine House at 3rd and Cherry Streets. In June 1846, the new group took the name the Second African Baptist Church, but when they later moved to a location on 8th Street, they took the name "the 8th St. Church." On August 3, 1846, the Second African Baptist church organized with 22 members. Harriet joined this church. Kennedy's St. Louis Directory (1860) lists 1851 as the date for erection of a building for the church on the corner of 8th Street, near Green. This church was headed by the Reverend John R. Anderson, a large, free black man, whose mother came west with the Bates family. As a young man, Anderson had worked for the Reverend Lovejoy in Alton and had witnessed his murder (John R. Anderson, 1818–1863, in Stevens, *History of Central Baptist Church*, 29–30).
99. Stevens, *History of Central Baptist Church*, 29–30.
100. Ibid.
101. See note 97.
102. Sandweiss, *St. Louis in the Century of Henry Shaw*, 63.
103. Payne, *History of the African Methodist Episcopal Church*, 171.
104. Shipley and Shipley, *The History of Black Baptists in Missouri*; Payne, *History of the African Methodist Episcopal Church*, iv, 11; Dodson, *Engendering Church*.
105. The five were the 8th Street Baptist Church, one Methodist (Wesley Chapel), and two AME churches: the First African Methodist Episcopal Church and St. Paul's Chapel of the AME Church.
106. Dodson, *Engendering Church*; Payne, *Recollections of Seventy Years*, 132.
107. *Missouri Republican*, February 19, 1854.

108. *Missouri Republican,* May 22, 1855, and July 19, 1855. "Mary Meachum, (colored) for enticing away a slave, was tried by a jury and acquitted. There was also another indictment against her for a similar offense, upon which a nolle prosequi was entered."

109. Revels, "The Autobiography of Hiram Rhoades Revels."

110. *Missouri Republican,* October 20, 1854. "Negro Riot—The locality of Eleventh and Green sts." "Accordingly going to an exhortation meeting which met on Wednesday night, many of them went armed, with sticks and clubs, anticipating a row. We learn that the house was full of members and those not members, and Revels was going on with his exhortation, when he mentioned in connection with the subject of the division which he was aware existed, that only thirteen of the members were dissatisfied with his course and manner of talking. Someone then responded— 'Turn them out' to which another rejoined 'They will put you out.' This reply was the signal for a general muss, which immediately took place, and ended in the rankest confusion. Of course, the sermon was broken off short and the preacher vanished."

111. *Missouri Republican,* October 27, 1854. The Negro Riot: "There are 16 cases on the recorder's docket, All that we could glean was that there are two parties in the church, and they had a fight 'in meeting.' . . . The preacher was knocked out of the pulpit, and fell according to some of the testimony, in one of the sister's laps. It was said afterwards that some parishioners had attended the meeting already armed with bricks and sticks."

112. *Missouri Republican,* October 20, 1854.

113. "The congregation were afraid of the police, and avoided any confusion outside. After a skirmish of about 15 minutes duration, in which little damage was done to either person or property, the church was vacated and cleared, and the combatants retired to their homes" (ibid.).

114. "[Revels] is not entitled to license, having come into the State only 13 months earlier.

115. Payne, *Recollections of Seventy Years,* 122.

116. Several of those arrested were charged with disturbing the peace or failure to have a license. One man was charged with "intent to kill" (*Missouri Republican,* October 28, 1854). *Missouri Republican* November 2, 1854: "The Negro rioters.—Ben Richards fined $10 . . . Geo. W. Early, was tried and discharged."

   Others getting licenses that month perhaps under the impetus of being arrested in the church dispute included Abraham Mills, age 50, a drayman. The 1854–55 St. Louis directory places Abraham Mills on the west side of 10th Street, between Franklin Avenue and Morgan. Also registering were Adam Nash, age 45, a carpenter, registered December 1854. Free Negro Bonds, Slavery Collection, Mo HS.

117. *Missouri Republican,* November 1, 1854.

118. Gross, *Double Character,* 127–28.

119. *Missouri Republican,* November 9, 1854.

120. *Missouri Republican,* November 14, 1854. "Discharged—Hiram R. Revels, the negro minister and pastor of the A.M.E. Church which was late the scene of riotous outbreak among its congregation was discharged from jail late Saturday night last by writ of habeas corpus." Ironically, Judge Scott of the Supreme Court, who had written the decision against the Scotts, issued the writ.

121. Payne, *Recollections of Seventy Years,* 122.

122. Ibid.

123. Revels, "The Autobiography of Hiram Rhoades Revels."

124. *Missouri Republican,* July 27, 1856.

125. Judge Robert Wells didn't even list a permanent address in the city according to the 1852 or 1853 St. Louis City Directories.

126. Walsh, *The Story Of An Old Clerk* (describing the federal court taking rooms outside the courthouse because of crowding); Scharf, *History of St. Louis,* vol. 1, 729–31.

127. *Missouri Republican,* July 24, 1855.
128. "Roswell M. Field . . . possessed the faculty in a greater degree than any other lawyer I recall of condensing in a small compass and making effective his pleadings in legal documents." *The Story of An Old Clerk.* The Scotts' attorney requested a directed verdict in his client's favor, which was refused. Dred Scott v. Sanford case files.
129. Bay, *The Bench and Bar of Missouri,* 538–44.
130. James Hardy was foreman of the jury (Byars memorandum). Dred Scott v. Sanford Case Files.
131. "Bleeding Kansas" was the nickname given to the state of Kansas after the Kansas-Nebraska Act of 1854 made the introduction of slavery into the state a matter of local sovereignty. John Brown's infamous massacre at Osawotamie occurred in May of 1856 (Goodrich, *War to the Knife: Bleeding Kansas*).
132. *Missouri Republican,* June 1, 1854.
133. See Chapter 24.
134. Kaufman, *Dred Scott's Advocate,* 198–99.
135. Charles Whittlesey, a young lawyer whose sister had married Lyman Norris, settled Garland's estate. Hugh Garland probate, PCDP.
136. Hugh Garland probate, PCDP. Slave Registry for 1850 Census lists 10 slaves in the Garland household.
137. Rutberg, *Mary Lincoln's Dressmaker*; Fleischner, *Mrs. Lincoln and Mrs. Keckley*; Keckley, *Behind the Scenes.*
138. August 10–November 13, 1855, Elizabeth Keckley and her son George were freed by Anne P. Garland for $1,200 Free Negro Bond registered May 5, 1859, for "Lizzie Keckley, John Finney: 39 5'2" occup mantuamaker." She was listed in the 1859 City Directory as "Keckley, Elizabeth, (col'd) dressmaker, North 5th between Washington Ave and Green."
139. Circumstances probably changed when Garland died. His widow may have needed cash from Keckley's purchase of her freedom.

    Hugh Garland's participation in the Scott's case as Sanford's lawyer and his refusal to allow enslaved Elizabeth Keckley to purchase her freedom have drawn criticism in the course of history.

    Two successive presidents of the college where Garland taught classical Greek at the time espoused similar views.
140. Garland, *A Life of John Randolph of Roanoke,* 127.
141. "There can be no doubt that the agitation of this slavery question had not been commenced and fermented by men who had no possible connection with it and who from the nature of the case could have no other motive but political ambition and a spirit of aggression had that subject been left as we found it under the compromises of the Constitution and the laws of God and conscience aided by an enlightened understanding of their true interests been left to work their silent yet irresistible influences on the minds of men there can be no doubt that thousands would have followed the example of John Randolph in Virginia, Maryland, Kentucky, and Missouri and that long ere this measures would have been adopted for the final though gradual extinguishment of slavery within their borders as it is that event has again been put off for another generation" (ibid., 152, 372).

Chapter 31

1. Benami Garland is not mentioned in his cousin's probate (Hugh Garland Probate, PCDP).
2. "Ben's father will go to see him in November or December as soon as our affairs permit." Ben was then in Europe (letter of P. Chouteau Jr. to wife, September 8, 1854, Chouteau Family Papers, Mo HS).
3. Kaufman, *Dred Scott's Advocate,* 146.
4. Ibid., 200.

5. Reverdy Johnson letter to Henry Chouteau, New Orleans, February 23, 1855, Chouteau Family Papers, Mo HS.

6. Kaufman, *Dred Scott's Advocate*, 12–13 (citing letter to Montgomery Blair dated December 24, 1854).

7. Ibid., 194.

8. Kaufman, *Dred Scott's Advocate*, 191–94.

9. See Chapter 26. After the trial, after Charlotte Blow Charless was widowed, she was to be found living at the St. Louis home of Frank Blair, Montgomery Blair's brother, suggesting a connection between Charlotte Charless and the Blairs. "1860 Kennedy's St. Louis City Directory."

10. Montgomery Blair, born in Franklin County, Kentucky, graduated from West Point in 1835. He served briefly as St. Louis's mayor in 1842 and as a judge in the Court of Common Pleas from 1843 to 1849. He moved to Maryland in 1852 (Lawson, *American State Trials*, 252).

11. *Missouri Republican*, March 24, 1855.

12. *Missouri Republican*, August 3, 1855: "Jail Statistics. During the month 65 prisoners committed to the county jail. 1 free negro without license, 20 negroes for safekeeping. Discharged during the same period 24. Number of Prisoners now confined in Jail 75.

13. A total of 39 were emancipated during the two months." *Missouri Republican*, December 4, 1855: "Slaves Emancipated–within a week or two past, 15–20 citizens of the city and county have had acts of emancipation recorded—taking opportunity to do so before the law just passed by the Legislature, and which embraces a clause prohibiting emancipation shall go into effect."

14. Manumission of Ophelia (daughter of Silvia McCoy) by will of Sarah Charless December 4, 1855 (executors Joseph Charless, C.T. Charless, Taylor Blow and E. A. W. Blow), vol. 25, St. Louis Circuit Court Record Book, p. 216. List of St. Louis manumissions on file with author.

15. Manumission of Nicene Clark (wife of Henry Clark), April 28, 1854 by Taylor Blow, vol. 24, St. Louis Circuit Court Record Book, p.161.

16. Not all were licensed to remain in the state.

17. He was elected on the American Party ticket to the 34th Congress and as a Republican to the 35th Congress March 4, 1855–March 3, 1859. Chaffee continued to be listed in the Springfield, Massachusetts, directory during his years in Congress.

18. President James Buchanan was known to enjoy vacationing there.

19. Fehrenbacher, *The Dred Scott Case*, 290.

20. Wilentz, *The Rise of American Democracy,* 689–92.

21. Green, *Springfield, 1636–1886,* 510.

22. Perhaps Dr. Jennings, whom they had called as a witness in a trial so long ago, was called to care for him. (Dr. Watts had disappeared from St. Louis.)

23. Minerva Blow letter to Henry Blow, from Carondelet, March 8, 1856. Blow Family Papers, Mo HS.

24. Arba Crane only arrived in St. Louis in 1856. So Roswell Field rather than Crane handled the case in federal court. Arba Crane, born in Walcott, Vermont, in 1834, graduated from Harvard Law School, and moved to St. Louis in 1856 (Lawson, *American State Trials*, 251).

25. Henry T. Blow sent in his objections to being identified with Benton and Blair (*Missouri Republican*, July 27, 1856). Another man published a similar disclaimer (*Missouri Republican,* January 25, 1857).

26. *Missouri Republican*, November 4, 1856.

27. John Fremont's last expedition with Joseph Nicollet was in 1839. From 1839 to 1846, Fremont led multiple He was appointed military governor of California by his superior officer but refused to step down when Gen. Kearny arrived to serve as governor on the orders of the president. Fremont was court-martialed and convicted of mutiny in 1848. He left the army because President Polk wouldn't lift the conviction despite Polk's request that he stay. From 1850 to 1851, Fremont

served briefly in the Senate as one of California's first senators. In 1856, he was nominated as the Republican candidate for president, becoming the only antislavery candidate in a campaign that included the Democrat James Buchanan and former president Millard Fillmore for the Whigs. Fremont proved to be a better leader of expeditions than of campaigns, and his campaign was bogged down in a multitude of scandalous charges. He finished second to James Buchanan, with Buchanan carrying Missouri (Chaffin, *Pathfinder: John Charles Fremont*, 66–74, 241, 367–78, 381, 417–20, 440–47; United States Department of the Interior, Printable Maps— Elections http://nationalatlas.gov/printable/images/pdf/elections/electo4.pdf [last visited May 31 2008]).

28. In 1856, in the three-way race, Fillmore, Fremont, and Buchanan, nationally Buchanan received, 1,839,642; Fremont received 1,342,069; Fillmore, 872,760.

29. October 4, 1856, letter of P. Chouteau to Julie Maffitt, Chouteau Family Papers, Mo HS.

30. Pierre Chouteau Jr. letter to Julie Maffitt, November 13, 1856, Chouteau Family Papers, Mo HS.

31. Vose, *Wealth of the World Displayed*, 116. J. F. A. Sanford is listed as residing at 138 Fifth Avenue.

32. Pierre Chouteau Jr. letter to Julie Maffit, Chouteau Family Papers, Mo HS.

33. Most of Sanford's letters are either in the Chouteau Family Papers of the Mo HS or indexed in Grace Nute, "Calendar of Papers of the American Fur Company." The single entry that suggests any sympathy for the Indians' plight is a letter of introduction that Sanford writes to Sibley to host a friend of his, who Sanford writes is interested in helping the Indians (letter of John F. A. Sanford to Henry Sibley, date, Henry H. Sibley Papers, Minn HS).

34. Letter of Pierre Chouteau Jr. to Julie Chouteau Maffitt, February 21, 1857, Chouteau Family Papers, Mo HS

35. This cannot be maintained definitely, but he died later that year in the same asylum and there are no letters at all indicating that he had traveled to Europe.

36. George Curtis had joined Montgomery Blair in arguing the Scott's appeal. George Curtis was the brother of Justice Curtis who sat on the bench and heard the appeal. There appears to have been no concern that the Justice recuse himself.

37. On December 16, 1856, the case was reported in the newspaper by name.

38. *Missouri Republican*, December 16, 1856 (emphasis added).

39. James M. McPherson, *Battle Cry of Freedom: The Civil War Era* (New York: Oxford University Press, 1988), 102–3.

40. *Missouri Republican*, January 1, 1857.

41. On January 3, 1857, Judge Daniels's wife burned to death in her dressing gown (*Missouri Republican*, January 6, 1857).

42. *Missouri Republican*, January 9, 1857, reporting an article from the *Herald Correspondence* of January 7.

43. Ibid.

44. Ibid.

45. *Missouri Republican*, January 9, 1857, reporting article from the *Herald Correspondence*, Washington. *Missouri Republican*, January 20, 1857, reporting article from *Jefferson City Examiner*.

46. Bolstering Justice Taney's majority opinion were the opinions of Justice Wayne of Georgia, 60 U.S. at 454, Justice Nelson of New York, ibid. at 457, Justice Grier of Pennsylvania, ibid. at 469, Justice Campbell of Alabama, ibid. at 493, Justice Catron of Tennessee, ibid. at 518. Writing dissents were Justice Mclean of Ohio, ibid. at 529 and Justice Curtis of Massachusetts, ibid. at 564. *Scott v. Sandford*, 60 U.S. 393 (1857).

47. *Scott v. Sandford*, 60 U.S. 393, 422 (1857).

48. Fehrenbacher, *The Dred Scott Case*, 337, 340.

49. Ibid., 340.

50. *Scott v. Sandford*, 403.

51. *Scott v. Sandford*, 406.

52. Fehrenbacher, *The Dred Scott Case,* 70.
53. In his 1831 unpublished attorney general opinion, Taney had written 4,000 words on the subject epigrammatically expressed as follows: "The African race in the United States, even when free, are everywhere a degraded race, and exercise no political influence. The privileges they are allowed to enjoy, are accorded to them as a matter of kindness and benevolence rather than of right.... And where they are nominally admitted by law to the privileges of citizenship, they have no effectual power to defend them, and are permitted to be citizens by the sufferance of the white population and hold what rights they enjoy at their mercy" (Litwack, *North of Slavery,* 53).
54. Scott v. Sandford, 60 U.S. at 475 (Justice Daniel concurrence).
55. Ibid.
56. *Missouri Republican,* December 16, 1856 (account of Geyer's argument).
57. Ibid., 403.
58. Howe, *What Hath God Wrought,* 702–8, 752, 762.
59. See Chapter 15.
60. Scott v. Sandford, 60 U.S. at 408–16 (Taney addressing mixed race through amalgamation statutes); VanderVelde and Subramanian, *Mrs. Dred Scott,* 1109–17.
61. Scott v. Sandford, 60 U.S. at 403.
62. White, Hoxie, and Salisbury, *The Middle Ground,* 70, 165.
63. Ibid.
64. Wozniak, *Contact, Negotiation and Conflict,* 43.
65. Goodwin and Goodwin, *Joseph R. Brown, Adventurer.*
66. See Chapter 7. Blegen, "The Unfinished Autobiography," 362.
67. This was one of the issues over which the Ojibwa bargained with Governor Dodge at the treaty of 1837; see Chapter 11.
68. Scott v. Sandford, 60 U.S. at 403.
69. *Missouri Republican,* July 27, 1856, discussed in Chapter 30.
70. Ibid., 404.
71. Satz, *Chippewa Treaty Rights,* 3–4.
72. Ibid., 18.
73. Ibid., 143–44.
74. See discussion in Chapter 15.
75. Scott v. Sandford, 60 U.S. at 404.
76. Scott v. Sandford, 60 U.S. at 403.
77. Because she helped the soldiers' wives with the laundry and had a darker skin, she was mistaken as an African slave. Nancy did prevail, but she was awarded the token one-penny damages that free blacks received when found to have been falsely enslaved. Nancy was not treated as if she were white upon moving to St. Louis, nor was she awarded what a kidnapped white immigrant would have expected. Nancy and Peggy Perryman in Nancy v. Steen, no. 4 (April 1848) and Perryman v. Philibert, no. 255 (November 1848), CCHRP.
78. The class of persons were only those "whose ancestors were negroes of the African race, and imported into this country, and sold and held as slaves" (Scott, 60 U.S. at 403). "The words 'people of the United States' and 'citizens' are synonymous terms, and mean the same thing. They both describe the political body who, according to our republican institutions, form the sovereignty, and who hold the power and conduct the Government through their representatives. They are what we familiarly call the 'sovereign people,' and every citizen is one of this people, and a constituent member of this sovereignty (Scott, 60 U.S. at 404).
79. Ibid.
80. Scott v. Sandford, 60 U.S. at 404.
81. Buckland, *The Roman Law of Slavery,* lists cases where a slave could be rewarded with manumission (ibid., 598) for denouncing bad acts or bearing witness to crime. In addition, "There are many instances of gifts of liberty as a reward...for revealing crime, or betraying the enemy, or for service...." Ibid., 589–90.
82. Justice Campbell picked on the stipulated set of facts to claim, "No evidence is found in the record to establish the existence of a domicile acquired by the master

and slave, either in Illinois or Minnesota," though Harriet's life story would have contributed that, for where a person marries and remains with her husband must be her domicile. *Scott v. Sandford*, 60 U.S. 393 (1857) at 494–95.

83. Ibid., at 410 and 407 respectively.

84. Ibid., at 404–5.

85. Ibid., at 404. Congress might have authorized the naturalization of Indians, because they were aliens and foreigners. But in their then-untutored and savage state, no one would have thought of admitting them as citizens in a civilized community.

86. This position was taken by dissenting justice Benjamin Curtis. *Scott v. Sandford*, 60 U.S. 393, 564 (1857). Fehrenbacher, *The Dred Scott Case*, 408.

87. Of course, the opinion did not articulate its ruling as to Harriet's status. Harriet's fate was being determined but she was just a derivative in the Court's order.

88. *Scott v. Sandford*, 60 U.S. 393 (1857) at 404.

89. Northwest Ordinance of 1787.

90. True, the Prairie du Chien trial in which John Bonga had testified was not an Article 2 court, under the U.S. Constitution's Article 2, but it was a federal territorial court rather than a state court.

91. George Bonga trading papers, Minn HS.

92. Maria Fasnacht, an African American woman in Prairie du Chien, had married one white man, divorced him, and married another.

93. Taney reasoned from an eighteenth-century Maryland enactment providing that interracial marriages enjoyed lesser privileges than other marriages. To discourage interracial marriage, a Maryland statute had provided that free blacks who married white spouses would become slaves.

    "The province of Maryland, in 1717 . . . passed a law declaring 'that if any free negro or mulatto intermarry with any white woman, or if any white man shall intermarry with any negro or mulatto woman, such negro or mulatto shall become a slave during life, excepting mulattoes born of white women, who, for such intermarriage, shall only become servants for seven years, to be disposed of as the justices of the county court, where such marriage so happens, shall think fit; to be applied by them towards the support of a public school within the said county. And any white man or white woman who shall intermarry as aforesaid, with any negro or mulatto, such white man or white woman shall become servants during the term of seven years, and shall be disposed of by the justices as aforesaid, and be applied to the uses aforesaid'" (Dred Scott v. Sanford, 60 U.S. 393, 407 [1857]).

94. The Court also cited a colonial Massachusetts law fining any one who solemnized an interracial marriage. Ibid., 408 (quoting a colonial law passed by Massachusetts in 1705).

95. McLaurin, *Celia, a Slave*, 29–31.

96. Thomas, *From Tennessee Slave to St. Louis Entrepreneur*, 2, 7, 60.

97. Brown, *From Fugitive Slave to Free Man*, 68–69.

98. Scott v. Sandford, 60 U.S. at 409.

99. Fehrenbacher, *The Dred Scott Case*, 365–66.

100. Allen, *Origins of the Dred Scott Case*, 25–30.

101. Graber, *Dred Scott and the Problem of Constitutional Evil*, 53–55.

102. This was the hallmark of Justice McLean's dissent. Scott v. Sandford, 60 U.S. 532–40.

103. Scott v. Sandford, 60 U.S. at 503.

104. Justice Curtis dissenting opinion, ibid., 573, 631.

105. Justice Curtis dissenting opinion, ibid., 583.

106. Justice Curtis dissenting, ibid.

Chapter 32

1. *Missouri Republican*, April 9, 1857; Fehrenbacher, *The Dred Scott Case*, 417–43.

2. Paul Finkelman, *Documents of the Dred Scott Case*.

3. *Missouri Republican*, March 22, 1857, 2: "Who Owns Dred Scott?" *Missouri Republican,* March 27, 1857, 2: "THE DRED SCOTT CASE—*WHOSE SLAVE IS HE?*"

4. *Frank Leslie's Illustrated Newspaper*, June 27, 1857.

5. Ibid.

6. *St. Louis News*, April 8, 1857.

7. Editorial correspondence of *Rochester American* reprinted in *Missouri Republican,* June 21, 1857, 1.

8. *St. Louis News*, April 8, 1857.

9. Ibid.

10. Ibid.

11. *Missouri Republican,* June 21, 1857.

12. *St. Louis News*, April 8, 1857.

13. *Frank Leslie's Illustrated Newspaper*, June 27, 1857.

14. The event was so newsworthy as to be photographed. Kilgo, *Likeness and Landscape*, 189.

15. *Frank Leslie's Illustrated Newspaper*, June 27, 1857.

16. *Missouri Republican,* June 21, 1857.

17. *Missouri Republican,* April 3, 1857.

18. J. F. A. Sanford Probate, PCCP.

19. May 26, 1857.

20. "Mr. Chaffee's political enemies were not slow in [attacking] his reputation... He was charged with the intent of making money out of the very slave system which upon the floor of the Congress he had condemned. With a twenty years anti-slavery record, he was compelled to deny these strictures and to say in public, 'There is no earthly consideration which could induce me to exercise proprietorship in any human being; and I regard slavery as a sin against God and a crime against man,' and he added, 'If in the distribution of the estate, of which the decision affirms, these human beings to be put, it appears that I, or mine, consent to receive any part of the thirty pieces of silver, then, and not till then, let the popular judgment, as well as the public press, fix on me the mark of a traitor to my conscience'" (Green, *Springfield, 1636–1886*, 510).

21. Kenneth Kaufman, *Dred Scott's Advocate*, 224–25.

22. Fehrenbacher, *The Dred Scott Case*, 48–50, 684.

23. Kenneth Kaufman, *Dred Scott's Advocate*, 226; May 27, 1857, Dred Scott v. Irene Emerson, Circuit Court record book 26, p. 267. "On the motion of the defendant's attorney, it is ordered that the Sheriff of St. Louis County... render his account... of the wages that have come to his hands of the earnings of the above named plaintiff and that Sheriff... pay the defendant at all such wages that now remain in his hands, excepting all commissions and expenses to which the said sheriff may be legally entitled."

24. May 27, 1857, Dred Scott v. Irene Emerson, Circuit Court record book 26, p. 267.

25. Letter of Pierre Chouteau Jr. to his son-in-law Dr. Maffitt, May 26, 1857, Chouteau Family Papers, Mo HS.

26. Taylor Blow had signed freedom papers for Frankey Cuterfoot and Tanny Overton on February 7, 1847; Nicene Clark (wife of Henry Clark, a free man of color) on April 28, 1854; and Ophelia (daughter of Silvia McCoy) by will of Sarah Charless (executors Joseph and Charlotte Charless, Taylor Blow and his wife) on December 4, 1855. He had been a witness for the emancipation of Hester Reed by Frances E. Twitchell on June 10, 1854, and he played some role in the support of Alexander Ball on December 29, 1846.

27. "For two or three years past Dred has been at large, no one exercising ownership over him, or putting any restraint upon his movements" (*St. Louis News*, April 8, 1857).

28. "Their whereabouts have been kept a secret, though no effort has been, and none probably would have been, made to recover them. Their father knew where they were, and could bring them back at any moment. He will doubtless recall them

now." "Dred Scott Free at Last: Himself and His Family Emancipated," *St. Louis Daily Evening News*, May 26, 1857, at 2.

29. An observer perceiving the Scott girls thought them to be only eight and 14. *Frank Leslie's Illustrated Newspaper*, June 27, 1857.

30. *Missouri Republican*, April 19, 1858.

31. *New York Times*, May 5, 1857.

32. "Mr. Sanford, we are here assured, was perfectly willing to give the negro his freedom any time, when the Massachusetts ownership permitted" (*Missouri Republican*, March 22, 1857). The truth is, Mr. Sanford never had anything to do with these slaves, except as executor of Dr. Emerson or agent of Mrs. Chaffee (*Missouri Republican*, April 3, 1857).

33. *New York Times*, June 28, 1878, 8. "Disposing of Two Millions: The Will of the Late Thomas E. Davis."

34. "Count A. DeSala, French Diplomat," *New York Times*, June 21, 1946 (obituary of their son).

35. Theron Barnum biography in Scharf, *History of St. Louis*, vol. 2, 1442–43.

36. Scharf, *History of St. Louis*, vol. 2, 1443.

37. Roswell Field, the Scott's attorney, was then boarding at Barnum's Hotel after giving up housekeeping in the city when his wife died (Kaufman, *Dred Scott's Advocate*, 227).

38. Thomas, *From Tennessee Slave to St. Louis Entrepreneur*, 81, note 23; *St. Louis News*, April 8, 1857; *Frank Leslie's Illustrated Newspaper*, June 27, 1857.

39. *St. Louis Evening News and Intelligencer*, September 20, 1858.

40. 1850 Bedford, Pennsylvania, census for the Taliaferro household includes three persons of color: "Eliza Johnston, 38 F. B., born Va.; Susan Johnston, 16 F. Mulatto, born Minnesota (1834); and John Johnston, 7 M. Mulatto, born Pa. (1843)."

   On August 29, 1852, young Master Horatio Dillon died in Panama on his way to California, still seeking his fortune: "In Panama, August 29th, of dropsy, Horatio N. DILLON, of Beaver County, Pa., aged 36 years." The Sacramento Daily Union, California September 25, 1852.

41. Anderson, *Kinsmen of Another Kind*.

42. Joseph Campbell participated in the uprising. Baptiste Campbell was tried (trial number 138), sentenced to death, and hanged on December 26, 1862, in Mankato. This was the largest mass hanging in American history—33 hanged out of 300 hundred and three sentenced to death. Anderson and Woolworth, *Through Dakota Eyes*.

43. May 31, 1857.

44. Vol. 7, p. 131, of the City of St. Louis Mortality register, June 17, 1876. She is listed as widowed, 61 years old. Place of death, between 7th and 8th Streets and between Locust and Olive Streets.

45. From 1854–55 Directory of Citizens and a Business Directory: "Scott, Dred (c) white washer. Alley between 10th and 11th, north of Wash."

   1859 Directory: "Scott, Harriet, wid. Dred, (col'd) laundress, alley Near Carr, between 6th and 7th."

   The 1860 census lists "Harriette Scott as living in the 7th ward of St. Louis, together with Elizabeth Scott 15, and Ellen Knox 50 In (Indian?)(Mulatto?) b. S. Ca. 1860."

   Kennedy's St. Louis Directory: "Scott Harriet (col'd) wid. Dred, resides alley between Franklin Ave and Wash, 7th and 8th."

   1864 Edward's St. Louis City Directory: "Scott, Harriet, (col'd) wid. Resides alley between 8th and 9th, Franklin Ave and Morgan."

   1866 Edwards's St. Louis Directory: "Scott Harriet, wid. Rear alley between 8th and 9th, Franklin Ave. and Morgan."

   1869 Edwards's St. Louis Directory, lists three different Harriet Scotts, one the widow of William, one designated as colored, and one not: "Scott, Harriet, Mrs. (col'd) resides rear 811 N. 8th Street and Scott, Harriet Mrs., resides 416 North 7th Street."

The 1870 City Directory lists "Scott Hattie Miss, r. 416 N. 7th." Unlike other entries, this person is not denominated colored, though she does not appear to be Harriet.

1874: "Scott Harriet, wid. Dred, resides alley between Wash and Franklin Ave, 7th and 8th Streets."

1875 Gould's St. Louis Directory: "Scott Harriet, resides alley rear 712 Wash." No designation as colored.

46. This was Block 181 of the official city map. Her death certificate is recorded by the city.

BIBLIOGRAPHY

U.S. Statutes

Act of Congress 1820, commonly known as the "Missouri Compromise."
The Northwest Ordinance of 1787.

Archival Documents

U.S. United States Census Records. Census records, 1860.
U.S. United States Census Records. Census records, 1850.
U.S. United States Census Records. Census records, 1840.
U.S. United States Census Records. Census records, 1830.
Treaty with the Chippewa 1837. Indian Affairs: Laws and Treaties, vol. 2. Edited by Charles J. Kappler. Washington, DC: Government Printing Office, 1904.
Treaty with the Sioux, August 19, 1825. Indian Affairs: Laws and Treaties, vol. 2. Edited by Charles J. Kappler. Washington, DC: Government Printing Office, 1904.
Treaty with the Sioux, 1837. Indian Affairs: Laws and Treaties, vol. 2. Edited by Charles J. Kappler. Washington, DC: Government Printing Office, 1904.
Roll of Mixed-Blood Claimants, 1856. Minnesota Historical Society Manuscripts Collection.

Papers and Letters Collections

Baker, B.F. Estate, in Kenneth McKenzie Papers. Missouri Historical Society, St. Louis.
Bates Family Papers. AMC96–000082. Missouri Historical Society, St. Louis.
Beaumont, William. William Beaumont Papers. AMC96–000090. Missouri Historical Society, St. Louis.
Beaumont, William. William Beaumont Collection. Washington University School of Medicine Library, St. Louis.
Bedford County, Pennsylvania, Recorder of Deeds. Slave Registry. Pioneer Historical Society, Bedford, PA.
Blow Family Papers. AMC96–000112. Missouri Historical Society, St. Louis.
Brown, Joseph R., and Samuel J. Family Papers, 1826–1956. Minnesota Historical Society Manuscript Collection, St. Paul.
Chouteau Family Papers. AMC93–000504. Missouri Historical Society, St. Louis.
Clouston, Robert. Journals 1846, 1850. Minnesota Historical Society Manuscript Collection, St. Paul.
Clark, William. *William Clark Papers.* Missouri Historical Society, St. Louis.

Edward E. Ayer Manuscript Collection. Letter of Stephen W. Kearny to E. A. Hitchcock. Newberry Library, Chicago.

Fort Snelling Sutler's Account Books and Mendota Account Books, 1836–39. Henry Sibley Papers. Minnesota Historical Society Manuscript Collection, St. Paul. Sutler's Account Books exist for Feb 28, 1837-July 1, 1837; Jan 1838–July 1838.

Fur Trade Collection. AMC93–000758. Missouri Historical Society, St. Louis.

Fur Trade Ledgers. AMC93–000759. Missouri Historical Society, St. Louis.

Garrioch, Peter. Diaries, 1837, 1843–1847. Minnesota Historical Society Manuscript Collection, St. Paul.

Geyer, Charles A. 1838 Botany Journal. Minnesota Historical Society Manuscript Collection, St. Paul.

Hitchcock, Ethan Allen. Hitchcock Family Papers. AMC94–000916. Missouri Historical Society, St. Louis.

Jarvis, Nathan S. "Letters of Nathan Jarvis," 1833–52. Minnesota Historical Society Manuscript Collection, St. Paul.

Kennerly Family Papers. Missouri Historical Society, St. Louis.

Lane, Anne E., The Lane Collection, William Carr Lane, 1837. Missouri Historical Society, St. Louis.

LeBeaume, Theodore. Theodore LeBeaume Papers. AMC94–000953. Missouri Historical Society, St. Louis.

LeClaire, Antoine. Antoine Le Claire Collection. Putnam Museum and Library, Davenport, Iowa.

Manumission Papers of Henry Dodge's five slaves, April 14, 1838, Circuit Court (Iowa County): Clerk of Court Papers, 1809–1868, Box 1, no. 20–22, Wisconsin Historical Society, Madison.

Napton, William Barclay. William Barclay Napton Papers. AMC93–000025. Missouri Historical Society, St. Louis.

Norris, Lyman Decatur. Letters, Norris Family Papers. Bentley Historical Library, University of Michigan, Ann Arbor.

O'Flaherty, Kate. Chopin Papers. AMC93–000503. Missouri Historical Society, St. Louis.

Pond Family Papers, Minnesota Historical Society Manuscript Collection, St. Paul.

Sanford, John A. Letters. The John F. A. Sanford letters and the Chouteau family letters cited in this book have been culled from a variety of different sources: the various manuscript collections of the Missouri Historical Society, the New-York Historical Society, the Minnesota Historical Society, and the National Archives. Most, but not all, are listed in Nute, Grace. "Calendar of Papers of the American Fur Company's Papers." *American Historical Review* 32 (1945). Nute did not include letters for her Calendar that were principally about family matters. The Nute index identifies the location of many of the letters. To simplify citation form for this book, citations to Sanford and Chouteau family letters are listed as "Sanford-Chouteau letter file," on file with the author.

Scott, Dred. Dred Scott Collection. Family Papers, AMC93–000616. Missouri Historical Society, St. Louis.

Sibley, H. H. Henry H. Sibley Papers (1815–1930). Minnesota Historical Society Manuscript Collection, St. Paul.

Southern Historical Collection. Edmund Kirby-Smith Papers. Wilson Library Manuscript Division, University of North Carolina at Chapel Hill.

Street, Joseph Montfort. Joseph Montfort Street Correspondence. Letters 1827–1840. Iowa Historical Society, Des Moines.

Taliaferro, Lawrence. Lawrence Taliaferro Papers, 1813–1868. Minnesota Historical Society Manuscript Collection, St. Paul.

Taliaferro, Lawrence. Lawrence Taliaferro Journals. Minnesota Historical Society Manuscript Collection, St. Paul.

Wells, Judge. Letter from Judge Wells. June 6, 1862, Colby College, Waterville, ME.

William A. Croffut Papers. E. A. Hitchcock Journal. Library of Congress, Manuscript Division, 813E.

U.S. Government Records (National Archives)

Lt. Darling Personnel File.

Dr. John Emerson Personnel File.

Dr. John Emerson's Weather Log for Fort Snelling.

Fort Crawford Court-martial Files, Old Army Files, JAG, RG 153.
Fort Snelling Court-martial Files, Old Army Files, JAG, RG 153.
Fort Snelling Post Muster Rolls. RG 217, Entry 516.
Jefferson Barracks Court-martial files, Old Army Files, RG–E–year.
Miscellaneous Reserve Papers: Sioux Affidavits, Roll of Mixed-Blood Claimants, 1856,
     Relinquishment by Lake Pepin Half-breed Sioux. RG 75.
Missouri Revised Statutes, Ch. 167, Art. II., 1845.
Post Returns for U.S. Army Posts: Fort Armstrong, Fort Snelling, Fort Crawford, Jefferson Barracks,
     and St. Louis Armory, organized by year.
Settled Pay Accounts of U.S. Army Officers, Record Group 217, Entry 516.
E. K. Smith Personnel File.
War Department, U.S. Adj. Gen'ls Office.
War Department, U.S. M217 U.S. War Department.
War Department, U.S. Roll 6, and after. Roll 5 ends in 1823.
War Department, US. Returns and Rolls, 5th Inf., 1815–1840.

St. Louis Court Records and Local Records

Krum, John. Revised Ordinances of the City of St. Louis (1850).
———.The Revised Ordinances of the City of St. Louis (1853).
Free Negro Bonds, Slavery Collection, Missouri Historical Society.
St. Louis Criminal Case Docket Files, on file with author.

Original Court Files

Affidavit by Miles H. Clark in Scott, Dred, a man of color in Emerson, Irene. 1 (Circuit Court Case Files,
     Office of the Circuit Clerk, City of St. Louis, Missouri, November 1846).
Alsey, a woman of color v. Randolph, William. 305 (Circuit Court Case Files, Office of the Circuit Clerk,
     City of St. Louis, Missouri, March 1841).
Angelique, a free woman of color v. Reynolds, John. 10 (Circuit Court Case Files, Office of the Circuit
     Clerk, City of St. Louis, Missouri, July 1828).
Barnes, Archibald, of color v. Meachum, John Berry. 120 (Circuit Court Case Files, Office of the Circuit
     Clerk, City of St. Louis, Missouri, November 1840).
Barnes, Brunetta, of color v. Meachum, John Berry. 121 (Circuit Court Case Files, Office of the Circuit
     Clerk, City of St. Louis, Missouri, November 1840).
Bascom, Caroline, a free mulatto woman v. Ferguson, John H. 20 (Circuit Court Case Files, Office of the
     Circuit Clerk, City of St. Louis, Missouri, April 1846).
Britton, Lucy Ann v. Mitchell, David D. 18 (Circuit Court Case Files, Office of the Circuit Clerk, City of
     St. Louis, Missouri, November 1844).
Celestine of Color v. Madame Julia Dumont. suit 15, Freedom Suits, Murdock and Field for Plaintiff
     (St. Louis Circuit Court, November 1844).
Charlotte (of color) v. Chouteau. II Mo. 193, Cobb for Appellant, Spalding and Tiffany for Appellee
     (St. Louis Circuit Court, October 1847).
Chouteau v. Pierre (of color). 9 Mo. 3 (St. Louis Circuit Court, January 1845).
Chouteau, Louis, a man of color v. Chouteau, Gabriel. 51 (Circuit Court Case Files, Office of the
     Circuit Clerk, City of St. Louis, Missouri, April 1844).
Chouteau v. Marguerite, 12 Pete 507 (1838).
Cloe Ann Smith of color v. Franklin Knox. Suit 120, Suit for Freedom (St. Louis Circuit Court,
     September 18, 1844, November 1844).
Diana Cephas v. Murray McConnell. (St. Louis Circuit Court, 1841).
Duty, Caroline v. Darby, John F., Administrator. 23 (Circuit Court Case Files, Office of the Circuit
     Clerk, City of St. Louis, Missouri, April 1850).
Duty, Ellen v. Darby, John F., Administrator. 18 (Circuit Court Case Files, Office of the Circuit Clerk,
     City of St. Louis, Missouri, April 1850).

Duty, Harry, of color v. Darby, John F., Administrator. 17 (Circuit Court Case Files, Office of the Circuit Clerk, City of St. Louis, Missouri, April 1850).

Duty, Jordan v. Darby, John F., Administrator. 20 (Circuit Court Case Files, Office of the Circuit Clerk, City of St. Louis, Missouri, April 1850).

Duty, Lucinda v. Darby, John F., Administrator. 22 (Circuit Court Case Files, Office of the Circuit Clerk, City of St. Louis, Missouri, April 1850).

Duty, Mary v. Darby, John F., Administrator. 24 (Circuit Court Case Files, Office of the Circuit Clerk, City of St. Louis, Missouri, April 1850).

Duty, Nelly, v. Darby, John F., Administrator. 19 (Circuit Court Case Files, Office of the Circuit Clerk, City of St. Louis, Missouri, April 1850).

Duty, Preston v. Darby, John F., Administrator. 21 (Circuit Court Case Files, Office of the Circuit Clerk, City of St. Louis, Missouri, April 1850).

Eaton v. Vaughan. 9 Mo. 743 (St. Louis Circuit Court, 1846).

Francis B. Murdoch v. Reliesan alias Melanie Christy, John Christy, Samuel Wiggins, Elias Langham and Archibal Carr. (St. Louis Circuit Court, In Chancery November term 1843).

Green Berry Logan, an infant, v. Berry Meachum, a free man of color. (St. Louis Circuit Court, 1836).

Hicks, Elsa, a mulatto girl v. McSherry, Patrick T. 121 (Circuit Court Case Files, Office of the Circuit Clerk, City of St. Louis, Missouri, November 1847).

In the Matter of Toney, alias William Morton—on habeas corpus. 11 Mo. 661 (St. Louis Circuit Court, July 1848).

Jackson, Henry, a person of color v. Fraser, James O. 103 (Circuit Court Case Files, Office of the Circuit Clerk, City of St. Louis, Missouri, July 1842).

Jane McCray v. William Hopkins. (St. Louis Circuit Court, 1845).

Jefferson, John v. McCutchen, William; McKnight, James. 23 (Circuit Court Case Files, Office of the Circuit Clerk, City of St. Louis, Missouri, November 1826).

Jesse, a man of color v. Coons, George W., Administrator. 32 (Circuit Court Case Files, Office of the Circuit Clerk, City of St. Louis, Missouri, November 1844).

Jonathan of Color v. Marshall Brotherton, Joil Dannah, Aza Willoughby, et al. Suit 32, Freedom Suits, King and Murdock appointed as attorneys (St. Louis Circuit Court, November 1841, September 17, 1841).

Judy (also known as Julia Logan) v. Meachum, John Berry. 11 (Circuit Court Case Files, Office of the Circuit Clerk, City of St. Louis, Missouri, March 1835).

Judy a/k/a Julia Logan v. Berry Meachum. (St. Louis Circuit Court, 1837).

Laban, a black man v. Price, Risdon H. 182 (Circuit Court Case Files, Office of the Circuit Clerk, City of St. Louis, Missouri, April 1821).

Logan, Green Berry, an infant of color v. Meachum, John Berry, a free man of color. 22 (Circuit Court Case Files, Office of the Circuit Clerk, City of St. Louis, Missouri, July 1836).

Malinda, a woman of color v. Coons, George W., Administrator. 220 (Circuit Court Case Files, Office of the Circuit Clerk, City of St. Louis, Missouri, November 1845).

Martha Ann, a person of color v. Cordell, Hiram. 9 (Circuit Court Case Files, Office of the Circuit Clerk, City of St. Louis, Missouri, November 1844).

Mary Charlotte, a woman of color v. Chouteau, Gabriel. 13 (Circuit Court Case Files, Office of the Circuit Clerk, City of St. Louis, Missouri, November 1843).

McCray, Jane, a mulatto woman v. Hopkins, William R.; Miller, William; Oliver, Eliza, et al. 162 (Circuit Court Case Files, Office of the Circuit Clerk, City of St. Louis, Missouri, November 1845).

Meachum v. Judy, alias Julia Logan, a woman of color. 4 Mo. 361 (St. Louis Circuit Court, 1836).

Merry, John, a free man of color v. Tiffin, Clayton; Menard, Louis. 18 (Circuit Court Case Files, Office of the Circuit Clerk, City of St. Louis, Missouri, November 1826).

Missouri marriages on line at Ancestry.com.

Nancy, a free woman of color v. Steen, Enoch. 4 (Circuit Court Case Files, Office of the Circuit Clerk, City of St. Louis, Missouri, April 1848).

Nat, a person of color v. Coons, George W., Administrator. 35 (Circuit Court Case Files, Office of the Circuit Court, City of St. Louis, Missouri, November 1844).

Pierre Chouteau, Senior v. Marguerite (a woman of colour). 12 Pete 507 (St. Louis Circuit Court, January 1838).

Pierre, a mulatto v. Chouteau, Gabriel. 125 (Circuit Court Case Files, Office of the Circuit Clerk, City of St. Louis, Missouri, November 1842).

Prescott v. Foote. Brown Docket (St. Louis, February 16, 1840).

Preston, a man of color v. Coons, George W., Administator. 34 (Circuit Court Case Files, Office of the Circuit Clerk, City of St. Louis, Missouri, November 1844).

Preston, Braxton; Mary; Nat, Beverly, et al v. Coons, George W., Administrator et al. 674 (Circuit Court Case Files, Office of the Circuit Court, City of St. Louis, Missouri, November 1841).

Rachel, a woman of color v. Walker, William. 82 (Circuit Court Case Files, Office of the Circuit Clerk, City of St. Louis, Missouri, November 1834).

Ralph, a free man of color v. Duncan, Robert; Duncan, James. 99 (Circuit Court Case Files, Office of the Circuit Clerk, City of St. Louis, Missouri, July 1833).

Rector, Molly, a free woman of color v. Bivens, John. 26 (Circuit Court Case Files, Office of the Circuit Clerk, City of St. Louis, Missouri, November 1827).

Scott, Dred, a man of color v. Emerson, Irene. 1 (Circuit Court Case Files, Office of the Circuit Clerk, City of St. Louis, Missouri, November 1846).

St. Louis Circuit Court Files: in notes as CCHRP.

St. Louis Probate Court Files, on the web at___. Noted as Krum, John. "Revised Ordinances of the City of St. Louis (1850). Docs no. 1681." July 17, 1846.

St. Louis Register of Deeds Volumes, St. Louis Registry of Deeds, St. Louis, Missouri.

Thomas Scott v. James Harrison. Number 90 (original in St. Louis Courthouse) (St. Louis Circuit Court, November Term 1848).

Winny v. Whitsides, Phebe. 190 (Circuit Court Case Files, Office of the City Clerk, City of Saint Louis, Missouri, April 1721).

Missouri Supreme Court Cases

Julia v. McKinney. 3 Mo. R. 270, 1833 WL 3254.

LaGrange v. Chouteau. 2 Mo. R. 20, 1828 WL 41.

Milly v. Smith. 2 Mo. R. 36, 1828 WL 1617.

Nat. v. Ruddle. 3 Mo. R. 400, 1834 WL 3555.

Rachael v. Walker. 4 Mo. R. 351, 1836 Wl 2300.

Ralph v. Duncan. 3 Mo. R. 194, 1833 WL 2662.

Wilson v. Melvin. 4 Mo. R. 592, 1837 2327.

Winny v. Whitesides. 1 Mo. R. 473, 1824 WL 1839.

Local Records

Circuit Court, St. Louis. St. Louis Circuit Court Clerk's Record Book.

Articles and Books

Ackermann, Gertrude W. (Gertrude Wilhelmine). "Joseph Renville of Lac Qui Parle." *Minnesota History* 12 (1931): 231–46.

Adams, Barbara Ann. *Early Days at Red River Settlement and Fort Snelling.* St. Paul, MN, 1894.

Address by the Colored People of the Missouri to the Friends of Equal Rights. NSTC Series: Series II 1816–1870. St. Louis: Missouri Democrat Print, Harvard University Library, 1865.

Adler, Jeffrey S. *Yankee Merchants and the Making of the Urban West: The Rise and Fall of Antebellum St. Louis.* New York: Cambridge University Press, 1991.

Albers, C., and William R. James. "Images and Reality: Post Cards of Minnesota Ojibway People 1900–80." *Minnesota History* 49 (1985): 229–40.

Allen, Austin. *Origins of the Dred Scott Case: Jacksonian Jurisprudence and the Supreme Court, 1837–1857.* Athens: University of Georgia Press, 2006.

Amar, Akhil Reed. *The Bill of Rights: Creation and Reconstruction*. New Haven, CT: Yale University Press, 2000.

Ambrosius, Lloyd E., ed. *Writing Biography: Historians and Their Craft*. Lincoln: University of Nebraska Press, 2004.

Anderson, Gary Clayton. *Kinsmen of Another Kind: Dakota-White Relations in the Upper Mississippi Valley, 1650–1862*. St. Paul: Minnesota Historical Society, 1997.

———. *Little Crow: Spokesman for the Sioux*. St. Paul: Minnesota Historical Society Press, 1986.

Anderson, Gary Clayton, and Alan R. Woolworth, eds. *Through Dakota Eyes: Narrative Accounts of the Minnesota Indian War of 1862*. St. Paul: Minnesota Historical Society Press, 1988.

Anti-Slavery Concert for Prayer. *Narrative of Facts, Respecting Alanson Work, Jas. E. Burr & Geo. Thompson, Prisoners in the Missouri Penitentiary, for the Alleged Crime of Negro Stealing*, Quincy, IL: Quincy Whig Office, 1842.

Appel, Livia. "Slavery in Minnesota." *Minnesota History Quarterly* 5 (February 1923): 40–43.

Association of Graduates U.S.M.A., et al. *Annual Register of Graduates and Former Cadets 1802–1990*. West Point, NY: West Point Alumni Foundation, 1990.

Babcock, Willoughby M., Jr. "Major Lawrence Taliaferro, Indian Agent." *Mississippi Valley Historical Review* 11, no. 3 (Dec. 1924), 358–75.

Bailey, John. *The Lost German Slave Girl: The Extraordinary True Story of Sally Miller and Her Fight for Freedom in Old New Orleans*. New York: Grove/Atlantic, 2005.

Baird, Elizabeth T., *O-De-Jit-Wa-Win-Ning, or Contes Du Temps Passe: The Memoirs of Elizabeth T. Baird*, Dennis Fredrick, ed. Green Bay, WI: Heritage Hill Foundation, 1998.

———. "Reminiscences of Life in Territorial Wisconsin 1810–1890." *Wisconsin Historical Collections* 15 (1900): 205–63. www.wisconsinhistory.org/turningpoints/search.asp?id=29 (accessed November 11, 2007).

Baird, Henry Samuel. "Recollections of the Early History of Northern Wisconsin 1800–1875." *Collections of the State Historical Society of Wisconsin* 4 (1859): 191–221. http://content. wisconsinhistory.org/u?/whc,437 (accessed November 11, 2007).

Baker, General James H. "Address at Fort Snelling in the Celebration of the Centennial Anniversary of the Treaty of Pike with the Sioux." *Minnesota Historical Society Collections* 12 (1908): 290–300.

Baker, H. Robert. *The Rescue of Joshua Glover: A Fugitive Slave, the Constitution, and the Coming of the Civil War*. Athens: Ohio State University Press, 2006.

Barr, Daniel P. *The Boundaries between Us: Natives and Newcomers along the Frontiers of the Old Northwest Territory, 1750–1850*. Kent, OH: Kent State University Press, 2006.

Bartlett, William W. "Jean Brunet, Chippewa Valley Pioneer." *Wisconsin Magazine of History* 33 (1921).

Baudissen, Graf Adelbert. *Der Ansiedler im Missouri-Staate*. Julius Badeser, 1854.

Bay, Mia. "In Search of Sally Hemings in the Post-DNA Era." *Reviews in American History* 34, no. 4 (2006): 407–26.

Bay, W. V. N. *Reminiscences of the Bench and Bar of Missouri*. St. Louis: F. H. Thomas, 1878.

Beltrami, A. *Pilgrimage in Europe and America*. 1823. Reprint, Carlisle, MA: Applewood Books, 2007.

Benedict, William A., and Hiram A. Tracy. *History of the Town of Sutton, Massachusetts, from 1704 to 1876*. Worcester, MA: Sanford, 1878.

Benton, Thomas Hart. *Historical and Legal Examination of the Part of the Supreme Court of the United States in the Dred Scott Case*. Kila, MT: Kessinger Publishing, 1857.

Berkeley, Edmund, and Dorothy Smith. *George William Featherstonhaugh, the First U.S. Government Geologist*. Tuscaloosa: University of Alabama Press, 1988.

Berlin, Ira. *Generations of Captivity: A History of African-American Slaves*. Cambridge, MA: Harvard University Press, 2003.

———. *Many Thousands Gone: The First Two Centuries of Slavery in North America*. Cambridge, MA: Harvard University Press, 1998.

Berry, Mary Frances. *My Face Is Black Is True: Callie House and the Struggle for Ex-Slave Reparations*. New York: Knopf, 2006.

Berthrong, Donald J. "John Beach and the Removal of the Sauk and Fox from Iowa." *Iowa Journal of History* 54 (1956): 289–310.

Billon, Frederic Louis. *Annals of St. Louis in Its Early Days under the French and Spanish Dominations*, 1886. Reprint, Bowie, MD: Heritage Books, 1971.

————. *Annals of St. Louis in Its Territorial Days from 1804 to 1821: Being a Continuation of the Author's Previous Work, the Annals of the French and Spanish Period.* St. Louis: Frederic Billion, 1888.

Bishop, Hariet E. *Floral Home: Or, First Years of Minnesota.* New York: Sheldon, Blakeman, 1857.

Blackstone, William, *Commentaries on the Laws of England,* volume 1. Chitty's edition, 1832.

Blassingame, John W. *The Slave Community: Plantation Life in the Antebellum South.* New York: Oxford University Press, 1979.

————, ed. *Slave Testimony: Two Centuries of Letters, Speeches, Interviews, and Autobiographies.* Baton Rouge: Louisiana State University Press, 1977.

Blegen, Theodore. "Slavery in Minnesota." *Minnesota History* 5 (1923): 40.

————. "The Unfinished Autobiography of Henry Hastings Sibley." *Minnesota History* 8 (1927): 329.

Bliss, John H. *Reminiscences of Fort Snelling.* St. Paul: Minnesota Historical Society Press, 1894.

Bloom, John Porter. *Territorial Papers of the U.S. Wisconsin Territory.* Vols. 27, 28. Washington, DC: National Archives, 1969.

Bogen, David S. *Privileges and Immunities: A Reference Guide to the United States Constitution.* Westport, CT: Greenwood Publishing, 2003.

The Book of St. Louisans: A Biographical Dictionary of Leading Living Men of the City of St. Louis and Vicinity. 2nd ed., rev., enl., and brought down to date. St. Louis, 1912.

Borchert, James. *Alley Life in Washington: Family, Community, Religion, and Folklife in the City, 1850–1970.* Champaign: University of Illinois Press, 1982.

Bornstein, Heinrich, *Funfundsiebzig Jahre in Alten and Neuen Welt, English Memoirs of a Nobody: The Missouri Years of an Austrian Radical, 1849–1866.* Detroit: Wayne State University Press 1997.

Bray, Edmund C., and Martha Coleman. *Joseph N. Nicollet on the Plains and Prairies: The Expeditions of 1838–39. With Journals, Letters, and Notes on the Dakota Indians.* St. Paul: Minnesota Historical Society Press, 1976.

Bray, Martha. *Joseph Nicollet and His Map.* Philadelphia: American Philosophical Society, 1980.

————, ed. *The Journals of Joseph N. Nicollet: A Scientist on the Mississippi Headwaters with Notes on Indian Life, 1836–37.* Translated by Andre Fertey. St. Paul: Minnesota Historical Society, 1971.

Breckinridge, S. M. *Emancipation in Missouri: Speech of S. M. Breckinridge Delivered in the Missouri State Convention,* University of Missouri-Kansas City, June 16, 1863. St. Louis: George Knapp & Co., 1863.

Brooks, Drex. *Sweet Medicine: Sites of Indian Massacres, Battlefields, and Treaties.* Albuquerque: University of New Mexico Press, 1995.

Brooks, James F. *Captives and Cousins: Slavery, Kinship, and Community in the Southwest Borderlands.* Chapel Hill: University of North Carolina Press, 2001.

Brown, B. Gratz. Freedom for Missouri. Letter to *Weekly New Era* (St. Joseph, MO), 1862.

Brown, Jennifer S. H., and Robert Brightman. *The Orders of the Dreamed: George Nelson on Cree and Northern Ojibwa Religion and Myth, 1823.* St. Paul: Minnesota Historical Society, 1988.

Brown, Jennifer S. H., W. J. Eccles, and Donald P. Heldman, eds. *The Fur Trade Revisited.* East Lansing: Michigan State University Press, 1994.

Brown, William Wells, *From Fugitive Slave to Free Man: The Autobiographies of William Wells Brown,* ed. William Andrews. Columbia: University of Missouri Press, 2003.

————. "My Southern Home," reprinted in *Brown, William Wells, From Fugitive Slave to Free Man: The Autobiographies of William Wells Brown,* ed. William Andrews. Columbia: University of Missouri Press, 2003.

————. "The Narrative of William Wells Brown," reprinted in *Brown, William Wells, From Fugitive Slave to Free Man: The Autobiographies of William Wells Brown,* ed. William Andrews. Columbia: University of Missouri Press, 2003.

Browne, Martha Griffith. *Autobiography of a Female Slave.* New York: Redfield, 1857. Reprint, Jackson: University of Mississippi Press, 1998.

Bruce, Henry Clay. *The New Man, Twenty-Nine Years a Slave; Twenty-Nine Years a Free Man: Recollections.* 1895. Reprint, Lincoln: University of Nebraska Press, 1996.

Brunson, Alfred. *A Western Pioneer: Or, Incidents of the Life and Times of Rev. Alfred Brunson, A.m.D.D., Written by Himself.* Cincinnati: Hitchcock and Walden, 1879.

Bryan, John A. "The Blow Family and Their Slave Dred Scott." *Missouri Historical Society Bulletin* 4 (1948): 223.

Buchanan, Thomas C. *Black Life on the Mississippi: Slaves, Free Blacks, and the Western Steamboat World.* Chapel Hill: University of North Carolina Press, 2004.

Buckland, W. W *The Roman Law of Slavery: The Condition of the Slave in Private Law from Augustus to Justinian.* Cambridge: Cambridge University Press, 1908.

Bundles, Alelia. *On Her Own Ground: The Life and Times of Madam C.J. Walker.* New York: Simon and Schuster, 2001.

Burr, Jason E., and George Thompson. *University of North Dakota, Narrative of Facts Respecting Alanson Work.* Quincy, IL: Quincy Whig Office, 1842.

Callender, John M. *New Light on Old Fort Snelling: An Archaeological Exploration, 1957–58.* St. Paul: Minnesota Historical Society, 1959.

Camp, Stephanie M. H. *Closer to Freedom: Enslaved Women and Everyday Resistance in the Plantation South.* Chapel Hill: University of North Carolina Press, 2004.

Carnes, Mark C., *Novel History: Historians and Novelists Confront America's Past.* New York: Simon and Schuster, 2001.

Cashin, Joan. "Black Families in the Old Northwest." *Journal of the Early Republic* 15 (1995): 449–75.

Castle, Henry Ansone. *Minnesota, Its Story and Biography.* Chicago: Lewis, 1915.

Catlin, George. *George Catlin's Letters and Notes of North American Indians.* New York: Gramercy, 1995.

———. *Letters and Notes on the Manners, Customs, and Conditions of North American Indians.* 2 Vols. (1832–1839). London, 1841. Reprint, Mineola, NY: Dover, 1973.

Catlin, George, George Gurney, Brian W. Dippie, and Renwick Gallery. *George Catlin and His Indian Gallery.* 2002. www.tfaoi.com/aa/4aa/4aa189.htm (accessed November 16, 2007).

Catterall, Helen Tunnicliff. "Some Antecedents of the Dred Scott Case." *American Historical Review* 30 (1924): 56–71.

Cayton, Andrew R. L., and Frederika J. Teute. *Contact Points: American Frontiers from the Mohawk Valley to the Mississippi, 1750–1830.* Chapel Hill: University of North Carolina Press, 1998.

Centennial History of Madison County, Illinois, and Its People: 1812–1912. Chicago: Lewis, 1912.

Chaffee, William Henry. *The Chaffee Genealogy.* New York: Grafton Press, 1909.

Chaffin, Tom. *Pathfinder: John Charles Fremont and the Course of American Empire.* New York: Farrar, Straus and Giroux, 2002.

Charless, Charlotte Taylor Blow. *A Biographical Sketch of the Life and Character of Joseph Charless.* Saint Louis: A. F. Cox, Printer, Office of the Missouri Presbyterian, 1869.

Chase, Levi B., *A Genealogy and Historical Notices of the Family of Plimpton or Plympton in America.* Hartford, CT: Plimpton Mfg Co. Printing, date.

Chevalier, Michael. *Society, Manners and Politics in the United States: Being a Series of . . .* Translated by Thomas Gamaliel Bradford. N.p.: Jordan Weeks, 1839.

Chittenden, Hiram Martin. *The American Fur Trade of the Far West.* Vols. 1 and 2. Place: publisher, 2006.

Chouteau, Auguste. *Fragment of Col. Auguste Chouteau's Narrative of the Settlement of St. Louis. A Literal Translation from the Original French Manuscript in Possession of the St. Louis Mercantile Library Association.* St. Louis: G. Knapp, 1858.

Christian, Shirley. *Before Lewis and Clark: The Story of the Chouteaus, the French Dynasty that Ruled America's Frontier.* New York: Farrar, Straus and Giroux, 2004.

Clamorgan, Cyprian. *The Colored Aristocracy of St. Louis.* Edited by Julie Winch. Columbia: University of Missouri Press, 1999.

———. *Notre Dame Archives Perpetual Calendar.* http://archives.nd.edu/calendar/cal1834.htm.

Clark, Christopher. *Social Change in America: From the Revolution to the Civil War.* Chicago: Ivan R. Dee, 2006.

Clark, Julius T. "Reminiscences of the Chippewa Chief, Hole-in-the-Day." *Wisconsin Historical Collections* 5 (1868): 378–409.

Clayton, Lawrence R., and Joseph E. Chance, eds. *The March to Monterrey: The Diary of Lieutenant Rankin Dilworth, U.S. Army: A Narrative of Troop Movements and Observations on Daily Life with General Zachary Taylor's Army during the Invasion of Mexico.* El Paso: Texas Western Press, 1996.

Clinton, Catherine. *Harriet Tubman: The Road to Freedom.* New York: Little, Brown, 2004.

———. "On the Road to Harriet Tubman." *American Heritage.* www.americanheritage.com/articles/magazine/ah/2004/3/2004_3_44.shtml, 2004.

Cullum, George Washington. *Biographical Register of the Officers and Graduates of the U.S. Military Academy,* United States Military Academy Association of Graduates. 3rd ed. West Point, NY: United States Military Academy, 1891.

Cobb, Thomas R. R. *An Inquiry into the Law of Negro Slavery in the United States of America*. N.p.: T. and J. W. Johnson, Negro Universities Press, 1858. Reprint, Athens: University of Georgia Press, 1968.

Coen, Rena Newman. "Edward K. Thomas, Fort Snelling Artist." *Minnesota History* vol. no. (1969): 317–26.

———. "Eliza Dillon Taliaferro: Portrait of a Frontier Wife." *Minnesota History* 52 (1990): 146–53.

———. "Taliaferro Portrait: Was It Painted by Catlin?" *Minnesota History* 42 (1971): 295–300.

Coffman, Edward M. *The Old Army: A Portrait of the American Army in Peacetime, 1784–1898*. New York: Oxford University Press, 1986.

Cooke, Philip St. George. *Scenes and Adventures in the Army; or Romance of Military Life*. Philadelphia: Lindsay and Blakiston, 1857.

Cooper, Zachary. *Black Settlers in Rural Wisconsin*. Madison: State Historical Society of Wisconsin, 1994.

Covey, Herbert C. *African American Slave Medicine*. Lanham, MD: Lexington Books, 2007.

Croghan, George, and Paul Prucha, eds. *Army Life on the Western Frontier: Selections from the Official Reports Made between 1826 and 1845*. Normal: University of Oklahoma Press, 1958.

Cross, Trueman. *Military Law of the United States*. Washington City, state: Geo. Templeman, 1838.

Dacus, Joseph A., and James W. Buel. *A Tour of St. Louis, or the Inside Life of a Great City*. St. Louis: Western Publishing Co., 1878.

Darby, John Fletcher. *Personal Recollections of Many Prominent People Whom I Have Known*. 1880. Reprint, New York: Arno Press, 1975.

Davis, David Brion. "The Significance of Excluding Slavery from the Old Northwest in 1787." *Indiana Magazine of History* 84, no. 1 (1988): 75–89.

DeCailly, Louis. *Memoirs of Bishop Loras, First Bishop of Dubuque, Iowa, and of Members of His Family, from 1792 to 1858*. City: Christian Press Association Pub. Co., 1897.

"Death of Mrs. C. C. Chafee." *The Springfield Republican*, February 12, 1903.

Delaney, Lucy. "From the Darkness Cometh the Light or Struggles for Freedom." In *Six Women's Slave Narratives*. 1891. Reprint, New York: Oxford University Press, 1988.

Delany, Martin R. *The Condition, Elevation, Emigration and Destiny of the Colored People of the United States*. City: Black Classic Press, 1993.

Delo, David Michael. *Peddlers and Post Traders: The Army Sutler on the Frontier*. Salt Lake City: University of Utah Press, 1992.

Densmore, Frances. *Chippewa Customs*. St. Paul: Minnesota Historical Society Press, 1979.

Deyle, Steven. *Carry Me Back: The Domestic Slave Trade in American Life*. New York: Oxford University Press, 2005.

Dibble, Ernest F. "Slave Rentals to the Military: Pensacola and the Gulf Coast." *Civil War History* 23 (1977): 101–13.

Diedrich, Mark. "Chief Hole-in-the-Day and the 1862 Chippewa Disturbance: A Reappraisal." *Minnesota History* (Spring 1987): pages.

———. *The Chiefs Hole-in-the-Day of the Mississippi Chippewa*. Minneapolis: Coyote Books, 1986.

Dietz, Charlton. "Henry Behnke: New Ulm's Paul Revere." *Minnesota History* (Fall 1976): pages.

DiNardo, Richard L., and Albert A. Nofi. *James Longstreet: The Man, the Soldier, the Controversy*. Cambridge, MA: DaCapo Press, 1998.

Dippie, Brian W. *Catlin and His Contemporaries: The Politics of Patronage*. Lincoln: University of Nebraska Press, 1990.

Dodson, Jualynne E. *Engendering Church: Women, Power, and the AME Church*. Lanham, MD: Rowman & Littlefield, 2002.

Donovan, Frank. *River Boats of America*. New York: Thomas Y. Crowell, 1966.

Dorsey, Bruce. *Reforming Men and Women: Gender in the Antebellum City*. Ithaca, NY: Cornell University Press, 2006.

Doubleday, Rhoda, ed. *Journals of Major Philip Norbourne Barbour, U.S. Inf. and His Wife Martha Isabella Hopkins Barbour*. New York: G. P. Putnam, 1936.

Drake, Charles D. "Immediate Emancipation in Missouri: Speech of Charles D. Drake, Delivered in the Missouri State Convention." St. Louis [s.n.] June 16, 1863.

Dubois, Laurent. "A Free Man." *The Nation*, April 16, 2007.

Du Bois, W. E. B. *Black Reconstruction 1860–1880*. 1935. Reprint, New York: Simon and Schuster, 1999.

Early, Sarah J. W. *Life and Labors of Rev. Jordan W. Early, One of the Pioneers of African Methodism in the West and South.* Nashville: Publishing House of the A.M.E. Church Sunday School Union, 1894.

Eastman, Charles. *The Soul of an Indian.* 1911. Reprint, New York: Dover Publications, 2003.

Eastman, Mary. *Dahcotah: Or Life and Legends of the Sioux around Fort Snelling.* 1849. Reprint, Minneapolis: Ross and Haines, 1962.

———. *Aunt Phillis's Cabin; or, Southern Life as It Is.* Philadelphia: Lippincott, Grambo, 1852.

Edwards, J. Passmore. *Uncle Tom's Companions: Facts Stranger than Fiction. A Supplement to Uncle Tom's Cabin: Being Startling Incidents in the Lives of Celebrated Fugitive Slaves.* London: Edwards, 1852.

Edwards, Laura F. "Domestic Violence and the Limits of Patriarchal Authority in the Antebellum South." *Journal of Southern History* 65 (1999): 733–70.

———. "Enslaved Women and the Law: Paradoxes of Subordination in the Post-Revolutionary Carolinas." *Slavery and Abolition* 26 (2005): 305–23.

———. *Gendered Strife and Confusion: The Political Culture of Reconstruction.* Champaign: University of Illinois Press, 1997.

———. "The Marriage Covenant Is at the Foundation of All Our Rights: The Politics of Slave Marriages in North Carolina after Emancipation." *Law and History Review* 14 (1996): 81–124.

———. *Scarlett Doesn't Live Here Anymore.* Champaign: University of Illinois Press, 2000.

Edwards, Richard, and M. Hopewell. *Edwards's Great West and Her Commercial Metropolis, Embracing a General View of the West, and a Complete History of St. Louis.* St. Louis: Edwards's Monthly, 1860.

Ehrlich, Walter. *They Have No Rights: Dred Scott's Struggle for Freedom.* Westport, CT: Greenwood Press, 1979.

Eichert, Magdalen. "Daniel Webster's Western Land Investments." *Historical New Hampshire* 26 (1971): 28–35.

Elderkin, James D. *Biographical Sketches and Anecdotes of a Soldier of Three Wars, as Written by Himself.* Detroit: Self-published, 1899.

Eliot, Charlotte C. *William Greenleaf Eliot, Minister, Educator, Philanthropist.* Boston: Houghton, Mifflin, 1904.

Ellis, Albert Gallatin. "Fifty-Four Years' Recollections of Men and Events in Wisconsin." *Wisconsin Historical Collections* 7 (1876): 219–22.

Eliot, William Greenleaf. *Discourse Preached at the Dedication of the First Congregational Church.* St. Louis, MO: Chambers, Harris and Knapp, 1837.

Engle, Stephen D. *Don Carlos Buell: Most Promising of All.* Chapel Hill: University of North Carolina Press, 1999.

Faherty, William Barnaby. *The Saint Louis Portrait: A Pictorial and Entertaining Commentary on the Growth and Development of Saint Louis, Missouri.* Tulsa, OK: Continental Heritage, 1978.

Featherstonhaugh, George W. *A Canoe Voyage Up the Minnay Sotor.* 2 vols. St. Paul: Minnesota Historical Society, 1970.

Feder, Norman. *Art of the Eastern Plains Indians: The Nathan Sturges Jarvis Collection.* Brooklyn, NY: Brooklyn Museum, 1964.

Federal Writers' Project. *The American Slave: A Composite Autobiography.* Arkansas Narratives Part 7, and Missouri Narratives, Part 11. Ed. George P. Rawick. Reprint, 1972.

Fehrenbacher, Don E. *The Dred Scott Case: Its Significance in American Law and Politics.* New York: Oxford University Press, 1978.

Ferguson, Eric. *The Eviction of the Squatters from Fort Snelling.* www.celticfringe.net/history/eviction. htm#links. 1998.

Ferrell, Robert H., ed. *Monterrey Is Ours! The Mexican War Letters of Lieutenant Dana 1845–1847.* Lexington: University Press of Kentucky, 1990.

Field, Ron. *Forts of the American Frontier, 1820–91: Central and Northern Plains.* Westminster, MD: Osprey, 2005.

Fields, Barbara Jeanne. *Slavery and Freedom on the Middle Ground.* New Haven, CT: Yale University Press, 1985.

Finkelman, Paul. *Documents of the Dred Scott Case* (city: publisher, date).

———. *An Imperfect Union: Slavery, Federalism, and Comity.* Chapel Hill: University of North Carolina Press, 1981.

———. "Slavery and the Northwest Ordinance: A Study in Ambiguity." *Journal of the Early Republic* 6 (Winter 1986): 343–70.

———. *Statutes on Slavery: The Pamphlet Literature.* 2 vols. New York: Garland, 1988.

Finkelnburg, Gustavus Adolphus. *Under Three Flags; or, The St. Louis Story Briefly Told.* 1911. Reprint, St. Louis: Helena, 1957.

Flandrau, Charles E. "Reminiscences of Minnesota during the Territorial Period." *Minnesota Historical Society* 9 (1901): 197–222.

Fleischner, Jennifer. *Mrs. Lincoln and Mrs. Keckly: The Remarkable Story of the Friendship Between a First Lady and a Former Slave.* New York: Broadway Books, 2003.

Foley, William E., and C. David Rice. *The First Chouteaus: River Barons of Early St. Louis.* Champaign: University of Illinois Press, 1983.

———. "Pierre Chouteau: Entrepreneur as Indian Agent." *Minnesota Historical Review* 72 (1978): 365–87.

Folsom, W. H. C. *Fifty Years in the North West.* St. Paul: Pioneer Press Co. 1887.

Folwell, William Watts. *A History of Minnesota.* 4 vols. 1921. Reprint, St. Paul: Minnesota Historical Society Press, 2006.

———. "The Sale of Fort Snelling, 1857." *Minnesota Historical Collections* 15 (1915): 393–410.

Fonda, John J. "Early Reminiscences of Wisconsin." *Wisconsin Historical Collection* 5 (1868): 205–84.

Foot, Samuel A. *An Examination of the Case of Dred Scott against Sanford, in the Supreme Court of the United States, and a Full and Fair Exposition of the Decision, and of the Opinions of the Majority of the Judges.* New York: W. C. Bryan, 1859.

Foreman, Grant. *Pioneer Days in the Early Southwest.* Cleveland, OH: Arthur H. Clark, 1926.

———, ed. *A Traveler in Indian Territory: The Journal of Ethan Allen Hitchcock, Late Major-General in the United States Army.* Cedar Rapids, IA: Torch Press, 1930. Reprint, Norman: University of Oklahoma Press, 1996.

Forsyth, Thomas. *Fort Snelling: Col. Leavenworth's Expedition to Establish It in 1819.* St. Paul: Minnesota Historical Society, 1880.

"Fort Snelling Calendar." *Minnesota Historical Society* 42 (Fall 1970): 116–17.

Fox Genovese, Elizabeth. *Within the Plantation Household: Black and White Women of the Old South.* Chapel Hill: University of North Carolina Press, 1988.

Frank, Louis Frederick. "Erastus B. Wolcott." In *The Medical History of Milwaukee: 1834–1914.* Milwaukee, WI: Germania Publishing Co., 1915.

Franklin, John Hope. *From Slavery to Freedom: A History of Negro Americans.* New York: McGraw-Hill, 1974.

Fraser, James W. *A History of Hope: When Americans Have Dared to Dream of a Better Future.* New York: Macmillan, 2002.

Frazer, Robert W. *Forts of the West, Military Forts and Presidios and Posts Commonly Called Forts West of the Mississippi River to 1898.* Norman: University of Oklahoma Press, 1965.

Frazier, Harriet C. *Runaway and Freed Missouri Slaves and Those Who Helped Them, 1763–1865.* Jefferson, NC: McFarland, 2004.

———. *Slavery and Crime in Missouri, 1773–1865.* Jefferson, NC: McFarland, 2001.

Fremont, John Charles. *Memoirs of My Life.* Chicago: Belford, Clarke, 1886. Reprint, Lanham, MD: Cooper Square Press, 2001.

Fridley, Russell W. "Fort Snelling, Military Post to Historic Site." *Minnesota History* 35 (December 1956): 178–92.

Fries, Robert F. *Empire in Pine: The Story of Lumbering in Wisconsin, 1830–1900.* Madison: State Historical Society of Wisconsin 1951.

Frost, Karolyn Smardz. *I've Got a Home in Glory Land: A Lost Tale of the Underground Railroad.* New York: Farrar, Straus and Giroux, 2007.

Gallay, Alan. *The Indian Slave Trade: The Rise of the English Empire in the American South, 1670–1717.* New Haven, CT: Yale University Press, 2002.

Garland, Hugh A. "A Course of Five Lectures, delivered in St. Louis on Protestantism and Government." In *Brownson's Quarterly Review,* 263. St. Louis: Benjamin H. Greene, 1852.

———. *Life of John Randolph of Roanoke.* New York: D. Appleton, 1851.

———. *The Second War of Revolution; Or The Great Principles Involved in the Present Controversy Between Parties.* Washington, DC: Office of the Democratic Review, 1839.

Gates, Henry Louis. *The Trials of Phillis Wheatley: America's First Black Poet and Her Encounters with the Founding Fathers*. New York: Basic Civitas Books, 2003.

Genovese, Eugene. *Roll, Jordan, Roll: The World the Slaves Made*. New York: Pantheon Books, 1974.

Gerteis, Louis S. *Civil War St. Louis*. Lawrence: University of Kansas Press, 2001.

Gillette, Mary. *The Army Medical Department, 1818–1865*. Washington, DC: Center for Military History, United States Army, 1987.

Gilman, Carolyn. "Grand Portage Ojibway Indians Give British Medals to Historical Society." *Minnesota History* 47 (Spring 1980): 26–32.

Gilman, Rhoda R. *Henry Hastings Sibley: Divided Heart*. St. Paul: Minnesota Historical Society Press, 2004.

———. "How Henry Sibley Took the Road to New Hope." *Minnesota History* 52 (Summer 1991): 220–29.

———. "Last Days of the Upper Mississippi Fur Trade." *Minnesota History* 42 (Winter 1970): 122–40.

Gilman, Rhoda R., Carolyn Gilman, and Deborah M. Stultz. *The Red River Trails: Oxcart Routes between St. Paul and the Selkirk Settlement, 1820–1870*. St. Paul: Minnesota Historical Society Press, 1979.

Gitlin, Jay. *Constructing the House of Chouteau: Saint Louis*. *Common-Place* 3 (July 2003): pages. www.common-place.org/vol-03/no-04/st-louis/.

Glickstein, Jonathan A. *American Exceptionalism, American Anxiety: Wages, Competition, and Degraded Labor in the Antebellum United States*. Charlottesville: University of Virginia Press, 2002.

Glymph, Thavolia. *Out of the House of Bondage: The Transformation of the Plantation Household*. New York: Cambridge University Press, 2008.

Golay, Michael, *The Tide of Empire: America's March to the Pacific*. New York: John Wiley, 2003.

Goodell, William. *The American Slave Code in Theory and Practice: Its Distinctive Features Shown by Its Statutes, Judicial Decisions, and Illustrative Facts*. 1853. Reprint, Ann Arbor: University of Michigan Press, 2005.

Goodman, Nancy, and Robert Goodman. *Joseph R. Brown, Adventurer on the Minnesota Frontier 1820–1849*. Rochester, MN: Lone Oak Press, 1996.

Goodrich, Thomas. *War to the Knife: Bleeding Kansas, 1854–1861*. Harrisburg, PA: Stackpole Press, 1998.

Goss, Dwight. *History of Grand Rapids and Its Industries*. Vol. 2. Chicago: C. F. Cooper, 1906.

Gowans, Fred. *Rocky Mountain Rendezvous: A History of the Fur Trade 1825–1840*. Layton, UT: Gibbs, Smith, 2005.

Graber, Mark A. *Dred Scott and the Problem of Constitutional Evil*. New York: Cambridge University Press, 2006.

Grant, Ulysses S. *Personal Memoirs of Ulysses S. Grant, 1822–1885*. 2 vols. 1885. Reprint, New York: Random House, 2002.

Green, Mason Arnold. *Springfield, 1636–1886: History of Town and City*. Springfield, MA: C. A. Nichols, 1888.

Grierson, Francis. *The Valley of Shadows*. Boston: Houghton-Mifflin, 1909. Reprint, Champaign: University of Illinois Press, 1990.

Griffiths, Martha. *Autobiography of a Female Slave*. New York: Redfield, 1857.

Grimsted, David, *American Mobbing, 1828–1861: Toward Civil War*. New York: Oxford University Press, 1998.

Grivno, Max L. "'Black Frenchmen' and 'White Settlers': Race, Slavery and the Creation of African-American Identities along the Northwest Frontier, 1790–1840." *Slavery and Abolition* 21 (December 2000): 75–93.

Gross, Ariela. "Beyond Black and White: Cultural Approaches to Race and Slavery." *Columbia Law Review* 640 (April 2001): 655–89.

———. *Double Character: Slavery and Mastery in the Antebellum Southern Courtroom*. Princeton, NJ: Princeton University Press, 2006.

Grossman, John F. *Army Uniforms at Fort Snelling, 1821–1832*. St. Paul: Minnesota Historical Society, 1974.

Haberly, Loyd. *Pursuit of the Horizon, a Life of George Catlin, Painter and Recorder of the American Indian*. New York: Macmillan, 1948.

Habermehl, John. *Life on the Western Rivers*. Pittsburgh: McNary and Simpson, 1901.

Hafen, Le Roy Reuben, and Harvey Lewis Carter. *Mountain Men and Fur Traders of the Far West: Eighteen Biographical Sketches*. Lincoln: University of Nebraska Press, 1982.

Hahn, Steven. *A Nation under Our Feet: Black Political Struggles in the Rural South from Slavery to the Great Migration*. Cambridge, MA: Harvard University Press, 2004.

Hall, Stephen P. *Fort Snelling, Colossus of the Wilderness*. St. Paul: Minnesota Historical Society, 1987.

Hamilton, Esley. "Winfield Scott Hancock at Jefferson Barracks." *Jefferson Barracks Gazette* 6, no. 4 (October–December 1998).

Hamilton, Holman. "Zachary Taylor and Minnesota." *Minnesota History* (June 1949): 97.

Hancock, Almira. *Reminiscences of Winfield Scott Hancock by His Wife*. New York: Charles L. Webster, 1887. Reprint, Scituate, MA: Digital Scanning, 1999.

Hansen, Marcus Lee. *Old Fort Snelling, 1819–1858*. Iowa City: State Historical Society of Iowa, 1918.

Hardeman, Nicholas Perkins. *Shucks, Shocks, and Hominy Blocks: Corn as a Way of Life in Pioneer America*. Baton Rouge: Louisiana State University Press, 1981.

Harper, Twelvetrees. *The Story of the Life of John Anderson, the Fugitive Slave*. London: William Tweedie, 1863.

Harris, Eddy L. "South of Haunted Dreams." In *Family Travel: The Farther You Go, the Closer You Get*. Edited by Laura Manske. Palo Alto, CA: Travelers' Tales, 1999.

Hart, Jim Allee. *A History of the St. Louis Globe-Democrat*. Columbia: University of Missouri Press, 1961.

Hasrick, Royal B. *The George Catlin Book of American Indians*. New York: Watson-Guptill, 1978.

Hawkinson, Ella. "The Old Crossing Chippewa Treaty and Its Sequel." *Minnesota History* 15 (1934): 282–300.

Heilbron, Bertha L. "Fort Snelling and Minnesota Territory." *Minnesota History* (December 1948): 316.

Heitman, Francis B. *The Historical Register and Dictionary of the U.S. Army from its Organization, September 29, 1789, to March 2, 1903*. 2 vols. 1903. Reprint, Champaign: University of Illinois Press, 1965.

Heneghan, Bridget T. *Whitewashing America: Material Culture and Race in the Antebellum Imagination*. Jackson: University Press of Mississippi, 2003.

Henig, Glen. "A Neglected Cause of the Sioux Uprising." *Minnesota History* 45 (Fall 1976): 107–10.

Henry, Guy V. Jr. *Military Record of Civilian Appointments in the United States Army*. New York: Carleton 1870.

Henry, William Seaton. *Campaign Sketches of the War with Mexico*. 1847. Reprint, New York: Arno Press, 1973.

Hess, Jeffrey A. Marx Swanholm, Susan Zeik, *Dred Scott from Fort Snelling to Freedom*. St. Paul: Minnesota Historical Society Press, 1975.

Hickerson, Harold. "William T. Boutwell of the American Board and the Pillager Chippewa: A History of Failure." *Ethnohistory* 12 (Winter 1965): 1–29.

Higginbotham, A. Leon, and F. Michael Higginbotham. "'Yearning to Breathe Free': Legal Barriers Against and Options in Favor of Liberty in Antebellum Virginia." *New York University Law Review* 68 (1993): 1213–71.

Higgins, Billy D. *A Stranger and a Sojourner: Peter Caulder, Free Black Frontiersman in Antebellum Arkansas*. Fayetteville: University of Arkansas Press, 2005.

Hill, Frederick Trevor. *Decisive Battles of the Law*. New York, 1907.

History of Bedford, Somerset, and Fulton Counties, Pennsylvania. Chicago: Waterman, Watkins, 1884.

Hitchcock, Ethan Allen. *Fifty Years in Camp and Field*. Edited by W. A. Croffut. New York: G. P. Putnam's Sons, 1909.

Hochschild, Adam. "The Black Napoleon." *New York Times Book Review*, February 25, 2007.

Hodder, Frank H. "Some Phases of the Dred Scott Case." *Mississippi Valley Historical Review* 16 (1929): 3–22.

Hoffman, M. M. "A Missionary Enterprise." *Palimpsest* 7 (June 1926): 184–92.

———. "New Light on Old St. Peter's and Early St. Paul." *Minnesota History* 8 (1927): 49.

Hofstadter, Richard. *Turner and the Sociology of the Frontier*. New York: Basic Books, 1968.

Hofstadter, Richard, and Seymour Martin Lipset, eds. *Turner and the Sociology of the Frontier*. New York: Basic Books, 1968.

Holmquist, Donald C. "Pride of the Pioneer's Parlor: Pianos in Early Minnesota." *Minnesota History* 39 (1965): 312–26.

Holmquist, June D. "Career of George Bonga." *Negro Digest*, May 1950.

Holt, Earl K. *William Greenleaf Eliot: Conservative Radical. Six Essays on the Life and Character of the 19th Century Unitarian Minister, Educator, and Philanthropist*. St. Louis: First Unitarian Church of St. Louis, 1985.

Holt, John R. *Historic Fort Snelling.* Fort Snelling, MN, 1938.

Home for the Friendless Centennial Report 1853–1953. St. Louis: Trustees of the Home for the Friendless, 1954.

Hopkins, Vincent C. *Dred Scott's Case.* 1951. Reprint, New York: Atheneum, 1957.

Horsman, Reginald. *Frontier Doctor: William Beaumont, America's First Great Medical Scientist.* Columbia: University of Missouri Press, 1996.

Howard, C. H. C. *Materials for a Genealogy of the Sparhawk Family in New England.* City: Higginson Book Company, 1999.

Howe, Daniel Walker. *What Hath God Wrought.* New York: Oxford University Press, 2007.

Humez, Jean M. *Harriet Tubman: The Life and the Life Stories.* Madison: University of Wisconsin Press, 2003.

Hunter, Louis C. *Steamboats on the Western Rivers: An Economic and Technological History.* North Chelmsford, MA: Courier Dover, 1994.

Hunter, Tera W. *To 'Joy My Freedom: Southern Black Women's Lives and Labors after the Civil War.* Cambridge, MA: Harvard University Press, 1997.

Hurd, John Codman. *The Law of Freedom and Bondage in the U.S.* 2 vols. Clark, NJ: Lawbook Exchange, 1858. Reprint, New York: Little, Brown, 2006.

Hurt, R. Douglas. *Agriculture and Slavery in Missouri's Little Dixie.* Columbia: University of Missouri Press, 1992.

Hurst, James Willard. *Law and Economic Growth: The Legal History of the Lumber Industry in Wisconsin, 1836–1915.* Cambridge, MA: Belknap Press, 1964.

———. "Lumber, Law, and Social Change: The Legal History of Willard Hurst." *American Bar Foundation Research Journal* 10, no. 1 (Winter, 1985): 138–44.

Ivey, Willie Catherine. *Ancestry and Posterity of Dr. John Taliaferro and Mary (Hardin) Taliaferro 1733–1821.* Tennille, GA, 1926.

Jackson, Mattie J. *The Story of Mattie J. Jackson; Her Parentage—Experience of Eighteen Years in Slavery—Incidents during the War—Her Escape from Slavery. A True Story.* Lawrence, state: Sentinel, 1866.

Jackson, Ronald Vern. *Iowa 1836 Territorial Census Index.* Bountiful, UT: Accelerated Indexing Systems, 1976.

———. *Iowa 1838 Territorial Census Index.* Bountiful, UT: Accelerated Indexing Systems, 1981.

———. *Iowa 1840 Territorial Census Index.* Salt Lake City, UT: Accelerated Indexing Systems, 1979.

———. *Michigan 1830 Index Census.* Bountiful, UT: Accelerated Indexing Systems, 1976.

———. *Minnesota 1840.* North Salt Lake, UT: Accelerated Indexing Systems, 1982.

———. *Wisconsin 1836 Census Index.* Bountiful, UT: Accelerated Indexing Systems, 1976.

———. *Wisconsin 1838 Census Index.* Bountiful, UT: Accelerated Indexing Systems, 1984.

———. *Wisconsin 1840 Census Index.* Bountiful, UT: Accelerated Indexing Systems, 1978. (Federal Censuses also available at Ancestry.com.)

Jackson, Ruby West, and Walter T. McDonald. *Finding Freedom, the Untold Story of Joshua Glover, Runaway Slave.* Madison: Wisconsin Historical Society Press, 2007.

Jacobs, Harriet A. *Incidents in the Life of a Slave Girl: Written by Herself.* New York: Cambridge University Press, 1987. Reprint, New York: Dover, 2001.

Jefferson Barracks Heritage History. City: Jefferson Barracks Heritage Foundation, year. www.jeffersonbarracks.org/JB_hist.html.

Johnson, Guion Griffis. *Antebellum North Carolina: A Social History.* Chapel Hill: University of North Carolina Press, 1937.

Johnson, Loren. "Reconstructing Old Fort Snelling." *Minnesota History* 42 (Fall 1970): 82–98.

Johnson, Richard W. "Fort Snelling from Its Foundation to the Present Time." *Collections of the Minnesota Historical Society* 8 (1898): 427–48.

Johnson, Thomas C. *St. Louis, Her Past, Present and Future and the Commercial Education of her Tradesmen, Manufacturers and Merchants.* St. Louis, MO: M. Niedner, 1860.

Johnson, Walter. *Soul by Soul: Life inside the Antebellum Slave Market.* Cambridge, MA: Harvard University Press, 1999.

Jones, Evan. *Citadel in the Wilderness; The Story of Fort Snelling and the Old Northwest Frontier.* New York: Coward-McCann, 1966.

Jordan-Lake, Joy. *Whitewashing Uncle Tom's Cabin: Nineteenth-Century Women Novelists Respond to Stowe.* Nashville, TN: Vanderbilt University Press, 2005.

Kane, Lucile M. *The Falls of St. Anthony: The Waterfall that Built Minneapolis.* St. Paul: Minnesota Historical Society Press, 1987.

———. "The Sioux Treaties and the Traders." *Minnesota History* 32 (Summer 1951): 65.

Kappler, Charles J., ed. "Treaty with the Chippewa 1837; Treaty with the Sioux, August 19, 1825." In *Indian Affairs: Laws and Treaties.* Vol. 3. Washington, DC: Government Printing Office, 1904. Also available at http://digital.library.okstate.edu/kappler/Vol2/treaties/.

Kargau, Ernst D. *The German Element in St. Louis. A Translation from the German of Ernst D. Kargau's "St. Louis in Fomer Years: A Common History of the German Element.* Edited by Don Heinrich Tolzmann. Translated by William G. Bek. Baltimore: Clearfield Company, 2004.

Kaufman, Kenneth. *Dred Scott's Advocate.* Topeka, KS: Tandem Library, 1996.

Keckley, Elizabeth. *Behind the Scenes, Formerly a Slave, and Four Years in the White House.* New York: G. W. Carleton, 1868. Reprint, Champaign-Urbana: University of Illinois Press, 2001.

Keillor, Steven J. *Grand Excursion: Antebellum America Discovers the Upper Mississippi.* Afton, MN: Afton Historical Society, 2004.

Kendrick, Stephen, and Paul Kendrick. *Sarah's Long Walk: How the Free Blacks of Boston and Their Struggle for Equality Changed America.* Boston: Beacon Press, 2004.

Kennedy, Cynthia M. *Braided Relations, Entwined Lives: The Women of Charleston's Urban Slave Society.* Bloomington: Indiana University Press 2005.

Kennedy, Roger G. *Mr. Jefferson's Lost Cause: Land, Farmers, Slavery and the Louisiana Purchase.* New York: Oxford University Press, 2004.

Kennerly, William Clark, as told to Elizabeth Russell. *Persimmon Hall, a Narrative of Old St. Louis and the Far West.* Norman: University of Oklahoma Press, 1948.

Keyser, James D., and Michael Klassen. *Plains Indians Rock Art.* Seattle: University of Washington Press, 2001.

King, Charles. *The True Ulysses S. Grant.* Philadelphia: J. B. Lippincott, 1914.

King, Wilma. *A Northern Woman in the Plantation South: Letters of Trypena Blanche Holder Fox, 1856–1876.* Columbia: University of South Carolina Press, 1993.

Kinzie, Juliet. *Wau-Bun: The "Early Day" in the Northwest.* Chicago: D. B. Cooke, 1856. Reprint, Philadelphia: Lippincott, 1873.

Kirschten, Ernest. *Catfish and Crystal.* 1965. Reprint, Toole, UT: Patrice Press, 1989.

Klement, Frank L. "The Abolition Movement in Minnesota." *Minnesota History* 32 (1951): 15–33.

Kutler, Stanley I. *The Dred Scott Decision.* Boston: Houghton Mifflin, 1967.

Lamm, Jane. "Dams and Damages: The Ojibway, the U.S., and the Mississippi Headwaters Reservoirs." *Minnesota History* 52 (1990): 2–15.

Landry, Donna, and Gerald Maclean, eds. *The Spivak Reader.* New York: Routledge, 1996.

Larson, Kate C. *Bound for the Promised Land: Harriet Tubman, Portrait of an American Hero.* New York: Ballantine, 2004.

Lass, William E. "Minnesota's Separation from Wisconsin: Boundary Making on the Upper Mississippi Frontier." *Minnesota History* 50, no. 8 (Winter 1987): 310–30.

———. "The Removal from Minnesota of the Sioux and Winnebago Indians." *Minnesota History* 38 (December 1963): 353–64.

Lavender, David S., and David J. Wishart, *The Fist in the Wilderness,* Lincoln: University of Nebraska Press, 1998.

Lawson, John D., ed., *American State Trials.* 17 vols. St. Louis: Thomas Law Book Co., 1914–36.

LeCompte, Janet. "Pierre Chouteau, Junior." In *The Mountain Men and the Fur Trade of the Far West.* 10 vols. Edited by Leroy Hafen. Lincoln: University of Nebraska Press, 1997.

———. "John F. A. Sanford." In *The Mountain Men and the Fur Trade of the Far West.* Lincoln: University of Nebraska Press, 1997.

Leigh, Edwin. *Bird's-Eye Views of Slavery in Missouri.* St. Louis: Keith and Woods, Bailey, Crawford, Witter, 1862.

Leonard, John W. *The Book of St. Louisians: A Biographical Dictionary of Leading Living Men of the City of St. Louis and the Vicinity.* St. Louis: St. Louis Republic, 1912.

Leopold, Aldo. *A Sand County Almanac.* 1949. Reprint, New York: Oxford University Press, 1989.

Levinson, Sanford, and Bartholomew H. Sparrow, eds. *The Louisiana Purchase and American Expansion, 1803–1898*. Lanham, MD: Rowman and Littlefield, 2005.

Lewis, Hugh M. *Robidoux Chronicles: Ethnohistory of the French-American Fur Trade*. Victoria, BC, Canada: Trafford Publishing, 2006.

Limerick, Patricia Nelson. *Desert Passages: Encounters with the American Deserts*. Albuquerque: University of New Mexico Press, 1985.

———. *The Legacy of Conquest: The Unbroken Past of the American West*. New York: W.W. Norton, 1987.

———. *Something in the Soil: Legacies and Reckonings in the New West*. New York: W.W. Norton, 2000.

Limerick, Patricia Nelson, Clyde A. Milner, and Charles E. Rankin, eds. *Trails: Toward a New Western History*. Lawrence: University of Kansas, 1991.

Litwack, Leon F. *North of Slavery: The Negro in the Free States*. Chicago: University of Chicago Press, 1961.

Livingston, James D., and Arthur Kelly, compilers. *A Livingston Genealogy for the Friends of Clermont*. Rhinebeck, NY: Co-sponsored by the Order of Colonial Lords of Manors in America, 1986 (original 1982 edition compiled by Clare Brant and Arthur Kelly).

Livingston, John. "Biographical Sketch of Verplanck Van Antwerp of Iowa." In *Portraits and Memoirs of Eminent Americans Now Living: With Biographical and Historic Memoirs of Their Lives and Action*. Vol. 2. London: Cornish, Lamport, 1853.

Louis, Billon Frederic. *Annals of St. Louis in Its Territorial Days from 1804 to 1821: Being a Continuation of the Author's Previous Work, the Annals of the French and Spanish Period*. St. Louis: printed for author, 1888.

Lowic, Lawrence. *The Architectural Heritage of St. Louis 1803–1891, from the Louisiana Purchase to the Wainwright Building*. St. Louis: Washington University Gallery of Art, 1982.

Luecke, Barbara K. *Feeding the Frontier Army 1775–1865*. Eagan, MN: Grenadier, 1990.

Luecke, Barbara K., and John C. Snelling. *Minnesota's First Family*. Eagan, MN: Grenadier, 1993.

Lyerly, Cynthia Lynn. "Religion, Gender, and Identity: Black Methodist Women in a Slave Society, 1770–1810." In *Discovering the Women in Slavery: Emancipating Perspectives on the American Past*. Edited by Patricia Morton. Athens: University of Georgia Press, 1996.

Lyman, George D. *John Marsh, Pioneer, the Life Story of a Trail-Blazer on Six Frontiers*. New York: Charles Scribner's Sons, 1930.

Lyons, Clare A. *Sex among the Rabble: An Intimate History of Gender and Power in the Age of Revolution, Philadelphia, 1730—1830*. Chapel Hill: University of North Carolina Press, 2006.

Lyons, Mary E. *Letters from a Slave Girl: The Story of Harriet Jacobs*. Reprint. New York: Simon Pulse, 1996.

Mabee, Carleton, and Susan Mabee Newhouse. *Sojourner Truth: Slave, Prophet, Legend*. New York: New York: New York University Press, 1993.

MacKaye, Percy. *Saint Louis; a Civic Masque*. Garden City, NY: Doubleday, Page, 1914.

Mahoney, Timothy R. *Provincial Lives: Middle-Class Experience in the Antebellum Middle West*. New York: Cambridge University Press, 2006.

———. *River Towns in the Great West: The Structure of Provincial Urbanization in the American Midwest, 1820–1870*. New York: Cambridge University Press, 1990.

Malone, Ann Patton. *Sweet Chariot: Slave Family and Household Structure in Nineteenth-Century Louisiana*. Chapel Hill: University of North Carolina Press, 1992.

Marcy, Randolph B. *Thirty Years of Army Life on the Border*. 1866 edition, unabridged. Reprint, New York: J. P. Lippincott, 1963.

Marryat, Frederick. *Diary in America: With Remarks on Its Institutions*. New York: Alfred A. Knopf, 1962.

———. "Minnesota as Seen by Travelers." Edited by Theodore C. Blegen. 1868. Reprint, *Minnesota History* 6 (1925): 168–84.

Marshall, Anna Maria, and Scott Barclay. "In Their Own Words: How Ordinary People Construct the Legal World." *Law and Social Inquiry* 28 (2003): 617.

Martin, John Hill. *Martin's Bar and Bench of Philadelphia, Together with Lists of Persons Appointed to Administer the Laws of the City and County of Philadelphia and the Province and Commonwealth of Pennsylvania*. Clark, NJ: Lawbook Exchange, 2006.

Martin, Jonathan D. *Divided Mastery: Slave Hiring in the American South*. Cambridge, MA: Harvard University Press, 2004.

McCandless, Perry, William E. Parrish, and William E. Foley, eds. *A History of Missouri: 1820 to 1860. The Missouri Sesquicenntenial History*. Columbia: University of Missouri Press, 2000.

McCann, Helen. "Frontier Feud: How Two Officers Quarreled All the Way to the Site of Fort Snelling." *Minnesota History* 42 (1970): 99–114.

McClure, Nancy. *Mrs. J. E. De Camp Sweet's Narrative of Her Captivity in the Sioux Outbreak of 1862*. Minnesota Historical Society Collections, Vol. 6. St. Paul: Minnesota Historical Society, 1894.

McDermott, John Francis. *The Early Histories of St. Louis*. St. Louis: St. Louis Historical Documents Foundation, 1952.

———. "J. C. Wild and Fort Snelling." *Minnesota History* 32 (March 1951): 12–14.

———. *A Glossary of Mississippi Valley French, 1673–1850* (1941).

McGinty, Brian. "Dred Scott's Fight for Freedom Brought Him a Heap O' Trouble." *American Illustrated* 16 (May 1981): 34–39.

McKenney, Thomas L. *Memoirs, Official and Personal; With Sketches and Travels among the Northern and Southern Indians*. 1846. Reprint, Lincoln: University of Nebraska Press, 1978.

McLaurin, Melton A. *Celia, a Slave*. New York, NY: Perennial, 1993.

Meachum, John B. *An Address to All the Colored Citizens of the United States*. Philadelphia: King and Baird, 1846.

Means, John, and R. E. Stanley. *$2,500 Reward! Ranaway from the Subscriber, residing in Mississippi County, Mo. My Negro named George...Also, from Radford E. Stanley, a Negro Man Slave, Named Noah...also, a Negro Man Named Hamp...also, Negro Man Slave Named Bob*. Advertisement, St. Louis. Richmond: Virginia Historical Society Library, August 23, 1852.

Menius, Joseph M., and Susan Blow. "Mother of the Kindergarten." St. Clair, MO: Page One Publishing, 1993.

Merrell, Henry. "Pioneer Life in Wisconsin." *Wisconsin Historical Collections* 7 (1876): 366–404.

Merrick, George Byron. *Old Times on the Upper Mississippi: The Recollections of a Steamboat Pilot from 1854 to 1863*. Cleveland: Arthur H. Clarke, 1909.

Mersman, Joseph J. *The Whiskey Merchant's Diary: An Urban Life in the Emerging Midwest*. Edited by Linda A. Fisher. Athens: Ohio University Press, 2007.

Miles, Tiya. *Ties that Bind: The Story of An Afro-Cherokee Family in Slavery and Freedom*. Berkeley: University of California Press, 2005.

"Missouri Broadside Collection, 75 pieces." Durham, NC: Duke University Libraries, 1836–1942.

Morgans, James Patrick. *John Todd and the Underground Railroad: Biography of an Iowa Abolitionist*. Jefferson, NC: McFarland, 2006.

Morton, Patricia. *Discovering the Women in Slavery: Emancipating Perspectives on the American Past*. Athens: University of Georgia Press, 1996.

Mueller, Richard. "Jefferson Barracks: The Early Years." *Missouri Historical Review* 67 (1972): 7–30.

Murphy, Lucy Eldersveld. "To Live among Us: Accommodation, Gender, and Conflict in the Western Great Lakes Region, 1760–1832." In *Contact Points: American Frontiers from the Mohawk Valley to the Mississippi*. Edited by Andrew R. L. Cayton and Frederika J. Teute. Chapel Hill: University of North Carolina Press, 1998.

Murphy, Lucy Eldersveld, and Wendy Hamand Venet. *Midwestern Women: Work, Community, and Leadership at the Crossroads*. Bloomington: Indiana University Press, 1997.

Musick, James B. *St. Louis as a Fortified Town: A Narrative and Critical Essay on the Period of Struggle for the Fur Trade of the Mississippi Valley and Its Influence upon St. Louis*. St. Louis: R. F. Miller, 1941.

Myer, Jesse S. *Life and Letters of Dr. William Beaumont, C.V.* St. Louis: Mosby, 1912.

Myer, Mrs. Max W. "Sarah Beaumont: Her Life and Loves." *Bulletin of the Missouri Historical Society* 17 (October 1960): 16–44.

Myers, William Starr, ed. *The Mexican War Diary of George B. McClellan*. Princeton, NJ: Princeton University Press, 1917.

Nacy, Michele J. *Members of the Regiment: Army Officers' Wives on the Western Frontier, 1865–1890*. Westport, CT: Greenwood Press, 2000.

Nagle, Liza. *The Buried History of the Sutler's Store*. St. Paul: Minnesota Historical Society, 1976.

Neely, Jeremy. *The Border between Them: Violence and Reconciliation on the Kansas-Missouri Line*. Columbia: University of Missouri Press, 2007.

Neill, Edward D. "Early Days at Fort Snelling." *Minnesota Historical Collections* 1 (1872): 420–38.

———. *Explorers and Pioneers of Minnesota in History of the Upper Mississippi Valley*. St. Paul: Minnesota Historical Society, 1881.

———. "Fort Snelling Echoes." *Magazine of Western History* 10 (1889): 604; and 11 (1889): 20.

———. "Fort Snelling, Minnesota: While in Command of Col. Josiah Snelling, 5th Infantry." *Magazine of Western History* 8, no. 2 (June 1888): 171–180; no. 4 (August 1888): 373–81.

———. *The History of Minnesota: From the Earliest French Explorations to the Present Time*. 4th ed. St. Paul: Minnesota Historical Company, 1882.

———. "Occurrences in and around Fort Snelling from 1819 to 1840". *Minnesota Historical Collections* 2. St. Paul: Ramaley, Chaney, 1872.

Nelson, Rodney B. *Beaumont: America's First Physiologist*. Geneva, IL: Grant House, 1990.

Nevins, Allan. *Fremont: Pathmarker of the West*. New York: Longmans, Green, 1955.

Newcombe, Barbara T. "A Portion of the American People: The Sioux Sign a Treaty in Washington in 1858." *Minnesota History* 45, no. 3 (Fall 1976): 82–96.

Newson, T. M. *Pen Pictures of St. Paul, Minnesota, and Biographical Sketches of Old Settlers, from the Earliest Settlement of the City, Up to and including the Year 1857*. 2 Vols. St. Paul: Author, 1886.

Nicollet, Joseph N. *Joseph N. Nicollet on the Plains and Prairies: The Expeditions of 1838–39 with Journals, Letters, and Notes on the Dakota Indians*. Edited by Edmund C. Bray and Martha Coleman Bray. St. Paul: Minnesota Historical Society, 1993.

———. *Report Intended to Illustrate a Map of the Hydrographical Basin of the Upper Mississippi River*. Printed for the Senate, 26th Congress, 2nd Session. Washington, DC: Blair and Rives, Printers, 1843.

———. *Report Intended to Illustrate a Map of the Hydrographical Basin of the Upper Mississippi River, Made by J. N. Nicollet, while in the Employ under the Bureau of the Corps of Topographical Engineers*. Washington: Blair and Rives, Printers, 1843.

Northup, Solomon. *Twelve Years a Slave*. 1968. Reprint, New York: Dover Publications, 2000.

Nute, Grace. "Calendar of Papers of the American Fur Company's Papers." *American Historical Review* 32 (1945): 1926–27.

———. "The Mississippi Valley from Prairie Du Chien to Lake Pepin: A Survey of Unpublished Sources." *Minnesota History* 7 (March 1926): 32–41.

Nylander, Jane C. *Our Own Snug Fireside: Images of the New England Home 1760–1860*. New Haven, CT: Yale University Press, 1993.

Obst, Janis. "Abigail Snelling: Military Wife, Military Widow." *Minnesota History* 54, no. 3 (Fall 1994): 98–111.

Ohler, Clara May Paine. *Frontier Life in the Old Northwest*. New Haven, CT: Yale University Press, 1908.

O'Leary, Elizabeth L. *At Beck and Call: The Representation of Domestic Servants in Nineteenth-Century American Painting*. Washington, DC: Smithsonian Institution Press, 1996.

Pacheo, Josephine F. *The Pearl: A Failed Slave Escape on the Potomac*. Chapel Hill: University of North Carolina Press, 2005.

Painter, Nell I. "Writing Biographies of Women." *Journal of Women's History* 9, no. 2 (Summer 1997): 154–63.

Parker, Donald Dean, ed. *The Recollections of Philander Prescott, Frontiersman of the Old Northwest 1819–1862*. Lincoln: University of Nebraska Press, 1966.

Parker, Joel. *Personal Liberty Laws, and Slavery in the Territories*. Boston: Wright and Potter, 1861.

Parsons, Charles Grandison, and Harriet Beecher Stowe. *Inside View of Slavery: Or, A Tour Among the Planters*. City: publisher, 1855.

Payne, Daniel Alexander. *History of the African Methodist Episcopal Church*. Edited by C. S. Smith. Nashville, TN: Publishing House of the A. M. E. Sunday School Union, 1891.

———. *Recollections of Seventy Years*. Edited by C. S. Smith. Nashville, TN: Publishing House of the A. M. E. Sunday School Union, 1888.

Pederson, Ken O. *The Story of Fort Snelling*. St. Paul: Minnesota Historical Society, 1966.

Peers, Laura. *The Ojibwa of Western Canada 1780 to 1870*. St. Paul: Minnesota Historical Society, 1994.

Pennsylvania Magazine of History and Biography 1915. Authored and published by the Historical Society of Pennsylvania, Philadelphia, PA, 29.

Peterson, Charles E. *Colonial St. Louis: Building a Creole Capital*. St. Louis: Missouri Historical Society, 1949.

Petersen, William J. *Steamboating on the Upper Mississippi*. 1937. Reprint, Mineola, NY: Dover Publications, 1996.

"Pioneer Journalist Stricken: Obituary: F. B. Murdoch." *The Pioneer*, San Jose, CA, May 10, 13, 1882: ——.

Podruchny, Carolyn, *Making the Voyageur Word: Travelers and Traders in the North American Fur Trade*. Lincoln: University of Nebraska Press, 2006.

Pond, Samuel W. *Dakota Life in the Upper Midwest*. St. Paul: Minnesota Historical Society, 2002.

——. *The Dakota or Sioux in Minnesota as They Were in 1834*. St. Paul: Minnesota Historical Society Press, 1986.

Pond, Samuel, and Gideon Pond. *Two Volunteer Missionaries among the Dakotas*. Boston: Congregational Sunday School and Publishing Society, 1893.

Powell, William H. *List of Officers of the Army of the U.S. from 1779–1900*. N.p.: N.Y.L.R. Hamersley, 1900. Reprint, New York: Gordon Press, 1972.

Pratt, Alexander F. "Reminiscences of Wisconsin." *Wisconsin Historical Collections* 1 (1855): 127–45.

Prescott, Philander. *The Recollections of Philander Prescott: Frontiersman of the Old Northwest, 1819–62*. Edited by Donald Dean Parker. Lincoln: University of Nebraska Press, 1966.

Primm, James Neal. *Lion of the Valley, St. Louis, Missouri, 1764–1980*. 3rd ed. Columbia: University of Missouri Press, 1981.

"Proceedings of a Council with the Chippewa Indians." *Iowa Journal of History and Politics* 9 (1911): 424–25.

Prucha, Francis Paul. "An Army Private in Old Fort Snelling in 1849." *Minnesota History* 36 (March 1958): 13–17.

——. "Army Sutlers and the American Fur Company." *Minnesota History* 40, no. 1 (1966): 22–31.

——. *Broadax and Bayonet: The Role of the United States Army in the Development of the Northwest 1815–1860*. 1953. Reprint, Lincoln: University of Nebraska Press, 1995.

——. *Documents of U.S. Indian Policy*. Lincoln: University of Nebraska Press, 1975.

——. *Indian Peace Medals in American History*. Madison: State Historical Society of Wisconsin, 1971.

——. "The Settler and the Army in the Frontier." *Minnesota History* 29 (September 1949): 231–46.

Quick, Henry, and Edward Quick. *Mississippi Steamboatin': A History of Steamboating on the Mississippi and Its Tributaries*. New York: Henry Holt, 1926.

Quigley, Martin. *St. Louis, The First Two Hundred Years*. St. Louis: First National Bank, 1964.

——. *St. Louis: A Fond Look Back: An Appreciation of Its Community by the First National Bank*. St. Louis: First National Bank, 1956.

Rammelkamp, Julian S. *Pulitzer's Post-dispatch, 1878–1883*. Princeton, NJ: Princeton University Press, 1967.

Rayman, Ronald A. "Confrontation at the Fever River Lead Mining District: *Joseph Montfort Street vs. Henry Dodge, 1827–28*." *Annals of Iowa* 44, no. 4 (Spring 1978): 278–95.

——. "Joseph Montfort Street: Establishing the Sac and Fox Indian Agency in Iowa Territory, 1838–40." *Annals of Iowa* 43, no. 4 (Spring 1976): 261–74.

Report of the Celebration of the Anniversary of the Founding of St. Louis, on the Fifteenth Day of February, A.D., 1847. St. Louis: Chambers and Knapp, 1847.

Ress, David. *Governor Edward Coles and the Vote to Forbid Slavery in Illinois, 1823–1824*. Jefferson, NC: McFarland, 2006.

Revels, Hiram, "The Autobiography of Hiram Rhoades Revels Together with Some Letters by and about Him." *Midwest Journal* vol. (1953): page.

Reynolds, Cugler. *Genealogical and Family History of Southern New York and the Hudson River Valley*. New York: Lewis Historical Publishing Co., 1914.

Reynolds, Daniel S. "North toward Home." *New York Times Book Review*, June 17, 2007. www.nytimes.com/2007/06/17/books/review/Reynolds-t.html?ex=1339473600&en=e0419b3ca0730e69&ei=5124&partner=permalink&exprod=permalink (newspaper published online).

Rhodes, James B. "The Fort Snelling Area in 1835: A Contemporary Map." *Minnesota History* (March 1956): 22.

Richter, August P. *The History of Davenport (German): Geschichte der Stadt Davenport und der County Scott: nebst Seitenblicken auf das Territorium und den Staat Iowa*. Davenport, IA, 1917.

Richter, Daniel K. *Facing East from Indian Country: A Native History of Early America*. Cambridge, MA: Harvard University Press, 2001.

Riggs, Mary. *A Small Bit of Bread and Butter*. Prairie Village, KS: Ash Grove Press, 1996.

Riggs, Stephen R. "In Memory of Rev. Thos. S. Williamson, M.D." 3 Collections of the Minnesota Historical Society, 1880, 372.

Riggs, Stephen R. *Mary and I: Forty Years with the Sioux*. 1880. Reprint, Gansevoort, NY: Corner House Publications, 1979.

Riley, Glenda. *Women and Indians on the Frontier 1825–1915*. Albuquerque: University of New Mexico Press, 1984.

Roark, James L. *Masters without Slaves: Southern Planters in the Civil War and Reconstruction*. New York: Norton, 1977.

Roberts, Robert. *The House Servant's Directory: An African American Butler's 1827 Guide*. Mineola, NY: Dover African-American Books, 2006.

Rodolf, Theodore. "Pioneering in the Wisconsin Lead Region." *Collections of the State Historical Society of Wisconsin* 15 (1900): 338–89.

Russo, Priscilla Ann. "The Time to Speak Is Over: The Onset of the Sioux Uprising." *Minnesota History* 45, no. 3 (1976): 97–106.

Rutberg, Becky. *Mary Lincoln's Dressmaker: Elizabeth Keckley's Remarkable Rise from Slave to White House Confidante*. New York: Walker, 1995.

Sachse, Nancy D. "Frontier Legend; Bennington's Martin Scott." *Vermont History* 34, no. 3 (1966): 157–68.

Sandweiss, Eric, ed., *St. Louis in the Century of Henry Shaw: A View beyond the Garden Wall*. Columbia: University of Missouri Press, 2002.

Salvatore, Nick. "Biography and Social History." *Labour History* 87 (2004): 187–92.

Satz, Ronald N. "Chippewa Treaty Rights: The Reserved Rights of Wisconsin's Chippewa Indians in Historical Perspective." *Transactions* (Wisconsin Academy of Sciences, Arts and Letters) 79, no. 1 (1991): page.

Savage, William Sherman. *Blacks in the West*. Westport, CT: Greenwood, 1976.

Saxton, Martha. "Lives of Missouri Slave Women: A Critique of True Womanhood." In *Contested Democracy: Freedom, Race and Power in American History*. Edited by Manisha Von Eschen and Penny Sinha. New York: Columbia University Press, 2007.

Schafer, Judith Kelleher. *Becoming Free, Remaining Free: Manumission and Enslavement in New Orleans, 1846–1862*. Baton Rouge: Louisiana State University Press, 2003.

Scharf, J. Thomas. *History of Saint Louis City and County, from the Earliest Periods to the Present Day: Including Biographical Sketches of Representative Men*. 2 vols. Philadelphia: L. H. Everts, 1883.

Schwartz, Marie Jenkins. *Born in Bondage: Growing up Enslaved in the Antebellum South*. Cambridge, MA: Harvard University Press, 2000.

Scott, Robert Garth. *Forgotten Valor*. Kent, OH: Kent State University Press, 1999.

Seymour, Flora Warren. *Indian Agents of the Old Frontier*. New York: D. Appleton-Century, 1941.

Shannon, James. *An Address Delivered before the Pro-Slavery Convention of the State of Missouri, Held in Lexington, July 13, 1855, on Domestic Slavery*. St. Louis: Republican Book and Job Office, 1855.

Shapiro, Fred R. and Joseph Epstein, *The Yale Book of Quotations*, Yale University Press: 2006.

Shepard, Elihu Hotchkiss. *The Early History of St. Louis and Missouri, from Its First Exploration by White Men in 1673 to 1843*. 8 vols. St. Louis: Southwestern Book, 1870.

Sherman, Nellie Cadle (Watson). *Taliaferro-Toliver Family Records*. 1960. Reprint, Salem, MA: Higginson, 1961.

Shipley, Alberta D., and David O. Shipley. *The History of Black Baptists in Missouri*. Nashville, TN: National Baptist Convention, 1976.

Shortridge, Wilson Porter. *The Transition of a Typical Frontier, with Illustrations from the Life of Henry Hastings Sibley, Fur Trader, First Delegate in Congress from Minnesota Territory, and First Governor of the State of Minnesota*. Menasha, WI: George Banta, 1922.

Sibley, Henry, "Memoir of Hercules L. Dousman." *Minnesota Historical Collections* 3 (1880): 192–200.

———. "Reminiscences of Early Days of Minnesota." *Minnesota Historical Collections* 3 (1880): 242–82.

———. "Reminiscences, Historical and Personal." *Minnesota Historical Society* 1 (1872): 457–70.

Silverman, Kenneth. "Biography and Pseudobiography." *Common-Place* 3, no. 2 (2003): pages.

Simson, Gary J. "*Dred Scott v. Sandford*: Right Result, Wrong Reasons?" *Stanford Law Review* 32, no. 879 (1980): pages.

Smith, E. Kirby. *To Mexico with Scott, Letters of Captain E. Kirby Smith to His Wife*. 1917. Reprint, Whitefish, MT: Kessinger, 2007.

Smith, Hubert G. "A Frontier Fort in Peacetime." *Minnesota History* 45, no. 3 (1976): 116–29.

Smith, Theodore Clark. *Parties and Slavery, 1850–1859*. New York: Harper and Brothers, 1906.

Smith, William Rudolph. *The History of Wisconsin In three parts, historical, documentary, and descriptive: compiled by direction of the Legislature of the State*. 1854.

———. *Observations on the Wisconsin Territory*. ca. 1838. Reprint, New York: Arno Press, 1975.

Snelling, Henry Hunt, Lewis Beeson, and Dorothy Kurtzman Phelps. *Memoirs of a Boyhood at Fort Snelling*. Private printing, 1939.

Snelling, William Jose. *Early Days at Prairie Du Chien*. Madison, WI, 1868.

———. *Running the Gantlet. A Thrilling Incident of Early Days at Fort Snelling*. St. Paul: Minnesota Historical Society, 1872.

Snyder, Charles E. "John Emerson, Owner of Dred Scott." *Annals of Iowa*. 3rd series, 21 (October 1938): 440–61.

Sorensen, Henri. *New Hope*. New York: HarperCollins, 1995.

Spangler, Earl. *The Negro in Minnesota*. Minneapolis: T. S. Denison, 1961.

Spencer, John W. "Reminiscences of Pioneer Life in the Mississippi Valley" [microform]. Davenport, IA: Griggs, Watson and Day, 1872.

Spivak, Gayatri Chakravorty. "Can the Subaltern Speak?" In *Marxism and the Interpretation of Culture*. Edited by Cary Nelson and Lawrence Grossberg. Urbana: University of Illinois Press, 1988.

St. Louis. New York: New Viewpoints, 1977.

St. Louis Business Research Council. *The Role of the Mississippi-Missouri River Systems in the Development of the St. Louis Region*. St. Louis, MO: Bardgett, 1961.

St. Martin, Thomas. *One Hundred Eighty Years of Weather: St. Snelling-St. Paul, MN, 1820–1999*. Woodbury, MN: T. St. Martin, 2000.

Stetson, Erlene, and Linda David. *Glorying in Tribulation: The Lifework of Sojourner Truth*. East Lansing: Michigan State University Press, 1994.

Stevens, Frank E. "Alexander Pope Field." *Journal of the Illinois State Historical Society* 14 (1911–1912): 7–37.

Stevens, George E. *History of Central Baptist Church*. St. Louis: King Publishing, 1927.

Stevens, Hiram F. *History of the Bench and Bar of Minnesota*. 2 vols. Minneapolis: Legal Publishing and Engraving, 1904.

Stevens, Thomas Wood. *The Book of Words of the Pageant and Masque of Saint Louis*. 2nd ed. Saint Louis Pageant Drama Association. St. Louis: Nixon-Jones, 1914.

Stevens, Walter B. *The Building of St. Louis, from Many Points of View by Notable Persons*. St. Louis: Lesan-Gould, 1908.

Stover, John F. *History of the Illinois Central Railroad*. New York: Macmillan, 1975.

Strand, Algot E. *A History of the Swedish Americans of Minnesota*. N.p.: Lewis Publishing, 1910.

Strasser, Susan. *Never Done: A History of American Housework*. New York: Dover Paperbacks, 2000.

Stratton, Joanna L. *Pioneer Women: Voices from the Kansas Frontier*. Simon and Schuster, 1981.

Street, Joseph Montfort. *1782–1840, Prairie Du Chien in 1827. Letters of Joseph M. Street to Gov. Cass Michigan Territory*. Madison, WI, 1888.

Stroud, George M. *A Sketch of the Laws Relating to Slavery in the Several States of the United States of America*. N.p., 1827.

Sunder, John E. *The Fur Trade on the Upper Missouri, 1840–1865*. Norman: University of Oklahoma Press, 1993.

Sweet, John Wood. *Bodies Politic: Negotiating Race in the American North, 1730–1830*. Philadelphia: University of Pennsylvania Press, 2007.

Taliaferro, Lawrence. "Autobiograpy of Major Lawrence Taliaferro." *Minnesota History* 6 (1894): 190–97.

Tanner, Helen Hornbeck, ed. *Atlas of Great Lakes Indian History*. Norman: University of Oklahoma Press, 1987.

"The Tate House: A Period Piece." *Pioneer* 3 (4): page.

Taylor, David Vassar. "The Blacks." In *They Chose Minnesota: A Survey of the State's Ethnic Groups*. Edited by June Drenning Holmquist. St. Paul: Minnesota Historical Society Press, 1981.

Taylor, Zachary. "Zachary Taylor to Thomas Lawson." *Minnesota History* 28 (March 1947): 15–19.

Thomas, Davis, and Karin Ronnefedlt, eds. *People of the First Man, Life among the Plains Indians in their Final Days of Glory: The Firsthand Account of Prince Maximilian's Expedition up the Missouri River, 1833–34*. New York: Dutton, 1976.

Thomas, James. *From Tennessee Slave to St. Louis Entrepreneur: The Autobiography of James Thomas*. Columbia: University of Missouri Press, 1984.

Thompson, George. *Prison Life and Reflections: Or A Narrative of the Arrest, Trial, Conviction, Imprisonment, Treatment, Observations, Reflections, and Deliverance of Work, Burr, and Thompson, Who Suffered an Unjust and Cruel Imprisonment in Missouri Penitentiary, for*

Attempting to Aid Some Slaves to Liberty. 1847. Reprint, New York: Negro Universities Press, 1969.

Thompson, Matilda G. "Mark and Hasty." In *The Child's Anti-Slavery Book Containing a Few Words about American Slave Children. And Stories of Slave-Life.* New York: Carlton and Porter, 1859.

Thornwell, Emily. *The Lady's Guide to Perfect Gentility.* New York: Derby and Jackson, 1856.

Tidball, Eugene C. *No Disgrace to My Country: The Life of John C. Tidball.* Kent, OH: Kent State University Press, 2002.

Tiffany, Francis. *Life of Dorothea Lynde Dix.* New York: Houghton Mifflin, 1918.

Tolzmann, Don Heinrich, ed. *The German Element in St. Louis, A Translation from German of Ernst D. Kargau's, St. Louis in Former Years: A Commemorative History of the German Element.* Translated by William G. Bek. 1893. Reprint, Baltimore: Genealogical, 2000.

Trautmann, Frederic, ed. and trans. "Johann Georg Kohl, a German Traveler in Territorial Minnesota." *Minnesota History* 49 (Winter 1984): 126–39.

Treacy, Patricia. *The Grand Hotels of St. Louis.* Mount Pleasant, SC: Arcadia Publishing.

Tregilis, Helen Cox. *River Roads to Freedom: Fugitive Slave Notices and Sheriff Notices Found in Illinois Sources.* Bowie, MD: Heritage Books, 1988.

Trexler, Harrison Anthony. *Slavery in Missouri, 1804–1865.* Baltimore: Johns Hopkins Press, 1914.

Troen, Selwyn K., and Glen E. Holt. *St. Louis.* New York: New Viewpoints, 1977.

Truettner, William H. *The Natural Man Observed: A Study of Catlin's Indian Gallery.* Washington, DC: Smithsonian Institution Press, 1979.

Tucker, Glenn. *Hancock, the Superb.* Indianapolis and New York: Bobbs-Merrill Company, 1960.

Tushnet, Mark. *The American Law of Slavery 1810–1860: Considerations of Humanity and Interest.* Princeton, NJ: Princeton University Press, 1981.

———. "Review of Mark S. Weiner, *Black Trials: Citizenship from the Beginnings of Slavery to the End of Caste.*" *Journal of American History* 92, no. 2 (September 2005): 647–48.

Ulrich, Laurel Thatcher. *A Midwife's Tale: The Life of Martha Ballard, Based on Her Diary, 1785–1812.* New York: Vintage, 1991.

Unrau, William E. *The Rise and Fall of Indian Country, 1825–1855.* Lawrence: University Press of Kansas, 2007.

Upham, Warren. "The Women and Children of Fort Saint Anthony Later Named Fort Snelling." *Magazine of History* 21 (July 1915): 25–39.

U.S. Military Academy. *Annual Register of Graduates and Former Cadets 1802–1990.* West Point, NY: United States Military Academy, 1990.

Usner, David H. Jr. *Indians, Settlers and Slaves in a Frontier Exchange Economy: The Lower Mississippi Valley before 1783.* Chapel Hill: University of North Carolina Press, 1992.

Van Antwerp, Verplank. "Reminiscences from Iowa." *Iowa Journal of History* 52 (1954): 343–64.

Van Cleve, Charlotte O. *"Three Score Years and Ten": Life-Long Memories of Fort Snelling, Minnesota, and Other Parts of the West.* Minneapolis: Harrison and Smith, 1888.

VanderVelde, Lea. "The Legal Ways of Seduction." *Stanford Law Review* 488 (1996):817.

———. "The Role of Captives in the Rule of Capture." *Environmental Law* 35 (2005): page.

VanderVelde, Lea, and Sandhya Subramanian. "Mrs. Dred Scott." *Yale Law Journal* 106 (1997): 1033, 1122.

Vexler, Robert I. *St. Louis: A Chronological and Documentary History, 1762–1970.* Dobbs Ferry, NY: Oceana Publications, 1974.

Vose, Reuben. *Wealth of the World Displayed.* New York: Reuben Vose 1859.

Wade, Richard. *Slavery in the Cities: The South 1820–1860.* New York: Oxford University Press, 1967.

———. *The Urban Frontier: Pioneer Life in Early Pittsburgh, Cincinnati, Lexington, Louisville, and St. Louis.* Chicago: University of Chicago Press, 1959.

Walker, Juliet E. K. *Free Frank: A Black Pioneer on the Antebellum Frontier.* Lexington: University Press of Kentucky, 1995.

Walkinshaw, Lewis Clark. *Annals of Southwestern Pennsylvania.* New York: Lewis Historical Publishing, 1939.

Walsh, Edward P. "The Story of an Old Clerk." Originally printed in *St. Louis Weekly Reveille*, Oct. 15, 1848; reprinted in *Glimpses of the Past*, St. Louis: Missouri Historical Society, Jefferson Memorial, 1934. www.umsl.edu/virtualstl/phase2/1850/events/perspectives/oldclerk.html.

Warner, Oliver. *Captain Marryat: A Rediscovery.* 1953. Reprint, New York: Hyperion Press, 1979.

Warren, William W. *History of the Ojibway People.* St. Paul: Minnesota Historical Society Press, 1885.

Washburne, E. B. *Sketch of Edward Coles, Second Governor of Illinois and Slavery Struggle, 1823–24.* New York: Negro Universities Press, 1882.

Washington, Booker T. *Up from Slavery.* New York: Doubleday, Page, 1901.

Wayman, Norbury L. *A Pictorial History of St. Louis.* St. Louis: Norbury L. Wayman, 1968.

Weber, Max. *General Economic History.* New York: Cosimo, 2007.

Weil, Tom. *The St. Louis Mercantile Library: Past, Present and Future.* St. Louis: St. Louis Mercantile Library Association, 1994.

Weiner, Mark. *Black Trials: Citizenship from the Beginnings of Slavery to the End of Caste.* New York: Knopf, 2004.

Weiner, Marli F. "Mistresses, Morality, and the Dilemmas of Slaveholding: The Ideology and Behavior of Elite Antebellum Women." In *Discovering the Women in Slavery: Emancipating Perspectives on the American Past.* Edited by Patricia Morton. Athens: University of Georgia Press, 1996.

Weisenburger, Steven. *Modern Medea: A Family Story of Slavery and Child-Murder from the Old South.* New York: Hill and Wang, 1998.

Welter, Barbara. "The Cult of True Womanhood: 1820–1860." *American Quarterly* 18, no. 2, 1art 1 (Summer 1966): 151–74.

West, Nathaniel. *The Ancestry, Life and Times of Hon. Henry Hastings Sibley.* St. Paul, MN: Pioneer Press, 1889.

Wetmore, Alphonso. *Gazetteer of the State of Missouri.* St. Louis: C. Keemle 1837.

Wheeler, Jacob D. *A Practical Treatise on the Law of Slavery Being a Compilation of All the Decisions Made on the Subject, in the Several Courts of the United States and State Courts.* 1837. Reprint, New York: Negro Universities Press, 1968.

Wheelan, Joseph. *Invading Mexico: America's Continental Dream and the Mexican War, 1846–1848.* New York: PublicAffairs, 2007.

Whelan, Mary K. "Dakota Indian Economics and the Nineteenth Century Fur Trade." *Ethno History* 40, no. 2 (1993): 246–76.

White, Bruce. "Encounters with Spirits: Ojibwa and Dakota Theories about the French and Their Merchandise." *Ethnohistory* 41, no. 3 (1994): 369–405.

———. "A Skilled Game of Exchange: Ojibway Fur Trade Protocol." *Minnesota History* 50 (Summer 1987): 229–40.

White, Deborah Gray. *Ar'n't I a Woman? Female Slaves in the Plantation South.* Rev. ed. New York: W.W. Norton, 1999.

White, Helen McCann. "Frontier Feud: How Two Officers Quarreled All the Way to the Site of Fort Snelling." *Minnesota History* 42 (Fall 1970): 99–114.

———. *Guide to a Microfilm Edition of the Lawrence Taliaferro Papers.* St. Paul: Minnesota Historical Society, 1966.

White, Richard. *The Middle Ground: Indians, Empires, and Republics in the Great Lakes Region, 1650–1815.* New York: Cambridge University Press, 1991.

White, Richard, and Patricia Nelson Limerick. *The Frontier in American Culture: An Exhibition at the Newberry Library.* Chicago: Newberry Library, 1994.

Wiggins, David S. *"Service in Siberia": Five Surgeons at Early Fort Snelling.* St. Paul: Minnesota Historical Society, 1977.

Wilentz, Sean. *The Rise of American Democracy.* W.W. Norton, 2005, 689–92.

Williams, J. Fletcher. "Memoir of Capt. Martin Scott." *Minnesota Historical Collections* 3 (1880): 180–87.

———. "Outlines of the History of Minnesota." In *History of the Upper Mississippi Valley.* Edited by Edward D. Neill. 1881. Reprint, Salem, MA: Higginson, 1994.

———. *A History of the City of Saint Paul and of the County of Ramsey, Minnesota.* 1876. Reprint, St. Paul: Minnesota Historical Society, 1983.

Williams, Michael Patrick. "The Black Evangelical Ministry in the Antebellum Border States: Profiles of Elders John Berry Meachum and Noah Davis." *Foundations* 21, no. 3 (1978): 223–41.

Winn, Kenneth. "Arsenic and Feminine Beauty in the Age of Henry Shaw (With a Little Murder on the Side)." Lecture presented at Tower Grove Park, St. Louis, April 2, 2006.

Wood, Kirsten E. *Masterful Women: Slaveholding Widows from the American Revolution through the Civil War.* Chapel Hill: University of North Carolina Press, 2004.

Wood, Peter H. *Black Majority: Negroes in South Carolina from 1670 through the Stono Rebellion.* New York: Random House, 1974.

Wood, Raymond W., and Thomas P. Thiessen. *Early Fur Trade on the Northern Plains*. Norman: University of Oklahoma Press, 1985.

Woodall, Allen E. *William Joseph Snelling and the Early Northwest*. St. Paul: Minnesota Historical Society, 1929.

Wozniak, John W. *Contact, Negotiation and Conflict: An Ethnohistory of the Eastern Dakota, 1819–1839*. Washington, DC: University Press of America, 1978.

Wyman, Mark. *The Wisconsin Frontier* Bloomington: Indiana University Press 1998.

Zeh, Frederick, William J. Orr Jr., and Robert Ryal Miller, eds. *An Immigrant Soldier in the Mexican War*. Translated by William J. Orr Jr. College Station: Texas A & M University Press, 1995.

Ziebarth, Marilyn, and Alan Ominsky. *Fort Snelling: Anchor Post of the Northwest*. St. Paul: Minnesota Historical Society, 1970.

Newspapers

Army and Navy Chronicle and Scientific Repository.
Army and Navy Chronicle, 1835–42.
Bedford Gazette.
Debow's Review, Agricultural, Commercial, Industrial Progress and Resources.
Frank Leslie's Illustrated Newspaper 4, no. 82 (June 27, 1857).
Missouri Republican, 1838–1856.
Northwestern Gazette and Galena Advertiser.
San Jose Telegraph, 1857.

Conversations

Ehrlich, Walter (January 30, 1996).
Shaw, Thomas (December 1, 2008).

Web Sources

Revised Dred Scott Case Collection, http://digital.wustl.edu/d/dre/.
U.S. Government Bureau of Land Management General Land Office Records, www.glorecords.blm/gov/.

City Directories for St. Louis

1836–37
1838–39 Keemles
1842, 1845, 1847, 1848, 1851, 1852
1854–55 St. Louis Directory of Citizens and a Business Directory
1857, 1858, 1859
1860 Kennedy's
1864 Edwards
1865 Edwards
1866 Edwards
1867 Edwards
1870
1871 Edwards
1872 Gould & Aldrich's
1873 Gould's
1875 Gould's
1876

CAPTIONS AND CREDITS

The following captions and credits pertain to illustrations that appear in the Dramatis Personae section.

Harriet Scott—Engraving from the daguerreotype taken for *Frank Leslie's Illustrated Newspaper*, 1857. *National Park Service, Jefferson National Expansion Memorial.*

Dred Scott—Albumen photograph, the only image remaining from the original daguerreotype plates taken for *Frank Leslie's Illustrated Newspaper*, 1857. *Photographs and Prints Collection, Missouri History Museum.*

Eliza and Lizzie Scott—From *Frank Leslie's Illustrated Newspaper*, 1857. *National Park Service, Jefferson National Expansion Memorial.*

Lawrence Taliaferro—Pictured in a uniform he is believed to have commissioned for himself, since no official uniform existed for Indian agents. An image of the Councilhouse appears to his left, and Fort Snelling is on his right. *Minnesota Historical Society.*

Elizabeth Dillon Taliaferro—*Minnesota Historical Society.*

George Catlin—The artist featured himself as a frontiersman in his self-portrait in Indian clothing. *National Portrait Gallery, Smithsonian Institution; gift of May C. Kinney, Ernest Kinney, and Bradford Wickes.*

Clara Catlin—*Smithsonian American Art Museum, Washington, DC / Art Resource, NY.*

Joseph Nicollet, George Featherstonhaugh—*Minnesota Historical Society.*

Henry Hastings Sibley—*Thomas Cantwell Healy / Minnesota Historical Society.*

Samuel Pond, Gideon Pond—*W. T. Bather / Minnesota Historical Society.*

Steven and Mary Riggs—*Minnesota Historical Society.*

Steven Bonga—Pictured in a fur hat and suit c. 1880, he served as a translator for the Ojibwa Treaty of 1837. *William D. Baldwin / Minnesota Historical Society.*

George Bonga—Was licensed as a fur trader to the Ojibwa. *Alfred Zimmerman / Minnesota Historical Society.*

William Bonga—Pictured about 1890. *Minnesota Historical Society.*

Jacob Fahlstrom—Reputed to be the first Swede in Minnesota. *Minnesota Historical Society.*

Joseph R. Brown—*Charles DeForest Fredericks / Minnesota Historical Society.*

Nathan Jarvis, William Beaumont—*National Library of Medicine.*

General D. C. Buell—*Library of Congress.*

Major E. A. Hitchcock, Pierre Chouteau Jr.—*Photographs and Prints Collection, Missouri History Museum.*

John F. A. Sanford—The only known portrait. *South Dakota State Historical Society.*

Julia Chouteau—Pictured with baby Ben Sanford, she showed a motherly interest in her nephew after her sister's death. *Photographs and Prints Collection, Missouri History Museum.*

Elizabeth Irene Sanford Emerson Chaffee, Dr. and Congressman Clifford C. Chaffee—*Connecticut Valley Historical Museum.*

B. S. Garland—*Lynchburg Museum System.*

Lucy Berry Turner Delaney— *National Park Service, Jefferson National Expansion Memorial.*

Hiram Rhoads Revels—He preached for the AME church in St. Louis and later became the first black congressman, as he is pictured here. *Brady-Handy Photograph Collection, Library of Congress.*

Reverdy Johnson, Montgomery Blair— *Brady-Handy Photograph Collection, Library of Congress.*

Chief Justice Roger Taney, Justices John McLean, Benjamin Robbins Curtis, James Moore Wayne—*Library of Congress.*

Justices John Archibald Campbell, John Catron—*Brady-Handy Photograph Collection, Library of Congress.*

Justice Peter Vivian Daniel—*Supreme Court Historical Society.*

Justices Robert Cooper Grier, Samuel Nelson—*Brady-Handy Photograph Collection, Library of Congress.*

INDEX